DEC 2014. TO [illegible]

CW00431605

[illegible] Will,
Natasha &
Liam
xxx

THE WORLD ENCYCLOPEDIA OF
AIRCRAFT CARRIERS
AND NAVAL AIRCRAFT

THE WORLD ENCYCLOPEDIA OF
AIRCRAFT CARRIERS
AND NAVAL AIRCRAFT

An illustrated history of aircraft carriers and the naval aircraft that launch from them, from the first airships and zeppelins through to today's modern warships and jets

Includes two specialist directories featuring over 130 aircraft and 170 aircraft carriers with full technical specifications, spanning from World War I up to the present day

BERNARD IRELAND AND FRANCIS CROSBY

LORENZ BOOKS

This edition is published by Lorenz Books,
an imprint of Anness Publishing Ltd,
Blaby Road, Wigston,
Leicestershire LE18 4SE

Email: info@anness.com

www.lorenzbooks.com; www.annesspublishing.com

Anness Publishing has a new picture agency outlet for
images for publishing, promotions or advertising.
Please visit our website www.practicalpictures.com
for more information.

Publisher: Joanna Lorenz
Senior Editor: Felicity Forster
Project Editor: Daniel Hurst
Copy Editor: Tim Ellerby
Designer: Design Principals
Production Manager: Pirong Wang

Previously published in two separate volumes, *The World
Encyclopedia of Aircraft Carriers* and *The World Encyclopedia
of Naval Aircraft*

PUBLISHER'S NOTE
Although the advice and information in this book are believed to
be accurate and true at the time of going to press, neither the
authors nor the publisher can accept any legal responsibility or
liability for any errors or omissions that may have been made.
The nationality of each submarine is identified in the specification
box by the national flag that was in use at the time of the
vessel's commissioning and service.

At Anness Publishing we believe that business should be conducted in an ethical and ecologically sustainable way, with
respect for the environment and a proper regard to the replacement of the natural resources we employ.

As a publisher, we use a lot of wood pulp in high-quality
paper for printing, and that wood commonly comes from spruce
trees. We are therefore currently growing more than 750,000
trees in three Scottish forest plantations: Berrymoss (130
hectares/320 acres), West Touxhill (125 hectares/305 acres) and
Deveron Forest (75 hectares/185 acres). The forests we manage
contain more than 3.5 times the number of trees employed each
year in making paper for the books we manufacture.

Because of this ongoing ecological investment programme,
you, as our customer, can have the pleasure and reassurance
of knowing that a tree is being cultivated on your behalf to
naturally replace the materials used to make the book you
are holding.

Our forestry programme is run in accordance with the UK
Woodland Assurance Scheme (UKWAS) and will be certified by
the internationally recognized Forest Stewardship Council
(FSC). The FSC is a non-government organization dedicated to
promoting responsible management of the world's forests.
Certification ensures forests are managed in an
environmentally sustainable and socially responsible way.
For further information about this scheme, go to
www.annesspublishing.com/trees

ǍPAGE 1: **The Sukhoi Su-27K**
PAGE 2: **The Invincible class**
PAGE 3: **The Blackburn Shark torpedo-spotter-reconnaissance plane**

Contents

398 DIRECTORY OF MODERN NAVAL AIRCRAFT: 1945 TO THE PRESENT DAY

Introduction

This comprehensive volume looks closely at the progress of aircraft carrier and naval aircraft design through history and offers readers a fascinating historical and global insight into the intriguing world of naval aeronautics. It is split into two clearly defined sections: the first looking at the history and development of aircraft carriers, and the second exploring the fascinating lineage of naval aircraft. Each section includes a detailed history of the most important developments in mechanical design and manufacture, and a comprehensive directory, giving an extensive global and chronological view of individual carriers and aircraft. Finally, there is a thorough glossary detailing the correct meanings of commonly used technical terms.

Aircraft Carriers

The first section of this book charts the fascinating history of the aircraft carrier. At the time of writing, it is over 100 years since Orville Wright provided "the proof which actual flight alone can give … [that] an engine-driven, man-carrying aerodrome [sic] had been constructed", at Kitty Hawk, North Carolina, USA. Within five years, brave young men were demonstrating to their respective navies that these fragile machines could actually be flown to and from warships. The promise of being able to loft a pair of keen eyes to several thousand feet to observe the movements of the opponent was the dream of every admiral, so it was a promise worth pursuing.

TOP: **A green-vested member of the catapult crew seems to be conducting the aircraft waiting to take off USS *Constellation* (CVA-64) in the South China Sea off Vietnam. Nearest is an F-4 Phantom while inboard and to the stern are RA-5C Vigilantes.** ABOVE: **The first of many, Britain's *Argus* (I), 1918, pioneered the functional combination of a "through flight deck" that was served by elevators connecting with the hangar below.**

For the British Royal Navy, Admiral Fisher's dictum had been simply "Hit first, hit hard and keep hitting" which, in the days before radar and reliable fire control, was not easy to satisfy. If an airborne observer could report enemy movement, he could equally well report fall of shot to enable his admiral to get on target just that little bit more quickly.

From duelling with pistols, pilots quickly progressed to hand-dropped bombs but knew that the difference between this and toting a torpedo was only a matter of lift and engine power.

Wartime development was rapid. In 1914, aircraft were still being set afloat to begin and end their flight. Four years later HMS *Argus* introduced the world to the through-deck aircraft carrier, a vessel of functional ugliness but of undoubted utility.

ABOVE: The Japanese carrier *Zuikaku*, together with her sister, *Shokaku*, spearheaded the task group that demonstrated, early in 1942, the potency of massed seaborne airstrikes. RIGHT: Although influential as the first "third generation" British carrier, *Ark Royal* (II) was a one-off. Her successors traded aircraft capacity for improved horizontal protection.

Before the peace, the Royal Navy lost the huge reserve of innovation and enthusiasm that had created the first-ever effective air arm, when it was transferred to the new, unified air force. During the inter-war years the Fleet Air Arm lapsed into near mediocrity compared with its major peers. Other nation's fleets were better appreciating the advantage of the big air wing, with its potential to deliver short-term force at a selected point. In this, they were far closer to adhering to Fisher's expressed aims.

World War II proved the concept of the deck-load air strike, confirming the carrier as the undisputed capital ship. However, many war-built vessels were soon rendered obsolescent as developments continued apace.

BELOW: The embodiment of seapower, virtually unchallengeable by conventional means, American carrier groups have enjoyed over a half-century of dominance at sea. RIGHT: Vast geopolitical changes near the end of the 20th century obliged major armed forces to redefine their missions. For the Royal Navy the big carrier made its comeback with the first of a new generation.

The Americans, with their steadily diminishing number of carrier battle groups, are now virtually alone in being able to influence local events around the world by simply appearing offshore. Such a latent threat, the contemporary equivalent of "gunboat diplomacy", is fully mobile, deployable at short notice anywhere that ships can float, and independent of costly, vulnerable and generally unpopular overseas bases.

From time to time, the large carrier, like the tank, has been written off as too vulnerable to survive in a missile-dominated battle environment. Like the tank, however, it continues to thrive and evolve, simply because there is nothing to replace it.

Naval Aircraft

In 1910, Eugene Ely became the first pilot to launch from a ship when he took off from the USS *Birmingham* and landed nearby after just five minutes in the air. On January 18, 1911, Ely became the first to land on a stationary ship – the USS *Pennsylvania* anchored on the waterfront in San Francisco. From these experimental beginnings was born one of the most potent manifestations of military might – naval air power.

The design and development of naval combat aircraft has always been challenging. In the early days of military aviation, naval aircraft were built by simply modifying existing land-based aircraft and making them suitable for the harsh environment of carrier operations. Unfortunately, the addition of essential equipment such as arrester hooks and beefed-up undercarriages as well as strengthened structures frequently eroded the performance an aircraft may have enjoyed as a landplane.

Purpose-designed naval aircraft such as torpedo-bombers, though potent in their own role, were vulnerable once within range of higher performance fighters. Only when naval aviation proved its strategic value in World War II, did purpose-designed high-performance combat aircraft start to appear that could hold their own over water or land. As a result, naval aviation has become a war-winning factor, although cost has also added to the difficulties faced by naval aircraft designers due to the comparatively low production runs associated with naval aircraft.

TOP: **A Royal Navy carrier showing what were, in their day, the most advanced aircraft in the Fleet Air Arm inventory – Sea Hawks and Sea Venoms.** ABOVE: **Early experiments on ships converted to aircraft carriers led to a new war-winning form of military might – naval air power.**

Nevertheless, nations like the United States can still project their military power anywhere they can sail their carriers. These vast ships, some as complex as cities, enable military planners to field some of the world's most potent aircraft types and, if required, launch strikes against potential enemies around the world without the need for land bases.

Carriers are free to roam – while not entering other countries' national waters – the seas, which make up 70 per cent of the Earth's surface. Aircraft carriers' speed and flexibility enable them to bring firepower in the form of naval air power anywhere in the world in a matter of days.

ABOVE: **The Merlin, a joint venture between Italy and Britain, is one of the most capable helicopters in military service today. The aircraft's two computers manage its mission system and the aircraft is controlled by a hi-tech glass cockpit. The helicopter is now a vital element of naval air power.**
LEFT: **The unique Harrier/Sea Harrier family of fighter and attack aircraft gave naval strategists the vertical take-off capability of helicopters but with the high performance of jet fighters. The type first saw action flying from ships during the Falklands War in 1982.** BELOW: **Flying boats like the Consolidated Coronado were able to patrol vast areas of ocean in search of enemy shipping and submarines. The heyday of the military flying boats was World War II but some types remain in service today.**

This section brings together information and data about naval aircraft from the earliest days to the present and indeed the next generation of naval combat aircraft such as the Lockheed Martin F-35. The reader will also find information about seaplanes, floatplanes and flying boats. Some could operate from carriers while others were far too big to do anything but take off from the sea, lakes or rivers under their own power. Aircraft such as the Short Sunderland and Consolidated Catalina were as vital a part of Allied naval air power as any carrier-borne aircraft and their presence could keep submarines and enemy shipping at bay. One of the most significant developments in post-war naval air power has been the increasingly important role played by helicopters. From novelty flying machines then flying ambulances, choppers were soon developed into rotary aircraft capable of carrying nuclear weapons.

The authors have had to make difficult choices and the A–Z listings do not claim to feature every aircraft carrier and naval aircraft ever built. They do, however, present the individual stories of the ships and aircraft that the authors believe to have been the most significant. The specifications are presented in a standard form to enable the reader to make comparisons of weight, speed, armament etc. Some early aircraft are given an endurance rather than a range and for other older, lesser known types, some of the details could simply not be found.

The book closes with an informative glossary of key naval and aviatory terms, that allow the reader to greater understand the full meaning of the technical information presented in the book.

Together the composite parts of this comprehensive volume provide the historian or military enthusiast with a fascinating overview of some of the world's most impressive aircraft carriers and naval aircraft and the part they have played in shaping history.

AIRCRAFT CARRIERS

IMAGE: **The *USS Constellation*.**

The History of Aircraft Carriers

An aircraft first flew from a ship just four years before the outbreak of World War I. History has left us no reason as to why this was attempted, except that the marriage of aircraft and ship appeared to be a promising idea. Indeed, the possibilities of what came to be naval aviation have depended ever since on the steady evolution of the technologies that support it. Early ambitions thus went no further than observation and reconnaissance, and the low-powered and unreliable aero engine of the time was rivalled by a variety of lighter-than-air craft. Of these, the long-endurance Zeppelin had a profound influence on developments by obliging warships to take high-performance fighters to sea.

Within nine years of that first flight from a ship's deck, the first true aircraft carrier was at sea. Already its aircraft were designed to reconnoitre, to protect the fleet, and to torpedo the enemy.

From here, it was the aircraft carrier's rapidly assumed capacity to deliver a concentration of destructive force that was the secret of it finally displacing the big-gun battleship as the undisputed arbiter of sea power.

LEFT: The USS *Intrepid* (CV-11) was an *Essex*-class carrier. These ships were the backbone of the US fleet in the Pacific war from 1943 to 1945.

First flights from ships

Observing Glenn Curtiss demonstrating aircraft to the US Army in 1908, naval officers were moved to suggest putting one aboard a warship, as yet for no clear purpose. Enthusiasm for flying was general at this time and an American newspaper offered a substantial prize for the first pilot to fly from a ship to a point ashore. The German HAPAG line took up the challenge but, as it happened, its failed attempt in November 1910 was upstaged by the US Navy, which had quietly been preparing its own.

Two months later, Captain Washington Irving Chambers had been appointed to liaise and cooperate with the experimenters. With modest funding he was able to engage Eugene Ely, an associate of Curtiss, to undertake a flight from a warship.

A temporary ramp, sloping downward from bridge to stemhead, was built over the forecastle of the scout cruiser USS Birmingham and, on November 14, 1910, Ely opened the throttle and launched himself into history. In gusty conditions, his wheeled undercarriage brushed the surface, but he recovered to fly the 3.2km/2 miles to shore.

Witnessing the feat, the acting Secretary of the Navy deemed it good publicity, immediately supporting a proposal to undertake the more difficult exercise of landing-on.

A temporary wooden platform was laid over the quarterdeck of the armoured cruiser Pennsylvania. It was complete with refinements such as "round-down" and a score of transverse ropes, weighted with sandbags, to arrest the aircraft. On January 18, 1911, Ely duly landed-on, remaining aboard for

TOP: **The first aircraft purchased for the US Navy, the Triad (A-1) being tested at Hammondsport by its designer Glenn Curtiss and Lt Theodore G. Ellyson, who was to become naval aviator No. 1. Able to operate from both water and land with its floats and wheels, the Triad was the first successful amphibian.** ABOVE: **Eugene Ely gets airborne from the deck of the USS Birmingham at Hampton Roads, Virginia on November 14, 1910. The historic first flight from ship to shore was about 3.2km/2 miles.**

an hour before "doing the double" by taking off again and flying ashore. Both Birmingham and Pennsylvania had been anchored.

In Europe, the British Admiralty, aware of activity on the part of both the French and Russian navies, had been training a first party of volunteer pilots through the good offices of the Royal Aero Club at Eastchurch, near Sheerness, and under the benevolent eye of the innovative then First Lord, Winston Churchill. The first two students gained their proficiency certification in April 1911. One of them, Charles Rumney Samson, not only taught Churchill himself to fly but went on to make the first flight from a British warship.

An inter-service committee had been considering the potential of aviation, the Royal Navy seeing its function as being to observe blockaded enemy harbours, "to ascend from a floating base" to scout for enemy forces at sea, to spot enemy submarines and minefields, and to direct naval gunfire.

Curtiss made a first flight in his "hydro-aeroplane" in February 1911 (the French had done it in 1910), the aircraft being symbolically hoisted by crane aboard the *Pennsylvania*. Two naval pilots, Schwann and Longmore, made the first British seaplane take-offs later in 1911.

During November 1911, Samson flew a Short S.27 off the forecastle ramp of the battleship *Africa* at a buoy off Sheerness. He used the same aircraft again in May 1912 for the next demonstration, staged during a Royal Fleet Review at Portland. Here, he made the first-ever take-off from a ship under weigh, flying from the battleship *Hibernia* to release a simulated 45kg/100lb bomb. Two months later, he made a similar flight from the battleship *London*, proceeding at 12 knots.

In the United States, the successes with Curtiss' wheeled aircraft had encouraged Chambers to talk in terms of "platform ships", i.e. with flight decks, but the growing potential of seaplanes sidetracked him from what would have been a promising direction of development.

TOP: **One of the great pioneers of manned flight, Glen H. Curtiss is seen here having just completed his record-making flight from Albany to New York in June 1910. He was to tell an interviewer, "Some day soon aeroplanes will have to start from the deck of battleships …"** ABOVE: **A Short S.38 on the flying-off platform of HMS *Africa*. Reports, unconfirmed, state that Charles Rumney Samson made the first British flight from the *Africa* in December 1911.** LEFT: **The first recorded flight by Samson from HMS *Africa*, on January 19, 1912.**

ABOVE: **Watched by crewmen crowding every vantage point, Eugene Ely makes the first ever touchdown on a warship's deck. The USS *Pennsylvania* was anchored off San Francisco on January 18, 1911.**

Zeppelins

The primary roles envisaged for early, low-powered heavier-than-air craft were based on observation and reconnaissance. In these, they were still inferior in many respects to lighter-than-air craft. Of these, the simplest were the tethered aerostats, of which the most common were kite balloons, deployed by many warships and auxiliaries.

Powered airships, capable of navigation, were properly termed "dirigibles". Those with an internal frame were termed "rigid", those without, "non-rigid". The latter, like balloons, were little more than inflated gas bags, and limited in size. As the British failed to master the technology of the rigid airship, they operated considerable numbers of non-rigids, popularly called "blimps". In naval service, their small size restricted them largely to coastal duties.

The most dominant airship was the large rigid, a category which, until after World War I, was virtually synonymous with "Zeppelin". These craft stemmed from the Friedrichshafen factory established by Graf Ferdinand von Zeppelin in 1898 to promote popular air travel as well as construct "air cruisers" for national defence.

Despite early setbacks and rivalry with the Schütte-Lanz company, Zeppelin's machines had been acquired for the German army by 1910 and, two years later, for the navy. Zeppelin had met the army's requirement for an operational endurance of 24 hours and it was this, together with its potential in long-range reconnaissance, which attracted naval interest. The placing of the naval order was, however, the

ABOVE: **Count von Zeppelin's main intention was to use his machines to popularize air travel. This pre-war impression emphasizes the more idyllic aspect of his enterprise.**

ABOVE: **An Italian non-rigid DE-type scouting airship communicating with an anti-submarine motor boat, or MAS. Of a total of 49 airships, the Italians lost seven in the course of the war, two of them as a result of accidents.**
LEFT: **With a volume of nearly 56,000m³/2,000,000cu ft, the L.53 was one of the largest types of Zeppelin to see service. She was a victim of an RNAS Camel fighter, flown from a high-speed lighter on August 11, 1918.**

effective end of Zeppelin's personal direction of company affairs. He was not a trained engineer and, with the navy insisting on imposing its own constructors and naval architects to improve and enlarge his products, he lost interest. By the outbreak of war in 1914, the Zeppelin Company was virtually a state concern.

The Royal Navy's airship aspirations were effectively wrecked along with its prototype rigid in 1911. This failure was exacerbated by Admiral Sir John Jellicoe (soon to become C-in-C, Grand Fleet) and Captain Murray Sueter (Director, Admiralty Air Department) separately travelling as civilians in commercial flights by Zeppelins and returning enthused with the craft's potential.

Lacking a similar force, it is perhaps not surprising that the Royal Navy, during the course of its North Sea operations of World War I, developed a phobia known commonly as "Zeppelinitis". Symptoms were widespread and took the form of a conviction that the fleet's every move was being observed. The truth was quite different as Admiral Tirpitz, father of the Imperial Navy, distrusted new technologies and was little interested in anything but his battle fleet. Fortunately for the British, he had neglected both the submarine arm and the Naval Airship Division, both of which began their war seriously below the approved establishment.

In the Royal Navy, long-range, high-angle, anti-aircraft gunnery was still in its infancy. The only true antidote to the Zeppelin was therefore the high-performance fighter for, by dumping ballast, the airship had a rate of climb which left it immune to interception by anything else unless surprised or otherwise caught unawares.

As a result the Zeppelin was the primary catalyst in the protracted and innovative process by which the Royal Navy produced the world's first through-deck aircraft carrier.

In practice, too many Zeppelins were diverted to unprofitable and costly bombing raids on England, while those allocated to fleet operation proved to be hostage to weather conditions. Requiring enormous dimensions for a modest payload, the airship eventually proved to be an evolutionary dead-end, the aircraft proving to be much more efficient.

TOP: **During operations in the Baltic, a reconnaissance Zeppelin overflies a German battleship, probably the *Markgraf*.** BELOW: **Another of the largest Zeppelins, the L.45 is here seen above two of the three sheds at Tondern. She was lost through forced-landing in France in October 1917.**

ABOVE: **A small, early example of a Zeppelin, L.9 had a volume of about 25,000m³/880,000cu ft and a length of 161.2m/529.3ft comparable with that of the armoured cruiser *Blücher*.**

Seaplanes versus landplanes

In February 1911, a month after Eugene Ely had shown that it was possible to land a landplane on a warship, Glenn Curtiss successfully took off in his "hydro-aeroplane", landed alongside the *Pennsylvania* and was briefly craned aboard. This then begged the question of which type of aircraft offered most for future progress. Superficially, the choice appeared simple. Take-off and landing platforms for landplanes were unwieldy and affected a warship's fighting power. On the other hand, a seaplane (as it came to be called) needed only to be transported, the water surface anywhere being its operating platform. This was attractive as an option but, perversely the sea is rarely calm and the aircraft was fragile. Further, its cumbersome float's and high undercarriage guaranteed that its performance would be inferior to that of an equivalent landplane.

From the outset, the Americans regarded the development of the catapult as a means to minimize the impact of aircraft on the launching ship. Their first successful launch of a seaplane from an improvised compressed air model occurred in November 1912, followed a month later by the launch of one of Curtiss' small flying boats. A practical catapult might be located more conveniently on a warship, but this still left unresolved the problem of alighting and recovery.

The British showed little initial enthusiasm for catapults and it was not until 1916 that they modified an Admiralty hopper, renamed *Slinger*, to conduct practical trials. For them, the

TOP: **Seen at Mitylene during the Dardanelles campaign, the *Ark Royal* (I) has a Short 166 "on the hook". Although designed to carry a 356mm/14in torpedo, the aircraft was capable of only 105kph/65mph. Note the Union Flag marking that pre-dated the familiar roundel.** ABOVE: **Originally an engines-aft, steam-driven hopper, the *Slinger* was converted for trials with catapults. Trials were suspended in 1919 as aircraft of the time took off equally well from a simple platform.**

simple, if ungainly, launching platform sufficed. As the average aircraft of the time could rise almost vertically from a standing position in as little as 45 knots relative wind speed, fast ships such as light cruisers needed no more than a platform. Capital ships began by locating platforms atop gun turrets, which could be trained to avoid having to steam into the wind.

The seaplane, launched on an expendable trolley and recovered from the sea, gave way to a wheeled landplane of higher performance, which alighted on the surface with the aid of temporary flotation bags.

It was obvious to all, however, that the ideal lay in a ship configured to both launch and recover wheeled aircraft. Even as the Americans were making their first successful catapult launches, the Beardmore yard approached the British Admiralty with proposals for a 15,000-tonner with sided superstructures and a straight-through deck along its central axis. Capable of accommodating, launching and recovering aircraft, she might have been the first true carrier had the Admiralty been bolder.

Instead, the small cruiser HMS *Hermes* was modified early in 1913 with a take-off ramp and canvas "hangars" for two seaplanes, a French Caudron G. III and a British Short S.64, the latter already fitted with folding wings and a radio. During fleet manoeuvres of 1913 the *Hermes* staged over thirty successful flights, demonstrating that seaplanes, at least, could be deployed at sea on a sustained basis. This led directly to the Admiralty acquiring a hull capable of being remodelled into a specialist seaplane carrier. It was this ship that was completed in 1914 as *Ark Royal* (I).

Up to this point the French had, if anything been slightly ahead with their conversion of the *Foudre*, while the Japanese had modified the *Wakamiya* to operate a mix of British and French-built seaplanes.

ABOVE: **The Italian Navy constructed several big-gun monitors to bombard Austrian shore installations. Dating from mid-1917 the *Faà di Bruno*, shown here being directed by a flying boat, boasted two 381mm/15in guns on a displacement of only 2,854 tonnes/2,809 tons.** BELOW: **First of the Royal Navy's seaplane-carrier conversions, the cruiser *Hermes* was, in 1913, given a launch platform forward and a canvas hangar aft. She is seen sinking after having been torpedoed in October 1914, the remains of the seaplane on her quarterdeck clearly visible.**

ABOVE: **One of three Gotha WD 20s built for long-range reconnaissance flight for the German Navy. Developed from the WD 14 torpedo-bomber, the WD 20 swapped weapon load for additional fuel to give it up to 10 hours of endurance.** LEFT: **Glenn Curtiss, having successfully flown his first flying boat early in 1912, developed his designs through a series of early prototypes. The F-Type, seen here, typifies the flimsy nature of early models.**

The Dardanelles Campaign

Strategically brilliant but tactically inept, the Dardanelles campaign of 1915 quickly mired into static warfare. Considerable Allied military forces were confined to the Gallipoli peninsula, where they were totally dependent upon support by sea. During the ten-or-so months of the campaign, the fleets were based on nearby islands.

The newly-completed *Ark Royal* (I), with six seaplanes, was involved from the outset but, although lacking nothing in enthusiasm, the infant Royal Naval Air Squadron (RNAS), was as the service expression has it, "thrown in at the deep end". During the initial naval bombardments, her aircraft were able to reconnoitre the many enemy fortifications but the boisterous February weather caused many flights to be aborted.

Hopes for the forts' destruction rested much on the 381mm/15in guns of the new battleship *Queen Elizabeth*. This was to be achieved through indirect fire across the peninsula, with fall of shot being corrected from the air. However, no trained observers yet existed, (a midshipman was usually selected on the basis of being the lightest!) and communications proved unreliable as no time had been

TOP: **HMS *Ark Royal* (I) is seen here soon after her arrival at Mudros in March 1915. The space abaft the cranes marks the hangar access hatch, while the long, unencumbered foredeck was intended for take-offs, although never used as such.** ABOVE: **Great things were expected from bombardment by HMS *Queen Elizabeth*'s 381mm/15in guns. Aerial spotting proved difficult, however, due to shortcomings in both aircraft and communications.**

allowed for testing, training or rehearsal. When aloft, the underpowered aircraft had to fly so low that they were continually struck by rifle fire.

In June 1915, the *Ark Royal* was relieved by the *Ben-my-Chree*, but for her the hot summer weather created its own problems. Seaplanes found it difficult to "unstick" from glassy water in the absence of wind, while the ever-present dust tormented already temperamental engines. Fortunately, enemy aircraft were few, however those that did appear were landplanes of higher performance and regularly reconnoitred the main fleet base at Mudros. "One of our lumbering seaplanes went up after it like an owl in sunlight" it was recorded, "but could rise no higher than the masts of the Fleet".

By dint of the round-the-clock efforts from its artificers, the RNAS averaged ten to twelve sorties daily, usually eight devoted to bombing (a Short 184 could lift 236kg/520lb) or

ABOVE: **One of the *Ark Royal* (I)'s Short 166 seaplanes is seen here taxiing across the harbour at Mudros. Note that the roundel marking has been adopted. The harbour was always packed with merchant shipping carrying naval supplies.**

spotting for naval gunfire, and only two to reconnaissance, for which just one modern camera was available.

There was an obvious need for higher-performance landplanes. However, because there was no point on the peninsula secure from enemy artillery fire, these had to operate from Mudros, which allowed them little time over Gallipoli.

During the initial landings and any littoral operations, the kite balloon proved to be more reliable for observation. However, even with their ship anchored close inshore the useful range of observation was limited. Their telephonic links were reliable, and despite their crews suffering badly from motion sickness, they usefully directed naval gunfire. In addition to those deployed by warships, there were those from the balloon ship *Manica*, later relieved by the *Hector*.

Great hopes had been placed on spotting enemy minefields from aircraft but conditions made this impossible. Known fields could not be swept because they were covered by artillery and unknown, short-term fields wreaked considerable execution.

A "first" achieved by the *Ben-my-Chree*'s Short 184s during August 1915, was the torpedoing and destruction of two enemy merchantmen in the strait.

Overall, naval aviation at the Dardanelles was poorly rated by the Admiralty, but this was due in great measure to senior officers not appreciating the still-primitive nature of the technologies involved and thus failing either to husband their very limited resources or to employ them efficiently within their obvious limitations.

TOP: **Another view of Mudros, dominated by the elegant lines of a *Cressy*-class armoured cruiser, with an *Eclipse*-class protected cruiser beyond. The blimp overhead was more useful than heavier-than-air craft in spotting, but was more vulnerable to enemy ground fire.** ABOVE: **Wing Commander Charles Rumney Samson with a French-built Nieuport Two-seater of his No.3 Wing at the Dardanelles. Note the observer's upward-firing Lewis gun. The extra-warm jacket, pistol and last cigarette are also noteworthy.** LEFT: **Lightly-built and not very suitable for operations in the North Sea, the Sopwith Schneider proved effective in the eastern Mediterranean, both at the Dardanelles and in the Aegean, as seen here. The anchored brigantines evoke an age that was about to disappear.**

Fighters aboard ships

The first three channel packets converted to seaplane carriers (*Engadine*, *Empress* and *Riviera*) were equipped only with hangar space and cranes. Their aircraft were of low performance and intended for reconnaissance, spotting, and bomber/torpedo roles. Lacking any flying-off ramps, the ships were required to heave-to to both despatch and recover their seaplanes. Already slow for fleet operations, they thus incurred further delay.

Their primitive level of capability was demonstrated on Christmas Day, 1914, when the three transported a total of nine aircraft to bomb the Zeppelin base at Cuxhaven. Only seven machines took the air, one found the target but inflicted no damage, and just three aircraft returned to their ships. The raid had historical significance in that it was the first-ever seaborne air strike, attracting in return the first-ever bombing attack on a warship at sea. It also demonstrated the still-rudimentary nature of naval aviation.

Packets converted later were improved by the addition of forward flying-off ramps. Initially, these were intended for launching seaplanes with the aid of expendable trolleys. These ships were supplemented by the rebuilt ex-Cunard ship, *Campania*. Aged, and arthritic with machinery problems, she was, nonetheless, considerably larger. In place of 18–24m/60–80ft launching platforms, hers was 50m/165ft in length and, importantly, she could maintain her speed in a seaway.

Frustration with the limitations of seaplanes led Admiral Jellicoe, C-in-C Grand Fleet to demand that "aeroplanes", i.e. landplanes, be introduced. On November 3, 1915, the first, a Bristol Scout "C" fighter flew from the *Vindex*, starting a sequence that would evolve through the Scout "D", the Sopwith Pup, the 1½-Strutter and the Camel.

The short ramp of the *Vindex* was copied aboard half-a-dozen light cruisers, the first of which, HMS *Yarmouth*,

ABOVE: **A Sopwith 2F.2 Camel lifts easily from the short launching platform of the Australian light cruiser *Sydney*. This picture dates from the latter part of World War I, the aircraft not being carried when the ship sank the celebrated German raider *Emden* in 1914. Note the 152mm/6in gun in an open mounting.**
BELOW: **Another view of a light cruiser's launch platform. From HMS *Yarmouth*'s bridge its limited dimensions are very apparent. Note that the guard rails and jack staff support have been lowered. The aircraft is a Sopwith Pup, piloted by Squadron Commander Frederick J. Rutland.**

successfully flew a Pup in June 1917 from a platform just 6m/20ft in length. This feat was quickly exploited for, on August 21, a Pup from the same ship intercepted Zeppelin L.23 near Terschelling, destroying it with "10 to15 shots".

Other launching platforms appeared atop the turrets of capital ships but, at this point, with recovery dependent upon flotation bags and the situation at the time, the aircraft was still very much an expendable item. Experience with the *Campania*, however, had led to a similar conversion on the new and fast "large light cruiser" *Furious*. She entered service in July 1917 and, on August 2, Squadron Commander Edwin Dunning used the Pup's excellent low-speed characteristics to make a risky side-slip and land on the *Furious*' forward flying-off deck. A repeat proved fatal but was instrumental in the ship being further modified with an after flying-on deck.

The Sopwith 2F.1 Camel was designed specifically as a shipboard fighter and on July 17, 1918, *Furious* launched seven of them against the Tondern Zeppelin base. Two airships were destroyed with bombs. A fortnight later, a Camel took off successfully from a specifically designed lighter, towed at high speed by a destroyer of the Harwich Force. Again, the stratagem was quickly exploited, the same pilot, the 18-year-old Lieutenant S.D. Culley, employing it on August 10 to bring down the L.53. The blazing, falling Zeppelin inspired Commodore Tyrwhitt to make the memorable signal, addressed to all ships, "See Hymns Ancient and Modern, Number 224, verse 7". Due consultation confirmed this to read:

"O happy band of pilgrims,
Look upward to the skies,
Where such a light affliction
Shall win so great a prize."

ABOVE: **In a scene that foreshadows the packed flight decks of later years, six of HMS *Furious*' Sopwith Camels are seen ranged forward in 1918. In the foreground is the hatch-like opening of the forward elevator. Note the palisade windbreaks, their paintwork continuing the ship's striped camouflage.**
BELOW: **Still wearing her wartime dazzle paintwork in this 1917 picture, the converted packet HMS *Pegasus* launches a Sopwith 1½-Strutter fighter. The crew members are standing on a portable platform section that permitted aircraft to be transferred from the hangar space below the goalpost mast.**

Air-dropped torpedoes

The idea of dropping torpedoes from seaplanes originated virtually with the seaplane itself, and can be attributed to no one person.

In the United States, the innovative Bradley Fiske, then a Rear Admiral, filed a patent for an air-dropped torpedo early in 1912. Although first favouring a weapon controlled by radio from an aircraft, he moved to the sounder idea of aiming the aircraft itself, increasing the probability of success through employing several simultaneously.

During the same year, Engineer Captain Alessandro Guidoni of the Italian Navy added floats to a French Henri Farman landplane to experiment with the dropping of deadloads to the limit of the aircraft's capacity. In 1913, he was given a more powerful, twin-engined seaplane, enabling him to demonstrate dropping a dummy 375kg/827lb torpedo on February 26, 1914.

Meanwhile at the Royal Naval Air Station at Eastchurch, Captain Murray Sueter enlisted the assistance of Thomas Sopwith to construct a rig for the evaluation of torpedo release gear at high speeds. This equipment Sopwith then incorporated into his Type "C" aircraft, with which he demonstrated that carrying a 363kg/800lb, 356mm/14in torpedo was feasible in 1913. Finally, on July 28, 1914, a first live drop was made by a Short Folder.

A 356mm/14in weapon had limited hitting power and, with his eye set on larger targets, Sueter set Sopwith the task of designing a landplane able to carry a 457mm/18in weapon. The existence of this project appears in minutes dated June 25,

TOP: **Designed from the outset to carry the harder-hitting 457mm/18in torpedo, the Sopwith Cuckoo needed to be a robustly constructed landplane in order to carry the load. The torpedo's propellers are here covered by a protective cap.** ABOVE: **An interesting "nuts and bolts" view of a Cuckoo, taken from an instruction manual. Of immediate note are the sturdy undercarriage, the small volume of the engine and the obviously poor forward view enjoyed by the pilot when putting down on a carrier's deck.**

1914, (and, therefore, pre-war) and was connected with the provision and location of coastal air stations. Inter alia, these stated that "the danger of raids would be greatly reduced by the prospect of torpedo-carrying aircraft stationed 80km/ 50 miles apart all along the coast … The detection and attack of hostile craft would be rendered much more rapid by the introduction of this type of coast defence". In view of the German fleet's shortly-to-be-adopted tactics of hit-and-run bombardments of English east coast towns, this appraisal was prescient but, unfortunately, well ahead of the technology to support it, for it would be 1917 before Sopwith could introduce the required aircraft.

The then First Lord, Winston Churchill, informed Sueter and his colleagues as early as April 3, 1915, that a very large fleet of aircraft was required. In place of individual "dashing exploits", it was necessary to deal "a decisive blow ... at the enemy's capital ships ... either in a fleet action or in his harbours".

The first successful "dashing exploits" were themselves still several months in the future, being the August 14 attacks by the *Ben-my-Chree*'s aircraft in the Dardanelles theatre.

As the British moved toward their objective of a mass torpedo attack on the German and/or Austrian fleet, the Germans themselves were not idle. By November 1916, their twin-engined Gothas were torpedoing merchant shipping off the English east coast. To lift them from the water, these aircraft required two 119kW/160bhp engines. In contrast, Sopwith's landplane, lifting from the flight decks that Sueter envisaged, required only a singe, 149kW/200bhp unit.

The Sopwith T.1 (later named the "Cuckoo") first flew in June 1917 but was a further year entering service. On October 19, 1918, the first operational squadron embarked on the new, flush-deck carrier *Argus*. Within a month the plan for the mass torpedo attack was terminated by the Armistice. By then, its gifted but outspoken champion, Murray Sueter, had joined Churchill in the dark outer regions of official favour.

TOP: **A Blackburn-built Cuckoo here makes a perfect release. Flying straight and low at about 90 knots made the aircraft vulnerable to return gunfire, however.** ABOVE: **The pioneer carrier HMS *Argus* manoeuvres in the Grand Harbour, not a straightforward task for a high-sided ship in a crosswind. Note the smoke from the problematical exhaust ducting, and the rows of scuttles, a legacy of her passenger liner origins.** LEFT: **Not driven by the same degree of urgency, the US Navy did not develop torpedo aircraft until after World War I. Here, a Liberty-engined Curtiss R-6L releases a weapon in 1922. The Curtiss R-series aircraft with floats or wheeled undercarriage, were also used by the RNAS, but in non-combat roles.** BELOW: **In what turned out to be an evolutionary dead-end Curtiss designed his Model 24 with twin engines to solve the problem of the heavy load of a torpedo. The US Navy ordered nine of the aircraft, designated the CT-1, but only one, seen here, was fitted in 1922 to actually carry a torpedo.**

The *Königsberg* operation

At the outbreak of World War I, several German cruisers were at large as commerce raiders. Operating in the Indian Ocean was the *Königsberg*, which having destroyed two ships, went to ground. On October 30, 1914, she was located by HM cruiser *Chatham*, hiding several miles inside the maze of waterways that form the delta of the Rufiji River, in what was then German East Africa.

Too deep in draught to ascend the river themselves, the *Chatham* and consorts instituted a blockade. The *Königsberg* shifted berth from time to time and, pending arrival of the promised Royal Naval Air Service (RNAS) flight, the senior British officer kept track of her through the services of a civilian pilot. From giving public exhibitions in his Curtiss "hydroplane", this gentleman found himself a temporary commission, his aircraft purchased and, with it, shipped north to the British base on Mafia Island. The aircraft's life was short but a second one was located and brought in.

Meanwhile, following rapid preparation, RNAS Expeditionary Squadron No. 4 arrived in early February 1915, together with two seaplanes and a party that included a Sopwith mechanic and a propeller expert. Presumably, the outfit also included a supply of bombs of up to 23kg/50lb. The RNAS task, however, was primarily to cooperate with naval gunners to encompass the enemy's destruction.

The agency for this was two small river monitors, *Severn* and *Mersey*, which, while drawing only 1.68m/5ft 6in of water,

TOP: **Seen here at Dar-es-Salaam, the 3,455-tonne/3,400-ton light cruiser *Königsberg* was the pre-war station ship for German East Africa. With war, her orders were to use these territories as a base and to act against allied shipping in the Indian Ocean. Having achieved little, however, she inexplicably "went to ground" in the remote and inaccessible Rufiji delta.** ABOVE: **Blockaded by the British, the *Königsberg*'s commanding officer established observation posts and gun positions along the approaches. Colonial duties at the time demanded innovative personnel and *Königsberg* crew are here seen manning a strongpoint.**

mounted two 152mm/6in guns and two 119mm/4.7in howitzers apiece. Laying in Malta, they had to be prepared and towed to East Africa, not arriving until early June.

In the interim, the RNAS had found that in the humid heat their aircraft could get aloft with only the pilot aboard and no observer, bombs, and a minimum amount of fuel. Even then,

ABOVE: The blockading forces made considerable use of aircraft for tracking the *Königsberg*'s movements and, finally, for spotting. They proved to be highly unreliable in the humid climate and here what appears to be a Short 827/830 is being towed by HMS *Severn*, one of the two small river monitors involved. ABOVE LEFT: One of the Short 827s of the expedition. Note the conspicuous top-mounted radiator and the forest of wire necessary to stiffen the large span of the wings.

they could only be coaxed to an altitude of 457m/1,500ft. Wooden propellers also warped and one aircraft was soon wrecked in a heavy landing. The other simply disintegrated as glue, rubber, and fabric failed in the conditions.

On April 23, three Short seaplanes were unloaded but these, too, were unable to climb sufficiently and all suffered damage from enemy fire; one being shot down.

Following the arrival of the monitors on June 3, four more aircraft were delivered, two Caudrons and two Henri Farmans. All were landplanes and had to be landed over the beach before being manhandled 2.4km/1.5 miles to an improvised air strip hacked out of the jungle by the now considerably enlarged RNAS party and native labour. The machines proved able to attain 1,219m/4,000ft but, again, two were soon lost.

On July 6 the monitors entered the river and, assisted by spotting aircraft, fired indirectly across the jungle. The enemy had long since established observation posts and a lively return fire ensued. Aircraft corrected about 80 of the 600-odd rounds fired by the British, who made three hits, suffering two in return.

Following repair, the monitors returned on July 11, and, after two hours and 200 more rounds, the Germans, low on ammunition, recognized the hopelessness of their situation, and scuttled their ship. Ironically, one of her final shots had brought down the sole remaining spotting aircraft, whose crew was rescued by the *Mersey*.

ABOVE LEFT: Before the *Königsberg* affair, the Germans drafted Bruno Buckner and his Pfalz-built Otto biplane into military service, shown here with Askari guard. ABOVE: Obsolete even by 1914 standards, this German floatplane could have operated under only ideal conditions. BELOW: With no prospect of escape and being systematically reduced by British indirect gunfire, the *Königsberg* was blown up by her own crew. The "petalling" of the shell plating around the two large nearer holes indicate that they were caused by internal explosions.

Arthur Balfour, Churchill's successor as First Lord, later felt able to announce (perhaps a trifle generously) to the War Committee that "the destruction of the *Königsberg* had been due almost entirely to the spotting of Naval aeroplanes".

Naval aviation at Jutland

The long-awaited trial of strength between the British Grand Fleet and the German High Seas Fleet finally came about off Jutland on May 31, 1916. For the former it proved to be a catalogue of disappointment and missed opportunity. On a day of fickle visibility, more and better aerial reconnaissance might well have made a significant difference to the outcome but, in truth, naval aviation was yet too fragile for such a major responsibility.

Admiral Jellicoe's Grand Fleet still had only the *Campania* and *Engadine* for air support and, farcically, the former failed to receive the signal to sail. Incorrectly assumed to be too slow to catch up, she and her ten seaplanes were ordered to remain at Scapa.

The action developed with the battle-cruiser squadrons of Beatty and Hipper heading for each other. Beatty had *Engadine* in company but, aware of the frailties of her aircraft, he refused to commit them to general reconnaissance. Only when the opposing cruiser screens had come into contact was the *Engadine* ordered to put up an aircraft. At 15:08 hours, therefore, "Seaplane No.8359" (a Short 184) took off to make history as the first aircraft to be involved in a naval battle. The pilot, Flight Lieutenant F.J. Rutland, was thereafter known widely as "Rutland of Jutland", and would go on to make a name in naval aviation.

With the cloudbase in places down to 274m/900ft and visibility of 1.6-6km/1-4 miles, Rutland had to get uncomfortably close to the enemy, attracting shrapnel bursts. His observer was able to radio one of the enemy cruisers'

TOP: **What with ineffective anti-aircraft fire and hopelessly inadequate bombs, ships and aircraft of World War I posed little mutual threat.** ABOVE: **Converted from a cross-channel packet, the seaplane carrier HMS *Engadine* became the first warship to launch an aircraft in the course of a naval action. One of her Short 184s is here visible abaft the box-like hangar.**

course changes before, at 15:45 hours, "a petrol pipe leading to the left carburretter [sic] broke". Forced to alight, Rutland "made good the defect with rubber tube" and reported that he could continue, only to be recalled by his ship.

Already too slow to remain in contact with Beatty's hard-pressed squadron, the *Engadine* now completely lost touch with it and played no further active part in the action (although she would encounter the stricken armoured cruiser *Warrior* and, unable to prevent her foundering, took off her entire surviving crew).

Admiral Scheer, commanding the German High Seas Fleet, enjoyed little better support from the Naval Airship Division. His thrust into the North Sea was to have been preceded by a line of five Zeppelins, scouting in a bold arc from southern Norway to a point off East Anglia. Poor visibility and crosswinds so delayed their departure, however, that none would observe any aspect of the daylight action of May 31.

Bent on returning to Wilhelmshaven, Scheer's fleet broke through the tail of Jellicoe's forces during the ensuing night. This triggered a series of desperately fought skirmishes, observed by at least two of a second group of five airships ordered out at dusk. Another, L.11, discovered Jellicoe's main body in the early light of June 1. For about 100 minutes, she held contact, coming under fire from all calibres of gun, at one stage from over 20 ships simultaneously. The bombardment by the frustrated British included main battery fire – "the line of ships could be made out from the muzzle flashes when the ships themselves were invisible". L.11 was not hit but "the

ABOVE LEFT: **Beyond his epic flight at Jutland, Frederick Rutland was decorated for gallantry. His later career was clouded through his subversion by the Japanese and his eventual suicide.** TOP: **Short 184 No. 8359, "the aircraft that flew at Jutland", is here seen alongside her mother ship, HMS** *Engadine*. **Parts of the original aircraft survive to this day at the Fleet Air Arm Museum, Yeovilton.** ABOVE: **A German propaganda postcard purporting to show a British battle cruiser under fire at Jutland.**

passage of the big shells and the bursting of shrapnel nearby caused such heavy vibrations in the framework that it seemed advisable to increase the distance…"

Zeppelin L.11 was, therefore, the only aircraft to contribute significantly to the operation. It is a misfortune of history that, by then, the action was over.

LEFT: **Jutland was, for the British, a material defeat. Realizing, however, that they could never defeat the Grand Fleet in battle, the German High Command was forced to resort to submarine warfare. It was the brutality of this that brought the United States, following several warnings, into World War I. This, on top of privations resulting from the British naval blockade, reduced Germany to despair, revolution and, ultimately, defeat.**

The first naval air strikes

Probably because they themselves lacked experience of large rigids, the British overestimated the capabilities of German Zeppelins, both in reconnaissance and in their capacity to inflict targeted damage by bombing. The scale of the Zeppelin "bogey" is evident in the resources devoted by both the Royal Naval Air Service (RNAS) and the Royal Flying Corps (RFC) in dealing with it.

Thus, on October 25, 1914, not three months into the war, the Harwich Force crept deeply into the Heligoland Bight in order to cover its seaplane carriers, whose objective was the Zeppelin base at Nordholz, near Cuxhaven. A heavy rainstorm was sufficient to prevent their seaplanes rising from water, however and, disgusted at the outcome ("I am sick to death of everything connected with aviation…", wrote Commodore Tyrwhitt to his wife) the force was obliged to withdraw. Taking a broader view, Churchill, the First Lord, noted, "It is no use trying these enterprises with overloaded machines. Either aeroplanes or seaplanes with wheels instead of floats must be used." Probably in these few words lay the genesis of the true aircraft carrier.

As Tyrwhitt awaited a further opportunity, a flight of RNAS landplanes was moved to Belfort whence, on November 21, they flew the 193km/120 miles to the Zeppelin works at Friedrichshafen. Their 9kg/20lb bombs narrowly failed to destroy the new L.7.

On Christmas Day 1914, the Harwich Force was again in the Heligoland Bight where, in totally calm conditions, the three seaplane carriers (*Empress*, *Engadine* and *Riviera*) hoisted out nine aircraft, all Shorts, but of three types. Only seven were

TOP: **Completed in July 1916, the Zeppelin L.31 had a life of just 12 weeks, being shot down by a British fighter. The latter's pilot reported her engulfed in flames, and just evading her "as she shot past me, roaring like a furnace".**
ABOVE: **Bomb damage inflicted upon innocent homes by Zeppelins, as here in Kings Lynn, aroused national anger.**

able to take off and these encountered fog and low cloud over the target area. Just one aircraft located the Nordholz site and its bombs caused no damage.

Nonetheless, the presence offshore of a powerful British force caused considerable German consternation. Tyrwhitt's waiting ships came under bombing and machine gun attack from two seaplanes and a Zeppelin. This, the first example of air attack on hostile warships at sea, caused some excitement but, again, no damage. Extended beyond their endurance, however, only two of the British raiders returned, although the missing crews were eventually recovered.

These disappointments set the tone for other attempts. As Churchill had observed, what was required was to operate landplanes directly from a ship's deck, implicitly with the necessary facilities for landing them on again. However, the development and provision of such would take time.

As an interim measure, the new "large light cruiser" *Furious* was converted in two stages. Between March 1917 and March 1918 she acquired a 69m/228ft flying-off deck forward and a 87m/284ft landing-on deck aft. With hangar space below for up to 16 landplanes, elevators and a rudimentary arrester system, she embodied the major features of a true aircraft carrier, although turbulence from the remaining superstructure left the landing deck too hazardous to use.

By 1918, ever-larger Zeppelins were able to carry 3.01 tonnes/ 3 tons of bombs, the largest of 300kg/661lb. Raids on England were becoming increasingly damaging and public indignation ran high. The Navy, under pressure to "do something", was now able to deploy the *Furious* against the more-distant Zeppelin facility at Tondern in Schleswig-Holstein.

On July 19, 1918, she duly despatched seven, bomb-armed Sopwith 2F.1 Camels in two flights, separated by ten minutes. The first arrived at 04:30 hours, achieving complete surprise. Two Zeppelins, L.54 and L.60, together with an aerostat, were destroyed by 23kg/50lb bombs. It was history's first successful naval air strike.

ABOVE: **Zeppelins were the direct stimulus for the extraordinary efforts made by the Royal Navy to take high-performance fighter aircraft to sea. Here, ship's routine goes on beside three Sopwith Camels ranged on the foredeck of HMS *Furious*.**
LEFT: **HMS *Furious*' foredeck, looking aft, this time with Sopwith Pups. Note the two mercantile-style posts and derricks for hoisting aircraft from the hangar below. Elevators were fitted only in 1918.**
BELOW LEFT: **On November 21, 1914, four RNAS Avro 504s sortied from a French airfield at Belfort to bomb the Zeppelin factory at Friedrichshafen. One aircraft was lost and the small damage inflicted was outweighed by the consternation caused.**
BELOW: **The wreckage of L.54 and L.60, destroyed by *Furious*' aircraft. The airships burned without exploding and so, incredibly, their enormous shed at Tondern survived, blackened but intact.**

British shipborne aircraft of World War I

As the British nation went to war in 1914 the Royal Naval Air Service (RNAS) operated an eclectic assortment of 78 aircraft types, including 20 of landplane, 12 of seaplane and 7 of non-rigid airship. Still largely experimental, it operated from shore bases, having only in the previous year sent aircraft to sea in HMS *Hermes* for evaluation in manoeuvres.

The functions of the service which had been defined by the Admiralty were observation, scouting and spotting. These duties could be undertaken by small, two-seater seaplanes, whose presence aboard a warship caused minimal impact and which, at least in theory, could use the sea for take-off and recovery, when conditions permitted.

However, the possibilities of using aircraft as torpedo carriers demanded a second category of larger seaplane for, with the low-powered engines available, the accommodation of such a load required far greater wing areas to provide the necessary lift.

From the outset, much of the RNAS' resources were mobilized to assist those of the Royal Flying Corps (RFC) in the defence of home soil against incursions by Zeppelin airships. Operations were, of course, land-based, using high-performance landplanes. Therefore, when the same Zeppelins began to dog the fleet in an observational role, the RNAS turned to solving the problems of operating landplanes from ships. A third category of aircraft had thus been added and modes of operation had been extended from neutral to both offensive and defensive. The problem, however, revolved not about launch but about recovery.

TOP: **Despite its diminutive size – its span was only 7.8m/25.8ft – and low power, the Sopwith Baby served until July 1917, when it was superseded by the Pup.** ABOVE: **Both British and German fleets explored the possibilities of aircraft working with submarines. Here, in May 1916, the E22 trims down to float off two ramp-mounted Sopwith Schneiders, instantly recognizable from their distinctive bull-nosed engine cowling.**

Radio communication between aircraft and ship had been demonstrated up to a range of 145km/90 miles, but the equipment remained fragile and unreliable.

The introduction of the folding wing by the Short brothers made for more compact stowage aboard ship. However, they were detrimental to a biplane's performance and easily removable wings were also tried.

Recreational flying was already popular before the war, with small seaplanes competing for the Schneider Trophy. Sopwith's design for a Schneider competitor provided the basis for his Tabloid. Even loaded, it weighed only 771kg/1,700lb and pioneered the evolution of launch and recovery routines, particularly in the use of flying-off ramps. Development of a more powerful engine saw the Tabloid evolve into the widely used Baby.

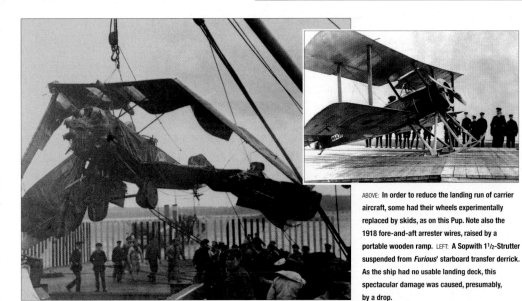

ABOVE: **In order to reduce the landing run of carrier aircraft, some had their wheels experimentally replaced by skids, as on this Pup. Note also the 1918 fore-and-aft arrester wires, raised by a portable wooden ramp.** LEFT: **A Sopwith 1½-Strutter suspended from *Furious'* starboard transfer derrick. As the ship had no usable landing deck, this spectacular damage was caused, presumably, by a drop.**

In contrast, the torpedo-carrying Short 184 appeared enormous, with over twice the wingspan and weighing in at over 3.01 tonnes/3 tons. Equipped with successively uprated engines, about 650 were built by a range of sub-contractors, and they saw service throughout the war.

Sopwith designs predominated for RNAS fighters, with Bristol and Parnall also of note. Introduced late in 1915, Sopwith's 1½-Strutter set a new standard, serving either as a two-seat fighter or as a single-seat bomber.

From early in 1916, the smaller Sopwith Pup complemented the 1½-Strutter. Agile, but with a low landing speed, the Pup served widely with the fleet. In turn, however, it was superseded by the 2F.1 Camel. Slightly larger and more powerful, the Camel had a greater useful payload and two forward-firing machine-guns.

By April 1918, when the RNAS and RFC were amalgamated into a single, unified Royal Air Force (RAF), over 100 aircraft were being carried by cruisers and capital ships, the Sopwith Cuckoo torpedo aircraft was in service and a new, anti-submarine role had been added.

ABOVE: **Out of her element; a Fairey Campania at a Royal Naval Air Station. As the name implies, the aircraft was designed specifically to operate from the ship of that name. Note the four-bladed propeller.**

Typical British shipborne aircraft of World War I

	Wing span	Speed	Power	Machine-guns	Payload
Sopwith Schneider	7.8m/25ft 8in	140kph/87mph	75kW/100hp	1	29.5kg/65lb
Sopwith Baby	7.8m/25ft 8in	161kph/100mph	97kW/130hp	1	59kg/130lb
Short 184	19.4m/63ft 6in	143kph/89mph	194kW/260hp	1	236kg/520lb
Fairey Campania	18.8m/61ft 8in	137kph/85mph	205kW/275hp	1	59kg/130lb
Sopwith 1½-Strutter	10.2m/33ft 6in	164kph/102mph	97kW/130hp	1	118kg/260lb
Sopwith Pup	8.1m/26ft 6in	180kph/112mph	60kW/80hp	1	29.5kg/65lb
Sopwith 2F.1 Camel	8.2m/26ft 11in	200kph/124mph	112kW/150hp	2	45kg/100lb
Sopwith Cuckoo	14.2m/46ft 9in	167kph/104mph	149kW/200hp	0	386kg/850lb

Rigid airships after World War I

For navies other than the German, the large rigid was very much a useful-looking invention that never found an application. Following the failure of its first effort in 1911, the Royal Navy did not begin again until 1914, its technology now well behind that of Germany. The first, R.9, went operational in April 1917 and, between then and 1919, when the Admiralty decided that no more would be built, a total of ten was produced, all considered experimental.

In 1918, R.23 was the first to carry its own defensive fighter aircraft. R.31 and R.32 were built to German Schütte-Lanz principles but the laminated wood frames were heavy and difficult to fabricate. R.33 onwards followed closely the design of the captured Zeppelin L.33, the R.34 making a celebrated first-ever double crossing of the Atlantic in July 1919.

Although a conference of December 1918 minuted that rigids were still considered to be valuable for fleet reconnaissance, the general lack of clarity over manning and responsibility following the establishment of the unified Royal Air Force in the previous April, led the Admiralty to cease further development. Some existing rigids soldiered on through the 1920s but never progressed beyond the experimental stage for military application. The R.101 disaster of October 1930 finished British involvement for good.

American naval aviation may be said to date from October 7, 1913, with the establishment by the Secretary of the Navy of a board to "prepare a comprehensive plan for the organization of a Naval Aeronautic Service". Although an unspecified "fleet

TOP: The Armstrong Whitworth-built R.33 was a straight copy of the German L.33, which force-landed and was burned-out on the Essex coast. With the Admiralty losing interest in airships in 1919, the craft was transferred to the Air Ministry. ABOVE: The control car of the USS *Akron* was a beautiful example of American 1930s streamlined styling.

dirigible" was listed as a requirement from the outset, resistance by many to "big bags" kept wartime dirigibles to non-rigids.

A more specific requirement of November 1916 nonetheless specified one "experimental Zeppelin" for which the starting point would prove to be the acquisition of the German L.49,

LEFT: **Zeppelin technological know-how was used by Goodyear in the design and construction of the USS** *Akron* **(seen here) and** *Macon*. **Giant airship hangars became an architectural form in themselves.**

ABOVE: **To explore the possibilities of airship co-operation with the fleet, the US Navy fitted the oiler** *Patoka* **with basic facilities, including a mooring mast, as depicted on this modern postage stamp.**

BELOW: **Both to extend visual reconnaissance range and for a measure of protection, the** *Akron* **and** *Macon* **carried the compact Curtiss F9C/09C Sparrowhawk. Carried within the airship's envelope, the aircraft could be lowered on a trapeze for launch and eventual recovery.**

captured in October 1917. To gain experience a close copy, even down to its Maybach engines, was constructed by the US Navy. Completed as the ZR.1 in 1923, but named USS *Shenandoah*, the craft was something of a disappointment. This was due mainly to her being inflated with helium, a safe gas but not as buoyant as the hazardous hydrogen used by the Germans. Vulnerability to weather was, as ever, the greatest danger and the craft was destroyed in a storm in September 1925 due, it was concluded, to ruptured gas cells.

This was already the US Navy's second such disaster. The epic flight of the British R.34 had resulted in the purchase of R.38, designated ZR.2, in 1921. Still on trials with an Anglo-American crew, she crashed in British waters in August 1921 with the loss of most of those aboard.

Delivered in October 1924, the US Navy's third large rigid was built by the Zeppelin company as war reparation. Officially ZR.3, but named USS *Los Angeles*, she operated successfully until retired in 1932.

ZRS.4 and ZRS.5, USS *Akron* and *Macon* respectively, were built by Goodyear jointly with Zeppelin. Their lives, too, were short. *Akron* was completed in 1931 and lost in April 1933, the *Macon* commissioned in 1933 and was lost in February 1935, both being destroyed in storms at sea.

All three later American rigids could launch and recover their own defensive fighter aircraft but, by the 1930s, they no longer had any military application. With the demolition of the *Los Angeles* in 1939 the large rigid airship, at least as a vehicle of war, passed into history. Feared, misunderstood, over-evaluated, it had proved to be an evolutionary dead-end for naval aviation.

ABOVE: **Based on the late Zeppelin L.49 design, the ill-fated USS** *Shenandoah*, **here seen moored to the** *Patoka*'s **mast, was built in the United States. Her buoyancy depended upon helium, giving her an inferior performance.**

37

The Sempill mission and Japanese naval aviation

At the end of the 19th century, British and Russian interests in the Far East differed sharply. The Russians also had differences with Japan which, having defeated China over Korea in 1894–95, was an up-and-coming regional power. Russia and Japan would themselves go to war in 1904–5 but during 1901, they had begun serious negotiations aimed at rapprochement, a development that caused great concern to the British, who feared an alliance between them.

Despite the size of Britain's late-Victorian navy, its resources were not infinite and many of its ships were far from up to date. Its representation in the Far East could probably have matched that of the Russians but not in combination with the Japanese who, in defeating the Chinese at the Battle of the Yalu, had demonstrated their ability to successfully fight a "modern" naval action.

Thus, with the first signs of Russo-Japanese understanding in 1901, the British made discrete diplomatic moves to pre-empt any formal treaty. The result, signed on January 30, 1902, was an Anglo-Japanese agreement, valid initially for five years. The new alliance agreed, inter alia, that if either were to be

TOP: **Dating from the turn of the century, the *Idzumo* (seen here) and her sister *Iwate* were 9,906-tonne/9,750-ton armoured cruisers from the renowned Elswick yard of Armstrong Whitworth. Following long and useful careers they were destroyed together at Kure by US naval aircraft in July 1945.** ABOVE: **With the virtual annihilation of a Russian squadron at Tsushima in May 1905, Japan became the primary sea power of the western Pacific. In a classic Japanese rendering, a Russian capital ship is overwhelmed by gunfire.**

attacked by a third power, the other would remain neutral. The other would assist if requested only if a fourth power was involved. Thus it was that Britain did not intervene during the Russo-Japanese War of 1904–5, but Japan assisted militarily during World War I.

To Japan's advantage, Britain built her capital ships and trained her personnel to the point where she could proceed independently. In return, the British were content to have a strong Far Eastern ally, allowing the Royal Navy to build up its

RIGHT: **Seen aboard an unidentified carrier, the Nakajima A2N2 of the early 1930s was the first Japanese naval fighter capable of holding its own against any foreign competition. Used extensively against China, it was already obsolescent.**

BELOW: **In order to establish its own naval air arm, the Japanese government sought British assistance. A team of 30 experts, headed by Sir William Forbes-Sempill, here seen second from left, accordingly arrived in Japan in 1921.**

strength in home waters, where the naval race with Germany was gathering momentum. In 1905, both partners were pleased to tighten the terms of the alliance and to renew it for ten years. By this date, however, the United States was viewing Japan as an increasingly unfriendly power, and the new agreement caused considerable disquiet.

In 1914 the Japanese Navy modified the *Wakamiya* similarly to the early Royal Navy seaplane conversions, later adding a flying-off deck forward, in connection with which it acquired Sopwith Pup fighters.

At the close of hostilities the Japanese made a formal request for British assistance in setting up a naval air arm. Well aware of American hostility, Britain agreed, but only on a "semi-official" basis. Consequently, in 1921, a party of 30 experienced officers travelled to Japan under the leadership of Sir William Forbes-Sempill, late Deputy Director of the new Air Ministry (later Baron Sempill).

Japan, although well behind Britain in naval air aviation technique, was at this time little behind the United States. Her first carrier, *Hosho*, was nearly ready to launch and the British quickly trained-up their charges, so that the first deck landing was made in February 1923.

By this time, strong American opposition to the Sempill mission had been largely instrumental in bringing about the abrogation of the Anglo-Japanese Alliance at the Washington Conference, to the deep offence of the Japanese.

ABOVE: **Consequent to the Sempill mission, Japan acquired the designs of several British aircraft. Here Japanese ratings are seen with a licence-built Sopwith Cuckoo, produced by Mitsubishi as the B1M1 (Type 13).**

The Americans, it transpired, had good reason to distrust the mission for, although it was also a commercial success, with British products and designs being acquired, several of its members, including the renowned "Rutland of Jutland", were successfully subverted by their hosts.

The verdict of history is that, while the Japanese would eventually have caught up with American expertise in the field, the British considerably expedited the process.

The Washington Treaties (1921–22)

The British wartime policy of containment resulted in the German battle fleet being neutralized rather than defeated. In the Mediterranean, much the same could be said of the Austro-Hungarian fleet.

Following Jutland, the Germans switched emphasis to the submarine war but although considerably slowed, their capital ship construction programme still proceeded. Yet to be finished were two *Bayern*-class battleships and four *Mackensen*-class battle-cruisers. Already formidable ships, the latter were even more exaggerated by the conflicting and sketchy intelligence reports. Unsurprisingly, therefore, both the British and Americans embarked on new classes of super-dreadnoughts to counter them.

ABOVE: **The limits of 10,160 tonnes/10,000 tons and 203mm/8in guns set for cruisers by the Washington Treaty unintentionally triggered a "cruiser race". The Japanese *Kumano* was one of a long series that cheated on limitations.**

ABOVE: **Built to implement remaining carrier tons, the USS *Wasp* (here seen commencing builder's trials in late 1939) proved to be too small, her operational capability limited by inadequate speed and flight deck dimensions.**

Determined to be the dominant western Pacific sea power, Japan was not to be outdone, commencing her ambitious "8/8" programme. In the Mediterranean, the French and Italians were building as much in competition with each other as in the necessity to counter the largely inactive Austro-Hungarians.

The wartime alliance of the five powers had appeared solid enough, but this solidarity disguised deep divisions, suspicions, and rivalries that surfaced again all too readily once the primary, mutual threat was overcome. Because of these, and for reasons of national pride, a new and ruinously expensive "naval race" was quickly developing. Sensing that public opinion was broadly hostile, the Americans pre-empted a developing British initiative by inviting all five powers to a Conference on Limitation of Armament. This duly opened in Washington on November 12, 1921, and, on their home ground, the Americans were at a distinct advantage, their code breakers eavesdropping on communications between the delegations and their governments.

The powers surprised even themselves with their readiness to consign their new construction programmes and many existing warships to oblivion. It was agreed that Great Britain, the United States, Japan, France and Italy should limit their

LEFT: Special clauses had to be built into the agreement to allow the oversized *Lexington* and *Saratoga* to be converted to aircraft carriers. *Lexington*'s fine entry is shown well here. ABOVE: The treaties allowed carriers to carry guns of up to 203mm/8in in the mistaken belief that they could, and should, be able to fight off cruisers. The *Saratoga*, which survived the war, had these useless appendages removed in favour of a 127mm/5in dual-purpose armament.

global capital ship tonnage to a fixed ratio of 5:5:3:1.75:1.75, the respective maxima being 533,425:533,425:320,055: 177,808:177,808 tonnes or 525,000:525,000:315,000: 175,000:175,000 tons.

Aircraft carriers were also specifically limited. Defined as vessels of at least 10,160 tonnes/10,000 tons displacement, designed for the *specific and exclusive* purpose of carrying aircraft, they were subject to the same ratio of construction. In this case, the overall tonnages should not exceed 137,166: 137,166:82,300:60,963:60,963 tonnes or 135,000:135,000: 81,000:60,000:60,000 tons. Carriers in existence, or building, on November 21, 1921, would be deemed "experimental" and not count against global totals.

No new carrier could exceed 27,433 tonnes/27,000 tons except that two, of up to 33,530 tonnes/33,000 tons, might be converted from hulls that would otherwise be scrapped. Like capital ships, carriers could be replaced only 20 years after their date of completion.

The Japanese came away resentful. They had pressed for a 10:10:7 ratio but had failed, and their valued Anglo-Japanese Alliance had been diluted to a face-saving but ineffective Four-Power Pact. The British had agreed to this only under considerable pressure from the United States, Australia and New Zealand.

> "I am convinced that a war with Japan is about as likely as a war with Mars." Senator Thomas Walsh of Montana. Debate following President Coolidge's address to Congress, December 1923

Concerned that the Japanese had been given mandate of many ex-German, western Pacific island groups, the Americans negotiated a general non-fortification clause, but with specified exceptions.

By agreeing to the aforementioned ratios Great Britain had also agreed to the abandonment of her traditional naval superiority. Since 1915, the US Navy had been pursuing a "second to none" policy and the British now accepted its demands for parity.

Ratified in 1923 and not to be terminated until 1936, the limitations imposed by the Washington Treaties would have a profound effect on the development and design of aircraft carriers in particular.

ABOVE: The first battleships ever to mount 406mm/16in guns, the two Japanese *Nagato*-class survived the severe culls imposed by the Washington Treaties. Surprisingly, neither was sunk by hostile action.

ABOVE: By concentrating the main battery, the designers of the British *Nelsons* were able to work in thicker armour over a limited area in order to comply with treaty limitations.

Carrier operational philosophies

Argus was the 100-eyed messenger of mythology and the name was entirely appropriate for Britain's first true aircraft carrier whose primary roles had been seen as spotting and reconnaissance as well as flying anti-Zeppelin patrols. So fast was naval aviation developing, however, that by the time of the ship's completion in 1918, mass airborne torpedo attack had been added. The objective here was specifically to neutralize a reluctant enemy fleet in its own ports. The attack never materialized because the necessary numbers of flight decks or aircraft were never available.

As it was accepted that capital ships at sea could not be destroyed by the small warheads of air-dropped 457mm/18in torpedoes, the objective was to use the weapon to slow an enemy sufficiently to be finished by gunfire – as would be demonstrated at Matapan and in the sinking of the *Bismarck*.

Thus, throughout the 1920s, the British carrier remained firmly wedded to the battle fleet, providing long-range reconnaissance, fighter air-cover and limited torpedo-bomber capacity. Only in the 1930s, and probably influenced by the Americans, did the Royal Navy start to look at operating carriers as a group, and independently of the battle fleet.

At the close of the Washington Conference in 1922, the British were well ahead in expertise but their ships were eclectic and not of efficient design. Unlike the United States and Japan, Britain had none of her planned super-dreadnoughts under construction and, therefore, was unable to take advantage of the treaty clause that permitted the conversion of two large hulls.

TOP: **Fairey III Fs aboard HMS** *Courageous* **in the 1930s. Arrester wires were not then in use and these aircraft were not fitted with hooks. Note the "planeguard" destroyer, positioned to assist in the event of a flying accident.**
ABOVE: **As, by far, the largest carriers in the world the USS** *Lexington* **(seen here) and** *Saratoga* **were able to establish and develop operational philosophies based on large air wings and high ship speeds.**

Flanking the Pacific, the fleets of America and Japan surveyed each other with thinly disguised hostility. With respect to the vast distances involved, each thought in terms of long endurance, with operational time extended by replenishment at sea.

The American Plan Orange was based on a battle fleet with a strong amphibious element advancing steadily through the presumed fortified Japanese-mandated island groups in order to recover lost territories. Land-based aerial opposition could be expected but the principal threat emanated from the Japanese fleet, specifically its carriers.

LEFT: Seen here in 1930, the *Saratoga* has much of her air wing ranged on deck. Her battle cruiser origins are evident in the fine stern configuration and the enormous casing that was four funnels in one.
BELOW LEFT: One of the best-known Fleet Air Arm aircraft between the wars was the Fairey III F. Although its first flight was made in 1926 it was not finally phased out until 1940. It served also as a float-fitted seaplane.
BELOW: Within days of Pearl Harbor, Japanese air power again proved its potency when the British capital ships, *Prince of Wales* (seen here leaving Singapore) and *Repulse* were caught without air cover, overwhelmed and sunk off the Malayan peninsula. BOTTOM: Seen here being catapulted, the Japanese Kawanishi E7K (Type 94) was widely used for reconnaissance flying from capital ships and cruisers. Known to the Allies as "Alf", it had a very distinctive engine note.

> "[The Japanese aircraft carrier] must be prepared
> to be impaled as it impales the enemy."
> Japanese Staff College study of November, 1936

The two big *Lexingtons* allowed the US Navy to examine the merits of large air wings and how they should be composed, not least to provide fighter cover for the fleet. Not impressed with the average pilot's ability to hit a freely-manoeuvring warship by either level bombing or torpedo, the Americans pioneered the later deadly technique of dive-bombing.

For the Japanese, the American fleet was the primary target. Much of the reconnaissance role was assumed by the float planes carried aboard all major warships, leaving the carriers the maximum capacity for offensive aircraft.

In order to strike first, the Japanese emphasized range as a paramount factor in aircraft specification. The major barrier to the destruction of an American fleet would then be its carriers, which therefore became the primary objective. Their neutralization meant that the Japanese carriers (fewer than the Americans because of the limitations imposed by the Washington Treaties) would be freed from the need to directly support the battle fleet and could operate either alone or in mutually supportive groups. The increased risk implicit in this mode of operation was understood and accepted.

Interestingly, it was generally accepted wisdom that a carrier's aircraft could not sink a battleship, the torpedo warheads being too small and dive-bombers achieving insufficient dive velocity. Yet, at the outset of the Pacific war, the British *Prince of Wales* and *Repulse* were destroyed primarily by air-dropped torpedoes, although this was achieved with land-based aircraft.

"Billy" Mitchell and the US Navy bombing trials

Unlike the British, who amalgamated Army and Navy aviation into a single, unified service in 1918, the Americans kept theirs separate. To avoid overlapping responsibilities and wasteful duplication, a Joint Army and Navy Board on Aeronautics had been formed in June 1919, but this did not prevent much agitation and politicking from those who supported the formation of an independent air force. These were mainly army personnel and none was more vociferous than Brigadier General William "Billy" Mitchell, despite President Harding's ruling before Congress in April 1921, that aviation was "inseparable from either the Army or Navy".

In January 1921, the Secretary of the Navy had announced that various ex-German warships would be expended as targets to evaluate the effectiveness of aerial bombing. In this, the Army was invited to participate, but an immediate Army demand for ship targets to conduct its own trials was turned down by the Navy as superfluous and unnecessary.

For the Navy, the exercise was designed to establish three major points: the ability of aircraft to locate ships in coastal waters; the probability of hitting ships with bombs while under

TOP: **Last of the "pre-Dreadnoughts", HMS *Agamemnon* was demilitarized post-war and converted into a radio-controlled target ship. In this role, she was employed in both bombing and gunnery trials. She was scrapped in 1926.** ABOVE: **William Mitchell's publicly avowed aim was to erase the US Navy's function of the nation's "first line of defence", arrogating the role to an air force independent of either army or navy. He is seen here (right) with fellow Army flier L.J. Maitland (left).**

weigh; and ascertaining the damage that such hits might inflict. It was therefore imperative that observers board the target vessel after each stage in order to note the cumulative damage and to make recommendations for improvement in future designs.

Mitchell's forte was to use exaggeration and innuendo to gain press publicity. To the Navy's anger he had recently published the unsubstantiated claim that aircraft could "destroy or sink any ship in existence today". With such an unscrupulous operator, the Navy should have been forewarned, but exercised no authority over him.

In June 1921, the bombing trials were staged off the Virginia Capes with the ex-German targets all anchored, stationary and unmanned. To warm up, Navy aircraft sank three U-boats without difficulty. The Army fliers then took some 20 minutes to dispose of a destroyer. On July 18, interest grew with the light cruiser *Frankfurt*, which took aircraft of both services six hours to sink, using 113–272kg/250–600lb bombs.

The "star turn" was the battleship *Ostfriesland*. To allow naval observers to assess progressive damage, it was specified that only two 113–136kg/250–300lb bombs could be dropped at a time and that only one 454kg/1,000lb bomb could be dropped between each inspection.

On the first day, the ship suffered superficial damage from only light bombs. With the second day, however, Mitchell played his trump. Ignoring the rules and all Navy attempts to call a halt, he sent in a continuous stream of aircraft. The ship was hit from low level with three out of five 454kg/1,000lb bombs and an unspecified number out of six 907kg/2,000lb bombs. It was the near misses that sank the ship, their concussive strength staving-in her hull plating.

As there had been no assessment, the *Ostfriesland* sinking proved nothing other than the obvious truth that stationary ships, with incomplete watertight integrity and no damage control parties, might easily be sunk. Any Navy attempt to point this out, however, was drowned by the blare of Mitchell trumpeting to the press and to the world in general that he had been right all along. Spectacular pictures, released to the press, easily misled an uninformed public.

Accepting that Mitchell had staged a coup, the Navy gritted its teeth and got down to the necessary task of improving horizontal and torpedo protection in its ships. Mitchell himself escaped official censure but, while strengthening the case for aircraft carriers, failed to prove that for an independent air force.

ABOVE LEFT: **As a Brigadier General, William "Billy" Mitchell, like Trenchard in Great Britain and Douhet in Italy, was firmly committed to the concept of the heavy bomber as arbiter of future wars. The means by which he pursued his aims were, however, less than scrupulous.** ABOVE: **Dating from 1893, the USS *Indiana* (BB.1) was sunk by the US Navy in explosives trials, simulating bombing, on November 1, 1920. Details were leaked to the international press by, it was believed, Mitchell for his own purposes.** BELOW: **Effectively hijacking the Navy's 1921 bombing trials, Mitchell demonstrated that a battleship (the ex-German *Ostfriesland*) could be destroyed by the concussive mining effect of near misses.** BOTTOM: **The ex-German light cruiser *Frankfurt* was expended in the same series of bombing trials as was the *Ostfriesland*. While the sinkings gained extensive publicity, they proved nothing.**

"Day of the battleship ended."
Newspaper headline after the *Ostfriesland* sinking

Catapults and arresters

Not as ready as the British to accept simple, but effective, flying-off platforms, the Americans worked on catapults from an early stage. From 1916, the British trials ship *Slinger* was evaluating two separate patterns while the US Navy had fixed quarterdeck units on several armoured cruisers. Both programmes were fraught with technical problems, although the USS *North Carolina* made a first under-weigh launch on July 12, 1916.

With the introduction of the through flight deck aircraft carrier there was adequate space for the light aircraft of the time to make rolling take-offs and catapults (or "accelerators") were not fitted to HMS *Argus*. Not completed until 1922, the USS *Langley* had a catapult from the outset. Other patterns were also evaluated but all were removed by 1928 as not being much used.

Arrester gear was a different matter. First tried as transverse wires with deadloads when Ely made his pioneer landing on the *Pennsylvania* on January 18, 1911, it reappeared in 1917 in HMS *Furious'* second rebuild. Although her after flying-on deck was to prove virtually unusable, it was fitted with fore-and-aft arrester wires. These, raised slightly from the deck, were designed to engage in hooks protruding from the skids that served her Sopwith Pups in place of wheeled undercarriages. A transverse wire system with deadloads was also tried out,

ABOVE: **A Curtiss Model F, AB-3, gets airborne from the fixed catapult installation on the afterdeck of the armoured cruiser USS *North Carolina* (CA-12) on July 12, 1916.** BELOW: **Catapulted from the British escort carrier HMS *Empress*, a Grumman Avenger torpedo-bomber releases the strop as it gets airborne.**

but so few landings were attempted that meaningful comparisons could never have been made. As a crash barrier, the *Furious* had a transverse frame strung with vertical cables.

Initially with an arrester system, the *Argus* was quickly fitted with a fore-and-aft wire arrangement, mainly to avoid wind gusts sweeping a landing aircraft over the side. Experiments

RIGHT: **Before aircraft land-on, a crew member sets up the barrier aboard an escort carrier of World War II. The torpedo-like object is a paravane streamed to divert mine cables.**

ABOVE: **Despite the longitudinal arrester wires, this skid-fitted Sopwith Pup has still slewed. Note the barriers used for these trials, the one in the foreground to prevent overshooting, the other (together with the handling party) to prevent the aircraft toppling overboard.**

involved the use of paired ramps that served both to elevate the wires and to slow the aircraft. It was soon found necessary to alter the cables so that they could be lowered to the deck to allow aircraft to taxi freely. A further refinement was introduction of a Landing Signals Officer, to indicate to a pilot when he was engaged with the wires and, by extension, to give him alignment on his approach to touch-down.

Fore-and-aft wires were far from satisfactory, not least in tending to cause aircraft to pitch on their noses. From 1925 until 1931, the Royal Navy abandoned them altogether on carriers. After the close of hostilities in 1918, the Americans no longer enjoyed the result of British experience and, in going their own way, benefited by the early adoption of transverse wire systems, retarded with friction brake-drums.

With no brakes and in the absence of wires, a carrier aircraft relied mainly on headwind to come to a halt. Heavier aircraft demanded the reinstatement of arresters as well as the installation of catapults. In the Royal Navy the first carriers so fitted on a permanent basis were the *Courageous* and *Glorious* in 1934. These were able to launch a 3,175kg/7,000lb aircraft at 56 knots. The aircraft themselves were also by now strong enough to withstand the considerable forces involved.

American carriers placed considerable importance on astern speed so that, in an emergency, aircraft could be landed over the bows. This entailed a second set of arrester wires forward. Large air strikes meant "spotting" ready aircraft on deck, and the technique was to catapult aircraft away until such time as there was sufficient free space to allow the remainder to make the slightly faster rolling take-offs.

TOP: **An artificer conducts a pre-launch check on a catapult. Note how the Japanese dolly runs along a raised track, the wheels of the aircraft's undercarriage remaining on the deck.** ABOVE: **How it should be done. The hook of an F6F Hellcat has engaged with the transverse arrester wire which, damped by hydraulic cylinders, has decelerated the aircraft without damage. Note the light construction of the flight deck on wartime American carriers.**

LEFT: **The only British submarine designed to accommodate and operate an aircraft on a permanent basis was the** *M2* **of 1927. Note the haze of diesel smoke as she charges batteries while laying alongside in Haslar Creek.** ABOVE: **Despite the size of the** *M2,* **her aircraft, the two-seater Parnall Peto, was very small. It is recorded that its crew enjoyed both submarine** *and* **flying allowances!**

ABOVE: **Low forward freeboard made the** *M2*'s **aircraft arrangements vulnerable to damage. Terribly slow to dive, she was difficult to handle once submerged.**

Aircraft aboard submarines

Although by no means "aircraft carriers", submarines of most major fleets have carried aircraft, mainly with a view to extending their limited horizons.

No World War I U-boat appears to have been intended for such a function but, on January 6, 1915, the *U-12* of the Flanders flotilla carried a Friedrichshafen FF-29a floatplane on its casing to a point within range of the English coast. The boat was flooded down to float off the aircraft, which then made a symbolic flight over enemy territory. The risk to boat and crew was considerable, attracting official opprobrium.

This, however, was a time of considerable aviation innovation and several companies – Hansa-Brandenburg, LFG and Heinkel – were moved to build prototypes for use aboard submarines. None entered German service.

After the 1918 armistice, the US Navy acquired German U-boat technology. It was impressed by the big *U-142*-class cruiser submarines, apparently well-suited to Pacific operations. At some stage it appears that a small aircraft had

been considered for these boats and the Americans conducted trials aboard their submarine *S-1*, using a Caspar-Heinkel U-1 floatplane. The results were not encouraging, so plans to incorporate a pressure-tight, topside hangar on the cruiser submarines *V-5* and *V-6* of 1926, were abandoned.

In 1927, the British converted the big minelaying submarine *M2* to carry a specially-built Parnall Peto floatplane. A cylindrical, pressure-tight hangar was built into the forward side of the superstructure, its door opening directly on to the catapult which ran the length of the forward casing. The arrangement was cumbersome, slow in operation and not judged a success. Its complexity and vulnerability probably caused the loss of the boat by foundering in 1932.

The *M2* experiment was quickly taken up by the French who, between 1927 and 1934, built their monster *Surcouf*, for a long time the world's largest submarine. She was large enough to incorporate two 203mm/8in guns into her forward superstructure and, at its after end, a cylindrical hangar for a knocked-down Besson MB.411 "observation seaplane". Although the submarine operated, and was lost, under the Free French flag during World War II, there is no evidence that either aircraft or guns had ever been of significant use.

Ever committed to the deployment of reconnaissance floatplanes from all conceivable platforms, it was the Japanese that most fully exploited the concept of aircraft aboard submarines. Experimentation with a small Heinkel aircraft began as early as 1923. Given folding wings, this design was developed as the Yokosuka E6Y1 and flew from the large minelaying submarine No.48 in 1927.

When other fleets had dropped the practice, the Japanese persevered. In 1935 they produced the little Watanabe E9W1 ("Slim"), superseded in 1941 by the more capable E14Y1 ("Glen"). These were intended for reconnaissance but, as the war moved against the Japanese, a new, offensive role was explored. During 1944, the first of the I-400 class submarines was completed. These dwarfed even the French Surcouf and held the record as world largest until the advent of nuclear power. Their designed function was to attack high-value targets on American soil, using a new, high-performance floatplane, the Aichi M6A1 Seiran. Three of these, plus spares, were accommodated in an enormous cylindrical topside hangar which gave on to a foredeck catapult.

In the event, Japan's desperate straits by 1945 saw the craft used for cargo-carrying. Only two were completed as Seiran carriers, and both of these too late to be of any use.

ABOVE: For a long time the world's largest submarine, the French *Surcouf* was designed around an observation aircraft and a pair of 203mm/8in guns.

ABOVE AND BELOW: During 1923 the US Navy also explored the possibilities of submarines carrying seaplanes. A knock-down Martin MS-1, derived from a wartime German design, was stowed in a pressure-tight canister abaft the conning tower. The facilities were not as elaborate as those of the *M2* but, like the British, the Americans saw little value in the venture and future development was abandoned.

LEFT: Probably the ultimate in aircraft-carrying submarines, the Japanese I-400 class of World War II copied the layout of the British *M2* in that the centrally located pressure-tight hangar gave directly on to a foredeck catapult. As three floatplanes could be accommodated, however, the scale was considerably greater. ABOVE: An I-400 type in profile with an Aichi M6A1 floatplane on the catapult. Note the crane, which could be folded down into the casing, and the 139.7mm/5.5in gun aft.

Inter-war development in carrier aircraft

During 1918–39, the undisputed lead in naval aviation enjoyed by the Royal Navy was emphatically lost to the fleets of the Japanese and the United States. Operating philosophies and, later, ship design resulted in too few aircraft aboard each carrier, so each aircraft design was multi-purpose. For navigation purposes, each usually was at least a two-seater, and most had to be interchangeable between floats and wheeled undercarriage, all of which reduced performance. A cash-strapped Royal Air Force, now responsible for the provision of Fleet Air Arm (FAA) aircraft and personnel, could afford only the minimum of either. By 1939, the FAA was back under naval control but damage already done was sufficient to adversely affect the service's performance during World War II.

British carrier aircraft were defined as spotter/reconnaissance, fighter/reconnaissance and torpedo/bomber (later torpedo-dive-bomber). The run of Sopwith fighters was broken in 1923, when the Camel was superseded by the Fairey Flycatcher. The Fairey III F three-seater spotter/reconnaissance aircraft served until replaced by the Hawker Osprey (fighter/reconnaissance) and the Fairey Swordfish (torpedo/spotter/reconnaissance). Only in 1937 did the FAA receive an effective dive-bomber in its first monoplane, the Blackburn Skua. Its poor performance as a fighter, however, saw it replaced largely by the still-ineffective Fairey Fulmar, with eight guns but insufficient speed.

American naval aviation received a tremendous boost in 1926 when the Morrow Board recommended the acquisition of 1,000 aircraft. Unlike in Britain, naval aviation remained fully under naval control. Aircraft were thus not "navalized" land designs but robust machines designed for the hard life aboard a carrier.

The first fighter *was*, however, modified from an existing design but this, the Boeing FB-2, then progressed to be FB-5 before being replaced in 1928 by the F2B. The series continued until 1937 with the F3B and the well-remembered F4B. From

ABOVE: **Converted from a battleship hull and designed with a single hangar, HMS *Eagle* was beamy and moved comfortably, but could manage barely 21 knots on a continuous basis. The aircraft on the hook is a Fairey III F floatplane.**

1935, Grumman effectively took over the stubby F2F and F3F. In 1940 came the first monoplane fighter, the highly effective Grumman F4F (Wildcat), immediately ordered also by Britain and France.

The first torpedo-bomber, the Curtiss CS, was superseded in 1926 by the Martin T3M, then the T4M before the very similar 204kph/127mph Great Lakes TG.2. In 1937 came the first monoplane torpedo-bomber, the 332kph/206mph Douglas TBD Devastator. All of these could also act in the scouting role.

The first purpose-designed dive-bomber, the Great Lakes BG-1, entered service in 1934 and could carry a 454kg/1,000lb bomb. In 1938 came the monoplane Northrop BT, which was refined to the Douglas SBD Dauntless by 1941.

Starting with no experience, the Japanese acquired mainly British designs. The Nakajima A1N1 (Type 3) was thus a Gloster-designed fighter, but was improved by 1930 to the A2N1 (Type 90). Replacements passed successfully through

ABOVE: **Designed as a fighter/dive-bomber, the Blackburn Skua was hopeless in the former role but, in its limited existence in the latter, made history by sinking the German cruiser *Königsberg* in Bergen in April 1940, the first major warship to be destroyed by dive-bombing.**

ABOVE: **Introduced in 1936, the Fairey Swordfish has been dismissed by too many wartime writers as "antiquated". It was, however, an aircraft with very special qualities, proving lethal to surface ship and submarine alike. Particularly, Swordfish are associated with Taranto, Matapan and the *Bismarck* pursuit.**

LEFT: **Properly known as the Curtiss Falcon, a multi-purpose dive-bomber/fighter/observation aircraft, the F8C became firmly associated with the first role, adopting the popular name of Helldiver.** BELOW: **One of a trend to "tubby" fighters, the Grumman F2F entered carrier service in 1935, but in 1938 was superseded by the slightly enlarged and more powerful F3F. This had departed squadron service by the end of 1941.**

the 352kph/219mph A4N1 (Type 95) to the first monoplane fighter, the Mitsubishi A5M4 (Type 96) "Claude" to the legendary A6M (Type O) "Zeke" or "Zero".

The first dedicated attack bomber was the Mitsubishi B1M1 (Type 13) which could carry a 457mm/18in torpedo or 500kg/ 1,102lb of bombs at 209kph/130mph. Its 1930 replacement, the B2M1 (Type 89), also a Blackburn design, carried a heavier load but was unreliable. It was superseded in succession by the smaller Yokosuka B3Y1 (Type 92), its derivative, the B4Y1 (Type 96) "Jean" and, by the outbreak of war, the monoplane Nakajima B5N2 (Type 97) "Kate".

As a first dive-bomber, the Japanese licence-built the Heinkel He 66 from 1934 as the Aichi D1A1 (Type 94), refining it to the D1A2 (Type 96) "Susie". The Aichi D3A1 (Type 90) "Val" was the first monoplane dive-bomber, serving well into World War II, but proving vulnerable to American fighters.

ABOVE: **The Japanese became interested in dive-bombing in 1930 and, in 1933, acquired rights to the German Heinkel He 66. This was developed successively as the Aichi D1A1, then the improved D1A2 (seen here). Known to the Allies as "Susie", this rugged dive-bomber saw second line war service.** LEFT: **With echoes of a Fairey III D, the Mitsubishi B1M series was conceived by British designers in Japanese employ.**

Armoured versus "open" construction

With tight limitations on individual and global carrier displacement imposed by the 1921–22 Washington Treaties, hard decisions had to be made with respect to carrier design.

The British took the view that a carrier's aircraft comprised her only offensive asset and, therefore, required the maximum reasonable protection. All aircraft were thus to be accommodated internally, protected above from bombing and, to the side, from shellfire. In the early days, the bombing threat was comparatively slight but, with a carrier still expected to be engaged in opposed reconnaissance, that from cruiser gunfire was real. For purpose-designed ships (as opposed to conversions) this led to an arrangement where the flight deck constituted the main strength deck, the hull being continuously plated up to that level and creating an enclosed "box" hangar.

The Americans and, to a lesser extent, the Japanese were influenced by the sheer size of their initial carrier conversions and the obvious advantages that large air wings would confer in a long-range Pacific war. Deck parks were accepted at an early stage but, to maximize below-deck capacity, an "open" design predominated. In this, the hangar (or lower hangar) deck became the strength deck, the hangar walls and flight deck being a relatively light structure that added little to structural strength. Because of their greater depth, British-style hulls suffered lower stresses and could be made lighter. On the other hand, in order to ship an acceptable number of aircraft, British

ABOVE: **The surprisingly elegant lines of HMS** *Ark Royal* **(II) are seen to advantage following her launch on April 13, 1937. Still in position is the poppet that supported the bows during launch.** BELOW: **The launch of the USS** *Ranger* **(CV-4) in February 1933. Her very fine lines are apparent, as are the light flight deck substructure and the apertures for three elevators and two groups of three folding funnels.**

LEFT AND BELOW: Views of *Illustrious* (left) and *Ark Royal* (below) show several points to advantage. Vertical protection of hangar walls was set inboard to allow for a large number of side apertures to accommodate boats, harbour handling arrangements, etc. The aerial view shows how the British arrangement of armament, although giving good all-round coverage, intrudes into the flight deck area.

carriers required two hangars. The resulting high freeboard kept the flight deck drier but placed it at a height where its weight, hence thickness, became critical.

British operational doctrine between the wars was expressed in terms of small, six-aircraft formations, for which the carriers were adequate. Elsewhere, full deck-load strikes called for much pre-warming of aircraft engines. This had largely to be conducted below and only an open design could provide the necessary ventilation.

From the early 1930s, the dive-bomber emerged as a major threat to carriers. Level bombing from a considerable height could result in horizontal protection being penetrated by relatively small bombs, but accuracy was low. Dive-bombing was accurate and the lower-level release of the bomb was compensated by its far larger weight.

The need to protect against this weapon had a dramatic effect on British carrier design. The 1937 *Ark Royal* (II) had two hangars, a light splinter-proof flight deck, an armoured lower hangar deck and an air wing of 54 aircraft. The following 1940 *Illustrious* had a flight deck armoured over the extent of the hangar, but only one hangar and an air wing of 36. Their size and displacements were comparable. The lower flight deck of the "armoured" carrier made it wetter, while the heavier elevators made operations slower.

The contemporary American view was that the British approach was too "defensive" and that the price to be paid in aircraft numbers was unacceptable.

Wartime experience duly showed British ships' resistance to both dive-bombing and kamikaze strikes, where American and Japanese carriers succumbed or were disabled by comparatively few hits. Conversely, the latter's carriers, with their large air wings, consistently inflicted far more damage.

There is, of course, no simple answer and, as with most ship design, the answer lies in compromise. Sufficient to say that British fleet carriers designed following war experience (*Ark Royal* (III), *Malta*) did not change in philosophy whereas the American equivalents (*Coral Sea*) did, with a corresponding huge rise in displacement.

> "[T]he British gave up almost 50 per cent of their aircraft capacity to obtain partial protection of the carrier."
> US Navy liaison officer aboard HMS *Formidable*, June 12, 1941

ABOVE: As an experiment in small fleet carrier design the USS *Ranger* (CV-4) was not a success and was not repeated. Note the funnel arrangements.
BELOW: The great hull of the USS *Midway* (CVB-41) takes shape at Norfolk, Virginia. Larger, and more, aircraft, together with a measure of protection demanded a leap in size compared with the preceding Essex class.

LEFT AND BELOW: **An old postcard invites a visit to the great Italian naval base at Taranto, an invitation taken up by the British Mediterranean Fleet in November 1940. The reconnaissance photography shows clearly how the arsenal fringes the grid of the old town, how ships anchored in the shallow harbour are vulnerable to torpedo attack, and how smaller vessels moored in a row, "Mediterranean fashion", make an excellent target for a bombing pass.**

BELOW: **Completed in 1915, the *Conte di Cavour* was reconstructed to modern standards in 1933–37. Although salvaged following her sinking at Taranto, she required such extensive refurbishment that she saw no further action.**

Taranto

During 1917, the Royal Navy developed plans to hit the German High Seas Fleet in its base with 120 torpedo aircraft. The plan never materialized but the concept survived. In 1938, therefore, with the prospect of war becoming a probability, the British Mediterranean Fleet trained for a moonlight air strike against the Italian fleet in its base at Taranto. In November 1940, the raid took place but on a far more modest scale than envisaged, for the Royal Navy never had sufficient carriers, of which two had already been lost.

Late in the evening of November 11, the new "armoured" carrier *Illustrious* was positioned off the Greek coast, some 274km/170 miles from Taranto. She had a close escort, with distant cover being provided by the Alexandria-based Mediterranean Fleet. The carrier's air group had been reinforced by aircraft from the elderly *Eagle*, temporarily inoperative following a severe shaking by high-level bombing. Even so, the combined strike force comprised just 21 Swordfish biplanes, organized in two waves of 12 and 9 respectively.

> "Manoeuvre well executed."
> Signal from C-in-C Mediterranean Fleet to HMS *Illustrious* on her rejoining the fleet the morning after the Taranto raid

Taranto had been under almost hourly surveillance by Malta-based reconnaissance aircraft and, suspecting a reason, the Italians were on high alert. For the raiders, the primary targets were the five battleships reported anchored in the outer harbour, the Mar Grande, protected by anti-torpedo net defences and by barrage balloons. The night selected would silhouette the targets against a three-quarter moon but, in case of overcast weather, the torpedo aircraft would be accompanied by flare-droppers. Further aircraft would provide distraction by dive-bombing ships and facilities in the neighbouring inner harbour, the Mar Piccolo.

In what was known as Operation "Judgement", the *Illustrious* launched her two formations at 20:40 and 21:30 hours. The first achieved surprise but the defences were quickly in action – Italian guns claiming to have fired 13,500 rounds. The cables of the barrage balloons were a considerable hazard to the torpedo aircraft, which came in

LEFT: **Like moths to a flame,** *Illustrious*'s **Swordfish orbit as they prepare to land-on. Note how flight deck area is maximized by a pronounced overhang at either end.**

ABOVE: **Dating from 1915, the extensively modernized** *Caio Duilio* **lacked effective sub-division and was put on the bottom by a single 457mm/18in torpedo. She returned to service within a year. The extra elevation of her modernized 320mm/ 12.6in armament allowed it to outrange the 381mm/ 15in of equally venerable British battleships.**

"Twenty aircraft had inflicted more damage upon the Italian fleet than was inflicted upon the German High Sea Fleet in the daylight action at the Battle of Jutland."
Admiral Cunningham, C-in-C Mediterranean Fleet, writing of the Taranto raid

very low over the outer breakwater, but the open cockpits of the Swordfish and its superb low-speed performance allowed the pilots to see and avoid them in the confused illumination of flares, searchlights and exploding ordnance.

Only about one-third of the planned anti-torpedo netting was actually in place, but this hung to a depth of nearly 10m/33ft, sufficient to protect the battleships from torpedoes fitted with standard contact pistols. However, the British were using newly developed duplex pistols, which would also be actuated by a target's magnetic field if the torpedo were set to run deep, below the target's keel and, by definition, beneath the protective net.

Low speed allowed the well-trained Swordfish aircrews to take their time and to launch accurately. Of eleven torpedoes expended, three hit the battleship *Littorio*, one the *Conte di Cavour* and another the *Caio Duilio*. Surprisingly, considering the small warheads of 457mm/18in torpedoes, all three were put on the bottom. The anchorage was so shallow that none was submerged to much more than upper deck level. All were therefore salvaged, but this operation and subsequent refitting took six months and the *Cavour* saw no further service.

For the loss of just two aircraft, a most economical raid had totally changed the balance of naval power in the Mediterranean at a critical juncture where the French fleet, expected by the British to be a powerful ally, had been immobilized by the unexpected collapse of France and the resulting armistice with the Germans.

ABOVE: **Brand new, the 15-inch battleship** *Littorio* **succumbed to three 457mm/ 18in torpedoes. She re-entered service in August 1941. The Italians riposted brilliantly in December 1941, using "human torpedoes" to put the British battleships** *Queen Elizabeth* **and** *Valiant* **on the bottom of Alexandria harbour.**

The *Bismarck* operation

One of the earliest functions prescribed by the British Admiralty for the Fleet Air Arm was that of slowing an enemy ship or formation to permit a decision to be reached by a classic gun action. Two such successful examples are afforded by the *Bismarck* episode and the battle of Matapan.

On May 21, 1941, the new German battleship *Bismarck*, accompanied by the heavy cruiser *Prinz Eugen*, sailed from Norway to raid commerce in the North Atlantic. Correctly guessing their intentions, the Admiralty quickly made fleet dispositions to intercept them.

In thick weather, the pair passed north of Iceland but on entering the Denmark Strait (between Iceland and Greenland) late on May 23, they were located by the patrolling cruisers *Norfolk* and *Suffolk*. These tracked and reported their progress southward, enabling British heavy units to intercept them early on the 24th. These, the veteran battle cruiser *Hood* and the brand new battleship *Prince of Wales*, opened fire at 05:53 hours. At 06:00 hours, with the range down to about 12,802m/14,000 yards, the *Hood* was destroyed by a massive explosion. Not yet battleworthy, the *Prince of Wales* broke off the action.

Herself damaged, *Bismarck* signalled her intention to make for a French port. The British cruisers remained in touch, their tracking reports bringing the carrier *Victorious* (also brand new) into range late on the 24th. At 22:00 hours she launched nine

TOP: **HMS *Ark Royal* (II) with one of her Swordfish squadrons. During the *Bismarck* operation, both *Ark Royal* and *Victorious* deployed two Swordfish squadrons. Their admirable low-speed characteristics enabled their carriers to operate them safely in borderline weather conditions.** ABOVE: **The destruction of the battle cruiser HMS *Hood*, unofficial flagship of the Royal Navy, triggered a massive hunt to avenge the loss.**

partially-trained Swordfish, which attacked by radar just after midnight. They obtained one torpedo hit that caused little damage.

The *Bismarck* then made radical changes of course to disguise the detachment of the *Prinz Eugen*. These also caused the cruisers to lose touch. It was now 03:00 hours on the 25th, when Admiral Tovey with the battleship *King George V* and the *Victorious* were barely 161km/100 miles distant.

LEFT: World War I had adequately demonstrated that sending warships on commerce-raiding cruises was an uneconomic proposition. The loss of the *Bismarck*, not long after that of the *Graf Spee*, proves that some lessons are never learned. ABOVE: In the conditions, the *Bismarck* proved to be a difficult target for aerial torpedoes. A single hit at a critical point was, nonetheless, sufficient to slow her and see her brought to battle. BELOW LEFT: The pleasing profile of the *Bismarck* was so similar to that of her consort, the heavy cruiser *Prinz Eugen*, that British gunlayers were confused. BELOW: Admiral Somerville's Force H, formed around the battle-cruiser *Renown*, the carrier *Ark Royal* (II) and the cruiser *Sheffield* operated with success out of Gibraltar. As such it was able to intervene decisively in the apprehension of the fugitive *Bismarck*.

Throughout the 25th the British searched blindly, and only at 10:30 hours on the following morning did a patrolling RAF Coastal Command PBY Catalina re-establish contact. The *Bismarck* was under 1,127km/700 miles from Brest and had to be slowed.

Fortunately, the Gibraltar-based Force H had been ordered north and found itself right on the German's projected track. With the group was the carrier *Ark Royal*, whose own aircraft made visual contact by 13:00 hours on the 26th. The cruiser *Sheffield* was detached to sight her and continue tracking.

In a full gale and low, thick overcast weather, *Ark Royal* despatched 14 Swordfish at 14:50 hours. An hour later these attacked blind by radar, only to discover that their target, mistakenly, was the *Sheffield*, then 32km/20 miles from the *Bismarck*. By dint of skilful manoeuvring, the cruiser survived.

It was not until 19:10 hours that a second strike, of 15 Swordfish, could be launched. In truly appalling weather conditions they commenced their attack at 20:47 hours, scoring two hits. One damaged *Bismarck*'s steering and a propeller shaft. Slowed and with her manoeuvrability impaired, she was now doomed.

Throughout the night of the 26th–27th British destroyers worried at her but were unable to inflict further torpedo damage. Before daybreak, however, Admiral Tovey arrived with the battleships *King George V* and *Rodney*. Waiting until full daylight, Tovey divided his ships and pounded the *Bismarck* to a wreck. Refusing to sink, she was despatched by a cruiser's torpedoes.

The *Hood* had been avenged but it had taken the combined efforts of seven battleships, two aircraft carriers and twelve cruisers to bring the *Bismarck* to book, and then only by virtue of a single aircraft torpedo.

The Battle of Matapan

During March 1941, the British intervention in Greece generated a succession of convoys from the south and, following sustained pressure from their German allies, the Italians despatched a battle group. Sailing on March 26, Admiral Iachino wore his flag in the battleship *Vittorio Veneto* that headed towards eastern Crete in a loose formation, which included 6 heavy cruisers, 2 light cruisers and 13 destroyers.

Aware of the enemy foray, the C-in-C Mediterranean Fleet, Admiral Cunningham, temporarily suspended all convoy movements and sailed late on the 27th with his three veteran battleships, the aircraft carrier *Formidable* and nine destroyers. Already at sea near Crete were his "light forces", four light cruisers and four destroyers. These were ordered to rendezvous with Cunningham late on the 28th but at 06:30 hours that day, they were sighted by the *Veneto*'s catapulted search aircraft. Assuming this to be an isolated group, Iachino decided to engage.

At about 08:00 hours a reconnaissance aircraft from the *Formidable* was reporting the scattered elements of the Italian force at about the same time as three of its heavy cruisers established visual contact with the British light forces. These, outranged, went about and headed south-eastward at maximum speed to draw the enemy on to Cunningham's main body.

Suspicious, the Italians broke off and headed off westward. The British light cruisers complied, only to find that they had been lured on to the *Veneto*.

TOP: **The *Vittorio Veneto*, Italian flagship at Matapan. Although badly damaged by a Swordfish torpedo, she was not sufficiently slowed to allow the veteran British battleships to make an interception.**
ABOVE: **A later British air strike missed the *Veneto*, the primary target, but hit and stopped the heavy cruiser *Pola*. This brought about the battle of Matapan.**

The Italian flagship opened fire at 10:56 hours and, now under 381mm/15in shellfire, the British made a contact report and again fell back. Fortuitously, at this point six *Formidable* Swordfish made a first attack on the *Veneto*. It was unsuccessful but persuaded the Italian admiral to abandon his operation. At 11:30 hours, therefore, he too ceased fire and turned westward for home.

The far slower British battle group, some 105km/65 miles astern but apparently unsuspected, appeared unlikely to be able to intercept Iachino. Then, at 15:20 hours, five more Swordfish from the *Formidable*, supported by high-level RAF bombers from Crete, put a torpedo into the *Veneto*'s port quarter. Still about 644km/400 miles from Taranto, the battleship slowed to 10, then 15 knots.

LEFT: **Sister ship to the *Illustrious*, the *Formidable* flew the critical air strikes that brought about the battle. Like the *Illustrious*, the *Formidable* also survived a later ordeal by dive-bombing that would have destroyed lesser ships.** BELOW: **The widely separated funnels of the Italian cruiser *Pola* show that her machinery spaces were likewise separated. However, a single 457mm/ 18in torpedo was sufficient to bring her to a halt.**

Further air attacks from Crete inflicted no further damage on the enemy but, by 19:00 hours, Cunningham had closed to about 72km/45 miles. To protect the flag the whole Italian force was now tightly grouped and steaming in five columns. Between them, they put up a concentrated barrage of fire when, between 19:35 and 19:45 hours, eight *Formidable* and two Crete-based Swordfish attacked out of the failing light. Only one torpedo found a target, bringing the heavy cruiser *Pola* to a complete halt.

Not appreciating Cunningham's proximity, Iachino pressed on but directed the *Pola*'s two divisional colleagues, *Zara* and *Fiume*, together with four destroyers, to stand by her.

Formidable's aircraft had wrongly claimed to have again hit the *Veneto* so when, at 20:30 hours, the light cruiser *Ajax* reported a radar contact on a stationary ship, Cunningham assumed that it was the Italian flagship which, in reality, was 80km/50 miles further on and making 19 knots.

At 22:30 hours, assisted by radar, the British battleships were just 2,743m/3,000 yards from the preoccupied Italians. Instantaneously, searchlights snapped on and heavy salvoes crashed into the *Zara* and *Fiume* which, with their guns still trained fore-and-aft, were converted in to blazing wrecks. Accompanying destroyers finished off the still-immobile *Pola* and two Italian destroyers.

Although Cunningham was unhappy at the *Veneto*'s escape, what came to be known as the Battle of Matapan established a moral ascendancy that the Italians were increasingly reluctant to challenge. Their fleet remained a powerful threat, but suffered from a deficiency in bold leadership.

ABOVE: **A training session aboard a British escort carrier. The warrant officer and pilot discuss the arming of the torpedo below the Swordfish while crew lie awaiting the order to remove chocks. Note the American-style decking and helmets.** BELOW: **Commander-in-Chief, Mediterranean Fleet at the time of Matapan, Sir Andrew Cunningham is seen here, as Admiral of the Fleet, inspecting the crew of a cruiser. Note the torpedo tubes on the left.**

Pearl Harbor

TOP: **Destroyed by explosion, the wreck of the battleship** *Arizona* **burns at her berth in Pearl Harbor. Searing images such as this galvanized the United States from its isolationist detachment.** ABOVE: **Standard torpedo-bomber with the Japanese carrier force, a Nakajima B5N2,Type 97 "Kate" leaves the deck of the** *Shokaku.* **Its torpedo was specially adapted to function in the shallow waters of the American base.**

Aware that any war with the United States would be decided principally on the question of sea control, the Japanese decided to make a pre-emptive strike on the US Pacific Fleet at its forward base of Pearl Harbor. Located on the small Hawaiian island of Oaho, the base was effectively immune to attack except from the air.

All six available Japanese fleet carriers were unobtrusively assembled at a remote anchorage before departing with their escort on November 26, 1941. Having crossed 5,633km/3,500 miles of the lonely north Pacific, the force commanded by Vice Admiral Nagumo Chuichi arrived at its launch point, 443km/275 miles north of its objective, at 06:00 hours on December 7. A first strike of 40 torpedo-bombers, 49 high-level bombers, 51 dive-bombers and 43 fighters was immediately despatched.

Oahu is irregular and mountainous, with Pearl Harbor on its south coast. The first wave approached down the western side, some of its number peeling away to suppress potential interference from the several military airfields.

The island had been well reconnoitred, the plan well rehearsed. It being a Sunday morning, the bulk of the fleet was alongside for the weekend. To the approaching enemy the view was as had been expected, the anchorage dominated by the line of seven battleships, berthed in pairs. There had been no formal declaration of war and surprise was absolute. In the absence of opposition, the aircraft arrived at 07:55 hours and were able to select their targets with deadly precision.

Armour-piercing bombs, fashioned from heavy naval projectiles, drilled through the battleships' horizontal protection, all but one being hit. Specially developed, shallow-running torpedoes lanced the calm harbour waters to devastate all five capital ships on the outer berth. Only rudimentary anti-aircraft armaments were mounted at this time, and return fire was uncoordinated. At each of the airfields and naval air stations aircraft, parked neatly in rows, were wrecked by bombing and low-level strafing.

At shortly before 09:00 hours the first strike was pulling out as the second arrived, having skirted the island's eastern side. Comprising 54 high-level bombers, 81 dive-bombers and

> "[A]n unwarranted feeling of immunity from attack... seems to have pervaded all ranks at Pearl Harbor, both Army and Navy."
> Admiral Ernest J. King, Chief of Naval Operations to
> Naval Court of Inquiry, November 6, 1944

ABOVE: Dry dock No.1 at Pearl Harbor after the attack. The battleship *Pennsylvania* was only lightly damaged but, in the foreground, the destroyer *Downes* is sitting on the blocks, flooded, while the destroyer *Cassin* has toppled. The smoke is from a distant fire.

ABOVE: Smoke from burning ships forms a backdrop to the devastation at Naval Air Station, Ford Island. An undamaged PBY Catalina patrol amphibian is parked at left. LEFT: Architect of the attack was Admiral Yamamoto Isoroku. An intelligent and gifted leader, he undertook the task only with the gravest of misgivings. He knew that Japan could sustain only a short war. BELOW: "Battleship Row" under attack. From left to right: *Nevada*, *Vestal* outboard of *Arizona*, *West Virginia* outboard of *Tennessee*, *Maryland* outboard of *Oklahoma*, and *Neosho*.

36 fighters, this force again hit the already stricken "Battleship Row" and the dockyard. The airfields took a further working-over and few American aircraft were able to get airborne.

By 09:45 hours the attack was over. With losses of only 29 of their number, Nagumo's jubilant pilots were returned, still unopposed, to their waiting carriers. They left behind 18 sunken ships, 4 of them battleships. The US Navy had lost 92 aircraft, the Army 96 and over 2,300 servicemen were dead.

The attack on Pearl Harbor was universally condemned as an act of treachery yet, whatever the ethics of the Japanese action, it is undeniable that as a military coup the attack was boldly conceived and efficiently executed. However, it was not a total success. The battleships were elderly yet still commanded too much respect at a point when it was apparent to many that the aircraft carrier had already assumed capital ship status. The enemy's concentration on the battleships resulted in most of the dockyard facilities and oil storage area being left unscathed. By the removal, albeit temporarily, of the battleships from the order of battle, the US Navy was obliged to accept its carriers as more relevant to its interests than the battle line.

Most significantly, Nagumo had struck on a day when no American carriers were in port. They survived through being at sea and would eventually prove to be his nemesis.

The Doolittle Raid and the
Battle of the Coral Sea

TOP: **Army Air Force B-25s crowd the deck of the carrier USS *Hornet*. Their wingspan was too great to allow them to be struck below, so sixteen was the maximum that could be handled. Note the escorting cruiser *Nashville* in the background.** ABOVE: **In a 1992 re-enactment aboard the USS *Ranger*, a veteran B-25 lifts off without difficulty. It may be remembered, however, that where the *Ranger*'s flight deck measures 319 x 72.5m (1,047 x 238ft), that of the *Hornet* was 251.3 x 33.4m (824.8 x 109.5ft) and encumbered with other aircraft.**

Carriers had inflicted the pain on Pearl Harbor and it was by carriers that the United States responded. Sixteen Army B-25 Mitchell bombers, led by Lt Col James H. Doolittle, were transported across the Pacific on the *Hornet*'s flight deck and on April 18, 1942, were launched at long range. Hitting Tokyo and three other cities, they flew on to Chinese airfields. Immortalized as "Thirty Seconds over Tokyo", the raid caused only symbolic damage but huge embarrassment to the Japanese authorities. It also served notice that their home soil was no longer beyond reach.

The southward Japanese advance continued, meanwhile, with the despatch of an invasion convoy, bent on doubling the "tail" of New Guinea to take Port Moresby, thereby directly threatening Australia. Forewarned by code breakers, however, the Americans had despatched Rear Admiral Jack Fletcher with the carriers *Yorktown* and *Lexington*.

As a preliminary move, the Japanese made unopposed landings on Tulagi and Guadalcanal in the Solomons. Hitherto unsuspected, Fletcher broke his cover on May 3, 1942, by an ineffective air strike against Tulagi. Approaching to cover the

invasion force were the two large Japanese carriers *Shokaku* and *Zuikaku* whose commander, Vice Admiral Takagi Takao, now knew of Fletcher's presence.

A belt of heavy frontal cloud lay over the area on May 6, beneath which three separate groups manoeuvred, searching. Early on May 7, Japanese search aircraft located the American oiler and her escorts. Wrongly reporting her as a carrier, they caused Takagi to waste a full and massive air strike in their destruction.

Fletcher, not far distant, had meanwhile located the Port Moresby invasion convoy. This, accompanied by the small carrier *Shoho*, was so over-reported that it was assumed to be Takagi's main force. A maximum air strike duly despatched the *Shoho*, the first carrier casualty of the Pacific war.

LEFT: **Heavy with maximum fuel and a token bomb load, a B-25 leaves the *Hornet's* deck. Special guidelines, painted well to the port side, ensure that the bombers' wingtips miss the island.**

ABOVE: **An escort's view as *Hornet* launches her B-25s. The operation brought together Halsey in the *Enterprise* and Mitscher in the *Hornet*, two men who were to dominate the American carrier operations.**

"From Shangri-La."
President Roosevelt's response to reporters demanding
to know from where Doolittle's aircraft had flown to bomb Tokyo

Both admirals were now aware that neither had discovered his major opponent, both of whom had about 120 aircraft. Daylight on May 8, found Fletcher in clear weather, whereas Takagi was still under low cloud. Nevertheless, by 08:30 hours, each had located the other and, in short time, 90 Japanese and 84 American aircraft were airborne.

Yorktown's torpedo aircraft enjoyed no luck but her dive-bombers hit the *Shokaku* twice, leaving her unable to launch aircraft. Many of the *Lexington's* aircraft failed to find their objective but one further bomb hit was made on the *Shokaku*.

In return, the Japanese torpedo aircraft attacked *Lexington* simultaneously from either bow. Unable to avoid all the torpedoes, she was hit by two of them. Two bomb strikes added to her problems but, within the hour, her damage control teams appeared to be winning just as the ship was wracked by an explosion caused by aviation fuel vapour. It was the first in a devastating series that finally caused her destruction. The *Yorktown* had also been hit by a single heavy bomb.

The Battle of the Coral Sea was significant in that it was the first fought by carrier groups seeking each other's destruction without ever coming within sight of each other (this action was fought at a range of about 322km/200 miles). In material terms, the Japanese came off better in having destroyed the much heavier US carrier, even though the damaged *Shokaku* had to withdraw for major repair. Strategically, however, the Americans won as, with the destruction of the *Shoho*, the invasion convoy turned back. Port Moresby was never to be taken and the mountainous tail of New Guinea would mark the southern limit of what had appeared to be an unstoppable Japanese advance.

TOP: **Dauntless SBD scout/dive-bombers ranged on the *Yorktown*. They were instrumental in the destruction of the Japanese carrier *Shoho* at the Coral Sea, the first carrier loss of the Pacific War.** ABOVE: **The major loss of the Coral Sea action was the American carrier *Lexington*. Severely hit by Japanese torpedo aircraft, she suffered further from dive-bombers. She was destroyed finally by massive internal explosions.**

The Battle of Midway

The Japanese wished to provoke a decisive battle with the US Pacific Fleet before it gained in strength. Their plan was to seize Midway Island, west of Pearl Harbor but close enough to be a threat. On coming to its defence the Americans would be ambushed by Admiral Yamamoto Isoroku and the main Japanese battle fleet. A brilliant leader, Yamamoto had a weakness for very complex plans, that for Midway dissipated his otherwise overwhelming strength.

American intelligence was, however, extraordinarily detailed, enabling the Pearl Harbor-based Admiral Chester Nimitz, C-in-C Pacific to make counter-dispositions in good time, deploying his smaller forces to the best advantage. Once again, carrier groups would be both spearhead and major target. Lacking the two damaged at the Coral Sea action, Vice Admiral Nagumo would use his remaining four carriers to soften-up the defences prior to the assault landing. For the Americans, the *Yorktown*, another Coral Sea casualty, was rapidly patched up and joined by the *Enterprise* and *Hornet*, commanded by Rear Admiral Raymond A. Spruance.

At first light on June 4, 1942, Midway radar detected an incoming strike of over 100 aircraft, half of Nagumo's strength. In a fierce air battle, defending fighters prevented major damage to installations, obliging Nagumo to prepare for an unscheduled second raid. His force had already been located by Midway reconnaissance and was subject to sporadic but ineffective attack by island-based aircraft.

The attack aircraft held back by Nagumo had been fully armed with torpedo and armour-piercing bombs to meet a hoped-for intervention by the American navy. Now there was a requirement for a second strike against Midway and the machines were being rearmed with light-explosive bombs.

ABOVE: **SBD Dauntless dive-bombers ranged aboard the *Enterprise* at Midway. Two squadrons of these were carried, together with one of F4F Wildcat fighters and one of TBD Devastator torpedo-bombers.**

At this juncture, Japanese reconnaissance reported American warships to the north of the island. They might, it indicated, include a carrier. There were, in fact, three and they were about to launch their own strike against Nagumo's force.

Following anxious deliberation, the Japanese admiral decided that the warships had to be the priority target. Once again, his armourers unloaded bombs to rearm the aircraft with torpedoes. Below, ordnance unavoidably littered the hangars while, topside, the flight decks were cleared for the imminent return of the Midway strike.

LEFT: **Working with strong intelligence regarding Japanese intentions, Pearl Harbor-based Admiral Nimitz was able to ignore enemy feint movements and concentrate his forces to maximum advantage.**

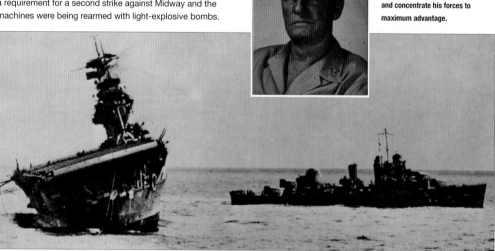

ABOVE: **Bombed, torpedoed and listing badly, the *Yorktown* was abandoned. A day later, however, she was still afloat (as seen here with the destroyer *Gwin* standing by). Taken in tow, she fell victim finally to submarine torpedoes.**

"I felt bitter. I felt like swearing."
Admiral Nagumo's Chief of Staff on losing four carriers
at Midway, June 1942

At this vulnerable point the American air strike arrived, its formations somewhat scattered. The torpedo-bombers suffered severe loss but their attack, although without result, drew down Nagumo's top cover. This left the following dive-bombers virtually unopposed and, within minutes, three Japanese carriers were fatally damaged.

The fourth ship of Nagumo's force, the *Hiryu*, put up her own dive-bomber force that followed the bearing taken by the jubilant, returning American fliers. This led it directly to the *Yorktown* which, in turn, was totally disabled by three bomb hits. (Still immobile, she was later despatched by two submarine torpedoes). *Yorktown*'s search aircraft had, however, already located the *Hiryu*, which was then destroyed by a dive-bomber force from the *Enterprise*.

Spruance remained in the area, his aircraft sinking the heavy cruiser *Mikuma* of the invasion force on June 6. He wisely held back, however, as the dispirited Yamamoto decided to abandon his operation.

The Japanese had suffered a major defeat despite the near presence of a substantial battle fleet that was powerless to change the course of the action. With Nagumo's group had been lost over 100 carrier-trained aircrew, continuing the haemorrhage of experienced personnel which the Japanese were never able to correct and which, ultimately, was to prove decisive.

ABOVE: **Nagumo's flagship *Akagi* is here seen manoeuvring violently to frustrate air attack. It availed her little for, in the words of her Flag Captain "we were unable to avoid the dive-bombers because we were so occupied in avoiding the torpedo attacks".** BELOW: **Disintegrating following a 127mm/5in hit from the *Yorktown*, a Nakajima B5N2 "Kate" sears a fiery trail to mark her passage. Note the torpedo falling away.** BOTTOM: **One of three Japanese bomb hits on the *Yorktown* exploded in the funnel, with the spectacular result shown here. It eventually made the island untenable and brought the ship to a standstill. Note the "not under control" balls.**

ABOVE: **The British escort carrier** *Chaser*, **seen from a catapulted Swordfish. Her mercantile origins are very evident in the hull and post-war, she was reconverted to a Dutch-flag general cargo ship. Note how the island is totally outboard of the flight deck edge.** LEFT: **Seen on her delivery voyage, the American CVE** *Kwajalein* **is carrying a deck-load of some seventy F4U Corsairs to Espiritu Santo in July 1944. All her short life was devoted to ferrying replacement aircraft.** BOTTOM: **An essential component to the US Navy's success in the Pacific was its adequate and highly efficient logistics service. Background to this scene of activity is the CVE** *Casablanca*, **name ship of a 50-strong class that was completed in under one year.**

Escort carriers

Following the fall of continental Europe in 1940, Great Britain's very survival depended upon transatlantic convoys. By 1943, with Germany increasingly fighting on the back foot, the convoys were equally vital to the military build-up prior to the necessary invasion of Europe.

Throughout, the major threat to the convoys was the U-boat while, in the initial stages at least, British and Allied escorts were too few, their speed and endurance being too low. Fortunately, the workhorse of the German submarine service, the Type VII, although continuously improved, had a poor submerged performance, typically 1,287km/800 miles at four knots. It was sufficient, therefore, for an escort to keep a submarine submerged until her convoy had passed, for the submarine could not catch up again unless she hazarded herself by surfacing. The answer was a single patrol aircraft that could force down all U-boats in the convoy's vicinity.

Auxiliary to the U-boat was the Luftwaffe's long-range maritime aircraft, initially the Focke-Wulf Condor, which acquired a Zeppelin-like reputation for circling a convoy beyond gun range, transmitting its position, course, and speed to marauding submarines. As with the Zeppelin, the antidote was the high-performance fighter. History, having repeated itself, demanded a similar solution, aircraft carriers. Fleet carriers were too few and too valuable to be so employed except for specific operations, so the auxiliary carrier (officially "escort carriers" from August 1942) was reborn.

Both American and British navies had pre-war plans to convert specific large merchant vessels to auxiliary carriers (few of them were, in fact, so converted) but it was only when faced with the realities of convoy warfare in 1940 that both fleets produced prototype escort carriers based on freighter-type hulls of, typically, only 7,000 gross registered tons. Small though their flight decks were and meagre or non-existent their facilities, they could deploy Swordfish ASW and/or Martlet (F4F Wildcat) fighter aircraft. For suppression of U-boats or Condors they were immediately effective.

British yards concentrated on ship repair, so escort carriers (CVE) were series-built in dedicated American construction facilities. Successive classes grew in size and capability, the larger types being retained by the US Navy for the Pacific war. For convoy escort, those under the White Ensign increasingly deployed the F6F Hellcat and the TBF/TBM Avenger, the latter very effective in ASW, carrying bombs, depth charges and rocket projectiles.

Before the arrival of the CVE, U-boats in the so-called mid-Atlantic air gap were untroubled from the air except by the all-too-few specialist VLR (very long range) aircraft, typically Liberators of RAF Coastal Command. The escort carrier, however, could maintain near-continuous, radar-equipped air patrols, denying U-boats the freedom to work around a convoy on the surface, and effectively defeating their integrated "wolf-pack" tactics.

With increasing numbers, CVEs could be spared to form the core of dedicated hunter-killer groups. Armed with Ultra-based intelligence, these especially targeted the enemy's resupply submarines, used to extend the patrols of longer-range operational U-boats.

During the North African landings, at Salerno and, increasingly, in the Pacific, escort carriers took on the task of providing air cover during the assault, followed by close air support for those ashore. The main drawback to their effectiveness in these roles was their limited speed and, in windless conditions, particularly in the tropics, attrition in high-performance aircraft could be considerable. CVEs were also used widely in the endless task of ferrying replacement aircraft.

ABOVE: **Vast wartime programmes resulted in huge numbers of redundant warships post-war. Here, lines of nearly new escort carriers lay in Boston Naval Shipyard in April 1946 awaiting disposal. The nearest, CVE-67, was earmarked for transfer to the Royal Navy but, instead, entered service as the** *Solomons.*

ABOVE: **Until early 1944, F4F Wildcats in Fleet Air Arm service were known as Martlets. Over 300 of these aircraft were acquired for the Royal Navy, giving its carriers a fighter at last equal to the enemy's shore-based machines.** LEFT: **By the close of the European war, the German fleet was largely neutralized. British fleet and escort carriers were thus increasingly able to target essential enemy seaborne supplies. Here, just days before the close of hostilities, aircraft from the CVEs** *Queen, Searcher* **and** *Trumpeter* **attack shipping near Narvik.**

LEFT: **Grumman Avengers on British service.** Although designed to carry a 533mm/21in torpedo internally, the aircraft was more often employed by the Royal Navy in a bomber or anti-submarine role, carrying depth charges, bombs or rockets. BELOW AND BOTTOM: **Entering service in 1940, the Fairey Albacore was a logical refinement of the Swordfish, which it complemented rather than replaced. In flight, the Albacore showed a much less angular appearance than the Swordfish. Both could carry a 680kg/1,500lb bomb load, shown here as six 113kg/250lb bombs.**

Carrier aircraft development during World War II

British-designed Fleet Air Arm (FAA) aircraft continued to be hedged by requirements for multi-purpose capability, for at least two seats and for very low stall speeds. Fortunately, therefore, the existing and hopeless Blackburn Roc fighter was quickly superseded by the American-sourced Grumman F4F Wildcat. Serving as the Martlet it could, along with the shorter-ranged Seafire and Sea Hurricane, take on high performance enemy land-based fighters and bombers. The F4F, like its successor, the F6F Hellcat, was a dedicated fighter, not encumbered with a secondary function. From mid-1943, the magnificent Chance-Vought F4U Corsair was acquired to work in parallel as a fighter-bomber.

Contemporary two-seat fighter-reconnaissance aircraft were the Fairey Fulmar, then the Firefly. Attempts to utilize more powerful engines in a fighter/torpedo aircraft met failure in the Blackburn Firebrand.

Oft derided, but much respected, the Fairey Swordfish served throughout as a reconnaissance/torpedo aircraft and even, in the absence of fighters, as a dive-bomber. Its successor, the Albacore, was only ever regarded as a less-draughty alternative. From early 1943, the Fairey Barracuda was the FAA's choice dive/torpedo-bomber, serving alongside the excellent Grumman TBF/TBM Avenger, a combination ASW aircraft and torpedo-bomber.

For the US Navy, the single-role F4F and F6F were produced in what, by British standards, were prodigious numbers. With the large *Midway*-class carriers under

construction, Grumman progressed to the twin-engined F7F Tigercat. Essentially a fighter-bomber, valuable in ground support, it entered service only in 1944 and would soon be displaced by jet aircraft.

Later than the Royal Navy, the Americans recognized the merits of the F4U Corsair, yet even these were surpassed by the remarkable Douglas AD-1 Skyraider, which entered service too late to make an impact on World War II.

Until 1943 the standard dive-bomber was the Douglas SBD Dauntless, it being superseded by the Curtiss SB2C Helldiver, capable of carrying a bomb load of up to 1,361kg/3,000lb.

The Japanese began the war with excellent aircraft of all three major categories. Although good performers, however, they had been designed close to their limits and were not

LEFT: **In Royal Naval service the Martlet/ Wildcat was associated mainly with escort carriers where, despite the increasing availability of Hellcats after 1943, it served until the end of hostilities. Robust and reliable, it flew well and, in its six 12.7mm/0.5in machine-guns, packed an adequate punch. Note that deck crew were by now being colour-coded, flight decks being extremely noisy places.**

amenable to further improvement. Under war conditions their successors were too long in development and problem-prone in service, a situation exacerbated by the deteriorating quality of aircrew training.

Introduced in mid-1940, the standard naval fighter was the Mitsubishi A6M (Type O), known as the "Zeke", or "Zero". A light armament, no armour and a fragile airframe were here combined with good aerodynamics to produce a low-level fighter of superb manoeuvrability and exceptional range. It eventually met its match in the F6F, and its successor, the Mitsubishi J2M Raiden, came too late to be of use.

Also introduced in 1940, the Nakajima B5N2 (Type 97) "Kate" proved to be an excellent torpedo-bomber, directly derived from the B5N1. Again, however, its time in service saw it become ever more vulnerable to defences. Its eventual successor, the B6N Tenzan, proved to have only marginally better performance.

Last of the carrier trio, the Aichi D3A1 (Type 99) "Val" was a satisfactory dive-bomber which, in time, proved deficient in both speed and armament. Its intended replacement, the Yokosuka D4Y1 Suisei, proved to be the fastest carrier-based dive-bomber but was subject to continual technical problems and was difficult for poorly trained pilots to handle.

Ultimately, the Americans prevailed with greater numbers, better organization, and superior design. As importantly, they had plentiful and well-trained aircrew.

LEFT: **Introduced in 1943 as a replacement for the Douglas SBD Dauntless, the Curtiss SB2C Helldiver could deliver three 454kg/1,000lb bombs. Despite the amount of glazing, the crew comprised only pilot and observer/rear gunner.**
ABOVE: **Light and manoeuvrable, the Mitsubishi A6M "Zeke" was deadly in a one-on-one, low-level dogfight. It remained in service too long, however, and was defeated by American second-generation fighters employing manoeuvres and formations based on experience.**

The Battle of Santa Cruz

By October 1942, the island of Guadalcanal marked the southern limit of the Japanese advance. It was being bitterly contested, but the Americans held the initiative with their possession of the only airstrip, Henderson Field. The Japanese army was ordered to storm and take the airstrip on October 25, whereupon the Japanese fleet would close to facilitate the island's capture and, it was hoped, to engage the American carrier force that was providing deep cover.

Early on October 26, a shore-based PBY Catalina located and reported the waiting carrier *Zuikaku*, some 322km/ 200 miles north-west of the Santa Cruz islands. About the same distance to the south-east was Rear Admiral Thomas C. Kinkaid with the American carriers *Enterprise* and *Hornet*. At 05:00 hours these launched 16 dive-bombers on an armed reconnaissance and these, at 06:50 hours, found the smaller enemy carrier *Zuiho*. She, together with the *Shokaku* and *Zuikaku*, were operating in company, once again under the experienced Admiral Nagumo.

At 07:40 hours, two 227kg/500lb bombs wrecked the *Zuiho*'s flight deck, but she had already launched her contribution to Nagumo's opening strike of 65 aircraft. One of his reconnaissance aircraft had located Kinkaid at about 06:30 hours and the strike was away inside 40 minutes. A second strike, of 44 aircraft, was immediately prepared as back-up, using the two larger carriers.

TOP: **The *Enterprise* with two of her SBDs. Although the dive-bombers badly damaged two enemy carriers at Santa Cruz, the ships survived.** ABOVE: **Under attack from dive-bombers and torpedo-bombers, simultaneously, the *Hornet* fights for her life.**

Between 07:30 and 08:15 hours the *Enterprise* sent away 29 aircraft, the *Hornet* 44, which flew in three groups. En route, they encountered the Nagumo strike, both losing aircraft to the escorting fighters.

Awaiting the onslaught, both of Kinkaid's carriers had their escorts close in a tight, protective ring in order to concentrate defensive fire. Overhead were 38 F4Fs of the combat air patrol (CAP). This was poorly directed, and failed to intercept the first enemy wave at a safe range.

ABOVE: **The *Enterprise* (seen here) and the *Saratoga* were the only two pre-war American fleet carriers to survive hostilities.** LEFT: **Wreathed in the smoke from her own anti-aircraft weapons, the battleship *South Dakota* manoeuvres to avoid the attentions of enemy torpedo aircraft while covering the carrier *Enterprise*.** BELOW LEFT: **An American heavy cruiser, probably *Northampton*, threatened by a low-flying "Kate", whose torpedo is clearly visible.**

At 09:00 hours the *Enterprise* was screened by a providential rain squall, so that the *Hornet* attracted the attack. First hit on the flight deck aft, she was then shaken by two near misses. A crippled aircraft clipped her funnel, crashed and penetrated her flight deck, then exploded. Two torpedoes from low-flying "Kates" hit her amidships. As the ship came to a halt, she took three further bombs and was crashed by another aircraft.

In return, the American dive-bombers caught up with the *Shokaku* in company with the already damaged *Zuiho*. Five 227kg/500lb bombs now put the larger carrier out of the action. Both, however, survived.

Nagumo's second blow, of 44 aircraft, concentrated on the yet undamaged *Enterprise*. Despite a doughty defence she took three bombs but succeeded in evading nine torpedoes.

Beyond Nagumo lurked a fourth Japanese carrier, the *Junyo*. Her own 29-plane strike hit the *Enterprise* group at 11:20 hours but succeeded only in damaging the escort. Unable to return to their carrier, *Hornet*'s aircraft landed either on the *Enterprise*, or flew to nearby Espiritu Santo.

Throughout the afternoon, crews battled to save the stricken *Hornet*, now under tow. Repeat small-scale formations from the *Zuikaku* and the *Junyo* hit her piecemeal with a further torpedo and two bombs. With the enemy fleet uncomfortably close, she

ABOVE: **Deck crews on the *Enterprise*, damaged by three bombs, work furiously to refuel, resupply and reposition her own aircraft and those from the stricken *Hornet*. Note the gun crew, closed-up in the foreground.**

could not be saved and was abandoned. Defying all efforts by her escort to sink her, her hulk had to be abandoned to the enemy, who sank her with torpedoes.

Although the Japanese lost other tonnage, all their carriers survived the Santa Cruz action. They had failed in their objective of seizing Guadalcanal, now of symbolic importance to both sides, but had claimed the valuable scalp of the *Hornet*. She had died hard, but her loss left the Americans desperately short of carriers.

Battle of the Philippine Sea

The year 1943 had transformed the situation in the Pacific, with a sequence of island-hopping Allied amphibious operations that gathered even more momentum in the following year. In June 1944, it was the turn of the Marianas, with the island of Saipan the objective.

By this time, too, the US Navy had established a powerful preponderance of aircraft carriers, nine *Essex*-class carriers (CVs) having been completed in parallel with nine *Independence*-class light carriers (CVLs).

Covering the amphibious fleet off Saipan was Admiral Raymond A. Spruance's Fifth Fleet, which included seven battleships, seven CVs and eight CVLs, deploying nearly 900 aircraft in total. With orders to destroy this armada "with one blow" was Vice-Admiral Ozawa Jisaburo's Mobile Fleet, whose five battleships were complemented by five fleet and four light carriers, with some 430 aircraft.

On June 18, Ozawa's fleet was crossing the Philippine Sea to attack Spruance from the west. Having aircraft of longer endurance, his plan was to stay beyond American range and to loose a series of air strikes that would hit the Fifth Fleet and fly on to Marianas airfields, there to refuel and rearm before raiding the Americans a second time in returning to their carriers.

Spruance's deputy, Vice Admiral Marc A. Mitscher had tactical control of the defence, his Fast Carrier Task Force (FT58) being divided into four task groups, typically of four carriers with a cruiser/destroyer escort.

Alerted to Ozawa's distant approach, Mitscher arranged his four groups in an "L" configuration with Vice Admiral Willis A. Lee's battleship task group TG.58.7 located in the angle.

TOP: **Riding at anchor at Majuro Atoll in the Marshalls, the Third/Fifth Fleet carriers are prominent. In the foreground is one of the distinctive *Independence*-class CVLs; in the distance is the veteran *Enterprise* and, beyond, *Essex*-class CVs.** ABOVE: **Desperately short of fuel, Fifth Fleet aviators are guided to their carriers by Admiral Mitscher famously burning their searchlights.**

All anti-aircraft guns were now supplied with proximity-fused ammunition and the carriers had, between them, 450 fighters. These were controlled by a fighter direction team experienced in meeting any combination of threat.

On June 19, between 10:00 and 15:00 hours, the Japanese hurled four waves of aircraft against this defence, which dissipated their efforts as a rock does a breaking sea. The first strike lost 42 aircraft from 69, the second 97 from 128. Those that went on to the island airfields found American intruder patrols overhead. The third wave became disorientated and, barely attacking, lost only 7 aircraft from 47, but the disastrous fourth lost 73 of 82. In the course of this massacre, Ozawa ran into an American submarine concentration, losing the carriers *Taiho* and *Shokaku*.

Having recovered about 100 aircraft Ozawa headed westward, followed by Spruance, less one carrier group. Finally sighting Ozawa at 15:40 hours on June 20, Mitscher launched 216 aircraft. These sank the carrier *Hiyo* and some tankers but, returning in darkness from maximum range, 80 aircraft ran out of fuel and ditched.

Ozawa had just 35 operational aircraft left but, mindful of his primary duty to protect the Saipan landings, Spruance did not press the pursuit to a conclusion, for which he attracted criticism.

Although the Japanese had lost three carriers, their greatest loss were the aircrew that manned the total of 426 aircraft destroyed. So overwhelming was Mitscher's success that his crews referred to it disparagingly as the "Marianas Turkey Shoot". In return, the Fifth Fleet suffered no losses in ships but 130 aircraft had been destroyed, together with a comparatively modest 76 aircrew.

The Americans were producing not only thousands of replacement aircraft but similar numbers of aircrew. The Japanese could nowhere near match this, and the situation was that their remaining carriers were effectively inoperable until more aircrew could be trained. This, the Americans had no intention of giving them time to do.

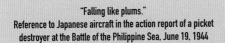

"Falling like plums."
Reference to Japanese aircraft in the action report of a picket destroyer at the Battle of the Philippine Sea, June 19, 1944

TOP: **The *Essex*-class *Bunker Hill* suffers a near miss from an enemy aircraft (upper left) that has apparently had its tail shot off. A year later the carrier would be so damaged as to be beyond economical repair.** ABOVE: **An F6F Hellcat of the later, *Essex*-class *Yorktown* is readied for launch. Note that the pilot receives instructions by hand signal and by chalk board.** BELOW LEFT: **Having survived every major carrier battle to date the *Zuikaku* once again puts her faith in a smart use of the helm to come through. In the foreground, assisting in providing flak cover, is the rarely photographed cruiser *Oyodo*.**

ABOVE: **A distant view shows the *Shokaku* damaged and under concentrated attack. She survived this only to be destroyed by submarine torpedo.**

Leyte Gulf

Just four months after the Battle of the Philippine Sea, the Americans landed on the island of Leyte in the Philippines themselves. The Japanese mustered their full available fleet in an all-out effort to dislodge them. As ever, their plan involved complex moves but in essence depended upon the invasion beaches being hit simultaneously by heavy surface warfare groups issuing from straits to the north and south.

Covering the American operation was the Third Fleet, which was the Fifth Fleet's title when under its alternative C-in-C, Admiral William F. Halsey. To prevent its intervention, Halsey was to be lured away by the irresistible bait of the remaining Japanese carriers which, in the near-absence of aircrew after the Philippine Sea debacle, were effectively useless. Vice Admiral Ozawa's mission, therefore, was to use his carrier group to trail its coat well to the north-east of the islands, attracting Halsey away to allow Vice Admirals Kurita and Nishimura to advance through the archipelago from the west.

Both the latter groups were detected early and, on October 24, 1944, subjected to prolonged air attack, Kurita by Mitscher's carriers, Nishimura by the lesser power of the Seventh Fleet, Vice Admiral Kinkaid's shore support force and land-based aircraft.

TOP: **The Battle of Samar. Taffy 3's escort carriers and their escort attempt concealment with funnel and chemical smoke as salvoes from Admiral Kurita's force fall among them. The carriers had been left uncovered once Admiral Halsey allowed himself to be enticed away by Ozawa's Northern Force.** ABOVE: **Alone on a wide sea; a pilot's view of his ship. A second aircraft, a Curtiss SB2C Helldiver, can be seen leaving the deck of this unnamed Essex-class ship.**

During the night of October 24–25, Nishimura's force was eliminated in a crushing gun and torpedo action in the Surigao Strait. However, the northern arm of the Japanese pincer advanced as planned.

The Japanese strategy had succeeded brilliantly, for Halsey, believing his pilots' reports that they had effectively destroyed Kurita's group, headed north after Ozawa, failing to leave behind even a precautionary covering force.

Ozawa could muster about a score of fighters, whereas Mitscher had about 500 aircraft of all types. Four carriers, *Zuikaku*, *Zuiho*, *Chiyoda* and *Chitose*, were easily destroyed during October 25, but annihilation of the whole group was prevented by urgent calls for Halsey's return.

> "It was like a puppy being smacked by a truck."
> Officer of destroyer USS *Johnston* sunk by 356mm/14in salvo at the Battle of Samar, October 25, 1944

LEFT: **Kamikazes continued their depredations following the main actions. On October 29, off Leyte, the CVL *Belleau Wood* suffered 92 fatalities and lost 12 aircraft in this spectacular incident.** BELOW: **Apparently armed with a 500kg/1,102lb bomb a kamikaze A6M "Zeke" readies for take-off in October 1944. As the aircraft made one-way trips, their range was effectively doubled.**

LEFT: **Admiral Halsey's legendary aggressive nature got the better of him at Leyte Gulf, only his national popularity saving him from censure. Admiral Fisher's dictum "Hit First, Hit Hard, Keep Hitting" has been paraphrased on this wartime poster.** BELOW: **Trailing defensive gun smoke, the *Zuikaku* and a *Terutsuki*-class destroyer are seen under attack at the Battle of Cape Engaño. Both the *Zuikaku* and the CVL *Chitose*, in the background, were sunk.**

Far to his south, the still-potent surface group of Kurita was, in the absence of the Third Fleet, heading southward down the coast of Samar. Between it and the vulnerable amphibious fleet lay only the unsuspecting escort carrier force of Rear Admiral Thomas L. Sprague. Attached to the Seventh Fleet, Sprague's 16 escort carriers (CVEs) were tasked mainly with close air support for forces ashore, but on the morning of October 25 they found themselves under fire from a force that included three battleships and six heavy cruisers.

One CVE is a useful unit but of limited potential. However, 16 CVEs together are much more formidable, deploying about 250 F4F Hellcats and 190 TBF/TBM Avengers. Organized in three groups, the force overcame its initial shock to hurl every available aircraft, armed or unarmed, against the apparently overwhelming force of Kurita. Their attacks gradually became more coordinated and were supported valiantly by Sprague's destroyer escort.

The scale and fury of Sprague's defence convinced Kurita that he was, after all, facing Mitscher's Third Fleet carriers and, after indecisive and largely ineffective action, he withdrew.

During this, the Battle of Samar, the Americans lost two CVEs and three escorts, the Japanese three heavy cruisers. For the first time, the Americans were then subjected to organized kamikaze tactics by land-based enemy aircraft.

Halsey, having been recalled, arrived too late to intercept Kurita's retreat but the Leyte landings had been saved from interference by Sprague's action.

After Leyte Gulf, the Imperial Japanese Fleet ceased to be a factor that could influence the outcome of the Pacific War. It had been defeated, not in classic surface action but by the medium of carrier-based air power.

ABOVE: **Although a decade in development, the Douglas A3D Skywarrior did not enter service as a carrier-based, nuclear-capable bomber until 1956. Its size and weight was a convincing argument for larger carriers.** LEFT: **Considered cramped even by 1945 standards, the *Essex*-class carriers nonetheless continued to be valuable assets, and most were subjected to one or more modernizations. This is *Intrepid* (CV-11) in October 1968, having been fitted with a full angled deck.**

Post-war aircraft carrier developments

As World War II ended, the pressure to increase the size of carriers was as strong as ever. Bristling arrays of 40mm/1.57in and 20mm/0.79in anti-aircraft (AA) weapons had proved inadequate to stop the kamikaze which, often shredded and with the pilot dead, still had the momentum to follow a ballistic course to its target. The short-term solution was the adoption of the fast-firing 76.2mm/3in 70-calibre gun which could disintegrate the machine but this was only a stop-gap pending the introduction of the surface-to-air missile (SAM), with its associated bulky directors, launchers, storage and loading gear.

In 1945 the Cold War began and, during its earlier years, the prospects of nuclear war were very real. Before the introduction of the nuclear submarine (1952) and the nuclear-tipped Polaris intercontinental ballistic missile, or ICBM (1960), the most practical means of delivering a nuclear weapon into Soviet Russian heartland was the carrier-based bomber. Such aircraft were seriously large, the original being the 23,977kg/52,860lb North American AJ Savage, delivered from 1949. From 1956, this was superseded by the 37,195kg/82,000lb, jet-propelled Douglas A3D Skywarrior. Their spans, respectively, were 22.91m/75ft 2in and 22.1m/72ft 6in.

Even before the introduction of these monsters, with their increased demands on catapults and landing space, much thought was being devoted to the optimization of flight deck

ABOVE: *Ark Royal* (III)'s new steam catapult being proofed by a Westland Wyvern from a shore-based trials unit. The extra power of steam catapults enabled smaller carriers to launch heavier aircraft.

procedures, the importance of which had been demonstrated in the pre-1945 "deck-load" air strikes.

The revolutionary, but simple, answer was first proposed in August 1951. By angling the flight path from starboard quarter to port bow, aircraft would no longer be at risk in fouling the island. A large parking area was also created, starboard side forward, and any aircraft that jumped the arresters or crash barrier no longer ran on into the deck park. Indeed, the pilot could simply hit the throttle and go around again. This "angled deck" was also clear of the forward-mounted catapults, which could be used even while aircraft were landing-on.

First trials of the angled deck were conducted during 1951 by HMS *Triumph*, which had it simply painted on to her axial deck. Similar work with the *Midway* led the Americans in 1952 to make the first physical conversion, aboard the *Antietam*.

Existing hydro-pneumatic and cordite-powered catapults were also nearing their practical limits. The idea of using steam power had been proposed during the 1930s and this concept, allied to wartime German work on long, slotted cylinders, led to a prototype steam catapult being trialled aboard HMS *Perseus* in 1951. Again the US Navy quickly took up the idea, the USS *Hancock* being the first recipient of a steam catapult in 1954, this being capable of launching a 31,751kg/70,000lb aircraft at 200kph/124mph.

Introduced in 1954 was the third British innovation to be universally adopted. Faster approaches and the nose-up landing attitude of some aircraft made it difficult for pilots to see and act upon the signals of the Deck Landing Officer (DLO), or "Batman". The Mirror Landing Aid replaced the DLO with a stabilized assembly which reflected his own landing light back to a pilot in the approach path. Suitable mirror/lens arrangements made it possible to inform the pilot that his line was correct, not high or low, nor to one side.

The latter three innovations together revolutionized deck operations and in particular facilitated the emergence of the American "super carrier".

ABOVE: **The *Essex*-class *Lexington* (CV-16) seen in a late conversion to an attack carrier. With a full angled deck she could operate A-3 Skywarriors, A-4 Skyhawks and F-8 Crusaders. Prominent here are the Rotodomes of two early-warning E-2 Hawkeyes.**

LEFT: **A welcome sight to returning aviators, the Deck Landing Officer (DLO), otherwise the "Batman", used a standard range of signals (with personal variation depending upon the heat of the moment) to guide an aircraft to safe touchdown. Note the windbreak/sightscreen, the "steadier" and the communications number.** ABOVE: **The Mirror Landing Aid replaced the DLO. From the reflection of his landing lights a pilot could verify his altitude and height, while the two lateral rows of lights indicated his axial alignment.**

LEFT: **For peacetime operation and under conditions of limited warfare the British Light Fleet Carrier proved to be flexible and economical. The Royal Navy could never maintain more than one off Korea. The** *Ocean,* **here seen with a deck-load of Sea Furies and Fireflies, arrived for her first tour in May 1951.** BELOW: **The Hawker Sea Fury was the last piston-engined fighter to be operated by the Fleet Air Arm. It also served in Korea aboard the Australian carrier** *Sydney* **and the example shown here is in Australian colours.** BOTTOM: **The** *Boxer* **(CV-21) was one of several** *Essex***-class carriers to serve in Korea. Seen here largely as she was in 1945, before the days of angled decks, it is apparent how vulnerable the massed forward deck park was to any overshoot on the part of a landing aircraft.**

Carriers in the Korean War

North Korea's invasion of the Republic of Korea (South Korea) on June 25, 1950, precipitated the first war to involve a coalition fighting under the United Nations (UN) flag. The war was primarily land-based and its course is not, therefore, relevant to this account. Korea, however, has an extensive coastline for its size, permitting warships to intervene effectively, particularly as the invaders possessed no reckonable navy.

Already in the theatre were the Japan-based US Seventh Fleet and the forces of the British C-in-C, Far East. Both services were now Cold War oriented and had run down their Far Eastern presence to token levels. Initially, the Americans

Planeguard duty for British carriers off Korea was, for destroyers, a boring and repetitive chore. When so detailed, the Canadian destroyer *Athabaskan* signalled "St Luke, Chapter 22, Verse 42." This turned out to be "Father, if thou be willing, remove this cup from me; nevertheless, not my will, but thine be done."

there could muster little more than a carrier group, built around the solitary *Valley Forge* (CV-45). Even more thinly supported was the British "Light Fleet" carrier *Triumph.*

Greatly outnumbered, the forces ashore required close air support, with deeper incursions to hit strategic targets, particularly communications. Airfields for land-based aircraft were practically non-existent so that the US Air Force had to work from bases in Japan or Okinawa. Cross-service agreement made the Air Force responsible for strategic targeting, but post-war training had emphasized air combat, so that aircraft carriers assumed the tasking.

On July 3, 1950, the two carriers operated in concert for a first operation, although it was largely symbolic for the ships as aircraft and operating procedures differed markedly.

Post-war, the British Fleet Air Arm (FAA) had shifted back to mainly home-produced aircraft, the usual mix being Seafire fighters (later, Sea Fury) and Firefly strike aircraft. Larger and faster, the *Valley Forge* deployed the then standard American combination of Grumman F9F Panthers (the first navy jet-

LEFT: **Utilitarian in looks but a superlative performer, the Vought F4U Corsair was arguably the best-ever carrier-borne piston-engined fighter. Due to the propeller's enormous torque and the pilot's far-back location, the aircraft could provide anxious moments on landing.** BELOW: **Winter off Korea is remembered without any great affection. Embalmed in a cheerless murk, the British "Light Fleet"** *Theseus* **has a non-flying day. Note the banded recognition markings and the rails for 27kg/60lb rocket projectiles on the nearest aircraft.**

propelled fighters to see combat), F4U Corsairs and AD Skyraiders. Both latter types were piston-engined but robust and versatile.

Despite experiences of World War II, the FAA still manifested relative matériel shortcomings. The Light Fleet could more economically deploy much the same air group as an armoured fleet carrier but proved to be too slow, cramped, and prone to weather damage and mechanical breakdown following extended tours on duty. Their aircraft, especially the Seafire, lacked the robustness of the Americans and, being of shorter range, were more limited in choice of targets. In contrast, the F4U and AD would stagger into the air hung about with bombs, rockets and napalm, yet still give four or more hours of close support.

Both navies operated helicopters for the first time in war. The Americans used the Sikorsky S-51 and S-55, the British only the former, known by them as the Dragonfly. Despite their limited performance, these early machines provided a new level of versatility, not least in their releasing an escort from the restricting duty of planeguard (i.e. to rescue pilots following overside flight deck accidents).

During the 37-odd months of the Korean War the Royal Navy was able to maintain just one Light Fleet on station at a time (and was pleased to accept Australia's offer of HMAS *Sydney* for one stint) for periods of up to seven months. Activity on-station was all-weather and unremitting, and the Light Fleets functioned so well because the enemy threat at sea was light to non-existent.

The US Navy's contribution was greater, building up to three, or even four, *Essex*-class carriers or light carriers (CVLs) on overlapping deployments, supported by escort carriers (CVEs) as available.

ABOVE: **Replenishment-at-sea (RAS) greatly extends the period that a warship can remain operational. Having simultaneously delivered to the carrier** *Antietam* **(CV-36) and the battleship** *Wisconsin* **(BB-64), the ammunition ship** *Rainier* **(AE-5) accelerates away.**

Carriers for sale

With the close of hostilities in 1945, the major powers all too quickly repolarized into East and West. The Cold War took grip, resulting by 1949 in the armed camps of the maritime-oriented North Atlantic Treaty Organization (NATO) and the predominantly military Warsaw Pact.

Greatly expanded during World War II, the navies of Britain and the United States were reluctant to dispose of their many, recently constructed capital ships, particularly the invaluable carriers, of which there had been too few to deter war.

Britain, impoverished by two major wars in thirty years, was in the grip of austerity yet still had obligations toward her remaining empire and NATO. The Naval Staff could justify two dozen and more "Light Fleet" or Intermediate carriers yet had not the funds to keep more than three or four in the active field. The large armoured fleet carriers, with their small aircraft capacity and large, expensive crews were thus phased out comparatively quickly. Surplus Colossus-class Light Fleets found their way into the Reserve Fleet trots, it being the intention of the Admiralty to complete the improved Majestics in slow time, releasing Colossus-class units for sale to offset the cost. With the rapid development of jet-propelled naval aircraft, however, the limitations of the Light Fleets in a shooting war became apparent and, with successive demands for fiscal cutbacks, ships of both classes were sold off, no Majestic ever serving in the Royal Navy.

TOP: **The *Independence*-class carriers were, for the US Navy, a means of creating further flight decks with fleet speed. They were too limited for peacetime use, however, and all were discarded or transferred. The *Cabot* went to Spain as the *Dédalo*, seen here in later years with V/STOL fighters forward.** ABOVE: **With the British government failing to provide the maritime strength necessary to protect Far Eastern imperial interests during World War II, Australia strengthened her own fleet post-1945. Two British "Light Fleets" were acquired on a permanent basis, the *Melbourne* being seen here.**

In accordance with the original plan, the Colossus herself went to France in 1946 as the Arromanches. In 1948 Australia took the Terrible (renamed Sydney) and Canada the Magnificent. Naval aviation appeared to have taken root when Australia then acquired the Majestic (renamed Melbourne) in

ABOVE: The Indian carrier *Vikrant* (ex-HMS *Hercules*) enters Grand Harbour, Malta, her new ownership evident from a modified radar fit and the mix of British and French-sourced aircraft. RIGHT: Following a period on loan to the Australian Navy, the British *Colossus*-class *Vengeance* was sold to Brazil in 1956 as the *Minas Gerais*. Used primarily for ASW, she is shown carrying Grumman S-2G Trackers, Agusta-built SH-3A Sea Kings and two Aerospatiale UH-13 Ecureuils.

1955 and Canada the *Powerful* (renamed *Bonaventure*) in 1957. Canada, however, abandoned carrier operation in 1970, and Australia in 1985. The French, having also acquired the light carriers (CVLs) *Lafayette* and *Bois Belleau* from the United States, went on to design and build their own carriers.

Having gained experience with Merchant Aircraft Carriers (MAC) and an escort carrier (CVE), the Dutch purchased the *Venerable* (renamed *Karel Doorman*) in 1948. However, she was sold-on to Argentina in 1969. Here she joined the ex-*Warrior*, which had gone south in 1958. Traditional rivalries had already seen Brazil acquire the *Vengeance* (renamed *Minas Gerais*) in 1960, although Chile never joined this "club".

A final Light Fleet transfer was that of the *Hercules* to India in 1961. Renamed *Vikrant*, she proved to be the foundation for a permanent air-arm as India developed into the regional naval power.

While smaller British carriers thus proved valuable to many other fleets worldwide, the equivalent American ships, the CVLs, were not, in general, sold out. Besides the aforementioned pair purchased by France only one more, the *Cabot*, went foreign, being acquired by Spain in 1967 and renamed *Dédalo*.

That so few fleets went on to develop permanent air arms demonstrates the high cost of conventional fixed-wing carrier operation, a situation hardly changed by the introduction of V/STOL and helicopters.

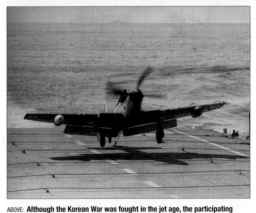

ABOVE: Although the Korean War was fought in the jet age, the participating "Light Fleets" of the British and Australian navies were still limited to Fireflies and Sea Furies which, nevertheless, gave an excellent account of themselves. Here, a Firefly AS5 of 817 Squadron touches down on the *Sydney*.

Suez

When, following years of nationalist agitation against foreign presence in Egypt, President Nasser nationalized the Suez Canal on July 26, 1956, it provoked strong Anglo-French reaction. A plan was concocted whereby Israel would attack Egypt, whereupon Britain and France would demand a ceasefire and a withdrawal of the warring forces to lines ten miles from either side of the canal. Anglo-French elements would then occupy key positions. Failing agreement on these points, Britain and France would intervene militarily.

During a long build-up period, Britain reinforced the Mediterranean Fleet and assembled her sadly run-down amphibious warfare vessels at Malta, the nearest "friendly" point with adequate facilities. The Royal Air Force was also reinforced on its Cypriot bases, although their distance from Egypt meant that fighter cover would be practicable only if carrier-based. To intimidate the Egyptians, there was little attempt at concealing concentrations and considerable international opposition to the plan resulted, notably in Britain and the United States.

The British assembled three jet-capable carriers (*Eagle*, *Albion* and *Bulwark*) with a mix of nearly 90 Sea Hawk ground attack fighters, Sea Venom all-weather strike fighters and

TOP: **Preliminary bombing of strategic targets, such as oil storage tanks in Port Said, sent a clear message to the Egyptians of the futility of prolonged resistance.** ABOVE: **Royal Marine Commandos wait on the flight deck of the *Theseus* as the ship's 11 Navy Whirlwinds operate a short shuttle service to shore.**

turbo-prop Wyvern strike aircraft. The French carriers *Arromanches* and *Lafayette* added about 59 F4U Corsairs and TBF/TBM Avengers. None of these aircraft could match the performance of the Soviet-supplied MiG-15s of the Egyptian air force.

To the British force were added the Light Fleet carriers *Ocean* and *Theseus*. As training ships they were not equipped to operate aircraft, and their task would be to implement the strategy of "vertical envelopment", as being experimented with by the US Marine Corps. This involved the use of helicopters to insert spearhead troops, in conjunction with parachute drops, ahead of a main amphibious assault. To transport and land men of 45 Commando, the *Ocean* embarked six Sycamores and six Whirlwinds of the joint army/navy experimental helicopter unit, and the *Theseus* eleven FAA Whirlwinds.

Israel duly attacked on the evening of October 29. Twenty-four hours later Nasser rejected the Anglo-French ultimatum and RAF bombing began, together with selective light naval bombardment. With Egyptian resistance continuing, the strike carriers hit airfields on November 1, wiping out all aircraft on the ground not already evacuated.

Stiffening resistance brought forward the amphibious landing and, in a change of plan, it was to be preceded by an Anglo-French parachute drop with the, as yet, untried helicopter landing down-graded to reserve. The carrier strikes continued, meanwhile, seeking out troop, supply, and vehicle concentrations. Their aircraft then switched to close support during and following the parachute assault of November 5. On the following morning, 40 and 42 Commando went ashore and, with some armoured assistance, moved into the outskirts of Port Said.

The beaches had too shallow a declivity to permit Tank Landing Ships (LSTs) to use them. Wharfage was essential, therefore, and the helicopter assault was thus directed at placing 45 Commando in a suitable position to secure the fishing harbour. Despite the total inadequacy of these early helicopters for the task in hand, over 400 men and 20 tons of equipment were put ashore in a continuous shuttle.

At midnight on the same day, international pressure enforced a ceasefire. The operation was wound down as United Nations forces assumed control, the canal remaining closed for the ensuing six months due to the necessity of salvaging the many Egyptian block-ships.

Militarily, the campaign was successful and the extemporized helicopter assault led directly to the conversion and building of "commando carriers".

ABOVE LEFT: **Seen from an inbound LST (Landing Ship, Tank) assault landing craft and the *Ocean*'s six Whirlwind helicopters ferry troops ashore at Port Said.**

ABOVE: **Alongside in Port Said the *Ocean*, with a French hospital ship beyond, is seen with the Whirlwind helicopters that successfully proved the principle of "vertical envelopment" in an opposed situation.**

RIGHT: **As three Whirlwinds head shorewards from the *Ocean*, a second wave awaits the signal to lift off. A Royal Marine officer can be seen sitting in the door, with his map case and cradling his submachine-gun.**

ABOVE: **Sea Hawk fighters provided very effective close support to ground forces during the Suez operation. Two 227kg/500lb bombs could be carried on underwing hardpoints and armourers are here seen "bombing up" on one of the British carriers.**

The impact of helicopters

The advantages of aircraft supported by rotors rather than wings were apparent very early, the US Navy's first recorded interest being in 1916. At this stage, however, the concept was well ahead of practical reality and it would be the late 1930s before innovators such as Cierva, Focke-Achgelis and Sikorsky produced practical prototypes.

On May 13, 1940, the latter flew his VS-300 in free flight in a United States not yet involved in the European war. Circumstances, however, soon encouraged the helicopter's rapid development. By 1943, Sikorsky's VS-316 had become the world's first production model and, as the R-4, recorded a first under-weigh landing aboard the carrier *Bunker Hill* on May 7, 1943.

Still lacking power, early helicopters had little useful payload margin and, like early aircraft, were limited largely to observation. Extensive trials were conducted in flying from the deck of freighters to spot surfaced U-boats in the vicinity of convoys. Focke-Achgelis built wind-powered, man-carrying observation helicopters that could be assembled and towed behind surfaced U-boats.

Immediately post-war it was the R-4, as the Hoverfly I, which gave the British Fleet Air Arm (FAA) its first experience of rotor aircraft. Able both to hover and to cover large areas rapidly, there was obviously potential as an offensive anti-submarine warfare (ASW) platform. It needed little in the way

TOP: **A string of *Bulwark*'s Westland Wessexes positions itself about its "spots" while a Type 82 frigate stands planeguard. Ships and helicopters have greatly influenced each other's design.** ABOVE: **Intended primarily for observation duties, the US Navy's Sikorsky HO3S-1 gave yeoman service during the Korean War and peacetime in the rapid rescue of ditched aviators, as of this F6F Hellcat.**

of flight deck, as demonstrated in 1946 by a successful landing on a destroyer. With the emerging Cold War emphasizing ASW, a whole new line of development was instigated.

An early success was the Bell HTL/HUL of 1946, widely used as a utility aircraft, for casualty evacuation and for transfers between ships. In the following year, the British firm of Westland began to build Sikorsky designs under licence, its Dragonfly corresponding to the American S-51, which saw considerable service in the Korean War. By now more reliable for use over water, helicopters appeared on aircraft carriers, their utility functions doubling with planeguard duty, thus releasing an escort ship for more appropriate employment.

Although the Sikorsky S-55 and S-58 (Westland's Whirlwind and Wessex) demonstrated considerable advances in capability during the 1950s and 1960s, they were too large to be considered for general ASW aboard flotilla ships.

For a frigate, the helicopter promised rapid, stand-off response to a submarine contact, but early machines such as the Westland Wasp were too small to carry the combined weight of sensors, weapons and data systems. The Americans sought to circumvent the problem by removing the crew, but the resulting Drone Anti-Submarine Helicopter (DASH) system was ahead of then-current technology, and proved unreliable.

The solution could lie only in either larger machines or in the operation of multiple smaller ones working as a team. This resulted in divergent development paths, with frigates being designed around ever-larger helicopters, ideally paired, and other aviation-capable ships such as the ASW helicopter carriers, commando carriers and amphibious warfare ships deploying them in numbers. The latter categories are also well able to fly ground attack helicopters such as the Apache, to compensate for their lack of the dedicated strike aircraft found aboard a conventional carrier. With their growing ability to operate V/STOL, and other novel forms of aircraft, such as the tilt-rotor V-22 Osprey, such ships are now blurring the once clear definition of what constitutes an "aircraft carrier".

TOP LEFT: Carried for planeguard and utility duties, the Piasecki Vertol HUP-2 was also adapted for anti-submarine warfare. This picture, of Korean War vintage, shows an Essex class in near-original configuration and a McDonnell F2H Banshee. ABOVE LEFT: US naval interest in helicopters began late in 1943 with the acquisition (from the Army!) of 25 Sikorsky R-4Bs. Known in naval service as HNS-1s, they were used for pilot training. ABOVE: The latest British Iron Duke class of frigate is designed to carry a single anti-submarine Merlin in contrast to previous classes that had the advantage of carrying two of the smaller but less capable Westland Lynxes. The impact of the Merlin's size can be seen in the design of this frigate. BELOW: Carried typically aboard Leander-class frigates such as the Aurora, the Westland Wasp HAS.1 comprised the ship's major anti-submarine system. Note the two torpedoes carried by this machine, of 829 Squadron.

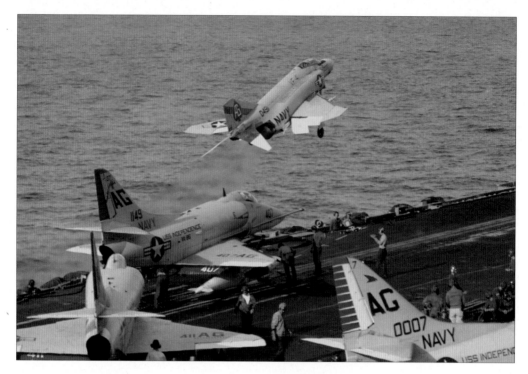

Carrier jet aircraft developments

Although the first official all-jet landings were made soon after World War II (December 3, 1945, by a Sea Vampire on HMS *Ocean*, and July 21, 1946, by a McDonnell FH-1 Phantom I on USS *Franklin D. Roosevelt*) propeller-driven strike aircraft, at the peak of their development, remained in front-line service until after the Korean War (1950–53).

The first standard American jet carrier fighters were the McDonnell F2H Banshee and the F3H Demon. These would also have served alongside the big strategic bombers with augmented turboprop propulsion aboard the cancelled *United States* attack carrier (CVA-58).

The nuclear-capable attack bomber which actually entered service was the all-jet Douglas A3D (later A-3 Skywarrior), a 37,195kg/82,000lb aircraft which was introduced in 1957 and ended its time in reconnaissance and tanker roles. It operated from *Essex*- and *Midway*-class carriers as well as the giant Forrestal. Its supporting F3H Demons were superseded from 1962 by the outstanding F4H Phantom II, which acted both as fighter and as tactical strike aircraft.

The F4H (later F-4) served in tandem with the F8U (later F-8) Crusader, complementing an attack wing of "heavy" A-3s and "light" McDonnell Douglas A-4 Skyhawks. Already, the heavy investment required for developing new aircraft was forcing joint company projects, but the A-4 was particularly

TOP: **Dating from the early 1960s, the McDonnell Douglas F-4 Phantom was one of the best-ever carrier aircraft, being purchased also for the Royal Navy. This example has just been catapulted from the waist position aboard the American carrier *Independence* (CVA-62).** ABOVE: **In July 1950 the Grumman F9F Panther became the first Navy jet aircraft to see combat. Two Panthers are seen here on the catapults of the *Leyte* (CV-32). This *Essex*-class vessel is still in her original configuration: note the 127mm/5in gunhouses to the right.**

durable. By the late 1960s the offensive element was widened with a new medium attack aircraft, the Grumman A-6 Intruder, a 1,043kph/648mph twin-seat bomber that came also in tanker and electronic warfare variants.

From 1973 the F-4 was gradually superseded by another superlative Grumman fighter, the twin-seat F-14 Tomcat, the first to feature variable wing geometry. Ten years later it was complemented by the small and lighter McDonnell Douglas F/A-18 Hornet, a multi-purpose machine.

During the Korean War, the smaller British carriers operated only piston-engined aircraft alongside their jet-equipped American allies. Nonetheless, there were by 1953 four Fleet Air Arm (FAA) squadrons flying the 950kph/590mph Supermarine Attacker, an interim jet fighter based on the RAF's Spiteful. It was quickly superseded by the successful but slower Hawker Sea Hawk, a single-seat ground attack fighter.

By the late 1950s, the Supermarine Scimitar had been introduced. Although multi-role and nuclear-capable, it represented a major improvement in performance and range, but at the cost of twice the weight. It flew alongside a new Blackburn design, the Buccaneer, a low-level nuclear-capable strike aircraft of exceptionally strong construction. It served until the Royal Navy's carrier force was controversially eliminated with the retirement of the *Ark Royal* (III) in 1978. For her final decade in service the *Ark Royal* had to operate American-sourced F-4 Phantoms, due to the cancellation of a new British fighter.

Where, owing to the limited numbers involved, the British government no longer considers domestically developed carrier aircraft a viable proposition and has purchased the American Joint Strike Fighter for its projected new carriers, the French have no such inhibitions. For their new carriers of the early 1960s they produced the durable Dassault Etendard fighter-bombers. More recently, for their confident new *Charles de Gaulle* carrier they have introduced the Dassault Rafale fighter, although production has been much delayed.

With the end of the Cold War, carrier-on-carrier actions have become only remote possibilities. The accent is now upon intervention and it may be assumed that future carrier aircraft will continue the priorities of air superiority and ground support, but with an increasing emphasis on stealth.

TOP: **On December 3, 1945 a converted deHavilland Vampire I made the first-ever landing by a pure jet aircraft aboard a carrier. Further strengthened, the aircraft went into limited production as the F.20 Sea Vampire. The carrier was the** *Ocean*, **a British "Light Fleet".** ABOVE: **Another Grumman success story was the F-14 Tomcat, the US Navy's first variable-geometry fighter. Designed to establish "air superiority", this example is carrying six Phoenix air-to-air missiles, long-range weapons capable of reaching beyond 180km/110 miles.**

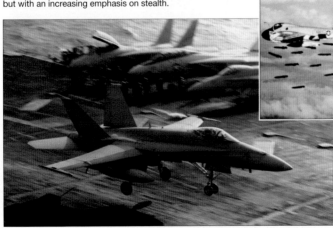

ABOVE: **In various configurations, the Grumman A-6 Intruder has served in the US Navy long and well. Its primary role was as an attack bomber, in which service it could carry a 7,855kg/17,280lb bomb load.** LEFT: **Touchdown. The elegant McDonnell Douglas F/A-18 Hornet is a multi-role fighter flown by both Navy and Marine pilots. Capable of Mach 1.8 speed, it entered squadron service in 1983.**

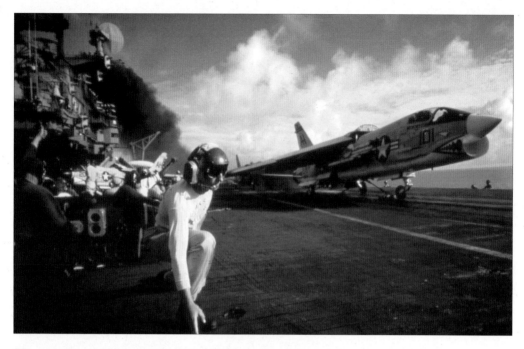

Naval air power in Vietnam

During the early 1960s, Communist insurgents from North Vietnam were freely infiltrating neighbouring South Vietnam via the contiguous border with Laos. To buttress the South's democratic government, and to register overt disapproval, the United States maintained a naval presence offshore. Its frequent reconnaissance overflights and inshore incursions in pursuit of signal intelligence finally provoked North Vietnamese light forces to tangle with American destroyers in August 1964. A retaliatory two-carrier air strike opened what was to prove a ten-year, unwinnable conflict.

With widespread public approval, Congress authorized President Johnson "to take all necessary measures … to prevent further aggression". Rapid reinforcement of two further carriers resulted in the immediate transfer of Chinese MiG jet fighters to bases around the North's capital, Hanoi.

As North Vietnamese activities continued unabated, the president, in December 1964, authorized a structured action plan. Air strikes against the Laotian infiltration routes would first warn Hanoi. If the hint were to be ignored, these would be extended to lines of communication inside North Vietnamese

TOP: **An LTV F-8 Crusader fighter awaits catapulting from the *Constellation* (CVA-64). Squadron deliveries for the aircraft were between 1957 and the late 1960s, with many earlier machines being successively modernized.**

ABOVE: **One result of the carrier operations off Vietnam was the life extension of the Douglas AD-1 Skyraider. By 1957 this highly versatile design was 12 years old. Universally known as the Spad, it is seen here in the A-1H single-seat low-level bombing version.**

> "Two SAMs, two o'clock low. Break right! Break right!"
> One naval pilot warning another during a low-level
> incursion over North Vietnam

borders. A final escalation, if proved necessary, would target the North's airfields and fuel resources, while ports would be mined and blockaded. From the outset, however, for fear of Chinese or Soviet intervention, rules of engagement were suffocatingly constricting.

TOP: **As in Korea, air power in Vietnam was vested in the aircraft carrier. Here, the** *Enterprise* **(CVAN-65) is seen launching an air strike. The world's first nuclear-powered carrier, she is still in her original configuration.** LEFT: **While it seemed improbable that the AD could ever be replaced by a jet-powered aircraft with similar versatility, McDonnell Douglas succeeded with the A-4 Skyhawk. It entered service in 1956 and, many variants later, was still giving a good account of itself in the 1982 Falklands War.** ABOVE: **The extensive mining of Haiphong and essential Vietnam waterways entailed, following cessation of hostilities, the massive Operation Endsweep. Aboard the** *Inchon* **(LPH-12) can be seen RH-53As, CH-53A Sea Stallions, re-equipped for mine clearing, June 1973.**

This was to be an aerial offensive, to be shared between the Seventh Air Force and carriers of Task Force 77 (TF77). To avoid overlap, North Vietnam and Laos were divided into target areas, or "route packages". Those "Up North" would be hit by carriers based on the so-called "Yankee Station", just south of Hainan Island, while those in Laos would receive attention from "Dixie Station" off the South Vietnamese coast.

The opening phases, "Barrel Roll" and "Steel Tiger", comprised armed reconnaissance missions over Laos. Their main result was that surface-to-air missile (SAM) sites began to appear. Because Soviet and Chinese technicians were likely to be involved, attacks during the vulnerable installation phase were banned.

SAMs, particularly the SA-2, became a major threat. They enforced high-speed, low-level flying, beneath radar coverage but within range of barrage fire from automatic weapons. This was far more deadly than enemy MiGs.

Yet having no effect, the American policy was extended to phase two in February 1965. This, code-named "Rolling Thunder", was a sustained bombing campaign of selected strategic targets, avoiding Hanoi and the principal port of Haiphong. For the first time, guided bombs were deployed against precision targets and cluster bombs on soft-skinned targets such as transport concentrations or dumps. On several

occasions, the campaign was stood down to give the enemy an opportunity to negotiate. Each time, with no response, it was resumed with the "bomb line" extending ever nearer to the Chinese border and to ever more sensitive targets.

With the proliferation of SAM and associated flak sites, "Iron Hand", highly hazardous suppression strikes, had to be undertaken frequently.

In March 1972, the North Vietnamese army invaded the South in strength and now-President Nixon ordered Haiphong and strategic waterways to be mined. Over 11,000 were laid.

The ceasefire of January 1973 brought a generally unsatisfactory campaign to a close. TF77 carriers' contribution had been enormous, with 21 separate ships making a total of 86 deployments. A total of 859 aircraft were lost from all causes and some 620 aircrew were listed dead, missing or captured. Many more were saved by the crews of the Helicopter Combat Support Squadrons. In terms of operational experience, the campaign was invaluable.

Carrier battle groups and tactics

Even by the onset of World War II, it was realized, particularly by the Japanese and American navies, that the aircraft carrier was no longer just the handmaiden of the battle line but an offensive unit in her own right. Her independence was emphasized by her requirement even when equipped with catapults, to "chase the wind" to launch and recover her aircraft. Needing thus to leave the mutual security of the main group, she also needed her own dedicated escort.

As we have seen, the naval war in the Pacific became, increasingly, one of carriers seeking mutual destruction. Their mighty blows, each hoping to be the first to land, were aimed at each other, leaving the gun-armed fleet as bystander if not actively involved in the carrier's defence.

The carrier battle group became the choice tactical formation but, in the early days, when just two to four carriers were available, an admiral had to choose whether to concentrate them for maximum offensive effort or to disperse them for improved concealment and survivability. This could depend simply on the available number of escorts. The Japanese might place a small carrier group ahead in order to divert the initial strike from the major group following some distance behind.

A full deck-load strike was reckoned to stand a good chance of disabling an enemy through damaging her flight deck if not actually sinking her. This is reflected in the composition of air wings for, as the disparity in carrier strength grew ever more decisively in the American's favour, their proportion of fighters grew from 25 to 65 per cent.

With fifteen or more carriers at his disposal, Mitscher grouped them in threes and fours with common escort. Three

TOP: **With no fixed-wing, conventional carriers remaining, the Royal Navy was reduced by the early 1980s to forming task groups around a V/STOL carrier. The *Invincible* is seen here in 1983, supported by a Type 12 frigate, two Leanders, a tanker and two multi-purpose store ships.** ABOVE: **Altogether a more formidable proposition, US Navy carrier battle groups, here centred on the *Kitty Hawk* (CVA-63), have the benefit of three-dimensional radar, airborne early warning and aircraft the equal of anything ashore. Trailing the group, unadvertised, will be a supporting nuclear submarine.**

of four Task Groups thus comprised a Task Force which was, effectively, the whole fleet less the fast battleships, to be used as a sort of mobile reserve.

At the time of the Battle of the Philippine Sea the sheer number of carriers, although deploying two-thirds fighters, could still muster an adequate offensive power while maintaining a defensive cover that simply overwhelmed the attackers.

ABOVE: **Despite post-World War II fleet rundown, Task Force 77, the US Navy's main presence off the Korean peninsula, was boosted with the arrival of new carriers. The *Philippine Sea* (CV-47) and another Essex class are visible over the deck park of the *Boxer* (CV-21).** LEFT: **Hard to believe, but 37 years separate the commissioning dates of the conventionally powered *Independence* (CV-62/1959) and the nuclear-powered *John C. Stennis* (CVN-74/1996). In terms of dimensions and aircraft capability, they differ little.** BELOW LEFT: **A lone Liberty ship stands silhouetted against the result of one of the post-war Bikini tests. The weight alone of the water in the column was sufficient to crush and swamp a conventional ship, and the possible use of tactical nuclear weapons required task groups to be more dispersed.** BELOW: **The atomic explosion to the left could easily encompass this 1955 task group. Here, the *Platte* (AO24) simultaneously refuels the *Essex*-class *Philippine Sea* (CV-47) and a *Fletcher*-class destroyer, the *Watts* DD-567.**

Radar now detected an incoming strike early enough for the escort, now often including a battleship, to close in a defensive ring. If the attackers escaped the Combat Air Patrol (CAP) at a distance, they then ran into a close-in barrage of proximity-fused ammunition.

The resulting attrition in Japanese aircrew led directly to the kamikaze. With a pilot no longer concerned for his survival, probability swung again in favour of the attacker. This strengthened arguments in favour of the larger carrier, supporting improved horizontal protection and a "beefed-up" armament, with greater inherent survivability.

By 1945, the big tactical groups of carriers and amphibious warfare craft dominated the Pacific war. A rethink was, however, in order with the advent of the Cold War and the very real possibility of nuclear weapon deployment. Even without particularly accurate delivery, its blast could sink or disable an entire group. Greater dispersion, although a solution, only increased the vulnerability to more likely conventional attack. This conundrum has a solution which must depend upon the nature of the threat at any specific time.

With the gradual diminishing of the number of available carriers, each becomes more significant. Her offensive capacity is eroded if her mission requires her also to deploy a credible anti-submarine component, in addition to airborne early warning, tankers, electronic warfare and utility aircraft. Accommodating all this, however, forces up the size of the carrier and, fortuitously, the larger the dimensions the greater the ability to absorb punishment while remaining operational.

The introduction of V/STOL

For a proven concept with obvious application, Vertical or Short Take-Off and Land (V/STOL) had a slow and difficult transition to naval use. It began with the Cold War assumption that the West's airfields and fixed aerial assets would be targeted and made unusable. Although some small supersonic aircraft could then still operate from suitable lengths of highway a V/STOL aircraft, using vectored thrust, could in theory require an area no larger than a tennis court. On this basis, the British Hawker company produced the prototype P.1127 (later "Kestrel") in 1960 and this, refined to the GR.1 version of the Harrier, entered RAF squadron service in October 1969.

In February 1966 an economy-driven Defence Review precipitated a run-down of British military presence "East of Suez", with the specious corollary that there would be no future role for aircraft carriers. The attack carrier CVA-01 was cancelled and no existing carrier would be replaced on its retirement. From the "mid-1970s" the Fleet Air Arm (FAA) would become all-helicopter.

Three years before, however, the prototype Kestrel had been demonstrated aboard the *Ark Royal* and, perhaps more significantly, had landed in 1966 aboard the commando carrier *Bulwark*, which could no longer handle conventional fixed-wing aircraft, deploying only helicopters.

Studies began for a ship combining the required facility for command and control with an area-defence SAM system and flight deck and accommodation for Sea King anti-submarine

warfare (ASW) helicopters. The navy quietly extended the studies to complement the helicopters with V/STOL. Because the government could no longer consider a "carrier", the ship became a "command carrier", or "through-deck cruiser". Surprisingly, the project survived to the stage of the ordering, in 1973, of the ship that would become the *Invincible*.

It was fortunate that, in 1969, the less cash-strapped US Marine Corps had placed a substantial order for modified Harriers, maintaining the aircraft's high profile, but it was to be 1975 before studies were funded into what would become the Sea Harrier. The prototype made a first landing aboard the *Hermes* in November 1978 and entered FAA squadron service in good time to join the *Invincible*, completed in July 1980.

BOTTOM: **In February 1963 the new Hawker P.1127, provisionally named the Kestrel, landed aboard the *Ark Royal* (III) and, four months later, operated from the commando carrier *Bulwark*. The long-term future of the Royal Navy's conventional carriers was already doubtful and the slow metamorphosis of the Kestrel to the Sea Harrier was one of great significance.** BELOW: **By its adoption of the aircraft, the United States Marine Corps rescued the Harrier from politically induced oblivion. This example gets airborne from the flight deck of the amphibious assault ship *Nassau* (LHA-4).**

Britain's last fixed-wing carrier, *Ark Royal*, had paid off in 1978 but the *Invincible*, carrier-manqué, together with the *Hermes*, proved the continuing validity of fighter cover for the fleet during the Falklands War of 1982. Here, they operated RAF ground-attack Harriers alongside FAA fighter variants.

V/STOL (or, better, STOVL, for that is the preferred mode of operation) is no substitute for the high-performance, purpose-designed fighter. Its engine, designed to deliver sufficient vectored thrust to support the aircraft's weight, is over-large and uneconomical for long-duration cruising as, necessarily, is the aircraft's configuration.

Limited-performance fighters are, however, infinitely superior to no fighters at all, and the concept is therefore appealing to fleets that cannot afford the cost of developing and sustaining large conventional carriers. Importantly, as far as evolution is concerned, V/STOL has enabled a whole range of hybrid vessels, particularly in amphibious warfare, to deploy significant air defence and ground attack capability.

During the Falklands emergency of 1982 large roll-on, roll-off ships and container ships were also proven to be capable of carrying and, if necessary, deploying Harriers. The associated Arapaho project embraced the "containerization" of all related support services and the provision of sectioned, prefabricated take-off pads. Between them, V/STOL and rotor flight have effectively blurred the definition of what constitutes an "aircraft carrier", enabling specialist large assault ships to provide organic close air support for their operations.

ABOVE: The need to justify the *Invincible* as a "through-deck cruiser" left her flight deck area significantly reduced by the Sea Dart area defence surface-to-air missile launcher and its guidance radars. LEFT: With the dissolution of the old Soviet Union, its armed forces suffered sudden reduction and a starvation of funding. The navy and its rapidly evolving conventional carrier capability were not spared and the future of such technologically advanced aircraft as the Yak-141 is far from certain. BELOW LEFT: The United Kingdom government is no longer willing to support an aviation industry capable of producing novel military aircraft. New aircraft are thus either the result of participation in international partnerships or are, like the F-35 Joint Strike Fighter, purchased directly. BELOW: The *Tarawa*-class amphibious assault ships are multi-purpose and, weighing-in at nearly 40,642 tonnes/40,000 tons full load, have a spacious flight deck capable easily of undertaking V/STOL operation. Here, a Marine Corps AV-8B leaves the *Belleau Wood* (LHA-3).

Argument – large or small carriers?

Naval aviation, in the shape of Conventional Take-Off and Land (CTOL) carriers, is staggeringly expensive, yet it is abundantly clear that any fleet with pretensions to "blue water" capability cannot function without it. Once the decision is made to acquire carriers, however, battle is joined and argument rages – what represents the best value for money, one or two large vessels or several smaller? Here, the American experience is enlightening, for the US Navy has been building large carriers in an unbroken line of development for a half century. With almost each new acquisition, another but similar argument erupts and, again, the big ship has to be justified.

In studies, four sizes of carrier were considered: (1) a 91,444-tonne/90,000-ton or more carrier or nuclear carrier (CV/CVN); (2) a 40,642–60,963-tonne/40,000–60,000-ton carrier, vertical take-off and land (CVV), capable of operating conventional and vertical or short take-off and land (V/STOL) aircraft; (3) a 20,321–35,562-tonne/20,000–35,000-ton VSS capable of operating V/STOL in all modes; and (4) a less than 20,321-tonne/20,000-ton ship unclassified, capable of operating V/STOL only in the vertical mode.

Category (1) ships can include about nine types of aircraft in their inventory, and a reduction in size to category (2) would mean the loss of heavy long-range interceptors of the size of the F-14 Tomcat.

All else being equal, a 335m/1,099ft, 91,444-tonne/90,000-ton ship compared with a 275m/902ft, 50,802-tonne/50,000-ton

TOP: **Large carriers are more cost effective and more survivable, but are staggeringly expensive to acquire and maintain.** ABOVE: **Short take-off, vertical land (STOVL) is allied to small waterplane area, twin hull (SWATH) in this concept small carrier, designed to give a steady platform in poor weather.**

vessel will have only 22 per cent greater dimensions yet 82 per cent more volume. Volume is the most critical parameter when designing to accommodate aircraft, magazine/fuel stowage and propulsion machinery.

Larger hulls are more easily driven. At 30 knots, a 91,444-tonne/90,000-ton vessel requires only one-third the horsepower per ton of a destroyer. A larger ship can continue to operate her aircraft in a higher sea state than a smaller one, while her overall accident rate is about half.

ABOVE: **This Thornycroft concept for a STOVL carrier dates from 1976, before ski-jumps were introduced. In comparison with a large carrier, her cost per ton would be significantly greater.** LEFT: **Concept drawings of STOVL fighter and airborne early warning AEW aircraft. The extra machinery weight, its complexity and its effects on aerodynamics will always mean that a STOVL aircraft will be an inferior performer compared with a conventional one.** BELOW: **An American concept for a small STOVL carrier. Note the landing spots aft and the angled take-off path which gives parking space forward of and abaft the island.** BOTTOM: **Resurrecting the old airship "skyhook" concept, this idea for a Harrier carrier entails the aircraft using excessive fuel in the hover mode. It also seems to be an awful lot of ship for very little aviation.**

In establishing sea superiority, the VSS compares badly with the CVV, its air wing being 30 against 50. Able to ship an anti-submarine warfare (ASW) component, the CVV could operate singly in all but a high-threat environment. In contrast, the VSS could operate singly in only low-threat situations and would require an ASW escort.

A 40,642-tonne/40,000-ton VSS could deploy about 30 aircraft, but a 20,321-tonne/20,000-ton ship only 8. Her capacity for self defence is low and she would require a capable, missile-armed escort. Ships of the smallest size would be able to operate V/STOL only in the uneconomical vertical take-off and land (VTOL) mode, reducing mission capability by nearly 50 per cent. The demands of a flight of, say, four aircraft would effectively squeeze out other roles for the ship.

Nuclear propulsion puts about 30 per cent more on the initial price of a ship but internal space thus saved enables her to stow four times as much aviation fuel and three times the ordnance. A nuclear ship can steam at high speed almost indefinitely and, while being free of tanker support herself, can offer limited fuel oil for her escorts. She has no smoke problem. Extra support costs appear to be of the order of three per cent.

In the face of enemy action, the larger carrier is the less vulnerable. Her extra size and compartmentalization enable her better to absorb penetration and shock. Her torpedo protection is more comprehensive and, if damaged, she has greater stability margins and more watertight subdivision. Not least, her extra aircraft make it less likely that she will be damaged in the first place. Initial cost per ton will be less but both air wing and through-life expenditure are considerable.

TOP: **Helicopters and V/STOL are complemented in the large assault ship, the one to give assault mobility, the other to provide limited ground support and fighter cover. This example is the *Nassau* (LHA-4).** ABOVE: **Even as the *Albion* and *Bulwark* proved the "commando carrier" concept for the Royal Navy, so did the *Essex*-class *Boxer* (CV-21) for the US Navy. Beyond landing most of her light anti-aircraft weapons, she appears little modified.**

Assault carriers

For amphibious warfare, the introduction of atomic weapons made speed of operation paramount, to clear the beach and to disperse shipping. The US Marine Corps (USMC) saw in the helicopter the means of, eventually, putting ashore a complete division but, in the early 1950s, the vision was ahead of the technology. Nonetheless, by 1956, Sikorsky had produced the HR25 helicopter, capable of lifting 20 equipped troops.

For the envisaged division, considerable sea transport would be required and the USMC requested the conversion of suitable reserve escort carriers (CVEs). Only one, however, was forthcoming, the *Thetis Bay* (CVE-90) emerging as the helicopter assault carrier CVHA-1 in July 1956 following limited modification for what was a temporary role.

In Britain these developments had been followed with interest and, in November 1956, the first such "vertical envelopment" operation was undertaken during the Suez intervention. Here, using an ad hoc collection of totally inadequate helicopters, two unconverted Light Fleet carriers took just 82 minutes to put ashore over 400 men and 23.4 tonnes/23 tons of stores at a selected point. This resulted in the conversion of the *Bulwark* and *Albion* to "commando carriers" in 1960 and 1962 respectively. In this role they could accommodate 750–900 troops and 16 helicopters.

The *Thetis Bay* could carry 22 helicopters but "spot" only five at a time. Exercises showed the unsuitability of CVEs for more elaborate conversion. Three *Essex*-class carriers (CVs)

thus acted as interim assault carriers until a designed-to-task ship could be produced. This was the Amphibious Assault Helicopter Carrier (LPH) of which the *Iwo Jima* and six sisters were completed between August 1961 and June 1970. At 17,273 tonnes/17,000 tons they were smaller than the British pair yet could support a full marine battalion of 2,100 men together with 32 assorted helicopters. The Bulwarks did, however, carry four vehicle and personnel landing craft (LCVPs) under davits, allowing heavy material to be put ashore. Lacking these, the Iwo Jimas were limited to the 2,858kg/6,300lb that could be slung beneath a CH-46 helicopter.

The last of the class was fitted for a pair of LCVPs but the ships' general limitations for assault operations in poor weather resulted in a rethink. What emerged in 1976 to 1980 was the

ABOVE LEFT: **An unusual view of the after end of the *Nassau* (LHA-4's) flight deck, seen from flight control. It will be apparent that the superstructure, unlike the island of a conventional carrier, extends almost to the centreline.**
ABOVE: **Sikorsky HUS-1/UH-34D Seahorses of US Marine Corps Squadron HMM-262 take off from an *Iwo Jima*-class LPH in the early 1960s during a training exercise.** LEFT: ***Nassau* participating in Desert Storm. Ships such as these, carrying 2,000 troops, their transport, helicopters and aircraft, are hugely versatile, yet represent an all-eggs-in-one-basket vulnerability.**
BELOW: **LHAs are named after actions significant to US Marine Corps history. Here, the *Saipan* (LHA-2) has her communications antennas lowered for flight operations.**

25,401-tonne/25,000-ton *Tarawa*-class LHA (Amphibious Assault Ship), combining the floodable docking well and vehicle deck of an LPD (Landing Platform, Dock) with an LPH's hangar space and flight deck. These could accommodate four Landing Craft, Utility, (LCU) in the well, together with smaller landing craft under davits.

A Tarawa was soon involved in satisfactory operation of Marine Corps V/STOL Harriers, while under development at the time was the fast Landing Craft, Air Cushion (LCAC). Both were seen as having potential and the LHA was stretched to accommodate them.

The resulting Helicopter/Dock Landing Ship (LHD) of the Wasp class weighs in at over 28,449 tonnes/28,000 tons. Still designed around the transportation of a marine battalion, her well is dimensioned to accommodate three LCACs and her flight deck is strengthened for routine V/STOL operation. In addition, she was designed with an eye to conversion to anti-submarine warfare (ASW) duties.

With the demise of the commando carriers in the 1970s, Britain deployed only the *Hermes*, which doubled as an ASW carrier, and a pair of LPDs. However, with the catastrophic run-down of the British merchant fleet it is no longer possible to simply charter suitable ships in an emergency. Considerable investment has, therefore, been required to create a coherent assault squadron comprising the *Ocean,* the two Albions and four *Bay*-class auxiliaries, the latter fitted with wells.

Carriers in the Falklands War

When, in April 1982, the Royal Navy had urgently to form a task group to take an expeditionary force to reclaim the invaded Falkland Islands, only two carriers remained to it, neither capable of deploying high-performance, CTOL aircraft. These, the *Invincible* and *Hermes*, sailed on April 5 with a total of 20 Sea Harriers and 28 Sea King helicopters. Ahead lay the whole hostile Argentine air force with one carrier of its own.

Following regrouping of participating ships at Ascension Island the now-organized Carrier Task Group 317.8 (CTG 317.8) left for the 322km/200-mile Maritime Exclusion Zone declared about the islands. Further aircraft, including RAF ground-attack Harriers and troop-carrying Chinook helicopters, followed aboard roll-on, roll-off (ro-ro) merchantmen.

On April 25, with deceptive ease, a small Argentine garrison on South Georgia was persuaded to surrender, four ship's helicopters having sunk a submarine alongside their jetty.

On May 1, the task group entered the Argentine-declared exclusion zone and set about establishing sea superiority, opening with bombardments of selected targets. The carriers remained further to the north-east, their distance attracting endless ribaldry from those at the firing end. Nonetheless, the operation's success depended upon air cover and the loss of

TOP: **Despite furious fitting-out work at Wallsend, second-of-class *Illustrious* was completed just too late to participate in the Falklands War. She is seen here (nearest) taking over from the hard-worked *Invincible* in September 1982.**

ABOVE: **A Type 42's best defence against an Exocet was to deflect it by passive means. The *Sheffield* reacted too slowly to a clear warning of an approaching air-launched missile.**

either carrier would have enforced its abandonment. This could not be risked.

The short-legged Sea Harriers had some local advantage as the enemy A-4 Skyhawks, Daggers and Mirages had to undertake a 1,127km/700-mile round trip, from the mainland, which left them no loiter time over the islands. The island-based Pucara ground-attack aircraft were no match for the British fighters.

One of three nuclear submarines in the area, HMS *Conqueror*, torpedoed and sank the Argentine cruiser *General Belgrano* on May 2. A controversial action, it was designed,

> "Every single Falklands casualty ... 778 is the official total — spent some part of his life in a helicopter."
> Surgeon Cdr Rick Jolley, interview of October 24, 1989

> "You learn down here to weep silently in your cabin at man's folly."
> Rev Charles E. Stewart, Scottish Free Church chaplain
> to HMS *Hermes* at the Falklands

successfully, to establish a clear moral ascendancy. The enemy fleet, including its carrier *25 de Mayo*, played no further part in the campaign.

The Argentine air force, on the other hand, redoubled its efforts. Ship after ship was hit by conventional low-level bombing. Many bombs fortunately failed to explode but ships were sunk and others severely damaged.

With a fair measure of sea control established, the army was put ashore on May 21 at San Carlos, nearly 97km/60 miles from its objective, the capital, Port Stanley.

Beyond the range of direct air attack, the enemy air force could reach the carriers only with their Super Etendard fighter-bombers flying to maximum range to release air-launched Exocet anti-ship missiles. In seeking to do this they failed, but succeeded in destroying the large ro-ro *Atlantic Conveyor*, together with her Chinook helicopters. The troops would now have to "yomp" to Port Stanley. This would take time, leaving the navy to hang on with minimal support, 12,875km/8,000 miles from home bases and in the depths of the Southern winter. It was with relief, therefore, that several brisk actions later, troops re-entered Port Stanley on June 14 enforcing the Argentine surrender.

A short but unpleasant war had cost about 1,000 lives, 75 per cent of them Argentine. From all causes, the British lost 10 V/STOL and 24 helicopters. About 100 Argentine aircraft are believed to have failed to return. Four Royal Navy ships, a fleet auxiliary, and a merchantman were sunk.

The Sea Harrier fighters were remarkably successful, as were their Sidewinder air-to-air missiles (AAMs). These aircraft flew over 1,400 defensive sorties, the RAF a further 150 in ground attack. Without the two aircraft carriers, however, they would not have been there.

ABOVE: **A view from *Hermes* of her "minder", the Sea Wolf-armed Type 22 frigate *Broadsword*. Type 22s were also paired with Sea Dart-armed Type 42s to form "missile traps".**

Directory of Aircraft Carriers

The overall total of true aircraft carriers, ships that conform to the treaty definition of being "designed for the specific and exclusive purpose of carrying aircraft ... [and] so constructed that aircraft can be launched therefrom and landed thereon", is not large, not least because that same treaty limited their proliferation. Space here is, therefore, available to review the many other forms in which aviation has served the world's navies at sea. The following directory is comprehensive in including all conventional aircraft carriers and many of the peripheral vessels that appeared along the way – balloon and seaplane carriers, CAM and MAC ships, helicopter carriers and, latterly, helicopter/V/STOL-capable assault ships. All, in the widest sense, are aircraft carriers and form a rich variety. The directory explores the background to each design and the degree of its success in service. Comparison between ships or classes is facilitated by the addition of a standard data panel. Space considerations have required the grouping together of carriers with similar functions but varying characteristics. Data panels for such groupings logically refer to the most significant of the vessels treated.

LEFT: *Invincible*. The V/STOL carrier now symbolizes the smaller navy. Fleets that can afford it will inevitably acquire large conventional carriers (CTOL), using V/STOL for special purposes.

LEFT AND FAR LEFT: **Two views of the raised catapult installation aboard the *North Carolina* (CA-12) with a Curtiss pusher flying boat embarked and taking off. The boat-handling crane has been fitted with a lightweight extension to deal with the 1-ton aircraft. Designated AB-3, the "A" represented Curtiss, the "B" a flying boat and "3" the third in the series.**

BELOW LEFT: **Taken at Pensacola in 1917 this picture shows the *Huntington* (CA-5) putting aloft a rather under-inflated kite balloon. Note the long stabilizing tail on the balloon. Forward of the mainmast, to which a horizontal swinging derrick has been added, can be seen a Curtiss N-9H floatplane.**

North Carolina (CA-12)

Built: Newport News, Virginia
Commissioned: May 7, 1908
Displacement: 14,760 tonnes/14,500 tons (standard); 16,160 tonnes/15,870 tons (deep load)
Length: 152.9m/502ft (at waterline); 153.7m/504ft 5in (overall)
Beam: 22.2m/72ft 11in
Draught: 7.6m/25ft (mean)
Aircraft: Up to 5, no hangar
Armament: 4 x 254mm/10in, 16 x 152mm/6in and 22 x 76mm/3in guns
Machinery: 2 sets vertical triple expansion, 2 shafts
Power: 17,150kW/23,000ihp
Speed: 22 knots
Fuel: 2,000 tonnes/1,960 tons
Range: Not known
Armour: 76–127mm/3–5in (belt); 25–89mm/1–3.5in (deck)
Complement: 914 men

North Carolina (CA-12) and *Huntington* (CA-5)

US naval aviation effectively began in September 1910 with the nomination of Captain Washington Irving Chambers as contact for all bodies concerned with or interested in the exploitation of flying in a service context. Although his appointment initially lacked official status, Chamber's engineering expertise and enthusiasm quickly resulted in the Navy Department acting upon his recommendations. It was his cooperation with Glenn Curtiss that resulted in Eugene Ely's pioneering flights to and from ships in November 1910 and January 1911.

Chambers did not favour specialist "aviation ships", believing that an aircraft should be treated as just another piece of essential shipboard equipment. Consequently, he showed an early interest in catapults powered by the compressed air available in all ships equipped with torpedo tubes.

The first working catapult was demonstrated aboard a barge as early as November 1912, but considerable further work preceded the fitting of the first catapult aboard a warship in October 1915. This was to the armoured cruiser *North Carolina*, attached to the naval air station at Pensacola, Florida, USA.

Following a series of static firings, the first under-weigh launch, that of a Curtiss flying boat, was made in July 1916. The aircraft still had to be recovered from the water by crane. Although the structure was fixed, and impeded the ship's after turret, it was repeated in the cruisers *Seattle* (CA-1) and *Huntington* (CA-5). In June 1917, *Huntington* was also fitted for the deployment of a kite balloon, which by then was widely used in already combatant navies.

From the American declaration of war in April 1917 onwards, the ships operated in the North Atlantic, where weather conditions disappointingly dictated that the equipment had to be removed.

LEFT: Seen transitting the Panama Canal in about 1930 the *Langley* (CV-1) shows clearly her original hull with flight deck erected above. The aircraft appear to be a mix of Boeing F2B and F4B and, beyond them, can be made out the tips of the two fold-down funnels. ABOVE: Obsolete by the 1930s, the *Langley* was converted to a seaplane tender, and redesignated (AV-3). With her forward flight deck and structure removed she was able to ship large, knocked-down aircraft such as the Consolidated P2Y flying boats seen here.

Langley (CV-1)

When, in 1918, the British pioneer *Argus* demonstrated that wheeled aircraft could operate successfully from through-deck ships, the US Navy quickly acquired its own for experimental conversion. Although superficially an unlikely choice, the large (and slow) fleet collier *Jupiter* (AC.3) had favourable characteristics. Her bridge structure was located well forward, separated by six capacious cargo holds from the machinery spaces, which were sited aft. She was twin-screwed, and her boilers exhausted unusually through a pair of tall, sided funnels.

Renamed *Langley*, she retained her bridge structure, her near full-length wooden flight deck being carried over on a lofty steel framework. This was open beneath, permitting a pair of gantry cranes to serve any of the original holds. Of these, No.1 was dedicated to aviation fuel stowage and No.4 to the elevator that connected the former weather deck with the flight deck. In the remaining holds, aircraft were stowed in a knocked-down condition. The cranes would retrieve them for assembly, before their transfer by lift to the flight deck, which had two catapults.

The starboard-side uptakes were cross-connected to the port and exhausted through a single (later two) port-side funnel. This hinged downward during flight operations to leave an unobstructed flight deck.

Modified more than once, the *Langley*'s arrester system combined fore-and-aft with transverse wires. Known, from her odd appearance, as the "Covered Wagon", she entered service in 1922. The service learned much from her but, obsolete by 1936, she was converted to a seaplane tender. In February 1942 she was fatally damaged by Japanese aircraft off Java.

Langley (CV-1)

Built: Mare Island Dockyard, California
Commissioned (as carrier): March 22, 1920
Displacement: 11,250 tonnes/11,050 tons (standard); 14,970 tonnes 14,700 tons (deep load)
Length: 158.1m/519ft (at waterline); 165.2m/542ft 2in (overall)
Beam: 19.9m/65ft 4in
Draught: 5.0m/16ft 6in (standard); 6.7m/22ft (deep load)
Aircraft: About 33
Flight deck: 159.3 x 19.8m/523 x 65ft
Armament: 4 x 127mm/5in guns
Machinery: Turbo-electric, 3 boilers, 2 shafts
Power: 5,250kW/7,000shp
Speed: 14.5 knots
Fuel: 2,040 tonnes/2,000 tons
Range: 22,680km/12,250nm at 10 knots
Armour: None
Complement: 425 men

ABOVE: In her final configuration as a seaplane tender the *Langley* looked even more odd. Note the now-visible original bridge structure, the lack of structure below the flight deck and the fold-down funnels.

Lexington (CV-2) class

That the 11,177-tonne/11,000-ton, 14-knot *Langley* could be succeeded by the 36,578-tonne/36,000-ton, 33-knot *Lexington* in just five years was a dramatically ambitious step but, in proving successful, greatly facilitated the advance of naval aviation in the US Navy.

Stemming from the post-World War I naval race, the six 44,198-tonne/43,500-ton *Lexington*-class battle-cruisers were laid down in 1920–21. Sacrificed to the ensuing Washington Treaty, four were cancelled. Two hulls were retained, however, for conversion to aircraft carriers in accordance with treaty provisions. Their size greatly influenced the parameters written into treaty limitations.

Driven by consideration of speed the hull form was long and slender, with boiler spaces consuming a significant proportion. *Argus*-style ducted exhaust was out of the question, the necessary solution being a vast stack, some 24.4m/80ft in height and dwarfing the island proper.

For its day, the new hangar was large and capacious, supplemented by a deep hold for the storage of knocked-down aircraft. Reconstruction was slow, the ships not completing until 1927. Nonetheless, they anticipated later British practice in fully enclosing the hangar, the side plating extending right up to the flight deck, the main strength deck.

Cruisers were, at this time, considered a major threat to carriers, resulting in considerable vertical and horizontal protection as well as a substantial medium-calibre gun battery. At the Washington Conference the American delegation insisted on the 203mm/8in gun as the maximum allowable

ABOVE: The two Lexingtons were near-identical but, where both had their 203mm/8in turrets removed, only the *Saratoga* had 127mm/5in armament substituted. She is seen here in September 1942, listing at 9.5 degrees after a torpedo attack, while being repaired at Tongatapu in the Pacific.

BELOW: Because of the two ships' similarity, the *Saratoga* was marked by a broad vertical black stripe on the funnel until the loss of her sister. This image thus probably shows *Lexington* (CV-2) as completed, with 203mm/8in turrets and a narrow forward end to the flight deck.

on a carrier. Only the *Lexington* (CV-2) and her sister, *Saratoga* (CV-3), were ever to carry such a battery. Its mass exacerbated the problems of asymmetric weight distribution while it was of doubtful value in being unable to fire across the flight deck. It was removed during 1940 in favour of the new dual-purpose 127mm/5in 38-calibre gun mounting (which only the *Saratoga* ever received).

Although widely criticized for consuming too great a proportion of the 137,166 tonnes/135,000 tons carrier tonnage permitted by treaty to the United States, the two ships convincingly demonstrated the superiority of the large carrier. Flight operations were facilitated by reduced ship motion and drier flight deck (notwithstanding higher transverse angular acceleration).

Above all, at a time when the exact role of the carrier was still being defined, the two proved the advantages of large air wings in the offensive strike role, an area also being explored by the Japanese.

During 1941, both ships were given widened flight decks forward but, as the *Lexington* was lost at the Coral Sea action in May 1942, only *Saratoga* received further modification. Her stability and survivability were enhanced by enlarged hull blisters and a lowering of the vast funnel casing. Larger blisters also increased the overall buoyancy to counteract the extra weight of years of additions and modifications, besides creating space for extra fuel oil. Asymmetry in the blisters also partially corrected the chronic problem of permanent list due to the island. The penalty was a quarter-knot loss in speed.

Worn out and obsolete, the ship was expended in 1946 at the Bikini atomic bomb trials.

LEFT: **The fine lines of the *Saratoga* (CV-3) are evident in this fine image. Note the unusual plan of the forward elevator and the line of palisades, or wind breaks, folded down. The 203mm/8in main battery is supported by twelve 127mm/5in weapons, disposed in groups of three in side pockets.** BELOW: **To the sorrow of many old "*Saras*", the *Saratoga*, shaken, patched and worn out by war, was expended as a "guinea pig" ship at the 1946 Bikini atom bomb tests.**

LEFT: **Considerable glamour was attached to naval aviation between the wars, a fact not lost on the recruitment service. The *Lexington*-class carrier is more obvious than the somewhat stylized aircraft, possibly Boeing F2Bs, flown from the *Saratoga* in the late 1920s.**

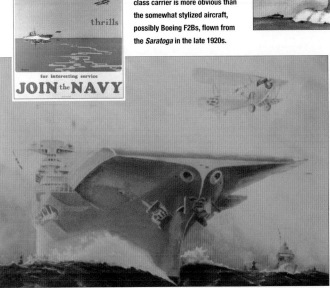

ABOVE: **The *Lexington* received a widened forward flight deck in her major 1936 refit. Note how the transition from the fine forward hull has resulted in distinctive knuckles. The stubby biplane fighter is a Grumman F2F, which flew from the ship until 1940.**

Lexington (CV-2) class

Built: *Lexington*, Bethlehem Steel, Fore River, commissioned December 14, 1927; *Saratoga*, New York Shipbuilding, Camden, commissioned November 16, 1927
Displacement: 39,450 tonnes/38,750 tons (standard); 48,500 tonnes/47,650 tons (deep load)
Length: 250m/822ft (bp); 270.5m/888ft (overall)
Beam: 32.1m/105ft 6in
Draught: 8.4m/27ft 6in (standard); 9.9m/32ft 6in (deep load)
Aircraft: About 80
Flight deck: 263.8 x 32.3m/866 x 106ft
Armament: 8 x 203mm/8in and 12 x 127mm/5in guns (as completed)
Machinery: Turbo-electric, 16 boilers, 4 shafts
Power: 134,300kW/180,000shp
Speed: 33 knots
Fuel: 2,700 tonnes/2,650 tons (original)
Range: 18,520km/10,000nm at 10 knots
Armour: 127–178mm/5–7in (vertical belt); 50mm/2in (deck)
Complement: 2,750 men

LEFT: **Despite the extreme fineness of her hull, the *Ranger* proved to be too slow. Note how far aft the flare is continued and the bulb, which can show maximum efficiency at only one speed.** ABOVE: ***Ranger* seen soon after her completion. Designed originally with no bridge structure, its late addition gave weight distribution problems. Note the sided sets of three fold-down funnels, an idea carried over from the *Langley*.**

Ranger (CV-4)

The first American carrier designed as such, the *Ranger* was considered unsuccessful, suffering from the limitations of both design inexperience and the restrictions imposed by the Washington Treaty.

Against the treaty global limit of 137,166 tonnes/135,000 tons carrier tonnage, the *Langley* was classed as "experimental" and did not count, but the giant Lexingtons consumed 33,530 tonnes/33,000 tons apiece. Only 70,107 tonnes/69,000 tons thus remained. American policy emphasized getting the maximum number of aircraft to sea and debate centred on whether this would be achieved best by building three ships, each of 23,369 tonnes/23,000 tons, four of 17,527 tonnes/17,250 tons or five of 14,021 tonnes/13,800 tons. Smaller vessels were considered ineffective.

The final choice of size needed to encompass the optimum number of existing and projected aircraft and how their accommodation and operation affected requirements for speed, protection, and armament, together with the dimensions and disposition of elevators.

Having experience only with the *Langley*, naval aviators insisted on a clear, obstruction-less flight deck. Current tactical doctrine also saw a carrier as an integral part of a force of scout cruisers but which, due to the speed and range of her aircraft, did not require to match their maximum speed. In terms of displacement tons per aircraft embarked, studies indicated that a flush-decked 14,021-tonne/13,800-ton ship of 29 knots offered the best compromise.

The ship that became the *Ranger* thus had her boiler spaces vulnerably concentrated and located well aft to minimize ducting and to allow exhaust via two groups of three small funnels, sided and capable of folding down during flight operations. The recently completed pair of British *Courageous*-class ships, however, resulted in a reassessment of the *Ranger* design that belatedly received a small island. This exacerbated a tight weight problem, which already demanded a very light construction. There was no armour built in and underwater protection was considered deficient. The hangar deck was the strength deck, the hangar being a light

LEFT: The only American fleet carrier not to participate in the Pacific war, the *Ranger* nonetheless proved her worth during the North African landings in November 1942. She is seen here soon afterward in what appears to be Measure 12 camouflage and with enhanced anti-aircraft armament. BELOW LEFT: Seen here almost edge-on, the large antenna of the *Ranger*'s CXAM-1 long-range air search radar did nothing to solve her increasing topweight problems. With a "K-ship" blimp hovering above, three Grumman TBM/TBF Avengers are seen with bomb bay doors open. BELOW: A somewhat informal photograph shows SBD Dauntless dive-bombers aboard the *Ranger*, possibly during the North African operations. In company with just three escorts, *Ranger* contributed 496 of the 1,078 sorties flown over the American sector in four days.

construction built on top and roofed by a wooden flight deck carried after the fashion of the *Langley*.

Recent exercises had highlighted the danger posed by the dive-bomber. This resulted in an armament biased to anti-aircraft warfare and an air wing that did not include torpedo aircraft, thus saving space on specialist facilities.

To achieve the required speed, the *Ranger* had fine lines but, in order to have a flight deck of useful width, had to adopt excessive flare. In poor conditions this made her wet, while her lack of length found her liable to pitch excessively in long-crested seas, a problem by no means unique.

Ranger's "open" hangar certainly pointed up advantages hitherto unsuspected but the design was too tight, necessitating that any catapult was fitted at hangar deck level, launching aircraft transversely through openings in the hangar walls, but eventually these were omitted as an economy measure.

Restricted to second-line duties during World War II, the ship went for disposal in 1947. She had been the only vessel of her size to be authorized and a rethink was obviously required for the definition of the ships that, similarly treaty-restricted, should succeed her.

Ranger (CV-4)

Built: Newport News, Virginia
Commissioned: June 4, 1934
Displacement: 14,021 tonns/13,800 tons (standard); 17,870 tonnes/17,550 tons (deep load)
Length: 222.4m/730ft (at waterline); 234.3m/769ft (overall)
Beam: 24.4m/80ft
Draught: 6m/19ft 8in (standard); 6.9m/22ft 6in (deep load)
Aircraft: About 76
Flight deck: 216 x 26.2m/709 x 86ft
Armament: 8 x 127mm/5in guns and 40 x 12.7mm/0.5in machine-guns (as completed)
Machinery: Geared steam turbines, 6 boilers, 2 shafts
Power: 39,900kW/53,500shp
Speed: 29 knots
Fuel: 1,595 tonnes/1,567 tons
Range: 18,520km/10,000nm at 15 knots
Armour: None
Complement: 2,140 men, including 760 aircrew

Yorktown class (CV-5, CV-6, CV-8)

All warship design is a compromise, and that of the Yorktowns shows the effects of both experience and the straitjacket of the Washington Treaty rules. By September 1931, when the small, one-off *Ranger* was laid down, the two Lexingtons had accumulated nearly eight ship-years of intensive fleet operations. Their speed margin over the battle fleet had enabled them to maintain station while flying had been continued in adverse conditions. This was largely a function of their great size, as were the large air wings that highlighted their offensive potential. It appeared that while a *Ranger*-sized carrier could satisfactorily augment a cruiser squadron in an opposed reconnaissance role, large carriers could enhance the striking power of the fleet itself. Even before the *Ranger* began to take shape it was therefore successfully argued that she should be followed by a pair of larger carriers.

Allowing for the *Ranger*'s planned displacement, the treaty permitted a further 55,883 tonnes/55,000 tons or so to the US Navy. This could conveniently be expended on a pair of 27,433-tonne/27,000-ton vessels, the largest ships permitted. Three ships were, however, more desirable.

The *Ranger* had been virtually unprotected but the new ships would be fitted with a horizontal armoured deck to counter the threat of dive-bombing, together with vertical protection to defeat cruiser gunfire. As the weight of the

TOP: **The only survivor of the trio, the *Enterprise* (CV-6) came through despite participating in nearly every Pacific carrier battle. An interesting design point, visible here, is the widening of the flight deck towards the centre to compensate for the intrusion of the island structure.** ABOVE: **American carrier air wings were maximized by suspending knocked-down aircraft from the hangar deckhead. Here, an F4F is being assembled aboard the *Enterprise*, late in 1941.**

Lexingtons' 203mm/8in battery was prohibitive, the ubiquitous 127mm/5in was adopted, it having to be accepted that the carriers' defence would be vested in their escort and in their own aircraft (the latter concept not yet combat-proven).

Studies showed that this level of protection, together with improved anti-torpedo protection and a 32.5-knot speed could, in fact, be achieved within a 20,321-tonne/20,000-ton displacement. The resulting power requirement demanded a conventional funnel arrangement.

In the hope of circumventing flight deck damage, arrester wires were fitted at either end to permit aircraft recovery over the bow or stern. Two catapults permitted athwartships launch to either side from the hangar deck and three elevators were provided. Continuing the "open-hangar" concept, with deck park, an impressive total of 96 aircraft could be accommodated. An additional bonus was the ability to warm-up aircraft engines in the hangar before transfer to the flight deck.

Two ships, *Yorktown* (CV-5) and *Enterprise* (CV-6), were laid down in 1934. Their near-sister, *Hornet* (CV-8), followed only in late 1939, when war in Europe was a reality. Treaty restrictions now abandoned, she could be built quickly with existing drawings.

The trio saw intensive service in the Pacific, notably at the critical battle of Midway in June 1942, at which the *Yorktown* was lost. The *Hornet*, which had launched the famous "Doolittle Raid" on Tokyo, was sunk at Santa Cruz in October 1942. The *Enterprise* survived and was scrapped as late as 1958. She had two major upgrades in anti-aircraft armament which in combination with much other accumulated weight obliged her to be bulged (or "blistered") to increase displacement.

ABOVE: **With what appears to be an F4U Corsair flying directly above, this ship has to be the *Enterprise*, for the aircraft did not enter carrier service with the US Navy until 1944, by which time *Hornet* and *Yorktown* had been sunk.** RIGHT: **This picture shows well the "open" construction typical of American carriers. The hull is flared over its entire length in order to maximize flight deck width.**

ABOVE: ***Enterprise*, probably during running trials in 1937 or early 1938. The large stack was necessary to receive uptakes from three boiler rooms. Note the shutter doors enclosing side openings to the hangar.** RIGHT: **A group of Avengers warms up on deck as the deck crew await another coming up on the elevator. Note the depth of the deck beams, necessary to maintain stiffness in a large open structure.**

Yorktown class (CV-5, CV-6, CV-8)

Class: *Yorktown*, Newport News, Virginia, commissioned September 30, 1937; *Enterprise*, Newport News, Virginia, commissioned May 12, 1938; *Hornet*, Newport News, Virginia, commissioned October 20, 1941
Displacement: 20,240 tonnes/19,875 tons (standard); 25,960 tonnes/25,500 tons (deep load)
Length: 234.6m/770ft (at waterline); 246.6m/809ft 6in (overall)
Beam: 25.4m/83ft 3in
Draught: 6.5m/21ft 6in (standard); 7.9m/26ft (deep load)
Aircraft: About 96
Flight deck: 244.3 x 26.2m/802 x 86ft
Armament: 8 x 127mm/5in and 16 x 28mm/1.1in guns, 24 x 12.7mm/0.5in machine-guns (as completed)
Machinery: Geared steam turbines, 9 boilers, 4 shafts
Power: 89,500kW/120,000shp
Speed: 32.5 knots
Fuel: 4,380 tonnes/4,300 tons
Range: 22,220km/12,000nm at 15 knots
Armour: 64–102mm/2.5–4in (vertical belt); 38mm/1.5in (deck)
Complement: 1,875 men

Wasp (CV-7)

As only about 15,241 tonnes/15,000 tons of treaty-permitted carrier tonnage remained to the Americans once the size of the Yorktowns had been decided, a second small carrier was inevitable. Although considerable design experience had been accumulated by this time, it was not yet operationally proven, as can be judged through the following summary of key dates:

	Laid down	Launched	Commissioned
Ranger (CV-4)	September 1931	February 1933	June 1934
Yorktown (CV-5)	May 1934	April 1936	September 1937
Enterprise (CV-6)	July 1934	October 1936	May 1938

The order for what became the *Wasp* (CV-7) was placed in September 1935. At this time, the Yorktowns were not even in the water and even though the *Ranger* had seen a year or more of service, the design process for the *Wasp* had preceded her completion. The *Ranger* had already pointed-up some of the deficiencies of small carriers, but further (albeit unproven) design work had highlighted desirable features possible in a larger hull. Inevitably, therefore, the *Wasp* would emerge as a small ship overburdened with large-ship features.

The policy of maximum-sized air wings resulted in hangar and aviation-related facilities dominating the ship above hangar

TOP: **Superficially similar to the Yorktowns, the one-off *Wasp* was significantly smaller and can be identified easily through her far taller funnel casing. Above the attendant tug the hangar side door is half open.** ABOVE: **Initially restricted by her size to the Atlantic Fleet, the *Wasp* assisted during the siege of Malta in ferrying in two loads of British Spitfires. Although lacking folding wings, these fitted comfortably on to an elevator.**

deck level, leaving space below it at a premium. To keep to the mandatory displacement, major dimensions were tightly circumscribed, leaving little volume for machinery. Boiler rooms were thus vulnerably grouped, and sandwiched between two engine rooms.

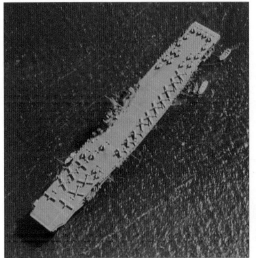

ABOVE: **Like the preceding Yorktowns, the *Wasp*'s flight deck extended further on the port side in way of the island structure, a feature clearly visible in this overhead shot.**

ABOVE: **Personnel of an escorting British ship watch as the *Wasp* prepares to fly off a deck-load of Spitfires for Malta in April or May 1942. Shortly after, she sailed for the Pacific.** BELOW: **Struck by three submarine torpedoes as she was engaged in refuelling aircraft, the *Wasp* was rapidly engulfed in uncontrollable fire and explosion.**

With the *Ranger* already overweight and the *Yorktown* realistically expected to be so, there was immense pressure on the *Wasp's* designers to cut weight. The light scantlings of flight deck and supporting structure were again adopted. To increase deck area and to counteract the offset load imposed by the island without using weight-consuming permanent ballast, both flight deck and hull beneath were asymmetrically extended on the port side.

Although the hangar was generous in proportion to ship size, the air wing was boosted, as in the *Ranger*, by the omission of larger, torpedo-carrying aircraft. To optimize launch rates, upon which American operational doctrine placed a premium, and without the multiple flying-off decks then favoured by the British and Japanese, four catapults were fitted, two forward on the flight deck and two athwartships at hangar deck level. The third elevator was of a skeletal, weight-saving deck-edge design, the first of its type.

Further, unseen economy in weight resulted in a deficiency in anti-torpedo protection and a side belt that was more nominal than actual. Despite considerable pressure, however, the *Wasp's* armament was kept in line with that of her larger contemporaries, but planned later upgrades of her ineffective pre-war automatic weapons were not carried out before her loss.

Considered too small and too slow, the *Wasp* joined the *Ranger* in the Atlantic early in the war. She rendered valuable assistance to the British in running two loads of fighters into Malta during the siege. Then sent to the Pacific, she was hit by three submarine torpedoes in September 1942. Like the *Lexington* before her, uncontrollable aviation fuel vapour explosions destroyed her.

Wasp (CV-7)

Built: Bethlehem, Quincy
Commissioned: April 25, 1940
Displacement: 14,970 tonnes/14,700 tons (standard); 19,100 tonnes/18,750 tons (deep load)
Length: 209.9m/689ft (at waterline); 225.8m/741ft 4in (overall)
Beam: 24.6m/80ft 8in
Draught: 6.1m/20ft (standard); 7.5m/24ft 6in (deep load)
Aircraft: About 74
Flight deck: 221.5 x 28.3m/727 x 93ft
Armament: 8 x 127mm/5in and 16 x 28mm/1.1in guns, 24 x 12.7mm/0.5in machine-guns
Machinery: Geared steam turbines, 6 boilers, 2 shafts
Power: 52,200kW/70,000shp
Speed: 29.5 knots
Fuel: 3,410 tonnes/3,350 tons,
Range: 22,220km/12,000nm at 15 knots
Armour: 16–19mm/0.63–0.75in (vertical belt); 32mm/1.25in (deck)
Complement: 2,165 men

Hybrid carrier studies

The essential features of an aircraft carrier have now been consistent for so long that it requires an effort of mind to visualize the situation at the time of the Washington Conference.

Aviation at sea was still a new concept and although the Royal Navy was, by virtue of being at the "sharp-end", well ahead in the associated technologies, no immutable ground rules had been laid.

True the British had already produced the world's first flush-decked carrier in the *Argus*, mainly as a platform for the deployment of torpedo-carrying aircraft, but they remained hostage to the traditional "big gun" lobby, which viewed aviation in a supporting role for the battle fleet.

The idea of heavy gun armament was still firmly entrenched, and it was not yet established whether carriers should be large or small, heavily armed and protected, or "soft", depending upon their escorts and aircraft for protection, a role in which aircraft were not yet proven.

Arguments persisted in all major fleets with respect to a carrier's exact role and, therefore, form. It occupied the US Navy for a decade, resulting in a series of design studies for ships with a flight deck overlaying a hangar and also a cruiser's armament and (nearly) a cruiser speed.

The two requirements co-existed awkwardly. Eight or nine 203mm/8in guns required three or four large turrets. Satisfactory firing arcs for these demanded either a cruiser-style forward end with a truncated flight deck and hangar, or to site the armament at a sufficient height to safely over-fire the flight deck without causing blast damage.

The idea that a carrier could successfully fight off a "treaty" cruiser bent on destroying her persisted even to the point where such a ship was

BELOW: **Ideas abounded for adding aviation to cruisers to improve their efficiency in the particular roles of reconnaissance in force and in commerce raiding. This design would have experienced weight distribution problems.**

ABOVE: **In a single hull, the marriage of air operations and a heavy surface armament was doomed to incompatibility. Each of these major requirements interferes catastrophically with the other.**

considered as an alternative contender to the design that became the *Yorktown*. The overriding argument, however, was that a carrier's principal weapon was her air wing. This could not operate with a damaged flight deck and therefore a carrier had no business engaging in a gun action with a heavy cruiser. A typical hypothetical design was proposed with the parameters that are shown in the specification box.

Hybrid carrier

Displacement: 27,490 tonnes/27,000 tons (standard)
Length: 233.4m/766ft (at waterline)
Beam: 27.4m/90ft
Draught: 8.3m/27ft 1in (mean)
Aircraft: About 75
Flight deck: Not known
Armament: 8 x 203mm/8in (4 double) and 12 x 127mm/5in (12 single) guns
Machinery: Turbo-electric, 4 shafts
Power: 104,450kW/140,000shp
Speed: 32.5 knots
Fuel: Not known
Range: 18,520km/10,000nm at 10 knots
Armour: 76mm/3in (vertical belt)
Complement: Not known

Long Island (AVG-1), Wolverine (IX-64) and Sable (IX-81)

Proposals for the conversion of smaller mercantile hulls to auxiliary carriers appear to have originated independently in the United States and Great Britain. Where the latter, however, saw their usefulness in convoy protection, the former viewed them as a general force multiplier, with specific roles in aircrew training and in aircraft transport.

The enormous American aircrew training programme proved to be critical to wartime success, and great credit is due to two unsung "heroines", *Sable* and *Wolverine*, which trained thousands in deck landings in the safe waters of the Great Lakes. Both had been converted from multi-decked paddle-propelled passenger vessels. They had few facilities beyond large flight decks, and aircraft flew from shore bases to exercise on them.

The first American escort carrier, *Long Island*, commissioned in June 1941, the same month as the pioneering British *Audacity*, and was converted

from an existing C-3 merchant ship. She had much in common with the still-extant *Langley*, retaining her original superstructure block with the flight deck erected above it on a high, open-sided framework. Plated-in only abaft the late superstructure, the space encompassed a small hangar equipped with a single elevator. There was no island and, as originally built, the flight deck was only 110.3m/362ft in length, long enough to land observation aircraft on, which would need to be launched by the forward-mounted catapult.

Experience soon highlighted shortcomings and subsequent upgrades included lengthening the flight deck, relocating the catapult, and improving the sub-division and the protection for the magazines.

Although the *Long Island* design was quickly improved upon, she formed the basis of the first group of escort carriers to be supplied to the British.

Long Island (AVG-1)

Built: Sun Shipbuilding
Converted: Newport News
Commissioned: June 2, 1941
Gross tonnage: 7,880 tons
Displacement: 14,250 tonnes/14,000 tons (deep load)
Length: 141.7m/465ft (at waterline), 149.9.m/492ft (overall)
Beam: 21.2m/69ft 6in
Draught: 7.8m/25ft 6in (mean)
Aircraft: 16
Flight deck: 127.3 x 21.6m/418ft x 70ft 10in
Armament: 1 x 127mm/5in and 2 x 76mm/3in guns, 4 x 12.7mm/0.5in machine-guns
Machinery: Busch-Sulzer 7-cylinder diesel engine, 1 shaft
Power: 6,340kW/8,500bhp
Speed: 16 knots
Fuel: 1,415 tonnes/1,390 tons
Range: Not known
Armour: None
Complement: 410 men

BELOW: **Seen later in the war, when she operated as an aircraft transport, the *Long Island* still shows her early features, particularly the short hangar right aft, the open underdeck forward structure and the total lack of superstructure. The lightly loaded mercantile hull required large quantities of ballast to immerse the single propeller and to impart a stable ship movement.**

Bogue-class escort carriers

American experience with the *Long Island*, and British with the very similar *Archer*, quickly exposed shortcomings in the conversions having been too austere. The flight deck was shorter than it needed to be, and the volume below it under-utilized for hangar space. Although deliberately chosen for ease of rearrangement of exhaust ducting, the diesel propulsion proved to be unreliable.

A specific American complaint was that their ships were too slow. Merchant ships are built for long-haul service, requiring that their most economical speed be maintained. A C-3, typically, was thus designed to run at 16.5 knots at a deadweight of 12,193–13,209 tonnes/12,000–13,000 tons. As carriers, they displaced nothing like this figure and, unless comprehensively ballasted, required a large increase in propulsive power to achieve a very small increase in speed.

An unforeseen problem had also arisen in building the existing hangar over a deck which retained its original sheer and camber. The slope and curvature resulted in considerable difficulty with the movement of aircraft about the space. Later ships were therefore built with hangar decks both plane and horizontal.

Early remedial measures included the addition of considerable quantities of permanent ballast and increasing the scantlings of added top-hamper. This not only gave better immersion but also reduced an earlier tendency to excessive stiffness and consequent rapid movement.

A further improvement was to switch to steam propulsion, technology with which the Americans were more familiar. At the comparatively low powers involved, this was not expected to cause any great exhaust problem.

The last of the first batch, which would have become HMS *Charger*, was retained by the US Navy for evaluation and training purposes. She had a diminutive island, sponsored out over the starboard side, because watch-keepers on earlier, flush-decked ships reported station-keeping and general ship control very difficult, with no points of reference.

BELOW: **On October 1, 1941 the Seattle-Tacoma Shipyard launched the freighter *Steel Advocate* for the Isthmian Steamship Company of New York. As can be seen from the temporary name, she had already been requisitioned for conversion to the escort carrier *Bogue* (CVE-9).**
BOTTOM: **The *Bogue*, as converted. The original forecastle and line of the upper deck can still be discerned and it is apparent that, to give adequate freeboard for the flight deck, the hull, in mercantile terms, is permanently in the ballast condition.**

American requirements for large air wings had to be matched by adequate fuel stowage. To achieve this, it was accommodated in tanks integrated with the ship's structure. From the outset the British were heavily critical of this practice, preferring to accept a much lower factor in favour of accommodating fuel in cylindrical tanks, de-coupled from the structure and, where possible, immersed in water. The conflicting views of what the British viewed as safe working practice, and what the Americans saw as unacceptably high standards in time of emergency, was never satisfactorily resolved.

The eleven *Bogue*-class escort carriers addressed most of the above points, together with the luxury of a second elevator. Essentially identical with the British Attacker class, all stemmed from the same yard.

Continued refinement in escort carrier design soon left the Bogues looking relatively unsophisticated. They were used very effectively in the Atlantic and where supported by a division of destroyer escorts, they exploited high-grade Ultra information to become efficient U-boat killers.

TOP: **Although, of course, the flight deck has to be flat, without sheer or camber, the upper deck of the original hull had both. The small galleries projecting from the ship's side followed the original curve, only later ships having them in a horizontal line as indicated here.** ABOVE: **An anonymous ship in an anonymous yard. No carrier, either new or returning from repair or refit, was allowed to sail empty. This one is being loaded with TBF/TBM Avenger sections to meet the endless attritional demands of the Pacific fleet carriers.**

ABOVE: *Bogue*'s war service was in anti-submarine warfare in the Atlantic. Seen here from a patrol aircraft, she is in Measure 22 camouflage. Note how the small island is completely outboard of the flight deck edge, so that it appears deeper from starboard than it does from port.

Bogue class

Class: Altamaha (CVE-18); *Barnes* (CVE-20); *Block Island* (CVE-21); *Bogue* (CVE-9); *Breton* (CVE-23); *Card* (CVE-11); *Copahee* (CVE-12); *Core* (CVE-13) *Croatan* (CVE-25); *Nassau* (CVE-16); *Prince William* (CVE-31)

Built: All by Seattle-Tacoma Shipbuilding

Commissioned: June 1942–April 1943

Gross tonnage: 8,400 tons

Displacement: 16,900 tonnes/16,600 tons (deep load)

Length: 141.8m/465ft (at waterline); 151.2m/ 495ft 8in (overall)

Beam: 21.2m/69ft 6in

Draught: 7.1m/23ft 3in (standard); 8.0m/26ft 3in (deep load)

Aircraft: About 24

Flight deck: 133.2 x 24.4m/436ft 8in x 80ft

Armament: 2 x 127mm/5in and 10 x 20mm/ 0.79in guns

Machinery: Geared steam turbine, 2 boilers, 1 shaft

Power: 6,340kW/8,500shp

Speed: 17 knots

Fuel: 3,260 tonnes/3,200 tons

Range: 48,710km/26,300nm at 15 knots

Armour: None

Complement: 900 men

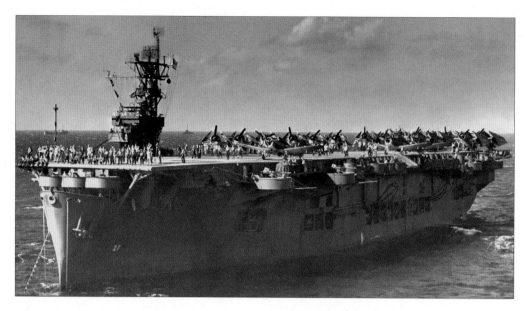

Sangamon-class escort carriers

Once the American auxiliary aircraft carrier programme moved into top gear, early in 1942, every available C-3 hull, the preferred basis for conversion, was soon allocated. To overcome an immediate shortfall, four T-3 tanker hulls were substituted. This decision was not popular with the US Navy, for these were to be fast, twin-screw fleet oilers, urgently required for extended Pacific operations and always in short supply.

Except for their continuous sheerline, which had to be built over to provide a flat hangar deck, the ships made excellent carriers, the four being known as the Sangamon class. Being longer than the C-3-derived carriers, they incorporated a larger hangar and flight deck. Their twin screws enhanced manoeuvrability and provided a measure of redundancy, although machinery spaces were common to each. They were inherently well subdivided, while their size enabled them to retain some tanks for fuel which could be freighted or transferred to smaller and ever-thirsty escorts. Their own bunker spaces were 80 per cent larger than those of a C-3, giving them the theoretical ability to steam around the world at 15 knots without refuelling.

No other tankers were so converted but they were regarded as very successful, their design becoming the starting point for later classes. In appreciation, they looked long and lower, continuously plated up to flight deck level but with a characteristic line of rectangular openings below hangar deck level providing access for hose-handling facilities.

Like the preceding Bogues, the Sangamons had two elevators and a single catapult. Despite the need for maximum-sized flight decks, American practice was to terminate them

TOP: **The four Sangamons were modified from twin-screw, *Cimmaron*-class fleet oilers. Larger and more powerful, they were the best of the early escort carriers but further hulls were too scarce to be spared.** ABOVE: **The diminutive size of a Sangamon bridge structure is here well shown, with the blocks of the aircraft-handling derrick. Judging by the dress of the "goofers" watching the Avenger, the picture was taken on an open day.**

short of bow and stern, to allow free arcs for the armament located there.

Although they saw considerable action, no Sangamons were lost, so that they received intermittent upgrades as opportunity offered. This included a second catapult, much improved electronics and considerable enhancement to the

LEFT: **A Sangamon was instantly recognizable by the row of rectangular recesses in the side shell plating, their lower edge following the line of the tankers' original upper decks. The class made its mark during the North African landings of November 1942, possibly the venue for this shot.**

ABOVE: **The distant mass of shipping suggests the North African landings. The aircraft to the left are Douglas SBD Dauntless dive-bombers. These were carried aboard only the *Sangamon* and *Santee*. The flight deck markings remain a mystery.** ABOVE RIGHT: **A deck crew races to release a hooked Avenger, fold wings and remove quickly from the landing area to free the deck for the next incomer.**

armament, which reflected the increased threat from air attack, particularly that of the kamikaze after October 1944.

As new ships, the four covered the American landings in North Africa in November 1942. At this point their armament comprised two 127mm/5in guns and two twin 40mm/1.57in mounts on the quarterdeck, with two further twin 40mm/1.57in and a dozen single 20mm/0.79in guns disposed in sided sponsons and on the forecastle. By the war's end the 40mm/1.57in weapons had increased to two quadruple and ten twin mountings. Only the close of hostilities prevented a further increase, with each of the 127mm/5in guns being traded for a further twin 40mm/1.57in, and all single 20mm/0.79in weapons being exchanged for twins. This enormous increase in top-weight was possible only because of their inherently stable tanker origins.

Compared with the C-3s, the Sangamons had greater survivability. Action damage included two kamikaze strikes, four bomb hits, one submarine torpedo and an internal explosion, yet all survived.

Sangamon class

Class: *Chenango*, converted Norfolk Navy Yard, commissioned September 19, 1942; *Sangamon*, converted Newport News, commissioned August 25, 1942; *Santee*, converted Puget Sound Navy Yard, commissioned August 24, 1942; *Suwannee*, converted Bethlehem Steel, Staten Island, commissioned September 24, 1942

Gross tonnage: 10,500 tons

Displacement: 24,500 tonnes/24,100 tons (deep load)

Length: 160.1m/525ft (at waterline); 168.7m/553ft (overall)

Beam: 22.9m/75ft

Draught: 9.3m/30ft 6in (deep load)

Aircraft: Up to 36

Flight deck: 153.1 x 25.9m/502 x 85ft

Armament (as designed): 2 x 127mm/5in, 8 x 40mm/1.57in (4 double) and 12 x 20mm/0.79in (12 single) guns

Machinery: Geared steam turbines, 4 boilers, 2 shafts

Power: 10,100kW/13,500shp

Speed: 18 knots

Fuel: 5,850 tonnes/5,750 tons

Range: 44,450km/24,000nm at 15 knots

Armour: None

Complement: 940 men

Casablanca-class escort carriers

In tropical conditions, escort carriers suffered from insufficient speed. A torpedo-laden Avenger required a relative wind speed of 30 knots to get airborne safely and, even when lightened by emptied tanks and ordnance racks, 25 knots to alight safely on a small carrier's crowded decks. Sometimes unable to raise 20 knots of relative wind in calm conditions, an escort carrier could be affected operationally, for to persevere with flying meant a high aircraft attrition rate.

Among the US Navy's enormous construction programmes, the President personally favoured those for escort carriers and destroyer escorts. When the industrialist Henry Kaiser proposed in mid-1942 to devote one of his yards to series production of escort carriers, he was quickly awarded a contract for 50. As good as his word, Kaiser produced these, the Casablanca class, in twenty months from the commencement of the first in November 1942 to the completion of the last in July 1944.

The Sangamons had been completed in August/September 1942 and were impressing people with their capability. It was decided to continue the less efficient Bogue type for British use, as they were adequate for anti-submarine warfare and convoy escort. Kaiser would build a new type for the US Navy, whose requirements differed.

To make a volume-critical hull of a given size go 3 knots faster requires a combination of greater power and improved lines, necessitating greater length. Time was saved by using

TOP: **Laid down as the *Alava Bay* (CVE-103), the *Roi* was completed in August 1944. Redesignated AVB-103 she spent her life ferrying aircraft and repatriating prisoners of war. Having seen just 20 months of service she was, like many others, discarded, and was scrapped in 1947.** ABOVE: **In contrast, those of her sisters commissioned early enough to provide ground support at Leyte Gulf saw more than enough action. Here, off Samar, a stricken Japanese aircraft dives at the *Kitkun Bay* (AVG-71).**

the fore and after ends of an existing fast transport design and inserting a longer mid-body.

Heavy machinery manufacturers were booked to the extent that both the favoured steam turbine and the unloved diesel were unavailable in the required timescale. The choice of an

ABOVE: **This profile shows features unique to the** *Casablanca*-**class ships, the wide, flat transom stern and the "open" elevator serving the after end of the flight deck. The curves of the disruptive camouflage suggest a variant of Measure 32.**

ABOVE: **Another unit subjected to change of name is seen here as the** *Tripoli* **(AVG-64) but was laid down as the** *Didrickson Bay*. **The vertical bands of camouflage colour comprising Measure 32/4A are blended at their forward edges by spray painting.** BELOW: **During the Battle of Samar in October 1944 escort carriers of the US Seventh Fleet found themselves under fire from Japanese battleships and cruisers. This carrier has been nearly straddled by a salvo of heavy projectiles.**

Casablanca class

Class: *Admiralty Islands* (CVE-99); *Anzio* (CVE-57); *Attu* (CVE-102); *Bismarck Sea* (CVE-95); *Bougainville* (CVE-100); *Cape Esperance* (CVE-88); *Casablanca* (CVE-55); *Corregidor* (CVE-58); *Fanshaw Bay* (CVE-70); *Gambier Bay* (CVE-73); *Guadalcanal* (CVE-60); *Hoggatt Bay* (CVE-75); *Hollandia* (CVE-97); *Kadashan Bay* (CVE-76); *Kalinin Bay* (CVE-68); *Kasaan Bay* (CVE-69); *Kitkun Bay* (CVE-71); *Kwajalein* (CVE-98); *Liscombe Bay* (CVE-56); *Lunga Point* (CVE-94); *Makassar Strait* (CVE-91) *Makin Island* (CVE-93); *Manila Bay* (CVE-61); *Marcus Island* (CVE-77); *Matanikau* (CVE-101); *Mission Bay* (CVE-59); *Munda* (CVE-104); *Natoma Bay* (CVE-62); *Nehenta Bay* (CVE-74); *Ommaney Bay* (CVE-79); *Petrof Bay* (CVE-80); *Roi* (CVE-103); *Rudyerd Bay* (CVE-81); *Saginaw Bay* (CVE-82); *Salamaua* (CVE-96); *Sargent Bay* (CVE-83); *Savo Island* (CVE-78); *Shamrock Bay* (CVE-84); *Shipley Bay* (CVE-85); *Sitkoh Bay* (CVE-86); *Solomons* (CVE-67); *St. Lo* (CVE-63); *Steamer Bay* (CVE-87); *Takanis Bay* (CVE-89); *Thetis Bay* (CVE-90); *Tripoli* (CVE-64); *Tulagi* (CVE-72); *Wake Island* (CVE-65); *White Plains* (CVE-66); *Windham Bay* (CVE-92)
Built: All by Kaiser, Vancouver
Commissioned: July 1943–December 1944
Displacement: 8,350 tonnes/8,200 tons (standard); 10,750 tonnes/10,550 tons (deep load)
Length: 149.5m/490ft (at waterline); 152.2m/ 499ft (overall)
Beam: 19.8m/65ft
Draught: 6.3m/20ft 9in (mean)
Aircraft: About 27
Flight deck: 144.6 x 24.4m/474 x 80ft
Armament: 1 x 127mm/5in, 8 x 40mm/1.57in (4 double), and 12 x 20mm/0.79in (12 single) guns
Machinery: Steam reciprocating engines, 4 boilers, 2 shafts
Power: 6,700kW/9,000ihp
Speed: 20 knots
Fuel: 2,040 tonnes/2,000 tons
Range: 18,980nm/10,250nm at 15 knots
Armour: None
Complement: 815 men

alternative fell on the Skinner Uniflow reciprocating steam engine. This five-cylinder, multi-expansion unit was very compact and was also used in amphibious warfare ships.

Kaiser's ships were designed without the sheer that complicated early conversions, and their fine after run with twin screws resulted in a distinctive, broad transom stern. They were still too small to have adequate protection worked around magazines, a shortcoming that led directly to the violent explosion that destroyed the *Liscombe Bay* following a single torpedo hit.

Commencement Bay-class escort carriers

During 1942, the President had declared that one hundred escort carriers would be built for the US Navy and, despite the already overwhelming Allied naval superiority by the autumn of 1944, this pledge would have been realized with the addition of 35 ships of the Commencement Bay type. This number, however, was simply not required and, with the hugely expanded service already experiencing personnel shortages, only 19 were actually completed. With hostilities ending, 4 more were dismantled in an incomplete state, while the other 12 were not laid down.

The very successful Kaiser production line for the Casablanca class saw the concept repeated by the award of 27 to the Todd organization. These, however, had to be spread between three yards and, with spare capacity emerging, Kaiser was given the other eight, only to have them cancelled.

It had been the size and adaptability of the Sangamons that had most impressed the navy but, with fleet oilers too few and too valuable for further conversions, it had to await a new design derived from the same characteristics.

The redundancy of twin shafts in the Sangamons was valued, but was offset somewhat by the grouping of the machinery spaces to mercantile standards, and vulnerability to a single torpedo. Redesigned, they were spread as far as the aviation facilities allowed.

With extreme urgency no longer a driving factor, the general specification could also be upgraded to accommodate larger and heavier aircraft. Larger and faster elevators were matched by a flight deck stressed to accept 7.7-tonne/17,000lb (as opposed to 6.35-tonne/14,000lb) aircraft. More generous flight deck dimensions permitted the use of a second catapult, although this partly overlapped the forward elevator. Modified from the model used in fleet carriers, this equipment could accelerate a 7.3-tonne/16,000lb aircraft to a speed of 145kph/90mph in a 30m/95ft run.

BELOW: **Purpose-designed and more sophisticated, the Commencement Bays came late in World War II, saw little action and, for the most part, were retained. The *Palau* (ACV-122) is seen here, probably about 1950, with an experimental Marine squadron of Piasecki HRP tandem-rotor helicopters.** BOTTOM: **The *Palau* again. Note the supports for the overhung weight of the bridge structure and the lofty mast, necessary to accommodate a comprehensive suite of electronics.**

Externally, the Commencement Bays could be recognized by their more generously proportioned superstructure, with the lattice mast of earlier classes replaced by a solid lower mast, topped-off by a lighter, pole topmast. Pronounced tables supported the proliferating antennas of radar and communications.

The bulk of the class remained active after the end of the war for, being the only small carriers able to operate the latest aircraft types, they were assigned anti-submarine warfare (ASW) duties. As such, some were early recipients in the deployment of helicopters.

Some of the class were discarded in the large clear-out of reserve fleet escort carriers (CVEs) in 1959–61 but the majority of the survivors served on until the early 1970s.

ABOVE: *Commencement Bay* (CVE-105) shows off to advantage the sweeping curves of Measure 32/16A which used matt black with up to four shades of green or grey. Note the large stern galleries, each accommodating a quadruple 40mm/1.57in mounting.

Commencement Bay class

Class: *Badoeng Strait* (CVE-116); *Bairoko* (CVE-115); *Block Island* (CVE-106); *Cape Gloucester* (CVE-109); *Commencement Bay* (CVE-105); *Gilbert Islands* (CVE-107); *Kula Gulf* (CVE-108); *Mindoro* (CVE-120); *Palau* (CVE-122); *Point Cruz* (CVE-119); *Puget Sound* (CVE-113); *Rabaul* (CVE-121); *Rendova* (CVE-114); *Saidor* (CVE-117); *Salerno Bay* (CVE-110); *Siboney* (CVE-112); *Sicily* (CVE-118); *Tinian* (CVE-123); *Vella Gulf* (CVE-111)

Built: Todd (Tacoma, Portland, Willamette)

Displacement: 19,250 tonnes/18,900 tons (standard); 26,200 tonnes/24,000 tons (deep load)

Length: 160.1m/525ft (at waterline); 169.9m/557ft (overall)

Beam: 22.9m/75ft

Draught: 8.5m/28ft (deep load)

Aircraft: About 33

Flight deck: 152.8 x 24.4m/501 x 80ft

Armament: 2 x 127mm/5in, 36 x 40mm/1.57in (3 quadruple, 12 double), and 20 x 20mm/0.79in guns

Machinery: Geared steam turbines, 4 boilers, 2 shafts

Power: 11,950kW/16,000shp

Speed: 19 knots

Fuel: 3,300 tonnes/3,250 tons

Range: 15,740km/8,500nm at 15 knots

Armour: None

Complement: 1,050 men

LEFT: **The *Sicily* (ACV-118) saw service throughout the Korean War, flying F4U Corsairs in ground support. She is seen here a little later, probably 1953–54, still retaining her armament and deploying Sikorsky S-55s, probably in the HRS troop-transport version. The change of category from CVE to ACV also brought changes of name, the *Sicily* having originally been allocated the name *Sandy Bay*.**

ABOVE: Names such as Kwajalein, Eniwetok and Majuro cement the connection between the Marshall Islands and the US Navy, hence this not over-accurate rendering of the *Essex*-class *Lexington* (CV-16).

LEFT: Sporting a full deck-load, this Essex is probably seen during the 1950s, but is much the same as her World War II configuration. The pronounced concave flare of the stern reflects the design requirement for an astern speed high enough to allow aircraft recovery over the bows, for which eventuality a second set of arrester wires was specified.

Essex class

The Vinson-Trammell Act of 1934 provided for the US Navy to be expanded to the maximum tonnage allowed by treaty. Four years later, with international agreements collapsing, it was decided to increase American carrier tonnage from the treaty-limited 177,808 tonnes/175,000 tons to 218,450 tonnes/215,000 tons. This permitted construction of the *Hornet* (CV-8) and for another, CV-9, of about the same size, although limitation was, by now arbitrary.

Even before CV-9 was laid down, however, the war in Europe in April 1941 had triggered a new, emergency American naval expansion. In May 1940, CV-10 to CV-12 were added, followed by CV-13 to CV-19 in August. Rapid carrier production on this scale demanded that the design be tightly controlled. Desirable features included a high speed, an expanded air group, better protection and enhanced armament. No longer limited by treaty, this package demanded over 27,433 tonnes/27,000 tons displacement which, although considerably larger than the Yorktowns, was still greatly influenced by them.

The extra displacement allowed for greatly improved horizontal protection, the longer hull having space to arrange machinery compartments for maximum survivability. Longer hulls are also a factor in higher speed and, of course, in larger flight decks. The Americans were less tolerant than the British of armament, etc intruding into deck space, which was

ABOVE: In this apparently featureless view of an Essex after flight deck it is, nonetheless, possible to discern arrester wires, the after elevator and the reduction in flight deck width in way of the port quarter armament. Note the small screen sheltering the Deck Landing Officer. The carrier is proceeding slowly in a stiff chop that is causing her planeguard destroyer some discomfort.

prioritized for aircraft manoeuvring and parking. Eight of the class's twelve 125mm/5in guns were thus grouped, *Lexington*-fashion, fore and aft of the island.

Named USS *Essex,* the first-of-class could accommodate an air group of 37 dive-bombers, 18 torpedo-bombers and 36 fighters (typically Helldivers, Avengers and Hellcats respectively). Three elevators were fitted, the first being a port-side deck-edge unit which folded into the ship's side when not in use. Two flush-mounted catapults were provided forward, but some early ships also received a transverse catapult located in the open-style hangar. Later ships had their bow section stretched by 4.88m/16ft to allow better arcs for the forecastle-mounted 49mm/1.93in battery.

ABOVE: **A picture-postcard Pacific day, but with sufficient cloud to make hostile aircraft difficult to spot. The ship is one of the earlier, short-hulled Essex class, a group which comprised CV-9–13, 16–18, 20 and 31. Later units were nearly 5m/16ft 5in longer with bow and stern gun positions extending from beneath the flight deck.**

BELOW: **Although it appears posed, this picture of** *Yorktown* **(CV-10) gives a good impression of a hangar space that seems vast – until aircraft are put in it. The F6Fs in the foreground enjoy about 1.37m/4ft 6in of clearance beneath the 5.33m/17ft 6in deckhead but the larger TBF/TBM had barely 0.3m/1ft.**

Essex class

Class: *Antietam* (CV-36); *Bennington* (CV-20); *Bon Homme Richard* (CV-31); *Boxer* (CV-21); *Bunker Hill* (CV-17); *Essex* (CV-9); *Franklin* (CV-13); *Hancock* (CV-19); *Hornet* (CV-12); *Intrepid* (CV-11); *Kearsarge* (CV-33); *Lake Champlain* (CV-39); *Lexington* (CV-16); *Leyte* (CV-32); *Oriskany* (CV-34); *Philippine Sea* (CV-47); *Princeton* (CV-37); *Randolph* (CV-15); *Shangri-La* (CV-38); *Tarawa* (CV-40); *Ticonderoga* (CV-14); *Valley Forge* (CV-45); *Wasp* (CV-18); *Yorktown* (CV-10)

Commissioned: December 1942–May 1946; *Oriskany* (CV-34), September 1950

Displacement: 28,000 tonnes/27,500 tons (standard); 37,050 tonnes/36,380 tons (deep load)

Length: 250.1m/820ft (at waterline); 266m/872ft (overall)

Length (later ships): 255m/836ft (at waterline); 270.8m/888ft (overall)

Beam: 28.4m/93ft

Draught: 7m/23ft (standard); 8.4m/27ft 6in (deep load)

Aircraft: 90–100

Flight deck: 262.9 x 32.9m/862 x 108ft

Armament: 12 x 127mm/5in (4 double, 4 single), 32 x 40mm/1.57in (8 quadruple), and 46 x 20mm/0.79in guns

Machinery: Geared steam turbines, 8 boilers, 4 shafts

Power: 111,900kW/150,000shp

Speed: 33 knots

Fuel: 6,450 tonnes/6,330 tons

Range: 37,040km/20,000nm at 15 knots

Armour: 64–100mm/2.5–4in (vertical belt); 38mm/1.5in (hangar deck); 38mm/1.5in (protective deck)

Complement: 2,630 men

Although not beyond criticism, the Essex class proved effective, the class being enlarged by the ordering of CV-20 and CV-21 in December 1941, CV-31 to CV-40 in August 1942, CV-45 in June 1943 and, finally, CV-50 to CV-55 early in 1945. In all, 24 were completed by a total of five builders, forming the largest-ever series of fleet carriers.

From the Pacific war, the class went on to serve in Korea and Vietnam. Overcrowded even in 1945, the ships nonetheless proved amenable to modernization, notably with angled decks, for service in the jet age. This, fortunately, reduced crew numbers, which had grown from an initial estimate of 2,386 to 3,385 by 1945. Some of the class survived until the 1980s by which time there was a wide variation, no two ships being alike.

Independence class

When contracts were signed for the early *Essex*-class fleet carriers, it was anticipated that deliveries would not begin before 1944. The President, as ever closely involved in naval affairs, was concerned. With war looming he considered that the fleet's few available carriers, CV-2 to CV-8, would, with losses, be insufficient to sustain operations until 1944. In the summer of 1941, he therefore proposed paralleling the escort carrier (CVE) programme with the rapid conversion of cruiser hulls into light carriers (CVL), fast enough to accompany the fleet in most weather conditions.

Having examined the proposal, the technical department responsible were united in their opposition to it. Besides disrupting the cruiser construction programme, hulls removed for the purpose would, they advised, be fundamentally unsuitable for the purpose, any carrier of this size being too lively and of inadequate freeboard to operate her aircraft in anything but favourable conditions.

A cruiser hull was of slender proportions so, built up with hangar and flight deck with necessary freeboard, it would present stability problems. To maintain speed in a seaway, cruiser hulls were given considerable sheer which, without major reconstruction, would result in the curved hangar deck

TOP: **The high, narrow-gutted cross section of the CVL in the foreground makes the *Essex* astern look squat and beamy. Note the funnel casings, cranked out beyond the line of the island structure and the distance to which the gun tubs are sponsoned from the hull.** ABOVE: **While this aerial shot emphasizes the original cruiser hull beneath the narrow flight deck, closer inspection reveals the large, faired blister, which follows a curve while the line of the hangar wall is straight.**

that was already proving troublesome in early CVEs. The four widely spaced boilers would require separate uptakes, all of which would impinge on an already narrow hangar. The fine run at either end would limit the dimensions of elevators, forcing them well towards the fuller mid-body.

TOP: The profile of the *Independence*-class CVLs was unique. In the initial design there would have been no island, navigation being conducted, Japanese-style, from below the forward edge of the flight deck. ABOVE: CVLs had narrow, cramped flight decks. Note here how the stern galleries appear to be "tacked-on", and the unusual supporting structure for the cranked funnel casings and the bridge. RIGHT: Working with the fleet, the CVLs required a full outfit of electronics, the main argument for including a bridge structure. The main input to the plan/position indicator shown here was from the standard SK air search radar, whose antenna was located on the stub mast between the two pairs of funnels.

The President persisted. Speed was the overriding priority and there were to be no frills. Under direct pressure, the Board reconsidered, agreeing that a *Cleveland*-class light cruiser hull, suitably bulged (or "blistered"), might work. It did. Bulging adds considerably more buoyancy than weight, and in this case for the sacrifice of 1½ knots in speed not only effected the necessary improvement in stability but also provided for a considerable increase in bunker capacity. The boiler uptakes were led via four externally supported casings to a distinctive row of small funnels.

Known, from the lead ship, as the Independence class, the CVLs were always weight-sensitive. The diminutive island was only partly balanced by a port-side flight deck extension to enable aircraft to be wheeled around the forward elevator. The ships tended to trim by the stern. Ordnance capacity was small while overcrowding was unavoidable, the projected 1,200 cruiser crew being swollen by some 25 per cent. The provision of a second catapult demanded a reduction in armament.

Despite the inevitable problems, the CVLs arrived in good time to supplement the fleet's carrier strength at a critical juncture. As four of the seven fleet carriers were, in fact, lost during 1942, the President was vindicated. In practice, the ships *were* lively but crew and fliers learned to live with it. They were able to operate torpedo aircraft as well as dive-bombers and fighters but they were never intended to be more than a stopgap. Their inferior characteristics were acceptable in war but they subsequently had little application.

Independence class

Class: *Bataan* (CVL-29); *Belleau Wood* (CVL-24); *Cabot* (CVL-28); *Cowpens* (CVL-25); *Independence* (CVL-22); *Princeton* (CVL-23); *Langley* (CVL-27); *Monterey* (CVL-26); *San Jacinto* (CVL-30)

Built: All by New York Shipbuilding, Camden

Commissioned: January 1943–December 1943

Displacement: 11,050 tonnes/10,650 tons (standard); 15,170 tonnes/14,900 tons (deep load)

Length: 183m/600ft (at waterline); 189.9m/622ft 6in (overall)

Beam: 21.8m/71ft 6in

Draught: 6.4m/21ft (standard); 7.5m/24ft 6in (deep load)

Aircraft: 31

Flight deck: 168.4 x 22.3m/552 x 73ft

Armament: 24 x 40mm/1.57in (2 quadruple, 8 double) and 16 x 20mm/0.79in guns

Machinery: Geared steam turbines, 4 boilers, 4 shafts

Power: 74,600kW/100,000shp

Speed: 31.5 knots

Fuel: 2,650 tonnes/2,600 tons

Range: 23,150km/12,500nm at 15 knots

Armour: 83–127mm/3.75–5in (vertical belt – except in CVL-22 and-23); 50mm/2in (protective deck)

Complement: 1,500 men

Midway class

The *Midway* had a difficult gestation as the President disliked the idea of "big" carriers, agreeing with much naval opinion that more, and smaller (i.e. *Essex*- and *Independence*-class) ships, were needed, not least because they were required urgently.

By 1940, however, the *Essex* design work was complete and studies began to define her successor. Much influenced by the Yorktowns, the *Essex* echoed current thoughts that carriers should be protected primarily against gunfire from heavy cruisers. The anti-torpedo defence of the *Essex* was subsequently thought deficient.

With the European war in progress, American designers were more conscious of the threat from aerial bombing but, by now, having access to British carrier practice, were equally aware that heavy flight deck protection on a limited displacement meant greatly reduced aircraft capacity. Then, in 1941, the British *Illustrious* and *Formidable* suffered and survived savage dive-bombing and their repair in American yards afforded graphic first-hand evidence of the value of horizontal protection.

The mere provision of large areas of armour required considerable increase in dimensions and displacement to float it. To keep this within bounds, the Americans decided on a soft-sided "open" hangar structure, topped-off with a heavy flight deck. There being no definitive answer as to whether

TOP: **Dwarfed by the yard's hammerhead crane the *Roosevelt*'s already low hull appears even lower. Note the revised disposition of the 127mm/ 5in armament and the wide stern gallery for automatic weapons.**

ABOVE: **The main argument for the big carrier was the deployment of strategic nuclear-capable bombers such as the Douglas A-3 Skywarrior seen here. This 37.2-tonne/82,000lb monster had, in extremis, to be stopped by the nylon crash barrier being sorted out in the foreground.**

one very thick deck gives more protection than several thinner ones, the designers in this case backed-up the heavy flight deck with 50mm/2in hangar deck *and* main deck. Although this was beneficial in lowering the ship's centre of gravity, they still had a flight deck with a comparatively low freeboard, which decreased further with later accumulations of weight.

Needing to be constructed in addition to the "production-line" Essex class, the big carriers, known as the Midways, did not receive presidential sanction until December 1942, resulting in their being completed too late to see combat.

The sheer size of the *Midway* resulted in an air group big enough to be considered unwieldy, a situation resolved by the rapidly increasing size and weight of aircraft.

ABOVE: **Newly completed, the *Midway* (CVA-41) leaves her builders. Her huge, rectangular flight deck would be much modified in her later career.**

BELOW: **Fully modernized, with angled deck and enclosed "hurricane" bow, a Midway appears squat compared with the later, and larger, Forrestal type in the background.**

ABOVE: **One of the world's three largest cruisers, the 17,273-tonne/17,000-ton *Des Moines* (CA-134), takes fuel from one of the world's three largest carriers. Note the side elevator lowered to hangar deck level.** BELOW: **Flanked by a row of McDonnell F2H Banshees, a Midway's crew of more than 2,100 assemble at divisions. The aircraft date the picture to the early 1950s.**

Only three of the planned six ships were ever built but post-war they proved to be good value for money. With the advent of the Cold War, the navy had the early responsibility for delivering strategic nuclear weaponry, and the Midways were the only carriers large enough to deploy the big "nuclear bombers" without extensive modification. They also trialled the launch of strategic missiles.

As naval aviation entered the jet age the class was much modified and modernized, gaining angled decks, up to four deck-edge elevators, steam catapults (including a third), and the plating-in of the bows up to flight deck level. Some compensation for the extra weight was achieved by the progressive elimination of the increasingly ineffective gun armament.

Impressive ships in their day, they were quickly made obsolescent by the new generation of "super carriers" and were paid off by 1992, after working lives that were comparatively short by American standards.

Midway class

Class: *Midway* (CVB-41), Newport News, commissioned September 10, 1945; *Franklin D. Roosevelt* (CVB-42), New York Naval Yard, commissioned October 27, 1945; *Coral Sea* (CVB-43), Newport News, commissioned October 1, 1947

Displacement: 48,250 tonnes/47,400 tons (standard); 61,000 tonnes/59,950 tons (deep load)

Length: 274.5m/900ft (at waterline); 295.2m/968ft (overall)

Beam: 34.5m/113ft

Draught: 9.9m/32ft 6in (standard); 10.6m/34ft 9in (deep load)

Aircraft: 136

Flight deck: 281.8 x 34.5m/924 x 113ft

Armament: 18 x 127mm/5in, and 84 x 40mm/1.57in (21 quadruple) guns

Machinery: Geared steam turbines, 12 boilers, 4 shafts

Power: 158,000kW/212,000shp

Speed: 33 knots

Fuel: 10,200 tonnes/10,000 tons

Range: 33,340km/18,000nm at 15 knots

Armour: 193mm/7.6in (vertical belt, port side), 178mm/7in (vertical belt, starboard side); 89mm/3.5in (flight deck); 50mm/2in (hangar deck); 44–50mm/1.75–2in (protective deck)

Complement: 3,550 men

United States (CVA-58)

During that period following World War II it appeared axiomatic that not only would the new enemy be the Soviet Union but also that any hostilities would involve atomic weapons. The only means of delivery at that time was the bomber and, assuming that it flew from a carrier's deck, an aircraft with a 3,704km/2,000nm combat radius could strike at any worthwhile target there. Carrying a bomb load of about 5.1 tonnes/5 tons and a huge fuel load, at a required 500 knots, the resulting aircraft would have a wingspan of over 35m/115ft and weigh 45 tonnes/100,000lb at take-off.

No existing carrier could routinely deploy such an aircraft. As a completely flush deck would be essential, the draft design for a new ship showed conning positions at the forward deck edge and no masts, it being required that major electronics be carried aboard dedicated escort vessels. No hangar was at first deemed necessary, but the resulting shallow hull of considerable length would have experienced excess stresses. For the first time in American practice, therefore, a hangar was overlaid with an armoured flight deck that was also the strength deck.

Four catapults would be fitted, two forward and two angled outward in the waist. Each was served by a deck-edge elevator. Between 16 and 24 bombers were to be carried, together with about 50 fighters, probably McDonnell F2H Banshees.

That the first-of-class had been named *United States* indicated the importance that the US Navy attached to the project. However within days of her laying-down in April 1949, a successful putsch by the rival Air Force lobby saw her cancelled by a new Secretary of Defense.

LEFT: For a vessel of such significance, the positioning of the first plate, the symbolic "keel-laying", appears remarkably low-key, the wider activity being lost to the solitary navy photographer. Today's initial laying would be of a complete module.

United States (CVA-58)

Built: Newport News, laid down April 18, 1949, then dismantled

Displacement: 68,250 tonnes/67,000 tons (standard); 80,500 tonnes/79,000 tons (deep load)

Length: 314.2m/1,030ft (at waterline); 331.8m/1,088ft (overall)

Beam: 39m/128ft

Draught: 10.5m/34ft 6in (deep load)

Aircraft: 70–80

Flight deck: 315.4 x 58m/1,034 x 190ft

Armament: 8 x 127mm/5in (2 double, 4 single), 16 x 76mm/3in (8 double) and 20 x 20mm/0.79in guns

Machinery: Geared steam turbines, 8 boilers, 4 shafts

Power: 209,000kW/280,000shp

Speed: 33 knots

Fuel: 11,200 tonnes/11,000 tons

Range: 22,220km/12,000nm at 20 knots

Armour: 38mm/1.5in (vertical belt); 19mm/0.75in (hangar walls); 50mm/2in (flight deck); 38mm/1.5in (hangar and protective decks)

Complement: 4,100 men

Forrestal class

Work expended on the aborted *United States* was not wasted. Firstly, the over-blown 45.4-tonne/100,000lb bomber actually entered service as the less ambitious 31.8-tonne/70,000lb Douglas A-3 Skywarrior, with only two-thirds the span but with a 6.94m/22ft 9in height that would demand a hangar of 7.62m/25ft headroom. Secondly, the navy's "floating" of more modest carrier studies coincided with the fortuitous outbreak of the Korean War in June 1950.

Within eight months a firm proposal was worked out, using the structure and layout of CVA-58 but with one less elevator. Psychologically, its design displacement was set at 102 tonnes/100 tons below 60,963 tonnes/60,000 tons. Scaled down, the flight deck remained flush but with a miniscule, retractable island. On either side amidships were four cranked "smoke pipes" that hinged after the fashion of those on the old *Langley*. In July 1952 the *Forrestal*, first of four, was laid down.

Major modifications were introduced during the construction process. British developments of steam catapults and angled decks were quickly exploited by the US Navy, in time for incorporation into the Forrestals. Adoption of the angled deck so altered the "ground plan" that it was possible to reinstate a conventional island, funnel and the customary masting and electronic arrays.

The four-ship programme spanned some seven years, during which time further developments resulted in significant variation between individual units. All experienced slamming problems in service from numerous sponsons and subsequent updates and service life extension programmes resulted in the exchange of conventional armament for missiles and close-in weapon systems. All four were decommissioned between 1993 and 1999, following about forty years' service.

ABOVE: **Only 39 months separate the laying down of the stillborn *United States* and the *Forrestal* (CVA-59) seen here, but a comparison of their deck plans shows considerable difference, the introduction of the angled deck allowing the reinstatement of the island structure. Note also that the bows have been enclosed.**

TOP RIGHT: **A planeguard helicopter keeps station on the *Saratoga* (CVA-60). In the foreground are parked an armed F/A-18 Hornet and an EA-6B Prowler electronics countermeasures (ECM) aircraft.** ABOVE: **Parked aircraft litter the vast deck of the *Saratoga* in an ordered confusion that leaves free only the port bow catapults. It can be appreciated from this view how the perennial design problem of weight distribution, caused by the island, has been largely solved by the adoption of the angled deck.**

Forrestal class

Class: *Forrestal* (CVA-59), Newport News, commissioned October 1, 1955; *Independence* (CVA-62), New York Navy Yard, commissioned January 10, 1959; *Ranger* (CVA-61), Newport News, commissioned August 10, 1957; *Saratoga* (CVA-60) New York Navy Yard, commissioned April 14, 1957

Displacement: 60,963 tonnes/60,000 tons (standard); 79,200 tonnes/77,800 tons (deep load)

Length: 302m/990ft (at waterline); 316.9m/1,039ft (overall)

Beam: 39.5m/129ft 5in

Draught: 11.4m/37ft 6in (deep load)

Aircraft (as designed): 32 A-3 Skywarrior bombers and 12 F3H Demon fighters

Flight deck: 310.5 x 72.3m/1,018 x 237ft

Armament (as designed): 8 x 127mm/5in (8 single) guns

Machinery: Geared steam turbines, 8 boilers, 4 shafts

Power: 194,000kW/260,000shp

Speed: 32.5 knots

Fuel: 7,940 tonnes/7,800 tons

Range: 18,520km/10,000nm at 20 knots

Armour: 38mm/1.5in (hangar walls); 50mm/2in (flight deck); 38mm/1.5in (hangar deck)

Complement: 4,500 men

129

Improved Forrestal class

During the time that it took to build the original Forrestals, technologies progressed to the point where each of the four exhibited significant variation. Their great size engendered new ideas in deck procedures. It also provoked hard criticisms on the grounds of cost. The question of successors was thus the subject of fierce debate.

Opponents argued that more, smaller and cheaper carriers were the sensible option. By the mid-1950s, however, the war-built Essex class were too limited to be considered viable attack carriers. Although still comparatively new, the Midways were having to undergo expensive and comprehensive updating. Large, capable carrier aircraft were a fact of life and the US Navy firmly believed that performance should never be compromised simply because they needed to operate from flight decks.

Attempts to design a replacement carrier of under 50,802 tonnes/50,000 tons displacement showed the impracticality of reconciling the likes of angled decks, high headroom hangar, and high speed within the limit. An updated, repeat Forrestal was obviously the best choice.

To encourage funding, it was advantageous not to increase displacement or, if possible, dimensions. This aim was assisted by a rapid decrease in the size of atomic weapons, arresting the explosive growth in that of the aircraft that carried them. A Forrestal hull remained adequate and, through being large, had better survivability than a smaller. A question mark remained over propulsion, however, for the prototype nuclear-powered

TOP: **In the course of four decades of service and various Service Life Extension Programs (SLEPS) the Improved Forrestals have been altered considerably over the years with, for instance, conventional gun armament being replaced in turn by Terrier and Sea Sparrow missiles.** ABOVE: **Carrier and escort replenish simultaneously, from a multi-purpose supply ship. However large the ship, continuous operation is dependent upon regular top-ups.**

carrier, *Enterprise*, then under construction, was years away from confirming that this was indeed the way forward.

Superficially similar, the second quartet incorporated improvements that placed it in a different class. The primary difference lay in flight deck layout, the wider centre section being lengthened to increase the area, the extra top-weight being compensated by the abandonment of gun armament.

Like the Forrestals, the new ships had three starboard-side, deck-edge elevators but, where the former had one forward of the island and two abaft it, the latter reversed this order, resulting in the island being located further aft. The port side elevator was also shifted to the after end of the flight deck sponson.

It was the intention to replace each former pair of 127mm/5in guns with a lighter twin Terrier SAM launcher, but individual fits varied. Able to be sited higher above the waterline, the missile systems reduced the wetness caused by the earlier gun sponsons impacting the sea. These early systems were, however, greatly dependent upon the ship for guidance, contributing greatly to the proliferation of masts and antennas.

Because of the danger of airborne nuclear attack, carrier task groups now observed considerable dispersion. With its escorts now necessarily more distant, a carrier needed a large, low-frequency sonar to meet the further threat posed by the fast enemy nuclear-propelled submarine.

With the nuclear-propelled *Enterprise* commissioning in 1961, the last of class, *John F. Kennedy*, was delayed but finally went ahead to a conventionally propelled, but further modified, design. *America* was decommissioned in 1996 and *Constellation* in 2003.

ABOVE: The *Constellation* (CVA-64) shows off her forward detail. The two projecting horns project from the catapult ends and catch the aircraft launching bridles. Between them are five scuttles opening from the forward emergency conning position.

BELOW: Including aircrew, an Improved Forrestal carried about 5,000 personnel, or about 5 people for each 0.3m/1ft of the ship's length. As submariners live among their torpedoes so do carriermen live among their aircraft.

ABOVE: One convincing argument for large carriers is their longevity, the average hull seeing 40 years. Although the design pressure of the large strategic bomber has passed in favour of the missile, there is no saying what future development will be.

Improved Forrestal class

Class: *America* (CVA-66), Newport News, commissioned January 23, 1965; *Constellation* (CVA-64), New York Navy Yard, commissioned October 27, 1961; *Kitty Hawk* (CVA-63), New York Shipbuilding, commissioned April 29, 1961

Displacement: 61,100 tonnes/60,000 tons (standard); 78,300 tonnes/76,900 tons (deep load)

Length: 302m/990ft (at waterline); 319.6m/1,048ft (overall)

Beam: 39.5m/129ft 5in

Draught: 11.2m/36ft 9in (deep load)

Aircraft: 8 x A-3 Skywarrior heavy bombers, 36 x A-4 Skyhawk light bombers, 44 x F-4 and F-8 (Phantom and Crusader) fighters, and 9 others (as designed)

Flight deck: 319.3 x 72.6m/1,047 x 238ft

Armament (as designed): Two twin Terrier SAM launchers

Machinery: Geared steam turbines, 8 boilers, 4 shafts

Power: 208,900kW/280,000shp

Speed: 33.5 knots

Fuel: 7,940 tonnes/7,800 tons

Range: 22,220km/12,000nm at 20 knots

Armour: 38mm/1.5in (hangar walls); 50mm/2in (flight deck); 38mm/1.5in (hangar deck)

Complement: 4,500 men

ABOVE: **Taking fuel on a sun-dappled sea,
the *Kearsarge* (CV-33) clearly demonstrates the
advantages of the angled deck, separating
the functions of launch, recovery and parking.**
ABOVE LEFT: **With the plated-in "hurricane" bow
and completely remodelled superstructure and
armament, a modernized Essex bears little
resemblance to an Essex of World War II.**

Essex class modernized

By the end of its building programme in 1946 there were 23 completed Essex class and the incomplete *Oriskany*. They represented a huge investment but faced an uncertain future, for it was yet to be determined how many would be retained for the peacetime navy. In addition, they already required expensive modification, for their pre-war design made few concessions to the new era of atomic weapons, jet aircraft and guided missiles.

Determined to retain as many as possible the US Navy conducted three major modernization programmes on the class, resulting in the upgrading of 15. Taking between 12 and 20 months to implement, the programmes were expensive at a time of greatly reduced budgets. Individual ships therefore tended to be completed with varying outfits. This was exacerbated by this being a period of great carrier innovation, with major developments occurring during the course of a programme.

In 1945, the piston-engined AD-1 Skyraider was the newly introduced state-of-the-art carrier strike aircraft. It was a magnificent machine but, within two years, Grumman was introducing the 933kph/580mph, jet-propelled F9F Panther. In the pipeline was the 24-tonne/53,000lb AJ-1 Savage, the designated carrier-based strategic nuclear bomber.

The incomplete *Oriskany* was selected for the pilot modernization, the need for which gained urgency with the June 1950 outbreak of the Korean War. Jet aircraft had little low-speed lift, resulting in higher launch and recovery speeds.

ABOVE: **Her landing area free, *Ticonderoga* (CVA-14) turns sharply into the wind to
accept aircraft in May 1961. Note how she appears to be towing a decoy. The A-3
Skywarriors were so large that they invariably occupied the slot abaft the island.**

More powerful catapults were required as was a reorganized deck procedure. These problems were soon to be firmly addressed by adopting the British steam catapult and angled deck, improvements so fundamental that early Essex updates were given a second spell in dockyard hands to retro-fit them.

Jet aircraft required far more fuel but it proved possible to blend it, using the ship's own bunkers, but at a cost in endurance. Vertical armour and most gun armament was removed to save weight while bulges ("blisters") were skilfully blended into the hull to increase buoyancy, stability and bunker space, though at a small cost in speed. The island was rebuilt to improve smoke clearance and to allow the bulk of the

ABOVE: The *Oriskany* (CV-34) was something of a prototype in the *Essex*-class modernization programme, receiving modified bows, angled deck and steam catapults. RIGHT: Name ship of the class, *Essex* (CV-9) shows off her new electronics suite to advantage. Limited space, and the avoidance of interaction, has obliged the antenna of the SPS 37A long-range, air search radar to be located well outboard while that of the smaller SPS 8 height finder set is opposite and inboard.

proliferating electronic antennas to be grouped satisfactorily on a substantial pole mast. The flight deck, elevators and catapults were all upgraded to suit the anticipated weight of the AJ-1. Heavier bomb lifts and greater magazine space were also required. Not all modernized units received the full, angled-deck configuration but all those that did had their after centreline elevator shifted to the starboard deck edge.

The original, overhanging forward end of the flight deck had proved vulnerable to storm damage, so all had their bow fully plated up to flight deck level (the so-called "Hurricane Bow") with a secondary, emergency conning position set into its forward edge.

Full modernizations stretched the basic Essex hull to its absolute limit with added displacement and high structural stress levels. Those that did not receive angled decks served usefully in non-strike roles such as helicopter carriers and in anti-submarine warfare. As a training carrier, the *Lexington* survived until the 1980s.

ABOVE: The *Shangri-La* (CV-38) was given a limited modernization but with enclosed bows, an angled deck and steam catapults, the latter evidenced by the forward-projecting horns. Note the after, deck-edge elevator in the lowered position.

Essex class modernized

(Typical data for late, angled-deck conversions)

Displacement: 31,350 tonnes/30,800 tons (standard); 41,950 tonnes/41,200 tons (deep load)

Length: 251.5m/824ft 6in (at waterline); 271.5m/890ft (overall)

Beam: 30.8m/101ft

Draught: 9.2m/30ft 2in (full load)

Aircraft: About 80 (typically F2H Banshee or FJ-2 Fury fighters, AD Skyraider strike aircraft and, occasionally, AJ Savage bombers)

Flight deck: 262.6 x 43.3m/861 x 142ft

Armament: 11 x 127mm/5in and 16 x 76.2mm/3in (8 double) guns (typically less)

Machinery: Geared steam turbines, 8 boilers 4 shafts

Power: 111,900kW/150,000shp

Speed: 32 knots maximum

Fuel: 6,410 tonnes/6,300 tons

Range: 20,740km/11,200nm at 20 knots

Armour: 38mm/1.5in (hangar deck); 38mm/1.5in (protective deck)

Complement: 2,970 men

Enterprise (CVAN-65)

Although studies for nuclear-propelled warships began as early as 1950, the then primitive state of the technology and the very obvious costs saw the necessary shore-based experimental reactors not being given the go-ahead until 1954. In 1955, however, the pioneer nuclear submarine *Nautilus* gave the process a fillip with her record-breaking undersea passages, and apparently unlimited stamina.

The major argument for nuclear propulsion centred upon virtually unlimited endurance and higher speed. It applied best, however, to smaller, low-endurance vessels, for a carrier had been driven to such large dimensions by aviation requirements that she was able to carry adequate bunkers. For carriers, replenishment-at-sea was more often concerned with aviation fuel, ordnance and the necessary provisioning of 5,000-plus personnel, of whom one-third were aircrew.

A major advantage was that, having no requirement for uptakes and funnel, a nuclear carrier could be flush-decked, with no island. With the earlier requirement for large, strategic carrier-based bombers this factor alone would have justified the extra cost but, with already huge flight decks and aircraft pegged to under 36.3 tonnes/80,000lb, it was no longer relevant. An island was preferred even though the "command cruiser" had shown that necessary major electronics could be carried elsewhere, aboard a dedicated escort. It gave important visual command over navigation and flight deck activities.

TOP: **Although greatly changed from its original configuration, the bridge structure of the *Enterprise* retained its small, square footprint with the upper levels jettied outward.** ABOVE: **The *Enterprise* was completed with an all-missile armament, updated to Sea Sparrows, one of whose launchers and its associated director can be seen sponsored out on the port quarter. The nearest aircraft is an anti-submarine S-3 Viking, by Lockheed.**

Ultimately, it was probably a mix of national prestige and the argument of "you'll never know until you've tried it" that moved the decision to build an experimental squadron of carrier, cruiser and escorts. Inter-service rivalry nonetheless caused the cost of the project to be endlessly reviewed, with naval concern that it would militate against future carriers, nuclear or conventional.

ABOVE: **The extreme flare necessary to support a large carrier's overhangs can lead to pounding in poor conditions and damage to projecting sponsons. Note the Vulcan/Phalanx CIWS located on the forward face of the bridge structure.** ABOVE RIGHT: **Arranging aircraft in tasteful displays occupies much of the peacetime carrierman's time, but can they be appreciated properly other than from the air?** RIGHT: **Manoeuvring a large carrier's bulk in restricted water is a task for tugs as the big ships lack side thrusters, a refinement common to merchantmen.**

Where later nuclear carriers would have only two reactors, the prototype *Enterprise* needed eight. To reduce the quantity of heavy shielding around them, they had to be grouped, vulnerably, together. Psychologically acceptable reductions were made where possible to reduce the ship's physical size but she was still to be 42.7m/140ft longer than an Improved Forrestal as laid down in 1958.

The island was made small and square at flight deck level. Above the height of aircraft tail fins, it was jettied-out to support the four great "billboards" of the experimental phased-array search radars. These, too, proved to be in advance of technology and, expensive to maintain, were eventually removed. Similarly, the unique conical structure supporting the 360-degree coverage of electronic support and counter-measures, gave way to a more conventional arrangement.

A considerable advantage of nuclear power was adequate steam for continuous operation of four catapults. Because it is incorporated in her anti-torpedo defence, *Enterprise* carries considerable quantities of fuel oil that can be used to top up escorts. Her aviation fuel capacity is 50 per cent greater than that of the preceding Improved Forrestals. She is scheduled to remain in service until 2013.

Enterprise (CVAN-65)

Built: Newport News
Commissioned: November 25, 1961
Displacement: 69,750 tonnes/68,500 tons (standard); 90,700 tonnes/89,100 tons (deep load)
Length: 317.2m/1,040ft (at waterline); 342.7m/1,123ft 6in (overall)
Beam: 40.6m/133ft
Draught: 11.3m/37ft
Aircraft: 99 (as designed)
Flight deck: 329.1 x 71.8m/1,079ft x 235ft 3in
Armament: 2 x octal Sea Sparrow SAM launchers and 3 x Vulcan/Phalanx CIWS (all fitted later)
Machinery: Geared steam turbines, 8 nuclear reactors, 4 shafts
Power: 209,000kW/280,000shp
Speed: 33 knots
Fuel: Nuclear
Range: Virtually unlimited between recoring
Armour: Not known
Complement: 5,500 men

John F. Kennedy (CVA-67)

In July 1960 the submerged submarine USS *George Washington* launched the Polaris intercontinental ballistic missile (ICBM) that effectively ended the career of the manned bomber as the chosen means of delivering strategic nuclear weaponry. It also had fundamental implications for the future form of the navy's carriers.

At this point in the carrier building programme, one Improved Forrestal (CVA-63) had been launched, a second (CVA-64) was soon to be, and a third (CVA-66) had been approved. The missing number in the series was borne by the prototype nuclear carrier *Enterprise* (CVAN-65) which was also about to be launched.

Fighting its own corner, the Air Force obliged the Navy to justify its continuing to build carriers of a size capable of deploying strategic bombers, as well as planning further hugely expensive nuclear-propelled carriers with a yet-unproven technology that might well be made redundant by the possibilities offered by a new generation of submarines. Once again, too, the air force resurrected the old and long-discredited argument that land-based air power, given the right aircraft, would offer a cheaper and equally effective alternative to carriers. The result of this agitation on a fiscally sensitive Congress was to delay the construction of the planned fourth Improved Forrestal (CVA-67) pending an exhaustive reappraisal of what form future carriers should take, an exercise useful also in delaying payments from over-stretched budgets.

TOP: **Although an intended bow sonar was never fitted to the *Kennedy*, it left its mark in the anchor located on the stemhead. Note how low the port side CIWS platform is situated.** ABOVE: **The *Kennedy*'s early air wing comprised the equivalent of 9 A-5 Vigilantes and 12 A-6 Intruders for heavy and medium attack, 24 A-4 Skyhawk light attack, 14 F-4 Phantom fighters, 6 E-2 Hawkeye electronic warfare and 3 RF-8 reconnaissance Crusaders.**

A starting point was the imminent entry into service of the A-5 Vigilante, an all-weather attack aircraft intended to replace the A-3 Skywarrior. Its take-off weight and dimensions were less than those of its predecessor. In particular, a folding tip to the tail fin reduced its stowage height by over one metre. As the 7.6m/25ft headroom of the hangars of current carriers was a dimension that very much influenced overall size, there was a possibility that it might be reduced to a money-saving 6.4m/21ft.

ABOVE: **Last of the conventionally propelled giant carriers, the** *Kennedy* **sports a uniquely canted funnel arrangement, reminiscent of late Japanese practice. Note the massive structure supporting the side elevator.** BELOW: **Designed for low-level attack, the long-lived Grumman A-6 Intruder can carry 7.85 tonnes/ 7.73 tons of external bombs and a centreline supplementary fuel tank.**

ABOVE: **Carrier superstructures have evolved an architecture of their own. The flood of data captured by the comprehensive electronics suite has to be presented in a form that can be rapidly understood while also being shared with other ships of a task group.**

Relieved of the responsibility of delivering strategic nuclear weaponry, the carrier force would assume tactical roles. This was reflected in other pending aircraft, such as the A-6 Intruder and the F6D air defence fighter, which were optimized as missile carriers rather than around high-speed performance. Take-off and landing speeds were actually being reduced.

It was argued, however, that, as far as CVA-67 was concerned, aircraft size and performance may have stabilized but, over the projected life of the ship, there was no guarantee that they would not, again, become demanding. The 7.6m/25ft hangar height was retained, for the smaller ship with a 6.4m/ 21ft hangar would be 2 knots slower, making her difficult to integrate with her sister carriers.

Short-term savings indicated long-term problems, so CVA-67, to be named *John F. Kennedy*, would be essentially a repeat Improved Forrestal, conventionally propelled, but with her design revised to take advantage of that of the *Enterprise*. She thus became a one-off, and the last boiler-powered "super carrier" of the US Navy. As if to underline the fact, her funnel was canted outboard, a distinctive recognition feature intended to improve smoke clearance. She is scheduled to be replaced (by CVN-22) in 2017.

John F. Kennedy (CVA-67)

Built: Newport News
Commissioned: September 7, 1968
Displacement: 61,850 tonnes/60,750 tons (standard); 84,200 tonnes/82,700 tons (deep load)
Length: 302m/990ft (at waterline); 320.6m/1051ft (overall)
Beam: 39.4m/129ft 4in
Draught: 11.2m/36ft 9in (deep load)
Aircraft: About 82
Flight deck: 313.5 x 72m/1,038 x 238ft 9in
Armament: 3 x octal Sea Sparrow SAM launchers, and 3 x Vulcan/Phalanx CIWS (all fitted later)
Machinery: Geared steam turbines, 8 boilers, 4 shafts
Power: 208,900kW/280,000shp
Speed: 33 knots
Fuel: Not known
Range: Not known
Armour: Not known
Complement: 5,400 men

Nimitz class

Having built a nuclear surface squadron of a carrier, cruiser and escorts, the US Navy had acquired experience and examples of three sizes of reactor. For the purpose of on-going studies aimed at the procurement of successors to the pioneer nuclear carrier *Enterprise*, this gave some flexibility in the design of the propulsion plant. Studies tended to favour proposals based on one overriding parameter, such as cost, size of air group etc, none of which could be enhanced except at the expense of the others. The most influential factors eventually proved to be the successful development of the A4W reactor (which avoided the complexity of the *Enterprise*) together with the length of

catapults capable of launching the following generation of aircraft, and the sheer amount of space required by personnel, numbering over 5,600.

With the accelerating demise of the war-built Essex class, specialist anti-submarine warfare (ASW) carriers with fleet speed were no longer available. Fleet carriers thus had to shoulder a wider range of roles, their old CVA/CVAN designators being changed to CV/CVN. Their air group now had to include such as AS aircraft and helicopters, airborne early warning (AEW), tankers etc. These not only reduced the number of attack aircraft but also demanded a greater range of specialist maintenance facilities and personnel, all of which

ABOVE: The *Nimitz* (CVAN-68) was the first of a long line of nuclear-propelled carriers. Her pristine trials condition emphasizes the considerable efforts that have been made to reduce hull protuberances.

LEFT: A contre-jour shot of a Nimitz engaged in replenishment. The mast and funnel of a supply ship are visible forward of the island while a UH-46 Sea Knight helicopter delivers at the carrier's after end.

added to the pressures on space. It therefore came to be accepted that a Forrestal derivative represented the *minimum* size of hull that would meet realistic requirements.

Back in 1950, the sudden outbreak of war in Korea had consolidated the post-World War II case for carriers. In 1964, Vietnam performed the same service. This campaign, which made heavy demands on carriers, saw the required force level being raised to 15 with a total of 12 interchangeable air groups. Of the 15, only the *Enterprise*, 8 Forrestals and 3 modernized Midways actually existed. An integrated procurement programme was thus initiated to acquire three post-Forrestals at two-year intervals. These became the first of the Nimitz class.

Carrier beam had long since ceased being constrained by Panama Canal dimensions but a new limitation now arose in the 40.9m/134ft width of the construction facility at Newport News.

Improvements incorporated into the Nimitz class are far from obvious to the superficial glance. Flight deck layout has been optimized to create the smoothest air flow downstream, consistent with the most practical alignment of the angled deck with respect to elevators and catapults, which have their own requirement for rapid and efficient aircraft handling.

The external hull surfaces have been considerably "cleaned up", obviating the need for many of the earlier sponsons that had enforced speed reduction due to their slamming in a head sea. So few sponsons do, however, reflect a considerable reduction in armament and, as none of the class has yet been exposed to operations involving a high risk of heavy counter-attack, this could well change.

Extended operations off Vietnam emphasized the advantages of nuclear propulsion, which released internal volume that could be utilized in larger magazines and aviation fuel storage facilities.

ABOVE LEFT: **Higher associated costs pay off when it comes to mobility. For a conventionally powered carrier, continuous high speed is very demanding on fuel but the nuclear ship has no such problems.** ABOVE RIGHT: **Primary defence for the carrier is vested in her aircraft and the capability of her escorts. If the ring is breached, however, she can still deploy the short-range Sea Sparrow (on either quarter) or the last-ditch CIWS systems flanking the transom.**

Nimitz class

Class: *Carl Vinson* (CVN-70), Newport News, commissioned March 13, 1982; *Dwight D. Eisenhower* (CVN-69), Newport News, commissioned October 18, 1977; *Nimitz* (CVN-68), Newport News, commissioned May 3, 1975

Displacement: 82,500 tonnes/81,000 tons (standard); 93,150 tonnes/91,500 tons (deep load)

Length: 317.2m/1,040ft (at waterline); 332.5m/1,090ft (overall)

Beam: 40.9m/134ft

Draught: 11.2m/36ft 8in (deep load)

Aircraft: About 87

Flight deck: 333.1 x 76.5m/1,092 x 250ft 9in

Armament: 3 x octal Sea Sparrow SAM launchers and 3 or 4 Vulcan/Phalanx CIWS

Machinery: Geared steam turbines, 2 reactors, 4 shafts

Power: 194,000kW/260,000shp

Speed: 31.5 knots

Fuel: Nuclear

Range: Virtually unlimited between recoring

Armour: Not known

Complement: 5,950 men

Improved Nimitz (CVN-71) class

Commencing with the *Forrestal* (CV-59), a full half-century ago, the American super-carrier has changed surprisingly little and must be one of the most successful programmes in warship history. Oil-fired boilers have been superseded by nuclear-powered heat exchangers, but well-trusted steam turbines still drive each shaft, with individual get-you-home diesel engines for emergencies.

Dimensions have risen but little and flight deck configuration has settled to a standard layout with four deck-edge elevators, two forward of the island and two on opposite sides aft. On the currently building *George H.W. Bush* (CVN-77), last of the present series, the angle of the flight deck has been marginally increased to permit both catapults to be utilized while aircraft are landing. It is claimed that an aircraft can be launched every 20 seconds, although the rate of steam consumption would be enormous.

Impressions of CVN-77 indicate a very clean upper hull, with minimum projections to invite slamming. Unusually, it incorporates a bulb forward, not for the purposes of housing sonar, but for improved hydrodynamic efficiency.

Of hull protection, little detail is available, but it appears to be based on a system of parallel longitudinal anti-torpedo bulkheads, divided into compartments. Usually void, some may be filled with aviation fuel to supplement the 8,636 tonnes/ 8,500 tons already carried but which can be consumed within 16 days.

Kevlar composition armour has long since replaced steel, but is incorporated only in specific areas and up to a reported thickness of 63mm/2.5in.

CVN-77 and a retrospective refitting programme will see the now elderly NATO Sea Sparrow SAM and Vulcan/Phalanx CIWS replaced, probably by four Rolling Airframe Missile

ABOVE: **The enormous overhang is now almost symmetrical, i.e. on both sides of the hull, giving a flight deck so wide that the "angled deck" has, as in the very earliest experiments, evolved into no more than an angled painted flight path. This is the *Washington* (CVN-73).**

LEFT: **Compared with the giant carrier, *Forrestal* (CVA-59), the Improved Nimitzes have waterline length and beam increased by 15.3m/50ft and 1.4m/4.7ft respectively. The hull is finer but capacity (the most important parameter) has increased by about 9 per cent.**

LEFT: **Note how the *Roosevelt*'s superstructure is positioned to suit the three starboard-side elevators, and how the separate mast, bearing the antenna of the long-range air search radar, is enlarging to become a structure in its own right.**

(RAM) launchers. These will be integrated into the so-called Ship Self-Defense System (SSDS) that in the Mk2 version links all sensors, command and control systems, and weaponry for the fastest response against incoming and anti-ship missiles. The system can also link with other ships so fitted.

Following the *Bush* will be the so far unnamed CVN-78, first of a modified "CVN-21" class. At a projected 101,605 tonnes/100,000 tons displacement, the new ships are likely to change little in the hull but the island, once again, will be configured around a four-quadrant, three-dimensional, phased array radar.

Nuclear propulsion, once questioned, is now confirmed although it is no longer indispensable for steam generation to power four catapults at maximum utilization. The CVN-78 will have electromagnetically powered catapults, working like giant linear motors and demanding vast peaks of electrical energy. This may be associated with the dispersed electrical drive system to be used in the pending British carriers.

To address overcrowding and to reduce manpower costs it is forecast that the current 5,750 or so crew will be reduced by about 10 per cent through automation and simplifying procedures.

CVN-78 is scheduled to be laid down in 2007 for 2014 completion, with her CVN-79 follow-on being 2011 and 2019 respectively. The earlier construction tempo has slowed to one every five years, no longer sufficient to maintain a ten-carrier fleet or, probably, to sustain the Newport News building facility.

ABOVE: **As in the days of explosive growth in battleships, the size of modern carriers limits the number of facilities that can accept them. They are also unable to transit the Panama Canal.**

ABOVE: **An F/A-18 Hornet is readied on the inboard waist catapult. It sits on the blast deflector panel which will be raised when it moves forward. Note the low dome at left, permitting local deck control.**

Improved Nimitz (CVN-71) class

Class: *Theodore Roosevelt* (CVN-71), commissioned October 25, 1986; *Abraham Lincoln* (CVN-72), commissioned December 16, 1989; *George Washington* (CVN-73), commissioned July 4, 1992; *John C. Stennis* (CVN-74), commissioned December 9, 1995; *Harry S. Truman* (CVN-75), commissioned July 25, 1998; *Ronald Reagan* (CVN-76), commissioned July 12, 2003; *George H.W. Bush* (CVN-77), commissioned April 2008

Displacement: 82,500 tonnes/81,000 tons (standard); 93,150 tonnes/91,500 tons (deep load)

Length: 317.2m/1,040ft (at waterline); 332.5m/1090ft (overall)

Beam: 40.9m/134ft

Draught: 11.2m/36ft 8in (deep load)

Aircraft: About 87

Flight deck: 333.1 x 76.5m/1,092ft x 250ft 9in

Armament: 3 x Octal Sea Sparrow SAM launchers and 3 or 4 Vulcan/Phalanx CIWS (but see notes)

Machinery: Geared steam turbines, 2 reactors, 4 shafts

Power: 194,000kW/260,000shp

Speed: 31+ knots

Fuel: Nuclear

Range: Virtually unlimited between recoring

Armour: Not known

Complement: 5,750 men

LEFT: **The LPH design proved deficient in not including assault landing craft but effective in assumed roles of helicopter-centred minesweeping and anti-submarine operations.** ABOVE: Derived from **experiment with converted** *Essex-*class carriers the Helicopter Carrier (LPH) was designed around the accommodation and transport of about 2,000 troops and the helicopters with which to put them ashore.

Iwo Jima class (LPH)

The helicopter revolutionized the landing of spearhead troops ahead of a main amphibious landing. Early carrier conversions during the 1950s proved the principle, leading to the construction of seven *Iwo Jima*-class Amphibious Assault Helicopter Carriers (LPH) during the next decade. They had a flight deck, hangar and two deck-edge elevators but no facilities for the launch and recovery of conventional aircraft.

Accommodation was provided for a Marine battalion landing team of about 2,100 personnel, together with their equipment and light vehicles. For landing purposes they depended upon an embarked Marine helicopter squadron, which normally comprises 24 CH-46 Sea Knight assault helicopters, 4 CH-53 Sea Stallion heavy-lift helicopters and 4 UH-1 Iroquois utility observation helicopters. The last-named could be replaced in specific roles by AH-1 Sea Cobra attack machines.

The Americans also placed much faith in aerial minesweeping, covering large areas using specially equipped sleds towed behind helicopters. This has

the advantage of speed; however, the benefit was, at best, superficial. For this role the LPH was temporarily equipped with the RH-53 and MH-53 variants of the Sea Stallion, fitted for aerial towage.

Later in their careers, the LPHs proved quite capable of operating Harrier V/STOL aircraft, which required no arrester gear, catapults or angled deck.

The LPH needed to be complemented by an LSD (Landing Ship, Dock) which had the facilities to transport and land associated heavy equipment such as armoured vehicles, artillery and bulldozers. Stowed forward on vehicle decks, these could be loaded into a variety of landing craft which were carried in a floodable after well, accessible through a wide, lowering stern gate. The well deck could be roofed with removable deck sections which, together, formed a clear area large enough to operate heavy-lift helicopters. No facilities, other than for refuelling, were incorporated for these machines, accommodated elsewhere.

All were decommissioned between 1993 and 2002.

Iwo Jima class (LPH)

Class: *Guadalcanal* (LPH-7), Philadelphia Navy Yard, commissioned July 20, 1963; *Guam* (LPH-9), Philadelphia Navy Yard, commissioned January 16, 1965; *Inchon* (LPH-12), Ingalls, Pascagoula, commissioned June 20, 1970; *Iwo Jima* (LPH-2), Puget-Sound Navy Yard, commissioned August 26, 1961; *New Orleans* (LPH-11), Philadelphia Navy Yard, commissioned November 16, 1968; *Okinawa* (LPH-3), Philadelphia Navy Yard, commissioned April 14, 1962; *Tripoli* (LPH-10), Ingalls, Pascagoula, commissioned August 6, 1966

Displacement: 17,300 tonnes/17,000 tons (standard); 18,680 tonnes/18,350 tons (deep load)

Length: 180.6m/592ft (at waterline); 183.6m/602ft (overall)

Beam: 25.6m/84ft

Draught: 7.9m/26ft (deep load)

Aircraft: 30–32 helicopters

Flight deck: 181.5 x 32m/595 x 105ft

Armament: 4 x 76.2mm/3in (2 double) guns, 2 x octal Sea Sparrow SAM launchers and 2 x Vulcan/Phalanx CIWS

Machinery: Geared steam turbines, 2 boilers, 1 shaft

Power: 17,150kW/23,000shp

Speed: 21.5 knots

Fuel: Not known

Range: Not known

Armour: None

Complement: 680 men

LEFT: **A Wasp has no angled flight deck but a wide island superstructure. Space has been gained by deleting former armament pockets on either side, right forward, where the CH-53 is here parked.**

ABOVE: **The *Wasp*-class LHD was designed to complement the *Whidbey Island*-class LSD and *San Antonio*-class LPD.**

Wasp class (LHD)

The reliance of the *Iwo Jima* LPH on a dock-type ship to transport its heavy equipment was obviously limiting. This quickly led to a new type of ship that sought to combine the characteristics of each. Built in 1971–80, these were the five *Tarawa*-class vessels, which were very expensive and, although undeniably flexible, were liable to be criticized for their "all eggs in one basket" approach.

Known as Amphibious Assault Ships (LHA) they also have accommodation for a Marine battalion, but differ fundamentally in incorporating a floodable docking well dimensioned to stow four Landing Craft, Utility. These can put 142 tonnes/140 tons of cargo directly on to the beach.

In exercises, the LHA has demonstrated that it can function efficiently and alternatively as a V/STOL carrier, deploying 20 AV-8A Harriers.

Although the final four Tarawas were cancelled, the concept was resurrected within five years with the laying-down in May 1985 of the *Wasp*, name ship of an improved class. These are termed

Helicopter/Dock Landing Ships, or LHD. Again configured around the requirements of a Marine battalion, their docking well accommodates three LCACS, or Air Cushion Landing Craft. Each can transport about 61 tonnes/ 60 tons at over 40 knots.

The Tarawas carry 127mm/5in guns, primarily for gunfire support, but these weapons have been suppressed in the Wasps to maximize flight deck area. Interestingly assuming names borne previously by regular carriers, the LHDs can deploy up to 36 helicopters. Equipped to operate ground-attack AV-8s, they can alternatively operate in the old escort carrier (CVE) role in providing close air support. They will also be able to deploy the MV-22 Osprey tilt-rotor aircraft which can be configured for either assault or ASW roles. LHAs can also function as Sea Control Ships or AS carriers (albeit expensive ones). To emphasize their versatility they have strengthened flight decks and incorporate lightweight Kevlar protection to limit splinter damage.

Wasp class (LHD)

Class: *Bataan* (LHD-5), commissioned September 20, 1997; *Bonhomme Richard* (LHD-6), commissioned August 15, 1998; *Boxer* (LHD-4), commissioned February 11, 1995; *Essex* (LHD-2), commissioned October 17, 1992; *Iwo Jima* (LHD-7), commissioned June 30, 2001; *Kearsarge* (LHD-3), commissioned October 16, 1993; *Wasp* (LHD-1), commissioned July 29, 1989; (LHD-8), due August 2007

Built: All by Ingalls Pascagoula (now Northrop-Grumman Ship Systems)

Displacement: 28,750 tonnes/28,250 tons (standard)/41,250 tonnes/40,500 tons (deep load)

Length: 237.1m/777ft 6in (at waterline); 257.3m/843ft 8in (overall)

Beam: 32.3m/105ft 10in

Draught: 8.1m/26ft 8in (full load)

Aircraft: Up to 36 helicopters or 20 Harrier V/STOL equivalents

Flight deck: 245 x 42.7m/803ft 3in x 140ft

Armament: 2 x 16-cell launchers for Sea Sparrow and RAM surface-to-air missiles, and 3 x Vulcan/Phalanx CIWS

Machinery: Geared steam turbines, 2 boilers, 2 shafts

Power: 57,500kW/77,000shp

Speed: 24 knots

Fuel: 6,300 tonnes/6,200 tons

Range: 17,590km/9,500nm at 20 knots

Armour: Kevlar only

Complement: 1,080 men

Balloon ships and early seaplane carriers

Kite balloons, which were configured to remain stable observation platforms in a wind, were deployed extensively from many classes of Royal Navy ship, but it was only the British that converted merchantmen to auxiliaries specifically for this purpose. Five such were taken up for service – the *Manica* and the *City of Oxford* from the Ellerman group, the *Hector* and *Menelaus* from Blue Funnel, and the *Canning* of Lamport and Holt.

Fairly standard in form, the conversion began with removal of the foremast and associated cargo gear. Ship's structure dividing the forward holds was then cut away to link the spaces, forming a continuous, unobstructed well. Collapsible wind breaks could be secured to the original hatch coamings to enable balloons to be safely inflated in a breeze.

Specialist equipment comprised a hydrogen gas generator and a compressor. Due to the explosive inflammability of hydrogen, routines were strictly observed.

Used mainly in service with the Grand Fleet, and in conjunction with coastal operations such as Gallipoli and in Belgium, their usefulness diminished as the war progressed and most reverted to cargo-carrying.

Empress

During 1913 the second-class cruiser *Hermes* had demonstrated the possibilities of taking seaplanes to sea and operating them on a continuous basis. Most thought of the aircraft in terms of observation and reconnaissance; others, such as the offensively minded Murray Sueter, regarded them as potential torpedo-carriers.

As war broke out in August 1914, it was Sueter who was instrumental in the requisitioning of three cross-channel packets of the South-Eastern & Chatham Railway Company. Too small for use as troop ships they were, nonetheless, fast and handy.

ABOVE: **Seen here aboard the light cruiser *Caradoc*, a kite balloon could extend the horizon for reconnaissance, but not at high speeds.**

RIGHT: **An unusually well-inflated specimen, this kite balloon has no observers in its basket, and may have just been transferred from a specialist balloon ship to a fleet unit with no facilities.**

LEFT: **Last of the three initial packet conversions, the *Empress* had the disadvantage of being four knots slower than her running mates. She can be identified by the short W/T (wireless telegraphy) spreaders aft.**

Like that of the *Hermes*, the initial "conversion" was primitive, involving little more than the clearance of afterdeck fittings and equipment, and the erection of a large, framed canvas "hangar" for three seaplanes, all of which were swung out and recovered by cargo derrick.

Completed in 1907, the *Empress* was the oldest of the three ships, all of which came from the specialist yard of Denny, at Dumbarton. Returned to commercial service in 1919, she was scrapped in 1933.

Engadine and Riviera

Together with the *Empress*, the Admiralty took up the slightly faster *Engadine* and *Riviera*. Once given the same initial, and very primitive, modifications, all three were attached to the Harwich Force. Their pioneer raid against the Zeppelin installations near Cuxhaven on Christmas Day, 1914 demonstrated both their potential and their limitations. It also highlighted the hazard of retaliatory enemy air attacks on the ships involved.

During 1915, therefore, all three ships were given a large, permanent, box hangar, together with cranes for aircraft handling. They also acquired a light anti-aircraft armament.

Once modified, however, they no longer operated as a coherent force but were attached to various commands to explore the possibilities of aerial cooperation. Serving with the Battle Cruiser Force, *Engadine* was thus able to make her modest, but historic, contribution to Jutland. *Riviera* was involved with army cooperation along the Belgian coast besides investigating the value of seaplane anti-submarine

ABOVE: **This early picture of the *Riviera* shows her in pre-war livery and equipped only with canvas protection for her embarked seaplanes.**

(AS) patrols. The slower *Empress* was employed, for the most part, in the Mediterranean. Proving small for the task, they were soon surpassed by larger ships, but all served throughout the war and were returned to commercial service during 1919.

Engadine survived until early 1941, being sunk by Japanese action in the Philippines, *Riviera* served the Royal Navy through a second war, not being scrapped until 1957.

ABOVE: *Engardine*'s permanent hangar extended well forward and involved demolition of the after end of the boat deck. No aircraft were carried on the foredeck.

ABOVE: *Engadine* following the installation of a permanent hangar and facilities in 1915. Except for landing most of her earlier lifeboats and receiving an enlarged bridge, her forward end remained unchanged. *Empress* was nearly identical.

Engadine

Built: Denny, Dumbarton
Gross tonnage: 1,675 tons
Displacement: 2,600 tonnes/2,550 tons (normal)
Length: 95.4m/313ft (bp); 96.3m/316ft (overall)
Beam: 12.5m/41ft
Draught: 4.1m/13ft 6in (mean)
Aircraft: Hangar accommodation for 4 seaplanes
Machinery: Three sets direct-drive steam turbines, 6 boilers, 3 shafts
Power: 8,206kW/11,000shp
Speed: 20.5 knots
Fuel: 407 tonnes/400 tons (coal)
Range: 1,570km/850nm at 10 knots
Armour: None
Complement: 144 men plus 53 aircrew

Ark Royal (I)

The *Hermes* trials with seaplanes brought about two avenues of progress. As noted previously, cross-channel packets were converted to get aircraft to sea with minimum delay. In parallel with this, the Royal Navy acquired a larger vessel, the first one to be specifically designed to carry and maintain seaplanes at sea. As a new build would have taken too long, the Admiralty purchased a merchantman in a very early stage of construction. She was a typical workhorse of

the time, a coal-fired, three-island single-decker with engine amidships. In her then-current state, it was not difficult to relocate engine, boilers, and bunkers aft. A resulting stern trim had to be countered by permanent ballast. In addition, capacious water ballast tanks were built in to adjust both freeboard and roll motion to facilitate the handling of the aircraft.

Occupying the central 40 per cent of the ship's length was a hold capable of stowing seven folded seaplanes. This was

ABOVE: **Seen entering Portsmouth Harbour during the 1930s, the *Ark Royal* has been fitted with a catapult for trials purposes. Her total lack of forward sheer is very evident.** LEFT: **Alongside at Portsmouth, the ship is seen with her jack half-masted. As she has already been renamed *Pegasus* the occasion could have been the death of King George V. The aircraft forward is a Fairey III F.**

accessed via a single large hatch served by two 3.01-tonne/
3-ton cranes and a cargo derrick. Forward of the hold, and
extending partly over it, were specialist workshops and
store rooms.

The ship was built without sheer and, with all anchor gear
relocated below, the foredeck was left clear and flat. The
intention was that aircraft could be flown directly from the ship
but, not least due to her very low speed, there is no evidence
that this was ever done. With its low freeboard and lack of solid
bulwarks, the forward end looked very prone to wetness.

Named *Ark Royal* (surely a peculiar use for an ancient
name), she was a very simple vessel, entering service as
early as December 1914. She was immediately sent to the
Dardanelles where her seaplanes were among the earliest to
support fleet activities in spotting and reconnaissance.

Losses consequent upon the eventual arrival of German
U-boats caused a hasty re-evaluation of the manner in which
the navy worked. The slow *Ark Royal* was considered too
vulnerable and, replaced by later conversions, she was
transferred to Salonika and the Aegean, where she spent the
remainder of the war.

Between the wars, she gave useful service in a couple of
low-level crises before being fitted with a catapult on the
foredeck for use as a trials ship. Late in 1935 she was renamed
Pegasus, her earlier name being passed on to the large new
fleet carrier which had just been laid down.

At the outbreak of her second war, the *Pegasus* had been
reduced to service as an aircraft transport. Naval-manned
Fighter Catapult Ships were, however, being urgently created
to supplement CAM ships in convoy escort. Despite her
unsuitability for North Atlantic conditions, the *Pegasus* made
several such trips before returning to a training role.

Sold out of service in 1946, she plied commercially until
being scrapped in 1950. From humble beginnings she served
the Royal Navy long and well.

TOP: **A trolley-mounted Sopwith Schneider ready for hoisting from the *Ark
Royal*'s hangar deck. With a span of only 8.7m/28ft 8in the aircraft could pass
through the hatch. Larger aircraft, such as the big Short seaplanes, had to have
their wings attached topside.** ABOVE: **Captured intact, apparently after having
force-landed due to an engine fire, a German seaplane is being put overside
from the *Ark Royal*.** BELOW: **Seen in Malta's Grand Harbour, probably in the early
1930s, the *Ark Royal* passes an Aberdeen & Commonwealth liner of the class
immortalized by the *Jervis Bay* in November 1940.**

Ark Royal (I)

Built: Blyth Shipbuilding, Blyth
Commissioned: October 12, 1914
Displacement: 7,210 tonnes/7,080 tons (standard);
    7,580 tonnes/7,450 tons (deep load)
Length: 107.4m/352ft 6in (bp); 111.5m/366ft
    (overall)
Beam: 15.5m/50ft 10in
Draught: 5.5m/18ft (full load, mean)
Aircraft: Hangar accommodation for 7
Armament: 4 x 12pdr guns
Machinery: 1 set vertical triple expansion,
    3 boilers, 1 shaft
Power: 2,240kW/3000ihp
Speed: 11 knots
Fuel: 509 tonnes/500 tons
Range: 5,560km/3,000nm at 10 knots
Armour: None
Complement: 120 men plus 60 aircrew

Ben-my-Chree, Vindex and Manxman

Rather larger than the earlier, Dover Strait vessels converted to aviation ships, the *Ben-my-Chree, Vindex* and *Manxman* were built for the Isle of Man Steam Packet Company. All three were converted with the addition of a seaplane hangar aft and a launch platform forward, intended mainly for wheeled landplanes.

Superficially, there was a strong resemblance, but they could be differentiated by the seaplane handling gear aft. The *Ben-my-Chree* had a simple post and cargo derrick, the *Vindex* had cranes which folded against the after superstructure when at sea, while the *Manxman* was fitted with a relatively heavy gantry crane which protruded beyond her counter.

Operating during the Dardanelles campaign, Short 184s from the *Ben-my-Chree* scored notable firsts with two successful torpedo attacks, one from the air, the other while taxiing.

Originally named *Viking*, the *Vindex* became the first Royal Navy ship to launch a landplane, a Bristol Scout, in November 1915. In August 1916, one attacked the Zeppelin L.17 with bombs, but without result.

The *Manxman* differed from her consorts in having a landplane added below her bridge structure. Serving with both the Grand Fleet and in the Mediterranean, she had the distinction of being the first Royal Navy ship to deploy the Sopwith Pup fighters.

Ben-my-Chree later had her forward launch ramp removed but while still operating as a seaplane carrier, she was hit by enemy artillery off the Turkish coast in January 1917. Aviation fuel caused an uncontrollable blaze that destroyed her.

Both of the other ships returned to commercial service in 1920 and went on to serve through World War II, the *Vindex* as a troopship (under her commercial name of *Viking*) and the *Manxman* as a radar training ship (renamed *Caduceus*).

LEFT: **The sided foremasts of the *Vindex* permitted a longer launch platform for landplanes to pass between while, aft, there was accommodation and cranage for five seaplanes.**

LEFT: **Although this profile shows the higher bridge and temporary forward launch platform, it is inaccurate in recording a derrick on the mainmast and a crows nest, neither of which were fitted. Funnels and masts should have a similar rake. Of all the packets similarly converted, the *Ben-my-Chree* was the only one lost to enemy action.**

ABOVE: ***Ben-my-Chree* could be instantly recognized by the tall derrick post right aft. Her mainmast would later be removed. The low bridge also indicates that the temporary forward launch platform has been landed.**

Ben-my-Chree

Built: Vickers, Sons and Maxim, Barrow
Completed: July 1908; commissioned as aviation ship January 2, 1915
Gross tonnage: 2,650 tons
Displacement: 3,970 tonnes/3,900 tons (standard)
Length: 114.4m/375ft (bp); 118.0m/387ft (overall)
Beam: 14.1m/46ft 2in
Draught: 4.6m/15ft (standard)
Aircraft: 4–6 depending upon type
Flight deck: Dimensions not known
Machinery: 3 sets direct-drive steam turbines, 4 boilers, 3 shafts
Power: 10,450kW/14,000shp
Speed: 24 knots
Fuel: 560 tonnes/550 tons (coal)
Range: Not known
Armour: None
Complement: 175 men

Nairana, Pegasus, Brocklesby and Killingholme

The *Nairana* and *Pegasus* brought to an end the line of development known to the Royal Navy as the "mixed carrier". Both ships were under construction when requisitioned in 1917, the *Nairana* for the Australian coastal service of Huddart, Parker and the *Pegasus* (as the *Stockholm*) for the Great Eastern Railway's North Sea route.

Modelled on the preceding *Manxman*, the two were very similar, except for the seaplane handling arrangements situated aft (gantry in *Nairana*, cranes in *Pegasus*). The forward launching ramp, extending from bridge front to stem head, had a removable section to allow cargo derricks to transfer fighter aircraft from forward hangar and hold.

By this point in the war, it was apparent that the future of naval aviation lay in larger, purpose-built vessels, as the smaller ships were seeing much activity but little action. The *Nairana* returned to commercial service in 1920 but the *Pegasus* was retained, serving as an aircraft transport until being scrapped in 1931.

Mention should be made of the *Brocklesby* and *Killingholme*, two of the Royal Navy's humblest aviation ships. These were specialist, shallow draught paddle steamers, built to operate the ferry service between Hull and New

ABOVE: Resplendent in dazzle camouflage, the *Pegasus* also shows facilities for both landplanes and seaplanes. Note the "PS" recognition letters atop the hangar and the Fairey Campania on the afterdeck.

BELOW: *Pegasus* served briefly on the China station during the 1920s and is seen here in the usual buff and white livery. Note that the launch facility has been removed but the forecastle remains built up.

Holland on the wide, lower estuary of the Humber. Their upper decks were spacious and open, designed to accommodate vehicles or indeed cattle.

Enemy Zeppelins were nightly crossing the English east coast on bombing missions that caused little damage but considerable public disquiet. It was the Navy's task to establish an outer defence line to intercept them.

Converted during 1916 to carry two small floatplanes apiece, the pair worked in conjunction with modified trawlers. The measure enjoyed no success, however, and both ships were returned to commercial service during 1917.

Pegasus

Built: John Brown, Clydebank
Commissioned: August 28, 1917
Displacement: 3,360 tonnes/3,300 tons (standard)
Length: 100.5m/329ft 6in (bp); 101.3m/332ft (overall)
Beam: 13.5m/44ft 3in
Draught: 4.7m/15ft 4in (standard)
Aircraft: Up to 9 (5 fighters and 4 floatplanes)
Machinery: Two sets geared turbines, 6 boilers, 2 shafts
Power: 7,250kW/9,700shp
Speed: 20 knots
Fuel: 367 tonnes/360 tons
Range: Not known
Armour: None
Complement: 255 men

Campania (I)

Having lost the Blue Riband of the North Atlantic in 1889, Cunard ordered two new express liners for the purpose of its recovery. The *Campania* and *Lucania* were delivered in 1893 and fully came up to expectations. In order to achieve their 21-plus knots, however, each was fitted with two enormous and complex "three crank triple engines", five-cylinder triple-expansion machinery delivering 22,371kW/30,000ihp. At speed, these demanded 488 tonnes/480 tons of coal per day.

Twenty years and 250 round voyages later the ship was worn out and sold for scrap. As HMS *Hermes* had just demonstrated that seaplanes could be operated at sea the Admiralty purchased the old vessel for a knock-down price for conversion to a "seaplane-carrying ship". This work was in hand by September 1914.

In April 1915 the *Campania* joined the fleet with a 36.6m/120ft flying-off ramp extending from bridge front to stem head. She could now manage only 18 knots, barely sufficient to work with the fleet.

As an experimental ship, her first six months proved disappointing. Exercising with the fleet on seven occasions, she had been able to fly seaplanes on only three of them. On these, engine and radio problems "had the result that the seaplanes have not been of much value". Difficulties with the ramp already meant that seaplanes were being both launched and recovered from the sea. For this, however, larger aircraft were required.

ABOVE: Following her second, and more comprehensive, rebuilding the *Campania*'s forefunnel has been divided to permit a longer forward platform. Her mainmast has been relocated forward of the after funnel to permit kite balloons to be deployed from a facility on the afterdeck.

Her continued employment was, nonetheless, supported by the C-in-C, Admiral Jellicoe, who noted that "the value of the ship will be immensely increased when machines … are supplied for the attack of enemy airships, and for scouting". The former role, he stressed, was "a most pressing necessity".

To correct her initial shortcomings, the *Campania* began a major remodelling in November 1915. Her bridge was removed and the forefunnel separated into two, sided casings. A new forward ramp, some 61m/200ft in length, passed between them. Beneath its after end was accommodation for "seven large seaplanes and three or four small fighting seaplanes suitable for attacking Zeppelins". On her afterdeck had been added facilities for operating a kite balloon.

Even before her recommissioning in April 1916, the navy's Director of Air Services noted that "the vulnerability and lack of speed of the *Campania* severely handicap her utility". Just two months later, the ship's great opportunity to prove that utility was squandered when she failed to receive sailing orders prior to Jutland. In February 1917, it was recommended the *Campania*'s Sopwith Baby seaplanes be changed for Pup landplane fighters and, soon afterward, a 1½-Strutter demonstrated a successful take-off.

By August 1917, new aviation vessels were being constructed and it was proposed to reduce the *Campania* to a training role with an "alighting deck" and a catapult. Probably in view of her condition, this was not put in hand.

Ever less than satisfactory, the *Campania*'s career was terminated just a week prior to the armistice. Dragging her anchors in a gale, she fouled other ships, was holed, and foundered quickly, due to poor subdivision.

TOP AND BELOW: **The poor subdivision of the *Campania* was always a source of anxiety to C-in-C, Grand Fleet. That his worries were well founded was confirmed by her rapid sinking following a collision in November 1918.**
ABOVE: **From 1917 the *Campania* deployed the Fairey F.17 (which also took the ship's name) an aircraft tailored in size to the ship's hatch. Here, one takes off with the assistance of a four-wheeled trolley.**

Campania (I)

Built: Fairfield, Govan
Commissioned: April 17, 1915 (into Royal Navy); originally completed April 8,1893
Displacement: 18,350 tonnes/18,000 tons (standard); 22,470 tonnes/20,600 tons (full load)
Length: 183.1m/601ft (bp); 189.5m/622ft (overall)
Beam: 19.8m/65ft
Draught: 7m/23ft (normal); 8.5m/28ft (full load)
Launching platform (in 1916): 74.7 x 13.4m/ 245 x 44ft) maximum
Aircraft: 10–12 plus 1 kite balloon
Armament: 6 x 119mm/4.7in (6 single) and 1 x 76.2mm/3in guns
Machinery: Two sets vertical triple expansion, 13 boilers, 2 shafts
Power: 22,380kW/30,000ihp
Speed: 23 knots/18 knots (sustained)
Fuel: 3,251 tonnes/3,200 tons (coal)
Range: 4,780km/2600nm at 21 knots
Armour: None
Complement: 443 men plus 157 aircrew

Furious (I) and (II)

The three extraordinary "large light cruisers" of the Courageous class were brainchildren of the controversial First Sea Lord, Sir John ("Jackie") Fisher. They fully embodied his theory that, if speed and firepower were adequate, protection could be greatly reduced since the ship could choose or decline action at will, while deciding her own range. This trio was conceived to be strong and fast enough to reconnoitre for the battle-cruiser force in any conditions.

Laid down in 1915, they were barely commenced when Fisher, their champion, resigned. Despite now being ceaselessly criticized, the two 381mm/15in armed ships, *Courageous* and *Glorious*, were completed in 1917 as designed. Their half-sister *Furious*, as yet unfinished, was due to be armed with a totally impractical single 457mm/18in gun forward and aft.

Sir John Jellicoe, C-in-C Grand Fleet, was keen to exploit the possibilities of aviation yet was continually frustrated by auxiliary carriers that were either too small and slow (*Engadine* etc) or unreliable (*Campania*). He had been demanding a carrier fast enough to maintain fleet speed and large enough to accommodate both high-performance fighters and seaplanes able to carry a torpedo. Jutland had largely discredited Fisher's ideas regarding battle-cruisers and the then unwanted *Furious*

TOP: **Following her second remodelling, the *Furious* had flight decks that completely surrounded her original funnel and superstructure. Note the palisade (wind-break) forward and the crash barrier aft, supported by a gallows structure.** ABOVE: **Extensive experiments were conducted with non-rigid airships ("blimps") in this case a "North Sea" type.**

was selected for conversion by a committee headed by the new C-in-C, Sir David Beatty.

Still incomplete, she had her forward turret removed in March 1917. It was replaced by a large box hangar with a flat top. From its forward edge a flying-off ramp sloped down to the stem head, similar to that fitted on the *Campania*. Apparently designed around accommodating eight seaplanes, the ship entered service in July 1917 with three Short 184 seaplanes and five Sopwith Pup fighters.

On August 2, 1917, encouraged by the ship's high speed and the excellent low-speed characteristics of the Pup, Squadron Commander Edwin Dunning of the RNAS

ABOVE: **As she first entered service in mid-1917, the *Furious* had lost her forward turret in favour of a flying-off deck and hangar. By the end of the year, her after turret was also removed.**

side-slipped around the bridge structure to effect a first landing on the hangar top. Five days later, he repeated the feat but a third attempt was fatal, the aircraft toppling overboard.

Suitable landing decks had frequently been proposed to obviate the need for fighters to alight on the sea, where they had to rely on the precarious assistance of flotation bags. Possibly influenced by Dunning's example, the *Furious* re-entered dockyard hands in November 1917. Four months of work saw her after 457mm/18in turret replaced by a second hangar and a flat, 91.4m/300ft landing deck. This communicated with the forward flight deck by elevated tracks flanking the remaining superstructure. Both flight decks were now served from the hangars by electric elevators, while the afterdeck was fitted with an embryonic arrester system comprising weighted transverse wires with longitudinal wires laid ahead of them.

Although by then-current standards, the *Furious* could successfully deploy aircraft, she remained unable to recover them for the remaining superstructure created violent and unpredictable eddying, which caused aircraft to lose control. A necessary third remodelling was only a matter of time.

ABOVE: **Even in calm conditions it was only just possible to manoeuvre a fully assembled Sopwith Pup through the *Furious*' access hatch.**
LEFT: **This view of the *Furious* at the fitting-out quay shows her aft 457mm/18in gun, which was of no practical use as a single weapon.**
BELOW LEFT: **A Sea Scout Zero, or SSZ, blimp hauled down on to *Furious*' afterdeck. The view shows interesting detail including the tracks interconnecting the forward and after flight decks.**

Furious (II)

Built: Armstrong, Whitworth, Newcastle
Commissioned: June 26, 1917
Displacement: 19,450 tonnes/19,100 tons (standard); 22,800 tonnes/22,400 tons (full load)
Length: 228.5m/750ft (bp); 239.6m/786ft 6in (overall)
Beam: 26.8m/88ft
Draught: 6.0m/19ft 9in (normal); 7.3m/24ft (full load)
Flight decks: 48.7m/160ft long (forward-ramp); 91.4 x 15.2m/300 x 50ft (aft)
Aircraft: 16 various
Armament: 10 x 140mm/5.5in (10 single), 5 x 76.2mm/3in (5 single) and 4 x 3pdr guns
Machinery: Geared steam turbines, 18 boilers, 4 shafts
Power: 70,100kW/94,000shp
Speed: 31.5 knots
Fuel: 3,450 tonnes/3,400 tons
Range: 11,110 km/6,000nm at 20 knots
Armour: 50–75mm/2–3in (vertical); 20–45mm/0.75–1.5in (horizontal)
Complement: 930 men

Vindictive

By mid-1917 the Royal Navy's need for purpose-built, through-deck carriers was fully established. The first two were in hand but the completion of the first was still a year away. Further conversions were therefore required to provide a stop-gap.

These needed to be reliable and fast enough to work with the battle fleet. The *Furious* had recently entered service following her first remodelling but, presumably because her utility was not yet proven, the choice for a second ship fell not upon one of her already operational sisters but on the last of the large, "Improved *Birmingham*"-class cruisers, HMS *Cavendish*, which would prove to be too small.

A wide-ranging aviation policy document of August 30, 1917, proposed that, because of the limited capacity of converted "carriers", each should deploy only one category of aircraft, i.e. reconnaissance, fighters, or torpedo/bombers. The addition of *Furious*' after landing deck must already have been anticipated, as she, the *Cavendish* and the just-ordered through-deck carrier *Hermes* were proposed to operate an aerial reconnaissance screen ahead of the fleet. A secondary role was to provide decks for the recovery of fighters from other ships, obviating the need for "ditching". The Admiralty's response to the paper was to direct that the *Furious* and *Cavendish* should be converted as seaplane and not standard aeroplane carriers.

Furious thus underwent her second remodelling, with the *Cavendish* very much her diminutive. Hangars were constructed forward and aft, connected by a single, port-side, elevated track. Atop the forward hangar was a 32.3m/106ft

TOP: **Very much a diminutive of the *Furious*, the *Vindictive* had only a short flying-off platform forward, enabling her to retain some of her main armament. The light mainmast was offset to the starboard side.**
ABOVE: ***Vindictive* in company with a Grand Fleet battle-cruiser, either *Indomitable* or *Inflexible*. Even by 1917, the use of disruptive colour schemes was far from universal.**

take-off platform, aircraft being brought up via a large hatch plumbed by a pair of derricks. The 58.8m/193ft after landing deck was served by an elevator. Depending upon type, six to eight seaplanes could be accommodated.

Renamed HMS *Vindictive*, in recognition of the old cruiser that had recently led the morale-boosting raid on Zeebrugge, the ship joined the Grand Fleet in October 1918, just a month before the close of hostilities. As with the larger *Furious*, the landing deck proved too hazardous to use, only one touch-down ever being made.

In the upper Baltic, hostilities continued beyond the armistice. Britain opposed the Bolshevik revolution and an active naval presence was maintained. Carrying a dozen assorted aircraft, in possibly the first use of a carrier in a ferrying role, the *Vindictive* arrived in support.

As the theatre was geographically small, the ship could more conveniently operate her aircraft from an inlet on the Finnish coast. In raiding the rather inactive Bolshevik fleet at Kronstadt, however, aircraft were flown from the ship, which also acted as "mother" to the Coastal Motor Boats (CMB) involved in penetrating the Russian base.

Following her return, the *Vindictive* had her ineffective after hangar arrangement removed but had a catapult fitted on the roof of the retained forward hangar. In this mode, she could deploy four floatplanes and proved ideal for the peculiarities of the then China station.

In 1928 the catapult was removed and, no longer in an aviation role, the ship served in various rear-echelon activities. She saw some combatant service during World War II and was scrapped in 1946.

TOP: **The substantial forward hangar is very obvious in this view, as is the port-side inter-connecting track between flight decks. Note that the forward platform has to be cantilevered in order to allow the forward 191mm/7.5in gun to retain its firing arc.** ABOVE: *Vindictive* **manoeuvring at Malta. Her after landing deck was a substantial structure which provided further hangar space. Only one landing is known ever to have been made on it.** BELOW: **Following her 1923 refit,** *Vindictive* **retained only her forward hangar, with a catapult on its roof and served by an offset crane.**

Vindictive	
Built:	Harland & Wolff, Belfast
Commissioned:	October 1918
Displacement:	9,930 tonnes 9,750 tons (standard); 12,170 tonnes/11,950 tons (full load)
Length:	172.1m/565ft (bp); 184.3m/605ft (overall)
Beam:	19.8m/65ft 1in
Draught:	5.3m/17ft 6in (light); 6.2m/20ft 3in (full load)
Flight decks:	32.3 x 14.9m/106 x 49ft (forward); 58.8 x 17.4m/193 x 57ft (aft)
Aircraft:	6+
Armament:	4 x 191mm/7.5in (4 single), 4 x 76.2mm/3in (4 single), and 4 x 12pdr (4 single) guns
Machinery:	Geared steam turbines, 12 boilers, 4 shafts
Power:	44,750kW/60,000shp
Speed:	29.5 knots
Fuel:	1,500 tonnes/1,480 tons
Range:	10,000km/5,400nm at 14 knots
Armour:	38–76mm/1.5–3in (vertical); 25–38mm/1–1.5in (horizontal)
Complement:	577 men plus 71 aircrew

Argus (I)

William Beardmore of Dalmuir had unsuccessfully proposed a dedicated aviation ship to the Admiralty back in 1912 and, by the time of Jutland, an exasperated Admiral Jellicoe was complaining of the low capability of the aviation ships serving with the Grand Fleet. The Admiralty therefore purchased the incomplete hull of the Italian passenger liner *Conte Rosso* for conversion, which was laying on the slip at Beardmore's yard, her construction suspended by the war.

Although the Admiralty's intention was to produce a more reliable version of the *Campania's* seaplane carrier, proposals for alternative configurations were also being aired. Two comparatively junior officers, with considerable naval aviation experience, were convinced that the way ahead was to provide a full length, unobstructed flight deck, capable of both launching and recovering high-performance landplanes. One, Lt Gerard Homes, proposed little or no superstructure, with all funnel gases being channelled aft for exhaust, via sided horizontal ducts. The other, Flight Commander Hugh Williamson, had separately interested Captain Murray Sueter in an alternative, with a narrow island superstructure offset to the starboard deck edge.

The responsible Admiralty Chief Constructor, J.H. Narbeth, was already supervising construction to a design combining a through-deck, sloping downward at the forward end and fitted with a Beardmore-style superstructure, with sided blocks connected by a bridge. The design incorporated Holmes' ducted funnel concept.

ABOVE: **A Sopwith 1¹/₂-Strutter making an early landing, probably when the *Argus* was fitted with a dummy island structure. Note the longitudinal arrester wires, raised by a transverse ramp.** BELOW: **The flight deck of the *Argus* retained the earlier feature of narrowing and sloping downward at its forward end. Her passenger liner origins are betrayed by the rows of scuttles, following the ship's original sheerline.**

In November 1916 and rather late in the day, wind tunnel tests indicated that the arrangement (and, incidentally, that of the *Furious*) would create severe turbulence, making landing-on impossible. To keep the project moving, all superstructure was therefore deleted, the final configuration being kept under review and subject to practical experience.

As completed, the *Argus* incorporated what would become regular carrier features. The hangar extended over about 60 per cent of the ship's length, its walls separated from the ship's sides by a run of compartments on either side. The hangar roof was a strength deck, continuous with the side shell plating and forming a coherent deep girder. The flight deck itself was a light structure, supported by a lattice, the equivalent of two decks higher.

LEFT: **Navigation in restricted waters was from a retractable wheelhouse set on the centreline of the flight deck, forward. Lacking the side apertures of later carriers, the *Argus* carried her boats at a considerable height.** BELOW: **A hangar view looking aft through the open roller door to the quarterdeck. For the aircraft of the day, the hangar deck had generous headroom but it was obstructed by centreline pillars.**

Beneath the after flight deck overhang, cranes could lift seaplanes from the water and transfer them directly, through a large roller door, to the hangar. Two large elevators connected the hangar with the flight deck.

Like the *Vindictive*, the *Argus* completed a month before the armistice and too late to see action. Embarked were the first squadron of Sopwith Cuckoo torpedo-carrying landplanes intended to pursue Sueter's project of attacking the reluctant German fleet in its own anchorages.

A first task was for the ship to model temporary structures which would decide the topside arrangements for the two follow-on ships (*Hermes* (II) and *Eagle*). An offset island superstructure proved to be beneficial, giving landing pilots a point of reference and vindicating Williamson's ideas.

The *Argus* also trialled arrester systems and, with her forward flight deck levelled, developed operational procedures. Ultimately, however, she proved to be too small and too slow. Serving throughout World War II as training carrier, aircraft transport and, when required, as a combatant, she was finally scrapped in 1946–47.

ABOVE: *Argus'* small retractable wheelhouse can be seen in the raised position. The configuration of the forward end of the flight deck is also more apparent.

Argus (I)

Built: Beardmore, Dalmuir
Commissioned: September 16, 1918
Displacement: 14,760 tonnes/14,500 tons (standard); 17,560 tonnes/17,250 tons (full load)
Length: 163.1m/535ft 3in (bp); 172.1m/565ft (overall)
Beam: 20.8m/68ft 3in
Draught: 6.4m/21ft (light); 7.6m/24ft 9in (full load)
Flight deck: 167.6 x 20.7m/550 x 68ft
Aircraft: About 20
Armament: 6 x 102mm/4in guns
Machinery: Geared steam turbines, 12 boilers, 4 shafts
Power: 15,480kW/20,750shp
Speed: 20.2 knots
Fuel: 2,290 tonnes/2,250 tons
Range: 6,670km/3,600nm at 10 knots
Armour: None
Complement: 375 men plus 120 aircrew

Hermes (II)

As the world's first aircraft carrier, designed-to-task from the keel up, HMS *Hermes* was a significant ship, yet displaying ample evidence that the British Admiralty was still not certain of what it expected a carrier to *do*.

At the time of her laying-down, in January 1918, conversion work was also in hand on the *Eagle* (nearly 22,353 tonnes/22,000 tons) and the *Vindictive* (less than 10,160 tonnes/10,000 tons). The former, capable of only 24 knots, would need to work directly with the battle fleet, but the latter, of about 30 knots, could use her reconnaissance aircraft to extend the useful visual range of a scouting cruiser force. The *Hermes* followed the *Vindictive* in having the size, scantlings and armament of a large cruiser, yet barely the speed of the *Eagle.* These mixed characteristics drew criticism from the then Admiral Commanding Aircraft. The unified Royal Air Force had been created in April 1918 and, in a spirit of cooperation, the Admiralty solicited interested opinion regarding the future employment of "heavier-than-air craft". In response (in

TOP: **With her enormous island and tripod mast, the *Hermes* was totally unlike the *Argus*. Note the lower freeboard and the pointed forward end to the flight deck. Anchors are housed in pockets to reduce slamming.** ABOVE: **What appear to be Fairey III Fs are seen here on *Hermes*' flight deck. Note the line of the flight deck, the 140mm/5.5in gun in the pocket and the 102mm/4in high-angle anti-aircraft gun.** BELOW: **The *Hermes* was the first carrier to present what might be termed a "modern" profile.**

September 1918), this Admiral adopted a chicken-and-egg approach by stating that this would depend largely upon "Their Lordships' building policy as regards Large Carriers. At present nothing is known of this policy after *Hermes*, which will be only a 25-knots craft, obviously too slow for most operations. As far as can be judged at present, no Aeroplane Carrier should be slower than *Furious* or *Vindictive…*"

LEFT: **Hermes'** low freeboard quarterdeck was at the same level as the hangar deck. It communicated with the hangar via vertical roller doors and with the overhanging flight deck via the after elevator, seen here in the "down" position. Note the "round down" of the flight deck.

With her machinery developing nearly twice the power of that installed in the *Argus*, it was thought impracticable to follow her system of horizontal exhaust ducting. Vertical uptakes and funnel casings were, therefore, accepted, apparently in a Beardmore-style double-island arrangement. As experiments in island configuration were still in progress, however, this was kept under review. *Hermes*' construction was well advanced when the failure of the *Furious*' layout convinced the Admiralty that a single, deck-edge island would be required. With no experience upon which to draw, designers created a massively proportioned superstructure block and failed, with the ship's slender underwater hull form, to compensate well for the asymmetry. Consequently, throughout her career, the ship was sensitive to any change in weight distribution.

The *Hermes* had a full-length flight deck, featuring a peculiar swell right aft, deemed aerodynamically beneficial. Like the *Argus*, her after flight deck overhung the quarterdeck,

allowing cranes to hoist floatplanes from the water and transfer them on trolleys to the hangar via a door, or to the flight deck by means of the only elevator. A second, forward, elevator was later added, along with arrester gear and a catapult.

Again, hull strength was maximized by continuing the shell plating right up to the flight deck, which formed the upper flange of the hull girder. As she was to operate with cruisers, however, the flight deck scantlings were increased to take account of aerial bombing. This exacerbated the existing weight problem, and bulges had to be added.

Criticism attended the size of her hangar that, again, did not extend to the sides of the hull. *Hermes* proved, in fact, that fleet carriers of this size were too small to be efficient.

Having spent much of her life in the Far East she was finally sunk there, Japanese carrier aircraft destroying her off Ceylon on April 9, 1942. She had never been large enough to function effectively as a fleet carrier.

ABOVE: **Caught without air cover, the *Hermes* was overwhelmed and sunk by Japanese carrier-based dive-bombers within 20 minutes.**

Hermes (II)

Built: Armstrong Whitworth, Newcastle
Commissioned: February 18, 1924
Displacement: 11,050 tonnes/10,850 tons (standard); 13,695 tonnes/13,450 tons (full load)
Length: 166.9m/548ft (bp); 182.8m/600ft (overall)
Beam: 21.4m/70ft 3in
Draught: 5.7m/18ft 9in (light); 6.8m/22ft 3in (full load)
Flight deck: 173.6 x 29.2m/570 x 96ft
Aircraft: About 20
Armament: 6 x 140mm/5.5in and 3 x 102mm/4in guns
Machinery: Geared steam turbines, 6 boilers, 2 shafts
Power: 29,850kW/40,000shp
Speed: 25 knots
Fuel: 2,040 tonnes/2,000 tons
Range: 10,370km/5,600nm at 10 knots
Armour: 76mm/3in (side belt)
Complement: 610 men

Eagle (I)

At the outbreak of war in August 1914, work ceased on two battleships being built by Armstrong Whitworth to Chilean account. Having promised that they would be returned at close of hostilities, the British Admiralty commandeered both. One, the *Almirante Latorre*, was completed as designed and served the war as the battleship HMS *Canada*.

Work on the second, *Almirante Cochrane*, was not resumed as her designated armament had been diverted to other new construction. Thus, when the Grand Fleet's post-Jutland needs for larger and faster seaplane carriers were considered, this hull was selected for conversion in January 1918. She was duly purchased outright and the name of HMS *Eagle* allotted. As the company was also working on the *Hermes* at this time, *Eagle* had to compete for materials and labour, and progress was slow.

Deletion of much heavy battleship armour saved over 2,032 tonnes/2,000 tons on displacement. She retained the hybrid coal/oil firing then common. Coal bunkers were arranged to give a measure of protection to machinery spaces and fired the boilers in normal conditions. For higher speed running, oil was used exclusively.

With the overall policy on carrier superstructures still unsettled, the *Eagle* was intended to receive a variant on the Beardmore proposals. She would have two, sided islands, each incorporating two funnels and a tripod mast. Each island would be arranged differently and they would be staggered. The resulting bizarre effect would make it virtually impossible

TOP: *Eagle* shared with *Hermes* the massive tripod mast and fire control top. Note the "battleship" features of bows and faceted hull. Note also the light, swinging platform for flight deck control. ABOVE: A World War II picture shows the *Eagle* little changed except for the addition of an aircraft housing beacon atop the fire control.

for an enemy submarine commander to estimate the ship's heading. Even before installation had begun, this was changed, the ship receiving a single, starboard-side island with two funnels and a massively proportioned tripod and fire control top, as installed in the *Hermes*.

With the post-war drawdown, work on the *Eagle* slowed until it was decided suddenly that flying trials were urgently required. Early in 1920, therefore, with one funnel, half boiler capacity and incomplete superstructure, the ship was transferred to Portsmouth Dockyard. Here she was completed with an experimental fore-and-aft arrester system, her flight

ABOVE: **From this angle, the** *Eagle*'s **original battleship hull is emphasized. Note the armoured belt. Two funnels were required due to the spread of the boiler rooms.** LEFT: **A good view of** *Eagle*'s **flight deck configuration. The aircraft are Fairey III Fs and Fairey Flycatchers. Note the latter's experimental markings.** BELOW: *Eagle* **and the looming mass of Gibraltar. The carrier spent much of her time in the Mediterranean and was eventually sunk there.**

deck was extended right forward and her hull bulged. The latter feature was an anti-torpedo measure rather than one to improve stability, and it cost the ship half a knot in speed.

Exhaustive trials with various types of aircraft established that the fore-and-aft system worked tolerably well once its form and position had been determined and the engagement fittings on the aircraft undercarriage improved. Although the large island proved to cause little problem, it was discovered that it was imperative to steam the ship dead into wind for flying operations, otherwise eddying became severe. A round-down on the flight deck, right aft, proved essential.

Larger, heavier aircraft, with high landing speeds, soon proved the arrester system inadequate, and it was removed in 1926. For ten years the ship proved large enough to land aircraft without arrester wires, but their continued growth dictated the fitting of a later, transverse system in 1936.

The *Eagle* was sunk by submarine torpedo on August 11, 1942, while covering the famous "August Convoy" to Malta.

ABOVE: **Always a most imposing vessel, the** *Eagle*'s **weakness was her low speed, but she had been designed as an inherently stable gun platform.**

Eagle (I)

Built: Armstrong Whitworth, Newcastle
Commissioned: February 20, 1924
Displacement: 22,250 tonnes/21,850 tons (standard); 27,180 tonnes/26,700 tons (full load)
Length: 191m/627ft 1in (bp); 203.4m/667ft 6in (overall)
Beam: 32.1m/105ft 2in
Draught: 6.6m/21ft 9in (standard); 8.1m/26ft 7in (full load)
Flight deck: 198.6 x 28.9m/652 x 95ft
Aircraft: About 20
Armament: 9 x 152mm/6in, and 4 x 102mm/4in guns
Machinery: Geared steam turbines, 32 boilers, 4 shafts
Power: 37,300kW/50,000shp
Speed: 24 knots
Fuel: 2,900 tonnes/2,850 tons
Range: 12,130km/6,550nm at 10 knots
Armour: 114.3mm/4.5in (vertical belt); 25mm/1in (horizontal)
Complement: 810 men

Courageous, Glorious and *Furious* (III)

With rapid post-war reduction of the Royal Navy, careful consideration needed to be given to the characteristics of the aircraft carriers that could be afforded and, subsequent to the Washington Treaty, permitted.

A battle-cruiser squadron had been retained and new doctrine called for a fast carrier to operate with it and to extend its reconnaissance capabilities. The obvious candidate was the *Furious* that was useless in her then-current configuration but capable of 30-plus knots. With the benefit of nearly two years' operation of the *Argus*, work began in 1920 to redesign the ship in her final through-deck form.

Balanced air wings, as now understood, had not yet evolved and carriers were still allotted separate roles. Aboard *Furious*, large three-seater spotter aircraft would need to be accommodated alongside reconnaissance aircraft and a number of fighters.

No definite result had yet stemmed from experiments with island structures and the *Furious* was redesigned, *Argus*-style, with none. On either side of the forward end of the flight deck was a partly recessed control position, one for navigational purposes, the other for flying operations. A totally retractable small wheelhouse for harbour manoeuvre was installed on the centreline.

TOP: **Seen in the mid-1930s, *Glorious* has had her quarterdeck raised by one level and the flight deck extended right aft. Note the bulge to the hull and the swung-out flight control platform.** ABOVE: **Note how the upper hangar is closed-off by roller doors. Opened, these allowed fighter aircraft to take off directly down the clear, sloping foredeck.**

To provide the required accommodation, hangars were arranged on two levels, but necessarily of lower headroom than that on *Argus*. The 175.7m/576ft flight deck formed the roof of the upper hangar that opened via large doors on to the flat forecastle deck. This was to allow fighters to respond rapidly by taking off directly from the hangar. The lower hangar similarly gave on to the quarterdeck, whence two cranes could transfer floatplanes to and from the water.

A longitudinal arrester system was included but proved unpopular and was removed in 1927. Forward of amidships the flight deck was given a pronounced ramp to encourage aircraft to get airborne.

The double hangar gave the *Furious* a greater freeboard than *Argus* resulting in a drier flight deck but one with higher levels of roll acceleration. To improve overall stability to the slender hull conspicuous bulges were added.

Like *Argus*, the *Furious* needed to have horizontal smoke ducting but, due to the far greater quantity of gases to be exhausted, this was not particularly successful. At high speeds, the after end of the upper hangar became extremely hot and some spaces were untenable.

Furious' final remodelling was successful enough to encourage a similar transformation of her erstwhile sisters, *Courageous* and *Glorious*. From the outset, both featured a starboard-edge island, essentially a large funnel casing, around which were arranged navigational and flying control facilities.

Reconstruction of the pair commenced in 1924–25. No arrester gear was initially provided, the retained feature of the deck ramp being sufficient to bring recalcitrant aircraft to rest. In the 1930s, however, increasing size and weight of aircraft saw a necessity to fit a transverse system. Two catapults were also added right forward.

All three proved to be efficient carriers. *Furious* served with distinction throughout World War II, but both her sisters were lost in controversial circumstances, *Courageous* to a submarine torpedo in September 1939, and *Glorious* to enemy gunfire in June 1940.

Courageous and *Glorious*

Class: *Courageous*, Armstrong Whitworth, Newcastle, commissioned (as carrier) May 5, 1928; *Glorious*, Harland & Wolff, Belfast, commissioned (as carrier) March 10, 1930
Displacement: 22,650 tonnes/22,250 tons (standard); 26,750 tonnes/26,250 tons (full load)
Length: 223.9m/735ft (bp); 239.9m/786ft 6in (overall)
Beam: 27.6m/90ft 6in
Draught: 7.4m/24ft 3in (standard); 8.5m/28ft (full load)
Flight deck: 175.7 x 31.6m/576 x 103ft 6in
Aircraft: About 48
Armament: 16 x 119mm/4.7in (16 single), and 24 x 2pdr pom-pom (3 octuple) guns
Machinery: Geared steam turbines, 18 boilers, 4 shafts
Power: 67,150kW/90,000shp
Speed: 30.5 knots
Fuel: 3,760 tonnes/3,700 tons
Range: 12,500km/6,750nm at 10 knots
Armour: 50–76mm/2–3in (vertical belt); 19–44mm/0.75–1.75in (horizontal)
Complement: 835 men

Ark Royal (II)

With the completion of the *Courageous*-class conversions in 1930, design studies began for the next large newbuild. The Washington Treaty had set the global limit for British aircraft carrier displacement at 137,160 tonnes/135,000 tons. Based on recent experience this was best devoted to half-a-dozen ships, each about 22,352 tonnes/22,000 tons. It was hoped that 60, even 72, aircraft and machinery for 30-plus knots might be accommodated.

To achieve the hoped-for aircraft strength, American-style deck parks would have to be adopted. These in turn would demand transverse arrester wire systems and a deployable safety barrier to prevent landing aircraft from bolting into the parking spaces. Accelerators/catapults would also be necessary to economize on take-off space. It was also agreed that, with assisted take-off and arrested landing, less wind-over-deck was required and so the carrier could be slower.

Overall dimensions were important for a volume-critical carrier tended to be larger than a weight-critical battleship of the same displacement. This reduced the number of docking facilities open to her.

The use of catapults, backed by an efficient deck organization could, it was reasoned, improve the launch rate of aircraft to the point where a second (forecastle) take-off deck was unnecessary. The bows could, therefore, be plated

TOP: **Bound for Mediterranean service at the time of the Spanish Civil War, the newly completed *Ark Royal* displays red-white-blue neutrality markings on her quarter gun mountings. Note how high-speed trials have scoured the forward paintwork.** ABOVE: **Located in sponsons just below flight deck level, the *Ark Royal*'s dual-purpose, high-angle guns had far better firing arcs than equivalent weapons in earlier carriers. What appears to be a de-gaussing cable has been cleated to the hull, suggesting that the date is 1940.**

continuously up to flight deck level. Supported by a smooth flare it was then possible to maintain a considerable width of flight deck to the forward extremity.

Floatplanes were, by now, diminishing in importance and, by handling them only by the amidships cranes, this allowed the quarterdeck to be enclosed, supporting a flight deck to a point right aft, its round-down cantilevered beyond.

Two hangars were again necessary. They were both enclosed, the upper having the unarmoured flight deck as its roof. Patches of protection were provided in way of magazines,

LEFT: The carrier's loss to a single submarine torpedo came as a shock. It led to the tightening up of damage control procedures and to future designs being less vulnerable to sequential flooding. BELOW LEFT: *Ark Royal*'s commissioned life was just 36 months and she was thus little modified. By incorporating larger overhangs, the deck plan more nearly approached a rectangle. BELOW: Not the best-ever portrait of the *Ark Royal*, this portrayal nonetheless emphasizes the close ties between the ship and the Gibraltar-based Force H. She was sunk almost in sight of the Rock.

and a limited 114.3mm/4.5in side belt flanked machinery spaces. The hull was not bulged, and the internal torpedo protection arrangement was configured as an air-fuel-air sandwich.

As a carrier was now deemed to rely upon her aircraft and her escort for protection, gun armament could be confined to anti-aircraft weapons. Sixteen 114.3mm/4.5in dual-purpose guns were provided, located in twin mountings, two to each "corner". They were set a fraction below flight deck level to maximize firing arcs. Much was also expected of the new multi-barrelled 2pdr pom-pom mountings.

A prestigious name being required for this, the first third-generation British carrier, the veteran *Ark Royal* had to relinquish hers. On trials in May 1938, the new ship achieved her designed speed with barely three-quarters full power, suggesting that she could have been built with two, rather than three, shafts.

Ark Royal's World War II career was brief but eventful, providing no opportunity for a major refit before her loss in November 1941. Due to an insufficient understanding of damage control, she disappointingly succumbed to a single submarine torpedo.

ABOVE: The conflicting demands of a relatively fine hull and a wide, straight-edged flight deck inevitably resulted in a strange and arresting geometry. Note the port side WT masts in the lowered position.

Ark Royal (II)

Built: Cammell Laird, Birkenhead
Commissioned: November 16, 1938
Displacement: 22,352 tonnes/22,000 tons (standard); 28,210 tonnes/27,710 tons (full load)
Length: 208.9m/685ft (bp); 244m/800ft (overall)
Beam: 28.9m/94ft 9in
Draught: 6.9m/22ft 9in (standard); 8.5m/27ft 9in (full load)
Flight deck: 237.9 x 29.3m/780 x 96ft
Aircraft: About 60
Armament: 16 x 114.3mm/4.5in (8 double), and 48 x 2pdr pom-pom (6 octuple) guns
Machinery: Geared steam turbines, 6 boilers, 3 shafts
Power: 76,100kW/102,000shp
Speed: 31 knots
Fuel: 4,500 tonnes/4,420 tons
Range: 20,740km/11,200nm at 10 knots
Armour: 114.3mm/4.5in (vertical belt); (horizontal – patches only)
Complement: 1,740 men

LEFT: The cost of a partly armoured deck was the acceptance of a single hangar, fewer aircraft and lower freeboard. Note the careful attention to streamlining on bridgefront and around the bow overhang to reduce eddies over the flight deck of the *Victorious*. BELOW LEFT: The British Pacific Fleet (BPF) in 1945 eventually included all six "armoured" carriers and the four surviving *King George V*-class battleships. The aircraft ranged in the foreground are F4U Corsairs. BELOW: BPF aircraft, such as this Grumman Avenger, had roundels without the red centre, to avoid any confusion with Japanese aircraft and "side tabs" to more nearly approximate American markings.

Illustrious class

Even as the *Ark Royal* was laid down a European war was appearing likely. Neither of the dictatorships possessed carriers but, to operate offensively against their maritime interests, the Royal Navy would be opposed by powerful land-based air forces. In those pre-radar days it was unlikely that a handful of carrier search aircraft could detect every incursion by enemy bombers, nor give sufficient warning for her fighters to intercept them. Exercises had shown that naval anti-aircraft gunfire could dispose of only a low proportion of attacking aircraft while single-seat fighters, lacking navigators, were unable to operate safely beyond horizon range of their carrier. It was obvious that some enemy bombers must get through to threaten the huge expanse of the flight deck.

Bombers, too, were faster and carried far heavier weapons, and the dangers of level bombing had been joined by those from dive-bombing. It was a matter of concern that the horizontal protection of *Ark Royal* was designed mostly to resist 9.1kg/20lb bombs where 100kg/220lb, even 250kg/551lb, weapons were now under development. As fleet carriers were so few, and they were so valuable in both attack and

defence, a new philosophy demanded that a carrier's main weapons system, i.e. her aircraft, be better protected. As a result, the concept of the armoured carrier emerged.

The 1936 programme funded the first two carriers designed to the new displacement limit of 23,369 tonnes/23,000 tons set by the recent London Treaty. These were to have flight decks capable of defeating a 226.7kg/500lb bomb dropped from 2,134m/7,000ft. This required 76mm/3in plate, weighing 586kg per m^2/120lb per sq ft. To resist cruiser gunfire beyond 6,401m/7,000yd, hangar side walls and transverse bulkheads required to be of 114.3mm/4.5in plate.

With an upper limit on displacement, this huge accumulation of weight had predictable consequences. Only one hangar was provided to minimize the area of vertical protection. This, in turn, reduced freeboard, compensating somewhat in stability terms for the heavy flight deck. It did, however, increase wetness on the flight deck and, of course, had a drastic effect on aircraft capacity, reduced from the *Ark Royal*'s 60-plus to only 33. Aviation fuel, the subject of elaborate precaution in the Royal Navy, was provided on this scale and when, later, American-style deck parks increased the air wing to 54, this proved a severe limitation on operational endurance.

The three ships of what became known as the Illustrious class were laid down within the space of eight weeks in 1937, and their completion in 1940–41 was a matter of huge relief to an overstretched Royal Navy.

Power had been increased by about ten per cent over *Ark Royal*, and the triple shafts were now a necessity. As the war progressed, new equipment and more aircraft increased displacement, while the associated extra crew members made for increasingly cramped accommodation.

It was the class's good fortune that severe damage incurred during World War II was all from the air (which it was designed to resist) rather than from the more dangerous torpedo. *Illustrious* and *Formidable* were able to survive savage bombing attacks while all three were later able to resist Japanese kamikaze attacks that would have disabled more lightly constructed vessels. All survived the war.

ABOVE: **Bleak and inhospitable, the** anchorage at Hvalfjord in Iceland was invaluable for the refuelling of escorts covering transatlantic convoys and for Anglo-American surface groups supporting Arctic convoys. *Victorious* is seen in company with British and American units. ABOVE RIGHT: **A Home Fleet ship,** *Victorious* came south on several occasions to support Malta operations. Note that the picture opposite was the inspiration for this impression. BELOW: **This is** a post-1943 picture, for the distinctive tub-like British homing beacon had been replaced by an American-type YE and the round-downs have been levelled to maximize deck space. The aircraft is a Fairey Barracuda dive-bomber.

HMS VICTORIOUS

Illustrious class

Class: *Illustrious*, Vickers-Armstrong, Barrow, commissioned May 25, 1940; *Victorious*, Vickers-Armstrong, Newcastle, commissioned May 15, 1941; *Formidable*, Harland & Wolff, Belfast, commissioned November 24, 1940
Displacement: 23,369 tonnes/23,000 tons (standard); 28,400 tonnes/27,900 tons (full load)
Length: 205.3m/673ft (bp); 226.9m/743ft 10in (overall)
Beam: 29.2m/95ft 9in
Draught: 7.5m/24ft 6in (standard); 8.5m/27ft 9in (full load)
Flight deck: 189.1 x 24.6m/620 x 80ft
Aircraft: About 36 in hangar
Armament: 16 x 114mm/4.5in (8 double) guns, and 48 x 2pdr pom-pom (6 octuple) guns
Machinery: Geared steam turbines, 6 boilers, 3 shafts
Power: 82,800kW/111,000shp
Speed: 30.5 knots
Fuel: 4,940 tonnes/4,850 tons
Range: 19,816km/10,700nm at 10 knots
Armour: 114.3mm/4.5in (belt); 38mm/1.5in (hangar wall); 76mm/3in (flight deck); 38–50mm/1.5–2in (hangar deck)
Complement: 1,180 men

Illustrious-class derivatives

Large and expensive in relation to their aircraft capacity, the three Illustrious class were laid down only months before a modified version, HMS *Indomitable*. Lower hull and machinery remained identical but, by adding 1.8m/6ft to the total depth of hull, two hangars were included, the lower of half length. This increased underdeck aircraft capacity to 45, but at some cost. Where the lower hangar could be given the preferred 4.9m/16ft headroom, the upper had to be reduced to 4.3m/14ft, a factor that later constricted the range of aircraft embarked, barring, for instance, the F4U Corsair.

Much the same area of flight deck retained its 76mm/3in armour but the vertical protection of the hangar was cut severely from 114.3mm/4.5in to only 38mm/1.5in plate. As with her three predecessors, the *Indomitable* was fitted with just one catapult, with consequent effect on launch rate.

Carrier design was now firmly dictated by larger and heavier aircraft. The high location of the ship's dual-purpose armament improved arcs, but only at the cost of reducing flight deck area and making its shape irregular. Considerable extra space was gained by virtually abolishing the round-down and extending the flight deck as a straight, cantilevered overhang. Outriggers were also introduced, supporting the tails of aircraft outboard of the deck edge to save further space.

For the final pair of derivatives (*Implacable* and *Indefatigable*) it was desirable to increase the maximum speed by a knot or so. This may not sound much but, nonetheless, required a one-third increase in installed power. This necessitated four propellers which, in turn, demanded modified hull lines with an extra 6.1m/20ft on waterline length. Redesign took some time and meant that the pair were not laid down until 1939, entering service very late in the war.

TOP: **The last two improved *Illustrious*-class ships were disposed of in 1955–56, but as training carriers still look pristine at the 1953 Coronation Review. Note the flag of Rear Admiral (Air).** ABOVE: ***Indefatigable* seen in her post-war training role. With peace, the lives of the big armoured carriers were short as the "Light Fleets" could be run far more economically while deploying as many aircraft.** BELOW: **By locating their main armament flush with the flight deck, British carriers had more effective firing arcs than did American. The cost was an indented flight deck plan that impinged on useful space.**

Even at this late stage Britain endeavoured to respect treaty displacement. As four sets of machinery occupied a greater proportion of hull length, a greater area of armour was required. To reduce this area both upper and lower hangar were given only 4.3m/14ft headroom, with the aforementioned consequence. Vertical protection remained at 38mm/1.5in but the vital horizontal protection was reduced to 64mm/2.5in. This was influenced by the acceptance that 500kg/1,102lb bombs would probably penetrate it in any case, leading to a proposal that future design should include thin flight deck protection to initiate the detonation of a bomb whose explosion would then be contained by a heavily armoured hangar deck.

Although the Royal Navy's armoured carriers became somewhat legendary in their ability to absorb punishment, the frequent battering took its toll. All spent considerable periods under repair, with the exception of *Implacable* that arrived in the Far East too late to be of much use.

Following hostilities these expensive ships, apart from the *Victorious*, all had very limited lives. For peacetime operations and in low-level conflict the "Light Fleets" could operate much the same air wing on half the complement. Except for the single modernization, which proved a very difficult task, all had been sold for scrapping by 1956.

ABOVE LEFT: **British Pacific Fleet carriers proved to be largely kamikaze-proof. This strike on the *Indefatigable* in April 1945 killed 14 and damaged the island, but disrupted flying operations for only half an hour.** ABOVE RIGHT: **A post-war picture of Sea Hornets and Sea Furies. The former type served afloat only between 1949 and 1951. The planeguard is a 1943-type *Battle*-class destroyer. Note that she has her seaboat ready swung-out for emergencies.**

BELOW: **A meeting of different worlds. The life of the average fellaheen and that of a fleet carrier crew member are about as far removed as can be imagined. *Indefatigable* transits the Suez Canal. The waterway was frequently mined by enemy aircraft.**

Illustrious-class derivatives

Class: *Indomitable*, Vickers-Armstrong, Barrow, commissioned October 10, 1941; *Implacable*, Fairfield, Govan, commissioned August 28, 1944; *Indefatigable*, John Brown, Clydebank, commissioned May 3, 1944

Details for *Implacable/Indefatigable*:

Displacement: 23,680 tonnes/23,250 tons (standard); 32,700 tonnes/32,100 tons (full load)

Length: 208m/682ft (bp); 233.8m/766ft 6in (overall)

Beam: 29.2m/95ft 9in

Draught: 7.8m/25ft 6in (standard); 8.5m/27ft 9in (full load)

Flight deck: 231.8 x 31.1m/760 x 102ft

Aircraft: About 55

Armament: 16 x 114.3mm/4.5in (8 double), 48 x 2pdr pom-pom (4 octuple, 4 quadruple) guns, and 53 x 20mm/0.79in (18 double, 17 single) guns

Machinery: Geared steam turbines, 8 boilers, 4 shafts

Power: 110,400kW/148,000shp

Speed: 32.5 knots

Fuel: 4,775 tonnes/4,690 tons

Range: 20,370km/11,000nm at 14 knots

Armour: 114.3mm/4.5in (belt); 38mm/1.5in (hangar wall); 76mm/3in (flight deck); 38–50mm/1.5–2in (hangar deck)

Complement: 1,375 men

LEFT: **With the Royal Navy already up to its treaty limit in carrier tonnage, the acquisition of an aircraft maintenance ship that looked like, and functioned as, a carrier was something of a bonus.**
BELOW: **Seen in the Far East during the Korean War, the *Unicorn* (left) with her double-hangar freeboard towers over the *Ocean* (right), a *Colossus*-class carrier.**

Unicorn

Putting the Mediterranean Fleet on a virtual war footing during the 1935–36 Abyssinian crisis was useful in exposing shortcomings. One such was the lack of heavy support for the existing, and planned, carrier force. This resulted in the one-off aircraft maintenance ship *Unicorn*.

To justify her cost, she would need to operate as a training carrier in peacetime. Topside, therefore, she would require carrier characteristics, much influenced by the completing *Ark Royal* (II). For her core business of storing, repairing and issuing aircraft (including floatplanes) she needed two, 4.9m/16ft headroom hangars. Her freeboard would be high but her draught was required to be limited, necessitating an unusually high power to ensure safe ship handling. An unlikely requirement

to mount aerial patrols to safeguard her location also provided a justification for weapons stowage. As the ship would have considerable value, she was given a 51mm/2in flight deck and was armed with a twin 102mm/4in mounting at each "corner", each pair with its own director.

Putting these requirements together the Naval Staff created what was called a Fleet Air Arm Maintenance Ship. This was however, to all intents and purposes, a light fleet carrier built outside treaty limitations, but not completed until 1943.

A feature was the pronounced overhang aft. This increased the useful length of the flight deck while providing a gantry for transferring floatplanes and aircraft transport lighters directly from sea to hangar.

The *Unicorn* had a distinctive appearance, although viewed beam-on,

her high freeboard gave the impression of a fleet carrier on a closing or receding heading. Delivered in 1943, she served as a regular carrier at Salerno before fulfilling a variety of roles in the Far East, including the Korean War.

Unicorn	
Built: Harland & Wolff, Belfast	
Commissioned: March 12, 1943	
Displacement: 15,900 tonnes/15,600 tons (standard); 20,700 tonnes/20,300 tons (full load)	
Length: 172m/564ft (bp); 196.1m/643ft (overall)	
Beam: 27.5m/90ft	
Draught: 6.3m/20ft 6in (standard); 7.4m/24ft 3in (full load)	
Flight deck: 183 x 28.8m/600 x 94ft 6in	
Aircraft: About 36	
Armament: 8 x 102mm/4in (4 double), 16 x 2pdr pom-pom (4 quadruple) guns, and 13 x 20mm/0.79in (4 double, 5 single) guns	
Machinery: Geared steam turbines, 4 boilers, 2 shafts	
Power: 29,850kW/40,000shp	
Speed: 24 knots	
Fuel: 3,050 tonnes/3,000 tons	
Range: 20,370km/11,000nm at 14 knots	
Armour: 38mm/1.5in (vertical longitudinal bulkhead); 51mm/2in (flight deck); 51mm/2in (protective deck)	
Complement: 1,100 men	

ABOVE: **Complete with catapult, arresters, two hangars and two elevators, the *Unicorn* could, and did, function efficiently as a light carrier.**

LEFT: **By locating the catapult along the forecastle and offset to the port side of No.1 hatch, it was possible to retain a CAM ship's full cargo capacity.** BELOW: **The launch of a CAM ship's fighter often caused consternation in neighbouring ships. The blast of the rocket-assisted take-offs required the bridge front and the control officer's cubicle to be suitably protected.**

CAM ships

From airfields in western France and Norway, German long-range Fw200 Condors made forays deep into the Atlantic to locate convoys for U-boats to attack. From the German naval viewpoint there were always too few of the aircraft, they were unreliable and their use was greatly restricted by a dog-in-the-manger Luftwaffe. Their navigation on long flights was frequently inexact, so that positions reported were usually inaccurate to a significant degree.

To the convoy crews, however, the seemingly omnipresent "snooper" had much the same effect as had the hated Zeppelin on the Grand Fleet a quarter century earlier. Circling beyond gun range it was truly a harbinger of death.

In the Air Ministry were men with long memories who suggested reacting similarly, but launching fighters now from merchantmen fitted with catapults. In November 1940 several hundred such modifications were proposed, the ships concerned remaining under the Red Ensign and carrying normal cargoes. As in World War I, a fighter would be launched upon an enemy reconnaissance aircraft being sighted. Following an engagement, the fighter would "ditch" alongside a convoy vessel for the pilot (only) to be recovered from often freezing water.

Catapults proved to be not only in short supply but also difficult to obtain. Therefore only 35 Catapult Aircraft (or "Armed") Merchantmen, or CAM ships, ever entered service and most by April

1941. As the hoped-for cheap, expendable fighter never entered production, the ships embarked early marks of Hurricane or Fulmar.

The aircraft was hurled into the air, further assisted by sequentially fired rocket clusters, whose white-hot blast enveloped the asbestos-clad Launch Officer's cabin and ship's bridge front alike. This sight should have been cheering to more convoys but, due to perceived risk, only eight CAM launches were made in 170 sailings. These resulted in six "kills", two damaged and only one pilot lost.

Together with the similar, but naval-crewed Fighter Catapult Ships, the CAMs were only ever an expedient and disappeared quickly with the introduction of the Escort Carrier (CVE).

LEFT: **A quick comparison with Royal Navy conversions of World War I will show that there was nothing revolutionary about the CAM concept. Nor was it any more hazardous to the pilots involved.**

LEFT: **The dry-cargo MACs retained their original mercantile hull with its long, unbroken sheerline. Even by escort carrier standards the conversion was spartan. The "A"-bracket at the bows was for the suspension of an acoustic hammer.** BELOW: **The tanker-MAC also retained its original hull, the raised "islands" of forecastle, bridge and poop still being clearly discernable. All original pipework remained accessible, bridged by the flight deck.**

MAC ships

Large programmes of escort carrier construction were initiated during 1941 for the purpose of convoy protection. Austere as these conversions were, it still took time to effect results, and alternative interim measures were suggested. As any and all shipping capacity was precious, the possibility of building a flight deck over a functioning cargo ship appeared attractive. Thus was born the Merchant Aircraft Carrier, or MAC ship.

The flight deck overlaid all conventional cargo access and, of course, required the removal of the usual cargo handling gear. As a result, the ships could carry only those cargoes that could be handled by pumping notably grain and oil. A tanker's upper deck is a complex of piping, so only the dry cargo type could be equipped with

a hangar and elevator. There was no catapult and, with a short flight deck and low speed, there was no question of operating fighters. All, therefore, were devoted to anti-submarine warfare (ASW), deploying up to four Fairey Swordfish to enhance the effectiveness of a regular convoy escort.

A first pair of conversions was ordered in June 1942. As building was at an early stage, it was possible to fit uprated machinery. Their flight decks were only 126.2m/414ft in length (later examples were longer) but equipped with arrester gear and safety barriers.

The hangar occupied only that space over the aftermost hold. General encumbrance and extra topweight reduced earlier cargo deadweight capacity by nearly 30 per cent.

Anglo-Saxon, the Shell oil company's then shipping arm, operated considerable numbers of economical, standard-design tankers, known popularly as "Three Twelves", from their ability to shift 12,000 deadweight tons (12,193 tonnes) at 12 knots on 12 tons (12.2 tonnes) of fuel per day. Ideal for conversion, they compensated for a lack of hangar by having a longer, 140.2m/460ft flight deck. For safety's sake only high flashpoint cargoes could be carried and less than 10 per cent capacity was lost.

As the escort carrier programmes came on stream, the MAC conversions were reduced from a projected 30 to just 19, with two of them being Dutch-flagged.

LEFT: **Only the dry-cargo MAC was able to be equipped with a hangar. As can be seen, its rudimentary elevator was tailored to the folded-dimensions of the ubiquitous Swordfish.**

Audacity

While there was no lack of proposals for the conversion of merchant shipping to auxiliary carriers, HMS *Audacity* had the distinction of actually being the first so converted.

Built as the NDL cargo liner *Hannover*, she was captured by the Royal Navy in March 1940, but in a damaged state resulting from her crew's efforts to destroy her. Following the initial proposal for a bare-bones conversion, she was taken in hand in January 1941. By June, she had been cut down to her weather deck and fitted with a 138.2m/453ft flight deck. This was a light structure, mounted on pillars, but represented a considerable addition in topweight. To establish the required stability range and roll period it was necessary to add about 3,048 tonnes/3,000 tons of permanent ballast.

No hangar was provided, while the flight deck was graced with just two arrester wires and a safety barrier. Although she was intended to operate fighter aircraft, no catapult was fitted, thus necessitating considerable re-spotting of aircraft on deck.

There was no island superstructure, with navigation being conducted rather primitively from projecting platforms. As the vessel was a relatively low-powered motor ship, redirecting the exhaust through the starboard side posed no particular problem.

Audacity was converted specifically to counter the threat posed by the German Fw200 Condor aircraft, and primarily to the UK–Gibraltar convoys. She carried no Swordfish, therefore, but six of the newly available Grumman Wildcat, known to the British as the Martlet. These were permanently parked topside.

Commissioned in June 1941 (with a part-Merchant Navy crew) she proved remarkably successful. She undertook three round trips before being sunk by U-boat, her aircraft being credited with the destruction of seven Condors. Equally importantly, she had established the case for the conversion of many other mercantile hulls. By coincidence and (it is claimed) an independent evolutionary process, the US Navy commissioned its prototype escort carrier *Long Island* in the same month.

TOP AND ABOVE: **Although the flying arrangements of the *Audacity* were extremely basic, nobody complained about the accommodation for, as can be made out, both original amidships accommodation decks were retained. No hangar was provided although the space above the existing No.4 hold was plated-in.**

Audacity

Built: Bremer-Vulcan, Vegesack
Commissioned (as carrier): June 1941
Displacement: 8,350 tonnes/8,200 tons (standard); 10,450 tonnes/10,250 tons (full load)
Length: 132.6m/434ft 9in (bp); 146.1m/479ft (overall)
Beam: 17.1m/56ft
Draught: 6.6m/21ft 8in (full load)
Flight deck: 138.2 x 18.3m/453 x 60ft
Aircraft: 6
Armament: 1 x 102mm/4in, 4 x 2pdr pom-pom (4 single) guns, and 4 x 20mm/0.79in (4 single) guns
Machinery: One 7-cylinder diesel engine, 1 shaft
Power: 3,880kW/5,200bhp
Speed: 15.5 knots
Fuel: 680 tonnes/670 tons
Range: 22,220km/12,000nm at 15.5 knots
Armour: None
Complement: 210 men

British-built escort carriers

During the 1930s, one of the Royal Navy's major tasks remained the protection of trade, a requirement both facilitated and complicated by the growing maturity of aircraft. Aircraft-equipped "cruisers" could more easily apprehend surface raiders, thought to be a major threat to convoys, while the other menace, the U-boat, was already known to be considerably deterred by patrolling aircraft. Thought had also been given to the provision of defensive air cover to prevent air attack on convoys, but the effect of such an attack was as yet difficult to visualize.

Small "trade protection" carriers might well have been built but for the very tight global tonnage limitations imposed by the 1921–22 Washington Treaty. The alternative Admiralty strategy was, once again, to convert suitable mercantile hulls. Suitable ships should have been identified pre-war and the necessary design work instituted, but this was an era of fiscal constraint and staff shortage, so little was actually done.

British owners operated a wealth of shipping; however, this was built to a wide variety of trading requirements. As there was little standardization, the Admiralty drew up very broad specifications for three separate classes of carrier.

Their major characteristics were as follows:

	Flight deck larger than	Speed	Aircraft
Type A	167.6 x 22.9m/550 x 75ft	20 knots	25
Type B	152.4 x 21.3m/500 x 70ft	18 knots	15
Type C	137.2 x 18.3m/450 x 60ft	16.5 knots	10

Type A conversions would be based on diesel-powered passenger liners. These, however, proved to be so valuable in wartime as troop carriers that only one, *Pretoria Castle*, was

TOP: **Swords into ploughshares. Little changed, the *Campania* lies in London docks in about 1950 promoting the Festival of Britain. Note her name, painted-up mercantile-style on her bows.** ABOVE: **Larger than the series-built American escort carriers, the *Campania* was a more comfortable ship to operate on the inhospitable Arctic convoy routes. In 1952 she acted as flagship for the British Monte Bello nuclear tests.**

ever converted. Although the rebuilding was a success the ship was not employed operationally, spending the war as a trials and training carrier.

With the recent experience of the massacre of merchant shipping during World War I it is surprising, in retrospect, that an auxiliary carrier conversion programme was not vigorously pursued from the opening of World War II. Even the substantial and increasing losses of 1940 appeared to make little difference. It took the rapid and effective conversion of the *Audacity* in January–June 1941 to demonstrate what could be done. By then, however, British hulls were in such short supply

LEFT: **Another escort carrier to repeat a World War I name was the** *Nairana*. **She, too, was employed mainly on Arctic convoy escort and in Atlantic anti-submarine operations.** BELOW: **Looks dramatic, feels uncomfortable but is quite safe. Any ship will pitch given the right combination of speed and wavelength. The remedy, if operations permit, is to adjust course and speed. This is** *Nairana*.

that the War Cabinet vetoed any large follow-on programme. Beyond the *Pretoria Castle*, only four others, all major cargo liners, were rebuilt as carriers. None entered service before 1943, by which time escort carriers (CVE) were being transferred from the large American construction programmes.

The four British examples, *Activity*, *Campania* (II), *Nairana* (II) and *Vindex* (II) were considered successful but, in view of the urgent situation at sea, were too few, too complex and too late. By adhering to tight, non-varying no-frills specifications, the Americans produced large numbers of simple, effective auxiliary carriers that combined a useful aircraft capacity on relatively small dimensions. This helped to permit British yards to concentrate on the enormous throughput of repairs to war-damaged ships.

LEFT: **Same ship, different paint scheme: the** *Pretoria Castle* **is seen in disruptive camouflage designed, not to conceal the ship, but to confuse her form and identity and, importantly, her heading.**

Pretoria Castle

Built: Harland & Wolff, Belfast
Commissioned as carrier: April 9, 1943
Displacement: 20,000 tonnes/19,650 tons (standard); 23,880 tonnes/23,450 tons (full load)
Length: 170.1m/560ft (bp); 181.3m/594ft 6in (overall)
Beam: 23.3m/76ft 3in
Draught: 8.7m/28ft 6in (full load)
Flight deck: 170.1 x 23.2m/560 x 76ft
Aircraft: About 21
Armament: 4 x 102mm/4in (2 double), 8 x 2pdr pom-pom (2 quadruple) guns, and 20 x 20mm/0.79in (10 double) guns
Machinery: Two 8-cylinder diesel engines, 2 shafts
Power: 16,000kW/21,500bhp
Speed: 18 knots
Fuel: 2,500 tonnes/2,450 tons
Range: 29,630km/16,000nm at 16 knots
Armour: None
Complement: 665 men

ABOVE: **Despite the pre-war plans, passenger liners were so valuable that only one, the** *Pretoria Castle*, **was ever converted to a carrier. Because of the ship's size she was employed almost exclusively for pilot training.**

Archer class

Archer class

Class: *Archer*, Sun Shipbuilding; *Avenger*, Bethlehem Steel; *Biter*, Atlantic Basin; *Dasher*, Tietjen & Lang
Commissioned: November 1941–July 1942
Displacement: 10,380 tonnes/10,200 tons (standard); 13,100 tonnes/12,850 tons (full load)
Length: 141.8m/465ft (bp); 150.1m/492ft (overall)
Beam: 21.2m/69ft 6in
Draught: 6.9m/22ft 6in (full load)
Flight deck: 125.1 x 23.8m/410 x 78ft
Aircraft: About 16
Armament: 3 x 102mm/4in, 16 x 20mm/0.79in guns
Machinery: 4 diesels, 1 shaft
Power: 6,340kW/8,500shp
Speed: 16.5 knots
Fuel: 1,425 tonnes/1,400 tons
Range: –
Armour: None
Complement: 540 men

ABOVE: **The first of the American conversions to be transferred to the Royal Navy, the *Archer* had no island superstructure. Except in way of the short hangar at the after end, the space below the flight deck was completely open.**

E ven before the entry of HMS *Audacity* into service, in July 1941, the Americans had begun work on six further auxiliary carriers to British account. Like so many that were to follow, they were based on the US Maritime Commission's standard C3 hull, the "C3" denoting a cargo vessel with waterline length of 137–152m/450–500ft.

First-of-class *Archer* differed from her near-sisters by having no island superstructure, but all were an advance on the *Audacity* in having a small hangar aft. Forward of this, the wood-on-steel flight deck was elevated on tall pillars.

Although they also had a catapult, this was incompatible with British-built aircraft. All of this group were diesel-propelled and suffered from chronic machinery problems.

Built to commercial, two-compartment standards, they did not meet British stability requirements, necessitating the addition of about 1,016 tonnes/1,000 tons of permanent ballast. Following the loss of *Avenger* and *Dasher*, major modifications were ordered in the stowage of ordnance and aviation fuel.

The usual aircraft mix was nine Swordfish or Avengers, and six Martlet (Wildcat) fighters. The flight deck (later lengthened) was of thin steel plate overlaid with wood, designed to be easy to repair. It was served by a single elevator.

LEFT: **Corresponding to the US Navy's Bogue class, the Attackers had a greatly extended hangar. This is *Ravager*, seen on an aircraft delivery trip. The tolerance of such small ships to large and varying topweight was remarkable.**

Attacker class

Class: *Attacker, Fencer, Stalker, Striker*, Western Pipe; *Battler, Hunter, Chaser, Pursuer*, Ingalls; *Searcher, Ravager*, Todd, Tacoma; *Tracker*, Willamette
Commissioned: October 1942–June 1943
Displacement: 10,380 tonnes/10,200 tons (standard); 14,650 tonnes/14,400 tons (full load)
Length: 141.8m/465ft (bp); 151.1m/495ft 6in (overall)
Beam: 21.2m/69ft 6in
Draught: 7.8m/25ft 6in (full load)
Flight deck: 134.2 x 25m/440 x 82ft
Aircraft: About 20
Armament: 2 x 102mm/4in,14 x 20mm/0.79in guns
Machinery: Geared turbine, 1 shaft
Power: 6,340kW/8,500shp
Speed: 18 knots
Fuel: 3,050 tonnes/3,000 tons
Range: –
Armour: None
Complement: 645 men

Attacker class

S ometimes referred to as the Tracker class, these 11 ships were a great advance on the Archers. Based on the American Bogue class they, too, were based on the C3 hull but were built from the keel up with a more comprehensive standard of subdivision. Sides were plated up to flight deck level, enclosing a hangar now large enough to accommodate a dozen Swordfish (or Avengers) and six Martlets. There was an elevator at either end of the hangar and a single catapult, port side forward.

With little experience of marine diesels the Americans also reverted to the tried and tested steam turbine. Offering no redundancy, the single shaft was a weakness in most escort carriers.

The Archers were transferred to the Royal Navy between November 1941 and July 1942, the Attackers following on between October 1942 and June 1943.

Ameer class

Modifications to earlier ships (improved subdivision, magazine protection and aviation fuel stowage), insisted upon by the British, created safer ships but at the cost of delays which Americans found unacceptable. Their rapid and efficient series production depended upon absolute conformation to a rigid specification. Unresolved differences probably influenced the decision not to transfer to the British any of the improved, but more complex, *Casablanca* (or "Kaiser") type. Further C3-based units therefore followed instead, these moving up to Vancouver for appropriate modifications to improving survivability, and taking six weeks per ship.

A further refinement of the basic type, the Ameers were transferred between July 1943 and February 1944 and featured a longer flight deck and hangar, as well as an all-American armament. The vexed question of aviation fuel safety was resolved only through shipping about one quarter of the ships' designed capacity, a severely limiting factor on extended operations.

ABOVE: **Effectively follow-on Attackers, the extensive Ameer class were built as carriers from the keel up and fitted out for their differing primary roles of convoy escort, ASW operations or aircraft transport.** LEFT: **A Wildcat and two Avengers aboard a British escort carrier. Note the painted version of Flag "F" in the foreground, displayed prominently during flight operations.**

All US-sourced escort carriers were returned at close of hostilities.

Ameer class

Class: *Ameer; Arbiter; Atheling; Begum; Emperor; Empress; Khedive; Nabob; Patroller; Premier; Puncher; Queen Rajah; Ranee; Reaper; Ruler; Shah; Slinger; Smiter; Speaker; Thane; Trouncer; Trumpeter*
Built: Todd, Tacoma, with the exception of *Queen Rajah*, Willamette; *Trouncer*, Commercial Iron Works
Commissioned: July 1943–February 1944
Displacement: 11,600 tonnes/11,400 tons (standard); 15,700 tonnes/15,400 tons (full load)
Length: 141.8m/465ft (bp); 151m/495ft (overall)
Beam: 21.1m/69ft 6in
Draught: 7.8m/25ft 6in (full load)
Flight deck: 133.6 x 26.8m/438 x 88ft
Aircraft: About 20
Armament: 2 x 127mm/5in,16 x 40mm/1.57in guns
Machinery: Geared turbine, 1 shaft
Power: 6.340kW/8,500shp
Speed: 17.5 knots
Fuel: 3,150 tonnes/3,100 tons
Range: –
Armour: None
Complement: 640 men

ABOVE: **Visible also at a distance in the picture above, the *Nabob* is seen after having survived a U-boat torpedo in August 1944. She was written off for further naval service but was converted to mercantile use postwar. Ironically, she was operated by the German Norddeutscher Lloyd company, retaining her RN name.**

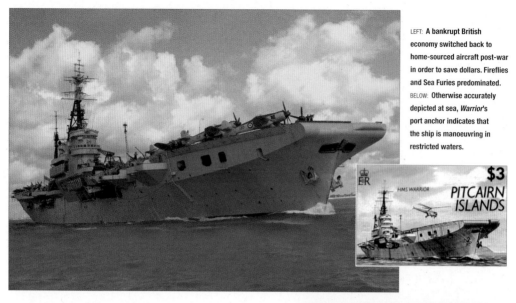

LEFT: **A bankrupt British economy switched back to home-sourced aircraft post-war in order to save dollars. Fireflies and Sea Furies predominated.** BELOW: **Otherwise accurately depicted at sea, *Warrior*'s port anchor indicates that the ship is manoeuvring in restricted waters.**

Colossus class

Experience in Norway and the Mediterranean by mid-1941 had demonstrated to the Royal Navy that the fleet required better defensive air cover. Fleet carriers were too few and too valuable to solve what was a pressing problem. Conversion of warships would prove less than satisfactory, while passenger liners, favourites for re-building, were already indispensable as troop carriers. New construction was therefore the only option.

Discussion centred upon a vessel intermediate between the complexity and expense of a fleet carrier and the limited capabilities of the escort carriers soon to enter service. Above all, this "intermediate" carrier had to be capable of being built in 21 months.

Naval design staff and specialist naval builders were already fully stretched, so Vickers-Armstrong, well-versed in both naval and mercantile practice, was made lead authority.

Several rapid draught proposals were considered, finalizing in February 1942 in a ship built generally to mercantile standards. Subdivision would, however, be greatly enhanced and all void spaces would be fitted with buoyant sealed drums. Standard cruiser machinery would be installed, powering twin shafts for 25 knots.

As only one hangar was considered, it could be given a headroom of 5.3m/17ft 6in which, later, allowed the ships to deploy aircraft that the fleet carriers could not. Armament was restricted to two

ABOVE: **As this late war picture shows, a Colossus' air wing was little inferior to that of a large British fleet carrier. The type's survivability was, however, never tested by kamikaze, bomb or torpedo.** BELOW LEFT: **Few of the Colossus class saw much in the way of modernization, soldiering on in their original form until their ultimate disposal, mostly in the early 1960s unless transferred.**

twin 102mm/4in mountings aft and a range of automatic weapons. An early alteration to the specification saw the flight deck enlarged, displacing the 102mm/4in guns. Urgency demanded that some important equipment had no back-up but, even so, the construction time had to be lengthened to 27 months.

Such was the strength of British shipbuilding that the orders for the first ten could be shared between eight yards. Two of the first three were completed within the target time but none could work-up and proceed to the Pacific in time to see action.

Majestic class

In all, contracts were issued for 16 of what became universally known as the "Light Fleets". However, as the programme and the war progressed, carrier aircraft developed rapidly. Physically larger, far heavier in loaded take-off, and with higher landing speeds, they demanded a general uprating of related equipment, in particular arresters, catapult and elevators, in addition to a strengthened flight deck.

At the same time, an improved Bofors and Oerlikon-based armament (the former with directors) was added, together with a new electronics outfit and fittings for replenishment-at-sea (RAS), so essential to extended Pacific operation. The final six differed sufficiently to form a subclass known as the Majestics.

Such modifications were facilitated by the lightness of construction but accommodation could not keep pace with the increase in crew numbers consequent upon the eventual introduction of deck parks and larger air groups.

Beyond 1945, the Light Fleets proved their worth during the Korean War. None, however, received battle damage to test the justification of their calculated

ABOVE: **Completed as the Canadian** *Bonaventure*, **the** *Powerful* **differed considerably in detail, the new funnel and masting being visible here. She also operated McDonnell Banshees and Grumman Trackers.** BELOW: **The name ship of the class,** *Majestic* **was completed in 1955 as the Australian** *Melbourne*. **Note that, even on a smaller carrier, an interim angled deck could be incorporated with advantage. The aircraft are A-4 Skyhawks, Trackers and Sea Kings.**

constructional shortcomings. Surplus to requirements, several were transferred abroad, proving to be highly durable, two still being extant at over 60 years of age.

Colossus and Majestic class

Colossus class: *Colossus; Glory; Ocean; Theseus; Triumph; Venerable; Vengeance; Warrior*
Majestic class: *Hercules; Leviathan; Magnificent; Majestic; Powerful; Terrible*
Built: Various
Commissioned: December 1944–May 1948
Displacement: *Colossus* 13,440 tonnes/ 13,200 tons (standard); 18,350 tonnes/ 18,000 tons (full load)
Majestic 16,050 tonnes/15,750 tons (standard); 19,850 tonnes/19,500 tons (full load)
Length: 192.2m/630ft (bp); 212m/695ft (overall)
Beam: 24.4m/80ft
Draught: *Colossus* 5.6m/18ft 6in (standard); 7.1m/23ft 3in (full load)
Majestic 5.9m/19ft 6in (standard); 7.5m/ 24ft 9in (full load)
Flight deck: 210.4 x 24.4m/690 x 80ft
Aircraft: About 48
Armament: *Colossus* 31 x 40mm/1.57in (10 double, 11 single), and 24 x 2pdr pom-pom (6 quadruple) guns
Majestic 30 x 40mm/1.57in (6 double, 18 single) guns
Machinery: Geared steam turbine, 4 boilers, 2 shafts
Power: 29,850kW/40,000shp
Speed: 25 knots
Fuel: *Colossus* 3,260 tonnes/3,200 tons
Majestic 3,230 tonnes/3,175 tons
Range: 22,220km/12,000nm at 14 knots
Armour: None
Complement: 1,050 men

Ark Royal (III) and *Eagle* (II)

Although treaty restrictions no longer applied, the design process for the *Implacable*'s successor began in 1940 with the same underwater hull form. The emphasis was laid on more and larger aircraft, together with even better protection from bomb attack. Only a small increase in target displacement was initially allowed, and it proved insufficient to permit the thickening of the flight deck, although the beam could be increased sufficiently to accommodate folded aircraft four abreast. A required increase in hangar headroom could be achieved only by reducing the depth of the overhead beams, which supported the heavy flight deck.

This "Improved Implacable", presented early in 1941, was poorly received and no order was placed. Within months, the *Formidable* and *Illustrious* survived heavy bomb damage. This led to more detailed design analysis, complicated further by the loss of the recently completed *Ark Royal* (II) to a single torpedo, due largely to poor design features.

A new design target was set for a 27,433-tonne/27,000-ton (standard) vessel with a 102mm/4in flight deck and provision for 72 aircraft. The necessary calculations and experiment demonstrated that the best attainable with this level of protection was a 32,105-tonne/31,600-ton ship stowing 57–69 aircraft. It was, by now, 1942 and, as the ship would be at least four years in build, it is interesting to speculate upon how long the Director of Naval Construction (DNC) thought the war would last.

Because of the anticipated new Barracuda multi-role aircraft and the need also to operate American-sourced aircraft, it was then decided to adopt American standards of

ABOVE: **Seen near the end of her career, the *Ark Royal* (III) is operating Phantoms and Buccaneers. Note how, at full power, the relatively full hull form is pushing water over the flight deck. The ship now is unarmed.**

BELOW: **The *Eagle* (II) was instantly distinguishable from her sister, when, in the course of her 1959–64 modernization, she gained an enormous Type 984, three-dimensional radar.**

5.3m/17ft 6in high hangars and elevators rated at 13.6-tonne/30,000lb capacity. The width of the hangars was further increased, requiring redeepening the deck beams and increasing the beam to 34.4m/112ft 9in. This, in turn, limited the number both of yards to build it and docks to stem it. The required 31.5 knots brought the overall length to about 243.8m/800ft and standard displacement to about 33,020 tonnes/32,500 tons.

Approval was given for four of the class and, at last, in October 1942, the first-of-class was laid down, the second not until May 1943. With now no hope of any completions during hostilities, the scarcely begun third unit was eventually abandoned and the fourth cancelled. (If the Americans had pursued their Essex programme in this dilatory fashion, they would have lost the Pacific war.)

The *Audacious* assumed the name of *Eagle* (II) from the abandoned unit and was launched in 1946, mainly to clear the slip. Her remaining sister, *Ark Royal* (III), was not put in the water until 1950.

With post-war austerity and an uncertain future, further progress was slow. *Eagle* was completed in a classic configuration in 1952 but the less advanced *Ark Royal* received substantial modifications, not being completed until 1955, but featuring an "interim" angled flight deck, steam-powered catapults and a third elevator placed, American-fashion, on the deck edge, a location not greatly favoured by British designers.

ABOVE LEFT: **The siting of the dual-purpose main armament always encroached upon flight deck space in British carriers. Adoption of the angled deck enforced a partial suppression of conventional gun armament, compensated by the addition of the Sea Cat missile.**

ABOVE: **Notice how the angled deck and aircraft deck parks are safely separated. Also the *Ark Royal* (III)'s pronounced "horn" to catch the aircraft launch bridles.**

RIGHT: ***Ark Royal* (III) on a port visit in company with a *Leander*-class frigate and a *Ness*-class supply ship. Note the two double-mattress Type 965 radar antennas for high definition air search.**

Ark Royal (III) and Eagle (II)

Class: *Eagle* (II), Harland & Wolff, Belfast, commissioned October 1, 1951; *Ark Royal* (III), Cammell Laird, Birkenhead, commissioned February 25, 1955

Particulars as built:

Displacement: 37,650 tonnes/36,970 tons (standard); 46,550 tonnes/45,720 tons (full load)

Length: 219.6m/720ft (bp); 245.1m/803ft 9in (overall)

Beam: 34.4m/112ft 9in

Draught: 10m/32ft 9in (full load)

Flight deck: 243.1 x 34.2m/797 x 112ft

Aircraft: 80

Armament: 16 x 114.3mm/4.5in (8 double), 64 x 40mm/1.57in (8 sextuple, 2 double. 12 single) guns

Machinery: Geared steam turbines, 8 boilers, 4 shafts

Power: 113,400kW/152,000shp

Speed: 30.5 knots

Fuel: 5,925 tonnes/5,820 tons

Range: 7,250km/3,915nm at 24 knots

Armour: 114.3mm/4.5in (vertical belt); 38mm/ 1.5in (hangar walls); 102mm/4in (flight deck)

Complement: 2,275 men

ABOVE: ***Ark Royal* (III) in the mid-1950s being overflown by a flight of Fairey Gannets. Although some of these aircraft were converted for airborne early warning duties, these are all ASW versions.**

Malta class

Although never realized, the Malta design is of great interest in showing how far the experience of four years of war and close cooperation with the US Navy altered British philosophy with respect to carriers.

The strike role had emerged as paramount, so that not only were large numbers of aircraft required but also the means to launch them at a high rate to maximize strike potential. American-style "open" hangars permitted aircraft engines to be warmed-up below while further elevators would facilitate rapid transfer to flight deck level. The largest feasible flight decks allowed for efficient "spotting", mass take-offs and landings, but their greater area militated against their being heavily protected. British-style "closed" hangars and heavy flight deck made, paradoxically, for a lighter ship because of the greater depth of the

continuously plated hull. Double hangars could also be provided, reducing the plan area (and, therefore, target area) for a given aircraft capacity.

A major argument against the "small area" ship, however, was the need for higher power, not only to maintain high speed when required but also to accelerate rapidly from cruising to launch speed.

With the design yet to be finalized, three (possibly four) Maltas were ordered in July 1943. Slightly larger than the American Midways then in build, the ships would have been of "open" design with two centreline and two deck-edge elevators. Over 149,140kW/200,000shp would have been dissipated over, probably, five propeller shafts, the centreline shaft being seen as less likely to incur torpedo damage. The number of rudders was not finally decided.

ABOVE: **The four projected *Malta*-class carriers were badly delayed by the Fleet Air Arm requesting that the design be recast along American, rather than British, principles.** BELOW LEFT: **In the words of the American official historian, kamikazes "crumpled like scrambled eggs" on the armoured flight decks of British carriers. This factor was hugely influential in later carrier design, both British and American.**

Even until their cancellation at the war's end, the Maltas were subject to continuous change, not least because the advent of the kamikaze and the heavy air-launched rocket challenged anew the acceptance of less well-protected ships.

Malta class	
Projected class: *Africa*, Fairfield, Govan; *Gibraltar*, Vickers-Armstrong, Newcastle; *Malta*, John Brown, Clydebank; *New Zealand*, Harland & Wolff, Belfast	
Commissioned: –	
Displacement: 47,350 tonnes/46,500 tons (standard); 57,680 tonnes/56,650 tons (full load)	
Length: 250m/820ft (bp); 273.6m/897ft (overall)	
Beam: 35.3m/115ft 9in (bp)	
Draught: 9m/29ft 6in (standard); 10.5m/34ft 6in (full load)	
Flight deck: 273.6 x 41.5m/897 x 136ft	
Aircraft: 80	
Armament: 16 x 114.3mm/4.5in (8 double) and 42 x 40mm/1.57in (7 sextuple) guns	
Machinery: Geared steam turbines, 8 boilers, 4 shafts	
Power: 149,140kW/200,000shp	
Speed: 32.5 knots	
Fuel: 6,110 tonnes/6,000 tons	
Range: Not known	
Armour: 102mm/4in (hangar walls); 102mm/4in (protective deck)	
Complement: 3,500 men	

LEFT: **Aircraft maintenance support ships resulted from the high attrition rates suffered during intensive operations by the British Pacific Fleet. Here, the *Pioneer* has a Supermarine Sea Otter perched forward. In the Far East, these aircraft were usually shore-based and used for air-sea rescue.**
ABOVE: **Although a new ship in this 1945 picture, the *Pioneer*, lacking all her carrier impedimenta, gives the impression of being stripped for disposal.**

Perseus and *Pioneer*

Intensive pre-war carrier operation indicated the high levels of aircraft attrition that might be expected under wartime conditions. This resulted in the one-off expensive Maintenance Carrier HMS *Unicorn*. Even before her completion, however, the Admiralty was having to plan the reconstruction of a British Eastern Fleet. With an estimated 1,000 attached aircraft, it would obviously require further forward maintenance ships for, in so vast a theatre, the use of fixed, shore-based repair facilities was not a practical option. Conversion of American-supplied (and owned) escort carriers (CVE) could not be considered, so the choice fell upon two hulls from the "Light Fleet" programme, retaining two hulls that could also have been reconverted in an emergency.

Perseus and *Pioneer* were two standard *Colossus*-type ships but, as their new role would see aircraft transferred only by crane, flying control facilities, arrester systems and catapult were deleted and hangar space reorganized for fuselage repair, high-level maintenance and system testing. Engines and major component repair and maintenance was the task of other ships in the fleet train. Much of their already light armament was suppressed and strange erections, including a large Scotch derrick, appeared topside.

Along with unconverted Light Fleets, *Perseus* and *Pioneer* arrived in the Pacific just too late to be of operational use. Post-war, there was an abundance of carriers, so neither was reconverted, and they were re-rated Ferry Carriers,

moving aircraft about the many extant British overseas bases and, on occasion, "topping-up" fleet carriers.

During 1951–52, the *Perseus* acted as floating test bed for the prototype steam catapult, under development since 1946. To generate sufficient speed for modern fleet aircraft without imposing dangerous acceleration forces, it was found that a 45.7m/150ft catapult was required. These could be fitted to fleet carriers but not to Light Fleets. Limited to a unit of only about 30.5m/100ft, the ships were thus always limited in their range of deployable aircraft.

The *Pioneer* was scrapped in 1954 and the *Perseus* in 1958, as the need for front-line aircraft heavy repair disappeared. For relevant data see under Colossus class.

RIGHT: **Looking rather more pristine, the *Pioneer* was fitted with only nominal armament and electronics. For her maintenance duties, she has been fitted with a Scotch derrick and an auxiliary accommodation block right aft.**

Centaur class

At the end of 1942, the requirements of future carrier aircraft were drastically reappraised. Maximum landing and take-off weight was nearly tripled, to 13.6 tonnes/30,000lb. Stall speed was increased to 75 knots, meaning that catapults had to accelerate them to this speed, and arresters had to stop them from it. Wingspan rose from 15.3m/50ft to 18.3m/60ft and take-off distance from 106.7m/350ft to 152.4m/500ft.

The planned 1943 building programme was to include eight "Improved Majestics", but it was clear that this design was simply too small to accept the new requirements. With an eye to the post-war fleet, it was also apparent that the six earlier armoured carriers would not be amenable to modernization. Assuming their enforced retirement, the planned Ark Royals would be the only modern fleet carriers. The new Majestic follow-ons would, therefore, need to work alongside them, necessitating a higher speed than that planned. A longer hull was, therefore, required on both counts and the installed power was doubled.

TOP: Until 1958 the *Centaur* deployed Sea Furies and Avengers then, with full angled deck and steam catapults, Sea Hawks. There was insufficient space to incorporate any armament of larger calibre than 40mm/1.57in.

LEFT: Steaming on a pristine sea, the *Bulwark* (nearer ship) and *Albion* present a very uncluttered appearance, mainly due to having much of their armament landed.

The new specification called for a single hangar, meeting the later criterion of 5.3m/17ft 6in headroom. Accommodation, stores, and fuel were to be sufficient for an air group of 24 attack aircraft and 16 fighters. Beyond splinter protection and small patches over vital areas, no armour was to be incorporated. Because of the ships' greater value, they were to be given four twin 114.3mm/4.5in mountings.

As final approval was given only in March 1944, and the proposed build time was 33 months, it was never likely that they would participate in the war against Japan that was expected to be resolved by the end of 1946. With hostilities ending

ABOVE: Completed to a revised, post-war design the three *Centaurs* presented unusually "clean" hulls, free of the many common protuberances except the crane support three-quarters aft. BELOW: British and American carriers conducted frequent "crossdecking" exercises to prove commonality. Here, a Douglas AD Skyraider, probably from the *Forrestal*, lands on *Centaur*.

16 months earlier than expected, contracts for four of the eight new *Centaurs* were therefore cancelled. Construction of the remainder slowed to a crawl, resulting in considerable design changes being introduced to accommodate new technologies and improved peacetime habitability standards.

Centaur class

Class: *Albion*, Swan Hunter, Wallsend, commissioned May 26, 1954; *Bulwark*, Harland & Wolff, Belfast, commissioned November 4, 1954; *Centaur*, Harland & Wolff, Belfast, commissioned September 1, 1953; *Hermes* (III), Vickers-Armstrong, Barrow, commissioned November 18, 1959

Displacement: 22,880 tonnes/22,470 tons (standard); 27,550 tonnes/27,050 tons (full load)

Length: 198.3m/650ft (bp); 224.5m/736ft (overall)

Beam: 27.5m/90ft

Draught: 7.1m/23ft 3in (standard); 8.3m/27ft 3in (full load)

Flight deck: 223.5 x 27.5m/732ft 9in x 90ft

Aircraft: 40–42

Armament: 32 x 40mm/1.57in (2 sextuple, 8 double, 4 single) guns

Machinery: Geared steam turbines, 4 boilers, 2 shafts

Power: 56,700kW/76,000shp

Speed: 28.5 knots

Fuel: 4,175 tonnes/4,100 tons

Range: 11,110km/6,000nm at 20 knots

Armour: None

Complement: 1,550 men

LEFT: **Looking most impressive**, *Victorious* checks responses with a zig-zag manoeuvre. Right forward is a de Havilland Sea Vixen, a very capable all-weather interceptor or strike fighter.

ABOVE: Sea Vixens and Buccaneers predominate in this view of *Victorious* at anchor. The intention of locating the forward elevator on the port-side deck edge was thwarted by the ship's relatively low freeboard.

Victorious modernized

There was a pressing post-war requirement to bring the six early armoured carriers up to a standard whereby they could operate modern aircraft. Designed with single hangars of 4.9m/16ft headroom, the three original (Illustrious) class were most suitable for a pilot reconstruction and, of these, *Victorious* was selected. It was estimated that the work, starting in October 1950, would take 43 weeks. The ship would be razed to hangar deck level and rebuilt with an increased beam and hangar height increased to 5.3m/17.5ft.

This, however, was a period of great innovation in carrier practice and the already considerable task was complicated by modifications and additions. Over 30 months into the job it was decided to install a full (8.5-degree) angled deck, although the ship's freeboard proved inadequate for the required deck-edge elevator.

Just two months later came the decision to add the huge new Type 984 three-dimensional radar. This would considerably uprate the ship's potential but greatly impacted on the layout of the superstructure and associated compartments below.

With much of the heavy horizontal structure replaced, it was belatedly forecast that the existing boilers (which now had also to provide steam for the two new catapults) could not last the extended life of the ship. Much work therefore had to be repeated in re-opening the hull for boiler replacement.

A final problem was that her planned British 76mm/3in 70-calibre armament was not ready, so that American-pattern 76mm/3in 50s had to be substituted.

The final result was judged successful but had been so difficult, so protracted (twice the estimated time) and so expensive (six times the first estimate) that the remaining five ships were phased out of service.

In her reconstruction, some of the *Victorious'* main statistics were changed. Length (overall) increased to 237.2m/778ft 4in, beam to 31.5m/103ft 4in. Standard displacement was now 30,886 tonnes/30,400 tons, full load 36,068 tonnes/35,500 tons. Main armament comprised six twin 76mm/

3in guns. Up to 38 modern aircraft could be accommodated (which does not suggest very good value for money).

Victorious modernized

Built: Vickers-Armstrong, Newcastle
Commissioned: May 15, 1941
Displacement: 30,886 tonnes/30,400 tons (standard); 36,068 tonnes/35,500 tons (full load)
Length: 205.3m/673ft (bp); 237.2m/778ft 4in (overall)
Beam: 31.5m/103ft 4in
Draught: 7.5m/24ft 6in (standard); 8.5m/27ft 9in (full load)
Flight deck: 189.1 x 24.6m/620 x 80ft
Aircraft: Up to 38
Armament: 12 x 76mm/3in (6 double) guns
Machinery: Geared steam turbines, 6 boilers, 3 shafts
Power: 82,800kW/111,000shp
Speed: 30.5 knots
Fuel: 4,940 tonnes/4,850 tons
Range: 19,816 km/10,700nm at 10 knots
Armour: 114.3mm/4.5in (belt); 38mm/1.5in (hangar wall); 76mm/3in (flight deck); 38–50mm/1.5–2in (hangar deck)
Complement: 1,180 men

ABOVE LEFT: **Most thorough of the commando carrier conversions that of the *Hermes* (III) saw her ponderous Type 984 radar replaced by a less capable 965. Although she has been fitted with a ski-jump for V/STOL operation only helicopters, transport and stores are here ranged on deck.**

TOP: **Amphibious group operation. As the carrier's Wessex helicopters wait to put their spearhead troops ashore, a flooded-down Fearless-type dock landing ship has her assault landing craft ready in support.** ABOVE: **As converted, the Centaurs carried variable numbers of Wessex and Sea King helicopters. The former were for lifting troops, the latter for anti-submarine operations.**

Centaur class as Commando Carriers

During the Suez campaign of November 1956 the *Colossus*-class *Ocean* and *Theseus* effectively demonstrated that special assault troops could be landed by helicopter to seize and hold key points ahead of a major amphibious landing.

It was decided to convert ships specifically for this role and between 1959 and 1962, the *Albion* and *Bulwark* were reconfigured as so-called Commando Carriers. In appearance they changed little but could now accommodate a full commando of about 750 men. In their new role, the ship's complement had been reduced by about 30 per cent and much hangar space had been freed so there was no problem with space.

The earlier air group was gone, in favour of 16 Whirlwind (later Wessex) helicopters. These required neither arrest gear nor catapults, which were removed. The interim angled-deck markings reverted to an axial configuration with nine widely spaced "spots" for helicopters.

To transport heavy gear, light transport and guns ashore, four assault landing craft were slung under substantial davits near the after end. All armament except four twin 40mm/1.57in guns was landed.

Between 1971 and 1973, with British fixed-wing carriers being phased out, the later and more capable *Hermes* (III) was converted to replace *Albion* which, with her never-converted sister, *Centaur*, went for scrap.

With extra experience, the *Hermes* (III) was given space for a second commando, although further troop-carrying helicopters were not provided. Fewer carriers, however, meant a diminished fleet anti-submarine warfare (ASW) capability. For this reason, *Hermes* (III) was reconfigured for ASW but acted also as a trials ship for V/STOL operation, with the Royal Navy seeking to acquire a marinized version of the Harrier. The wisdom of this was vindicated by the aircraft's versatile performance during the 1982 Falklands War.

Centaur class as Commando Carriers

Class: *Albion; Bulwark; Hermes* (III)
Displacement: 22,658 tonnes/22,300 tons (standard); 27,738 tonnes/27,300 tons (full load)
Length: 198.3m/650ft (bp); 224.5m/736ft (overall)
Beam: 27.5m/90ft
Draught: 7.1m/23ft 3in (standard); 8.3m/27ft 3in (full load)
Flight deck: 223.5 x 27.5m/732ft 9in x 90ft
Aircraft: 40–42
Armament: 8 x 40mm/1.57in (4 double) guns
Machinery: Geared steam turbines, 4 boilers, 2 shafts
Power: 56,700kW/76,000shp
Speed: 28.5 knots
Fuel: 4,175 tonnes/4,100 tons
Range: 11,110km/6,000nm at 20 knots
Armour: None
Complement: 1,550 men

CVA-01

By the mid-1960s it was becoming urgently necessary to lay down replacements for the Royal Navy's ageing carrier force. A design of a nominal 53,848 tonnes/53,000 tons was decided upon as being the maximum likely to receive Treasury approval, not least because of limitations in facilities at both builders and dockyards. It had also been conclusively demonstrated that a 10 per cent reduction in cost would result in 50 per cent reduction in capability. Dimensions were also driven by a demand for maximum commonality between naval and air force aircraft.

Coded CVA-01, the carrier would have been almost symmetrical in plan, the angled deck to port balanced by an access track outboard of the superstructure linking forward and after ends. The angled deck was offset at only 3.5 degrees, creating a three-zone working area. Two steam catapults and two elevators, one of them on the starboard-quarter deck edge, could handle aircraft of up to 34 tonnes/75,000lb weight.

Although essentially of closed design, the hangar opened out on to a quarterdeck to allow limited pre-warming of aircraft engines. The layout of the

ABOVE: **Innovative deck layout was a feature of the planned CVA-01, with the after (starboard quarter) elevator feeding aircraft to the forward catapult via the "Alaskan Highway" outboard of the island. This would interfere neither with landing operations nor deck parks.** Hangar space would be maximized by housing ASW helicopters aboard accompanying supply ships and replacing the CAP by missile defence. ABOVE RIGHT: **Faced with the expensive prospect of building three CVA-01s, the British government preferred the RAF's proposal of cheaper, land-based air power. However, the proposed means, the variable geometry F-111K, was never acquired by the British, though variants continue to give good service to the USAF and RAAF 40 years after the F-111's first flight.**

long, narrow superstructure was dominated by the requirement to efficiently separate the numerous and complex electronics systems.

The ship's strike capability would be maximized by operating in concert with a projected Strike Cruiser, which would incorporate all a task group's command facilities as well as deploying its force of ASW helicopters.

To guarantee the availability of one ship requires, ideally, three and the *Eagle*-sized CVA-01 was killed off by the 1966 Defence Review, which planned withdrawal from "East of Suez" and which capitulated to the RAF argument that the (stillborn) F-111 aircraft would be a cheaper and equally effective option. History, alas, proves invariably that the argument is specious.

CVA-01 (name never confirmed)

Built: Order never placed
Displacement: 50,900 tonnes/50,000 tons (standard); 55,650 tonnes/54,650 tons (full load)
Length: 271.5m/890ft (at waterline); 293.7m/963ft (overall)
Beam: 37.2m/122ft
Draught: 9.8m/32ft 3in (full load)
Flight deck: 283 x 58.3m/928 x 191ft
Aircraft: About 45
Armament: Twin Sea Dart SAM
Machinery: Geared steam turbines, 6 boilers, 3 shafts
Power: 100,700kW/135,000shp
Speed: 28+ knots
Fuel: 6,310 tonnes/6,200 tons
Range: 11,110km/6,000nm at 20 knots
Armour: Nominal
Complement: Not known

Argus (II)

The naval force despatched to recover the Falklands in 1982 included many "ships taken up from trade" (STUFT). One was the roll-on, roll-off/container ship *Contender Bezant*, whose spacious vehicle decks made her ideal as an aircraft transport. Subsequent to the hostilities, she was purchased and converted to a helicopter training ship by Harland & Wolff. Renamed *Argus* (II), she is a Royal Fleet Auxiliary (RFA), civilian-manned but carrying a permanent naval party.

Prior to conversion she had excess stability in the unloaded condition, making for an unacceptably lively motion. To raise her centre of gravity she was given a heavy superstructure and a flight deck formed from the original deck,

inverted and filled with reinforced concrete. The new hangar is divided into four by heavy doors and may be opened to allow engine warm-up. It is connected to the flight deck by two elevators. In peacetime the role of the *Argus* (II) is to train helicopter aircrew but, in hostilities, she can operate six to twelve ASW helicopters. She can also carry a dozen Harrier-sized V/STOL aircraft, although her configuration militates against their efficient use.

Argus (II) is a good example of how helicopters and V/STOL aircraft enable a variety of cargo vessels to act as auxiliary aircraft carriers.

Plans to similarly convert a sister ship were abandoned due to cost and, indeed, would be hard to justify in the long term.

Argus (II)

Built: Cantieri Riuniti "Breda", Venice, Italy
Commissioned: (as *Argus*): October 28, 1987
Displacement: 22,661 tonnes/22,256 tons (standard); 28,675 tonnes/28,163 tons (full load)
Length: 160m/525ft 3in (bp); 175.12m/574ft 10in (overall)
Beam: 30.4m/100ft
Draught: Not known
Flight deck: 113.52 x 28m/372ft 8in x 91ft 11in
Aircraft: A mix of up to 6 x Sea King helicopters and 12 x Harrier V/STOL
Armament: 4 x 30mm/1.18in (2 double) and 2 x 20mm/0.79in (2 single) guns
Machinery: Two diesels, 2 shafts
Power: 17,456kW/23,400bhp
Speed: 22 knots maximum
Fuel: 4,600 tonnes/4,527 tons (heavy oil); 1,590 tonnes/1,565 tons (diesel oil)
Range: 37,040km/20,000nm at 19 knots
Armour: 1.5m/4ft 11in reinforced concrete over flight deck
Complement: Not known

Invincible class

The aborted CVA-01 was planned to operate in concert with a Command Cruiser, which would have assumed command and control functions for a task group. This ship would also have housed a wing of helicopters and been responsible for the group's anti-submarine warfare (ASW) defence, numbers being more efficiently deployed and maintained by a single vessel.

The standard Sea King AS helicopter requires considerable headroom and design studies indicated that a carrier-style through-deck was the preferred configuration. Size was increased due to the need to incorporate the Sea Dart that would otherwise have been deployed by the similarly cancelled Type 82 escort.

Sea Dart, however, could not deal with the threat posed by Cold War-era Soviet fast bombers armed with stand-off air-to-surface missiles (ASM) whose optional nuclear warheads could lay waste a whole task group. Like the Zeppelin and the Fw200 before them, these needed to be countered by fast interceptors. The Admiralty was thus greatly interested in Hawker's P.1127 project, a V/STOL fighter able to operate from small decks.

The aircraft was demonstrated successfully aboard a carrier early in 1963 but, due greatly to the political decision to abandon "aircraft carriers", it was not acquired until 1975. Now in production as the Harrier, it had already been bought for the US Marine Corps and the Spanish Navy.

By the late 1960s, plans were already complete for a Helicopter/Command Cruiser of about 18,000 tonnes/ 17,716 tons, with hangar space for nine Sea Kings and three

TOP: The *Invincible* satisfactorily operated RAF ground-attack Harriers (airborne, right) in the Falklands and, at the time of writing, the Royal Navy is due to phase out its Sea Harriers (on deck). ABOVE: Removal of the Sea Dart and extending the parallel flight deck has considerably increased the viability of the Invincibles. Note the new-design mainmast and Goalkeeper CIWS right forward.

more on the through flight deck. Obviously, in confidence that the V/STOL argument would be won, the design was stretched to just below the psychologically important 20,000-tonne/ 19,684-ton mark in order to squeeze in a further five marinized Sea Harriers.

RIGHT: **Carriers never operate unsupported. It therefore made more practical sense to maximize the aircraft capacity of what is quite a small carrier and put Sea Dart systems (as that being tested here) aboard a dedicated escort.**

In April 1973, the resulting HMS *Invincible* was ordered "for but not with". For political purposes, the name was not a traditional carrier name, and the ship was termed a "through-deck cruiser". When common sense re-emerged her two sisters took the honoured names of *Illustrious* (II) and *Ark Royal* (IV).

Although the limited hybrid design has resulted in a hangar with a narrowed amidships section, the ships have proved flexible. Space has been saved by using scissors-type elevators, capable of being accessed from any side. The unobstructed flight deck permits fuel-saving rolling take-offs for the Harriers (RAF versions can also be deployed) and economy has been further enhanced by installing a "ski-jump" at the forward end.

Gas turbine propulsion has conferred great sprint potential and has reduced the size of machinery spaces, but has increased the silhouette and imposed the need for space-consuming removal paths for the regular replacement of gas turbines.

The V/STOL carrier cannot pretend to replace the conventional (CTOL) carrier in terms of potential but, having a scale not dictated by the likes of catapults and arresters, can be afforded by minor navies.

ABOVE: **Note how V/STOL and helicopter operation have no requirement for an angled deck, the flight path being effectively parallel with the ship's but offset to port. The original forward Vulcan/Phalanx CIWS was poorly sited with bad coverage to the port side.** BELOW: **Still lacking some equipment, the new *Ark Royal* (IV) arrives at her Portsmouth home port for the first time. Note that she is still in builder's ownership and wearing a Red Ensign prior to commissioning.**

Invincible class

Class: *Invincible*, Vickers-Armstrong, Barrow-in-Furness, commissioned July 11, 1980; *Illustrious* (II), Swan Hunter, Wallsend, commissioned June 20, 1982; *Ark Royal* (IV), Swan Hunter, Wallsend, commissioned November 1, 1985

Displacement: 17,150 tonnes/16,850 tons (standard); 20,970 tonnes/20,600 tons (full load)

Length: 192.5m/632ft (bp); 206.2m/677ft (overall)

Beam: 27.4m/90ft

Draught: 8.8m/28ft 10in maximum

Flight deck: 183 x 35m/600 x 114ft 9in

Aircraft: 8 x Sea Harriers, 9 x ASW and 3 x AEW Sea King helicopters

Armament: 1 x Sea Dart SAM system and 2 x Goalkeeper CIWS

Machinery: 4 Olympus gas turbines, 2 shafts

Power: 83,500kW/112,000hp

Speed: 28 knots

Fuel: Not known

Range: 11,110km/6,000nm at 18 knots

Armour: None

Complement: 1,000 men plus 320 aircrew

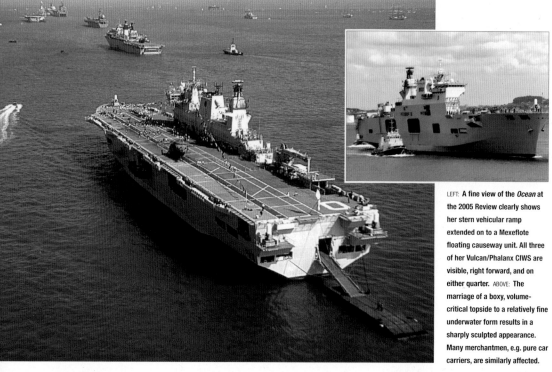

LEFT: A fine view of the *Ocean* at the 2005 Review clearly shows her stern vehicular ramp extended on to a Mexeflote floating causeway unit. All three of her Vulcan/Phalanx CIWS are visible, right forward, and on either quarter. ABOVE: The marriage of a boxy, volume-critical topside to a relatively fine underwater form results in a sharply sculpted appearance. Many merchantmen, e.g. pure car carriers, are similarly affected.

Ocean

Although not true aircraft carriers in the sense that their function is not primarily that of operating aircraft, modern large amphibious-warfare ships have, with the development of helicopters and V/STOL, become potent aviation-capable ships in their own right. In the helicopter carrier HMS *Ocean* (L12), supporting the assault ships *Albion* (L14) and *Bulwark* (L15), the Royal Navy has a capable group, able to transport and land up to three military battalions and their equipment.

The *Ocean* has a through flight deck and starboard-side island but, being intended to operate helicopters only, she has no angled deck, arrester gear, catapult or ski-jump. Six helicopter spots are provided but, although her elevators are dimensioned to accept V/STOL aircraft, there are currently no plans to deploy them.

A military battalion, with light vehicles and equipment, can be accommodated and landed by the ship's four LCVPs (Landing Craft, Vehicle, Personnel) carried under davits in deep pockets in the hull. Normally also carrying Sea King helicopters, the flight deck can support Chinooks. In the future, these will be joined or superseded by Merlins or even a marinized version of the army's Apache ground attack helicopter.

Diesel-propelled, the *Ocean* is good for only 20 knots and, although fitted with comprehensive electronics to fit her as a headquarters ship, has a very light defensive armament, making her very escort-dependent.

The two *Albions* can also each accommodate a battalion at a pinch. However, they have extensive superstructure forward and a flight pad aft with only two helicopter spots. They complement the *Ocean* in having a large, floodable well, closed by a stern gate and are able to accommodate four LCU

(Landing Craft, Utility) or two American-pattern LCAC (Landing Craft, Air Cushion). They also carry four LCVPs under davits. Like the *Ocean*, they are diesel-propelled and equipped only with light defensive armament.

Ocean

Built: Kvaerner, Govan
Commissioned: September 30, 1998
Displacement: 22,150 tonnes/21,750 tons (full load)
Length: 198.8m/651ft 10in (bp); 6.6m/21ft 8in (overall)
Aircraft: 12 x Sea King or 4 x Merlin plus 6 x Lynx/Apache helicopters
Flight deck: 170 x 31.7m/229ft 6in x 103ft 11in
Armament: 3 x Vulcan/Phalanx CIWS
Machinery: Two 12-cylinder diesel engines, 2 shafts
Power: 13,500kW/18,100bhp
Speed: 20 knots
Fuel: Not known
Range: 14,820km/8,000nm at 15 knots
Armour: Not known
Complement: 490 men, including aircrew

LEFT AND BELOW: **Current interventional policy demands that seaborne expeditionary forces have organic air power. The sheer cost of naval air, however, frightens successive governments into endless prevarication. Computer-generated images of what is a continuously evolving design are a poor substitute for the actual cutting of steel but, in lieu of action, may be expected for a while yet.**

Queen Elizabeth class

Long-planned, these carriers will be the largest warships ever to be operated by the Royal Navy. Because of the much-diminished condition of the British shipbuilding industry, and the politics inseparable from the allocation of naval orders, sections will be constructed at Govan, Portsmouth and Wallsend, and transported to Rosyth for final assembly.

Their strike component will comprise Lockheed Merlin F-35 Joint Strike Fighters (JSF) in their STOVL (Short Take-off, Vertical Land) variant. Although constructed with the requisite overhang for angled deck operations, the flight deck will not be so marked. No catapults, associated steam plant or arrester gear is fitted, although space for their possible later addition has been allocated.

For STOVL operations, the forward ski-jump is approached either axially from the after marshalling area or at an angle from the starboard side. This point, between the two islands (a new and unique arrangement) is served by one of the two deck-edge elevators. These are large enough to accept the non-folding wings of the F-35, the Merlin ASW helicopter and the as-yet unspecified airborne early warning (AEW) aircraft.

Propulsion is electric, both quiet and flexible. Generators, driven by gas turbines and/or diesel engines may be located where convenient, providing power for the motors that drive the shafts. Podded propulsion, much used in cruise ships, was considered but apparently rejected. The large electrical capacity may influence a later choice of catapult.

As currently planned, the forward island will be dedicated to navigation, the after one to flying control. Armament has not yet been finalized and all statistics are subject to change. Those for complement and speed appear, for instance, to be unrealistically low.

If the timetable suffers any further politically inspired delays, the existing Invincibles will be hopelessly inadequate by the time of their replacement.

Queen Elizabeth class

Class: *Queen Elizabeth*, laid down 2006, launched 2009, commissioned 2012; *Prince of Wales*, laid down 2009, launched 2012, commissioned 2015
Displacement: 59,000 tonnes/58,000 tons (full load)
Length: 284m/931ft 2in (overall)
Beam: Not known
Draught: Not known
Aircraft: About 35
Flight deck: Maximum width 75m/245ft 10in
Armament: Not known
Machinery: Gas turbines and/or diesel engines; electric drive
Power: Not known
Speed: 25+ knots
Fuel: Not known
Range: Not known
Armour: Not known
Complement: About 600 men plus aircrew

LEFT: Converted to a seaplane carrier, the *Wakamiya* was little changed externally. Note the more complex rigging of the derricks and the after section of the forward flying-off platform.
ABOVE: Commencing in 1932, the *Kamoi* underwent a bewildering number of modifications to best equip her for her dual role of seaplane carrier and fleet tanker. The experience contributed to the design of purpose-built ships.

Early seaplane carriers

During World War I, the vast island groups of the western Pacific were German territory and hostile to Japan which, following the peace, assumed a mandate. Given the scale of the area, it is not surprising that the Japanese Navy showed a lively interest in naval reconnaissance from its very inception. Floatplanes appeared on all major warships, but humbler ships were also converted to specialist seaplane carriers. Deploying floatplanes or flying boats, these could quickly establish a forward reconnaissance base from any suitable anchorage.

The first such ship was the *Wakamiya*, a 4,400 gross registered tons British-built cargo ship modified roughly

in 1914 by the addition of steel-and-canvas hangars for four seaplanes. These were handled by the ship's cargo gear. In the Japanese Navy's first-ever seaborne air strike, the *Wakamiya*'s aircraft attacked the German bases at Tsingtao in 1914. After the war she was fitted with a flying-off platform over the forecastle, from which she acquired Sopwith Pup fighters were flown. The ship was discarded in 1931.

Encouraged by the success of the *Wakamiya*, the Japanese modified two fleet tankers, *Notoro* and *Tsurumi*, in 1924. Covered accommodation was added for up to ten aircraft apiece before and abaft the central bridge structure, and conspicuous cranes were included

for their handling. Retaining their full tanker capacity, the pair acted simultaneously as aircraft transports, but were capable of independent operation such as during the campaign against China. Both reverted to tankers during World War II, in the course of which the *Tsurumi* was lost.

Before the Japanese began to design and build specialist seaplane carriers in the 1930s a third and larger tanker, the *Kamoi*, underwent similar, but more elaborate conversion for the deployment of up to a dozen aircraft. She, too, reverted to tanker duties from 1943 and became a war loss. Targeted specifically by American submarines, tankers had become more valuable than seaplane carriers.

LEFT AND BELOW: **Superimposition of seaplane facilities on the fleet oiler *Notoro* resulted in a complex and unlovely structure, as the ship was required to retain her designed functions. A light spar deck was constructed over the topside pipework for the seaplanes. A second light deck at bridge level served both as a handling area and a support for the canvas sides to the "hangars".**

Kamoi, as modified

Built: New York Shipbuilding, Camden, NJ; commissioned as carrier in 1933
Displacement: 17,300 tonnes/17,000 tons (standard); 19,960 tonnes/19,600 tons (full load)
Length: 151.3m/496ft (at waterline)
Beam: 20.4m/67ft
Draught: 8.4m/27ft 8in (full load)
Aircraft: 12 floatplanes
Flight deck: None
Armament: 2 x 140mm/5.5in, and 2 x 76mm/3in guns
Machinery: Turbo-electric, 2 boilers, 2 shafts
Power: 6,700kW/9,000shp
Speed: 15 knots
Fuel: 2,540 tonnes/2,500 tons (coal)
Range: Not known
Armour: None
Complement: Not known

Hosho

Assertions that the *Hosho*, Japan's first through-deck carrier, began life as a tanker seem unlikely to be correct. Her waterline length-to-beam ratio was a fine 9.15:1 and she was powered for a most unmercantile 25 knots. In addition, her upper deck (also the hangar and strength deck) dipped by a full half-deck towards the after end, a typical Japanese warship design feature. Whatever her origins, she was completed in a very creditable three years, the process facilitated somewhat by the very experienced British mission then present to transfer hard-won technological detail under the auspices of the 1902 Anglo-Japanese Alliance.

For smoke discharge, the *Hosho* followed the American *Langley*-style fold-down funnels rather than the *Argus'*

ducted arrangement. A diminutive island bridge, the first such, was located on the starboard deck edge but, being just forward of the funnels, created severe smoke eddying and was soon removed.

Hosho had a half-length hangar with an elevator at either end. Forward and aft, the flight deck was supported on an open structure, initially with a pronounced run-down at either end but later flattened forward and extended aft, overlapping the stern. Only over its after third was the hull plating continued upward to flight deck level and, over this length, the flight deck was of increased width.

Following the removal of the island, navigation and flight deck operations were conducted from sided open platforms, an unsatisfactory arrangement. A folding mast had also to be added.

ABOVE: **Probably a 1922 trials picture of *Hosho* which had its small island structure removed in the following year. Note that the hangar is only part length and of "open" construction, erected atop the hull proper.**

Although small, the *Hosho* (a planned sister was cancelled) taught the Japanese much. Classed as "experimental" she had an uneventful, if busy, career, even surviving the general massacre of the Japanese fleet during World War II. Following service in repatriating military personnel, she was scrapped in 1947.

ABOVE: **The extreme narrowness of the forward flight deck caused the removal of the island, while the effective area was increased by levelling the pronounced slopes at either end.** LEFT: **Interesting detail here includes the funnels and WT mast lowered for flying, and the series of ramps and bridges associated with the longitudinal arrester system.**

Hosho	

Built: Asano Shipbuilding, Tsurumi
Commissioned: December 27, 1922
Displacement: 7,585 tonnes/7,450 tons (standard); 9,930 tonnes/9,750 tons (full load)
Length: 155.5m/509ft 10in (bp); 168m/550ft 10in (overall)
Beam: 18m/59ft
Draught: 6.2m/20ft 3in (full load)
Aircraft: About 25
Flight deck: 158.3 x 22.7m/519 x 74ft 6in
Armament: 4 x 140mm/5.5in, and 2 x 76mm/3in guns
Machinery: Geared steam turbines, 8 boilers, 2 shafts
Power: 22,400kW/30,000shp
Speed: 25 knots
Fuel: 2,750 tonnes/2,700 tons (oil); 960 tonnes/940 tons (coal)
Range: 14,820km/8,000nm at 15 knots
Armour: Not known
Complement: 550 men

Akagi

As with other signatories to the Washington Treaty of 1921–22, Japan had to abandon her ambitious capital shipbuilding programme. Two incomplete hulls could, however, be converted to aircraft carriers. Compared to the 137,160 tonnes/135,000 tons carrier tonnage allowed to Great Britain and the United States, Japan was permitted only 82,296 tonnes/81,000 tons. The two rebuilds might displace up to 33,528 tonnes/33,000 tons but subsequent ships were limited to 27,432 tonnes/27,000 tons apiece.

At the time of the agreement there were under construction two *Kaga*-class battleships and four *Amagi*-class battle-cruisers. Longer and faster, two battle-cruisers, *Amagi* and *Akagi*, were selected for conversion. The former, however, was damaged on the slip by earthquake, and a battleship hull, that of the *Kaga*, had to be substituted as the only one sufficiently advanced to undergo what could be called "conversion".

TOP: **The *Akagi* as she was post-1938. Note that the extended flight deck slopes continuously in either direction from the centre and that the new island is located on the port side.** ABOVE: **As completed, the *Akagi* retained some elegance of line. The starboard-side funnel was divided curiously into two distinct sections.**

Reconstruction was a major task. The required air wing of 60 aircraft demanded a double hangar arrangement, imposing an unacceptable topweight on a slender hull. In order to reduce weight and to lower the centre of gravity, the main armoured deck was thinned from 96mm/3.8in to 80mm/3.15in and lowered by one level. As it linked with the upper edge of the side belt this, too, had to be lowered, simultaneously being reduced from 250mm/9.8in to 152mm/6in in thickness. This,

LEFT: **Although indistinct, this profile demonstrates the *Akagi*'s slightly hogged appearance, due to the sloping flight deck, also the considerable bulge and the substructure transferring the weight of the island to the hull.**

in turn, meant refashioning the bulge, earlier an anti-torpedo feature but now also enhancing stability.

Taking the design of the British *Courageous* a stage further, aircraft from either hangar could take off directly over the bows, the penalty for which was the flight deck being terminated over 61m/200ft from the forward end. Aft, the flight deck was supported on lofty pillars, beneath which a gantry crane could transfer floatplanes over the quarterdeck and into the lower hangar.

Article X of the treaty permitted carriers to be armed with up to ten guns not exceeding 203mm/8in in calibre. Armed to the limit, the *Akagi* had two twin cruiser-style turrets firing forward from upper hangar deck level and six armoured casemates well aft, but sited too low to be of any practical use. There was no restriction on the number of guns of less than 127mm/5in calibre, and 12 of 120mm/4.7in were installed.

There was no island superstructure, the many boilers exhausting through a curious, starboard-side casing, partly vertical, partly curved downward and outboard. A distinctive clipper stem set off a profile that was not inelegant. This did not persist, however, for operational shortcomings and the requirements of more and larger aircraft brought about further remodelling during 1936–38. This added a square, port-side island structure while the flight deck, which sloped downward in both directions from amidships, was continued right forward, supported on pillars and gaining two catapults. The forward 203mm/8in gun mountings were landed as the hangars were extended some distance forward. The complex funnel casing was simplified but enlarged. All improvements added further topweight and the bulges needed to be widened, costing about a half-knot in speed.

A Pearl Harbor veteran, the *Akagi* was sunk at Midway.

TOP: **This "as built" profile shows both the oddly configured funnel and the forecastle deck over which fighters could take off directly from the lower hangar. With the later forward extension of the flight deck, two forward-firing twin 203mm/8in turrets had to be sacrificed.** ABOVE: **An uncommon view of** *Akagi*'s **island from ahead. A most unusual feature is the wood-planked flight deck, with individual timbers correctly notched into the margin plank. The caulking, however, is none too tidy!**

ABOVE: **The** *Akagi* **is here seen lying off the Japanese Naval Academy at Yetajima, near Kure.**

Akagi	

Built: Kure Naval Dockyard
Commissioned: March 25, 1927
Displacement (in 1938): 37,150 tonnes/ 36,500 tons (standard); 43,500 tonnes/ 42,750 tons (full load)
Length: 235m/770ft 6in (bp); 261.2m/856ft 5in (overall)
Beam: 31.4m/102ft 10in
Draught: 8.7m/28ft 6in full load
Aircraft: 72
Flight deck: 190.3 x 30.5m/624 x 100ft
Armament: 6 x 203mm/8in, and 12 x 119mm/4.7in guns
Machinery: Geared steam turbines, 19 boilers, 4 shafts
Power: 98,500kW/132,000shp
Speed: 31.5 knots
Fuel: 5,850 tonnes/5,750 tons
Range: 15,190km/8,200nm at 16 knots
Armour: 152mm/6in (vertical belt); 80mm/3.15in (armoured deck)
Complement: 1,570 men

Kaga

The necessity to select the *Kaga* as a running mate to the *Akagi* caused considerable operational problems due to the speed difference, as designed, of 6 knots (26.5 against 32.5). Being a battleship, the *Kaga* had a waterline length-to-beam ratio of a relatively bluff 7.77:1 compared with the battle-cruiser *Akagi*'s 8.59:1. The latter was also nearly 20m/65ft 8in longer. Within the restrictions of available space, any uprating of *Kaga*'s machinery could have only small effect on speed. A first improvement, however, was the conversion to full oil-firing from an earlier mix of eight oil-fired boilers, and four boilers that burned coal under oil spray.

Externally, the conversion closely followed that of the *Akagi*. The truncated flight deck was repeated, with two lower flying-off levels forward. The upper of these, i.e. that serving the upper hangar, was very constricted, flanked as it was by twin 203mm/8in gun turrets and also accommodating the navigation position, there being no island structure.

Possibly because of difficulties experienced with the *Akagi*, or possibly to evaluate alternative arrangements, the *Kaga* was fitted with long ducts, running outside the hull, just below the level of the flight deck that exhausted either side, just short of the quarterdeck. The flight deck itself was built without the *Akagi*'s "hump" and with two elevators and no catapults.

With her inherently better stability, *Kaga* experienced fewer problems with armour distribution. The main protective deck was thinned from 102mm/4in to 40mm/1.57in but, as it did not require to be lowered, the position and configuration of the side belt and bulges were unaffected. The belt, nonetheless, was reduced in thickness from 280mm/11in to 152mm/6in.

Exhibiting the same in-service limitations as the *Akagi*, the *Kaga* underwent extensive modification during 1934–35. The confined nature of the navigational arrangements had already resulted in the addition of a diminutive pilot house on the starboard edge of the flight deck. This was now superseded by a modest island structure which, unlike the *Akagi*'s, was located on the starboard side.

New and more powerful machinery and boilers (only eight in number) were installed. Being also lighter, they exacerbated the effect of the extra weight of the extensive topside improvements. Larger bulges had to be added, with the major result that the stern section had to be rebuilt and extended by over 10m/32ft 10in to regain an acceptable after run.

With her lengthened stern, the *Kaga*'s new, full-length flight deck was of almost identical length to that of her running mate. In being extended forward it gained a third elevator and two

TOP: **Although *Kaga* was not a sister of *Akagi*, she shared a rakish elegance as completed. Note the 203mm/8in guns forward at upper hangar deck level and aft, located in very low casemates.** ABOVE: **As rebuilt in 1934–35, the *Kaga* gained a starboard-side island while the boilers now exhausted through a prominent funnel on the starboard side only.**

(later three) catapults. The exhaust ducts were replaced by a single, starboard-side, *Akagi*-style funnel casing.

The four 203mm/8in guns displaced by the forward extension of the hangars were relocated in two further casemates aft, as useless as the remainder. Sixteen 127mm/5in guns were located in sponsoned twin-mountings just below flight deck level.

Created together, the *Akagi* and *Kaga* operated together and, together, they were destroyed at Midway, where the loss of four carriers turned the course of the Pacific war.

ABOVE: **If this is truly a pilot's briefing, rather than a publicity picture, the practice compares poorly with those in Western carriers for over half the personnel can neither hear nor see what they are being told.**

Kaga

Built: Kawasaki, Kobe
Commissioned: March 31, 1928
Displacement (in 1935): 38,900 tonnes/ 38,200 tons (standard); 43,270 tonnes/ 42,500 tons (full load)
Length: 225.2m/738ft 3in (bp); 247.7m/812ft 2in (overall)
Beam: 32.5m/106ft 7in
Draught: 9.3m/30ft 6in (full load)
Aircraft: 72
Flight deck: 246.8 x 30.5m/809ft 2in x 100ft
Armament: 10 x 203mm/8in, and 16 x 127mm/ 5in guns
Machinery: Geared steam turbines, 8 boilers, 4 shafts
Power: 94,750kW/127,000shp
Speed: 28 knots
Fuel: 8,350 tonnes/8,200 tons
Range: 18,520km/10,000nm at 16 knots
Armour: 152mm/6in (vertical belt); 40mm/1.57in (armoured deck)
Complement: 1,460 men

Ise and *Hyuga*

Enlarged versions of the American Wyomings, the *Ise* and *Hyuga* also improved on the preceding Japanese Fuso class. They were completed in 1917–18 as 31,700-tonne/31,200-ton battleships carrying twelve 356mm/14in guns in six twin turrets of which one pair was superimposed in the waist. Originally two-funnelled, they lost the forward funnel in a 1934–37 modernization. In the course of this they acquired new machinery, extra horizontal armour and their distinctive "pagoda" bridge structure. Extra top-weight was compensated by enlarged bulges that, while improving resistance to torpedoes, required the stern to be rebuilt and extended by about 7.6m/25ft to comply with hydrodynamic requirements.

The loss of four front-line carriers at Midway shocked the Japanese Navy into emergency measures including the conversion of the *Ise* and *Hyuga* to hybrid battleship/carriers. Therefore,

during 1943–44, their after two turrets were removed and a new deck erected over the after end. This had 11 aircraft "spots", connected by rail to two waist catapults. Beneath the deck was hangar space for 11 more aircraft, to be transferred by elevator.

The arrangement was designed around the Aichi D4Y3 ("Judy") dive-bomber, with an intended launch rate of one aircraft every two minutes. At this stage of the war, however, the aircraft could not be supplied in sufficient numbers and, as the catapults obstructed the waist turrets, they were removed. The ships were thus reduced to deploying a few floatplanes, handled by crane, the handling deck occupied largely by light anti-aircraft weapons.

Having never been operated in their intended role, both ships narrowly escaped destruction as part of the

TOP: **Following their 1934–37 rebuildings the two Hyugas emerged with a single funnel and an imposing "pagoda" foremast structure. Note the quarterdeck catapult and handling crane for three floatplanes.** ABOVE: **Six centreline turrets were very ambitious, their weight resulting in massive stresses on a hull with relatively fine ends.**

decoy force at the battle of Leyte Gulf, only to be sunk in shallow water at Kure by American carrier aircraft during the final weeks of the war.

Ise and Hyuga

Class: *Ise*, Kawasaki, Kobe, commissioned December 15, 1917; *Hyuga*, Mitsubishi, Nagasaki, commissioned April 30, 1918
Displacement (in 1944): 36,000 tonnes/ 35,350 tons (standard); 39,400 tonnes/ 38,700 tons (full load)
Length: 195.8m/642ft (bp); 219.6m/720ft (overall)
Beam: 33.8m/110ft 10in
Draught: 9.3m/30ft 6in (full load)
Aircraft: 22
Flight deck: None
Armament: 8 x 356mm/14in, and 16 x 127mm/5in guns
Machinery: Geared steam turbines, 8 boilers, 4 shafts
Power: 60,500kW/81,000shp
Speed: 25.5 knots
Fuel: 4,330 tonnes/4,250 tons
Range: 17,590km/9,500nm at 16 knots
Armour: 127–305mm/5–12in (vertical belt); 119mm/4.7in (armoured deck)
Complement: 1,460 men

ABOVE: **After 1943–44, the ships carried an enormous box hangar, whose 22 aircraft were transferred for launch by two elevated waist catapults. The two central turrets were retained, but their firing arcs were greatly restricted by the catapults.**

Ryujo

Buried deeply in the Washington Treaty was a paragraph defining an aircraft carrier as having, *inter alia*, a standard displacement in excess of 10,160 tonnes/10,000 tons. Concerned that only 17,272 tonnes/17,000 tons of carrier tonnage were left to them, the Japanese decided to evaluate a sub-10,160-tonne/10,000-ton ship, which would not be reckonable. Laid down in 1929, the *Ryujo* would have worked satisfactorily with a modest air group but the 48 aircraft demanded required a double-hangared design that was over-ambitious on the displacement.

With weight restriction so tight, there was no margin for armour and the cruiser-style hull was built with low freeboard. To save weight, the upper deck sheerline undulated to follow the stress distribution in the lightly constructed hull. There was no island structure, the navigation bridge being located below the forward transverse edge of the flight deck, which terminated some 20m/65ft 7in short of the bows. Smoke was exhausted through two

downward-curved casings on the starboard side while sponsoned below the deck edges were six twin 127mm/5in gun mountings.

Weak in structure, tender in motion, the *Ryujo* returned to dockyard hands within a year of her completion. During 1934–36 she was bulged to increase her beam. Her hull was stiffened, ballast added and two of the 127mm/5in mountings suppressed to reduce weight at that height.

These improvements inevitably increased her standard displacement to a reckonable figure, but they also increased her immersion. Her freeboard forward was now inadequate and a further modification was required to raise the forecastle by one deck level.

Ever a problem, the *Ryujo* was restricted to lesser wartime operations. Still useful, she had a short career, being overwhelmed by American carrier aircraft at the Battle of the Eastern Solomons in August 1942.

ABOVE: **The conflicting requirements of maximum aircraft and minimum displacement resulted in the unsatisfactory** *Ryujo.* **Her very low forward freeboard was offset by considerable flare to prevent the bow plunging.** LEFT: **The port-bow view, looking aft, emphasizes the sheer complexity of Japanese ship design. Despite its massive appearance, the double-hangar top structure was of light scantlings and superimposed on a very low hull. Note the discontinuity in the latter's sheerline.**

Ryujo

Built: Yokohama Dockyard Company
Commissioned: May 9, 1933
Displacement (in 1936): 11,000 tonnes/ 10,800 tons (standard); 13,850 tonnes/ 13,600 tons (full load)
Length: 167.9m/550ft 4in (bp); 180.1m/590ft 6in (overall)
Beam: 20.8m/68ft 3in
Draught: 6.8m/22ft 6in
Aircraft: 48
Flight deck: 156.8 x 23.2m/514 x 76ft
Armament: 8 x 127mm/5in guns
Machinery: Geared steam turbines, 6 boilers, 2 shafts
Power: 48,500kW/65,000shp
Speed: 29 knots
Fuel: 2,550 tonnes/2,500 tons
Range: 18,520km/10,000nm at 14 knots
Armour: None
Complement: 660 men

Soryu and *Hiryu*

The Japanese Navy required further large carriers, but was limited by treaty to only 17,272 tonnes/17,000 tons more carrier-tons. Again, however, there was a possible means of circumvention in the treaty definition of an aircraft carrier which, while displacing at least 10,160 tonnes/10,000 tons, had to be "designed for the specific and exclusive purpose of carrying aircraft". Like the Americans and British, the Japanese were tempted into producing studies for hybrid cruiser/carriers with a limited air wing but a powerful main armament. All, however, proved to be unsatisfactory compromises.

Laid down in 1934, the *Soryu* was of conventional design therefore, and calculated to consume all the remaining tonnage allowance. Her cruiser-style hull was high-powered and capable of exceptionally high speed, but she was well designed in that the lower of her double hangars was recessed into the hull, keeping her overall profile low and avoiding the chronic problems being experienced by the still-new *Ryujo*. The main penalty for the high speed and large air wing was weak protection. A starboard-side island was fitted from the outset, with smoke exhausting through the preferred horizontal funnels on the same side.

During 1934, the Japanese had announced their proposed "Second Replenishment Programme" for their fleet, a programme which included a pair of *Soryu*-sized carriers. They hoped that the second of these could be built with Great Britain and the United States extending the Japanese allocation. However, the Japanese were to be disappointed at the Second London Naval Conference, from which their delegates walked out in January 1936. In the following July, and now in breach of treaty agreement, the second ship, *Hiryu*, was laid down. Feeling themselves no longer bound by tonnage restrictions, her designers increased her beam by one metre. In addition to improving her stability, this permitted a thickening of the belt armour and greater fuel capacity. Her island was on the port side.

Both ships were lost at Midway, early victims of dive-bombing.

Soryu and *Hiryu*

Class: *Soryu*, Kure Naval Dockyard, commissioned January 29, 1937; *Hiryu*, Yokosuka Naval Dockyard, commissioned July 5, 1939
Displacement: 17,600 tonnes/17,300 tons (full load); 22,350 tonnes/21,950 tons (standard)
Length: 209.9m/688ft 2in (bp); 230m/745ft 6in (overall)
Beam: 22.3m/73ft 3in
Draught: 7.9m/25ft 9in (full load)
Aircraft: 73
Flight deck: 217 x 27m/711ft 6in x 88ft 6in
Armament: 12 x 127mm/5in guns
Machinery: Geared steam turbines, 8 boilers, 4 shafts
Power: 113,400kW/152,000shp
Speed: 34.5 knots
Fuel: 4,430 tonnes/4,350 tons
Range: 19,080km/10,300nm at 18 knots
Armour (over machinery and magazine spaces only): 89–150mm/3.5–5.9in (vertical belt); 25–55mm/0.9–2.1in (protective deck)
Complement: 1,250 men

ABOVE: **Hiryu's bridge structure was located on the port side and almost exactly amidships. Soryu's starboard-side island was set further forward because of the two funnels.**

Zuiho class

A further means by which the Japanese could circumvent their treaty-agreed limits was through the construction of auxiliaries designed for rapid conversion to aircraft carriers in an emergency. Several such vessels were provided for by the 1934 "Second Replenishment Programme", with two of them being the submarine depot ships *Tsurugisaki* and *Takasaki*. The usual bulk associated with such ships was increased by a topside hangar, capable of accommodating three floatplanes, for which two catapults were provided.

Only the *Tsurugisaki* was ever completed in this configuration for, during 1941, the pair were transformed into the light carriers *Shoho* and *Zuiho*. In both size and aircraft capacity they matched the US Navy's *Independence*-class CVLs, though lacking their speed. Initially equipped with eight diesel engines, coupled four to a shaft, (the same arrangement, incidentally, as in the German so-called "pocket battleships") they acquired steam turbines during their conversion. There was no island superstructure, and the boilers exhausted through a horizontal, starboard-side funnel. Exceptionally slender ships, they nonetheless had the stability required for a single-hangar configuration and for four twin 127mm/5in gun mountings located in sponsons just below the deck edge. It was a feature of all Japanese carriers with horizontal funnels that only those gun mountings immediately abaft the casing were given enclosures to protect the crews.

The *Shoho* had the melancholy record of being the first Japanese carrier to be lost, being a casualty at the Coral Sea action in May 1942. *Zuiho* went on to give good service, having her flight deck extended almost to the bows. She, too, did not survive the war, being destroyed in the Leyte Gulf battles of October 1944.

TOP AND ABOVE: **Two views of the ships show them as originally converted, with the flight deck terminating well short of the bows. *Shoho* was sunk in this condition, only *Zuiho* surviving to undergo further modification.**

ABOVE: **Under overwhelming air attack in October 1944 the *Zuiho*, devoid of aircraft, manoeuvres at high speed. The thick, dark smoke is issuing from her downswept funnel while the light smoke from her forward end is from her defensive armament.**

Zuiho class

Class: *Zuiho*, Yokosuka Naval Dockyard, commissioned December 27, 1940; *Shoho*, Yokosuka Naval Dockyard, commissioned January 26, 1942
Displacement: 11,450 tonnes/11,250 tons (standard); 14,350 tonnes/14,100 tons (full load)
Length: 185m/606ft 7in (bp); 205.6m/674ft 2in (overall)
Beam: 18.2m/59ft 8in
Draught: 6.6m/21ft 6in (full load)
Aircraft: 30
Flight deck: 180 x 23m/590ft 2in x 75ft 5in
Armament: 8 x 127mm/5in guns
Machinery: Geared steam turbines, 4 boilers, 2 shafts
Power: 38,800kW/52,000shp
Speed: 28 knots
Fuel: 2,550 tonnes/2,500 tons
Range: 14,450km/7,800nm at 18 knots
Armour: None
Complement: 800 men

Ryuho

As with the two *Zuihos*, the *Ryuho* was converted from a submarine depot ship. In her case, it was the *Taigei*, a slightly larger predecessor of the two Tsurugisakis. Like them, she was exceptionally slender in her proportions (12.3:1 at the waterline) but proved to be structurally weak. In 1936, just two years after her completion, she was back in dockyard hands for stiffening and the addition of bulges to improve her stability. She was initially powered for only a 20-knot speed, which suggests that, unlike her follow-ons she really was intended to service submarines. She also carried three floatplanes, but in a more complex arrangement accessed by elevator.

Despite her less-than-satisfactory history the *Taigei* was taken in hand during 1941, along with the later pair, for conversion to a carrier, in this case the *Ryuho*. Not surprisingly, the end result looked very similar although, completed

later, in November 1942, she was equipped with larger elevators.

Still suspect, the *Ryuho* spent most of her career in the still-valuable role of training carrier aircrews who, despite their specialist calling, were used in a variety of roles, many shore-based. Such profligacy eventually proved disastrous.

During June 1944, the major part of the remaining Japanese fleet was mobilized to counter the American invasion of Saipan. Among the carriers was the *Ryuho*, on her first combat assignment. She emerged virtually unscathed, but her aircrews, along with those of sister carriers, had been slaughtered in what the Americans came to call the "Marianas Turkey Shoot". Reverting to her previous unexciting existence the ship managed to escape retribution, despite being caught at Kure by the massive American carrier-based air strikes of July 1945. She was scrapped in 1946.

TOP: **Converted from a submarine depot ship, the** *Ryuho* **gave the impression of immense length. The reconstruction was not a success, the ship proving structurally weak and, for the greater part of her career, demoted to the training of aircrew.**
ABOVE: **High freeboard contributes to an easy motion.**

Ryuho

Built: Yokosuka Naval Dockyard
Commissioned: March 31, 1934
Displacement: 13,600 tonnes/13,350 tons (standard); 16,450 tonnes/16,150 tons (full load)
Length: 197.4m/647ft 4in (bp); 215.8m/707ft 6in (overall)
Beam: 19.6m/64ft 3in
Draught: 6.6m/21ft 9in (full load)
Aircraft: 30
Flight deck: 185.1 x 23m/607 x 75ft 6in
Armament: 8 x 127mm/5in guns
Machinery: Geared steam turbines, 4 boilers, 2 shafts
Power: 38,800kW/52,000shp
Speed: 26.5 knots
Fuel: 2,950 tonnes/2,900 tons
Range: 14,820km/8,000nm at 18 knots
Armour: None
Complement: 875 men

Hiyo and *Junyo*

O f a size with the Italian *Aquila*, the *Hiyo* and *Junyo* were among the largest of carrier conversions, but where the *Aquila* had served as a liner but never as a carrier, the reverse was true of the Japanese pair. They were laid down in 1939 as the *Idzumo Maru* (*Hiyo*) and *Kashiwara Maru* (*Junyo*) for the Japan–United States service of Nippon Yusen Kaisha (NYK). Listed at the time as 28,000 gross registered tons (grt) motor liners, they were taken over before launch by the Japanese Navy. Doubts have been expressed that the ships were ever intended to be completed as liners, but their relatively poor subdivision and the necessity to change from diesel propulsion to steam suggests otherwise. Like many ships designed to mercantile standards, however, they probably incorporated design features intended to facilitate conversion.

Completed in good time to replace some of the carrier tonnage lost at Midway, the pair was unusual in incorporating islands of considerable size, built around uptakes that terminated in a funnel that was canted outboard. The whole structure was sponsoned beyond the edge of the flight deck, facilitating the path of boiler exhaust but creating a

mass that needed to be offset by asymmetric bulging. Their double hangar arrangement was possible only by restricting the headroom of each to 3.2m/10ft 6in. This proved acceptable only because the Japanese introduced few innovations in carrier aircraft during the war.

Operated as front-line units, they deployed air groups of 50-plus comprising the full range of dive-bombers, torpedo-bombers and fighters. Both were present at the disastrous Philippine Sea action of June 1944, during which the *Hiyo* was lost to American torpedo aircraft. Her sister survived being torpedoed by an American submarine in December of the following year.

BELOW: **This view gives a good idea of the substructure necessary to transfer the overhung weight of the island to the hull. A problem with the pair was underpowering, apparently caused by a mismatch between mercantile steam turbines and naval-pattern, destroyer-type boilers.**

TOP: **The massive hull of the *Junyo* betrays her passenger liner origins. As converted, this pair were the first Japanese carriers to incorporate funnel and island, although not without some idiosyncracy. Note the radar antennas, atop the bridge and on the light signal mast.** ABOVE: *Junyo* **was one of the few Japanese carriers to survive the war relatively intact. Despite the considerable weight of the funnel uptakes and island structure, it can be seen to be situated almost entirely outboard of the flight deck edge.**

Hiyo and Junyo

Class: *Hiyo*, Kawasaki, Kobe, commissioned July 31, 1942; *Junyo*, Mitsubishi, Nagasaki, commissioned May 5, 1942
Displacement: 24,600 tonnes/24,150 tons (standard); 28,300 tonnes/27,800 tons (full load)
Length: 206.1m/675ft 9in (bp); 219.5m/719ft 8in (overall)
Beam: 26.7m/87ft 7in
Draught: 8.1m/26ft 8in (full load)
Aircraft: 53
Flight deck: 210.5 x 27.3m/690 x 89ft 6in
Armament: 12 x 127mm/5in guns
Machinery: Geared steam turbines, 6 boilers, 2 shafts
Power: 41,800kW/56,000shp
Speed: 24 knots
Fuel: 2,950 tonnes/2,900 tons
Range: Not known
Armour: None
Complement: 1,200 men

Shokaku class

Having failed to gain agreement for equality of tonnage with the fleets of Great Britain and the United States, the Japanese delegation walked out of the Second London Naval Conference in January 1936. It was the end of naval limitation by mutual agreement, initiating new building programmes by the one-time signatories.

As with the US Navy, the early carrier conversions had demonstrated to the Japanese the advantages of larger vessels, and the *Akagi* design was in the process of being updated. During 1937–38, the two Shokakus were laid down to this design. No longer trammelled by limited displacement and indisputably the best of the Japanese carriers, they were so central to naval planning that the date for opening hostilities at Pearl Harbor was determined by their completion.

Slightly shorter than the *Akagi*, they were even finer-lined yet deployed an air group of comparable size. The double hangars that gave the *Akagi* a high profile were more fully incorporated into the Shokakus' main hull structure.

Outline statistics show that the design philosophy was closer to that of the Americans than to that of the British:

It will be noted that the British ship, more heavily protected, needed to be proportionately broader in the beam so that, although given greater propulsive power per ton, she was significantly slower and with a much smaller air group. The *Shokaku* compared more closely with an Essex, although the price of the latter's larger air group and superior protection was lower installed power.

TOP: The *Zuikaku*, reputedly on her commissioning day in September 1941. A feature of Japanese carriers, visible here rigged right aft, was a collapsible mast and derrick for transferring aircraft. ABOVE: Not the sharpest of pictures, this photograph shows a ready A6M Type 0 "Zeke" ahead of several D3A Type 99 "Val" dive-bombers.

Comparison of major carrier classes

	Length (wl)	Beam (wl)	L/B	Displacement	Power	SHP/ton	Speed	Aircraft
Shokaku	250m	26m	9.6	25,700 tons	160,000shp	6.2	34+ knots	84
Essex (US)	249.9m	28.4m	8.8	27,200 tons	150,000shp	5.5	32.5 knots	91
Implacable (UK)	222.7m	29.2m	7.6	23,450 tons	148,000shp	6.3	32 knots	54

The Shokakus' meagre weight allowance for protection needed to be devoted to covering machinery and magazine spaces, leaving the enclosed hangars and flight deck unprotected. Topwide weight-saving in all Japanese carriers was evident in the pronounced narrowing of the forward flight deck. In contrast, American and British flight decks were more nearly rectangular in plan.

Like the *Akagi*, the Shokakus had three elevators and two catapults, and featured starboard-side, horizontal funnel casings. Both Shokakus had starboard-side islands.

From the Japanese perspective, both ships had fine war records. Both formed part of the carrier force that devastated Pearl Harbor before going on to ravage the Indian Ocean. In May 1942, they were at the Coral Sea action, where the *Shokaku* survived three hits by dive-bombers. They participated in the Battle of the Eastern Solomons (August 1942) and at Santa Cruz (October 1942), during which the *Shokaku* took four more hits. The ship was finally sunk, not by aircraft but by submarine torpedoes, at the disastrous Battle of the Philippine Sea (June 1944). The *Zuikaku* was also severely damaged, and now the last survivor of the six Pearl Harbor raiders, she lasted a further four months, being expended as part of Ozawa's decoy force during the Leyte Gulf battles of October 1944, a Japanese ruse that nearly succeeded.

TOP: **The somewhat bland appearance of the class belies their true size, which can be gauged from the white-uniformed crew men visible against the shell plating.** ABOVE: **Loaded with thousands of tons of aviation fuel and ordnance, lightly built carriers are particularly vulnerable to the attentions of dive-bombers.** BELOW: **This particular incident is the bombing of the *Shokaku* at the battle of the Coral Sea in May 1942. A fierce blaze of aviation fuel has erupted right forward.**

Shokaku class

Class: *Shokaku*, Yokosuka Naval Yard, commissioned August 8, 1941; *Zuikaku*, Kawasaki, Kobe, commissioned September 25, 1941
Displacement: 26,150 tonnes/25,700 tons (standard); 32,700 tonnes/32,100 tons (full load)
Length: 236.2m/774ft 6in (bp); 257.7m/845ft (overall)
Beam: 26m/85ft 6in
Draught: 8.9m/29ft 3in (full load)
Aircraft: 84
Flight deck: 198.3 x 23m/650 x 75ft 6in
Armament: 16 x 127mm/5in guns
Machinery: Geared steam turbines, 8 boilers, 4 shafts
Power: 119,400kW/160,000shp
Speed: 34+ knots
Fuel: 5,350 tonnes/5,250 tons
Range: 17,590 km/9,500nm at 18 knots
Armour (over machinery and magazine spaces only): 165–210mm/6.5–8.3in (vertical belt); 100–130mm/3.9–5.1in (protective deck)
Complement: 1,650 men

Taiho

Japan's only purpose-built armoured carrier, the *Taiho* was laid down in July 1941. This pre-dates the navy's own battle experience, but the ship departed so drastically from domestic mainstream design that she was probably an experiment in response to well-publicized reports of the resilience of British carriers to German dive-bombing in the Mediterranean. Longer and finer-lined than a British Illustrious, she was of higher power, significantly faster and of far greater endurance. The fully plated bows, and the substantial island dominated by a massive funnel, gave her profile a passing resemblance to that of the British ship, but she boasted a far larger air wing. Although the armour was on a substantial scale, it did not run to protection of the hangar walls. This measure to reduce topweight was complemented by the elimination of a deck, compared with the Shokakus, resulting in a lower flight deck forward.

In the main battery, the earlier standard 127mm/5in gun was replaced by the new-pattern 100mm/3.9in, which possessed a higher rate of fire.

Up to seven follow-ons are believed to have been considered but, as none was ever commenced, it is likely that it was decided to build more, but smaller and simpler, vessels.

With an operational life of barely three months, the *Taiho* was never able to fully prove her utility. Neither her heavy horizontal nor vertical armour could protect her from the submarine torpedo that found her during the Philippine Sea battle of June 1944. Struck by this single weapon, she should have survived but, being in action, continued to be run hard. Ruptured aviation fuel lines resulted in the collection of vapour pockets and her destruction by catastrophic explosion was only a matter of time.

In order to operate at high tempo for maximum periods a carrier is a floating repository of fuel and explosives. Operational safety and survivability in action depend upon careful attention to design detail. Time contstraints meant that prolonging the design and construction process was not possible under war conditions, and the results were to prove fatal in the case of the *Taiho*.

ABOVE: **The enclosed bows and large, rectangular stack cause the *Taiho* to immediately be compared with a British Illustrious. She was also, however, the first Japanese carrier to have armour worked into flight and hangar decks. Ironically, she was sunk by submarine torpedo. BELOW: Previous Japanese carriers were armed with the standard destroyer-type 127mm/5in gun. Although dual-purpose, its rate of fire was insufficient to deal with air attack. The *Taiho* introduced a new and more effective 100mm/3.9in weapon.**

Taiho

Built: Kawasaki, Kobe
Commissioned: March 7, 1944
Displacement: 29,850 tonnes/29,300 tons (standard); 38,000 tonnes/37,300 tons (full load)
Length: 238.2m/781ft (bp); 260m/852ft 6in (overall)
Beam: 27.7m/90ft 9in
Draught: 9.6m/31ft 6in (full load)
Aircraft: Up to 75
Flight deck: 257.4 x 30m/844 x 98ft 6in
Armament: 12 x 100mm/3.9in guns
Machinery: Geared steam turbines, 8 boilers, 4 shafts
Power: 119,400kW/160,000shp
Speed: 33.5 knots
Fuel: 5,800 tonnes/5,700 tons
Range: 14,820km/8,000nm at 18 knots
Armour: 100mm/3.9in (flight deck); 125mm/4.9in (lower hangar deck); 150mm/5.9in (vertical belt)
Complement: 1,750 men

Chitose class

A further pair of ships designed for ready conversion were the seaplane carriers *Chitose* and *Chiyoda*. Extraordinarily lean in hull, they were laid down in 1934 and 1936 respectively as mother ships for up to 24 floatplanes. These were accommodated mainly below deck, and the after 60 per cent of the hull was dedicated largely to their handling and transfer by rail about the upper deck to any one of four catapults. A large, covered structure, supported on four pillars, dominated the centre section. Used for pre-flight preparation, it also supported several derricks and the diesel engine exhaust. The diesels were installed for economic cruise propulsion, a lower speed alternative to the main steam turbine installation.

Completed in 1938, both served in their original role in Chinese waters. During 1941, however, the below-deck seaplane accommodation was converted for the stowage and deployment (through the transom stern) of a dozen midget submarines, craft in which the Japanese Navy always showed great interest.

With the general shortage of carrier tonnage after Midway both ships were razed and rebuilt as single-hangar light carriers, re-entering service in 1943 (*Chiyoda*) and 1944 (*Chitose*). For this purpose, their hulls required to be bulged to restore an acceptable stability range.

Except for their unusual sterns, configured primarily for seaplane recovery, the pair appeared typical of Japanese carriers, totally flush-decked and conned from a difficult location beneath the forward overhang of the flight deck. The original machinery was retained, both groups exhausting through the customary starboard-side, horizontal funnel.

As carriers, the pair re-entered service as the Japanese Navy was in its twilight phase. They were called from training aircrew for the full mobilization that culminated in the Philippine Sea action. They survived this with no more than bomb damage to the *Chiyoda*, but

TOP: **Reconnaissance floatplanes were an essential part of Japanese forward strategy in the Pacific. The navy's seaplane carriers were of unusual design and effective, but built for simple conversion into light aircraft carriers.**

ABOVE: **Although valuable in their original role, both were converted in 1942–43. Essential for aircrew training, they were then pressed into front-line service as carrier losses mounted.**

both were expended in October 1944 in the successful decoy operation conducted during the Leyte Gulf battles.

Chitose class

Data as carriers:

Class: *Chitose*, Kure Navy Yard, commissioned July 25, 1938; *Chiyoda*, Kure Navy Yard, commissioned December 15, 1938
Displacement: 11,400 tonnes/11,200 tons (standard); 14,800 tonnes/14,500 tons (full load)
Length: 174.1m/570ft 9in (bp); 192.6m/631ft 6in (overall)
Beam: 20.8m/68ft 3in
Draught: 7.4m/24ft 2in (full load)
Aircraft: 30
Flight deck: 180.4 x 23m/591ft 6in x 75ft 6in
Armament: 8 x 127mm/5in guns
Machinery: Geared steam turbines, 4 boilers, 2 shafts
Power: 32,800kW/44,000shp plus 9,550kW/12,800bhp
Speed: 28.5 knots
Fuel: 3,660 tonnes/3,600 tons
Range: 19,450km/10,500nm at 18 knots
Armour: None
Complement: 990 men

LEFT: **A detail from a Chitose, as built. The aircraft are Nakajima E8N Type 95 two-seat reconnaissance seaplanes. Used successfully in the Sino–Japanese War, production ended in 1940 when it gained the Allied codename "Dave".**

LEFT AND BELOW: *Mizuho* and *Nisshin* were never converted to carriers as they might have been because they were both sunk. *Nisshin* lacked the two waist catapults of her sister and differed in having three centreline gun mountings forward. Being diesel-driven, both could increase useful deck area by dispensing with conventional funnels, exhaust ducts being built into the vertical pillars of the forward gantry.

Mizuho and *Nisshin*

Chitose and *Chiyoda* represented a first solution to the Japanese Navy's requirement for high-endurance seaplane tenders but, even before their completion a third ship, *Mizuho*, was laid down. Where the lead pair were steam-propelled, with auxiliary diesel cruising engines, the *Mizuho* was all-diesel, with a direct-drive unit coupled to each shaft. As total developed power was barely one third that of the *Chitose*, while displacement and hull parameters were virtually identical, it has to be assumed that the resulting modest speed of 22 knots was intended. Puzzlingly then, it appears a contradiction that the fourth, and last, of these unusual ships should be fitted with diesel engines of comparable power to *Chitose*'s steam plant, resulting in a similar, 28-knot sustainable sea speed.

Although their deck arrangements for aircraft were identical, the ships differed in detail. The most obvious was that the second pair lacked the large funnel required by the steamers, their diesels exhausting via the forward pair of pillars that supported the aircraft handling gear. Neither did the second pair have this area roofed-in.

The *Chitose* pair had two twin 127mm/5in gun mountings forward, superimposed destroyer-fashion. *Mizuho* added a third but as two were now disposed flanking the bridge structure, could still use only two on targets other than straight ahead. The *Nisshin*, therefore, had her three all located on the centreline, with the aftermost superfiring the others.

All except *Nisshin* were modified with a type of stern chute for launching midget submarines. The *Nisshin*'s auxiliary function was, however, minelaying, with a reported capacity of 700. For this purpose, her stern was rounded, with minelaying doors on either quarter.

As the *Mizuho* was lost in May 1942 and the *Nisshin* in July 1943, neither was converted into a through-deck aircraft carrier, as were their predecessors.

Mizuho and *Nisshin*

Class: *Mizuho*, Kawasaki, Kobe, commissioned February 25, 1939; *Nisshin*, Kure Naval Yard, commissioned February 27, 1942
Displacement: 11,500 tonnes/11,300 tons (standard); 13,950 tonnes/13,700 tons (full load)
Length: 174.1m/570ft 9in (bp); 194.1m/636ft 6in (overall)
Beam: 19.7m/64ft 8in
Draught: 7.1m/23ft 2in (full load)
Aircraft: 25
Flight deck: None
Armament: 6 x 127mm/5in guns
Machinery: Two 6-cylinder, direct-drive diesel engines, 2 shafts
Power: 35,000kW/47,000bhp
Speed: 28 knots
Fuel: Not known
Range: 20,370km/11,000nm at 18 knots
Armour: None
Complement: Not known

LEFT: With space both topside and below these ships could transport about two dozen aircraft to establish and maintain a forward reconnaissance base. An instance of this was at Tulagi in the Solomons in August 1942, an event that triggered the dour struggle for neighbouring Guadalcanal.

Shinano

The shock of losing four fleet carriers at Midway stimulated the Japanese Navy to extraordinary measures for their replacement, none more so than the *Shinano*. Still under construction as the third *Yamato*-class battleship, the largest such ever built, she was converted to a carrier before her completion. Although relatively slow for her adopted role, she was robust and beamy, being able to retain much of her hull armour despite having a single, "open" hangar and armoured flight deck superimposed.

Despite her exceptional size, she was intended to deploy a relatively small air wing, the bulk of her great capacity being devoted to carrying spare aircraft, ordnance, etc for other carriers, thus extending their endurance. In retrospect, this would appear to be a very expensive and inefficient alternative to the Americans' highly-effective fleet train.

As completed, the *Shinano* bore more than a passing resemblance to the late *Taiho*, with a substantial island structure, offset well to the starboard edge of the flight deck and incorporating a large, rectangular funnel, again canted outboard. Unlike the *Taiho*, she lacked the plated-in bows, her forward flight deck being supported on the more usual open structure.

By the end of 1944, at the time of her completion, the threat of large-scale carrier-borne air strikes was such that every peripheral space was occupied by light automatic weapons. Standard issue was the small calibre 25mm/1in gun of obsolete Hotchkiss design. Where *Taiho* had carried over 70 of these, *Shinano* had twice as many.

The largest-ever carrier until the arrival of the American Forrestals, the *Shinano* never went operational. Moving between shipyards in order to complete fitting-out, she was hit by a full salvo of submarine torpedoes. Still riddled with openings, her bulkheads not yet watertight, she defeated all efforts at damage control, slowly foundering.

Shinano

Built: Yokosuka Navy Yard
Commissioned: October 8, 1944
Displacement: 66,000 tonnes/64,800 tons (standard); 73,200 tonnes/71,900 tons (full load)
Length: 244.1m/800ft 6in (bp); 266.1m/872ft 6in (overall)
Beam: 36.3m/119ft 2in
Draught: 10.3m/33ft 10in (full load)
Aircraft: About 50 (120 maximum)
Flight deck: 256.2 x 40.3m/840 x 132ft
Armament: 16 x 127mm/5in guns
Machinery: Geared steam turbines, 12 boilers, 4 shafts
Power: 112,000kW/150,000shp
Speed: 27 knots
Fuel: 9,060 tonnes/8,900 tons
Range: 18,520km/10,000nm at 18 knots
Armour: 80mm/3.15in (flight deck); 200mm/7.9in (hangar deck); 205–350mm/8.1–13.8in (vertical belt)
Complement: 2,400 men

ABOVE AND BELOW: **Constructed in great secrecy and destroyed before even being formally commissioned, the *Shinano* remains something of a mystery. The extent to which she was aircraft carrier, as opposed to aircraft transport and maintenance ship, is unclear. Her vast flight deck was fitted with arresters at either end, similar to American practice and on other large Japanese carriers, yet the disposition of catapults (if any) is unclear.**

LEFT: **US carrier aircraft hit Kure and Kobe on July 24 and 28, 1945 in an effort to account for the remaining heavy units of the Japanese Navy. Just three weeks before the end of the war, the attackers met little opposition.** ABOVE: **Hit by two carrier-based strikes and by US Army B-24s, the *Amagi* keeled over in shallow water. Note the many gun tubes and the pair of downswept funnel casings.**

Unryu class

The Pacific war was won by carrier strength, the Americans succeeding by adhering to a basic design and allowing no variation in specification. Despite holding the initiative, the Japanese had no such discipline, and the nearest to a standard class that they produced were the Unryus, for which the sorry record was of two variants and only three completed of a planned 17.

The class had little enough opportunity to prove itself but, if specifications can be believed, its designers had done a good job. Far smaller than an American fleet carrier, an Unryu equated approximately in dimensions and displacement to a British Centaur. There, however, the comparison finishes, for the Japanese vessel enjoyed nearly twice the installed power, 4 knots greater speed, heavier armament, and nearly 50 per cent larger air wing.

Superficially, there was a strong visual resemblance to the *Soryu*, but experience had improved the layout, allowing an Unryu to function with two elevators rather than three. Its similar main battery of six twin 127mm/5in gun mountings was also disposed more symmetrically.

Where the American war effort became ever more powerful, that of the Japanese soon began to falter, its resources simply inadequate to sustain a prolonged war. An example was the cruiser machinery that powered the Unryus. Unavailable for two units (*Aso* and *Katsuragi*) destroyer machinery had to be substituted. Such is the price of speed, however, that the loss of one-third designed power resulted in a reduction of only 2 knots.

Six of the initial design were laid down, but only three were completed. Three more were never laid down, nor a planned batch of eight with larger dimensions. Four major yards were involved in the programme but, subjected to changes in priority and specification, and short of materials, were unable to complete it. The carrier war was, however, already lost beyond redemption.

Unryu class ●

Class: *Amagi* (II), Mitsubishi, Nagasaki, commissioned August 10. 1944; *Aso*, Kure Naval Yard, launched November 1944, not completed; *Ikoma*, Kawasaki, Kobe, launched November 1944, not completed; *Kasagi*, Mitsubishi, Nagasaki, launched October 1944, not completed; *Katsuragi*, Kure Naval Yard, completed but not commissioned; *Unryu*, Yokosuka Naval Yard, commissioned August 6, 1944

Displacement: 17,450 tonnes/17,150 tons (standard); 22,900 tonnes/22,500 tons (full load)

Length: 207.2m/679ft 3in (bp); 227.5m/745ft 10in (overall)

Beam: 22m/72ft 2in

Draught: 7.6m/25ft 9in (full load)

Aircraft: 64

Flight deck: 217.2 x 27m/712ft x 88ft 6in

Armament: 12 x 127mm/5in guns

Machinery: Geared steam turbines, 8 boilers, 4 shafts

Power: 113,400kW/152,000shp

Speed: 34 knots

Fuel: 3,720 tonnes/3,650 tons

Range: 14,820km/8,000nm at 18 knots

Armour (over machinery and magazine spaces only): 45–150mm/1.8–5.9in (vertical belt); 25–55mm/1–2.2in (protective deck)

Complement: 1,590 men

LEFT: **The Unryus were the nearest that the Japanese came to constructing a standard series of carriers. Even these, however, differed between units, nullifying the benefits of strict standardization.**

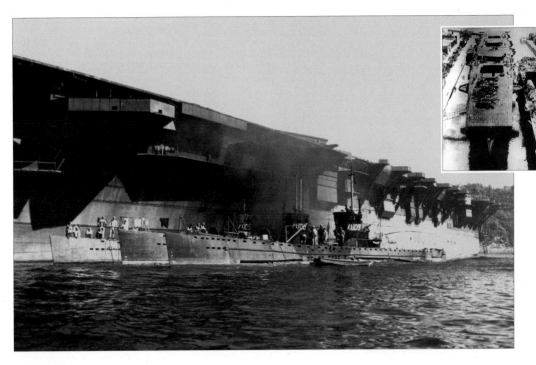

Ibuki

The final pair of a long series of Japanese heavy cruisers, *Tone* and *Chikuma,* were unique in concentrating a four-turret main battery all forward, leaving the after one-third of the upper deck totally clear for the deployment of five floatplanes. These were permanently stowed topside, being transferred by rail to one or other of the sided catapults. Their function was to provide a reconnaissance service to extend a cruiser squadron's visual range.

Two more of the type were laid down in 1942 but as battle experience had questioned the earlier ships' utility, it was decided to complete the new ships as improved versions of the earlier Suzuya class, to be named *Kurama* and *Ibuki*.

Victim of yet another policy shift, one hull was dismantled, but the other was launched as the *Ibuki* in May 1943. Work then stopped on her as well, it being proposed to convert her into a fast fleet oiler before the decision was made to complete her as a light carrier. For four

months, work progressed swiftly until, in March 1945, it halted for good with the ship complete to flight deck level. Never finished, she was broken up post-war.

If completed, the *Ibuki* would have been the only Japanese light carrier with an island superstructure. Otherwise, although the original line of the now heavily bulged cruiser hull remained obvious, her appearance was fairly standard, with a starboard-side horizontal funnel and with either end of the flight deck supported on an open structure, a measure to reduce weight and stress at the hull extremities.

With light anti-aircraft weapons proliferating, a feature of Japanese carriers was by now the ranks of deck-edge gun tubs with their deep, bracket supports. To the large number of standard 25mm/1in guns, of which the *Ibuki* had 48, were now being added multiple-barrelled rocket projectors, in a largely vain attempt to counter the menace of the mass air strike.

ABOVE: **Never completed, the *Ibuki* was surrendered at Sasebo in August 1945. Here, US personnel are seen aboard three small supply submarines, moored alongside. Note the carrier's pronounced bulge.**
TOP: **Soon afterward, the hull was transferred to the Sasebo Navy Yard's No. 7 Dock and was broken up.**

Ibuki

Built: Kure Naval Yard
Commissioned: Not commissioned
Displacement: 12,750 tonnes/12,500 tons (standard); 16,550 tonnes/16,250 tons (full load)
Length: 188m/616ft 4in (bp); 203m/665ft 6in (overall)
Beam: 21.2m/69ft 7in
Draught: 6.3m/20ft 7in (full load)
Aircraft: 27
Flight deck: 205.1 x 23m/672ft 4in x 75ft x 6in
Armament: 4 x 76mm/3in guns
Machinery: Geared steam turbines, 4 boilers, 2 shafts
Power: 53,700kW/72,000shp
Speed: 29 knots
Fuel: Not known
Range: Not known
Armour (may have been removed on conversion): 100–125mm/3.9–4.9in (vertical belt); 35–60mm/1.4–2.4in (protective deck)
Complement: 1,000 men

Taiyo class

Between May 1938 and January 1940 the Mitsubishi yard at Nagasaki laid down three 17,100-gross registered ton (grt) cargo-passenger liners to the account of Nippon Yusen Kaisha (NYK). They were launched 1939–40, but work then appears to have been halted. Not until May 1941 (still seven months before Japan entered the war) was construction resumed, the *Kasuga Maru* being transferred to the Sasebo Navy Yard and the other pair, *Yawata Maru* and *Nitta Maru*, going to Kure Navy Yard, all for conversion to escort carriers. When it is recalled that the pioneering British and American equivalents (HMS *Audacity* and *Long Island*) were first commissioned only in June 1941, it will be appreciated that the Japanese were well abreast of developments.

Even by escort carrier standards, however, the conversions were very basic. The hulls were larger and faster than Allied examples and could have made excellent carriers had they been fitted with the necessary catapult and

arrester gear. As it was, their careers were limited largely to ferrying aircraft and training aircrew. For the former role, a large, port-side post and derrick were added.

The hulls possessed adequate stability without bulges and the original upper deck line remained clearly visible. There was no island and the somewhat truncated flight deck was served by two elevators. A respectable armament was shipped, but varied between vessels in both calibre and number of barrels, the ships obviously having to accept what was available.

Their occupation left them vulnerable to submarine attack. All three were thus sunk by submarine attack, only one of them in home waters.

BELOW: **At about 18,290 tonnes/18,000 tons, the three Taiyos should have made useful carriers but their speed was inadequate. Without either catapult or arrester gear, they were employed mainly for aircraft transport, the aircraft being loaded alongside but flown off.**

ABOVE: **The *Taiyo*'s original passenger liner hull is very obvious in this picture. Note the straight rake to the bows, the sheerline, the paired scuttles and lack of bulges. There is no island structure, the ship being navigated from a position beneath the forward overhang. By naval standards, commercial hulls are inadequately subdivided.**

Taiyo class

Class: *Taiyo* (ex-*Kasuga Maru*), Mitsubishi, Nagasaki, commissioned September 15, 1941; *Unyo* (ex-*Yawata Maru*), Mitsubishi, Nagasaki, commissioned May 31, 1942; *Chuyo* (ex-*Nitta Maru*), Mitsubishi, Nagasaki, commissioned November 25, 1942

Displacement: 18,290 tonnes/18,000 tons (standard); 22,200 tonnes/21,800 tons (full load)

Length: 168.1m/551ft 2in (bp); 180.4m/591ft 6in (overall)

Beam: 22.5m/73ft 10in

Draught: 6.3m/20ft 8in (standard); 7.8m/25ft 6in (full load)

Aircraft: 27

Flight deck: 172.2 x 23.6m/564ft 6in x 77ft 3in

Armament: 6 x 119mm/4.7in guns (*Taiyo*); 8 x 127mm/5in guns (all others)

Machinery: Geared steam turbines, 4 boilers, 2 shafts

Power: 18,650kW/25,000shp

Speed: 21 knots

Fuel: Not known

Range: 12,040km/6,500nm at 18 knots

Armour: None

Complement: 800 men

TOP AND ABOVE: **This unusually fine image of the** *Kaiyo* **clearly betrays the passenger liner beneath the flight deck. Note the mercantile forecastle and complete original bridge front with prominent wings. She, too, was employed as an aircraft transport before being sunk in shallow water by carrier aircraft.**

Shinyo and *Kaiyo*

Modern cargo-passenger liners were of great value to the Japanese for the movement of troops and supplies around their sprawling "co-prosperity sphere". It says much, therefore, for the urgency of the need for further flight decks that such ships were continually being withdrawn for conversion to escort carriers and aircraft transports.

Not to be confused with the regular warships of similar name, the *Scharnhorst* and *Gneisenau* were 18,200-gross registered ton (grt) liners built for Norddeutscher-Lloyd's Far East service.

Stranded in Japan by the outbreak of the European war, the former ship was purchased early in 1942 for the Japanese Navy. Early plans to use her as a transport were overtaken by the disaster at Midway, and she was put in hand for a carrier conversion in September 1942. The task was apparently complex, for it occupied 15 months. Renamed *Shinyo*, she emerged as a standard Japanese escort carrier, but recognizable immediately

through her semi-Maierform bow profile and her prominent, angular bulges. A brief 11-month operational career was terminated by submarine torpedo.

Built in 1938–40 for Osaka Syosen Kabusiki Kaisha's (OSK) Japan–South America service were the appropriately named *Argentina Maru* and *Brazil Maru*. At 12,750grt, they were smaller than most taken for conversion, and they were diesel-powered for economy on their exceptionally long sea passages. The *Brazil Maru* being sunk by submarine early on in the war, her sister alone was taken in hand late in 1942. Her superstructure was razed and her diesel engines removed in favour of steam turbines. This considerable boost in propulsive power predictably increased her maximum speed by only 2 knots.

Another standard conversion, she was renamed *Kaiyo* and, lacking arresters and catapults, spent her career ferrying aircraft. She was scrapped, having been beached, badly damaged post-war.

Shinyo

Built: Bremer-Vulkan, Breman
Commissioned: May 28, 1936
Displacement: 19,100 tonnes/17,500 tons (standard); 23,250 tonnes/22,850 tons (full load)
Length: 185.1m/606ft 11in (bp); 195.8m/642ft 2in (overall)
Beam: 25.6m/84ft
Draught: 8.2m/26ft 10in (full load)
Aircraft: 33
Flight deck: 181 x 24.6m/590ft 6in x 80ft 6in
Armament: 8 x 127mm/5in guns
Machinery: Geared steam turbines, 4 boilers, 2 shafts
Power: 19,400kW/26,000shp
Speed: 22 knots
Fuel: Not known
Range: Not known
Armour: None
Complement: 950 men

LEFT: **The** *Shinyo*'s **forward sheerline, clearly visible, caused the hangar deck to be carried higher. This, in turn, required bulges to be fitted to restore the required stability range. Note the water disturbance around the leading edge of the bulge.**

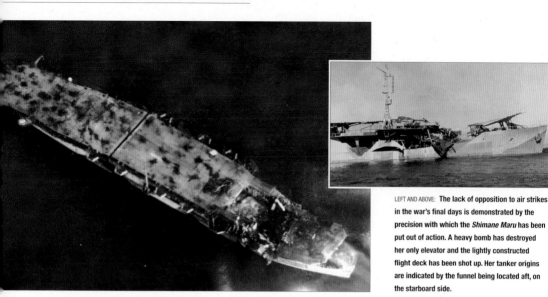

LEFT AND ABOVE: **The lack of opposition to air strikes in the war's final days is demonstrated by the precision with which the *Shimane Maru* has been put out of action. A heavy bomb has destroyed her only elevator and the lightly constructed flight deck has been shot up. Her tanker origins are indicated by the funnel being located aft, on the starboard side.**

Yamashiro Maru and *Shimane Maru*

Despite needing her merchant fleet both to supply her many garrisons and to import basics and raw materials, Japan began by expending it heedlessly. No convoy strategy existed and there were few escorts. The strongly offensively minded Japanese Navy viewed such policy as "defensive", actively resisting it. Small wonder, therefore, that the highly focussed American submarine campaign caused a crisis before action was taken. Following the Allied lead, Japanese yards were directed at the series production of simple, standard designs. These particularly included tankers, which had been specifically targeted.

With a growing convoy network established, the Japanese adopted another Allied initiative in the adaptation of tankers at MAC ships. These retained their full liquid cargo capacity but had a flight deck built above.

Two conversions, the *Yamashiro Maru* and *Chigusa Maru*, were known to have been made to 2TL-type tankers of 10,000 gross registered tons (grt). At 15 knots, they were very slow for tropical conditions. They had no hangar, up to eight light Army aircraft being permanently ranged topside for the purpose of convoy air cover. The first-named was sunk in 1945 but it is doubtful if the other was ever completed as a carrier, trading as a tanker post-war.

From the slightly larger and fast 1TL type, four conversions were scheduled. Marginally more sophisticated, these featured a small hangar and single elevator. The *Shimane Maru* was thus converted by February 1945, only to be

BELOW: **Like the American Sangamon class, the *Yamashiro Maru* had a line of apertures in the shell plating amidships, marking the level of the upper deck of the original tanker hull.**

sunk by aircraft just five months later. Her sister, *Otakisan Maru* was never completed as a carrier and the final pair were never commenced.

Neither type had an island but their tanker origins were evident in that the familiar, starboard-side horizontal funnel was located well aft. Few tankers were fast enough to be considered as carriers.

Shimane Maru

Built: Kawasaki, Kobe
Commissioned: February 28, 1945
Displacement: 12,000 tonnes/11,800 tons (standard)
Length: 150m/491ft 9in (bp); 160.6m/526ft 6in (overall)
Beam: 20m/65ft 8in
Draught: 9.1m/29ft 10in (mean)
Aircraft: 12
Flight deck: 155.1 x 23m/508ft 6in x 75ft 6in
Armament: 2 x 119mm/4.7in guns
Machinery: Geared steam turbines, 2 boilers, 1 shaft
Power: 6,400kW/8,600shp
Speed: 18 knots
Fuel: Not known
Range: 18,520km/10,000nm at 15 knots
Armour: None
Complement: Not known

Akitsu Maru class and *Kumano Maru*

A wide variety of shipping, even cargo-carrying submarines, came under the control of the Japanese Army, but even the outstandingly successful campaign of early 1942 was undertaken by many with only ad hoc arrangements for amphibious warfare.

Exceptions to this were the *Akitsu Maru* (9,200 gross registered tons – grt) and *Nigitsu Maru* (9,550 grt), designed as small cargo-passenger liners but acquired and converted from the outset. Their uptakes were rerouted to the starboard side, but the amidships structure was retained as troop accommodation. To put the troops and light equipment ashore the ships carried a score of the ubiquitous Daihatsu landing craft on deck, which were effectively motorized sampans fitted with a bow ramp. These were handled by the ships' cargo gear.

Overall, a through flight deck extended from the bows to a point about 80 per cent aft. Up to 20 light Army

aircraft were stored beneath and transferred by a simple after-end elevator. There was no provision for flying-on, it being presumed that a shoreside airstrip had been secured.

Akitsu Maru was completed as early as January 1942, her running mate some 14 months later. Both fell victim to submarine attack during 1944.

Of more workmanlike appearance, but not completed until March 1945, the *Kumano Maru* was converted from a standard dry-cargo vessel. Her through flight deck, which extended over the centre 80 per cent of her length, could accommodate about three dozen light Army aircraft. What appeared to be a partial hangar had no elevator, the flight deck being served by cargo derrick. Flanking the hangar was troop accommodation. The deck below gave

storage for up to 25 Daihatsus of two varieties, which were discharged and recovered via stern doors.

Surviving the war, the ship was reconverted for commercial use.

TOP: **The simple nature of the *Akitsu Maru*'s conversion is evident in this view, the mercantile hull extending forward and aft. Note the lack of elevators and arrester gear.** ABOVE: **This early picture of *Kumano Maru* shows what appears to be a relocated original funnel.**

Akitsu Maru

Built: Harima Shipbuilding, Harima
Commissioned: January 30, 1942
Displacement: 12,000 tonnes/11,800 tons (standard)
Length: 143.8m/471ft 7in (bp); 159m/521ft 4in (overall, approximately)
Beam: 19.5m/64ft
Draught: 7.9m/26ft 3in (mean)
Aircraft: 20 light aircraft
Flight deck: 123 x 22.5m/403ft 2in x 73ft 8in
Armament: Up to 12 Army 76mm/3in guns
Machinery: Geared steam turbines, 4 boilers, 2 shafts
Power: 5,600kW/7,500shp
Speed: 20 knots
Fuel: Not known
Range: Not known
Armour: None
Complement: Not known

BELOW: ***Kumano Maru* with her funnel angled downward. Army-controlled, with many boats and stern doors, the ship was among the earliest assault carriers.**

Akitsushima

The Seaplane Tender was a very specific type of aviation ship that, while it could vary considerably in size, was always identified through the outsize, trademark crane(s) at the after end. Many types of ship, mostly conversions, could deploy floatplanes but the seaplane tender was tailored to the heavy flying boat. In the context of a Pacific war, both the Japanese and United States navies were interested in the provision and maintenance of forward flying boat bases. These were required to be self-sufficient for considerable periods of time and, above all, mobile.

From 1940, American examples were configured around the Consolidated PBY Catalina and the 16.3-tonne/ 16-ton-plus Martin PBM Mariner, being able to lift them bodily from the water for repair or maintenance. The ships were mostly in the 8,128–9,144-tonne/ 8,000–9,000-ton bracket.

Newly introduced, Japan's large flying boat was the Kawanishi H8K2 Type 2. Known to the Allies as "Emily", it closely resembled the British Sunderland

and conferred an increased medium-range potential in both reconnaissance and attack. Five specialist ships were ordered for its support but, like so many Japanese programmes, it was severely curtailed; only one ship, the *Akitsushima*, ever being completed.

Little more than half the displacement of her American equivalents, she resembled a large destroyer forward. Her second twin 127mm/5in mounting was poorly located, between the funnel and mast, commanding limited arcs. On a revolving base right aft was a long-jibbed crane with an "Eiffel-tower" profile. This served a heavy cradle which may (or may not) have been built to act as a trainable catapult for smaller floatplanes.

Japan's further territorial expansion after 1942 was obviously most unlikely, and the cancellation of the final four units probably resulted from a revised assessment of the future course of the war as much as by priorities in shipbuilding.

Akitsushima herself was sunk by air attack during 1944.

TOP: **Although published plans suggest a trainable catapult on the afterdeck of the *Akitsushima*, there seems little evidence of it in this profile. The disruptive camouflage includes false bow and stern waves of a magnitude hardly likely on a 19-knot ship.** ABOVE: **Well armed and protected, the Kawanishi H8K ("Emily") was considered the most difficult Japanese aircraft to shoot down.**

Akitsushima

Built: Kawasaki, Kobe
Commissioned: 1942
Displacement: 4,750 tonnes/4,650 tons (standard); 5,700 tonnes/5,600 tons (full load, approximately)
Length: 109.1m/357ft 7in (bp); 118m/386ft 10in (overall)
Beam: 15.8m/51ft 9in
Draught: 5.4m/17ft 9in (mean)
Aircraft: 1
Flight deck: None
Armament: 4 x 127mm/5in guns
Machinery: Four diesel engines, 2 shafts
Power: 5,970kW/8,000bhp
Speed: 19 knots
Fuel: Not known
Range: Not known
Armour: None
Complement: Not known

ABOVE: The *Foudre* is seen here soon after her completion and still in her original configuration as mother-ship and carrier of torpedo craft. Her funnels were later raised and a temporary hangar erected aft.

ABOVE: Seen soon after conversion, the *Foudre* has acquired her garage-like hangar but retains her three short funnels. The take-off platform forward was later replaced by a square assembly platform.

Foudre

Completed in the unrealistic role of cruiser-sized torpedo boat, carrier and mother ship, the *Foudre* had little use (although equipped with facilities for an observation balloon) and served as a multi-purpose auxiliary until, in 1911–12, she was converted for experimental naval aviation purposes. Much of the earlier top-hamper was removed and a large, permanent hangar erected. This could house about four of the eight floatplanes carried.

During 1914 a temporary platform was built over the forecastle and, on May 8, Réné Caudron used it to make the first-ever flight from a French ship. The aircraft was one of his own G.III amphibians.

The *Foudre*'s main contribution was in cooperation with similarly converted British seaplane carriers in the eastern Mediterranean. Naval aviation moved on quickly, however, and by 1917 the ship was again working as an auxiliary. She was scrapped in 1922.

Following British practice, the French requisitioned other ships for wartime aviation service. Largest of these was the 3,320-gross ton cargo-passenger ship *Campinas*, modified simply by protecting the forward and after well decks with canvas sides and roofing to

accommodate about eight floatplanes. These were handled with the ship's cargo gear. She also worked in the eastern Mediterranean. Two cross-channel packets, *Nord* and *Pas de Calais*, were also pressed into service. Unusually, each was paddle-propelled and both worked in the English Channel as seaplane carriers.

All three latter ships alternatively deployed small, pusher-engined flying boats. These were the so-called FBAs, built on both sides of the Channel by the Franco-British Aviation Company.

Following hostilities, the mercantile naval sloop *Bapaume* was fitted with a launch platform extending from bridge to stem head. Although only experimental, it saw the first flight from a French ship of landplanes, fighters with wheeled undercarriages.

Foudre

Built: At. et Ch. de la Gironde, Bordeaux
Commissioned: September 17, 1896
Displacement: 6,080 tonnes/5,975 tons (standard); 6,210 tonnes/6,100 tons (full load)
Length: 118.9m/389ft 10in (overall)
Beam: 19.1m/62ft 6in
Draught: 7.2m/23ft 6in (full load)
Aircraft: Up to 8 floatplanes
Flight deck (launch platform): 34.5 x 8m/113ft 2in x 26ft 3in
Armament: 8 x 100mm/3.9in, 4 x 65mm/2.6in, and 4 x 47mm/1.85in guns
Machinery: Two sets triple expansion steam engines, 24 boilers, 2 shafts
Power: 8,650kW/11,600ihp
Speed: 19 knots
Fuel: 800 tonnes/786 tons (coal)
Range: Not known
Armour: 120mm/4.7in (protective deck), also protected casemates
Complement: 450 men

Béarn

Following the Washington Treaty of 1921–22, four of the incomplete hulls of the *Normandie*-class battleships were scrapped and the fifth, *Béarn*, was earmarked for conversion to a fleet carrier. However, she was not a good choice due to her low speed and her outer shafts being driven by vertical steam reciprocating engines, whose height resulted in the ship's high profile. This odd mix of machinery was for cruise economy, the steam turbine-driven inner shafts being coupled only for high speed boost.

Before reconstruction began, in August 1923, the hull was partially decked for static flying trials. As completed there was a near full-length flight deck which, in plan, narrowed significantly at either end. Here, it was supported on an open structure, the after end with a pronounced round-down and the forward end modified likewise following sea experience to improve airflow over the deck. There were three elevators, all on the centreline.

As with contemporary foreign carriers, the massive funnel casing dominated the island structure, all of which was located outboard of the flight deck's starboard edge. Abaft it was a prominent gooseneck crane.

Although her original armour plan was considerably reduced during her reconstruction, the *Béarn* remained well

ABOVE: **These sketches depict the *Béarn* in her original carrier configuration. Refitted in the United States, 1943–44, she lost either end of her flight deck in being reduced to aircraft transport status.**

protected. Uniquely, her main battery of eight 155mm/6.1in guns was casemated.

During World War II, the ship was blockaded in the French Antilles until 1943 when the islands finally declared for the Allies. Refitted and rearmed in the United States she served as an aircraft transport, for which service her flight deck was truncated and a second prominent crane installed. Following post-war service in French Indochina she was withdrawn in 1948 but continued in static harbour service until 1966. Scrapping began in the following year.

TOP LEFT AND ABOVE: **Too slow to be an efficient fleet carrier, the *Béarn* nonetheless possessed considerable "presence". The round-down to the forward end of the flight deck dates these pictures to the early 1930s. The massive island was completely outboard of the flight deck edge and, like those of Japanese carriers, was heavily buttressed beneath.** LEFT: **Biplanes such as these Morane-Saulniers were soon displaced by a succession of parasol-winged aircraft such as the Loire Gordou-Leseurre 32, the Morane-Saulnier MS225 and the Dewoitine D373.**

Béarn

Built: F. et Ch. de la Méditerranée, La Seyne
Commissioned: May 28, 1927
Displacement: 22,200 tonnes/21,800 tons (standard); 28,450 tonnes/27,950 tons (full load)
Length: 170.6m/559ft 4in (bp); 182.6m/598ft 8in (overall)
Beam: 27.1m/88ft 10in
Draught: 8.4m/27ft 6in (standard); 9.3m/30ft 6in (full load)
Aircraft: 35–40
Flight deck: 177 x 21.3m/580ft 9in x 69ft 11in
Armament: 8 x 155mm/6.1in, 6 x 75mm/2.9in, and 8 x 37mm/1.46in guns
Machinery: Two sets steam reciprocating engines and two sets geared steam turbines, 12 boilers, 4 shafts
Power: 29,850kW/40,000shp
Speed: 21.5 knots
Fuel: 2,250 tonnes/2,210 tons
Range: 12,960km/7,000nm at 10 knots
Armour: 83mm/3.25in (vertical belt); 25mm/1in (flight deck); 25–119mm/1–4.7in (protective deck)
Complement: 880 men

Joffre class

Perhaps because of the disappointingly low speed of the *Béarn*, perhaps from a need to establish the ideal size of carrier for its requirements, the French Navy proposed during the early 1930s several designs based on hybrid cruiser technology. The ideas came to nought but the thinking influenced two new ships eventually authorized in 1936. France was permitted 60,963 tonnes/60,000 tons total carrier displacement by virtue of the Washington Treaty and, with an eye to an eventual third ship, the size was fixed at a target of 18,289 tonnes/18,000 tons each. Much of a size with a

British *Courageous* but even finer-lined for greater speed, the ships, named provisionally *Joffre* and *Painlévé*, were of novel layout. The superstructure was long and narrow, and not cantilevered beyond the starboard side of the hull. Its considerable offset weight, however, allowed the flight deck to be built parallel and separate, extending beyond the port side of the hull. Two hangars, the lower of half length, would have been provided, accommodating up to 40 unspecified aircraft. Barely commenced, the ships were scrapped after France's occupation in 1940.

Joffre class

Built: At. Et Ch. de St. Nazaire
Laid down: November 1938, 1939
Displacement: 18,289 tonnes/18,000 tons (standard); 20,350 tonnes/20,000 tons (full load)
Length: 228m/747ft 6in (at waterline); 236m/773ft 9in (overall)
Beam: 25.5m/83ft 7in
Draught: 6.5m/21ft 3in (approximately)
Aircraft: 40
Flight deck: 200 x 28m/655ft 9in x 91ft 3in
Armament: 8 x 130mm/5.1in, and 8 x 37mm/1.46in
Machinery: Geared steam turbines, 8 boilers, 4 shafts
Power: 89,500kW/120,000shp
Speed: 32.5 knots
Fuel: Not known
Range: Not known
Armour: Not known
Complement: 1,200 men

LEFT: **The Joffre design grouped its main armament similar to that of the later American Essex class. Aircraft appear to be taken aboard at upper hangar deck level and transferred within via roller doors at either end.**

Commandant Teste

Although described as a Seaplane Carrier, the *Commandant Teste* could accommodate both floatplanes and flying boats. Her generous freeboard enclosed a capacious hangar that was served either by a stern ramp or by any of four heavy cranes. Each crane also served an adjacent catapult, two ahead and two abaft the central funnel casing.

Her utility in a Far Eastern colonial context is obvious but nevertheless she

spent her life mainly in the Mediterranean supporting flights from battleships and cruisers, and developing strike/reconnaissance roles. Scuttled at Toulon in 1942, she was salvaged and repaired, only to be broken up in 1950.

Commandant Teste

Built: F. Ch. de la Gironde, Bordeaux
Commissioned: November 17, 1932
Displacement: 10,200 tonnes/10,000 tons (standard); 11,900 tonnes/11,700 tons (full load)
Length: 156m/511ft 6in (bp); 167m/547ft 6in (overall)
Beam: 27m/88ft 6in
Draught: 6.9m/22ft 8in (full load)
Aircraft: Up to 26
Flight deck: None
Armament: 12 x 100mm/3.9in, and 8 x 37mm/1.46in guns
Machinery: Geared steam turbines, 4 boilers, 2 shafts
Power: 15,600kW/21,000shp
Speed: 20.5 knots
Fuel: 295 tonnes/290 tons (oil); 735 tonnes/720 tons (coal)
Range: 11,110km/6,000nm at 10 knots
Armour: 30mm/1.18in (partial protective deck)
Complement: 640 men

ABOVE LEFT: **Depot and repair ships have impressive freeboards due to on-board workshops, and accommodation for both their own and visiting crews. Note the paravane chains rigged at the bows and the half-masted jack.**

ABOVE: **The isolated single funnel, massive cranage and low freeboard aft combined to give the *Commandant Teste* a unique profile.**

LEFT: Little altered post-war, the *Dixmude* performed useful service in what was then French Indochina. Note how the box-like island has the appearance of being supported by neither flight deck nor hull.

Dixmude

Built: Sun Shipbuilding, Philadelphia
Commissioned: May 4, 1942
Length: 141.8m/465ft (at waterline); 150m/492ft (overall)
Beam: 21.2m/69ft 6in
Draught: 7.7m/25ft 2in (full load)
Aircraft: 20+
Flight deck: 134.2 x 24.1m/440 x 79ft
Armament: 3 x 102mm/4in, and 12 x 20mm/0.79in guns
Machinery: Two 6-cylinder diesel engines driving 1 shaft
Power: 6,350kW/8,500bhp
Speed: 16.5 knots
Fuel: 3,260 tonnes/3,200 tons
Range: Not known
Armour: None
Complement: 850 men

Dixmude

One of the original *Avenger*-class escort carriers built in the United States for the Royal Navy, the *Biter* was returned in April 1945. She was immediately transferred on loan to the French Navy, being renamed *Dixmude*.

As the French were also acquiring more capable carriers on transfer, the *Dixmude*, herself an early type of CVE, was employed mainly in training. Then, disarmed, she assumed the role of aircraft transport, collecting machines from the United States, many for use in the Far East.

By 1960 she had been relegated to static harbour duties and, six years later, was returned to the Americans for scrapping. She was by then the last of the early escort carrier conversions still afloat. Where her two Royal Navy sisters had lives each of 9 months, hers had been of 24 years.

LEFT: With elevators lowered, probably to ventilate the hangar, the *La Fayette* transits the Suez Canal in the early 1960s, the date fixed by the additional lattice mast between the funnel pairs.

La Fayette class

Class: *La Fayette*, New York Shipbuilding, Camden, commissioned August 31, 1943; *Bois Belleau*, New York Shipbuilding, Camden, commissioned March 31, 1943
Displacement: 10,850 tonnes/10,650 tons (standard); 15,000 tonnes/14,750 tons (full load)
Length: 183m/600ft (at waterline); 189.9m/622ft 6in (overall)
Beam: 21.8m/71ft 6in
Draught: 6.4m/21ft (standard); 7.5m/24ft 6in (full load)
Aircraft: About 30
Flight deck: 165.9 x 22.3m/544 x 73ft
Armament: 28 x 40mm/1.57in guns
Machinery: Geared steam turbines, 4 boilers, 4 shafts
Power: 75,000kW/100,000shp
Speed: 32 knots
Fuel: 2,350 tonnes/2,300 tons
Range: 20,370km/11,000nm at 15 knots
Armour: 50mm/1.97in (vertical belt)
Complement: 1,200 men

La Fayette class

With little post-war potential, most American *Independence*-class CVLs were quickly discarded. Three, however, were transferred abroad, two of them to the French Navy. In January 1951, the *Langley* (CVL-27) hoisted her new colours as the *La Fayette* (R96) followed in September 1953, by the *Belleau Wood* (CVL-24), which became the *Bois Belleau* (R97). Transferred under the wide-ranging Mutual Defense Assistance Program, both ships assumed names redolent of Franco-American alliance.

Altered by the addition of a tall lattice mast amidships, both saw service in the Far East, the *La Fayette* at the Suez intervention. Both were returned for disposal in the early 1960s, leaving the Spanish *Dédalo* as the sole remaining CVL.

FAR LEFT: **Toward the end of her life, the** *Arromanches* **worked as an ASW carrier deploying Breguet Alizé aircraft, of which one is seen here. Note the considerably altered masting and new funnel cap.** LEFT: **British carrier design always favoured the fully enclosed bow for its superior weatherliness.** BELOW: **Despite the alternative of compact whip aerials, British-built carriers still favoured the more efficient wire aerial strung between light lattice masts, here seen in the raised position.**

Arromanches

Designed and built for wartime exigencies, the British Light Fleet Carriers proved to be capacious and economical for peacetime use. They also lent themselves to a degree of modernization and proved to be surprisingly durable. These qualities were best seen in those examples which were acquired by foreign fleets, for they invariably served longer than those in the Royal Navy, which were superseded by later classes. Such was the *Colossus*, name ship of the original group, which was loaned to France in August 1946 and which was bought outright five years later.

Already impoverished by World War II, France was involved in a protracted struggle to regain authority over her former territory of Indochina. Initially, this benefited her armed forces by increased funding but, in the long term, it had the opposite effect with new equipment and, indeed, a planned new carrier, being cancelled due to the continued financial drain.

With the French aircraft industry still to re-establish itself, the ex-*Colossus*, renamed *Arromanches* (R95), deployed

American-built aircraft of World War II vintage both in the Far East and at Suez in 1956. By this date, however, the first of two new carriers was, at last, on the stocks but, as these would be six years in build, it was worthwhile to modernize the *Arromanches* during 1957–58.

Remodelled, she gained a moderate angled deck of four degrees but no steam catapult. Not fully jet-capable, she could deploy the Breguet Alizé AS aircraft and, indeed, with the new carriers in service, she was further modified and redesignated a full anti-submarine carrier, with an air wing of two dozen helicopters.

Following final service as a training carrier, the *Arromanches* was laid up for four years prior to her scrapping in 1978.

Arromanches

Built: Vickers-Armstrong, Newcastle
Commissioned: December 16, 1944
Displacement: 13,600 tonnes/13,350 tons (standard); 18,550 tonnes/18,200 tons (full load)
Length: 192.2m/630ft (bp); 212m/695ft (overall)
Beam: 24.4m/80ft
Draught: 5.6m/18ft 6in (standard); 7.2m/23ft 6in (full load)
Aircraft: 35–40
Flight deck: 207.4 x 24.4m/680 x 80ft
Armament: 31 x 40mm/1.57in guns
Machinery: Geared steam turbines, 4 boilers, 2 shafts
Power: 29,850kW/40,000shp
Speed: 25 knots
Fuel: 3,300 tonnes/3,250 tons
Range: 22,220km/12,000nm at 14 knots
Armour: None
Complement: 1,450 men

ABOVE: Cadet accommodation flanks the long, narrow hangar and is marked externally by the long "promenade" decks. LEFT: The *Jeanne d'Arc*'s light armament has been considerably strengthened in recent years through the addition of six Exocet MM38 canister launchers, located in two angled groups of three between the forward 100mm/3.9in guns.

Jeanne d'Arc

Laid down in 1960 with the temporary name of *Résolue*, this ship commissioned as the *Jeanne d'Arc* (R97), assuming the name of a training cruiser that had just paid off. The primary function of both was the sea training of officer cadets but the new ship, to be cost-effective, was required to be capable of multiple roles. Of pleasing appearance she is, therefore, conventional warship forward and aviation vessel aft. This unusual combination bears comparison only with the Italian *Vittorio Veneto* and the Russian Moskvas.

Training (of nearly 200 cadets) is a peacetime activity, so that the accommodation that flanks the long, narrow hangar is allowed to encroach on its space. In an emergency, this could be removed to give accommodation for up to eight Supter-Frélon transport helicopters, or more WG-13 Lynx AS helicopters if the ship is required to lead an anti-submarine task group. Alternatively, the full accommodation could be retained for a 700-strong assault battalion, with its equipment.

The limitations of a multi-role ship are, however, evident. The American *Iwo Jima*-class LPHs were widely criticized for shipping no landing craft to move heavy equipment ashore. Only two are carried by the *Jeanne d'Arc*. With the superstructure as a barrier across the forward end of the flight deck,

V/STOL aircraft can be operated only in the fuel-thirsty vertical mode. Forward, the ship's six Exocets are of use only against other ships, not as shore gun support, for which the ship's four 100mm/3.9in weapons are both lightweight and poorly located.

The already comprehensive range of electronics – radar, sonar, and control and command facilities – could well be supplemented to give the ship what would probably be her best combat role, as a Headquarters Ship. The "Jeanne" is scheduled to run until 2010.

Jeanne d'Arc		
Built: Brest-Arsenal		
Commissioned: June 30, 1964		
Displacement: 10,180 tonnes/10,000 tons (standard); 12,570 tonnes/12,350 tons (full load)		
Length: 172m/563ft 10in (at waterline); 182m/596ft 9in (overall)		
Beam: 24m/78ft 8in		
Draught: 6.9m/22ft 7in (full load)		
Aircraft: 8+ helicopters		
Flight deck: 62 x 21m/203ft 3in x 68ft 10in		
Armament: 6 x MM38 Exocet SSM, and 4 x 100mm/3.9in guns		
Machinery: Geared steam turbines, 4 boilers, 2 shafts		
Power: 29,850kW/40,000shp		
Speed: 26.5 knots		
Fuel: 1,385 tonnes/1,360 tons		
Range: 12,500km/6,800nm at 16 knots		
Armour: None		
Complement: 740 men (crew only)		

ABOVE: **In company with four French destroyers, the *Jeanne d'Arc* lies alongside the Landungsbrücken for a port visit to Hamburg, probably in the early 1970s.**

LEFT: **This view shows well the short-range Crotale SAM launcher on the port quarter sponson, shipped in exchange for two 100mm/3.9in guns. The prominent dome abaft the funnel houses the antenna of the aircraft landing-air radar.** ABOVE: **A Super Etendard fighter on the *Clemenceau's* port-side steam catapult.** BELOW: **This earlier picture of the *Clemenceau* shows the original armament of eight 100mm/3.9in guns in single mountings. Unusually the ship was deploying a mix of Lynx and Super-Frélon helicopters.**

Clemenceau class

After several false starts, the French Navy finally laid down its first two modern carriers, the *Clemenceau* (R98) in 1955 and *Foch* (R99) in 1957. They were late enough to incorporate an 8-degree angled deck and steam catapults from the outset. French ships tend to speed, the necessary power demanding space, a long hull and fine lines. Jet aircraft also require length but, being thirsty, also need considerable capacity for fuel storage. The usual design trade-offs still applied, however, for budget restraints required the smallest ship to meet the specification.

As designed, the pair therefore had a standard displacement comparable with that of a British Illustrious but with a length (between perpendiculars) greater by over 30.5m/100ft yet with less than 0.91m/3ft more on the beam. Even without the same degree of protection, and with armament reduced to save topweight, the first-of-class proved tender, and both needed to be bulged by nearly 1.82m/6ft. This measure increases freeboard, improves stability and increases fuel capacity, thought at the cost of a knot or so in speed.

Hangar design tends towards the fully enclosed, but one of the two elevators is a space-saving deck-edge

unit, located immediately abaft the island. The carriers' strike component comprises 16 Dassault Super Etendards, trans-sonic aircraft capable of carrying tactical nuclear weapons or the air-launched AM 39 variant of the Exocet.

During their life under the French flag, both ships underwent two major upgrades of heavy equipment, structure and electronics. Four of the original eight 100mm/3.9in guns were landed in favour of two Crotale short-range SAM systems, although the sponson of the forward mounting looks vulnerable to heavy seas.

In 2000, the *Foch* was sold to Brazil, becoming the *Sao Paolo*, but the *Clemenceau* was scrapped in 2003. This left the French Navy with just one fleet carrier.

Clemenceau class

Built: Brest-Arsenal (Hull of *Foch* sub-contracted to Ch. de l'Atlantique, St. Nazaire)
Displacement: 22,400 tonnes/22,000 tons (standard); 33,300 tonnes/32,700 tons (full load)
Length: 238m/780ft 4in (bp); 265m/868ft 10in (overall)
Beam: 31.7m/103ft 11in
Draught: 7.5m/24ft 7in (standard); 8.6m/28ft 3in (full load)
Aircraft: 38–40
Flight deck: 257 x 28m/842ft 8in x 91ft 10in
Armament: 2 x octal Crotale SAM launchers, and 4 x 100mm/3.9in guns
Machinery: Geared steam turbines, 6 boilers, 2 shafts
Power: 94,000kW/126,000hp
Speed: 32 knots
Fuel: 3,800 tonnes/3,700 tons
Range: 13,800km/7,500nm at 18 knots
Armour: "Light protection"
Complement: 1,350 men

LEFT: **Seen running builder's trials the** *Charles de Gaulle* **is still devoid of topside clutter. Great efforts on the part of the French Navy to lower the radar signature of its ships has left them increasingly bland in appearance.** ABOVE: **Late acquisition of two Grumman E-2C Hawkeye airborne early warning (AEW) aircraft (see here forward of the island and right aft) caused last-minute modifications to the** *de Gaulle***'s design.** BELOW: **Despite the prestige attached to the** *de Gaulle***, her expensive new Rafale fighter-bombers are being procured very slowly. Four are seen here with two variants of Etendard beyond.**

Charles de Gaulle

The *Charles de Gaulle* is very much a prestige project and since the disposal of the two Clemenceaus, one in serious need of a running mate to guarantee the availability of at least one flight deck. However, a second ship is not planned before 2014 and may be constructed in the same programme and to the same basic design as the two British Queen Elizabeths. She will probably, therefore, be conventionally propelled and, despite the *de Gaulle* sharing much commonality with French nuclear submarine technology she will alone have to bear considerable infrastructure costs.

By modern standards, her layout is conventional but with a larger than usual island structure located well forward to allow space for two starboard-side, deck-edge elevators to be sited abaft it. There is no centreline elevator. To maximize flight deck area there is a very pronounced overhang to the angle deck. Two US-sourced catapults are fitted, one forward and one set obliquely across the angled deck. Some modification proved

necessary to accommodate the late purchase of two E-2C Hawkeye airborne early warning (AEW) aircraft.

The customary composition of the air group-attack/bombers, fighters and AEW, reflects the downgrading of anti-submarine warfare (ASW) since the end of the Cold War. Only two helicopters are thus usually carried, and neither necessarily fitted for ASW.

The primary area defence SAM systems are located in deep, box-like sponsons that appear to be vulnerable to slamming in heavy seas.

Electronics are comprehensive, the suite including air and surface search radar, missile fire control, navigation and a laser-based deck landing system. The only guns are four multiple 20mm/0.79in Giat mountings for close-in defence.

The stern configuration is unusual, housing towed-array and variable-depth sonars as well as towed-decoy/anti-torpedo devices.

The much-delayed Rafale fighter programme will see final deliveries only in 2007, to finally replace the Etendards.

Charles de Gaulle

Built: DCN, Brest
Commissioned: May 18, 2001
Displacement: 37,250 tonnes/36,600 tons (standard); 42,750 tonnes/42,000 tons (full load)
Length: 238m/780ft 4in (at waterline); 261.5m/857ft 4in (overall)
Beam: 31.5m/103ft 3in
Draught: 8.7m/28ft 6in (mean)
Aircraft: 34 plus 2 helicopters (currently 20 x Super Etendard, 12 x Rafale F1, 2 x E-2C Hawkeye, and 2 x AS 322 or equivalent)
Flight deck: 261.5 x 64.4m/857ft 4in x 211ft 2in)
Armament: 4 octuple SAAM/F launchers, 2 sextuple Matra Sadral PDMS launchers
Machinery: 2 K15 reactors, 2 sets geared steam turbines, 2 shafts
Power: 61,200kW/82,000shp
Speed: 27 knots
Fuel: Nuclear
Range: Indefinite between recoring at 25-year intervals
Armour: Not known
Complement: 1,910 men, including aircrew

Balloon and seaplane carriers

Despite its nation's poor industrial base, the Imperial Russian Navy was always ready to embrace new technologies. Mine and torpedo warfare was thus followed by several, uncoordinated ventures involving the lofting and towing of balloons by warships (not to mention man-lifting kites). Stated objectives were the direction of gunfire, spotting for mines and to experiment in signalling.

The Russo-Japanese War of 1904–05 gave added impetus and, in May 1904, the armoured cruiser *Rossia* became the first warship to routinely use a kite balloon to extend her horizon while on an operational cruise.

Later that year the veteran passenger liner *Russ* was comprehensively modified for the deployment of nine balloons of three types. Dedicated and fully equipped for this function, she may lay claim to being the world's first true aviation ship. She was also a platform in the pioneering use of aerial photography.

On their arrival, heavier-than-air machines were greeted by the navy in equal fashion. Flying was conducted from 1910, with the first aircraft acquired soon after. Early reliance on small Curtiss-built flying boats was broken by the introduction of the domestically designed Grigorovich, which served aboard ship and from shore stations.

ABOVE: **The M-5 was one of an evolving series of flying boats designed by Dmitri Pavlovich Grigorovich. Production runs of several hundred were made of the M-5, M-9 and M-15. Each type had a tail fin of distinctive shape.**

During World War I, a single but very active seaplane carrier served with the Baltic Fleet. She was the 3,800-gross registered ton *Orlitza*, a converted merchantman with steel-and-canvas hangars covering either well deck to give accommodation for half a dozen aircraft.

Based on Sevastopol, however, and part of the Black Sea Fleet, was a properly constituted aviation squadron of three Russian and, later, several Romanian vessels. Their aircraft were used offensively as well as in fleet and military cooperation. The best equipped was thought to have been the *Romania*.

ABOVE: **M-5s were used in reconnaissance, spotting and bombing missions. They had an endurance approaching five hours maximum but, being poorly armed, needed to fly with escort, making single, ship-based aircraft vulnerable.**

Romania

Built: At. et Ch. de la Loire, St. Nazaire
Commissioned: 1904
Registered tonnage: 3,793grt; 1,340 net
Length: 108.9m/356ft 10in (overall)
Beam: 12.8m/41ft 10in
Draught: 4.4m/14ft 6in
Aircraft: Up to 4 flying boats
Flight deck: None
Armament: Possibly 4 x 152mm/6in, and
  4 x 76mm/3in guns
Machinery: 2 sets vertical triple expansion,
  5 boilers, 2 shafts
Power: 5,369kW/7,200ihp

227

Moskva class

Given the known range of the early Polaris missiles, it was apparent that to target the west Russian heartland, a western SSBN would need to operate either in the hostile and shallow White Sea (effectively a Soviet lake) or in the safer and more benign waters of the eastern Mediterranean. The *Moskva* design was therefore developed to operate primarily with the Soviet Black Sea Fleet, deploying a powerful force of anti-submarine (AS) helicopters to isolate and destroy an SSBN at the very earliest opportunity. As the landlocked Mediterranean would be dominated by hostile air power, a considerable anti-aircraft (AA) armament was shipped for the area defence of both ship and her support group. For defence against a surface threat, a Moskva would depend upon her escort.

These ingredients resulted in a unique design solution, comparable only with the more conventional French *Jeanne d'Arc* or the Italian *Vittorio Veneto*. Like them, however, the after end is dedicated to aviation, the forward end to multi-purpose armament.

To maximize the after-end capacity on limited dimensions, designers developed a hull which attained its maximum waterline width aft of amidships, maintaining this width to a point well aft. The resulting hangar was wide and spacious as, through moderate flaring, was the flight deck above. Although

ABOVE: The *Moskva*'s Kamor Ka-25 ("Hormone") helicopters were of three variants; Type A for ASW, Type B for mid-range targeting of long range ship-to-ship missiles (SSM) and Type C for general utility activities.

bold, the solution was not entirely satisfactory for the forward end, with its narrow waterplane, supported the considerable mass of armament, while the broad waterplane of the after end bore only the far lesser weight of hangar and aircraft. The result was a persistent trim by the bows, giving the pair, despite their prestigious names, a reputation as poor seakeepers in adverse sea states.

Their career, however, was most effectively circumscribed by the apparently unanticipated arrival of V/STOL. The introduction of the Harrier *doppelgänger*, the Yak-36 ("Forger"),

ABOVE: The duel functions of the *Moskva* design are sharply demarcated. Note how the plan attains its maximum width well aft in order to maximize flight deck area. LEFT: Known to the West as Top Sail, the enormous antenna of 3-D radar dominates the profile. The general impression is one of a huge fort-like superstructure.

LEFT: **Forward and below the Top Sail antenna are a Head Net C air search radar and two Head Light director radars for the SA-N-3 launchers. Note one SA-N-3 ("Goblet") launcher in the elevated position. Pendant numbers were often changed.** ABOVE: **The wave formation around the bows does not indicate the presence of a large bulb. Any installation is, therefore, likely to be small, of medium frequency and of limited range.**

saw the *Moskva* acting as trials ship for its evaluation. The massive superstructure, a barrier across the forward end of the flight deck, totally precluded any fuel-saving rolling take-off, stamping the ships as "helicopter only".

Forward, the ships fairly bristled with both AA and AS weaponry. In the superfiring positions were two, twin-pedestal launchers for the SA-N-3 ("Goblet") area defence AA missile with a 30km/18.6-mile range. Further redundancy was provided through each launcher having its own director.

Further forward was the smaller, twin-pedestal launcher of the SUW-N-1 AS stand-off system, capable of targeting a submerged target with a conventional or nuclear charge at

ranges of up to 24km/14.9 miles. This was backed by AS torpedo tubes amidships (later removed) and, right in the eyes of the ship, two of the venerable and well-trusted, 12-barrelled RBU-6000 AS rocket launchers (although, if the ship was close enough to use them she, herself, would be in dire danger from the submarine being hunted).

The dipping sonars deployed by the helicopters were backed by a medium/low-frequency unit mounted at the ship's forefoot and variable-depth sonars deployed from the stern gallery, below the flight deck.

Condemned by reduction in the Russian Fleet, the *Moskva* was discarded in 1995 and the *Leningrad* in 1992.

ABOVE: **Accommodation and maintenance facilities for helicopters are located in the superstructure and beneath the flight deck. Note the towed, variable-depth sonar (VDS) housed in the transom.**

Moskva class

Class: *Moskva*, Nikolaev South, commissioned 1967; *Leningrad*, Nikolaev South, commissioned 1968
Displacement: 15,200 tonnes/14,900 tons (standard); 18,950 tonnes/18,600 tons (full load)
Length: 179m/586ft 10in (at waterline); 190m/622ft 11in (overall)
Beam: 26m/85ft 3in
Draught: 7.6m/24ft 10in (standard); 8.5m/27ft 11in (full load)
Aircraft: 14 "Hormone" (Ka-25) helicopter equivalents
Flight deck: 86 x 34.1m/282ft x 111ft 9in
Armament: 2 x SA-N-3, 1 x SUW-N-1, 2 x RBU-6000, and 4 x 57mm/2.24in guns
Machinery: Geared steam turbines, 4 boilers, 2 shafts
Power: 74,600kW/100,000shp
Speed: 30 knots
Fuel: 2,800 tonnes/2,750 tons
Range: 25,930km/14,000nm at 12 knots
Armour: Not known
Complement: 830 men

LEFT AND BELOW: **A major development of the Moskva design, that of the Kievs includes a through flight deck to allow V/STOL operation and an armament more heavily oriented toward anti-surface ship warfare.**

Kiev class

Although an extrapolation of the Moskva, the leap in scale to the Kiev was very bold for a fleet that had never previously specified a through-deck carrier. Best appreciated by her Russian categorization as a Large Anti-submarine Cruiser she was designed to operate only helicopters and V/STOL aircraft. There were no catapults or arrester gear, precluding the deployment of conventional, higher-performance machines. As with the Moskvas the forward end was dedicated to armament and the after end to aviation.

To operate efficiently, V/STOL fighters require a rolling take-off. With the forward end fully populated, the preferred design solution was an angled flight deck and an island superstructure. Contrary to normal practice, the flight path was all on the port side so that, even with a moderate, 4.5-degree

angle, the deck had a considerable overhang, thought to be simply counterbalanced by the island, which was massive by usual carrier standards. The layout left the starboard side and the centreline area abreast the island free for parking and marshalling. The outfit lacked some redundancy in that only one of the elevators was large enough for a V/STOL aircraft.

The ship's main weapon system was her AS helicopters, for which seven "spots" were provided on the flight path. They were, of course, only the sharp end of an AS suite that included also a large, bow-mounted, low-frequency sonar, variable-depth sonar (VDS) deployed from a stern gallery, and, on the foredeck, a SUW-N-1 stand-off system and two RBU-6000 rocket projectors.

Intended to hunt down SSBNs in the open ocean, a Kiev could expect to be opposed by American carriers. As her dozen or so V/STOL fighters would have availed her little, her major weapon was the SS-N-12 ("Sandbox") anti-ship missile, eight canister launchers for which were located forward. This

LEFT: **A Kiev bow wave is typical of that resulting from a large sonar bulb, housing a physically large, low-frequency, long-range unit. This is complemented by a higher-frequency VDS, deployed from the stern. In a submarine hunt, helicopters would deploy their "dunking sonars" and share data with the ship via a single data link.**

weapon's 500km/311-mile range required specialist helicopters to give mid-course correction to target. Two reload missiles were provided for each launcher.

As in the Moskvas, two SA-N-3 area defence anti-aircraft (AA) systems were provided. In the first two Kievs, these were complemented by the short-range SA-N-4 ("Gecko") AA missile, whose launcher retracted down into a small silo. As "last-ditch" defence against incoming anti-ship missiles, each quadrant of the ship was covered by a pair of 30mm/1.18in Gatling-style guns, each group working independently with its own adjacent-director.

Typical of Soviet designs, that of the *Kiev* gave the impression of being over-armed and overcrowded despite her not inconsiderable displacement. Certainly, the flight deck enjoyed limited freeboard and was probably wet by usual standards. Refits saw various baffles and windbreaks being provided to protect one weapon system from the effects of another. Redundancy in radar and director systems also allowed selection to avoid the effects of interaction.

Completed later, and to an improved specification, the *Admiral Gorshkov* (ex-*Baku*) currently awaits transfer to India. The remainder were discarded, the *Minsk* in 1992, *Novorossiysk* in 1993 and *Kiev* in 1994.

ABOVE: **Compared with the *Kiev* opposite, the *Minsk* has had the port sponsons extended and an improved leading edge fitted to the angled deck. The squared-off stem head houses a retractable radar associated with the guidance of the SS-N-12 ("Sandbox") anti-ship missiles.**

ABOVE: **With the superstructure mass to one side and the assorted large weaponry in front, the leading end of the angled deck has suffered problems with turbulence, evidenced by the addition of wind deflector plates and altered configurations. Note what appears to be an adjustable flow plate fitted transversely.**

Kiev class

Class: *Kiev*, Nikolaev South, commissioned May 1975; *Minsk*, Nikolaev South, commissioned February 1978; *Novorossiysk*, Nikolaev South, commissioned September 1982

Displacement: 36,650 tonnes/36,000 tons (standard); 43,250 tonnes/42,500 tons (full load)

Length: 249.5m/818ft (at waterline); 273.5m/896ft 9in (overall)

Beam: 32.7m/107ft 3in

Draught: 8.5m/27ft 10in (standard); 10m/32ft 9in (full load)

Aircraft: 14 or 17 "Hormone" (Ka-25) or "Helix" (Ka-27) helicopter equivalents and 12/13 "Forger" (Yak-38) V/STOL equivalents

Flight deck (irregular): 185 x 20m/606ft 6in x 65ft 7in (flight path)

Armament: 8 x SS-N-12, 2 x SA-N-3, 2 x SA-N-4, 1 x SUW-N-1, 2 x RBU-6000, and 4 x 76mm/3in and 8 x 30mm/1.18in guns

Machinery: Geared steam turbines, 8 boilers, 4 shafts

Power: 149,000kW/200,000shp

Speed: 32 knots

Fuel: 7,640 tonnes/7,500 tons

Range: 24,080km/13,000nm at 18 knots

Armour: Not known

Complement: Not known

Admiral Kuznetsov

Conceived during the Communist era, the *Admiral Kuznetsov* began life as the *Leonid Brezhnev*, then briefly becoming the *Tbilisi*. Although she was completed, her only sister, *Varyag*, was abandoned in 1993 when a reported 70 per cent complete, and acquired by Chinese interests.

Her design stems directly from that of the Kiev class, enlarged and with the major difference that the earlier anti-ship missile container/launchers that demanded the whole foredeck on the Kievs have been replaced by vertical launch silos. This improvement has permitted a through flush deck for the first time in Russian naval practice.

Despite her size and conventional layout, the ship is limited in the size and weight of aircraft embarked through the lack of a catapult. Nonetheless, she operates high-performance fighters; whole loaded take-off is assisted by a prominent forward "ski-jump". For their recovery, the angled deck is equipped with conventional arrester wires.

At a time when Western fleets are moving away from old, Cold War imperatives to equip for more flexible amphibious and littoral warfare, the Russian fleet has not assumed any discernable new role. The *Kuznetsov*, therefore, is still geared to leading a powerful ASW surface group, for which she provides reconnaissance, fighter cover, and long-range, anti-ship missile defence. Half of her aircraft accommodation is devoted to ASW helicopters.

Her current air wing comprises, typically, Su-27 ("Flanker") fleet air defence fighters and Su-25 ("Frogfoot") fighters in their hook-equipped UTG variant. These two-seaters are intended for ground attack. There are nine spots on deck for helicopter operations.

TOP: **Capable of operating in conventional take-off and land (CTOL) as well as V/STOL modes, the *Kuznetsov* was a fully-developed fleet carrier that had been evolved in a very short space of time from the Moskvas.** ABOVE: **Known to NATO as the "Flanker", the Sukhoi Su-27K is also known, somewhat confusingly, as the Su-33. It first operated from the ship in November 1989.**

The *Kuznetsov* has the usual layered armament encountered in Russian ships. The vertical launch silos for the SS-N-19s are beneath the forward flight deck and normally closed-off with flush-fitting covers. With its 483km/300-mile range, the missile requires aerial mid-course correction to position it for its terminal active radar homing phase.

The SA-N-9 missile ranges only to about 97km/60 miles, the ship being dependent for area defence on either her escorts or her aircraft. She has no less than eight point-defence systems, comprising short-range 7km/4.5-mile SAMs in a common mounting with a pair of 30mm/1.18in Gatling-type guns. These are backed by six sextuple 30mm/1.18in mountings, each with its own director.

FAR LEFT: **Besides attack fighters such as Su-27K (Su-33), seen here, and the Su-25 ("Frogfoot"), the *Kuznetsov* carried up to 18 Ka-27 ("Helix") helicopters, of which** half a dozen appear here. Of two variants, those embarked were the Ka-27 PL ("Helix-A") ASW and Ka-27 PS ("Helix-D") planeguard/search and rescue. ABOVE: Su-27Ks (Su-33s) demonstrating non-catapult-assisted take-off from the *Kuznetsov*. Outer wings, horizontal tail surfaces and tail cone all fold to reduce aircraft size for stowage.

The massive island is configured around the many electronics systems and follows closely the design of that of the *Baku*, the much-delayed fourth unit of the Kiev class. Much of its available area is devoted to the location, one per quadrant, of the four large, rectangular planar arrays of the ship's 3-D air search radar.

A full 7-degree angled flight deck is provided, with a pronounced overhang. There are no centreline elevators, both of those fitted being deck-edge units, one forward of, and one abaft, the island. The freeboard appears to be rather low although the ski jump would largely prevent loose water on the forward flight deck. The deep sponsons housing the four SA-N-9 groups look vulnerable to slamming.

In 1988, the Russians laid down the *Ulyanov*, the first of a new class of 75,000-tonne/73,815-ton vessels. She may have been nuclear powered but would certainly have had steam catapults, permitting her to deploy heavier aircraft. She was approaching launching stage when scrapped in about 1993.

RIGHT: **A philatelic miniature sheet commemorating 300 years of the Russian Navy, founded by Peter the Great, who had studied as a practical shipwright in Deptford and Zaandam.** BELOW: **Seen still wearing her completion name of *Tbilisi*, the *Kuznetsov* is fitted with a ski-jump bow of almost caricature proportions. She also carries a heavy anti-surface ship punch in the shape of the 12 vertical-launch SS-N-19 ("Shipwreck") missiles.**

Admiral Kuznetsov

Built: Nikolaev South
Commissioned: January 21, 1991
Displacement: 46,750 tonnes/45,900 tons (standard); 59,550 tonnes/58,500 tons (full load)
Length: 280m/918ft (at waterline); 304.5m/998ft 4in (overall)
Beam: 37m/121ft 4in
Draught: 10.5m/34ft 5in (mean)
Aircraft: 60 maximum; usually 18 x Su-27, 4 x Su-25, 15 x Ka-27, 2 x Ka-31
Flight deck: 304.5 x 70m/998ft 4in x 229ft 6in
Armament: 12 x SS-N-19 ("Shipwreck"), 4 x sextuple SA-N-9 ("Gauntlet"), 8 x CADS-N-1 PDMS, 6 x sextuple 30mm/1.18in CIWS, and 2 x RBU-12000 ASW mortars
Power: 150,000kW/200,000shp
Speed: 30 knots
Fuel: Not known
Range: 15,740km/8,500nm at 18 knots
Armour: Not known
Complement: 2,950 men, including aircrew

Albatross

Built: Cockatoo Docks & Eng. Pty, Ltd, Sydney
Commissioned: January 17, 1929
Displacement: 4,890 tonnes/4,800 tons (standard); 6,210 tonnes/6,100 tons (full load)
Length: 128.7m/422ft (bp); 135.3m/443ft 6in (overall)
Beam: 18.6m/61ft
Draught: 5m/16ft 6in (full load)
Aircraft: Up to 9 floatplanes or amphibians
Flight deck: None
Armament (as built): 4 x 119mm/4.7in (4 single), and 1 x quadruple 2pdr pom-pom guns
Machinery: Geared steam turbines, 4 boilers, 2 shafts
Power: 8,950kW/12,000shp
Speed: 22 knots
Fuel: 1,020 tonnes/1,000 tons
Armour: None
Complement: 370 men

Albatross

Built in Australia, the *Albatross* was an aviation ship forward and a colonial sloop aft. Vaguely modelled on the British *Ark Royal* (I) she was given a generous forward freeboard, the high forecastle containing a hangar for up to nine aircraft. These were accessed *Ark Royal* fashion via a hatch served by two cranes. A third crane transferred the aircraft to a centreline catapult.

Her ability to patrol and police large areas caused the Royal Navy to acquire her late in 1938. She spent much of World War II employed in this role in the relatively peaceful Indian Ocean. Postwar, she was sold for commercial use.

Vengeance

Built: Swan, Hunter, Wallsend
Commissioned: January 15, 1945
Displacement: 13,750 tonnes/13,500 tons (standard); 18,850 tonnes/18,500 tons (full load)
Length: 192.2m/630ft (bp); 211.4m/693ft 7in (overall)
Beam: 24.4m/80ft
Draught: 6.5m/21ft 4in (standard); 7.5/24ft 6in (full load)
Aircraft: 30+
Flight deck: 207.4 x 24.4m/680 x 80ft
Armament: 16 x 40mm/1.57in, and 24 x 2pdr pom-pom guns
Machinery: Geared steam turbines, 4 boilers, 2 shafts
Power: 29,850kW/40,000shp
Speed: 25 knots
Fuel: 3,260 tonnes/3,200 tons
Range: 22,220km/12,000nm at 14 knots
Armour: None
Complement: 1,320 men

Vengeance

Although the Royal Australian Navy had acquired both the *Sydney* (ex-*Terrible*) and *Melbourne* (ex-*Majestic*) from the British, the latter ship remained in European waters for the duration of the Korean War. Hard worked, the *Sydney* required a consort, so the Australians took the *Vengeance* on loan for two and a half years (1953–55). This allowed sea training for aircrew to continue pending the arrival of the *Melbourne*. As the *Vengeance* was never purchased, she received no change of name under Australian colours.

Worked-up again to operational status, she returned briefly to British service before being purchased by the Brazilian Navy as the *Minas Gerais*.

ABOVE: **An early picture of** *Sydney*
**at Portsmouth. She retained her
tripod mast and plain bridge
front but later acquired a light
mast by the funnel, supporting
the antenna of a homing beacon.**
FAR LEFT: *La vie quotidienne.*
**Later-model, clipped-wing
Fireflies await their turn for
catapulting on what looks like
a leisurely day's practice flying.**
LEFT: *Sydney* **wears her number
as a Sea Fury, resplendent in Korean War stripes,
awaits take-off. The piston-engined Sea Fury found
itself fighting Soviet-built MiGs while supporting
Fireflies in ground attack.**

Sydney

The Pacific war of 1942–45 was fought uncomfortably close to Australia, and its being decided principally by carrier-borne air power was not lost on the Royal Australian Navy (RAN), which therefore acquired the *Majestic*-class Light Fleet Carrier *Terrible* in December 1948. Renamed *Sydney*, she arrived in home waters during the following May, about a year before the outbreak of the war in Korea.

The greatest immediate contribution that the Western allies could make to stem the enemy onslaught was through air power and, lacking facilities ashore, this was necessarily carrier-based. Drastic post-World War II reductions in fleet strengths, however, had left few operational Allied warships in the Far East. For its part, the Royal Navy managed to maintain a single light carrier off the Korean west coast and, during 1951, invited the Australians to take a four-month shift.

In severe winter weather, *Sydney* operated her composite air group of two squadrons of Fireflies (two-seat, anti-submarine, reconnaissance and strike aircraft) and one of Hawker Sea Furies (single-seat, fighter-bomber). There was also aboard a lone US Navy helicopter and crew, the first helicopter to work from an Australian ship.

Of 64 days on station, 43 were flown, the *Sydney* chalking up 2,366 sorties for the loss of three pilots and 16 aircraft to enemy action.

In April 1955, shortly before the commissioning of the *Melbourne* into the RAN, the *Sydney* was reduced to training status. By 1962 she was in reserve, but was re-activated as a transport to assist the Australian army's involvement in Malaya. She repeated this service in Vietnam but, at the end of that war, she was sold out and scrapped in 1976, a further example of the longevity of what began as an emergency design.

Sydney

Built: HM Dockyard, Devonport
Commissioned: February 5, 1949
Displacement: 15,375 tonnes/15,100 tons
(standard); 19,850 tonnes/19,500 tons (full load)
Length: 192.2m/630ft (bp); 212m/695ft (overall)
Beam: 24.4m/80ft
Draught: 6.6m/21ft 6in (standard); 7.6m/25ft
(full load)
Aircraft: About 36
Flight deck: 207.4 x 24.4m/680 x 80ft
Armament: 30 x 40mm/1.57in guns
Machinery: Geared steam turbines, 4 boilers,
2 shafts
Power: 29,850kW/40,000shp
Speed: 25 knots
Fuel: 3,540 tonnes/3,480 tons
Range: Not known
Armour: None
Complement: 1,230 men

ABOVE: **The year of 1977, and** *Melbourne*'s **men are mustered for a special occasion. Note the American-style "21" identification on the flight deck, forward.** RIGHT: **As with other things naval, the Australians steadily moved away from British-sourced equipment. Following her major 1969 refit, the** *Melbourne* **emerged with uprated catapult, Philips electronics and an air wing comprising A-4 Skyhawks, S-2 Trackers and Sea King helicopters.**

Melbourne

Of the six incomplete *Majestic*-class Light Fleet Carriers, the name ship had to wait until 1949 before being taken in hand to remodel her as a "jet-capable" carrier. This being a period of significant innovation in carrier technology, the completion process took some six years and several changes of plan, eventually including the major advances of angled deck, steam catapult and mirror landing sight.

Early angled decks such as these were set at a shallow offset of only 5 degrees or so to the centreline, the flight path still involving much of the ship's length and, therefore, deck parking space. One advantage for a small carrier, however, was that it limited the size of the port-side overhand and consequent weight distribution problems.

Jet aircraft had poorer low-speed characteristics than earlier piston-engined machines, their higher landing speed requiring upgrading of the ship's

arrester gear. Launch velocities also needed to be higher, demanding the steam catapult.

Rechristened *Melbourne*, the ship was completed in 1955 as the new flagship of the RAN. She was able to deploy the Sea Venom, the first British all-weather jet carrier fighter/strike aircraft. Most of her remaining aircraft were turbo-prop Gannets, reflecting the importance attached to AS operations during the Cold War.

Helicopters were now becoming widely accepted and, during the 1960s, replaced fixed-wing AS aircraft in the *Melbourne*'s air wing. With the increasing "Americanization" of the RAN, however, her flight deck was strengthened during the 1970s and catapult replaced in order to re-equip with A-4 Skyhawk fighters

and the 12.2-tonne/27,000lb S-2 Tracker twin-engined AS aircraft. Sea King helicopters were also shipped in numbers proportional to mission.

At the end of the ship's operational life in 1983, the Australian government decided that she would be scrapped without replacement.

Melbourne

Built: Vickers-Armstrong, Barrow
Commissioned: November 8, 1955
Displacement: 16,400 tonnes/16,100 tons (standard); 20,620 tonnes/20,250 tons (full load)
Length: 192.2m/630ft (bp); 214m/701ft 6in (overall)
Beam: 24.4m/80ft
Draught: 8.0m/26ft 3in (full load)
Aircraft: About 24
Flight deck: 210.5 x 32m/690 x 105ft
Armament: 25 x 40mm/1.57in guns
Machinery: Geared steam turbines, 4 boilers, 2 shafts
Power: 29,850kW/40,000shp
Speed: 24 knots
Fuel: 3,050 tonnes/3,000 tons
Range: Not known
Armour: None
Complement: 1,250 men

ABOVE: **Alterations and additions to the** *Melbourne*'s **island, particularly the acquisition of a lattice mast, did nothing for the previously classic "Light Fleet" profile.**

Warrior

Starting almost from scratch, the Royal Canadian Navy (RCN) evolved, largely by its own magnificent effort, into one of the world's largest fleets between 1939 and 1945. Although remembered largely as a small-ship navy, inseparable from the North Atlantic convoy war, the RCN was already operating modern cruisers by 1945 and, with first-hand experience of the effect of naval air power on the conduct of the Atlantic war, was keen to acquire its own carrier. Its eventual choice, the Royal Navy's *Majestic*-class Light Fleet Carrier *Powerful*, had to be completed to Canadian requirements, and so in the interim the brand-new *Colossus*-class *Warrior* was loaned for training purposes. In this role, she served 1946–48.

TOP AND ABOVE: **Almost certainly taken at the same time, this pair of pictures is particularly interesting in accurately recording the *Warrior*'s unusual counter-shaded camouflage scheme, applied despite her completion early in 1946. Four shades appear to have been used, with near-white around the counter (and even below boats) ranging to darkest grey over normally illuminated surfaces. On this particular day, however, the light has defeated the planned effect.**

ABOVE: **A Fairey Firefly Mk.4 in Royal Canadian Navy (RCN) colours. It probably belongs to No.825 Squadron, which was on detachment to the RCN at this time.**

Warrior

See also *Independencia* (Argentina)
Built: Harland & Wolff, Belfast
Commissioned: January 24, 1946
Displacement: 14,250 tonnes/14,000 tons (standard); 19,950 tonnes/19,600 tons (full load)
Length: 192.2m/630ft (bp); 212m/695ft (overall)
Beam: 24.4m/80ft
Draught: 6.6m/21ft 6in (standard); 7.2m/23ft 6in (full load)
Aircraft: 35
Flight deck: 207.4 x 22.9m/680 x 75ft
Armament: 24 x 2pdr pom-pom guns, and 17 x 40mm/1.57in guns
Machinery: Geared steam turbines, 4 boilers, 2 shafts
Power: 29,850kW/40,000shp
Speed: 25 knots
Fuel: 3,250 tonnes/3,190 tons
Range: 15,740km/8,500nm at 20 knots
Armour: None
Complement: 1,100 men

LEFT: **Only ever serving under Canadian colours, here the *Magnificent* edges into an empty Grand Harbour in Malta. Note how the wings of the lone Sea Fury, right aft, fold upwards, while those of the line of Fireflies fold backwards.**

Magnificent

Built: Harland & Wolff, Belfast
Commissioned: March 21, 1948
Displacement: 14,760 tonnes/14,500 tons (standard); 19,950 tonnes/19,600 tons (full load)
Length: 192.2m/630ft (bp); 212.8m/698ft (overall)
Beam: 24.4m/80ft
Draught: 6.1m/20ft (standard); 7.2m/23ft 6in (full load)
Aircraft: About 36
Flight deck: 208.9 x 22.9m/685 x 75ft
Armament: 28 x 40mm/1.57in guns
Machinery: Geared steam turbines, 4 boilers, 2 shafts
Power: 29,850kW/40,000shp
Speed: 25 knots
Fuel: 3,510 tonnes/3,450 tons
Range: 17,320km/9,350nm at 12 knots
Armour: None
Complement: 1,170 men

L oan of the *Warrior* to the Royal Canadian Navy had to terminate in 1948, before the Canadian government finalized the sale of the incomplete *Powerful*. For continuity in training and experience, therefore, a second Light Fleet Carrier, the *Majestic*-class *Magnificent*, was lent from 1948. Because the *Powerful*'s remodelling was to full current standards, it was subject

to several changes of design. The process being protracted, it was necessary eventually to extend the loan of the *Magnificent* until 1957. Although the RCN was active during the Korean War, the carrier was not committed. The ship never served in the Royal Navy for, following her return, she remained in reserve until, lacking any foreign buyer, she was scrapped.

LEFT: **The remodelled *Bonaventure* makes an interesting comparison with the *Magnificent* (above). She was unique in acquiring the faired sponsons, forward and aft on either side, to support her new twin 76mm/3in mountings.**

Bonaventure

Built: Harland & Wolff, Belfast
Commissioned: January 17, 1957
Length: 192.2m/630ft (bp); 214.9m/704ft 6in (overall)
Beam: 24.4m/80ft
Draught: 7.6m/25ft (full load)
Aircraft: 30+
Flight deck: 208.9 x 34.3m/685 x 112ft 6in
Armament: 8 x 76mm/3in (4 double), later 4 x 76mm/3in guns
Machinery: Geared steam turbines, 4 boilers, 2 shafts
Power: 29,850kW/40,000shp
Speed: 24.5 knots
Fuel: 3,150 tonnes/3,100 tons
Range: Not known
Armour: None
Complement: 1,200 men

P urchased outright by the Canadian government in 1952, the *Majestic*-class Light Fleet carrier *Powerful* then underwent a five-year transformation into the *Bonaventure.* She acquired a strengthened, 8-degree angled deck, upgraded arrester gear and steam catapult to operate American-sourced jet fighters and heavy anti-submarine aircraft. Her armament comprised American 76mm/3in 70s and her

enlarged island supported two lattice masts carrying a full range of American radars. Stretched to her limits, she could not efficiently operate later carrier aircraft and, by the early 1960s, had downgraded to a pure anti-submarine carrier, operating only helicopters. With the continued drawdown of the navy due to changing political imperatives, she was discarded shortly after a major refit in 1970 and was not replaced.

Giuseppe Miraglia

During 1924–27, the Spezia yard refashioned the incomplete coastal liner *Cittá di Messina* as the aviation ship *Giuseppe Miraglia*. The Italian Navy's first such, she was built up amidships with hangars before and abaft her superstructure. These were accessed by doors in the transverse screen bulkheads and were served by four folding cranes. Forward and aft were prominent catapults.

Besides undertaking experimental work, the *Miraglia* serviced the catapult flights found aboard all major Italian warships. She served spells as a fleet transport and, towards the end of her life, as a depot ship. The *Miraglia*'s period of greatest utility was in the mid-1930s, during the Italian conquest of Abyssinia (now Ethiopia). She is believed to have been scrapped following World War II.

Giuseppe Miraglia

Built: Not known
Commissioned: 1927
Displacement: 4,970 tonnes/4,880 tons (standard)
Length: 115m/377ft (unspecified)
Beam: 15m/49ft 2in
Draught: 5.2m/17ft (standard)
Aircraft: About 20
Flight deck: None
Armament: 4 x 102mm/4in guns
Machinery: Geared steam turbines, 8 boilers, 2 shafts
Power: 8,950kW/12,000shp
Speed: 21 knots
Fuel: Not known
Range: Not known
Armour: None
Complement: 180 men

LEFT: Seen from a British battleship, the *Miraglia* is near the end of her career. Her catapults and aircraft derricks have been removed and she is carrying a deck cargo.

Bolzano, proposed

Torpedoed and fire-damaged, the heavy cruiser *Bolzano* was stripped for conversion to a fast transport for carriage of supplies to North Africa. With all armament except light anti-aircraft weapons removed, her defence lay in a dozen Reggiane fighter aircraft. All top-hamper forward of the after funnel would be razed, the aircraft being parked along

the centreline and moved forward sequentially for launch from two catapults set in the bows. There was no means of recovery, aircraft being expected to land ashore. Despite the loss of her forward boiler space, the *Bolzano* would still be capable of 25 knots. The ship was destroyed by "human torpedoes" before completion.

Bolzano, proposed

Built: Ansaldo, Genoa
Commissioned: August 19, 1933
Displacement: 11,250 tonnes/11,050 tons (standard); 14,150 tonnes/13,900 tons (full load)
Length: 194.3m/637ft (bp); 197m/645ft 10in (overall)
Beam: 20.6m/67ft 6in
Draught: 6.1m/20ft (standard)
Aircraft: 12
Flight deck: None
Armament: 10 x 89mm/3.5in, and 20 x 37mm/1.46in guns
Machinery: Geared steam turbines, 8 boilers, 4 shafts
Power: 89,500kW/120,000shp
Speed: 25 knots
Fuel: Not known
Range: Not known
Armour: 70mm/2.7in (vertical belt); 25–50mm/ 1–2in (protective deck)
Complement: Not known

LEFT: Stemmed in dry dock, the *Bolzano* is seen shortly before her near-fatal torpedoing. Note the extensions built along either side of the upper deck, probably for minelaying.

TOP: **Structurally near-complete, but lacking vital equipment including catapults and compatible aircraft, the *Aquila* lies at Genoa in 1943.** ABOVE: **Although guarded by German soldiers following the Italian capitulation of September 1943, the *Aquila* was destroyed by a combination of Allied bombing and sabotage.**

Aquila and *Sparviero*

Allied with Germany, buoyed with confidence, Mussolini announced in 1938 a supplementary naval construction programme to protect Italy's "rights and interests in the Mediterranean". He emphasized the fleet's duties in "maintaining communications with Italy's immense overseas possessions" and winning access to the oceans beyond the "encircled" Mediterranean. Having thus effectively defined the need for a true blue-water navy, the Duce and his naval staff resolutely ignored their planners' advice by excluding aircraft carriers. Given its central geographical location, they repeatedly pointed out, "Italy *was* an aircraft carrier".

Following June 1940, naval action with the Royal Navy adequately demonstrated the folly of reliance on land-based naval air support, yet it still took a further year for the Duce to relent and to authorize conversion of a passenger liner.

During the 1930s wiser heads had tentatively identified the liners *Roma* (32,583 gross registered tons – grt) and *Augustus* (32,650grt) as suitable for this purpose and the former was taken in hand by her original builders during July 1941. The result, renamed *Aquila*, was a stylish vessel with full flight deck and cantilevered, starboard-side island that showed some influence from the designers of the *Graf Zeppelin*. Her appearance was marred somewhat by prominent bulges, added for both stability and protection. Incomplete at the Italian capitulation, the *Aquila* was sabotaged, scuttled, raised and scrapped by 1952.

Renamed *Sparviero*, the diesel-propelled *Augustus* would have received an austere, *Argus*-style conversion, flush-decked with no island. To avoid the necessity of remodelling her rather fine bow sections, the forward 25 per cent of the flight deck was narrowed to a mere take-off platform, supported on an open

structure. Work commenced as late as September 1942, however, and never progressed beyond the razing of the original upper decks. Like the *Aquila*, she was scuttled and then scrapped by 1947.

Aquila

Built: Ansaldo, Sestri Ponente
Commissioned: September 21, 1926
Displacement: 23,900 tonnes/23,500 tons (standard); 28,300 tonnes/27,800 tons (full load)
Length: 203.1m/666ft (bp); 231.2m/758ft (overall)
Beam: 29.5m/96ft 9in
Draught: 7.3m/24ft (standard)
Aircraft: About 36
Flight deck: 213.5 x 25m/700 x 82ft
Armament: 8 x 135mm/5.3in, and 12 x 65mm/2.6in guns
Machinery: Geared steam turbines, 8 boilers, 4 shafts
Power: 29,800kW/40,000shp
Speed: 20 knots
Fuel: 2,800 tonnes/2,750 tons
Range: 7,410km/4,000nm at 18 knots
Armour: 80mm/3.15in patches over magazines etc
Complement: About 1,500 men

ABOVE: **Reminiscent of that on the *Argus* (I), the conversion of the *Sparviero* would have been in no way as thorough as that of the *Aquila*. The forward section was no more than a flying-off ramp.**

Andrea Doria (I) class

Class: *Andrea Doria* (I), (C553), Tirreno, Riva Trigoso, commissioned February 23, 1964; *Caio Duilio* (C554), Navalmeccanica, Castellammare, commissioned November 30, 1964

Displacement: 6,620 tonnes/6,500 tons (standard); 7,430 tonnes/7,300 tons (full load)

Length: 144m/472ft 2in (bp); 149.3m/489ft 6in (overall)

Beam: 17.3m/56ft 9in

Draught: 5m/16ft 5in (standard); 7.5m/24ft 7in (full load)

Aircraft: 2/3 Augusta AB-212 ASW helicopters

Flight deck: 30 x 16m/98ft 4in x 52ft 6in

Armament: 1 x Standard SM-1 SAM system, 8 x 76mm/3in guns, 6 x ASW TT

Machinery: Geared steam turbine, 4 boilers, 2 shafts

Power: 44,750kW/60,000shp

Speed: 30 knots

Fuel: 1,120 tonnes/1,100 tons

Range: 11,110km/6,000nm at 15 knots

Armour: None

Complement: 480 men

Andrea Doria (I) class

Contemporary with the French *Jeanne d'Arc* and the Soviet Russian Moskvas, the Andrea Dorias reflected the powerful anti-submarine bias of Cold War warship design in the marriage of a cruiser-style forward end to an after end dedicated to helicopter aviation. The small helicopter of the day, the Agusta AB-212, was limited in capacity, and the fuel, data links, sonars and weaponry necessary to conduct a protracted submarine hunt were best shared between a flight of two aircraft with one stand-by. Accommodation for these and the bulky early guidance, storage and launch systems for the Standard SM-1 area defence SAM drove the ships' design parameters. Both ships were discarded in 1991–92 as their systems became obsolete.

Vittorio Veneto

Built: Navalmeccanica, Castellammare

Commissioned: April 30, 1969

Displacement: 8,300 tonnes/8,150 tons (standard); 9,620 tonnes/9,450 tons (full load)

Length: 170m/557ft 4in (bp); 179,6m/588ft 10in (overall)

Beam: 19.4m/63ft 7in

Draught: 5.5m/18ft (standard); 7.8m/25ft 7in (full load)

Aircraft: 6 Augusta AB-212 ASW helicopters

Flight deck: 40 x 18.5m/131ft 2in x 60ft 9in

Armament: 1 x Standard SM-1/ASROC launcher, 4 x Otomat SSM launchers, 8 x 76mm/3in and 6 x 40mm/1.57in guns

Machinery: Geared steam turbines, 4 boilers, 2 shafts

Power: 54,450kW/73,000shp

Speed: 31 knots

Fuel: 1,270 tonnes/1,250 tons

Range: 11,110km/6,000nm at 20 knots

Armour: None

Complement: 550 men

Vittorio Veneto

Carrying twice the number of helicopters, the *Vittorio Veneto* (C550) derives directly from the preceding Andrea Dorias. Having under-deck (as opposed to superstructure) hangaring, her after end has its freeboard raised by one deck. Fitted to coordinate a major submarine hunt, the ship can participate with AS torpedoes deployed either by ASROC launcher, or directly by torpedo tube. The ASROC launcher also handles Standard SM-1 SAM missiles. In the waist are four canister-launchers for Otomat SSMs. Space has also been found for no less than 14 single gun mountings. Space is saved by combining funnels and masts. She is to be retired in 2007.

Giuseppe Garibaldi

Built: Italcantieri, Monfalcone
Commissioned: September 30, 1985
Displacement: 9,570 tonnes/9,400 tons (standard); 13,440 tonnes/13,200 tons (full load)
Length: 162,8m/533ft 9in (bp); 180.2m/590ft 10in (overall)
Beam: 23.7m/77ft 9in
Draught: 6.7m/21ft 11in (full load)
Aircraft: Up to 12 (Sea King or Sea Harrier equivalents)
Flight deck: 173.8 x 30.4m/569ft 10in x 99ft 9in
Armament: 4 x Otomat SSM launchers, 2 x Octal Aspide SAM launchers, 6 x 40mm/1.57in guns, and 6 x ASW TT
Machinery: 4 gas turbines (LM 2500), 2 shafts
Power: 59,700kW/80,000shp
Speed: 30 knots
Fuel: Not known
Range: 12,960km/7,000nm at 20 knots
Armour: None
Complement: 575 men

Giuseppe Garibaldi

Designed primarily as an anti-submarine helicopter carrier, this very neat vessel can equally well deploy V/STOL aircraft. She is Italy's first through-deck carrier. Her flight deck is served by two elevators and, forward, has pronounced sheer as opposed to a "ski-jump". For her AS role she mounts a large low/medium-frequency sonar in a bulbous bow, but also has four canister-launched Otomat SSMs located on the quarters. At either end of the monolithic superstructure are octal launchers for Aspide/Sea Sparrow SAM missiles. The *Garibaldi*'s funding was facilitated by giving her a disaster-relief capability.

Andrea Doria (II)

The new carrier *Andrea Doria* (II) is intended to replace the *Vittorio Veneto* in 2007. Designed only for V/STOL and helicopter operation, she has a non-angled flight deck, no catapult or arrester gear. Two elevators are provided, one of them a starboard-side, deck-edge unit. Port-side, forward there is a "ski-jump".

Fitted to act as a command ship, the *Doria* can also assist in amphibious assault. On-board equipment includes four landing craft, two cranes, three lifts, and two roll-on, roll-off ramps. In this mode, aircraft would be carried only in deck parks. Future air wings will comprise the JSF (after 2012) and EH-101 helicopters.

Andrea Doria (II)

Built: Fincantieri, Riva Trigoso
Commissioning: 2007
Displacement: 27,000 tonnes/26,500 tons (full load)
Length: 215.8m/707ft 3in (at waterline); 234.5m/769ft (overall)
Beam: 29.5m/96ft 10in
Draught: 7.5m/24ft 8in (full load)
Aircraft: 8 Sea Harrier/JSF and 12 Sea King/ EH-101 equivalents
Flight deck: 184 x 34m/603ft 3in x 111ft 6in
Armament: 4 x 8-cell vertical-launch systems for Aster 15 SAM, 2 x CIWS
Machinery: 4 x LM 2500 gas turbines, 2 shafts
Power: 88,000kW/118,000shp
Speed: 30 knots
Fuel: Not known
Range: 12,960km /7,000nm at 16 knots
Armour: Not known
Complement: 700 men as a private ship

Seaplane carriers, mercantile

During World War I, the German High Seas Fleet (HSF) observed an overall policy different to that of the British Grand Fleet. The anticipated decisive arena was the North Sea and as the HSF was numerically the inferior force, its intentions were to let the British take the offensive, while stimulating the occasional set-piece action where a British formation might be caught at a disadvantage. There was, however, a secondary theatre of operations in the Baltic, where the German Navy worked offensively against a somewhat passive Russian fleet.

Possessing only one Zeppelin airship in 1914 and recognizing that land-based aircraft could as yet patrol only a limited distance offshore, the navy chartered commercial tonnage for the deployment

of seaplanes. This policy owed nothing to British initiatives, being undertaken completely in parallel and embracing an entirely different approach.

The British took up small, speedy vessels that, initially only primitively converted, worked directly with sections of the battle fleet. Only with time did the conversions become more sophisticated. In contrast, the Germans viewed aerial reconnaissance either as a routine measure or as a service to be undertaken ahead of a fleet operation. The choice of chartered ships reflected this. Not expected to cruise with the fleet, they were standard cargo carriers of anything between 2,500 and 7,500 gross registered tons (grt), and none with a speed exceeding 11 knots.

ABOVE: **Conversion of the *Santa Elena* involved the erection of steel-framed canvas hangars over No.2 and No.3 hatches, the relocation of cargo derricks for seaplane handling and the addition of powerful searchlights, sited on mast tables.**

Conversion of each was similar with large, canvas-covered, steel-framed hangars erected in way of existing hatch areas, usually in well decks. Cargo derricks were re-sited as required to handle up to six aircraft and large searchlights mounted on prominent mast platforms.

The Grand Fleet noted very little evidence of these ships but they were both active and aggressive in the Baltic.

Santa Elena

Built: Blohm & Voss, Hamburg
Owner: Hamburg-Süd
Completed: 1907
Registered tonnage: 7,415grt; 4,732 net
Length: 131.4m/430ft 10in (overall)
Beam: 16.7m/54ft 9in
Draught: Not known
Aircraft: Hangar space for 6 floatplanes
Flight deck: None
Armament: 2 x 88mm/3.46in guns
Machinery: 1 set quadruple expansion steam engines, 3 boilers, 1 shaft
Power: 2,250kW/3,000ihp
Speed: 11 knots
Fuel: Not known
Range: Not known
Armour: None
Complement: 120 men

ABOVE: **The *Answald* was a five-hatch ship with temporary hangars erected over Nos. 2 and 5. The sail effect of these considerable erections made her difficult to manage in a breeze.**

Seaplane carriers, warship

German minelaying and minesweeping operations in the strategically important Heligoland Bight were constantly threatened by British incursions. To assist in giving advance warning, the German Navy decided to convert a pair of older light cruisers as seaplane carriers, specifically to accompany light forces in the Bight. In spring 1918, the *Stuttgart* had her mainmast moved further aft and the space between it and the aftermost funnel cleared for the installation of a steel-and-canvas hangar to accommodate two seaplanes. A third aircraft, with handling derrick, was located on the afterdeck. In compensation, armament was substantially reduced. The second ship, *Stettin*, was never modified.

Stuttgart

Built: Danzig Naval Dockyard
Commissioned: February 1, 1908
Displacement: 3,530 tonnes/3,470 tons (standard); 4,070 tonnes/4,000 tons (full load)
Length: 116.8m/383ft (at waterline); 117.4m/384ft 11in (overall)
Beam: 13.3m/43ft 8in
Draught: 5.4m/17ft 9in (full load)
Aircraft: 3
Flight deck: None
Armament: 4 x 105mm/4.13in, and 2 x 88mm/3.46in guns
Machinery: 2 sets vertical triple expansion steam engines, 11 boilers, 2 shafts
Power: 10,370kW/13,900ihp
Speed: 24 knots
Fuel: 410 tonnes/400 tons (coal)
Range: 7,590km/4,100nm at 12 knots
Armour: 50mm/2in (protective deck)
Complement: 350 men

Auxiliary carriers (World War I), proposed

Intelligence of British progress on the through-deck carrier *Argus* stimulated the German Navy to propose similar conversions. Hulls considered were those of Norddeutscher Lloyd's (NDL) *Bremen* (1897, 11,570 gross registered tons – grt), the *Konigin Luise* (1896, 10,711grt), and the *Ausonia* (11,300 grt) which, like the *Argus*, was still in build for an Italian company.

Sketch plans for the *Ausonia* indicated a starboard-side funnel and island and a landing deck occupying two-thirds the length of the ship. The hangar below opened directly on to a forecastle take-off platform. Below the hangar was indicated accommodation for seaplanes, handled aft by two derricks.

Had the *Ausonia* conversion ever been implemented, her long landing deck and funnel/bridge, starboard-side island layout would have worked well and pre-empted the island superstructure on the British *Hermes* and Japanese *Hosho*.

Ausonia, proposed

Built: Blohm & Voss, Hamburg
Launched: April 15, 1915
Displacement: 12,800 tonnes/12,580 tons (standard)
Length: 149.6m/490ft 6in (bp); 158m/518ft (overall)
Beam: 18.8m/61ft 8in
Draught: 7.4m/24ft 3in (standard)
Aircraft: 13+
Flight deck: 121 x 17.3m/396ft 9in x 56ft 9in (landing, approximately); 37 x 9.3m/121ft 3in x 30ft 6in (take-off, approximately)
Armament: Not indicated
Machinery: Geared steam turbines, 2 shafts
Power: 11,950kW/16,000shp
Speed: 20.5 knots
Fuel: 1,530 tonnes/1,500 tons (coal)
Range: Not known
Armour: None
Complement: Not known

Graf Zeppelin

Operating as part of a commerce-raiding group, a German carrier could have provided the means to both find and attack convoys, while being able to defend her own force against enemy air attack. Under the terms of the 1935 Anglo-German Naval agreement, the German Navy was allowed about 42,672 tonnes/42,000 tons carrier tonnage, and two ships, each of a nominal 20,320 tonnes/20,000 tons, were authorized.

German lack of experience in carrier design was now evident, as requirement for high speed, good protection *and* a heavy armament progressively escalated design parameters to levels comparable with those of an American Essex.

High speed and good sea keeping demanded a long hull with generous freeboard. An air group of reasonable size required double hangars, resulting in a high flight deck. The flight deck was heavy, being lightly armoured and serving as the strength deck, resulting in the hull needing to be compensated with bulges to ensure adequate stability.

Horizontal protection comprised an armoured flight deck and protective deck, while a vertical belt was proof against cruiser gunfire. Three major calibres of defensive armament were provided. Fitted with three elevators and two catapults, the flight deck terminated

a little short of the bows, for, at one stage, aircraft were to have been able to take off directly from the upper hangar and over the forecastle.

The lead ship, *Graf Zeppelin*, was launched in 1938; however, the project was bedevilled by design problems, particularly with catapults and aircraft, the latter not assisted by a Luftwaffe high command antagonistic attitude toward aircraft being operated under naval control.

Further problems arose through constant changes in naval construction priorities. Progress on the carriers was thus spasmodic. The second hull was never launched while the *Graf Zeppelin* was shunted between ports. Incomplete still in 1945, she was captured by the Russians. Also unable to complete her, they scrapped her in about 1949.

ABOVE: **A probably unofficial shoulder patch for a ship that never even came within a year of completion.** BELOW: **The design displacement of the *Graf Zeppelin* conformed initially to international agreement but, in the course of construction, increased by a factor of nearly 50 per cent.**

ABOVE: **Following her launch in December 1938, Germany's first aircraft carrier, *Graf Zeppelin*, is ready for transfer to her fitting-out berth.**

BELOW: **To assist in achieving her relatively high maximum speed, the *Graf Zeppelin* was fitted with a bulbous bow. Note the overhang of the short flight deck and the carefully profiled embrasures for the casemates of two of the ship's 15cm/5.9in guns.**

Graf Zeppelin

Built: Deutsche Werke, Kiel

Launched: December 8, 1938

Displacement: 23,620 tonnes/23,200 tons (standard); 28,600 tonnes/28,100 tons (full load)

Length: 250m/819ft 9in (at waterline); 262.5m/860ft 8in (overall)

Beam: 31.5m/103ft 3in

Draught: 6.4m/21ft (standard); 7.4m/24ft 3in (full load)

Aircraft: 42 (12/30 dive-bombers and 30/12 fighters)

Flight deck: 240 x 27m/786ft 10in x 88ft 6in

Armament: 8 x 15cm/5.9in, 10 x 10.5cm/4.13in, and 22 x 8.8cm/3.46in guns

Machinery: Geared steam turbines, 16 boilers, 4 shafts

Power: 149,200kW/200,000shp

Speed: 33.5 knots

Fuel: 6,860 tonnes/6,740 tons

Range: 14,750km/8,000nm at 19 knots

Armour: 20–45mm/0.8–1.8in (flight deck); 60mm/2.4 in (protective deck); 100mm/3.9in (vertical belt)

Complement: About 1,750 men plus aircrew

LEFT: **On paper, the reconstruction of the express liner *Europa* should have resulted in a formidable carrier. In practice, however, the structural, engineering and stability problems combined to make the project non-viable.**
BELOW LEFT: **Code-named "Elbe" (not her final planned name), the NDL liner *Potsdam*'s conversion was possible only by building on to both sides of the hull over 60 per cent of its length.**

Auxiliary carriers (World War II), proposed

Having failed to produce a useful auxiliary aircraft carrier during World War I, the Germany Navy did no better the second time around. As progress on the fleet's first regular carrier was only intermittent, with technical difficulties besetting both ship and her intended aircraft, it is difficult to provide a rationale for the later (1942) proposals to convert a number of passenger liners and warships to auxiliary carriers, which presumably would have encountered the same problems.

Three Norddeutscher Lloyd passenger liners were selected, the late Blue Riband holder *Europa* (49,746 gross registered tons – grt), the *Gneisenau* (18,160grt) and the *Potsdam* (17,528grt). In addition was the German heavy cruiser *Seydlitz* and the captured French cruiser *de Grasse*. Conversion of the latter ships should have resulted in carriers equivalent to American *Independence*-class CVLs.

The *Gneisenau* and *Potsdam* as auxiliary carriers would have been larger than any beyond a few Japanese conversions but would, themselves, have been dwarfed by the rebuilt *Europa*. Razed to her upper deck, she would have received a near full-length flight deck, overhanging at its after end. The comparatively large island superstructure proved impossible to balance within the narrow-gutted hull of the express liner, a problem not fully resolved by comprehensive bulging. To fashion a hangar also meant cutting deeply through the passenger decks, including the strength deck, necessitating complex structural compensation. Beyond the stripping of passenger fittings, none of the liners were rebuilt.

Very nearly complete, the cruiser *Seydlitz* had, in contrast, most of her superstructure removed before the project was abandoned in 1943. The *de Grasse* lay at Lorient, where priority for labour and materials was always directed at the U-boat facility. The hull of the *Seydlitz* was eventually scuttled, whereas the *de Grasse* survived to be completed for the post-war French Navy.

Europa, proposed

Built: Blohm & Voss, Hamburg
Completed: March 19, 1930
Displacement: 44,800 tonnes/44,000 tons (standard); 57,520 tonnes/56,500 tons (full load)
Length: 280m/918ft (at waterline); 291.5m/955ft 9in (overall)
Beam: 37m/121ft 4in
Draught: 8.5m/27ft 10in (standard); 10.3m/33ft 9in (full load)
Aircraft: About 42 (18–20 dive-bombers, 20–24 fighters)
Flight deck: 276 x 30m/904ft 10in x 98ft 4in
Armament: 12 x 10.5cm/4.13in, and 20 x 37mm/1.46in guns
Machinery: Geared steam turbines, 24 boilers, 4 shafts
Power: 74,600kW/100,000shp
Speed: 26.5 knots
Fuel: 8,650 tonnes/8,500 tons
Range: 18,520km/10,000nm at 19 knots
Armour: None
Complement: Not known

LEFT: **Having served the British and Canadian navies for some 12 years already, the *Independencia* was well up to date when acquired by Argentina in 1958. Her disposal in 1971 terminated a life short by the standards of the *25 de Mayo* (below).**

Independencia

Built: Harland & Wolff, Belfast
Commissioned: January 14, 1946
Displacement: 14,250 tonnes/14,000 tons (standard); 19,950 tonnes/19,600 tons (full load)
Length: 192.2m/630ft(bp); 212m/695ft (overall)
Beam: 24.4m/80ft
Draught: 6.6m/21ft 6in (standard); 7.2m/23ft 6in (full load)
Aircraft: 20–30, depending upon type
Flight deck: 207.4 x 22.9m/680 x 75ft
Armament: 24 x 40mm/1.57in (1 quadruple, 10 double) guns
Machinery: Geared steam turbines, 4 boilers, 2 shafts
Power: 29,850kW/40,000shp
Speed: 25 knots
Fuel: 3,250 tonnes/3,190 tons
Range: 15,650km/8,500nm at 20 knots
Armour: None
Complement: 1,075 men

Independencia

Built as the British Light Fleet Carrier HMS *Warrior*, the *Independencia* served in the Royal Canadian Navy during 1946–48. Following her return to the Royal Navy she was twice upgraded receiving, besides new electronics and bridgework, an interim angled deck, improved arrester gear, a more powerful catapult and a flight deck strengthened for 9.1-tonne/20,000lb aircraft.

Before this, the *Warrior* had been used in unsuccessful experiments to operate jet aircraft on skids rather than conventional wheeled undercarriages. For these, the forward end of the flight deck was covered in rubber sheeting supported by airbags.

Sold to Argentina, she operated piston-engined aircraft until her disposal in 1971.

Veinticinco de Mayo (25 de Mayo)

Like the *Independencia*, the *25 de Mayo* is an ex-British *Colossus*-class Light Fleet Carrier. Completed as the *Venerable,* she was sold to the Netherlands in 1948. Modernized during 1955–58, she gained an angled deck and a distinctive new superstructure with extensive electronics suite. Badly damaged by fire in 1968, she was rebuilt with components cannibalized from British reserve carriers and sold on to Argentina. Considerable sums were then devoted to updating her data and information systems and in increasing her flight deck area. The intention was to operate French-built Super Etendards but this proving impracticable, A-4Q Skyhawks were substituted. Mechanically worn out, she was not fully operational after 1985, but was not deleted until 1997.

Veinticinco de Mayo

Built: Cammell Laird, Birkenhead
Commissioned: January 17, 1945
Displacement: 14,250 tonnes/14,000 tons (standard); 19,950 tonnes/19,600 tons (full load)
Length: 192.2m/630ft (bp); 211.4m/693ft 2in (overall)
Beam: 24.4m/80ft
Draught: 6.5m/21ft 4in (standard); 7.5m/24ft 6in (full load)
Aircraft: 22–34, depending upon type
Flight deck: 208.9 x 32m/685 x 105ft
Armament: 12 x 40mm/1.57in (12 single) guns
Machinery: Geared steam turbines, 4 boilers, 2 shafts
Power: 29,850kW/40,000shp
Speed: 25 knots
Fuel: 3,260 tonnes/3,200 tons
Range: 22,220km/12,000nm at 14 knots
Armour: None
Complement: 1,400 men

ABOVE: **The existence of the *25 de Mayo* was prolonged beyond her useful life. The Argentinian Navy was greatly disappointed that the ship's limitations did not permit the effective operation of its Super Etendard fighter-bombers.**

Vikrant

Launched in 1945 as HMS *Hercules*, the *Vikrant* was a *Majestic*-class Light Fleet Carrier.

Incomplete, she was purchased by the Indian government in 1957 and finished with angled deck, steam catapult, and air conditioning. Her original air wing comprised Sea Hawk ground-attack jet fighters and Breguet Alize ASW aircraft, used to effect in the short war against Pakistan.

ABOVE: **With a career of 35 years, the *Vikrant* demonstrated the extraordinary longevity of the ex-British Light Fleet carrier. For the Indian Navy charged with oceanic operations, she proved the necessity of naval aviation, her Seahawks being invaluable during the dispute with Pakistan.**

During the 1980s, she was updated in electronics and armament, and her facilities were reorganized for the Sea Harrier V/STOL. These operated alongside an ASW component of Sea King helicopters, whose overall height prevented their being struck below.

Vikrant

Built: Vickers-Armstrong, Newcastle
Commissioned: March 4, 1961
Displacement: 16,000 tonnes/15,700 tons (standard); 19,850 tonnes/19,500 tons (full load)
Beam: 24.4m/80ft
Draught: 7.2m/23ft 7in (full load)
Aircraft: About 20
Flight deck: 207.4 x 32m/680 x 105ft
Armament: 15 x 40mm/1.57in guns
Machinery: Geared steam turbines, 4 boilers, 2 shafts
Power: 29,850kW/40,000shp
Speed: 24 knots
Fuel: 3,200 tonnes/3,150 tons
Range: 22,220km/12,000nm at 14 knots
Armour: None
Complement: 1,300 men

She finished her career as an all-V/STOL attack carrier, being discarded in 1996, having been fitted with a "ski-jump".

Viraat

As fourth and much–delayed unit of the British *Centaur* class, the *Hermes* (III) was greatly modified in the course of her career. First completed in 1959 she was converted from 1971 to a commando carrier, operating helicopters and stowing four assault landing craft under davits (a facility that she retains). Five years later she was modified to an ASW carrier, deploying mainly Sea Kings. In 1980–81, in a further role change, she received a ski-jump forward and new facilities to operate V/STOL aircraft. These modifications were timely, permitting the ship to play a prominent role in the recovery of the Falklands in 1982.

Paid off in 1984, she was purchased by India in 1986 and, little changed beyond updated major electronics, continued to operate Sea Harrier and Sea King squadrons.

Viraat

Built: Vickers-Armstrong, Barrow
Commissioned: November 18, 1959
Displacement: 24,282 tonnes/23,900 tons (standard); 29,220 tonnes/28,700 tons (full load)
Length: 198.1m/650ft 3in (bp); 226.9m/744ft 7in (overall)
Beam: 27.4m/90ft
Draught: 8.80m/28ft 10in
Aircraft: Up to 30; usually 6 V/STOL and 9 helicopters
Flight deck: 226.9 x 48.8m/744ft 7in x 160ft 2in
Armament: 2 Sea Cat quadruple short range SAM launchers
Machinery: Geared steam turbines, 4 boilers, 2 shafts
Power: 56,700kW/76,000shp
Speed: 28 knots
Fuel: 4,275 tonnes/4,200 tons
Range: 10,400km/5,610nm at 14 knots
Armour: None
Complement: 1,170 men

LEFT: **Wearing the dark grey of the Indian Navy, the *Viraat* gives the impression of being larger than her 24,282 tonnes/23,900 tons. She was the only Royal Navy carrier to retain a deck-edge elevator, here seen in the raised position. Note the completely revised range of electronics. As the Royal Navy's last operational fixed-wing carrier, she was heavily used, not least during the Falklands War. Her hull and machinery are now over 60 years old and must have only limited remaining life.**

LEFT: **As built, the *Gorshkov* shipped an advanced and very comprehensive electronics suite. If retained by the Indians its maintenance will prove expensive.** BELOW: **Although revised in its layout, the armament of the *Gorshkov* still occupied the complete foredeck. As the Indian Navy's objectives are very different from the Russian Navy's it will probably be removed in its entirety.**

Ex-*Admiral Gorshkov*

Currently due to be transferred to India is the Russian carrier *Admiral Gorshkov*. Damaged by fire, the ship is currently undergoing a refit.

The only survivor of four *Kiev*-class ships, the *Gorshkov* commissioned late in order to incorporate the then new Sky Watch planar radar, whose fixed arrays dictate the size and configuration of a large island superstructure. Whether this and the remainder of the comprehensive "command ship" electronics suite will be transferred with the ship, is, as yet, unknown.

Apparently evolved from the early *Moskva*-class ships in order to utilize the new concept of V/STOL, the Kievs had a through-angled deck that suggested that they could operate conventional fixed-wing aircraft, although they were never fitted with arrester gear or catapults.

The Indian Navy requires carriers, and the 17-year-old *Gorshkov* is young compared with the *Vikrant*, which has seen 45 years of use. To maximize her

carrier potential, the service will have little interest in the massive offensive armament of canister-launched SSN-12 SSMs, silo-launched SA-N-9 SAMs and AS rocket launchers that crowd the foredeck. Cleared, they will vacate useful flight deck parking space, space that could be increased by widening the forward flight deck by giving the bow sections greater above-water flare.

Effectiveness of the earlier large force of Helix-A (Ka-27) ASW helicopters was greatly enhanced by a massive low/medium-frequency sonar housed in the ship's bulbous forefoot, and variable-depth sonar deployed aft.

It is reported that the ship's future armament will comprise only six combination gun/close-range missile CIWS mountings.

The Indian Navy has long harboured a desire to build indigenous carriers and has been commissioning foreign design studies. It is likely that orders for one or more of 38,608 tonnes/38,000 tons from

home yards will be confirmed in the near future to underline India's status as a major regional power.

Ex-*Admiral Gorshkov*	⊛

Built: Nikolaev South
Commissioned: January 11, 1987
Displacement: 38,900 tonnes/38,200 tons (standard); 46,200 tonnes/45,400 tons (full load)
Length: 249.5m/818ft (at waterline); 283.2m/ 928ft 6in (overall)
Beam: 32.7m/107ft 4in
Draught: 8.5m/27ft 10in (standard); 9.9m/32ft 6in (full load)
Aircraft: About 30 (Sea Harrier equivalents and Sea King equivalents)
Flight deck: 283.2 x 51m/928ft 6in x 167ft 2in
Armament (revised): 6 Kortik/Kashtan CIWS mounts
Machinery: Geared steam turbines, 8 boilers, 4 shafts
Power: 130,500kW/175,000shp
Speed: 32 knots
Fuel: 7,130 tonnes/7,000 tons
Range: 24,080km/13,000nm at 18 knots
Armour: Not known
Complement: About 1,500 men

ABOVE: **Stripped of its foredeck clutter, the ex-*Gorshkov* could emerge as a very capable carrier, as seen in this impression. The implication here is that the electronics will be retained to allow her to act as a command ship. Compatibility with other units could be a problem.**

Karel Doorman (I)

Following wartime experience with MAC tankers and the consequent formation of the Fleet Air Arm's 860 (Royal Netherlands) Squadron the Netherlands acquired the British-built escort carrier *Nairana* (II) in 1946. She was renamed after Rear Admiral Karel W.F.M. Doorman who, as Allied Flag Officer at the Battle of the Java Sea (February 1942), went down with his ship. Being of riveted construction, the *Nairana* had been preferred for Arctic service and differed further from American CVEs by having the flight deck as main strength deck. She served the Netherlands Navy until 1948, when she was returned and converted for commercial service.

Karel Doorman (I)

Built: John Brown, Clydebank
Commissioned: September 27, 1943
Displacement: 14,050 tonnes /13,800 tons (standard); 17,400 tonnes/17,100 tons (full load)
Length: 152m/498ft 3in (bp); 161.2m/528ft 6in (overall)
Beam: 20.7m/68ft
Draught: 7.8m/25ft 8in (mean)
Aircraft: 21
Flight deck: 153.1 x 20.1m/502 x 66ft
Machinery: Two 5-cylinder diesel engines, 2 shafts
Power: 8,000kW/10,700bhp
Speed: 16 knots
Fuel: 1,685 tonnes/1,655tons
Range: 24,080km/13,000nm at 15 knots
Armament: 2 x 102mm/4in (1 double), and 16 x 2pdr pom-pom (4 quadruple) guns
Armour: None
Complement: 640 men

Karel Doorman (II)

As they gained experience with the ex-*Nairana*, the Dutch negotiated the sale of the larger *Venerable* from the Royal Navy. On transfer in 1948 she assumed the same name of *Karel Doorman*. Until 1955 she operated British-sourced, piston-engined aircraft but was then given an extensive three-year modernization. She emerged with an 8-degree angled deck, steam catapults, improved elevators and a mirror landing sight. Her island structure had been completely re-modelled, with a lofty lattice mast, the better to locate a revised electronics outfit, all of domestic origin.

The upgrade permitted the operation of the jet-propelled Hawker Sea Hawk, a ground-attack fighter which remained in Royal Navy front-line service until 1958. These were partnered by the anti-submarine AS.4 variant of the Grumman Avenger. In addition, there was a flight of Sikorsky HSS-1N helicopters, configured for nocturnal ASW operations.

By 1965, with the Cold War emphasizing ASW, the *Doorman* lost her strike and air defence role, carrying only helicopters and the heavy Grumman S-2 Tracker. A single, obsolete carrier, her future was already doubtful when, in 1968, she suffered a serious fire. Still worth refitting, however, she was purchased by Argentina, beginning a new career as the *25 de Mayo.*

Karel Doorman (II)

Built: Cammell Laird, Birkenhead
Commissioned: January 17, 1945
Displacement: 14,250 tonnes/14,000 tons (standard); 19,950 tonnes/19,600 tons (full load)
Length: 192.2m/630ft (bp); 211.4m/693ft 2in (overall)
Beam: 24.4m/80ft
Draught: 6.5m/21ft 4in (standard); 7.5m/24ft 6in (full load)
Aircraft: 24
Flight deck: 208.9 x 32m/685 x 105ft
Armament: 34 x 40mm/1.58in guns
Machinery: Geared steam turbines, 4 boilers, 2 shafts
Power: 29,850kW/40,000shp
Speed: 25 knots
Fuel: 3,260 tonnes/3,200 tons
Range: 22,220km/12,000nm at 14 knots
Armour: None
Complement: 1,320 men

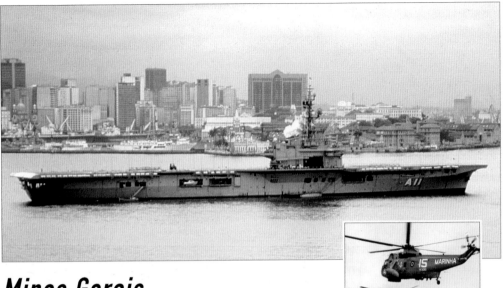

Minas Gerais

Named after one of the 20 Brazilian states, the *Minas Gerais* began life as HMS *Vengeance*, a *Colossus*-class Light Fleet Carrier. Purchased in 1956, she went to Rotterdam for a comprehensive modernization. Upgraded to operate 9,072kg/20,000lb aircraft, she received new elevators, arrester gear and steam catapult. A relatively large, 8.5-degree angled deck was counterbalanced by an access track outside the new island. Replacing the austere good looks of the original structure, this arrangement was topped by a raked

funnel casing and a substantial lattice mast. The ship was deleted in 2001, having been replaced by the French carrier *Foch* which was purchased and renamed *Sao Paolo*. At the time of writing, it has been announced that plans are afoot to acquire this last working example of a "Light Fleet" for exhibition in the UK.

BELOW: **Plans to acquire A-4 Skyhawk fighter-bombers from the United States came to nought and the ship's usual fixed-wing component was limited to Grumman S-2 Trackers.**

TOP: **A huge nation of enormous potential wealth, Brazil needs carriers, or "air-capable" ships, to police her extensive offshore waters.**

ABOVE: **Reduced effectively to an ASW carrier, the *Minas Gerais* operated several types of helicopter in a variety of roles. These are two naval SH-3 Sea Kings.**

Minas Gerais

Built: Swan Hunter, Wallsend
Commissioned: January 15, 1945
Displacement: 16,200 tonnes/15,900 tons (standard); 20,250 tonnes/19,900 tons (full load)
Length: 192.2m/630ft (bp); 212m/695ft 3in (overall)
Beam: 24.4m/80ft
Draught: 6.6m/21ft 6in (standard); 7.4m/24ft 3in (full load)
Aircraft: 20–30
Flight deck: 207.4 x 32m/680 x 105ft
Armament: 10 x 40mm/1.57in (4 double, 2 single) guns
Machinery: Geared steam turbines, 4 boilers, 2 shafts
Power: 29,850kW/40,000shp
Speed: 24 knots
Fuel: 3,260 tonnes/3,200 tons
Range: 22,220km/12,000nm at 14 knots
Armour: None
Complement: 1,300 men

Dédalo (I)

Converted during 1921–22 from an ex-German merchantman, Spain's first aviation ship, Dédalo, was officially classified as an Aviation Transport. She was more than that, however. From centre island aft, she was decked over, creating space for four Italian-built flying boats. These were handled by derricks stepped to a goalpost structure. Below, the previous hold space, now accessed by elevator, housed and supported two kite balloons. Right forward, a single, tall

mast acted as a mooring point for either of two especially built, 40m/131ft 2in dirigibles. These could also alight on the cleared forward end. The ship was scrapped in 1940.

BELOW: Reconstructed from a 20-year-old cargo ship the Dédalo was equipped with an afterdeck large enough for four to six flying boats, handled by derricks, and a forward well to accommodate a large kite balloon, which could be moored to the foremast.

Dédalo (I)

Built: Wigham Richardson, Newcastle
Completed: May 1901
Displacement: 11,000 tonnes/10,800 tons (standard)
Registered tonnage: 5,510grt
Length: 128.1m/420ft (overall)
Beam: 16.8m/55ft 2in
Draught: 6.3m/20ft 6in (mean)
Aircraft: Up to 25 floatplanes, or 7 flying boats plus 1 airship
Flight deck: None
Armament: 2 x 100mm/3.9in, and 2 x 57mm/2.24in guns
Machinery: 1 set quadruple expansion steam, 3 boilers, 1 shaft
Power: 2,390kW/3,200ihp
Speed: 10 knots
Fuel: 920 tonnes/900 tons (coal)
Range: 5,560km/3,000nm at 10 knots
Armour: None
Complement: 400 men

Dédalo (II)

Following a long period in reserve, the Independence-class light carrier Cabot (CVL-28) was reactivated by the Americans for a five-year loan to the Spanish Navy. Transferred in 1967, and assuming the name Dédalo, she was purchased outright in 1973. Reconstruction had left her with only two of her earlier four funnels and, although now with strengthened flight deck,

up-rated catapult and classed as an aircraft carrier with a nominal capacity of 20 aircraft, she appears to have operated from the outset as an anti-submarine (ASW) carrier, deploying only helicopters. In preparation for the entry into service of the new Principe de Asturias, the Dédalo acted as a V/STOL training ship.

She was sold out in 1989, the last example of an effective emergency class.

Dédalo (II)

Built: New York Shipbuilding, Camden, N.J.
Commissioned: July 24, 1943
Displacement: 14,750 tonnes/14,500 tons (standard); 16,750 tonnes/16,450 tons (full load)
Length: 183m/600ft (at waterline); 190m/623ft (overall)
Beam: 21.8m/71ft 6in
Draught: 7.9m/26ft (mean)
Aircraft: 7 Harrier V/STOL equivalents plus 16 Sea King helicopter equivalents, or 22 Sea Kings
Flight deck: 166.2 x 32.9m/545 x 108ft
Armament: 26 x 40mm/1.57in guns
Machinery: Geared steam turbines, 4 boilers, 4 shafts
Power: 74,600kW/100,000shp
Speed: 30+ knots
Fuel: 1,830 tonnes/1,800 tons
Range: 13,330km/7,200nm at 15 knots
Armour: 83–127mm/3.25–5in (vertical belt); 50mm/2in (protective deck)
Complement: 1,100 men plus aircrew

LEFT: Although the US Navy had little use for its Independence-class CVLs after 1945, the reactivated Cabot (CVL-28), renamed Dédalo, gave the Spanish Navy over 20 years' service.

ABOVE LEFT: **The *Principe de Asturias'* three gas turbines are located in the superstructure, driving electrical generators which power the propulsion motor, connected to a single shaft.** ABOVE: **No angled deck is fitted, but the flight path, as is evident here, is angled from port quarter to centreline. The ship is usually very lightly armed.**

Principe de Asturias

During the early 1970s, the US Navy developed the Sea Control Ship (SCS) as a replacement for escort carriers (CVE). Heading an escort group in the defence of a convoy, the SCS's helicopters would follow up contacts made by the towed sonar arrays of frigates. Her V/STOL fighters would deal with aerial threats, both direct and from horizon-distance "snoopers" charged with the mid-course correction of incoming surface-to-surface missiles (SSM) launched by submarines or by surface ships. For these duties, the air wing comprised 11 anti-submarine (ASW) helicopters, 3 airborne early warning (AEW) helicopters, and 3 V/STOL fighters. In US Navy circles, the SCS's deliberately austere design attracted powerful opposition, which also emphasized its supposed vulnerability to battle damage. It was thus never adopted but the design was purchased by the Spanish Navy as an affordable replacement for the ageing *Dédalo*, somewhat similar in size.

An angled deck is not fitted, but the marked flight path is angled to starboard, extending from the port quarter and culminating in a 12-degree "ski-jump" right forward. A low quarterdeck is linked to the flight deck by elevator and to the hangar via doors. A second elevator is fitted forward of the island. Armament is limited to four 12-barrelled 20mm/0.79in "Meroka" guns, forming the close-in weapon systems (CIWS) for use against anti-ship missiles.

A pair of repair-by-replacement gas turbines generate the power to drive a single shaft, the perceived vulnerability of which is offset by two retractable, self-contained "get-you-home" propulsion units.

The Spanish Navy's remit for the *Principe de Asturias* is far wider than any envisaged for an SCS. Her air group of approximately 20 aircraft will therefore vary considerably in its constitution, dependent upon the ship's current role.

Principe de Asturias

Built: Bazán, et Ferrol
Commissioned: February 17, 1989
Displacement: 11,700 tonnes/11,500 tons (standard); 16,500 tonnes/16,200 tons (full load)
Length: 187.5m/614ft 9in (bp); 195.1m/639ft 8in (overall)
Beam: 24.4m/80ft
Draught: 6.7m/22ft (full load)
Aircraft: About 20, usually 12/14 ASW/attack helicopters and 6/8 V/STOL fighters
Flight deck: 175.3 x 29m/574ft 9in x 95ft 1in
Armament: 4 x 12-barrelled 20mm/0.79in "Meroka" CIWS guns
Machinery: 2 LM 2500 gas turbines, 1 shaft, plus 2 retractable Pleuger directional thrusters
Power: 34,300kW/46,000hp or, 2 x 600kW/800hp
Speed: 26 knots
Fuel: Not known
Range: 12,000km/6,500nm at 20 knots
Armour: None
Complement: 775 men

ABOVE: **Known as Matadors in Spanish service, the Harrier IIs were built in the United States by McDonnell Douglas as the EAV-8B. Deliveries began in 1976.**

Balloon ship

Not noted, in modern times at least, for the size or bellicosity of her navy, Sweden can nonetheless claim to have constructed the first-ever craft redesigned purely for aviation purposes. Inasmuch as it was not self-propelled, it was termed a "barge", although a sophisticated barge. The shallow hull boasted ship-shaped fore-and-after-end, and conventional ground tackle. A long,

rectangular central well was surrounded by a very deep (about 4m/9ft 10in high) coaming, creating a sheltered box for the inflation of a German-supplied kite balloon.

LEFT: **It is not clear why the Swedish Navy chose to design its first balloon vessel without means of propulsion for this limited the utility of an otherwise useful asset.**

Balloon ship	
Built: Lindholmens Mek. Verkstad, Göteborg	
Commissioned: 1904	
Displacement: 224 tonnes/220 tons	
Length: 47m/154ft (overall)	
Beam: 10m/33ft	
Draught: 1.8m/6ft	
Aircraft: 1 kite balloon	
Flight deck: None	
Armament: None	
Machinery: Non-propelled	
Armour: None	
Complement: 25	

Accommodation/workshops occupied the hull's wing spaces flanking the central well. Hydrogen generation and compression equipment was powered by petrol-driven generators, as were the lofting winches. Although the craft operated until 1924, its utility must have been very limited by its lack of any means of self-propulsion.

Gotland

Light cruiser forward and aviation ship aft, the Gotland's concept pre-dated those such as the Japanese Ise and Tone classes, and more modern hybrids such as the Moskvas, *Jeanne d'Arc* and *Vittorio Veneto*.

Her six 152mm/6in guns were disposed in twin turrets forward and aft (the latter with restricted arcs) and two singles flanking the bridge structure in the last known use of casemates.

A light spar deck aft was laid with three tracks, bearing eight self-propelled trolleys, each of which could support a float plane with wings folded. Three more aircraft could be stowed below. Forward of the tracks was a turntable-mounted, compressed-air catapult which could be aligned with any of the tracks.

Following the transfer of an aircraft, the catapult was trained on the beam for launching. The system was designed around the Hawker Osprey, which aircraft were recovered from the water by a crane located right aft. With the aircraft landed, the tracks could be used to load up to 100 mines, released over the stern.

By 1943, the ship was obsolete and the Swedes (neutral during World War II) removed all aviation-related equipment, converting the Gotland Into an anti-aircraft/training cruiser. Ten years later she received an up-grade, acquiring new secondary and automatic weapons, together with up-to-date control equipment. She finally went for scrap in 1962.

Gotland	
Built: AB Götaverken, Göteborg	
Commissioned: December 16, 1934	
Displacement: 4,850 tonnes/4,750 tons (standard); 5,650 tonnes/5,550 tons (full load)	
Length: 130.1m/426ft 6in (at waterline); 133.4m/437ft 6in (overall)	
Beam: 15.4m/50ft 7in	
Draught: 5.0m/16ft 6in (standard); 5.5m/18ft (full load)	
Aircraft: 11 floatplanes	
Flight deck: None	
Armament: 6 x 152mm/6in, and 4 x 75mm/2.95in guns	
Machinery: Geared steam turbines, 4 boilers, 2 shafts	
Power: 24,600kW/33,000shp	
Speed: 27.5 knots	
Fuel: 855 tonnes/840 tons	
Range: 7,410km/4,000nm at 12 knots	
Armour: 28–50mm/1.1–2in (protective deck); 28–50mm/1.1–2in (turrets)	
Complement: 450 men	

LEFT: **In pre-helicopter days, a floatplane-carrying light cruiser made sense for the policing of Sweden's long and complex coastline. Observation of strict neutrality during World War II was never an easy task for the Swedish Navy, and the *Gotland*'s aircraft helped cover large areas.**

Chakri Naruebet

Having built the Spanish *Principe de Asturias* to the basic American Sea Control Ship (SCS) design, the Bazán yard went on to produce a diminutive for the Thai Navy. The *Chakri Naruebet* bears a strong family resemblance but is far more simply equipped, mainly on a "for but not with" basis.

As her main task is the patrol of Thailand's considerable coastline, she is fitted with an economical CODOG installation, cruising usually on diesel engines but with the ability to change to gas turbines for high speed.

Six ex-Spanish-built Matador AV-8S V/STOL aircraft have been acquired but the ship usually works only with helicopters.

Her armament is defensive, an America-sourced Mk.41 eight-cell vertical launch system not yet fitted. There are a reported three French Matra Sadral point-defence systems (PDMS) and four Vulcan/Phalanx 20mm/0.79in CIWS. Very much a figurehead for an extensive but small-ship fleet, she still lacks a medium-range surface search radar and proper fire control. Electronic warfare support systems and countermeasures are also lacking, as is a planned hull-mounted sonar. Thailand plans to acquire submarines.

ABOVE: **Beyond acting as prestige flagship for the Thai Navy and also as royal yacht, it is difficult to envisage any role for the *Chakri Naruebet* that could not better be undertaken by smaller, helicopter-equipped warships. The key probably lay in growing rivalry with other regional fleets, such as those of Malaysia and Indonesia.**

Chakri Naruebet

Built: Bazán, Ferrol
Commissioned: March 27, 1997
Displacement: 11,700 tonnes/11,485 tons (full load)
Length: 164.1m/538ft (at waterline); 182.6m/598ft 8in (overall)
Beam: 22.5m/73ft 9in
Draught: 6.2m/20ft 4in (mean)
Aircraft: Up to 6 x AV-8S Matador V/STOL, 6 x S-70B-7 Seahawk helicopters
Flight deck: 174.6 x 27.5m/572ft 6in x 90ft 2in
Armament: 3 x Matra Sadral PDMS, or 4 x Vulcan/Phalanx CIWS, and 2 x 30mm/1.18in guns
Machinery: 2 x LM 2500 gas turbines or 2 x MTU 16-cylinder diesels, 2 shafts
Power: 33,000kW/44,250hp or 8,800kW/11,800bhp
Speed: 26/16 knots
Fuel: Not known
Range: 18,520km/10,000nm at 12 knots
Armour: None
Complement: 600 men, including aircrew

ABOVE: **A smaller version of Spain's *Principe de Asturias*, the *Chakri Naruebet* makes an interesting comparison. Compact and economical, the design would provide a good basis for a conventional trade-protection carrier.**

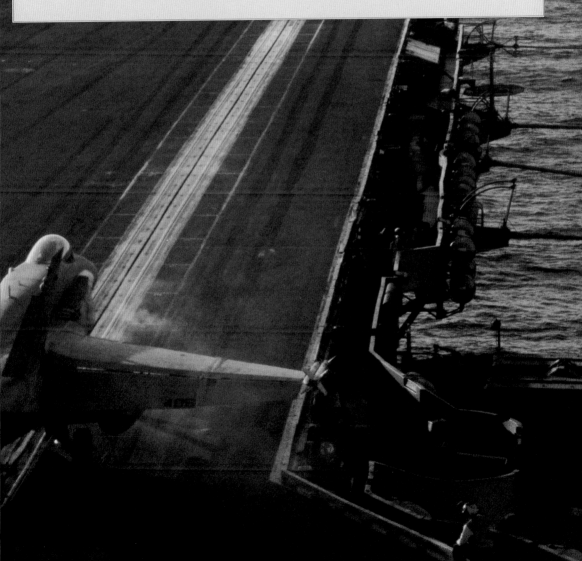

NAVAL AIRCRAFT

IMAGE: **FA-18 Hornets take off from the flight deck of the *USS Saratoga* aircraft carrier**

The History of Naval Aircraft

Combat aircraft have played an increasingly important role in conflict since they came into their own during the pioneering days of air warfare in World War I. Naval aviation, that is military aviation that takes place from fighting ships, was born in 1911 when a Curtiss biplane landed on a wooden platform built on the cruiser USS *Pennsylvania* and took off from it again. Although seen by most more as a stunt than a demonstration of the potential of naval air power, it proved the concept. The first true carrier with an unobstructed flight deck did not enter service with the Royal Navy until the last stages of World War I, but by the end of World War II the carrier was seen to be a mighty warship with the potential to project a nation's power more flexibly than the large battleships that once ruled the waves.

The importance of carriers today is best demonstrated by former US President Bill Clinton, who said, "When word of crisis breaks out in Washington, the first question that comes to everyone's lips is: 'Where is the nearest carrier?'" Nuclear-powered and nuclear-armed supercarriers were the ultimate development. These small floating cities are a far cry from the converted ships from the pioneering days of aircraft operating from naval craft.

LEFT: The photograph, taken on the deck of a World War II British carrier, shows over 20 Corsair fighters with wings folded to save space and carrying auxiliary fuel drop tanks. The Royal Navy was the first service to operate the bent-wing fighter from carriers.

Fleet fighters – the rise of naval air power

Naval air power has its origins in 1910, a key year in the development of military aviation. On November 14 that year, a Curtiss biplane became the first ever to take off from a ship. The aircraft, flown by Eugene B. Ely, flew from a 25.3m/83ft platform built over the bows of the US Navy cruiser USS *Birmingham*. Within two months, Ely had succeeded in landing a Curtiss on a ship, this time the USS *Pennsylvania*. Although these feats were seen by many as little more than stunts, Ely had shown that aircraft actually did not need to operate from dry land. By combining one of the oldest means of transport, the boat, with the newest, the aeroplane, a new means of waging war was born.

Britain's first deck take-off came on January 10, 1912, when the Royal Navy officer Lt C.R. Samson flew a Short biplane from staging erected over the gun turret of the cruiser HMS *Africa*. By 1915, Britain had two ships with 36.6m/120ft-long flying-off decks but they were far from operational. Flying-off platforms were, however, fitted to a handful of Royal Navy ships. A Sopwith Pup, using the HMS *Yarmouth* flying platform, was launched against and destroyed a German Zeppelin – this action is believed to have been the earliest use of a 'carrier-borne' fighter for air defence.

The first significant use of carrier-borne air power came in the 1931–32 war between China and Japan. In January 1932, carrier-borne aircraft operated in support of Japanese land forces in action near Shanghai. It was not, however, until World War II that aircraft carriers and their fighters came into their own.

The carrier was vital in the Japanese campaigns in World War II in the Pacific and enabled them to project power over vast distances. Carriers were able to make or break campaigns

TOP: **The Royal Navy was keen to field the best available fighters to counter the Zeppelin threat at sea. The foredeck of HMS *Furious* is seen here in 1918 with Sopwith Camels brought up from the below-deck hangar by the forward elevator, the opening for which can be seen in the foreground.**

ABOVE: **Aircraft were used for a variety of tasks at sea and on land from the earliest days of air power. Just as aircraft were used to 'spot' artillery on land, here an Italian flying boat helps an Italian Navy vessel direct its fire, circa 1918.**

by providing strike aircraft, and air cover for other ships, convoys and assault ships, and so their protection was vital. Each carrier had fighter aircraft to defend the ships and carriers from air attack. The US Navy developed defensive fighter 'nets' over carrier groups to protect them from enemy aircraft by a combination of radar early-warning and standing patrols of fighters, some up to 64km/40 miles away from the carrier. The carrier that could be protected from air attack was a massive strategic asset in any theatre of war.

While Britain at first had second-rate or obsolete aircraft deployed as carrier-borne fighters, other nations developed high-performance hard-hitting fighters designed from the outset as carrier aircraft. One of the first true fighters deployed by the Royal Navy was the Sea Hurricane, the navalized version of the famous Battle of Britain fighter. RAF Hurricanes had flown on and off HMS *Glorious* during the Norwegian campaign in 1940 and shown that high-performance fighters could be operated from carriers. It was followed into Royal Navy service by the American-built Grumman Martlet (known as the Wildcat in the US Navy and later in the Royal Navy). The Wildcat proved itself almost immediately in its first carrier deployment on convoy protection in September 1941 by driving away or destroying enemy aircraft. Meanwhile, the Sea Hurricanes soldiered on tackling German torpedo aircraft while newer high-performance fighters were awaited from America.

World War II Japanese carrier-borne air power was formidable. Six aircraft carriers took part in the devastating December 1941 attack on Pearl Harbor which decimated the US Pacific Fleet. In this and other attacks, Japanese strike aircraft were only able to carry out their deadly missions because they were escorted by fighters like the Mitsubishi Zero, which took on defending fighters. The Zero was a formidable fighter but its excellent manoeuvrability was achieved at the price of pilot safety. To save weight there was no armour protecting the pilot and often there was not even a radio fitted in the aircraft.

One carrier fighter in particular could be described as a war winner – the Grumman F6F Hellcat. Following its arrival in combat in August 1943, this tough fighter was able to turn the tables on the Zero and gave US Navy and Marine Corps pilots the upper hand until the war's end. Aircraft carriers were shown to be as good as their defences, and in particular the fighters that protected them.

TOP: **Naval air power was at first manifested by aircraft launched like this Sopwith Camel from a launching platform on the Royal Australian Navy ship HMAS *Sydney*, 1917.** ABOVE: **Another favoured method of getting the early naval fighter airborne was by launching them from high-speed lighters. The theory was that if the lighter and its aircraft were already travelling at speed, the wind would lift the aircraft into the air much quicker. The same principle applied to the lighters that were towed at around 25 knots behind a warship – this configuration is pictured with a Sopwith Camel getting airborne.** BELOW: **The Grumman Hellcat was the second-largest single-engine fighter of World War II after the land-based P-47. The Hellcat was so big because the US Navy needed a fast aircraft that could carry useful loads of weaponry over great distances – this required a large engine and room for lots of fuel.**

Naval aircraft technology up to 1945

When the Wright brothers built their pioneering Wright Flyer in 1903, the principal material used for the wings and fuselage was wood braced by piano wire for added strength. By the end of World War II, just over four decades later, most military aircraft were all-metal and could cover distances and achieve speeds of which the Wrights could have only dreamed.

As engine technology improved and aircraft speeds increased, drag on early aircraft became a serious design consideration and aircraft frames were increasingly covered and enclosed with taut fabric to achieve streamlining. This technique was used into the mid-1930s, but by the time of World War II most new aircraft were of all-metal 'monocoque' construction. Whereas the early fabric-covered aircraft got their structural strength from taut metal bracing wires, the metal skin of the monocoque fuselage, and in time the wings and tail, welded or riveted to a light metal interior framework provided an incredibly strong construction. The downside of this construction was the damage that would be caused by cannon shells hitting the metal structure – in fabric-covered aircraft the shells could have passed right through the aircraft causing little damage.

The Wrights chose a biplane configuration for their Flyer and this form was used in all early naval aircraft, as two pairs of wings generated much more lift than a monoplane. It was not until 1936, for example, that the Royal Air Force deployed a monoplane in front-line service and some time later that the Royal Navy's Fleet Air Arm followed suit.

Until World War II, most carrier-borne fighter aircraft were just navalized versions of proven landplanes. Undercarriages

had to be strengthened due to the great stresses generated as an aircraft slammed down on a pitching carrier deck – more early Seafires were written off by landing incidents than by enemy action. The addition of arrester hooks also required strengthening of the fuselage to cope with the violence of 'catching the wire'. As military planners came to realize the war-winning strategic value of aircraft carriers, dedicated purpose-designed naval types began to enter service.

In terms of space saving, wings needed to fold to minimize the room taken up by an aircraft on or below a carrier deck. Wing-folding was a labour-intensive manual task until complex

ABOVE: **The Fairey Swordfish is a naval aviation legend. The comparatively slow biplane carried out countless daring missions during World War II against the toughest odds and went on to outlast the aircraft developed to succeed it.**
LEFT: **The superstructure of HMS *Furious* shows just how skilled the pilots of the pictured Sopwith Pups had to be during these early deck operations. Equally primitive at this time was the use of cranes to lift the aircraft from and return them to the hangar below the deck. The development of hydraulic lifts changed this.**

LEFT: **Not all naval aircraft needed a flight deck. Many fighting ships carried small flying boats or amphibians like the Supermarine Walrus or floatplanes such as the Vought Kingfisher pictured. The aircraft would be craned over the side into the sea and then craned back on deck after its mission.**

ABOVE: **The arrester hook was a comparatively simple but effective means of stopping an aircraft in a controlled manner on a carrier deck. Failure to 'catch' any of the wires on landing would result in a punishing meeting with an emergency catcher 'net' that was deployed on later wartime carriers. The other possibilities were a disastrous collision with other aircraft on the deck or going over the side.**
LEFT: **The Grumman Wildcat. Initially known by the Royal Navy as the Martlet, this aircraft was the standard US naval fighter from 1942–43. In December 1940, the aircraft became the first US type in British service in World War II to down an enemy aircraft.**
BELOW: **The Supermarine Walrus served with both the Royal Navy and the Royal Air Force. RN aircraft were amphibian shipborne observation aircraft while the RAF machines were used mainly for Air Sea Rescue missions and saved many lives.**

hydraulic wing-folding systems were developed. Wings could fold a little, i.e. just the wingtips (such as on early Seafires), while others (such as on the Corsair) folded perhaps halfway along their length just outboard of the undercarriage. The Grumman Wildcat's innovative 'sto-wing' mechanism developed by Leroy 'Roy' Grumman was crucial to the US Navy's success in the Pacific in World War II. With the wings folded parallel to the aircraft fuselage in one sweeping motion, the aircraft's size was dramatically reduced. This allowed easier movement around the ship but most significantly increased the carrier's aircraft capacity by 50 per cent. One technical innovation dramatically increased US naval air power. This innovation was used on later Grumman aircraft including the Avenger and Hellcat.

Engine technology developed rapidly between the wars. The 1917 Sopwith Camel had a top speed of 188kph/117mph and was powered by a Clerget 130hp in-line piston engine. Just over a quarter of a century later, the Pratt & Whitney Double Wasp was producing 2,100hp and pushing the Grumman Bearcat along at 677kph/421mph.

At the end of World War I, air-cooled radials and in-line piston-engines were the dominant engine types and both had

much to commend them. They were developed to the maximum until the jet engine ultimately replaced them both, but naval jets were not introduced until after World War II.

Naval aircraft weaponry to 1945

In the early days of air warfare, aircraft armament was non-existent or locally improvised. The first fighters were armed with revolvers, rifles or shotguns carried by the pilots or observers but the importance of reliable hard-hitting armament was soon appreciated. Once weapons like the 0.303in Lewis machine-gun were proven, their use was then perfected. At first the guns were mounted on pivot pins or flexible mounts, aimed by the observers or pilots at enemy aircraft, but they became truly effective once the guns were fixed to the aircraft and were synchronized to fire between the spinning propeller blades. To aim at a target, the pilot simply had to fly straight at it.

During World War I, two rifle-calibre machine-guns were usually enough to inflict serious damage on fabric-covered, mainly wooden aircraft or enemy airships. By the mid-1930s this was clearly inadequate to destroy the larger metal aircraft coming off drawing boards at the time. Consequently, more and bigger guns were used to arm fighter aircraft, and wing-mounted guns and, later, cannon became more common.

During World War I, experiments had been carried out to see if large calibre weapons (cannon) firing explosive ammunition could destroy enemy aircraft. Early British tests found that the recoil of these comparatively large weapons was enough to stop a slow-moving firing aircraft in flight, never mind inflict damage on an enemy. French development work was more successful and a 37mm cannon was used in combat by French aces Guynemer and Fonck, both of whom destroyed German aircraft with the weapon.

TOP: **A Fleet Air Arm Fairey Albacore being armed with 113kg/250lb bombs. Although carrier-based aircraft were frequently used to attack land targets, strikes on shipping with free-fall bombs required great skill and nerve as the attackers were typically met with robust anti-aircraft defences.** ABOVE: **Many naval fighter aircraft, including this Grumman Hellcat, were armed only with machine-guns, in this case six 0.5in Brownings. The picture shows the barrels of the guns being 'pulled through' to ensure they are clear of any obstructions that might cause a jam in combat when failures could prove fatal.**

When the legendary Spitfire first went to war its original armament was eight 0.303in Browning machine-guns but as the Luftwaffe provided their aircraft with more armour and self-sealing fuel tanks it was apparent that eight machine-guns were not adequate to inflict enough damage on enemy aircraft. When the Seafire was developed for production it was

LEFT: **The Fairey Swordfish was typically armed with an 18in torpedo as shown but could also carry the equivalent weight in bombs or mines.**

cannon-armed. Although the machine-gun and cannon were the most significant air-to-air weapons in the period, unguided rockets were highly developed by the end of World War II.

Bombs of varying types and weights were carried from the earliest days of naval aviation. Britain's early bombing successes began on October 8, 1914, with the Royal Naval Air Service raids on the Zeppelin sheds at Dusseldorf and Cologne. The aircraft used were two Sopwith Tabloids. The aircraft attacking Cologne failed to find its target due to bad weather and bombed the railway station instead but the other Tabloid successfully dropped a small number of 9kg/20lb bombs on the airship shed destroying it and Zeppelin Z.9 in the process.

Dedicated carrier-borne torpedo-bombers existed almost exclusively prior to and during World War II in which they played a key role in many actions including the attack at Taranto and the Japanese attack on Pearl Harbor. Torpedo-carrying aircraft had first appeared during the later years of World War I. Generally, the torpedoes carried by these aircraft for attacks on shipping were designed specially for air launch and were smaller and lighter than those carried by submarines. Nevertheless, airborne torpedoes could weigh as much as 908kg/2,000lb, which was more than twice the typical bomb load of a contemporary single-engined bomber. The aircraft carrying it had to be bigger and needed to have a more powerful engine but none were high-performance aircraft and they were vulnerable to fighters. The introduction of improved torpedoes and anti-shipping missiles that could be carried by conventional long-range bombers led to the torpedo-bomber's general disappearance almost immediately after the war.

INSET ABOVE: **A Grumman Corsair shown firing rocket projectiles (RPs) at a Japanese ground target on Okinawa.** BELOW: **A Fleet Air Arm Fairey Firefly armed with cannon and RPs. The high-speed unguided rockets proved deadly on impact with aircraft but were equally devastating against ground targets, armour and surface vessels. Two British RP types were used in World War II – the 6in with 27kg/60lb warhead and the 3.44in with 11kg/25lb warhead.**

Pearl Harbor

The December 7, 1941, Japanese carrier-borne attack on the US naval base at Pearl Harbor was the culmination of ten years of deteriorating relations between the two nations. In 1937 Japan had attacked China as part of its plans to dominate the Far East and South-east Asia. When war broke out in Europe, Japan allied itself with Germany. Meanwhile, the US applied diplomatic pressure and used embargoes to try to resolve Japan's conflict with China. The US oil embargo was particularly badly received in Tokyo where the act was viewed as a threat to Japan's national security. The posturing and pronouncements by both Japan and the US escalated to dangerous levels by the summer of 1941 when the pride and prestige of both nations was in jeopardy. While they both apparently continued to pursue diplomatic means to resolve their differences, Japan already had plans for war.

The Japanese attack on Pearl Harbor was intended to immobilize the US Pacific Fleet so the US could not interfere with Japan's expansionist plans. The attack was conceived by Admiral Isoroku Yamamoto, Commander-in-Chief of the Japanese Combined Fleet, who knew that Japan's only hope of success against the United States and its industrial might was to achieve a swift and overwhelming victory thereby avoiding a prolonged war with a formidable foe.

"Yesterday, December 7, 1941 – a date which will live in infamy – the United States of America was suddenly and deliberately attacked by naval and air forces of the Empire of Japan."
President Franklin Roosevelt

TOP: Part of the armada of Japanese aircraft destined for Pearl Harbor prepare to take off from the deck of a Japanese carrier. Total surprise was achieved in the attack that came to be known as 'The Day of Infamy'. Using aircraft operating from more than 322km/200 miles away from the target, the attack required considerable co-ordination. ABOVE: Japanese planning for the attack was meticulous and took many forms. Reconnaissance and intelligence received from spies enabled the Japanese military planners to build accurate models with which to brief aircrew. However, this incredibly accurate scale model of Battleship Row was constructed after the attack for use in the making of a Japanese propaganda film.

On November 26, 1941, a Japanese fleet of 33 warships, including six aircraft carriers, sailed from Japan towards the Hawaiian Islands taking a route to the north to keep it clear of shipping that could alert the US of the Japanese activity. In the early morning of December 7 the fleet found itself about 370km/230 miles north of its target and at 06:00 the first wave of fighters, bombers and torpedo-bombers was launched. Their target at Pearl Harbor was the 130 ships of the US Pacific Fleet. Seven of the Fleet's nine battleships were conveniently berthed together on 'Battleship Row' on the south-east shore of Ford Island. At 06:40 a Japanese midget submarine was spotted and destroyed near the entrance to Pearl Harbor.

ABOVE: A Japanese Navy Nakajima B5N2 'Kate' takes off from the aircraft carrier *Shokaku*. Nearing the target, the Japanese force split so some of the aircraft could neutralize any attempted defence from US fighter aircraft. Few defending aircraft had the opportunity to leave the ground during the attack.

ABOVE RIGHT: Japanese Navy Aichi 'Val' dive-bombers prepare to take off on the morning of December 7, 1941. The carrier in the background is the *Soryu*. A mixed force of 183 bombers, dive-bombers, torpedo-bombers and fighters comprised the first Japanese attack wave that began its take-off at 06:00 hours.

A few minutes later a US radar station picked up a signal indicating a large formation of aircraft heading their way but interpreted it as a flight of B-17 bombers arriving from the mainland. Within an hour all became clear as the first wave of Japanese aircraft arrived and attacked. In all, 351 Japanese aircraft took part in the attack, including Aichi D3A dive-bombers, Nakajima B5Ns (carrying bombs and torpedoes) and Mitsubishi Zeros.

A large armour-piercing bomb penetrated the deck of the USS *Arizona* which caused one of the ship's ammunition magazines to explode at 08:10. Within nine minutes the *Arizona* sank, with the loss of 1,177 crew. The USS *Oklahoma*, subjected to continued torpedo attack, rolled over, trapping over 400 of her crew inside the hull. Meanwhile, the USS *California* and USS *West Virginia* both sank where they were moored. The USS *Utah*, a training ship, capsized with over 50 of her crew. The USS *Maryland*, USS *Pennsylvania* and USS *Tennessee* all suffered major damage. As well as attacking the harbour itself, Hickam, Wheeler and Bellows airfields, Ewa Marine Corps Air Station and Kaneohe Bay Naval Air Station were all attacked. By the end of the day, 164 US aircraft were destroyed with a further 159 damaged.

The second wave of the Japanese attack came at 08:40, this time destroying the USS *Shaw*, USS *Sotoyomo* and heavily damaging the *Nevada*. By 10:00 the second wave of attacking aircraft had departed having lost only 29 aircraft in the whole raid.

The attack was audacious and, as expected, achieved complete surprise. It also would not have been possible without carrier-borne attack aircraft. It inflicted massive material damage on the Pacific Fleet although the US aircraft carriers were not in port at the time of the attack. The major effect, however, was not what the Japanese had expected.

ABOVE: The attack on the US Pacific Fleet was intended to warn the US off but instead made the industrial giant more determined to quash Japan.

BELOW: Crippled and effectively destroyed by an armour-piercing bomb dropped from a Japanese aircraft, the USS *Arizona* was lost with 1,177 crew. Today, a 56m/184ft-long memorial to those who died during the attack is positioned over the mid-portion of the sunken battleship.

Tokyo had hoped that the US would take the message and not interfere with Japanese plans in the Western Pacific. Instead the attack on Pearl Harbor united a nation previously divided over the issue of military intervention. The US, incensed at the apparently mock negotiations going on while the attack was imminent, was at war with Japan. When he heard about the botched diplomatic activity that was still going on while the attack was underway, Admiral Yamamoto is supposed to have said, "I fear all we have done is to awaken a sleeping giant and fill him with a terrible resolve."

The Doolittle Raid

The April 1942 US air attack on Japan, launched from the aircraft carrier USS *Hornet* and led by Lieutenant Colonel James H. Doolittle, was at that point the most daring operation undertaken by the United States in the Pacific War. Though conceived as a diversion that would also boost American and Allied morale, the raid generated strategic benefits that far outweighed its limited goals.

The raid had its origins in a chance remark that it might be possible to launch twin-engined bombers from the deck of an aircraft carrier, making feasible an early retaliatory air attack on Japan that would not call for putting even more US warships at risk, close to Japan. On hearing of the idea in January 1942, US Fleet commander Admiral Ernest J. King and Air Forces leader General Henry H. 'Hap' Arnold, responded enthusiastically. Arnold assigned Doolittle to assemble and lead the air group. The well-tested and proven B-25 Mitchell medium bomber was selected and tests showed that it could indeed fly off a carrier while carrying bombs and enough fuel to reach and attack Japan, and then continue on to friendly China.

Recruiting volunteer aircrews for the top-secret mission, Doolittle began special training for his men and modifications to their aircraft. The new carrier *Hornet* was sent to the Pacific to carry out the Navy's part of the mission, which was so secret, her commanding officer, Captain Mitscher, had no idea of his ship's part in the operation until just before 16 B-25s

ABOVE: **Lt Col James H. Doolittle (centre) flanked by members of the crews who took part in the raid and Chinese officials pictured in China after the mission.**

LEFT: **Following the raid, Doolittle expected that the loss of all 16 aircraft, coupled with the relatively minor damage caused to the enemy would lead to his court martial. Instead Doolittle was awarded the Medal of Honor by President Roosevelt and was promoted straight to Brigadier General, missing the rank of Colonel. He went on to command the Twelfth Air Force in North Africa, the Fifteenth Air Force in the Mediterranean and the Eighth Air Force in the UK during the following three years.**

were loaded on his flight deck. *Hornet* sailed on April 2, 1942, and headed west to be joined in mid-ocean on April 13 by USS *Enterprise*, which would provide limited air cover.

The plan called for an afternoon launch on April 18, around 643km/400 miles from Japan but enemy vessels were spotted before dawn on April 18. The small enemy boats were believed to have radioed Japan with details of the American carriers heading their way, so Doolittle's Raiders were forced to take off immediately while still more than 965km/600 miles from their target.

ABOVE LEFT: **A B-25 leaves the flight deck of** *Hornet*, **heading for Japan. Note the personnel watching from the signal lamp platform on the right. For the duration of the voyage leading to the raid, the aircraft were ranged on** *Hornet*'s **flight deck in the order they were to leave as there was no room to rearrange them. The B-25's long non-folding wings meant they were too large to fit on the elevator to take them below. The lead aircraft, flown by Doolittle himself, had only a few hundred feet of deck to reach take-off speed.** ABOVE RIGHT: **Smoke pours from Japanese targets following the raid.** LEFT: **The B-25s were stripped of some of their defensive guns and given extra fuel tanks to extend their range. Wooden broom handles were placed in each plane's plastic tail cone, simulating extra machine-guns to deter enemy fighters. Each B-25 carried four 227kg/500lb bombs. One bomb was decorated with Japanese medals, donated by a US Navy Lieutenant who had received them during pre-war naval attaché service and now wished to return them.** BELOW: **The B-25 Mitchell went on to become one of the most widely used aircraft of World War II and served with many nations.**

Most of the 16 B-25s, each with a crew of five, attacked the Tokyo area, while some bombed Nagoya. Damage to Japanese military targets was slight, and none of the aircraft reached China although virtually all the crews survived.

Japan's military leaders were nevertheless horrified and embarrassed by the audacious raid. The Americans had attacked the home islands once and could do it again and so the Japanese were forced to keep more ships and aircraft near the home islands ready to repulse further US attacks. These significant military resources could otherwise have been used against American forces as they attacked island after island while making their way closer to Japan.

Combined Fleet commander Admiral Isoroku Yamamoto proposed that the Japanese remove the risk of any similar American raids by destroying America's aircraft carriers in the Pacific theatre. The Doolittle raid thus precipitated the Japanese disaster at the Battle of Midway a month and a half later.

Perhaps the most significant result of the logistically impressive Doolittle mission was the hard-to-quantify but very real effect that it had on the morale of the broader American public. The United States was finally hitting back after Pearl Harbor and the brave men who were the Doolittle Raiders raised the confidence of all Americans, civilians and military alike.

LEFT: **The deck of USS *Enterprise* during the Battle of Midway. The carrier's Dauntless dive-bombers are being readied for flight. The Douglas Dauntless had the lowest loss ratio of any US carrier aircraft of World War II.** ABOVE: **Admiral Chester W. Nimitz had a major advantage – cryptoanalysts had broken the Japanese Navy code and knew that Midway was the target of the impending Japanese strike, as well as a likely date and a Japanese Navy order of battle. This meant he was able to ignore the Japanese attempts to draw elements of his force away.**

The Battle of Midway

The Battle of Midway was among the most significant naval battles of World War II and carrier-borne aircraft played the major role. In mid-1942, the Japanese Navy sought to draw the US Pacific Fleet into a decisive battle that would tip the balance of naval power in Japan's favour once and for all. Their plan was to seize the island of Midway, which was close enough to Pearl Harbor to be a threat, and provoke a US naval response. The Japanese Navy then planned to ambush the US Fleet as it came to defend and retake Midway.

Unfortunately for the Japanese, the US Navy codebreakers had deciphered their enemy's coded transmissions and found that a trap had been set. This gave Admiral Nimitz, US Navy Commander-in-Chief Pacific, the opportunity to best deploy his smaller forces. Four Japanese carriers steamed towards Midway while Admiral Yamamoto's group remained behind waiting to ambush the American aircraft carriers that would make their way to defend Midway. Although the United States knew what Japan had planned, the US Navy did not know the exact location of the enemy ships.

At dawn on June 4, 1942, the Japanese began their air attack on Midway but met stiff resistance from the defending fighters. This called for a second raid and by this time Vice-Admiral Nagumo's ships were coming under limited attack by Midway-based USAAF B-17 and B-26 bombers as well as SBU Vindicator dive-bombers.

By this stage, the strike aircraft still available to the Japanese (the rest were on the way back from Midway) were configured to attack the expected intervening US ships. Instead the aircraft had to have different ordnance loaded

for a repeat attack on Midway. When Japanese patrol aircraft reported American warships to the north of the island, the order was given to again change the ordnance so the target would be the newly discovered US warships. This chaotic period inevitably resulted in all manner of ordnance laying around the below-deck aircraft hangars as orders changed and the decks were emptied for the aircraft returning from Midway.

It was at this time that the US air attacks against the Japanese fleet began. Three squadrons of TBD Devastator torpedo-bombers were decimated by anti-aircraft fire and defending Zero fighters. Of the 41 aircraft that attacked, only 4 made it back. While the Japanese were congratulating themselves, another formation of SBD Dauntless bombers from *Yorktown* and *Enterprise* arrived unnoticed. Lieutenant Commander Clarence Wade McClusky, air-group commander of the *Enterprise*, had led 32 of the Dauntless dive-bombers in search of Japanese naval targets.

Below him suddenly appeared the *Kaga* and *Akagi*. McClusky led his formation straight down at the carriers in a 70-degree dive. The *Kaga* took a direct hit and its deck, full of aircraft, ordnance and fuel, erupted. A second bomb crashed through the forward aircraft elevator and exploded among the fuelled aircraft on the hangar deck. A third bomb hit a fuel bowser, which exploded and destroyed the bridge, killing the captain and other senior officers. At 17:00 hours the surviving crew were ordered to abandon ship.

The *Akagi* took a bomb in the midship elevator, which exploded ammunition nearby while a second bomb struck the aircraft being rearmed and refuelled on the deck. The ensuing

LEFT: Hit by a shell from the *Yorktown* during a torpedo run, a Nakajima 'Kate' breaks up in mid-air before dropping its deadly torpedo which can be seen falling safely away. ABOVE: The flight deck of USS *Yorktown* looking aft shortly after she was hit by two Japanese torpedoes. Men are balancing themselves on the listing deck as they prepare to abandon the carrier – one crew member is already wearing a life jacket. The crew were ordered to abandon the ship at 14:55 hours but the carrier remained afloat a day later. The *Yorktown* was finally sunk by Japanese torpedoes while under tow for repair assessment. BELOW LEFT: An artist's impression of the action during the Battle of Midway. BELOW: *Akagi* was a 36,500-ton aircraft carrier that began life as a battlecruiser. She was completed as one of Japan's first two large aircraft carriers in March 1927. The *Akagi* was flagship for the Pearl Harbor attack in December 1941 and later took part in carrier raids into the Indian Ocean area. During Midway, as the flagship of Admiral Nagumu, the *Akagi* is pictured taking evasive manoeuvres while under attack by dive-bombers from the USS *Enterprise*. Although seriously damaged, the carrier did not sink but was scuttled by Japanese destroyer torpedoes early the following day.

fires raged out of control and the order to abandon ship was given at 19:00 hours.

Meanwhile, the carrier *Soryu* was attacked and hit by Dauntless squadron VB-3 from the USS *Yorktown*, led by Lieutenant Commander Maxwell F. Leslie. The resulting fire on the Japanese carrier was so intense that the armoured hangar doors melted. The carrier was out of action by 10:40 hours and sank around 19:20.

The fourth Japanese carrier, *Hiryu*, shrouded in haze, was spared at that stage and launched an attack against the *Yorktown*. One Japanese bomb smashed through the ship's side and destroyed five of the carrier's boilers. A number of torpedo hits sealed the *Yorktown*'s fate and the order to abandon ship was given at 14:55. Within a couple of hours, however, a US aircraft had found the *Hiryu* and ten minutes later the *Enterprise* launched a formation of dive-bombers against the Japanese carrier. The dive-bombers flew unprotected as the fighters had to remain to defend the

American ships against air attack. Thirteen dive-bombers struck at the carrier while her pilots were in the mess. Four bombs struck in quick succession, completely destroying the flight deck and setting the hangar deck below on fire. Although no bomb penetrated deep into the ship and it was still able to steam at 30 knots after the attack, the fires could not be controlled. The *Hiryu* was abandoned by its crew in the early hours of June 5.

In just one day, four of the six carriers that had launched the devastating air attack against the US at Pearl Harbor had been destroyed. Japan also lost more than 300 aircraft and 3,000 men, including many of Imperial Japanese Navy's most experienced aircrew.

Yamamoto still had a huge battle force that could outgun the US Pacific Fleet but, without the protection of his aircraft carriers, the Japanese admiral's gamble had not paid off and he had no option but to withdraw from the fight. From then on, Japan had to fight a largely defensive war.

The growth of naval aviation

In August 1914, Britain had no aircraft carriers, so four merchant ships were quickly converted to become seaplane carriers by the addition of a seaplane hangar. In December 1914, three of the carriers, the *Empress*, *Engadine* and *Riviera* participated in a strike against Heligoland. These ships were typical of most early Royal Navy seaplane carriers, which had to stop before they could lower their aircraft into the water for take-off. On their return the aircraft were craned back onboard. These ships remained the principal carrier type in British service at the end of World War I.

During World War I, the light battlecruiser *Furious* was converted into an aircraft carrier with a small forward take-off deck, and it was on this ship that the first successful deck landing occurred when Squadron Commander Dunning landed his Sopwith Pup on August 2, 1917. Dunning tried to repeat his achievement two days later but a burst tyre caused the aircraft to fall over the side of the carrier, drowning the pioneering naval aviator. Flying an aircraft is a complex undertaking, and becomes more so when other factors are added, such as darkness, bad weather and a carrier deck that could be moving in all three planes at once – up and down, side to side and rolling. The operation of aircraft from a carrier called for the development of special flying techniques.

The experiments on the *Furious*, however, proved that safe deck operations needed a deck free of obstructions. The Italian

ABOVE: **Naval aviation presents even greater hazards than land-based aviation, and this was more so when the techniques for operating from early carrier decks were being developed. Squadron Commander E.H. Dunning pioneered deck landings on Royal Navy ships in August 1917, to prove it could be done by flying around the inconveniently positioned funnel. Sadly, during the trials his Sopwith Camel went over the side of HMS *Furious*.**

liner *Conte Rosso* was bought and converted into a 'flat top' aircraft carrier and renamed *Argus*, while *Furious* was modified to take a full-length flight deck. In July 1918, *Furious* launched six Sopwith Camels against Zeppelin sheds on what became the first-ever carrier strike.

ABOVE: **This photograph, taken on a Royal Navy carrier, illustrates many of the elements of carrier operation. A variety of aircraft types, a cramped deck, the elevator in action taking aircraft below and the deck crew anxiously watching for the next aircraft to land.**

The first US aircraft carrier, the USS *Langley*, was commissioned in 1922, while the first purpose-designed aircraft carrier was Japan's *Hosho* of 1925. France's first aircraft carrier, *Béarn*, entered service in 1927. By 1939, Britain had six aircraft carriers in service and by 1941 the USA had eight aircraft carriers. Meanwhile, Japan had ten aircraft carriers.

Aircraft take off from a carrier to the bow, into the wind, and land from the stern. Carriers steam at speed into the wind during take-off to increase the wind speed over the deck, leading to more lift for the aircraft taking off.

Pilots making an approach would rely on the skill of a 'batsman' or landing signal officer to control the plane's landing approach. 'Bats' visually gauged the approaching aircraft's speed, altitude and attitude and relayed the information and corrections to the pilot using coloured paddles like ping-pong bats. When landing on a carrier, an aircraft would rely on its tailhook catching one of a number of arrester wires stretched across the deck to bring it to a stop in a shorter distance than if it was landing on a normal runway.

Into the 1950s, aircraft would land on the flight deck parallel to the ship's centreline. Aircraft already recovered would be parked at the bow end of the flight deck. A metal mesh safety barrier would then be raised behind the recovered aircraft in case the next aircraft to land missed the wires and overshot.

This problem was overcome by the later introduction of the angled deck, a British innovation introduced in the 1950s. In this configuration the runway was aligned off-centre a few degrees across the ship. Any aircraft missing the arrester cables on landing would then have the opportunity to employ maximum power to take off from an unobstructed deck and go around again as the other aircraft had left the 'runway' and parked in safety to the side.

ABOVE: **Two classic naval types in the air together. The Grumman Avenger (foreground) would never have sought out Japan's Mitsubishi Zero for combat, but often drew unwanted attention from the excellent fighter.**
BELOW: **The Grumman Wildcat (or Martlet as it was briefly known by the Royal Navy) typifies how advances in aircraft technology made carriers more potent. The unique Grumman wing-folding mechanism meant the fighter took up much less room in the hangar and on deck so more could be taken onboard.**

LEFT: **Carrier operations were and are still high-risk situations. Here a US Navy Grumman Hellcat burns following a landing accident. Incidents like this could prevent other aircraft landing or force them to head for another carrier, dry land or consider ditching. Aircraft coming in to land after combat were often low on fuel, so any delay in landing was feared.** ABOVE: **A deck crewman uses a variety of hand signals to tell the pilot what to do next, having taken the wire and landed on this carrier. An aircraft is taken below to the hangar deck on the elevator – the waiting Hellcat is next.**

Seaplanes and flying boats to 1945

Historians disagree over who first lifted off from water in an aircraft but it was possibly the Austrian Wilhelm Kress. His tandem winged aircraft, powered by a 30hp engine, reportedly took off, albeit briefly, from an Austrian reservoir in October 1901. The first proper take-off from water was made by Frenchman Henri Fabre in a seaplane named *Hydravion* on March 28, 1910.

While aircraft carriers were being developed to project military might, some aircraft designers were striving to perfect those frequently overlooked naval aircraft types, seaplanes and flying boats. 'Seaplane' is an American description for any kind of aircraft designed to operate from water, although they have been developed into many forms. Flying boats have a fuselage with an underside designed like a boat – a planing hull. Typically flying boats have wing-mounted floats to stabilize the aircraft while it is on or moving through the water, although manufacturers like Savoia-Marchetti produced large flying boats with twin parallel hulls and no floats. Amphibians are flying boats that also have an undercarriage so can operate from land or water – some versions of the Catalina were built this way.

Floatplanes were traditionally designed aircraft, often land-based designs, mounted on floating pontoons. Floatplanes were among the most pioneering of early aircraft, partly because so many record-breaking flights were made over great expanses of water and the ability to put down on water increased the pilot's chances of survival in an emergency such as a fuel shortage.

The cutting-edge reputation of floatplanes was helped in no small way by the famous Schneider Trophy races that took place between 1913 and 1931. The competition was intended

TOP: **The Farman Aviation Works founded and run by brothers Henry and Maurice Farman developed this floatplane version of their MF 11 Shorthorn. It was used for reconnaissance, bombing and training roles. This machine is pictured at Felixstowe.** ABOVE: **Fabre's Hydravion was a seaplane with a fuselage structure of two beams that carried unequal span biplane surfaces with a tailplane at the forward end and a monoplane wing at the rear. The Gnome rotary engine drove a pusher propeller mounted at the rear of the upper fuselage beam.**

to encourage technical advances in aviation but gradually became a contest of speed over a measured course. The Schneider Trophy significantly accelerated aircraft design, particularly in aerodynamics and engine development. It was a floatplane winner of the Schneider, the Supermarine S.6B, that led directly to the development of the Spitfire.

The streamlined advanced aircraft that took part and their low drag, liquid-cooled engines also influenced the designs of the North American P-51 Mustang and the Italian Macchi C.202 Folgore. Although floatplane versions of famous fighters such as the Mitsubishi Zero and the Spitfire were built during World War II, these developments were usually abandoned in favour of carrier-borne combat aircraft. It was, however, in the time before the arrival into service of helicopters that many warships carried their own floatplanes for reconnaissance. The Nakajima E8N2 was a short-range reconnaissance floatplane that could be launched from a catapult. Small flying boats were, however, also used in this way – the Supermarine Walrus was an air sea rescue/spotter amphibian that was carried on some Royal Navy cruisers during World War II. It 'lived' on the warship's deck with its wings folded to save space and then when required would be lowered by a deck crane into the sea. At the end of its sortie the process would be reversed.

Flying boats, however, were barely influenced by the developments driven by the Schneider Trophy. By their nature, these aircraft were built for range and endurance and generally grew larger and heavier until, like the dinosaurs some of the later, larger ones resembled, they became extinct. Germany's Blohm und Voss Bv 238 was the largest built by the country and was designed for long-range reconnaissance duties. With a wing span of over 60m/197ft it was powered by no less than six engines but only one prototype, weighing more than 80,000kg/176,000lb, was built. Britain's largest military flying boat was the Short Shetland of which only two prototypes were built and flown towards the end of World War II. Although these aircraft were at the evolutionary extreme for piston engine-powered flying boats, they had been preceded by many types that were extraordinarily successful such as the Short Sunderland and Kawanishi H8K2.

ABOVE: The Grumman Duck with its distinctive streamlined integral float served throughout World War II in a variety of roles and was used by the US Navy, Coast Guard and Marine Corps. The type is known to have attacked German U-boats as well as serving in the coastal patrol and reconnaissance roles.

BELOW: The Blackburn Shark was a versatile torpedo-bomber that could be equipped with an undercarriage or floats.

TOP: The Nakajima A6M2-N 'Rufe' was a floatplane development of the famous A6M Zero intended for use in support of amphibious operations.

ABOVE: The Short Shetland carried on the Short tradition of large flying boats established with the C-class boats that became the Sunderland. The Shetland, impressive as it was, was not needed in the post-war world when new large flying boats were considered to be surplus to requirements.

Naval air power and the Korean War

Shortly after World War II ended, the US Navy's plans for the next generation of 'supercarriers' were sidelined due to the influence of the US Air Force who at that time, with Strategic Air Command, dominated US military thinking. The Korean War, however, reinforced the value of carriers and the need for a larger, more capable 'supercarrier'.

The United Nations began carrier operations against North Korean forces on July 3, 1950, in response to the invasion of South Korea. UN Task Force 77 at that time consisted of the US Navy carrier USS *Valley Forge* and Britain's HMS *Triumph*. Although the UN had air supremacy, having effectively neutralized the threat posed by the North Korean Air Force, the North Korean ground forces virtually overran South Korea – only a small area in the south-east near the port of Pusan held out.

By mid-September 1950, three US Navy Essex-class aircraft carriers were available for Korean War operations: in addition to *Valley Forge*, *Philippine Sea* and *Boxer* were on station. *Valley Forge* and *Philippine Sea* each carried two squadrons of F9F Panther jet fighter-bombers and two of propeller-driven World War II-vintage F4U Corsair fighter-bombers as well as a squadron of Skyraider attack aircraft. *Boxer* had an all-propeller air group that comprised four squadrons of Corsairs and one of Skyraiders. Britain's HMS *Triumph* fielded two squadrons of Fireflies and Seafires. The US escort carriers *Badoeng Strait* and *Sicily* each also provided a base for US Marine Corps' F4Us, which were specialists in close-air support for ground forces.

On September 15, the UN made an amphibious landing at Inchon, some 160km/100 miles up the west coast from Pusan, as the UN forces at Pusan counter-attacked. The Inchon landing succeeded only because of the air support available from the UN's carriers, and by the end of September virtually all organized North Korean forces had been subdued or driven north of the 38th parallel.

TOP: **USS *Lake Champlain*. Fire was a major hazard on carriers and required prompt action to stop its spreading. Unignited fuel pouring from an aircraft jet pipe posed a major threat and any fire could prove deadly.** ABOVE: **The Vought Corsair, often thought of as only a World War II combat aircraft, was a key aircraft in the United States' Korean War inventory. In the first year of the war, the Corsair flew 80 per cent of all US Navy and US Marines close-support missions. Night-fighter versions were deployed and in a pure fighter role the Corsair tangled with and destroyed enemy jets.**

As the war progressed, the carriers continued to support UN ground troops together with land-based UN aircraft that could now operate from recaptured airfields. By early November 1950, UN troops were facing increasing numbers of Chinese troops who were now openly supporting North Korea. UN forces attempted to arrest the Chinese advance by destroying the crossings of the Yalu river. Between November 9 and 21, aircraft of a now greatly enlarged Task Force 77 – Skyraiders and Corsairs escorted by Panthers – flew 593 sorties against the road and rail bridges across the Yalu. On November 9 an F9F Panther flying from the USS *Philippine Sea* became the first US Navy jet to achieve an aerial victory in combat when it shot down a MiG-15 during a raid on a Yalu target.

In May 1951, United States Navy Skyraiders carried out the only aerial torpedo attack of the Korean War, but not against a maritime target. Despite attacks by ground troops and B-29 bombers against the strategically important Hwachon dam, the structure had remained intact. But on May 1, eight Douglas AD-1 Skyraiders from USS *Princeton* launched torpedoes against the dam and breached it.

Although the Royal Air Force played little part in the war, the Fleet Air Arm continued to provide a carrier presence and played a vital role in the United Nations strategy. The light carrier HMS *Theseus* as part of Task Force 77 was relieved by HMS *Glory* in April 1951 – this ship was in turn relieved by HMAS *Sydney*. These ships all carried Fairey Firefly and Hawker Sea Fury fighter-bombers. When HMS *Ocean* served in the theatre from May until October 1952, the ship launched 123 fighter-bomber sorties in a single day. It was a Sea Fury FB Mk 11 from *Ocean*, piloted by Lieutenant Peter Carmichael, that flew straight into the history books on August 9, 1952, when the aircraft destroyed a Communist MiG-15 in air-to-air combat. This was the first example of a jet being destroyed by a piston-engined fighter in air combat.

By the ceasefire of July 27, 1953, 12 different US carriers had served 27 tours in the Sea of Japan as part of the UN task force. During periods of intensive air action, up to four carriers were on station at the same time. A second carrier unit, Task Force 95, enforced a blockade in the Yellow Sea off the west coast of North Korea. Over 301,000 carrier strikes were flown during the Korean War: 255,545 by the aircraft of Task Force 77; 25,400 by the British and Commonwealth aircraft of Task Force 95; and 20,375 by the escort carriers of Task Force 95.

Carrier-based combat losses for the United States Navy and Marine Corps were 541 aircraft while Britain's Fleet Air Arm lost 86 aircraft in combat and the Australian Fleet Air Arm lost 15.

It was, however, the performance of the US Navy aircraft that proved so important in the history of naval air power. US Congress finally gave the US Navy funding for its 'supercarrier'.

ABOVE LEFT AND ABOVE: **Two views of Royal Navy carrier HMS *Ocean* with Fireflies and Sea Furies on the deck. *Ocean* was a Colossus-class light fleet carrier launched in July 1944, and on December 3, 1945, the ship became the first aircraft carrier to receive landings by a jet aircraft. The Royal Navy operated five carriers off Korea as part of the British and Commonwealth element of the United Nations forces and *Ocean* made two tours – May 5 to November 8, 1952, and the second from May 17, 1953, to the end of hostilities. It was during the first tour that Sea Fury pilot Lt Peter Carmichael from HMS *Ocean* achieved his historic victory over a MiG-15 jet** BELOW: **The Grumman F9F Panther was the US Navy's most widely used jet fighter in the conflict.** BOTTOM: **US Navy Corsairs on a snow-covered deck illustrate the challenging conditions in which deck crews and naval aviators have to operate.**

US Navy carriers and the Vietnam War

O n August 2, 1964, the USS *Maddox*, a United States Navy destroyer carrying out electronic surveillance in the Tonkin Gulf, was attacked by North Vietnamese patrol boats. The US Navy presence was there in support of democratic South Vietnam, which Communist insurgents were entering from North Vietnam. The ultimate consequence of the attack was massive.

Five days later US Congress passed the Tonkin Gulf Resolution that authorized President Johnson to "take all necessary measures" to protect US interests. The carriers USS *Ticonderoga* and *Constellation* arrived in the area within days, and their jet aircraft launched bombing raids against North Vietnamese patrol boat bases and an oil storage depot.

Although the raids were judged to be a success, one aircraft was lost and its pilot, Lt Everett Alvarez Jr, became the first of around 600 downed US airmen who became prisoners of war. Alvarez was not released until the peace treaty was signed eight years later.

These raids, launched from US Navy aircraft carriers, were the first air missions of the Vietnam War. What followed until August 15, 1973, was the longest (nine years), most costly (in terms of aircraft and crews) and probably the most difficult war in naval aviation history.

During the war, US aircraft carriers were based in the South China Sea on 'Yankee Station' (off North Vietnam) and 'Dixie Station' (off South Vietnam) and provided air support for US forces fighting south of the Demilitarized Zone (DMZ) in the Republic of (South) Vietnam. The carriers also served as bases for USN aircraft operating on bombing missions over North Vietnam and Laos.

TOP: **Carrier-borne air power was fundamental to the US air war conducted over Vietnam. Without the carriers and the role the US Navy and Marine Corps played, the US effort would have been limited to missions conducted from land bases.**
ABOVE: **A US Navy F-4 Phantom II prepares to launch followed by a North American Vigilante. Both aircraft served in the conflict but the F-4 served with the US Air Force and US Marine Corps, as well as the US Navy in the war. The Phantom was used for fighter, bomber, reconnaissance and 'wild weasel' jamming missions.**

Aircraft crews were bound by political constraints and targets were chosen carefully to avoid any action that would provoke Chinese or Soviet intervention. Despite all the air warfare in the sky over Vietnam, only five US pilots (USAF and USN) achieved ace status. This was because North Vietnamese pilots were careful to avoid dogfighting. The rules of engagement also specified that US pilots had to have visual confirmation of any enemy aircraft before engaging. By this point it was too close for air-to-air missiles like Sidewinders to be effective and it was not until later in the war that fighters were armed with effective guns. American pilots were found overall to have lost the air-fighting skills that proved so vital in Korea and World War II. This led to the establishment of the Top Gun programme for US Navy pilots.

The US Navy crews were also operating against an enemy equipped with sophisticated Soviet anti-aircraft defences. In 1965, the North Vietnamese began building a massive Surface-to-Air Missile (SAM) arsenal. After US raids, these SAM sites were always the first to be rebuilt but the rules of engagement specified that US aircraft could only attack them if the sites were a minimum of 48km/30 miles from a city and had their radar turned on. The presence of the SAM sites led US pilots to fly low and fast below enemy radar with the result that some, flying the most advanced combat aircraft in the world, were brought down by small arms fire.

US Navy aircraft operating from carriers suffered heavy losses in the war. In 1968 alone, the USS *Oriskany* lost half of its air complement, 39 aircraft, in just 122 days, a staggering attrition rate. Carriers expected to lose on average 20 aircraft for each cruise in the theatre.

The number of carriers deployed varied during the conflict, but up to six operated at one time during Operation Linebacker. Twenty-one US aircraft carriers deployed under the US Seventh Fleet and conducted 86 war cruises for a total of 9,178 days on the line in the Gulf of Tonkin. A total of 530 aircraft were lost in combat, (most to surface-to-air missiles or anti-aircraft fire) and 329 more in operational accidents. In all, 377 US naval aviators lost their lives, 64 were reported missing and 179 were taken prisoners-of-war. A further 205 officers and men of the ships' crews of three carriers (*Forrestal*, *Enterprise*, and *Oriskany*) were killed in major shipboard fires caused by accidents, not enemy action, and many more were injured.

ABOVE LEFT: **The Douglas A-4 Skyhawk was a vital element in the US Navy's war. All carrier wings had Skyhawk squadrons and the A-4s performed many of the Navy's and Marine Corps' light air attack missions over the jungles and mountains of Vietnam. Production of this remarkable naval aircraft did not cease until 1979.** ABOVE: **Napalm was widely used in the Vietnam War, and in this photograph is dropped by a Douglas Skyraider. Essentially a sticky incendiary petrol jelly, the substance is formulated to burn at a specific rate and stick to whatever it hits. Napalm also rapidly deoxygenates available air and creates large amounts of carbon monoxide. Apart from its use against troops and buildings, Napalm bombs were also used in the Vietnam War to clear landing zones for helicopters.** BELOW: **The Douglas Skyraider, in this case the A-1H version, was widely used in Vietnam. The versatile aircraft bucked the trend of switching to jet aircraft and remained in front-line use long after its expected retirement date. US Navy Skyraiders were even credited with the destruction of two Soviet-built MiG-17 jet fighters during the war. The type flew on until November 1972 when it was replaced by the A-7 Corsair II.**

Naval aircraft armament since 1945

Even before World War II ended it was clear that the jet fighter aircraft that would develop would need more effective armament than the machine-guns then available, some of which were based on World War I designs. The closing speeds of two jet aircraft and the area over which a jet dogfight could take place meant that pilots might get one passing chance to down an enemy aircraft – guns had to pack real destructive power. At the end of World War II, German fighter armament development was considered the most advanced and some of their weapons were adopted and improved by the Allies after the war. The advanced Mauser MG-213 cannon, for example, was copied by Britain, Russia, the US, Switzerland and France among others, and equipped most of the world's air forces in the post-war period. The British version of the Mauser, the Aden, is still used today. Some aircraft, Dassault's Super Etendard and Rafale for example, are armed with even larger calibre guns like the 30mm GIAT/DEFA cannon, but even highly evolved cannon have their limitations and cannot be effective over great distances.

Aircraft-launched guided and unguided missiles were used in World War II but the single most important development in aircraft armament since the war has been the guided Air-to-Air Missile (AAM) with its high-explosive warhead. Unguided missiles, many of them of World War II vintage, continued to be used into the 1950s.

Guided AAMs are now used by fighters to attack enemy aircraft from a minimum of 1.6km/1 mile away and up to 160km/100 miles. AAMs were first used in anger in 1958 when Taiwanese F-86 Sabres clashed with MiG-15s of the People's Republic of China. Armed with early examples of the AIM-9 Sidewinder, the F-86s downed a number of Chinese MiGs with the new weapon.

TOP: **A Royal Navy Sea Harrier FA.2 armed with four AIM-120 AMRAAMs (Advanced Medium-Range Air-to-Air Missiles). Weighing 154kg/340lb, each missile uses an advanced solid-fuel rocket motor to reach a speed of Mach 4 and a range in excess of 48km/30 miles. The AIM-120 can counter the electronic jamming of an enemy and on intercept an active-radar proximity fuse detonates the 40lb high-explosive warhead to destroy the target.**

ABOVE: **The AGM-65 Maverick is an air-to-ground tactical missile used against armour, air defences, ships, vehicles and fuel storage facilities. Using infrared tracking, the missile has a range of 27km/17 miles and can carry a warhead of up to 135kg/300lb.**

Modern air-to-air missiles are usually Infra-Red (IR) guided (in which the missile sensors make it follow a high-temperature heat source such as an engine exhaust) or radar-guided (in which the missile homes in on a target illuminated by a radar from the aircraft, and then follows on its own radar). The latter type of missile normally uses a technique called semi-active radar homing, which allows the radar to operate in pulses, to

FAR LEFT: **Armed with six long-range Phoenix air-to-air missiles, the F-14 Tomcat was a formidable air combat adversary. The potent missiles weighing 447kg/985lb could streak towards targets at speeds in excess of Mach 5.** LEFT: **Although modern combat aircraft like the F-18 Hornet/Super Hornet are still armed with guns, it is unlikely they would ever be used in a modern air-combat environment where missiles dominate.**

avoid making itself a target to radar-homing missiles. Some missiles use both the IR and radar guidance methods, being radar-guided to within a few miles' range, then IR-guided to terminate in destruction.

Whatever the guidance, the AAM must reach its target quickly as most only have enough fuel for a few minutes' run. In missiles with speeds of three or four times the speed of sound, the run can be counted in seconds.

AAMs are usually proximity armed, and having detected that they are within lethal range, explode without having to hit the target. This is to counter last-second evasive manoeuvres by the target aircraft and even if a missile just misses the target, the detonation will still cause substantial damage. Air-to-air missiles are categorized according to their range, into Short-Range Missiles (SRAAMs), Medium-Range Missiles (MRAAMs), and Long-Range Missiles (LRAAMs).

The SRAAM is designed for use in close air combat and distances up to 18km/11 miles, and a typical SRAAM would be the well-known and widely used American Sidewinder (AIM-9) series.

The MRAAM is mainly used to intercept targets beyond SRAAM range, and uses a radar homing system with a greater detection range and better all-weather properties than the infrared guidance system.

LRAAMs are truly remarkable weapons, and perhaps the most impressive of all was the Phoenix carried exclusively by the US Navy F-14 Tomcat. In its time the world's most sophisticated and expensive AAM, the Phoenix had a speed of five times the speed of sound, and could be launched from over 200km/124 miles distance from a target, before the F-14 had even appeared on an enemy aircraft radar screen.

With no real alternatives on the horizon, air-to-air missiles will remain the prime armament of naval and indeed land-based fighters for many years to come.

ABOVE: **A torpedo-armed Royal Navy Westland Wasp HAS.1, typifying the real destructive but versatile power that post-war helicopter development brought to naval military aviation. The light Wasp could carry two Mk 44 or 46 torpedoes or Mk 44 depth charges. Incredibly, it was also cleared to carry the WE177 272kg/600lb Nuclear Depth Bomb.** BELOW: **A Royal Navy Supermarine Scimitar could carry up to 96 unguided rockets. This large and heavy fighter could also carry four AGM-45 Bullpup air-to-ground missiles or four AIM-9 Sidewinder air-to-air missiles.**

Aircraft carriers of the Falklands War

When Argentine forces invaded the Falkland Islands in early April, 1982, Britain's Royal Navy had only two of its four aircraft carriers in service – HMS *Invincible* and HMS *Hermes*. It was, however, only due to these two carriers and the aircraft they carried, that Britain was able to win a conflict some 12,900km/8,000 miles away.

The 1960s and 70s had seen a gradual run down of Britain's carrier assets and, following a 1981 Defence Review, *Invincible* was to have been sold to Australia. *Hermes*, however, had undergone a £30 million refit and conversion to become a ski-ramp carrier capable of operating the new Sea Harrier fighters that were to prove so vital during the Falklands campaign. *Hermes*, the task force flagship, and *Invincible* both sailed from Portsmouth on April 5, 1982, after a rapid, remarkable and frantic period of preparation.

At this stage in the Cold War, *Invincible*'s air group typically consisted of nine Sea King HAS.5 Anti-Submarine Warfare (ASW) helicopters and perhaps just five Sea Harrier FRS.1 fighters. This was because the mission for which the ship had trained was that of anti-submarine warfare in the North Atlantic pitted against Soviet submarines. In this form of warfare, the ASW helicopters were the most important air assets while the Sea Harriers were there to deal with Soviet patrol aircraft that might have got too close to the carrier. The Falklands changed that and showed that even post-Imperial Britain still had to retain the capability to use carriers to project military power wherever needed around the world. After the Falklands, the typical Royal Navy carrier air group became three AEW Sea Kings, nine ASW Sea Kings and eight or nine Sea Harriers.

TOP: **The Royal Navy carriers HMS *Illustrious*, foreground, and HMS *Invincible* pictured in September 1982. *Invincible* and *Hermes* were the only British carriers available when the conflict developed.** ABOVE: **This picture of the hangar deck in a British carrier during the war epitomizes the versatility, organization and planning that is required to wage war from an aircraft carrier. Harriers, helicopters and troops all prepare for battle beneath the ship's armoured deck.**

Aircraft carriers were, however, not the only ships to carry aircraft during the Falklands war. The Ministry of Defence requisitioned many merchant navy ships to sail south to help retake the Falklands. Although some were converted for use as troop carriers or floating hospitals, several were also converted into basic aircraft carriers. The container ship SS *Atlantic Conveyer*, for example, had been laid up on the Mersey but was quickly taken to Devonport for conversion into a 'Harrier Carrier' and headed south. With containers stacked around the flight deck, the ship and others like it were able to operate the versatile V/STOL Sea Harrier. Unfortunately, on May 25, the *Atlantic Conveyer* was struck by an air-launched Exocet missile

FAR LEFT: **A Royal Navy Sea Harrier leaves the ski-ramp of HMS** *Hermes*. **Sea Harriers alone claimed 24 kills with no losses in air combat, although 2 were lost to ground fire and 4 in accidents. Fleet Air Arm unit 801 NAS achieved a sortie rate of 99 per cent for all missions tasked, fired 12 missiles, 3,000 rounds of 30mm cannon and dropped 56 bombs.** LEFT: **The biggest airborne threat to the British task force were the anti-shipping missiles carried by Argentine Super Etendards. The weapons proved deadly against a number of British ships.** BELOW: **Helicopters were a vital element of the British inventory and enabled troops and supplies to be moved ashore and around the Islands quickly. They were also used for covert operations and casualty evacuation as well as anti-submarine patrols.**

and was destroyed with the loss of twelve crew, three Chinook and six Wessex helicopters. During the conflict, Royal Navy helicopter support and assault ships had both also successfully landed Sea Harriers on their helicopter flight decks.

The Argentine Navy also had a carrier in operation during the Falklands war, the *Veinticinco De Mayo*. Formerly Royal Navy Light Fleet Carrier HMS *Venerable*, launched in December 1943, *Veinticinco De Mayo* was acquired by Argentina in 1961. The deployment of four Royal Navy nuclear-powered 'hunter-killer' submarines and the subsequent sinking of the cruiser *General Belgrano* kept most of the Argentine fleet including *Veinticinco De Mayo* in Argentina's shallow coastal waters. Accordingly the carrier played little part in the conflict although some of her aircraft later flew raids while operating from mainland Argentina.

When the war was over, *Hermes* sailed back to the UK on July 5 while *Invincible* remained on station until July 29 when

she was relieved by her brand-new, hurriedly completed sister-ship *Illustrious* on August 27, 1982. *Illustrious* was in fact completed three months ahead of schedule and after the quickest of sea trials sailed south, commissioning on the way. *Hermes* arrived back at Portsmouth on the July 21 while *Invincible* got home on September 17, having spent 166 days at sea, at that point a record for continuous Royal Navy carrier operations.

The sale of *Invincible* was then cancelled and the Australians were offered the older *Hermes* instead. *Invincible* went on to see operational duty again off the former Yugoslavia and later Iraq. *Hermes* was decommissioned in 1984, laid up at Portsmouth until 1986 and was sold to the Indian Navy who commissioned the ship on May 12, 1987, having renamed her INS *Viraat* (Giant). The *Viraat* is the flagship of the Indian Navy. The *Veinticinco De Mayo* was laid up in 1993 and was finally scrapped in India during 1999.

ABOVE: **The** *Atlantic Conveyor* **'Harrier Carrier' was a 15,000-ton Cunard roll-on roll-off container ship and is pictured here with Chinooks and a Sea Harrier landing on the deck. It was destroyed by an Exocet on May 25, 1982.**

ABOVE: **Britain fielded a mixed Harrier force during the Falklands War as seen in this carrier deck shot from the time. The Sea Harriers were tasked with air defence while the RAF Harriers were to specialize in ground attack.**

Naval aviation technology – 1945 to the present day

For most of the latter half of the 20th century, combat aircraft designers continued to do what their predecessors had done – improve performance through a better understanding of aerodynamics, more powerful engines and harnessing all available technology. Piston-engined fighters had virtually reached the end of their evolutionary line by 1945 although many remained in service for some years after the end of World War II. Jet-powered fighters began to make their mark towards the end of the war, and within a decade supersonic speeds were regularly achieved, albeit in dives. At the same time, the advent of nuclear weapons made the development of nuclear-capable carrier-borne jet aircraft a high carrier priority for land-based and carrier forces.

A greater understanding of 'area rule' – the design technique that produces a fuselage contour with the lowest possible transonic wave drag – came in the 1950s and helped aircraft designers break through the 'sound barrier' and produce aircraft capable of supersonic speeds in level flight.

Jet engine technology progressed rapidly in the 1950s resulting in engines like the Buccaneer's Rolls-Royce 5,035kg/11,100lb-thrust Spey. This engine generated more than twice the output of the Sea Hawk's 2,268kg/5,000lb Rolls-Royce Nene. Afterburner or reheat capability was developed in

TOP: **The development of the helicopter has given naval strategists much greater flexibility in the types of forces and responses they can create in times of tension. Here, Royal Navy Wessexes are seen landing on HMS *Bulwark* when it served as a commando carrier.**
ABOVE: **Space is always an issue on carriers, and among the features used to alleviate the problem is folding helicopter tails and rotor blades. The aircraft shown is a Sea King of the US Navy unit HS-5.**

the late 1940s to give fighters an emergency boost of energy if required. When a pilot engages afterburner, additional fuel is simply burned in the jetpipe to generate extra thrust. This does consume considerable amounts of fuel and is used sparingly.

At first, jet fighters continued to use the construction techniques and materials employed on piston-engined aircraft. With the dawn of high-speed flight and the extreme stresses places on an airframe, designers began to look beyond aluminium and magnesium alloys and used titanium alloys and specially developed steel. Carbon or graphite fibre composites are also now commonly used as they weigh half as much as aluminium alloys but have three times the strength. This major weight saving reduces the overall weight of combat aircraft and allows them to carry more fuel or weaponry.

RIGHT: **Two aircraft designs, both capable of vertical take-off but very different – the Harrier family and the helicopter technically do not require conventional flight decks.** BELOW: **A Westland Wyvern pictured during tests of** *Ark Royal*'s **new steam catapult, which enabled heavier aircraft to operate from carriers.** BELOW RIGHT: **This system, the Mirror Landing Aid (MLA), replaced the earlier entirely human paddle-waving Deck Landing Officer system. Pilots of faster jets with a nose-up attitude struggled with the old system, so the British developed the MLA, which reflected the pilot's own landing lights back to him and, with mirrors and lenses, instructed him on his altitude and attitude.**

Jet-aircraft designers have always grappled with the problem of trying to reduce the take-off and landing runs of high-speed combat aircraft and never more so than on carrier operations. A truly innovative solution was the development of swing-wing, or variable geometry, in which the wings can move automatically from the swept to the spread position to maximize the aircraft's aerodynamic performance as required.

On take-off, the spread position generates more lift and gets the aircraft off the ground or carrier deck sooner. Once in the air, the wings can be swept back for high-speed performance. On approach to landing, the aircraft spreads its wings. As more lift is generated, the aircraft's speed slows, reducing the violence of the landing as the carrier aircraft's hook catches the wire. Only a handful of swing-wing combat aircraft have entered service and only one for carrier operations – the F-14 Tomcat.

The ultimate solution to the short take-off requirement is the Harrier – the only single-engined Vertical or Short Take-Off and Landing (V/STOL) in service. The key to the Harrier's truly remarkable vertical take-off capability lies with the vectored thrust from the Harrier's Rolls-Royce Pegasus engine, directed by four jet nozzles. The nozzles swivel as one, directing thrust from directly to the rear to just forward of vertical. In air combat the nozzles can be used to rapidly decelerate the aircraft so that an enemy aircraft, previously on the Harrier's tail, shoots by, unable to stop thus becoming the Harrier's prey instead. The Soviet Union developed the Harrier-inspired Yak-38 which became the first Soviet combat aircraft designed purely for carrier operation to enter series production and also the first production

ABOVE: **During 1985 the first outline design for a navalized version of the Su-27 fighter was developed from a design first approved in 1985. The Su-27K (K for** *korabelny* **or shipborne) but later designated the Su-33, was conceived to provide the Soviet Navy's new carriers with a fighter for self-defence. The aircraft is a late example of a landplane design being modified for carrier use.**

vertical take-off/landing aircraft built by the Soviet Union. While the Harrier had one versatile engine, the Yak-38 had an engine in the rear used for forward flight while two other smaller, less powerful engines were housed to the rear of the cockpit.

Where fighters once had mechanical linkages from control columns to control surfaces, modern fighters have Fly-By-Wire (FBW). This form of electronic signalling eliminates the need for mechanical linkages and a control column. Computers are now as fundamental to naval and land-based combat aircraft as engines and weapons.

Target – Libya

In 1986, following a number of terrorist attacks on US citizens and interests, US intelligence cited "incontrovertible" evidence that the incidents were sponsored by Libya. Meanwhile, the US Sixth Fleet based in the Mediterranean, began a series of manoeuvres designed to keep the pressure on Libya. Two, sometimes three, aircraft carriers (the *Saratoga, America* and *Coral Sea*) conducted 'freedom of navigation' operations that would take the US warships up to and then southward through a line across the sea that Libya's leader Colonel Gaddafi had proclaimed to be the "line of death".

ABOVE: **The USS *Saratoga* was one of the US Navy carriers on station in the region at the time of the tension with Libya. During the exchanges the ship launched A-7s armed with AGM-88 missiles, A-6s armed with AGM-84 missiles and Mk 20 Rockeye II cluster bombs, and EA-6Bs from VAQ-132.**
BELOW LEFT: **The picture shows an aircrew pre-flight briefing taking place onboard the *Saratoga* on March 22, 1986.**

The line marked the northernmost edge of the Gulf of Sidra and the Libyan leader had warned foreign vessels that the Gulf belonged to Libya and was not international waters – they entered at their own risk and were open to attack by Libyan forces. On March 24, 1986, Libyan air defence SAM missiles were launched against two US Navy F-14s intercepting an intruding Libyan MiG-25 that was too close to the US battle group. Next day, a Navy A-7E aircraft struck the SAM site with AGM-88A HARM missiles. At least two of five threatening Libyan naval attack vessels were also sunk.

US President Ronald Reagan wanted to mount a strike against the Libyan leader's regime but sought cooperation from Western allies. The USAF's plans assumed that UK-based F-111s could fly through French airspace to strike at Libya. Speculation about the strike in the Western media alerted the Libyans and caused the plan to be changed to include support aircraft (EF-111 and US Navy A-7 and EA-6B) to carry out suppression of enemy defences. The US Navy role in the operation grew as the raid had to hit Gaddafi hard.

ABOVE: A US Navy pilot pictured with his A-7 Corsair II. RIGHT: A US Air Force F-111 takes off from RAF Lakenheath in Suffolk, England, heading for the attack on Libya after a 7-hour flight and a number of refuellings. Co-ordination was crucial for the attack involving US Navy, US Marine Corps and USAF aircraft.

Plans were further complicated when France, Germany, Italy and Spain all refused to cooperate in a strike. The F-111s now had to navigate over the ocean around France and Spain, pass east over the Straits of Gibraltar, and then over the Mediterranean to line up for their bombing run on Libya. It would be a gruelling round-trip of 10,300km/6,400 miles taking 13 hours. On April 14, 1986, the United States launched Operation 'El Dorado Canyon' against Libya.

US planners tabled a joint USAF/USN operation against five major Libyan targets. Two were in Benghazi: a terrorist training camp and a military airfield. The other three targets were in Tripoli: a terrorist naval training base; the former Wheelus AFB; and the Azziziyah Barracks compound, which housed the HQ of Libyan intelligence and also contained one of five residences that Gaddafi was known to have used. Eighteen F-111s were to strike the Tripoli targets, while US Navy aircraft were to hit the two Benghazi sites.

At 17:36 GMT on April 14, 24 F-111s left the UK, six of them spare aircraft set to return after the first refuelling. The US Navy attack aircraft came from carriers of the US Sixth Fleet operating in the Mediterranean. *Coral Sea* provided eight A-6E medium bombers and six F/A-18C Hornets for strike support. USS *America* launched six A-6Es plus six A-7Es and an EA-6B for strike support. They faced a hazardous flight as Libya's air defence system was very sophisticated and virtually on a par

with that of the Soviet Union. Timing was critical, and the USAF and USN attacks had to be simultaneous to maximize the element of surprise so that the strike aircraft could get in and out as quickly as possible. Of the eighteen F-111s that headed for Libya, five had aborted en route so at around midnight GMT, thirteen F-111s reached Tripoli and carried out their attack at speeds around 740kph/460mph and heights of 61m/200ft.

EF-111As and US Navy A-7s, A-6Es, and an EA-6B armed with HARM and Shrike anti-radar missiles flew in defence-suppression roles for the F-111s. Across the Gulf of Sidra, Navy A-6E aircraft attacked the Al Jumahiriya Barracks at Benghazi, and to the east, the Benina airfield. News of the attack was being broadcast in the US while it was underway. The Navy's Intruders destroyed four MiG-23s, two Fokker F-27s, and two Mil Mi-8 helicopters.

The operation was never intended to topple Gaddafi, but he was known to have been very shaken when bombs exploded near him. When he next appeared on state television he was certainly subdued. Most importantly, the raids demonstrated that even in those pre-stealth days and thanks to the support of aircraft carrier assets, the US had the capability to send its high-speed bombers over great distances to carry out precision attacks. The raid was considered a success, but the situation between the US and Gaddafi remained unresolved for another 17 years before an uneasy peace was agreed.

ABOVE: Although the Libyan Air Force had the high-performance MiG-25 fighter, as pictured, no fighter opposition was encountered during the US attacks. Anti-aircraft defences were, however, extensive and resulted in the loss of one USAF F-111 shot down over the Gulf of Sidra.

ABOVE: A Libyan Air Force Sukhoi Su-22 of the kind Libya operated at the time. The defences the attacking US aircraft did encounter were sophisticated long-range anti-aircraft missiles. Tripoli alone was protected by an estimated 214 anti-aircraft missiles at the time.

A 21st-century carrier at war

A recent deployment of the United States Navy carrier USS *Enterprise* – 'the Big E' – is a good illustration of the nature, scale and capability of current US naval air power. On November 18, 2006, more than 5,400 sailors assigned to USS *Enterprise* (CVN-65) returned to Naval Station Norfolk, Virginia, following a six-month deployment in support of the ongoing rotation of forward-deployed forces conducting "operations in support of the global war on terrorism".

Nuclear-powered aircraft carrier USS *Enterprise* was deployed on May 2, 2006, as the flagship of *Enterprise* Carrier Strike Group (ENT CSG) comprised of Carrier Air Wing One (CVW-1), Destroyer Squadron Two (DESRON-2), USS *Enterprise* (CVN 65), guided-missile cruiser USS *Leyte Gulf* (CG 55), guided-missile destroyer USS *McFaul* (DDG 74), guided-missile frigate USS *Nicholas* (FFG 47), and fast combat support ship USS *Supply* (T-AOE 6). On its cruise, the carrier supported operations in the US 5th, 6th and 7th Fleet areas of responsibility.

Carrier Air Wing (CVW) 1, embarked on the *Enterprise* included the 'Sidewinders' of Strike Fighter Squadron (VFA) 86, the 'Checkmates' of VFA-211, the 'Knighthawks' of VFA-136, the 'Thunderbolts' of Marine Strike Fighter Squadron (VMFA) 251, the 'Screwtops' of Airborne Early Warning Squadron (VAW) 123, the 'Rooks' of Tactical Electronic Warfare Squadron (VAQ) 137, the 'Maulers' of Sea Control Squadron (VS) 32, the 'Rawhides' of Carrier Logistics Support (VRC) 40, and the 'Dragonslayers' of Helicopter Anti-Submarine Squadron (HS) 11.

During the cruise, the squadrons of CVW-1 flew nearly 23,000 hours, including nearly 12,000 hours of combat

TOP: **The nuclear-powered aircraft carrier USS *Enterprise* (CVN 65) pulls into its homeport of Naval Station Norfolk, after a six-month deployment. The *Enterprise* was commissioned in November 1961 and is 342m/1,123ft long. It was built to accommodate 99 aircraft and its nuclear power provides steam for the operation of four catapults. It was completed with an all-missile armament.**
ABOVE: **An F/A-18C Hornet, attached to the 'Sidewinders' of Strike Fighter Squadron (VFA) 86, prepares to 'shoot' off the flight deck of the *Enterprise*.**

missions in Operations 'Iraqi Freedom' and 'Enduring Freedom'. During its deployment, the *Enterprise* steamed nearly 100,000km/60,000 miles, dropped 137 precision weapons over nearly 8,500 sorties flown, and spent nearly $10 million alone on feeding the crew. Around 15.6 million emails were sent and received aboard the *Enterprise*.

"Carrier Air Wing 1 and the entire *Enterprise* Strike Group team were prepared to flexibly and effectively support a variety of missions," said Captain Mark Wralstad, Commander, CVW-1. "Whether we operated carrier-based aircraft from

ABOVE LEFT: **An F/A-18C Hornet clears the** *Enterprise* **deck. Armed with a 20mm cannon and up to 7,000kg/15,500lb of weapons including air-to-air missiles, other guided weapons and rockets and tactical nuclear weapons, the Hornet is one of the world's most capable combat aircraft.** ABOVE RIGHT: **The** *Enterprise* **displaces 89,600 tons and at the commissioning was the world's first nuclear-powered aircraft carrier and simply the mightiest warship to ever sail the seas.** *Enterprise* **is the tallest (76m/250ft) carrier in the US Navy and the fastest. The ship was built with a distinctive square island supporting phased-array radars and a complex electronic warfare system.** LEFT: **Sailors aboard the** *Enterprise* **direct an HH-60H Seahawk helicopter, attached to the 'Dragonslayers' of Helicopter Anti-submarine Squadron (HS) 11, on the flight deck during a vertical replenishment (VERTREP) with the Military Sealift Command (MSC) fleet replenishment oiler USNS** *Laramie.*

land, engaged our nation's enemies from the sea, or engaged our friends and allies from the flight deck of *Enterprise*, the entire strike group helped to set the conditions for security and stability throughout the world."

During June and July 2006, *Enterprise* aircraft launched 781 aircraft sorties in direct support of troops participating in Operation 'Iraqi Freedom' and 237 aircraft sorties in support of Operation 'Enduring Freedom'.

On one day alone, September 20, 2006, aircraft assigned to CVW-1 stationed aboard USS *Enterprise* flew 14 missions in the skies over Afghanistan and provided their heaviest day of close air support to International Security Assistance Force (ISAF) troops and other coalition forces on the ground as part of Operation 'Enduring Freedom'.

F/A-18F Super Hornets from the 'Checkmates' of Strike Fighter Squadron (VFA) 211, supported both ISAF and other coalition ground forces in multiple locations north of Kandahar in Afghanistan. The Navy's latest generation of fighter/attack aircraft completed multiple strafing runs against the Taliban using the aircraft's M61A1 20mm gatling gun and ended the engagement by dropping Guided Bomb Unit (GBU)-12 weapons – general-purpose, laser-guided 226kg/500lb bombs.

Later that day, the *Enterprise*-based 'Checkmates' attacked a compound north of Kandahar believed to be a Taliban haven.

The compound was destroyed with GBU-12 weapons. After refuelling, 'Checkmates' aircraft flew multiple show-of-force missions north of Kandahar against the Taliban who were attacking coalition ground forces with small arms fire.

F/A-18C Hornets from the 'Sidewinders' of VFA-86 performed multiple strafing runs against Taliban positions near Kandahar. The *Enterprise*-based aircraft expended GBU-12 weapons against the extremists, ending the engagement.

The 'Sidewinders' continued their missions later that day as they provided support for ISAF ground convoys and coalition troops. When ground controllers notified the *Enterprise*-based aircraft of a Taliban compound used for offensive action against ISAF and coalition ground forces identified north of Kandahar, 'Sidewinders' Hornet aircraft expended multiple GBU-12 weapons against the fortification, destroying the target.

Speaking at the time, Rear Admiral Raymond Spicer, commander of the *Enterprise* Carrier Strike Group, said, "Whether *Enterprise* strike group is protecting coalition troops on the ground, conducting planned strikes on known terrorist sites, or providing airborne command and control for our coalition partners, we have demonstrated our ability to operate as a combat-ready naval force capable of sustained combat operations, deterring aggression, preserving freedom of the seas, and promoting peace and security."

Current and future carriers

Today, aircraft carriers remain the largest military ships operated by modern navies. By way of example, a US Navy Nimitz-class carrier, powered by a combination of two nuclear reactors and four steam turbines, is 333m/1,092ft long and costs about US$4.5 billion. The United States Navy is the world's largest carrier operator with eleven in service, one under construction, and one on order. It is these warships that are the cornerstone of the United States' ability to 'project power' around the world. During the 2003 invasion of Iraq, US aircraft carriers served as the primary base of US air power. As a result, and even without the ability to place significant numbers of aircraft on land bases, the United States was capable of carrying out significant air attacks from carrier-based squadrons. Although nations including Britain and France are looking to increase their carrier capability, the US will remain the dominant carrier operator.

At the time of writing, ten countries maintain a total of 20 aircraft carriers in active service. As well as the USA, Britain, France, Russia, Italy, India, Spain, Brazil, Thailand and China all have carriers that operate or are capable of operations. In addition, South Korea, Britain, Canada, China, India, Japan, Australia, Chile, Singapore and France also operate naval

TOP: **A BAE SYSTEMS proposed early design for the next generation of Royal Navy aircraft carriers, the CVF. Large new carriers require massive investment to bring into service and take so long to develop that the threat they are developed to counter can change in the meantime.**

ABOVE: **The USS _Abraham Lincoln_ (CVN-72) boasts all the amenities found in any American city with a comparable population. These include a post office (with its own post or 'zip' code), TV and radio stations, newspaper, fire department, library, hospital, general store, barber shops, and more.**

vessels capable of carrying and operating significant numbers of military helicopters.

Using techniques developed during World War II, aircraft carriers never cruise alone and are generally accompanied by a variety of other warships that provide protection for the carrier, which would be a prime target for any potential enemy. The collection of ships, with the carrier at its heart, is known as a battle group, carrier group or carrier battle group.

The Royal Navy plans to replace its current carrier fleet of three Invincible-class carriers operating Harriers and helicopters with two new larger STOVL 'CVF' aircraft carriers. HMS *Queen Elizabeth* and HMS *Prince of Wales* are scheduled to enter service in 2014 and 2016 respectively. Each ship will be a similar size and weight as the ocean liner the QE2. A CVF would weigh 65,000 tons (around 32,500 average family cars) at full displacement and measure 284m/931ft in length with a flight-deck width of 73m/239ft. With nine decks, the flight-deck could handle a maximum of 40 aircraft (36 Joint Strike Fighters and 4 AEW aircraft) and would be compatible with the aircraft of friendly nations. Each of the two huge lifts that move aircraft from hangar to flight deck can carry two aircraft apiece and are so big just one of them could carry the weight of the entire ship's crew.

A CVF will carry over 8,600 tons of fuel to support the ship and its aircraft, which would be enough for the average family car to travel to the moon and back 12 times. Crew numbers will be just 40 per cent larger than those of the current Royal Navy carriers although the new ships will be three times larger. The two ships will be the largest warships ever built for the Royal Navy.

Despite all the shipbuilding advances, improvements in the technology and capabilities of anti-ship missiles mean that the vulnerability of carriers will always be a concern for naval strategists. Though the carrier and the carrier group can defend itself against multiple threats, in time, the prime ships of navies may well become submarines. Already capable of unleashing formidable nuclear and conventional firepower, submarines remain difficult to attack when operating deep in the ocean. Although these submarines could launch and retrieve unmanned reconnaissance aircraft (drones), there would be no place for manned aircraft and naval aviation as we know it could become a matter for history books and aviation museums.

ABOVE LEFT: **The Nimitz-class supercarriers are a class of five nuclear-powered aircraft carriers in service with the US Navy and are the largest capital ships in the world. The ships are numbered with consecutive hull numbers starting with CVN-68. The letters CVN denote the type of ship – CV is the hull classification for aircraft carriers, while N indicates nuclear propulsion. The number after the CVN means that this is the 68th aircraft carrier.**

ABOVE: **USS *Enterprise* (CVAN-65) is manoeuvred by tugs in shallow water.** BELOW: ***Charles de Gaulle* (R91) is France's only serving aircraft carrier and is the flagship of the French Navy. It is the first French nuclear-powered surface vessel, and the first nuclear-powered carrier built for an operator other than the United States Navy.** BOTTOM: ***Admiral Kuznetsov* was launched in 1985 and was commissioned into the Soviet Navy but is now the flagship of the Russian Navy. The carrier has no catapult so cannot launch aircraft with heavy offensive loads but has got a ski-ramp.**

Top Gun

Immortalized by the 1986 Hollywood blockbuster of the same name, Top Gun, or more properly the United States Navy Fighter Weapons School (NFWS) was established in 1969. Although no longer based at Miramar in California or flying F-14s, the current incarnation of Top Gun remains a vital means of keeping the US Navy at the forefront of air fighting doctrine.

In the early years of the Vietnam war, the United States was not achieving the same level of air-to-air combat superiority that it had enjoyed in Korea. By 1968, concerns about the comparatively low kill ratio in South-east Asia prompted the formation of a US Navy air combat 'masters' course teaching Air Combat Manoeuvring (ACM) and weapons systems use. The first course commenced on March 3, 1969, and Top Gun was formally commissioned as a separate command at NAS Miramar on July 7, 1972. From then on, NFWS became the hub for Navy and Marine Corps tactics development and training. The school focused on teaching the art of Dissimilar Air Combat Manoeuvring using 'friendly' aircraft to replicate the handling and capabilities of enemy aircraft such as the MiG-17 and MiG-21.

Top Gun instructors initially operated the A-4 Skyhawk to replicate the MiG-17 and borrowed USAF T-38 Talons to 'be' the MiG-21 to instruct F-4 Phantom aircrews in dissimilar training. Top Gun swiftly established itself as a centre of excellence in fighter doctrine, tactics and training and soon every US Navy fighter squadron had its share of Top Gun graduates who served as Subject Matter Experts (SMEs) in their units passing on their expertise. US Navy win-to-loss ratios in South-east Asia climbed to 20:1 before standardizing at the target level of 12.5:1. The USAF, without a Top Gun

LEFT: **The expression 'Top Gun' is now used around the world in military aviation, and has come to epitomize, as the Hollywood blockbuster film starring Tom Cruise stated, the best of the best. The Top Gun programme keeps the US Navy's pilots among the best fighting aviators in the world.**

programme of its own, maintained its poor kill-to-loss ratio until it too set up a dissimilar air combat training programme of their own. Successful Top Gun graduates who achieved air combat victories over North Vietnam and returned to Top Gun as instructors included 'Mugs' McKeown, Jack Ensch and the first US 'aces' of the Vietnam War, Randy 'Duke' Cunningham and Willie Driscoll.

With the 1970s and 1980s came the introduction of the Grumman F-14 and the Northrop F/A-18 Hornet as the US Navy's primary fleet fighter aircraft flown by Top Gun students. Meanwhile, Top Gun instructors retained their A-4s and F-5s, but also added the General Dynamics F-16 to more accurately simulate the threat posed by the Soviet Union's latest MiG-29 and Sukhoi Su-27 fighters. During the 1990s, the students' syllabus was developed with greater emphasis on the air-to-ground strike mission to reflect the real missions flown by multi-role aircraft like the F-14 and F/A-18. Eventually the

ABOVE: **Twenty-five modified Israeli Kfir-C1s were leased to the US Navy and the US Marine Corps from 1985 to 1989 to act as adversary aircraft in dissimilar air combat training. Of these aircraft, which were designated F-21A Lion, the 12 F-21 aircraft leased to the US Navy were painted in a three-tone blue-gray 'ghost' scheme and were operated by VF-43, based at NAS Oceana. In 1988 they were returned and replaced by the F-16N.**

BELOW: **The now retired F-14 Tomcat, here shown with wings sweeping back, was one of the world's greatest combat aircraft. Top Gun made very good pilots even better.**

RIGHT: **A Tomcat with its wings spread and 'fires burning' just after take-off. The final Tomcat Top Gun class graduated in early October 2003 and the type was retired from US Navy service in 2006.**

instructors retired their A-4s and F-5s, which were replaced by F-14s and F/A-18s.

1996 saw the end of an era when Top Gun left its California base and was absorbed into the Naval Strike and Air Warfare Center (NSAWC) at NAS Fallon, Nevada. Today's Top Gun instructors fly the F/A-18A/B/C Hornet and the F-16A/B Falcon (aircraft destined for Pakistan but never delivered due to embargoes) that are assigned to NSAWC. Top Gun continues to refine fighter tactics in its Power Projection and Maritime Air Superiority modules to keep the Fleet aware of and trained in current tactical developments.

There are five courses each year, each 6 weeks in duration for 12 US Fleet fighter and strike fighter aircrews. This course is designed to train experienced US Navy and Marine Corps fighter aircrews at an advanced level in all aspects of fighter aircraft use including tactics, hardware, techniques, and the 'current world threat'. The course includes around 80 hours of lectures and a rigorous flight syllabus that sets student aircrews against adversary aircraft flown by Top Gun instructors. Just as Top Gun was originally conceived, each new graduate of the Navy Fighter Weapons School returns to their operational squadron as a training officer fully trained in the latest tactical doctrine.

Top Gun also runs an Adversary Training Course, flying with adversary aircrew from each Navy and Marine Corps adversary squadron. These pilots receive individual instruction in threat simulation, effective threat presentation, and adversary tactics.

Tactics being developed today at the US Navy Fighter Weapons School will enable US Navy aircrews to carry an aggressive and successful fight to the enemy and ensure that they remain Top Guns.

ABOVE: **Feeling the need for speed, an F-14 flies in formation with an A-4 Skyhawk, the latter being the favoured mount of Top Gun instructors for a number of years.** BELOW: **The A-4 had comparable handling to the MiG-17 and was a vital teaching aid used for tutoring the pilots who could have faced the best aviators the Warsaw Pact and other potential enemies could muster.**

Directory of World War Naval Aircraft

1914–45

The marriage of military aviation and sea power was a potent mix, perhaps best demonstrated by the devastating attack carried out on Pearl Harbor in December 1941 by Japanese aircraft operating from aircraft carriers. Without the carriers and the specialized aircraft that operated from the carriers, the Japanese could never have struck Pearl Harbor. These floating airfields carried fighters for defence and for attacking enemy aircraft, but could also carry purpose-designed attack aircraft such as dive-bombers that, in the hands of skilled pilots, could destroy enormous warships. The same was true of the torpedo-bomber, which could launch devastating attacks on surface vessels.

Prior to World War II, naval aircraft tended to be the poor relations of the high-performance land-based types. As the opposing sides squared up to fight in World War II, there was no room for second best in the battles that were fought, sometimes thousands of miles from major land masses. Modifications to aircraft like the Spitfire and Hurricane were a useful stopgap but these aircraft were in a different league to the tough, purpose-designed naval aircraft like the Grumman Hellcat that proved to be real war winners.

LEFT: **Two classic Grumman purpose-designed naval fighters flying in formation – the Bearcat (closest) and the Hellcat. The 'cat' series continued to the F-14 Tomcat.**

Aichi D3A

This two-seat low-wing monoplane dive-bomber, codenamed 'Val' by the Allies, came to prominence on December 7, 1941, during the attack on Pearl Harbor. When the Japanese naval task force launched its first wave of 183 aircraft from six aircraft carriers to attack Pearl Harbor's Battleship Row and other US Navy installations on the Hawaiian island of Oahu, among them were 51 Aichi D3As. This first wave of the attack was led by a formation of D3As, which became the first Japanese aircraft to drop bombs on American targets during World War II. One of the D3As' victims during the attack was the American Pacific Fleet flagship USS *Pennsylvania*. In all, 129 Aichi D3A aircraft were used as part of the Japanese Pearl Harbor task force.

After the attack and despite its relative obsolescence, the D3A took part in all major Japanese carrier operations

ABOVE: In mid-1936 the Imperial Japanese Navy issued a specification for a monoplane carrier-based dive-bomber to replace the D1A then in service. Aichi, Nakajima and Mitsubishi all submitted designs.

in the first ten months of the war. Prior to the 'Day of Infamy' at Pearl Harbor, the type had only seen limited action from land bases in China and Indochina.

The D3A was designed to replace the Aichi D1A2 Navy Type 96 Carrier Bomber and featured a fixed landing gear to eliminate extra weight as well as the maintenance demands of a retractable undercarriage. The outer 1.83m/6ft sections of the wing hinged up to save space during carrier stowage.

The type had first flown in January 1938, and between December 1939 and August 1945 the Aichi company built a total of 1,495 aircraft in two main variants.

ABOVE: Preparing to unleash the 'Day of Infamy', Aichi D3A1 'Val' dive-bombers get ready to take off from a Japanese aircraft carrier during the morning of December 7, 1941, to attack Pearl Harbor.

ABOVE: US Navy personnel prepare to remove a D3A that crashed during the attack on Pearl Harbor. The Japanese only lost 29 aircraft during the attack, but United States military losses were huge.

LEFT: **A crashed D3A being craned on to a salvage barge following the Pearl Harbor attack.**
BELOW: **This stamp shows the D3A1's fixed undercarriage fitted with streamlined fairings to reduce the drag. Weight saving and simplification were achieved at the expense of performance.**

The Type D3A1 entered service with the Imperial Japanese Navy in 1940. The production D3A1 featured a 1,000hp Mitsubishi Kinsei 43 or 1,070hp Kinsei 44 engine. A large dorsal fin was installed to correct directional stability problems and the aircraft was equipped with only two forward-firing 7.7mm Type 97 machine-guns and one flexible rear-firing 7.7mm Type 92 machine-gun. Typical bomb load was a single 250kg/551lb bomb carried under the fuselage. Two additional 60kg/132lb bombs could be carried on wing racks beneath each wing outboard of the dive brakes.

The D3A2, the main production version, had the more powerful 1,300hp Kinsei engine and increased fuel capacity of 1,079 litres/237 gallons which gave an increased range of 1,472km/915 miles. This version can be identified by the addition of a longer rear canopy section. Some 1,016 examples were built by the time it was considered obsolete at the end of 1942. Nevertheless, in April 1942, during attacks on the British cruisers HMS *Cornwall* and HMS *Dorsetshire* in the Indian Ocean, D3As are known to have released over 82 per cent of their ordnance on target. During this action, the British carrier *Hermes* also sank following attacks by 'Vals' – the only Royal Navy carrier lost to enemy air attack during World War II.

Commonwealth of
Dominica
$2
AICHI D3AI TYPE 99 'VAL'

The arrival of the faster Yokosuka Suisei relegated the D3A2s to land-based units and to smaller carriers too short for the Suisei's higher landing speed.

Over the following years, many 'Vals' were used as training aircraft but as the war progressed and the Americans moved closer to the Japanese mainland, most of the remaining aircraft were used in desperate kamikaze suicide attacks against US naval ships at Leyte and Okinawa.

ABOVE: **The 'Val' was credited with dive-bombing and sinking the only Royal Navy carrier lost during World War II. Inevitably, the type was also used for kamikaze attacks as the Japanese position worsened.**

Aichi D3A1 'Val'

First flight: January 1938
Power: One Mitsubishi 1,070hp Kinsei 44 radial piston engine
Armament: Two 7.7mm machine-guns in upper forward fuselage plus one in rear cockpit; external bomb load of 370kg/816lb
Size: Wingspan – 14.37m/47ft 2in
Length – 10.20m/33ft 5in
Height – 3.80m/12ft 7in
Wing area – 34.9m²/376sq ft
Weights: Empty – 2,408kg/5,309lb
Maximum take-off – 3,650kg/8,047lb
Performance: Maximum speed – 385kph/239mph
Service ceiling – 9,300m/30,510ft
Range – 1,470km/913 miles
Climb – 3,000m/9,845ft in 6 minutes

Arado Ar 196

From 1933, the German Navy (*Kriegsmarine*) operated shipborne reconnaissance aircraft – catapult launched in the harshest conditions and recovered by crane, the aircraft were carried by all major warships, including battleships. By 1936 the types in use were considered obsolete and, following a competition, Arado's twin-float Ar 196 was chosen to be the replacement aircraft in *Kriegsmarine* service. Following further testing and development, the Ar 196A-1 entered service in June 1939. Warships would launch the aircraft to scout ahead looking for danger or targets of opportunity.

Tirpitz and *Bismarck* carried six aircraft each while the *Scharnhorst* and *Gneisnau* had four. Heavy cruisers carried

ABOVE: **As well as its shipborne service, the Arado Ar 196 also served with coastal reconnaissance units. This Ar 196A-5 served in the eastern Mediterranean and Aegean Seas in 1943.** BELOW LEFT: **The type was the standard equipment of Germany's capital ships – the *Tirpitz* and *Bismarck* each carried six examples of the aircraft. The aircraft were catapulted off a launch rail when required and then hoisted back on deck on their return.**

three while smaller battleships and cruisers had two. The first operational cruise for two of these early aircraft was aboard the pocket battleship *Admiral Graf Spee* when it sailed for the South Atlantic in August 1939. The Arados took the warship's 'eyes' well over the horizon to look for prospective targets and located the majority of the ship's 11 British victims. During the Battle of the River Plate in December 1939, both of the *Spee*'s aircraft were destroyed on the ship's deck by British gunfire.

However, as well as equipping the fleet, the type also served widely with shore units on coastal reconnaissance duties. The Ar 196A-2 was designed to operate from shore bases looking for enemy shipping, although forward-firing cannon fitted within the wings gave the Arado a powerful punch against enemy aircraft as well as surface vessels. In addition the type had a 7.9mm forward-firing machine-gun in the fuselage nose and up to two 7.9mm flexible guns in the rear cockpit. A 50kg/110lb bomb could also be carried under each wing. On May 5, 1940, two Ar 196s operating from a shorebase in Denmark spotted Royal Navy submarine HMS *Seal*, damaged by a mine it was trying to lay. After repeated attacks by the two floatplanes the submarine, so damaged it was unable to dive, surrendered to one of the floatplanes as it landed next to it.

Other land-based Ar 196s operating along the French coast of the Bay of Biscay successfully intercepted RAF Whitley bombers attacking German U-boats sailing to and from their protective pens.

Each of the aircraft's two floats contained a 300-litre/ 66-gallon fuel tank while the aircraft's wings could be folded manually to the rear. A continuous greenhouse-style canopy covered the pilot and observer's positions – the latter crewmember was unable to completely close his section of canopy, ensuring the rear cockpit armament was always at readiness. Visibility was good from the cockpit and the type, easy to handle both in the air and on water, proved very popular with its crews. In all, 541 Ar 196s were built (of which 526 were production models) before production ended in August 1944. About 100 examples were built at SNCA and Fokker plants in France and Holland respectively. The Arado Ar 196 was the last fighting floatplane built in Europe.

Only three Ar 196 floatplanes survive. A machine preserved in Bulgaria is one of twelve the Bulgarian air force operated from coastal bases during World War II. Romania was the only other customer for the type. Two other aircraft, captured by the Allies when the battlecruiser *Prinz Eugen* surrendered at Copenhagen, are preserved in the US Naval Aviation Museum and the National Air and Space Museum in the USA.

ABOVE LEFT AND ABOVE: **Although the aircraft's basic design was decided early on, there was uncertainty regarding the best arrangement of floats. Accordingly prototypes were built using both single and twin floats, the single-float models pictured here having two smaller outrigger floats for stability. Some single-float aircraft did see limited service even though evaluation showed the twin-float configuration to be best.** BELOW: **The float rudders on the twin-float production model aided manoeuvring on the water and are clearly visible in this air-to-air study. The long floats also each contained a 300-litre/66-gallon fuel tank.**

ABOVE: **The Ar 196 was the last combat floatplane to be built in Europe, and the type also saw service with the Bulgarian and Romanian air forces through to mid-1944. The aircraft's wings were all metal but with fabric-covered control surfaces.**

Arado Ar 196A-3

First flight: Summer 1937 (prototype)
Power: One BMW 960hp 312K radial engine
Armament: Two 20mm cannon in outer wings, one fixed forward-firing 7.92mm machine-gun, one 7.92mm machine-gun aimed by observer and two 50kg/110lb bombs under wings
Size: Wingspan – 12.44m/40ft 10in
    Length – 10.96m/35ft 11in
    Height – 4.44m/14ft 7in
    Wing area – 28.3m²/305sq ft
Weights: Empty – 2,572kg/5,670lb
    Maximum take-off – 3,303kg/7,282lb
Performance: Maximum speed – 312kph/194mph
    Service ceiling – 7,000m/22,965ft
    Range – 800km/497 miles
    Climb – 414m/1,358ft per minute

LEFT: **Designed by Major F.A. Bumpus, the Blackburn Baffin was a conventional two-seat single-bay biplane torpedo-bomber of mixed metal and wood construction with fabric covering.**

Blackburn Baffin

First flight: September 30, 1932
Power: One Bristol 565hp Pegasus IM3 radial engine
Armament: One fixed 0.303in forward-firing Vickers machine-gun, one 0.303in Lewis machine-gun in rear cockpit and up to 907kg/2,000lb of bombs or one torpedo
Size: Wingspan – 13.88m/45ft 7in
Length – 11.68m/38ft 4in
Height – 3.91m/12ft 10in
Wing area – 63.45m²/683sq ft
Weights: Empty – 1,444kg/3,184lb
Maximum take-off – 3,452kg/7,610lb
Performance: Maximum speed – 219kph/136mph
Service ceiling – 4,570m/15,000ft
Range – 869km/540 miles
Climb – 146m/480ft per minute

Blackburn Baffin

The prototype Baffin, originally known as the Ripon V, differed sufficiently from the earlier Ripon marks to warrant a new name. Inspired by the local installation of radial engines in Finnish-built Ripons, Fairey pursued their own radial-engined version as a private venture. The successful tests of the two-seat torpedo-bomber prototype led not just to a new name but also to an order from the Fleet Air Arm who began replacing early mark Ripons with Baffins from January 1934. The first unit to re-equip was No.812 Squadron on HMS *Glorious*. Although only 29 aircraft were built from new as Baffins, over 60 more Ripons were 'upgraded' to Baffin standard by the installation of the Bristol Pegasus I.M3 radial engine. Upgrade is something of a misnomer as the performance was little improved over that of the Ripon and consequently the type was considered obsolete by 1937. In that year, New Zealand bought 29 of the surplus Baffins for coastal defence duties, some of them serving as late as 1941.

Blackburn Iris

The Iris was the first flying boat produced by the Yorkshire-based Blackburn Aeroplane and Motor Co Ltd. It was designed in response to a specification for an RAF long-range reconnaissance aircraft. June 19, 1926, saw the first flight of this five-man three-engined wooden biplane flying boat; its distinctive biplane tail had an elevator on the upper plane and three rudders. The two pilots sat side by side in an open cockpit while their fellow crew also sat in open cockpits to their rear.

Following evaluation, the prototype (the Iris I) was returned to Blackburn where an all-metal hull was fitted together with more powerful engines – the aircraft was then redesignated Iris II.

The aircraft's ruggedness is best demonstrated by the fact that on September 28, 1928, the Under Secretary of State for Air, Sir Philip Sassoon, embarked on a 15,929km/9,900-mile flight in a Blackburn Iris from Felixstowe to Karachi and back, to inspect Royal Air Force units in Malta, Egypt and Iraq. The aircraft returned to Britain on November 14, 1928.

Three improved production Iris IIIs entered RAF squadron service in 1930, becoming the largest type in the inventory. These were re-engined and became Iris IVs.

LEFT: **Looking as much boat as aircraft, the Blackburn Iris was a sturdy flying machine that served in the Royal Air Force from 1930–34.**

Blackburn Iris

First flight: June 19, 1926
Power: Three Rolls-Royce 570hp Condor IIIB piston engines
Armament: Three 0.303in machine-guns (nose, mid-fuselage and tail) plus up to 907kg/2,000lb of bombs
Size: Wingspan – 29.57m/97ft
Length – 20.54m/67ft 5in
Height – 7.77m/25ft 6in
Wing area – 207.07m²/2,229sq ft
Weights: Empty – 8,640kg/19,048lb
Maximum take-off – 13,376kg/29,489lb
Performance: Maximum speed – 190kph/118mph
Service ceiling – 3,230m/10,600ft
Range – 1,287km/800 miles
Climb – 184m/603ft per minute

LEFT: **The Firebrand's distinctive large fin was developed to counter directional instability caused by engine torque.**
ABOVE: **The Firebrand could carry a torpedo or 16 unguided rocket projectiles.**

Blackburn Firebrand

Outline designs for what became the Firebrand were first produced in response to a 1939 Admiralty requirement for a single-seat four-gun carrier-borne aircraft to replace the Gladiator, Fulmar and Skua. Designed around the Napier Sabre III 24-cylinder engine, the first flight of the first of three Firebrand prototypes took place on February 27, 1942. Nine production examples were completed as Firebrand F.1s while the second prototype was undergoing carrier trials on HMS *Illustrious*. The second prototype was modified with a wider wing centre section to improve the type's torpedo-carrying ability, leading to the production of 12 Firebrand TF.IIs. These aircraft served with trials unit No.708 Squadron, the only Fleet Air Arm unit to receive the type during World War II.

The Sabre engine was also used to power the Hawker Typhoon fighter and

this type was given priority for the engines. Consequently, a new powerplant was needed for the Firebrand and the Bristol Centaurus was chosen. This required some changes to the airframe to accommodate the new engine, and this version was designated the Firebrand TF.III. It had its first flight on December 21, 1943.

The new engine produced more torque than the Sabre and required an enlarged fin and rudder to counteract the resultant directional instability. The TF.III was considered unsuitable for carrier operations so the 27 production examples were confined to land duties while the improved TF.4 was developed.

The first Firebrand variant to see mass production, 102 examples of these TF.4 were built, and first entered FAA service in September 1945. The ultimate production Firebrand was the TF.5, featuring minor aerodynamic improvements.

The Firebrand was a classic compromise aircraft – a torpedo-fighter that excelled neither as a fighter nor torpedo-carrier. By the time the type's many faults were rectified, much more capable aircraft were available. Despite this, the type lumbered on in Royal Navy service until 1953.

The Firebrand was unusual in that there was an extra airspeed gauge mounted outside the cockpit so that during landing the pilot would not have to look down into the cockpit to take instrument readings – which is a clue to the poor low-speed handling characteristics of the type.

LEFT: **One of the early Sabre-engined Blackburn Firebrands. Its poor fighter performance led to its unfortunate development as a torpedo-fighter.**

Blackburn Firebrand TF.5

First flight: February 27, 1942
Power: One Bristol 2,520hp Centaurus IX radial piston engine
Armament: Four 20mm cannon, plus one torpedo or sixteen 27kg/60lb rockets
Size: Wingspan – 15.63m/51ft 4in
    Length – 11.81m/38ft 9in
    Height – 4.04m/13ft 3in
    Wing area – 35.58m²/383sq ft
Weights: Empty – 5,368kg/11,835lb
    Maximum take-off – 7,938kg/17,500lb
Performance: Maximum speed – 547kph/340mph
    Service ceiling – 8,685m/28,500ft
    Range – 1,191km/740 miles
    Climb – 701m/2,300ft per minute

Blackburn Perth

First flight: October 11, 1933
Power: Three Rolls-Royce 825hp Buzzard IIMS in-line piston engines
Armament: One 37mm automatic gun, three 0.303in machine-guns in nose, mid-fuselage and tail positions plus a bomb load of up to 907kg/2,000lb
Size: Wingspan – 29.57m/97ft
    Length – 21.34m/70ft
    Height – 8.06m/26ft 6in
    Wing area – 233.27m²/2,511sq ft
Weights: Empty – 9,492kg/20,927lb
    Maximum take-off –17,237kg/38,000lb
Performance: Maximum speed – 212kph/132mph
    Service ceiling – 3,505m/11,500ft
    Range – 2,414km/1,500 miles
    Climb – 244m/800ft per minute

Blackburn Perth

Derived from, and designed to replace, Blackburn's own Iris flying boat in service with No.209 Squadron at Mount Batten, the Perth entered service in January 1934. The Perth differed from the Iris by having an enclosed cockpit for the pilots and power provided by three Rolls-Royce Buzzard engines. The other significant difference was the Perth's primary armament – a bow-mounted 37mm automatic anti-shipping gun that could fire 0.68kg/1.5lb shells at the rate of 100 rounds per minute.

In addition to the pilot and co-pilot, the Perth's crew consisted of a navigator, wireless (radio) operator, an engineer gunner and a gunner. An interior 'cabin' included sleeping berths, a galley, mess, radio room, and a navigation compartment complete with a chart table which emphasized the 'boat' in flying boat.

Built in small numbers for the RAF (4), the Perth served until May 1936 and has the distinction of being the largest biplane flying boat ever operated by the RAF.

Blackburn Ripon

The two-seat Blackburn Ripon with its 12-hour endurance was a carrier-borne torpedo-bomber and reconnaissance aircraft developed from Blackburn's Swift, Dart and Velos design family and devised to replace the Dart in Fleet Air Arm service. Two prototypes flew in 1928, one a landplane, the other a floatplane. The first production version, the Ripon II powered by a 570hp Lion XI engine, began to enter service in July 1929 and first equipped units on board HMS *Furious* and *Glorious*.

The Ripon IIA could carry a range of offensive loads including a torpedo, while the last production variant, the Ripon IIC, introduced aluminium and steel in the wing construction in place of wood.

UK Ripon production ended in 1932 but a single example of an export version, the Ripon IIF, was sold to Finland as a pattern aircraft. Having interchangeable wheels and float landing gear, 25 examples were produced under licence in Finland. Some of these carried out reconnaissance of Russian forces in the winter of 1939–40 while others later flew night-time anti-submarine patrols. The last Finnish machine was retired in December 1944 and one of these machines survives in a Finnish museum. Fleet Air Arm Ripons were removed from front-line service in 1935 but some served in secondary roles until the start of World War II.

Blackburn Ripon IIA

First flight: April 17, 1926 (prototype)
Power: One Napier 570hp Lion XIA in-line piston engine
Armament: One fixed forward-firing 0.303in machine-gun and one 0.303in machine-gun in rear cockpit plus up to 680kg/1,500lb bombs or one torpedo
Size: Wingspan – 13.67m/44ft 10in
    Length – 11.20m/36ft 9in
    Height – 3.91m/12ft 10in
    Wing area – 63.45m²/683sq ft
Weights: Empty – 1,930kg/4,255lb
    Maximum take-off – 3,359kg/7,405lb
Performance: Maximum speed – 203kph/126mph
    Service ceiling – 3,050m/10,000ft
    Range – 1,706km/1,060 miles
    Climb – 155m/510ft per minute

Blackburn Skua

The Blackburn Skua was a departure for the Fleet Air Arm as it was an all-metal monoplane, which contrasted sharply with the fabric-covered biplanes that equipped the FAA for most of its history. It was also the Fleet Air Arm's first naval dive-bomber and their first carrier aircraft with flaps, a retractable undercarriage and a variable-pitch propeller. Despite these innovations, the two-seat fighter/torpedo-bomber was virtually obsolete when it entered service in August 1938.

The first Skua prototype had its maiden flight at Brough on February 9, 1937, but an order for 190 production aircraft (Skua II) had been placed months before, such was the urgency to bolster the FAA inventory as war clouds gathered in Europe.

As a fighter it was no match for contemporary enemy types but on September 26, 1939, a Skua of *Ark Royal's* 803 Squadron shot down the first enemy aircraft of World War II, a German Do18 flying boat. Its dive-bombing capabilities were also proven early in World War II. On April 10, 1940, 16 Skuas of Nos.800 and 803 Squadrons flew from the Orkneys to Bergen harbour in the night. Arriving at dawn they bombed and sank the German cruiser *Königsberg*, the first large warship sunk by Allied forces in the war. The returning aircraft (one was lost) were virtually empty of fuel having operated at the extreme of their range.

TOP LEFT: **Early production Skuas of No.803 Squadron in pre-war paint scheme.** TOP RIGHT: **It may be hard to believe today, but the all-metal monoplane Skua was considered very advanced for its time. It was the only naval dive-bomber in British use for the first two years of the war. It was, however, soon considered obsolete when pitted against the latest German fighter types.** ABOVE: **The Blackburn Skua was the first monoplane aircraft to enter service with the Fleet Air Arm and was still the only monoplane serving with the Fleet Air Arm at the start of World War II.**

Eleven days later most of the victorious aircraft and crews were lost on an attack on Narvik. On June 13, 1940, disaster occurred when the Skuas of 800 Squadron, attempting to dive-bomb the German ship *Scharnhorst* at Trondheim, were decimated by the Messerschmitt Bf 109s of II/JG77. Occasional air combat successes followed but the Skua was removed from front-line duties in 1941 when the Fairey Fulmar entered FAA service. The type continued to serve until the war's end as a trainer and target tug. No complete Skuas are known to survive.

Blackburn Skua II

First flight: February 9, 1937
Power: One Bristol 905hp Perseus XII radial engine
Armament: Four 0.303in machine-guns in wings, one 0.303in machine-gun on flexible mount in rear cockpit plus one 227kg/500lb bomb
Size: Wingspan – 14.07m/46ft 2in
    Length – 10.85m/35ft 7in
    Height – 3.81m/12ft 6in
    Wing area – 28.98m²/312sq ft
Weights: Empty – 2,490kg/5,290lb
    Maximum take-off – 3,732kg/8,228lb
Performance: Maximum speed – 362kph/225mph
    Service ceiling – 6,160m/20,200ft
    Range – 1,223km/760 miles
    Climb – 482m/1,580ft per minute

Blohm und Voss Bv 138

The Blohm und Voss Bv 138 was named *Seedrache* (Sea Dragon) but was unofficially referred to as 'the flying clog' by its crews. The type was the wartime Luftwaffe's principal long-range maritime reconnaissance aircraft, often flying for hours far out over the sea in search of Allied convoys and shipping. The Bv 138 served in the Atlantic, Arctic, Bay of Biscay, Mediterranean, Baltic and Black Sea equipping a total of around 20 squadrons. Fully loaded it could fly over

ABOVE: The Bv 138A-1 exhibits an impressive rotation from the water. This was an early example of the revised design rectifying the shortcomings of the Ha 138 prototype and featured an enlarged hull, as well as bigger fins and tail booms and a bow turret. BELOW LEFT: This study shows the relative positions of two of the aircraft's powerplants. Note the four propellers of the centre engine and the three blades of the engine to the left.

4,000km/2,485 miles and stay aloft for 16 hours but its range could be increased further by the use of RATO packs (rocket assisted take-off) or when launched by catapult from seaplane tenders. The aircraft could land on the sea close by the tenders, be refuelled and then take off from the water again or be craned on to the tender and then catapult-launched.

Following a lengthy development period the prototype, the Ha 138V1 (registered as D-ARAK) made its first flight on July 15, 1937 – this was one of the earliest aircraft designs to emanate from Hamburger Flugzeugbau GMBH, the aircraft subsidiary of shipbuilders Blohm und Voss. Instabilities and design flaws called for a redesign which led to the Bv 138A-1 with an improved hull which set the form of the production versions that followed.

The Bv 138 was unusual as it was powered by three engines – one was mounted high above the aircraft's centreline driving a four-bladed propeller while one engine on each wing drove three-bladed propellers. Equally unusual was the aircraft's twin boom tail unit.

Although the Bv 138 could carry a small bombload or depth-charges, most operations were purely reconnaissance. For self-defence the Bv 138 was equipped with gun turrets at the bow and the stern of the fuselage, as well as behind the central engine. Although different versions of the aircraft carried various armament, the standard included two 20mm cannon and four machine-guns – the type was credited with the destruction of an RAF Catalina and a Blenheim. As the Bv 138 could absorb a lot of battle damage and the diesel fuel rarely ignited when hit by enemy fire, the type was generally well liked by its crews. It could carry 500kg/1,102lb of bombs or depth charges or, in place of these, up to ten infantry troops and all of their associated equipment.

There were three principal versions. The Bv 138A-1 was the first production version and entered service in April 1940. Twenty-five were built and the type is known to have flown reconnaissance missions during the German invasion of Norway in 1940. The Bv 138B-1, of which 24 examples were produced, entered service in December 1940 and introduced a reinforced hull and floats as well as improved engines and armament.

The Bv 138C-1 had structural strengthening and improved armament. The standard service model of which 227 were built, the Bv 138C-1, began to enter service in March 1941. Most were equipped with catapult points for operation from seaplane tenders and some were equipped with a modified fuel filter to remove possible pollutants when refuelling from U-boats. Some C-1s were also equipped with the FuG 200 *Hohentwiel* or FuG 213 *Lichtenstein S* radars which made the task of searching out enemy ships and submarines somewhat easier. Of the 227 Bv 138C-1s that were built, 164 were equipped with bomb racks, which doubled the offensive payload of the earlier versions.

Some Bv 138s were later converted for the mine-sweeping role – the Bv 138 MS variant with all weaponry removed carried a large degaussing 'hoop' with a diameter the same as the aircraft's length to explode magnetic mines at sea. In total, 297 Bv 138s were built between 1938 and 1943.

ABOVE: With a 27m/89ft wingspan and weighing in at over 14,700kg/ 32,408lb, the Bv 138 was a large aircraft to be catapulted, but this was a fuel-saving option, as was rocket-assisted take-off. BELOW: A good study of a Bv 138 *Seedrache* (Sea Dragon) showing the hull and bow turret that housed a 20mm MG 151 cannon. Note the Blohm und Voss manufacturer's logo painted on the starboard side of the flying boat's nose.

ABOVE: Excellent study of the crew at work in a Bv 138. The *oberleutnant* at the centre was this aircraft's commander – note the rank patch on his left arm with the two pairs of wings and the white bar. The Bv 138 *Seedrache* (Sea Dragon) was unofficially referred to as 'the flying clog' by its crews.
ABOVE RIGHT: The commander (with the lifejacket) of a moored Bv 138 flying boat reports to his squadron commander after returning from a flight.

Blohm und Voss
Bv 138C-1

First flight: July 15, 1937 (prototype)
Power: Three Junkers 880hp Jumo 205D diesel piston engines
Armament: Two MG 151 20mm cannon, three MG 15 7.92mm machine-guns, one MG 131 13mm machine-gun plus up to 600kg/1,324lb of bombs or depth charges
Size: Wingspan – 27m/88ft 7in
Length – 19.9m/65ft 3in
Height – 6.6m/21ft 7in
Wing area – 111.9m^2/1205sq ft
Weights: Empty – 8,100kg/17,860lb
Maximum take-off – 14,700kg/32,413lb
Performance: Maximum speed – 275kph/171mph
Ceiling – 5,000m/16,400ft
Range – 5,000km/3,105 miles
Climb – 220m/722ft per minute

LEFT: The massive
Blohm und Voss
Bv 222 was
vulnerable to
attacks from
fighters, and two
of the 12 built
were shot down.

Blohm und Voss Bv 222

Blohm und Voss Bv 222C

First flight: September 7, 1940
Power: Six Junkers 1,000hp Jumo 207C
diesel engines
Armament: Three 20mm cannon in forward and
two overwing turret positions
Size: Wingspan – 46m/150ft 11in
Length – 37m/121ft 5in
Height – 10.9m/35ft 9in
Wing area – 255m²/2,745sq ft
Weights: Empty – 30,650kg/67,572lb
Maximum take-off – 49,000kg/108,027lb
Performance: Maximum speed – 390kph/
242mph
Service ceiling – 7,300m/23,950ft
Range – 6,095km/3,787 miles
Climb – 6,000m/19,685ft in 52 minutes

The Bv 222 Wiking (Viking) was the
largest production military flying boat
of World War II. At 46m/150ft 11in, the
six-engined giant had a wingspan greater
than that of the Boeing B-29 as well as
flying boat rivals the Short Sunderland
and Kawanishi H8K. The BV 222 was
designed to meet a Deutsche Lufthansa
requirement for a long-range passenger
transport for their North and South
Atlantic routes but, like so many German
'civil' aircraft of the time, its military
applications and potential were clear
to the Luftwaffe too. The unobstructed

interior floor area, due to bulkheads
being kept below that level, was both
useful for freight and was passenger
friendly – the wings' tubular main spar
contained fuel and oil tanks.

Construction of the first example, the
Bv 222 V1 (registration D-ANTE) began
in January 1938, but it was not until
September 7, 1940, that the first
prototype, flown by *Flugkapitan*
Helmut Wasa Rodig, took to the air.

The first Luftwaffe Bv 222 operation
using the prototype, by now fitted with
larger freight doors, was flown between

Hamburg and Kirkenes, Norway, on July
10, 1941. Defended only by escorting
Messerschmitt Bf 110 fighters, the
Bv 222 V1, still flown by a civilian crew,
began to fly regular supply missions
across the Mediterranean to the *Afrika
Korps* in North Africa. It was then
transferred to the Mediterranean theatre.
Only 12 were built.

LEFT: The sturdy
and reliable Boeing
biplane matched
low weight with a
great engine, and
was one of the
most widely used
American aircraft of
the inter-war years.

Boeing F4B/P-12

Boeing F4B-4/P-12E

First flight: June 25, 1928 (Boeing Model 83
prototype)
Power: Pratt & Whitney 550hp R-1340-16 Wasp
9-cylinder radial engine
Armament: Two fixed forward-firing 0.3in
machine-guns
Size: Wingspan – 9.14m/30ft
Length – 6.12m/20ft 1in
Height – 2.84m/9ft 4in
Wing area – 21.13m²/228sq ft
Weights: Empty – 1,068kg/2,354lb
Max loaded – 1,638kg/3,611lb
Performance: Maximum speed – 303kph/188mph
Ceiling – 8,200m/26,900ft
Range – 595km/370 miles
Climb – 1,525m/5,000ft in 2 minutes, 42 seconds

Boeing developed the F4B as a
private venture as a possible
replacement for the US Navy's Boeing
F2B and F3B fighters. Their new aircraft
was smaller and lighter than the earlier
Boeing machines but retained the Wasp
engine of the F3B and included some
design changes. Together this resulted in

improved performance which impressed
the US Navy who then ordered the F4B
in great quantities. Later, the US Army
followed suit, giving the aircraft the
designation P-12. Both the United States
Navy and Army utilized a host of different
variants (F4B-1, F4B-2, F4B-3, F4B-4
and P-12, P-12B, P-12C, P-12D, P-12E

and P-12F respectively) some of which
served early in World War II. Though
obsolete, some were hastily brought
back into front-line service for air
defence for a short period in the high
state of alert following Pearl Harbor.

Brazil was the only major customer
for the type outside the US.

Brewster F2A Buffalo

Having made carriages since 1810, in 1935 the Brewster Company decided to diversify and branched out into the aviation business. Some of the pilots who later had to go to war in this stubby fighter wished Brewster had stayed in the carriage business!

The F2A was designed to meet a US Navy specification for a carrier-based monoplane and was awarded the contract making it the Navy's first monoplane fighter. Of the 54 ordered only 11 made it into service, the rest being sold to Finland. Further contracts from the US Navy brought the F2A-2 and the more heavily armed and armoured F2A-3 into service. US Marine Corps aviators used the Buffalo to the best of their ability in the first Battle of Midway when 13 out of 19 were destroyed. This was the end of the type's US forces' use

as a front-line carrier-borne fighter as it was relegated to training duties.

Further orders placed by Britain (where the F2A was named Buffalo by the RAF and then found to be inadequate for the war in Europe) and the Netherlands East Indies brought more Buffaloes to the war in the Far East where they were thoroughly outclassed by the Japanese fighters. The aircraft's failure was due to its poor manoeuvrability, heavy weight and basic instability. In spite of this, by the time of the fall of Singapore in February 1942, RAF Buffaloes had destroyed 30 Japanese aircraft in the air, which says more about the skill and bravery of those RAF pilots than the design of the Buffalo.

Only in Finland did the Buffalo manage to hold its own when, for three years from mid-1941 until September

1944, it successfully opposed Soviet forces and then German forces until the end of the war.

LEFT: **The Brewster design that became the lacklustre Buffalo did, however, beat the Grumman XF4F1 (which led to the Wildcat) to the US Navy contract.**

Brewster F2A-3 Buffalo

First flight: December 1937
Power: Wright 1,200hp R-1820-40 Cyclone radial piston engine
Armament: Four fixed forward-firing 0.5in machine-guns
Size: Wingspan – 10.67m/35ft
Length – 8.03m/26ft 4in
Height – 3.68m/12ft 1in
Wing area – 19.41m²/209sq ft
Weights: Empty – 2,146kg/4,732lb
Maximum take-off – 3,247kg/7,159lb
Performance: Maximum speed – 517kph/321mph
Ceiling – 10,120m/33,200ft
Range – 1,553km/965 miles
Climb – 935m/3,070ft per minute

Consolidated PBY-5A Catalina

Few World War II military flying boats remain in the air today but the Catalina is a notable exception with a number still flying almost eight decades after the type was conceived. In February 1928, Consolidated received a contract for a prototype flying boat from the US Navy. The aircraft was designated XPY-1 and was unusually designed for installations of either two or three engines. It was, however, the initial configuration with two powerplants that was to ultimately develop into the most outstanding monoplane flying boat of the 1930s, the PBY Catalina.

The contract for the construction of the PBY prototype was issued to the Consolidated Aircraft Corporation in October 1933 and the aircraft flew for the first time in March 1935. Aircraft started to be delivered to the United States Navy's Patrol Squadrons in October 1936. As part of a training

TOP: **The PBY was a manifestation of many years of flying boat building experience by Consolidated. The Catalina was produced in greater numbers than any other flying boat of World War II and the type was serving with 21 USN Patrol Squadrons at the outbreak of the war.** ABOVE: **The Royal Air Force were aware of the PBY from the outset and evaluated an example at the Marine Aircraft Experimental Establishment, Felixstowe, in July 1939.**

exercise but most importantly to also demonstrate the aircraft's long-range endurance capabilities, Patrol Squadron VP-3 flew a non-stop round trip from San Diego, California, to the Panama Canal Zone in 27 hours and 58 minutes, covering a distance of 5,297km/3,292 miles.

The PB1s were powered by 850hp Pratt & Whitney R-1830-64 engines but in 1937 the engines were upgraded to 1,000hp and 50 aircraft were ordered with the designation PB-2. The third variant, the PB-3, was delivered to the Soviet Union in 1938 along with a manufacturing licence. The Soviet PB-3 was powered by two Russian-built 950hp M87 engines and designated GST. The PB-4 variant also appeared in 1938 with large mid-fuselage blister observation and gun positions.

In April 1939, the US Navy ordered a prototype amphibious version which was capable of landing on water or land (for

ABOVE: **This study gives an excellent view of the boat's two-stepped hull. Note the undercarriage wheel lying flush with the side of the fuselage and the large glazed blister forward of the tail.**

which it was fitted with an undercarriage that retracted into the fuselage) and was designated XPBY-5A. After service evaluation tests, orders were placed by the US Navy, with whom the type entered service in late 1936. Twenty-one USN Patrol Squadrons were equipped with PBYs when the USA entered World War II in December 1941.

The Royal Air Force had already shown interest in the type, aware of the gathering war clouds in Europe and the need to patrol British waters far from land. One aircraft was flown over from the US for RAF evaluation and as soon as war was declared, 30 examples of the amphibious version were ordered. These were delivered to the RAF in early 1941 and were in service almost immediately, named Catalina by the British – the US Navy also adopted the name Catalina in 1942. On a patrol on May 26, 1941, a Catalina of No.209 Squadron operating from Castle Archdale in Northern Ireland spotted the German battleship *Bismarck* after Royal Navy ships had lost the enemy ship.

Six hundred and fifty Catalinas were operated by the RAF and many served in the Atlantic. Two Royal Air Force Catalina pilots who operated in the Atlantic were awarded the Victoria Cross for gallant attacks on German submarines in the open sea. British 'Cats' also operated in Ceylon and Madagascar patrolling the Indian Ocean, while aircraft operating from Gibraltar were on station for the 1942 Allied landings in North Africa. The last U-boat sunk by RAF Coastal Command was destroyed by a No.210 Squadron Catalina on May 7, 1945.

The PBY-5A variant was used widely during World War II by a number of countries. Canadian-built versions of the flying boat were also produced and were known as Cansos in Royal Canadian Air Force service. Further development of the Catalina led to the fitting of more powerful 1,200hp engines, revised armament and search radar equipment. By the end of

ABOVE: The Catalina entered RAF service in early 1941 operating from bases in Northern Ireland. Royal Air Force Catalinas sank 196 German U-boats during World War II, the last of them in May 1945. BELOW: In one of its elements, the Catalina featured the innovative stabilizing floats under the outer wing, which retracted to form aerodynamic wingtips.

production in 1945, over 4,000 Catalinas had been made, making it the most-produced flying boat in history.

Catalinas were operated by many air arms around the world, including Australia, Brazil, France, the Netherlands, New Zealand, South Africa and the Soviet Union. A number remain in civilian use today and are popular attractions at air shows.

ABOVE: Early examples of the Catalina were pure flying boats, and the undercarriaged, amphibious version did not appear until 1939. Used by the Allies in all theatres, the Catalina excelled at mine-laying, bombing, air-sea rescue and anti-submarine duties. It was a classic combat aircraft.

Consolidated PBY-5A Catalina

First flight: March 1935

Power: Two Pratt & Whitney 1,200hp R-1830-92 Twin Wasp 14-cylinder radial engines

Armament: Two 0.5in machine-guns in bow turret and one in each beam blister; one 0.30in machine-gun in ventral tunnel; plus a war load of up to 1,814kg/4,000lb of bombs, mines or depth charges, or two torpedoes

Size: Wingspan – 31.70m/104ft
Length – 19.45m/63ft 10in
Height – 6.15m/20ft 2in
Wing area – 130m²/1,400sq ft

Weights: Empty – 9,485kg/20,910lb
Maximum take-off – 16,067kg/35,420lb

Performance: Maximum speed – 288kph/179mph
Service ceiling – 4,480m/14,700ft
Range – 4,095km/2,545 miles
Climb – 189m/620ft per minute

LEFT AND BELOW:
Consolidated and
Sikorsky were competing
to produce a Catalina
replacement with better
all-round performance
and capability.
Consolidated won with
the XPB2Y-1 (pictured)
but had to revise the tail
with B-24-type fins to
improve stability.

Consolidated PB2Y Coronado

The XPB2Y-1 prototype of what came to be known in British service as the Coronado first flew in December 1937 and within eight months was delivered to the US Navy for service evaluation. Six examples of the first production version, the PB2Y-2, went into service for trials in January 1941. The type was designed to meet a US Navy requirement for a larger and more powerful maritime patrol bomber to replace Consolidated's own PBY Catalina. Although the prototype had flown in 1937, the US Navy did not at that point have the funding to place a major order. Accordingly, it was not until 1941 that the type was ordered in quantity, resulting in the US Navy eventually acquiring 200 examples of the PB2Y-3 – this was an improved PB2Y-2 with self-sealing fuel tanks, more machine-guns and, on later production examples, ASV radar.

This impressive deep-hulled aircraft had a large cantilever wing and twin oval tail fins with a Consolidated family resemblance to those of the B-24 Liberator. Like the PBY Catalina, the PB2Y featured the innovative floats that retracted to become wingtips thus reducing drag and increasing range.

A number of Coronados, designated PB2Y-3R, were converted for transport duties by having most military equipment removed and turrets faired over. This version could carry 44 passengers and 7,257kg/15,999lb of cargo or 24 stretcher cases and 3,900kg/8,598lb of cargo. The PB2Y-5H, used in the Pacific, was a naval ambulance version of the Coronado that could carry 25 stretchers. US Navy PB2Ys also saw combat in the Pacific, carrying out anti-submarine and bombing missions.

In 1943, another ten examples of the PB2Y-3 were supplied under Lend-Lease

arrangements to the RAF and were designated Coronado I. These aircraft were operated by Coastal and then Transport Command who used them on transatlantic and Caribbean routes.

One PB2Y survives, preserved in the US at Pensacola's National Museum of Naval Aviation.

Consolidated PB2Y-5 Coronado

First flight: December 17, 1937 (prototype)

Power: Four Pratt & Whitney 1,200hp R-1830-92 radial engines

Armament: Six 0.50in machine-guns in three powered turrets, two machine-guns in waist positions, two torpedoes or up to 5,450kg/ 12,000lb of bombs or depth charges housed internally or beneath the wings

Size: Wingspan – 35m/115ft, 24.2m/79ft 3in
Height – 8.4m/27ft 6in
Wing area – 165m²/1,780sq ft

Weights: Empty – 18,530kg/40,850lb
Maximum take-off – 30,000kg/66,139lb

Performance: Maximum speed – 310kph/194mph
Ceiling – 9,181m/30,100ft
Range – 1,720km/1,070 miles
Climb – 174m/570ft per minute

ABOVE: **A PB2Y-3R on take-off. This was a transport conversion by the Rohr Aircraft Co. for Naval Air Transport Service from the PB2Y-3 with the turrets removed and a side hatch added.**

LEFT: **The model that featured a retractable undercarriage was passed over by the US Army but welcomed by the US Navy.**
BELOW: **The Curtiss Hawk family that included the US Navy BFC-2s spanned 15 years of production at a time when aviation technology was gathering real pace.**

Curtiss BFC-2/B2FC-1

The single-seat unequal-span Curtiss Hawk II biplane was part of the large family of aircraft that began with the Curtiss Models 34 and 35 in the mid to late 1920s. Developed from the P-6E, Hawk II demonstrator aircraft flew all over the world and secured a number of overseas orders. The US Navy acquired two examples for testing and decided they had development potential. The USN first ordered 28 examples of the F11C-2 production version powered by a 600hp Wright Cyclone and had them fitted with a bomb 'crutch' for a 227kg/500lb bomb beneath the fuselage – this was to be used for dive-bombing. This version entered USN squadron service with VF-1B aboard USS *Saratoga* in 1933 and was redesignated BFC-2 to reflect its fighter-bomber role. These aircraft, officially though rarely called Goshawks, were in service until 1938.

The US Navy also procured a variant with manually retracted landing gear. This version was designated XF11C-3 by the Navy and Model 67A by the manufacturer. The XF11C-3 was delivered to the US Navy in May 1933. Powered by a 700hp Wright R-1820-80 radial engine, tests found the -3 to be 27.5kph/17mph faster than the -2 though with reduced manoeuvrability due to the weight increase. Speed was the requirement so the type was ordered but changed from the XF11C-3 to the XBF2C-1.

Twenty-seven BF2C-1s were ordered by the US Navy, with a raised rear 'turtledeck' spine, a semi-enclosed cockpit, and a metal-framed lower wing. Armed with two Browning machine-guns and three hardpoints for up to 227kg/500lb of external stores, the aircraft were delivered in October 1934. Assigned to VB-5B aboard USS *Ranger*, the type only served until 1937 having been withdrawn due to incurable problems with undercarriage operation and the aircraft's wing becoming weakened by the accumulated stresses of dive-bombing.

This was a shabby end to the last Curtiss fighter accepted for service with the US Navy. Most were simply ditched in San Diego Bay. Export versions with wooden rather than metal wings continued to fly in China and Siam for several years, and Chinese machines saw action against the Japanese.

Curtiss BF2C-1

First flight: May 1933 (XF11C-3 prototype)
Power: One Wright 750hp R-1820F-53
Armament: Two 0.30in machine-guns and underwing racks for up to 210kg/464kg of bombs
Size: Wingspan – 9.58m/31ft 6in
   Length – 7.16m/23ft 6in
   Height – 3.05m/10ft
   Wing area – 24.34m²/262sq ft
Weights: Empty – 1,406kg/3,100lb
   Maximum take-off – 2,307kg/5,086lb
Performance: Maximum speed – 368kph/228mph
   Ceiling – 8,230m/27,000ft
   Range – 1,282km/797 miles
   Climb – 655m/2,150ft per minute

LEFT: **A Curtiss H-16 of the United States Navy.**
ABOVE: **UK flying boat pioneer Lt John Porte aboard the *America*, which led to the H series and Britain's Felixstowe flying boats. Porte was to have co-piloted the transatlantic aircraft.**

Curtiss H Series Flying Boats

Flying boat pioneer Glenn Curtiss was born in Hammondsport, New York, in 1878. After working as a bicycle mechanic he set up his own motorcycle factory in 1902. Curtiss became interested in aviation and his company began manufacturing airship engines then moved on to building aircraft. In 1908 Curtiss' *June Bug* completed the world's first one-kilometre flight and over the following years he set a series of high-profile records. Curtiss produced the world's first practical seaplane in 1911 then set about designing a flying boat with which he hoped to cross the Atlantic.

Record-breaking flights ceased when World War I broke out, but Curtiss managed to sell two of his H-12 aircraft – derived from the transatlantic flight attempt aircraft – to the Royal Naval Air

Service in Britain. The RNAS were so impressed, they ordered a total of 84 examples before the war's end. A further 20 were ordered for the US Navy – the latter machines were powered by 200hp Curtiss V-2-3 engines. The RNAS considered the H-12s to be underpowered for their size so the aircraft were re-engined first with 275hp Rolls-Royce Eagle Is and later with 375hp Eagle VIIIs, these variants being designated H-12A and H-12B. The US Navy machines were also re-engined but with 360hp Liberty engines and these aircraft were then known as H-12Ls. The US Navy aircraft did not see action in Europe, instead being held to patrol home waters looking for German submarines. The RNAS H-12s, operating from bases in Britain and Ireland, were tasked with anti-Zeppelin patrols and

containing the threat of German U-boats. Capable of flying long ocean patrols and armed with four machine-guns and bombs, the aircraft could easily destroy airships or U-boats. On May 14, 1917, an H-12 shot down a Zeppelin over the North Sea – this was the first ever enemy aircraft to fall to the guns of a US-built aircraft. It was just six days later that an H-12 became the first aircraft to win a victory over a submarine.

The Curtiss H-16 was a development of the H-12 and was built in greater numbers than any other twin-engined Curtiss flying boat. With a hydrodynamically improved hull and more armament, the first H-16 was flown on March 27, 1918. US Navy examples did see service in France, based on the coast to carry out long-range anti-submarine patrols.

LEFT: **The Felixstowe flying boats that were derived from the Curtiss H Series were widely used as patrol aircraft over the North Sea, often fighting enemy aircraft, as well as hunting U-boats and Zeppelins. Later versions served in the Mediterranean. The H Series were an important 'family' of flying boats that saw much action.**

Curtiss H-16

First flight: March 27, 1918
Power: Two 400hp Liberty 12A in-line piston engines
Armament: Six 0.303in machine-guns and up to 417kg/920lb of bombs
Size: Wingspan – 28.97m/95ft 1in
  Length – 14.05m/46ft 1.5in
  Height – 5.4m/17ft 9in
  Wing area – 108.14m^2/1164sq ft
Weights: Empty – 3,357kg/7,400lb
  Maximum take-off – 4,944g/10,900lb
Performance: Maximum speed – 153kph/95mph
  Ceiling – 3,030m/9,950ft
  Range – 608km/378 miles
  Climb – 3,050m/10,000ft in 29 minutes, 49 seconds

LEFT: **The very unusual means of operation meant that the Sparrowhawks were highly publicized even though only six production aircraft were delivered. One is preserved at the Smithsonian in the US.**

Curtiss F9C-2 Sparrowhawk

First flight: April, 1932 (XF9C-2)
Power: One Wright 438hp R-975-E radial piston engine
Armament: Two fixed fuselage-mounted 0.3in machine-guns
Size: Wingspan – 7.77m/25ft 6in
Length – 6.13m/20ft 1.5in
Height – 3.24m/10ft 7in
Wing area – 16.05m²/173sq ft
Weights: Empty – 948kg/2,089lb
Maximum take-off – 1,261kg/2,779lb
Performance: Maximum speed – 283kph/176mph
Ceiling – 5,850m/19,200ft
Range – 478km/297 miles
Climb – 515m/1,690ft per minute

Curtiss F9C Sparrowhawk

The F9C was designed to meet a 1930 US Navy requirement for a small carrier-borne naval fighter that could operate from existing carriers without the need for folding wings. Curtiss' response was the F9C. This aircraft, along with other contenders, was rejected for carrier operations by the Navy but was deemed suitable to operate from the US Navy's new giant airship, the USS *Akron*. Incredibly, the 240m/785ft-long airship that was designed for strategic maritime reconnaissance duties had a hangar built inside it, big enough to hold four F9Cs.

The aircraft were launched and recovered by a trapeze that was lowered through large doors which opened in the underside of the *Akron*. Entering service in September 1932, the aircraft had a hook fixed to the top of the fuselage that caught the trapeze, which would then raise the aircraft up into the hangar without the need to fold the small fighter's wings. The Sparrowhawk retained a standard undercarriage for land operations although experiments saw the removal of the landing gear and replacement with an extra fuel tank. The loss of the *Akron* and her sister ship the *Macon* in 1933 and 1935 put an end to this unique manifestation of naval air power.

LEFT: **Gruelling test-flying showed that the original parasol monoplane configuration was structurally unsuitable for a dive-bombing aircraft so the SBC bucked the trend of the time and the monoplane became a biplane again.**

Curtiss SBC-4 Helldiver

First flight: December 9, 1935 (XSBC-2)
Power: One Wright 900hp Wright R-1820-34 Cyclone 9 radial piston engine
Armament: Two 0.3in machine-guns plus one 227kg/500lb bomb
Size: Wingspan – 10.36m/34ft
Length – 8.57m/28ft 1.5in
Height – 3.17m/10ft 5in
Wing area – 29.45m²/317sq ft
Weights: Empty – 2,065kg/4,552lb
Maximum take-off – 3,211kg/7,080lb
Performance: Maximum speed – 377kph/234mph
Service ceiling – 7,315m/24,000ft
Range – 949km/590 miles
Climb – 567m/1,860ft per minute

Curtiss SBC Helldiver

The Curtiss SBC Helldiver was the last military biplane to enter US Navy service and was an aircraft whose role was changed not once but twice during its development, which saw the design alter from monoplane to biplane. Conceived as a two-seat monoplane fighter (the XF12C-1), it was then designated as a scout and finally as a scout-bomber. During dive tests for this latter role, the parasol monoplane configuration was found to be structurally weak for dive-bombing so a redesign led to a biplane layout. The eventual production aircraft, the SBC-3, was delivered to the US Navy in July 1937, some four years after the flight testing of the XF12C-1.

The more powerfully engined SBC-4 appeared in 1939 and some of these machines, destined for France before its invasion, were diverted to the RAF who designated them the Cleveland. One USMC and two USN front-line squadrons were still operating the SBC-4 when the US entered World War II but they were withdrawn in early 1942.

LEFT: **The Curtiss SB2C Helldiver was appropriately named according to some of its critics. Structural shortcomings and poor low-speed handling were its main faults, but the type packed a real punch and sank more enemy shipping than any other dive-bomber. It was a very important Allied naval aircraft in World War II.**

Curtiss SB2C Helldiver

The Curtiss SB2C was the third Curtiss aircraft supplied to the US Navy to be called Helldiver but this aircraft shared little in common with the earlier aircraft except its name. The SB2C was developed to replace the Douglas SBD Dauntless and was a much larger aircraft able to operate from the latest aircraft carriers of the time. It carried a considerable array of ordnance and featured an internal bomb bay that reduced drag when carrying heavy weapon loads. The SB2C Helldiver is another aircraft whose contribution to the final Allied victory in World War II is often underestimated.

Manufacturers faced demanding requirements from the USMC and USAAF, and responded by incorporating features of a 'multi-role' aircraft into the design. The first two prototypes crashed, one due to structural failure. This would have sealed the fate of many new aircraft, but as large-scale production had already been ordered in late 1940, a large number of significant modifications were identified for the production model.

Development and production was delayed to the point that Grumman's Avenger, which entered development two years later than the Helldiver, entered service before the Curtiss machine. The many modifications and changes on the production line meant that the Curtiss Helldiver did not enter combat until November 1943 with VB-17 operating from the USS *Bunker Hill*, when they carried out a strike against the Japanese-held port of Rabaul in Papua New Guinea.

Even though the Helldiver was in service, concerns about structural problems meant that crews were forbidden to dive-bomb in 'clean' conditions. This did nothing to endear it to the crews who had relinquished their lighter and smaller SBD Dauntless in favour of what came to be known as 'the beast', partly because of its poor handling at low speeds.

Curtiss Helldiver production at Columbus, Ohio, was supplemented by the output of two Canadian factories. Fairchild Aircraft Ltd (Canada) produced 300 aircraft all

ABOVE: **Some of the prototype's instability issues were resolved by the introduction of an enlarged tail, which led to one of its nicknames – the 'big-tailed beast'. Note the large glazed cockpits.**

ABOVE: **Despite a difficult start, the SB2C made a major contribution to the Allied victory in the Pacific. Its range of over 1,900km/1,200 miles meant it could cover great areas of the Pacific in search of its targets.**

LEFT: **The Helldiver was an all-metal, low wing cantilever monoplane. Its wings folded up to save space on carrier decks – note the arrester hook.**
BELOW: **The trailing edge flaps were perforated to act as dive-brakes and crews were not allowed to dive the aircraft unless it was carrying external ordnance.**

designated SBF while Canadian Car and Foundry built 894 examples all designated SBW.

Despite all the problems, the Helldiver became the most successful Allied dive-bomber of World War II and certainly made a major contribution to the successful outcome of the war in the Pacific. The aircraft eventually had good range, making it a very useful weapon for action in the great expanse of the Pacific. The aircraft also packed a significant punch and could carry 454kg/1,000lb of bombs under its wings while a torpedo or another 454kg/1,000lb of ordnance could be carried in the internal bomb bay.

Later improvements to this already more than capable combat aircraft included an uprated Wright Cyclone engine and hardpoints for carrying rocket-projectiles.

The Helldiver saw considerable action in the battles of the Philippine Sea and Leyte Gulf, and played a significant part in the destruction of the Japanese battleships *Yamato* and *Musashi*. As the Allies moved towards the Japanese home islands, Helldivers were active in the Inland Sea and helped deal the deathblow to the Japanese Navy.

Although 26 examples of the SBW-1 version were supplied to the Royal Navy under Lend-Lease, these Fleet Air Arm machines did not see operational service. A total of 450 were

in fact ordered but after FAA testing determined that the aircraft had "appalling handling", the order was cancelled.

Curtiss also built 900 examples of a Helldiver version for the USAAF, designated A-25A Shrike. None saw service with the USAAF and many were converted to SB2C-1 standard for the USMC.

Post-war, Helldivers were the only bombers in the US Navy and continued to equip USN units until 1948 when the Douglas Skyraider was introduced.

Other post-war operators of the Helldiver included the Italian, Greek and Portuguese navies. Helldivers fought on with the French Navy and were used by them in Indochina. Thailand took delivery of six Helldivers in 1951 and retired the aircraft in 1955.

ABOVE: **This aircraft is preserved in the US by the Commemorative Air Force and is the last Helldiver still flying. It is an SB2C-5, the last production variant of the aircraft, and served in the US Navy from 1945–48.**

Curtiss SB2C-4 Helldiver

First flight: December 18, 1940
Power: One Wright 1,900hp Wright R-2600-20 Cyclone radial engine
Armament: Two 20mm cannon in wings, two 0.3in machine-guns in rear cockpit; 454kg/1,000lb of bombs or a torpedo carried internally plus an additional 454kg/1,000lb of bombs and rocket projectiles carried under wings
Size: Wingspan – 15.16m/49ft 9in
  Length – 11.17m/36ft 8in
  Height – 4.01m/13ft 2in
  Wing area – 39.2m²/422sq ft
Weights: Empty – 4,784kg/10,547lb
  Maximum take-off – 7,537kg/16,616lb
Performance: Maximum speed – 434kph/270mph
  Service ceiling – 8,870m/29,100ft
  Range – 1,987km/1,235 miles
  Climb – 549m/1,800ft per minute

Curtiss SO3C-1 Seamew

The Curtiss SO3C was a two-seat scout monoplane developed in 1937 to replace the US Navy's Curtiss Seagull biplanes. For a time, the SO3C was also, imaginatively, called Seagull. From the outset the aircraft was designed with versatility in mind and could operate from land bases, carrier decks or from water thanks to easily interchangeable float and undercarriage assemblies. The aircraft never lived up to its early promise.

Having beaten competing prototypes for the sizeable contract, the type was found to have major stability problems, which the manufacturers tried to remedy by the addition of upturned wingtips and an enlarged tail surface. While the wingtip modification was a good idea, the enlarged fin was unfortunately not. The base of the enlarged fin extended over, and was in part attached to, the sliding rear cockpit canopy. As the canopy opened and closed, then so did the section of the fin thereby reducing its effectiveness. Most aircraft don't have their canopies open during flight but the SO3C was an observation aircraft and the crewman at the rear of the aircraft often slid his 'greenhouse' canopy forward for a clear view of the sea below. The type first entered service in July 1942 aboard USS *Cleveland*, and crews generally found the SO3C to be difficult and unpleasant to fly.

When the SO3C was chosen for Royal Navy service under Lend-Lease, it was named Seamew, a name which universally replaced the confusing and repetitive Seagull. Although 250 were destined for Fleet Air Arm use, only 100 were in fact accepted and the type never saw operational service. The Seamew (nicknamed 'Seacow' by British crews) entered RN service in January 1944 and was declared obsolete in September

ABOVE: **A pilot runs up the Ranger engine on his SO3C, a very unsatisfactory naval aircraft that saw just 18 months US Navy service. Note the upturned wingtips introduced to improve stability.**

the same year. Relegated to secondary duties, the majority of the British aircraft were used to train FAA crew in Britain and Canada.

Having survived in front-line United States Navy service for only 18 months, the Seamew was replaced by the Seagull biplanes – taken out of mothballs – that it was intended to replace.

LEFT: **After accepting only 100 examples of the SO3C Seamew, the Royal Navy refused to put the type into front-line service and instead used the Seamews as training aircraft for radio operators and gunners.**

Curtiss SO3C-2C (floatplane variant)

First flight: October 6, 1939 (XSO3C-1 prototype)

Power: One Ranger 600hp SVG-770-8 engine

Armament: One 0.3in forward-firing machine-gun, one 0.5in machine-gun on flexible mount in rear crew position plus up to 295kg/650lb of bombs or depth charges carried beneath the wings

Size: Wingspan – 11.58m/38ft
Length – 11.23m/36ft 10in
Height – 4.57m/15ft
Wing area – 26.94m²/290sq ft

Weights: Empty – 1,943kg/4,284lb
Maximum take-off – 2,599kg/5,729lb

Performance: Maximum speed – 277kph/172mph
Ceiling – 4,815m/15,800ft
Range – 1,851km/1,150 miles
Climb – 220m/720ft per minute

Curtiss F8C-4/02C-1 Helldiver

The aircraft that became the first of three different US Navy Curtiss aircraft called Helldiver was derived from the Curtiss Falcon series. It was designed from the outset as a dive-bomber and had two fixed forward-firing machine-guns fitted to the upper wing. The aircraft's fuselage was made of welded steel tubing while the wings were made of wood.

Although the first prototype crashed in testing, development continued. Among the special features was a bomb rack that launched the Helldiver's 227kg/ 500lb bomb away from the aircraft, as it dived, to avoid the bomb entering the propeller arc.

Like the Curtiss Falcon that inspired it, this aircraft's fuel tanks were 'saddle' tanks, carried on both sides of the aircraft fuselage – how any designer of a fighter aircraft thought that this was ever a good idea defies belief. A single bullet from an enemy aircraft or even small-calibre ground fire could have turned the Helldiver into a fireball.

The first production version was the F8C-4 of which 25 were built. These aircraft served from US Navy carriers from 1930 but were retired from service by the outbreak of World War II.

The US Marine Corps ordered 63 examples of the land-based F8C-5

ABOVE LEFT: **The robust Helldiver was a good aircraft and served the US Navy and Marine Corps for around a decade.** ABOVE: **Favoured for US Navy public relations activity, the type was immortalized on film as being the aircraft used to shoot King Kong as he clung on to the top of New York's Empire State Building.**

variant and a change in the aircraft's primary role from dive-bombing to observation led to their redesignation as the 02C-1. By the time that the US Navy ordered a further 30 examples of the type to operate from carriers, they too were designated 02C-1.

LEFT: **The Helldiver's performance was adequate but not exceptional, and its vulnerable fuel tanks could have cost the US Navy dear in combat. It was some years before self-sealing fuel tanks were developed.**

Curtiss F8C-5/02C-1

First flight: 1928
Power: One Pratt & Whitney 450hp R-1340-4 Wasp radial engine
Armament: Two 0.3in machine-guns and up to 227kg/500lb of bombs or depth charges
Size: Wingspan – 9.75m/32ft
　　Length – 7.82m/25ft 8in
　　Height – 3.12m/10ft 3in
　　Wing area – 28.61m²/308sq ft
Weights: Empty – 1,143kg/2,520lb
　　Maximum take-off – 1,823kg/4,020lb
Performance: Maximum speed – 235kph/146mph
　　Ceiling – 4,955m/16,250ft
　　Range – 1,159km/720 miles
　　Climb – 289m/948ft per minute

LEFT: The XO3C-1 prototype was a 'tube-and-fabric' aircraft with welded steel tubing fuselage and aluminum-framed wings and tail surfaces. Armament consisted of a single 0.30-calibre Browning machine-gun fitted in the forward cowling and fired by the pilot, while a similar weapon was stowed in the rear cockpit and could be operated from a swivel mount. The XO3C-1 cost $113,445, a great deal of money for the time. The 'Anacostia' on the aircraft side refers to the Naval Air Station where it was based.

Curtiss SOC Seagull

The SOC Seagull was the last Curtiss biplane to see front-line US Navy service. It was a single-engined scout/observation biplane that served on battleships and cruisers, being launched by catapult and recovered by crane after a sea landing. Its mission was to spot naval gunfire and scout ahead on behalf of its mother ship.

The SOC prototype, the XO3C-1 was ordered by the United States Navy in June 1933 and first flew in April 1934. It was ordered into production (135 built) and entered service in 1935 as the SOC-1. Although the prototype was an amphibian, this first production version was purely a floatplane – conversion from one to the other was, however, a straightforward undertaking.

The pilot and observer/gunner sat in tandem cockpits under a continuous canopy with individual sliding opening sections. The rear crewman had a 0.3in machine-gun on a flexible mount. The Seagull's wings folded back against the aircraft's fuselage for easier stowage on board carriers where deck and hangar space is always at a premium.

Land-based versions had an undercarriage in place of the distinctive float and the next production version,

powered by a Pratt & Whitney R-1340-22, was the SOC-2 model for land operations. Eighty-three examples of the SOC-3 fitted with arrester gear for carrier operations were also built. The Naval Aircraft Factory later built some

ABOVE: The SOC Seagull was capable of flexible applications, with folding wings and a float that could be exchanged for wheeled landing gear. The Seagull had good low-speed flight characteristics suitable for short-distance open sea landings in the relatively smooth-water 'slick' that its home turning ship could create.

of the same aircraft and these were designated SON-1.

Production ceased in 1938 and Curtiss worked on a successor aircraft named Seamew. The latter aircraft did not fare well in service and was withdrawn. The SOCs, by then in second-line roles, were swiftly reinstated and continued to serve until the end of World War II.

The Seagull, like Britain's Swordfish, lasted in service far longer than ever expected and the type even outlasted planned successor aircraft in service.

Curtiss SOC-1

First flight: April 1934 (prototype)

Power: One Pratt & Whitney 600hp R-1340-18 Wasp

Armament: Two 0.3in machine-guns and up to 295kg/650lb of bombs

Size: Wingspan – 10.97m/36ft
    Length – 8.06m/26ft 6in
    Height – 4.50m/14ft 9in
    Wing area – 31.77m²/342sq ft

Weights: Empty – 1,718kg/3,788lb
    Maximum take-off – 2,466kg/5,437lb

Performance: Maximum speed – 266kph/165mph
    Ceiling – 4,540m/14,900ft
    Range – 1,086km/675 miles
    Climb – 268m/880ft per minute

de Havilland Sea Mosquito

The Mosquito was one of the first true multi-role combat aircraft. It started life in late 1938 as a design for a bomber/reconnaissance aircraft that could fly so fast and high, no defensive armament was needed. The aircraft's construction did not require the use of strategic materials, instead using wood for virtually the whole aircraft, leading to the aircraft's 'wooden wonder' nickname.

Fighter, night-fighter, photo-reconnaissance and bomber versions were all produced and served with distinction during World War II.

Britain's Admiralty had drawn up a 1944 specification N.15/44 for a carrier-borne strike aircraft for use in what may have been a protracted carrier war against the Japanese in the Pacific. In March 1944, a modified Mosquito Mk IV, piloted by legendary British test pilot Eric 'Winkle' Brown, became the first British twin-engine aircraft to land on an aircraft

carrier. This trial, on board HMS *Indefatigable*, proved the feasibility of what came to be called the Sea Mosquito.

From early on in production, the Sea Mosquito T.R. Mk 33 featured hydraulically operated folding wings, long-travel Lockheed-designed hydraulic undercarriage legs (rubber was used in Mosquitoes), large-diameter four-bladed propellers and an arrester hook. All 50 production Sea Mosquitoes were equipped to carry a 45.7cm/18in torpedo and large drop tanks. Alternatively it could carry two 227kg/500lb bombs in the bomb bay, and two beneath the wings. American ASH radar was housed in a telltale thimble housing on the nose. Jet-assisted take-off was also an option for the type.

A small number of Sea Mosquito T.R. Mk 37s also entered service, differing from earlier models mainly by the

ABOVE: **The Mosquito was an obvious candidate for being navalized although not every carrier could accept the comparatively large aircraft. The prospect of a lengthy carrier war against Japan crystallized the idea into a 1944 Admiralty requirement.**

installation of British radar in a larger nose housing.

With the war's end and jet aircraft in the ascendancy, the original order for 97 Sea Mosquitoes was reduced to the 50 total that entered service. Sea Mosquitoes saw little service, first joining No.811 Squadron at Ford in 1946 and disbanding at Brawdy in July 1947, having simply replaced the land-based Mosquito F.B. Mk VIs that No.811 Squadron had operated.

de Havilland Sea Mosquito T.R. Mk 33

First flight: May 15, 1941 (Mosquito fighter prototype)

Power: Two Rolls-Royce 1,635hp Merlin 25 in-line piston engines

Armament: Four 20mm cannon, one 18in torpedo or four 227kg/500lb bombs, or rocket projectiles

Size: Wingspan – 16.5m/54ft 2in
Length – 12.35m/40ft 6in
Height – 3.81m/12ft 6in
Wing area – 42.19m²/454sq ft

Weights: Empty – 6,736kg/14,850lb
Maximum take-off – 10,833kg/23,850lb

Performance: Maximum speed – 605kph/376mph
Ceiling – 9,181m/30,100ft
Range – 2,035km/1,265 miles
Climb – 555m/1,820ft per minute

ABOVE: **After the success of the Mosquito, de Havilland produced the Hornet, which was inspired by the Mosquito but was an all-new aircraft. A navalized version, the Sea Hornet (pictured), was produced in limited numbers.**

Dornier Do 18

The Dornier Do 18 was designed to replace the military and civil (for Lufthansa) versions of Dornier's Do 15 *Wal* (Whale) flying boat, which had set a number of distance records in its class. The Do 18, first flight March 15, 1935, incorporated a number of innovations and interesting technical features. The flying boat's hull was comprised of seven individual watertight compartments, any two of which could be holed and filled with water without affecting the aircraft's operation. Understanding of aerodynamics and hydrodynamics was growing at the time and the Do 18, though clearly from the same stable, was aerodynamically advanced compared to its Dornier forerunners – its wing tapered, had rounded tips and had the Junkers-style 'double-wing' flap and ailerons.

The Do 18 also had an enclosed cockpit for the side-by-side pilot and co-pilot positions while the radio operator and navigator sat right behind them. A gunner sat in an open compartment between the wing's trailing edge and tail to provide defence against enemy air attack. The aircraft had unique water level sponsons, known as *stümmel*, located directly beneath the wings and joined to them by struts.

ABOVE: **Deutsche Lufthansa received six Do 18s to mainly carry mail across the Atlantic. This aircraft, D-ABYM was named *Aeolus* and was the third example built, hence the designation Do 18 V3.**

Compartmentalized to again minimize the effect of any damage, these stubby wing-like sponsons provided stability in the water and also generated lift in the air. Twin rudders were positioned behind the rear 'step' of the hull to aid steering on the water. Two tandem-mounted diesel engines, one pulling and one pushing atop the wing provided the power, bestowing great range and endurance. The upper rear of the engine housing was beautifully streamlined giving a perfect line to the tip of the propeller spinner. The engines' cooling radiators were housed in a central wing pylon over the aircraft's centreline.

Following its first flight in March 1935, the Do 18 prototype, together with other early examples, joined the Lufthansa fleet operating on South Atlantic services. As an illustration of the Do 18's capabilities, the third prototype, D-ABYM, undertook one test flight in July 1936 that lasted over 30 hours.

ABOVE: **The Do 18G-1 variant introduced a large gun turret on top of the rear fuselage for improved self-defence. Note the large and sturdy *stümmel* beneath the wings, clearly visible as the aircraft is craned.**

ABOVE: **As this Do 18D is preparing to launch, the rear-facing engine of the tandem pair can been seen in action. The D model was the first production series and equipped five front-line units.**

With three different factories involved in production, the Do 18 entered Luftwaffe service in 1936. By mid-1939, five Luftwaffe front-line units were equipped with Do 18s but by then the type was considered to be obsolete due to its comparatively poor performance and light armament. Nevertheless, it did carry out hazardous reconnaissance duties over the North Sea. On September 26, 1939, a Do 18 became the first German aircraft of World War II to be shot down by British aircraft when a formation of three Do 18s was caught over the North Sea by Royal Navy Blackburn Skuas flying from HMS *Ark Royal* – the victorious pilot was Lieutenant B.S. McEwan.

The Bv 138 was ordered as the Dornier boat's replacement in Luftwaffe service but due to problems with the Blohm und Voss aircraft, an improved version of the Do 18 was hurriedly developed as a stop-gap. The Do 18G-1 had the more powerful 880hp Jumo 205D engine and take-off could also be helped by the use of booster rockets. This version was also better able to defend itself with the addition of a 13mm machine-gun in the open bow position while a 20mm cannon was housed in a power-operated turret that replaced the open gun position over the rear step of the hull.

Production stopped in mid-1940, while the G-1 models replaced the D models still in Luftwaffe service, many of the later variants being shifted to air-sea rescue duties. The Do 18G-1 was gradually withdrawn from service with the last Norway-based machines known to have been withdrawn in the summer of 1941.

ABOVE: **This early production Do 18 shows the open bow position and the surface area of the *stümmel* which, as effectively short wings, gave the boat added lift. Note the streamlined engines.**

Dornier Do 18G-1

First flight: March 15, 1935 (prototype)
Power: Two Junkers 880hp Jumo 205D diesel piston engines
Armament: One 13mm machine-gun in nose position, one 20mm machine-gun in dorsal turret and up to 100kg/220lb of bombs carried beneath wings
Size: Wingspan – 23.7m/77ft 9in
Length – 19.38m/63ft 7in
Height – 5.32m/17ft 6in
Wing area – 98m²/1,055sq ft
Weights: Empty – 5,978kg/13,180lb
Maximum take-off – 10,795kg/23,800lb
Performance: Maximum speed – 267kph/166mph
Ceiling – 4,200m/13,800ft
Range – 3,500km/2,175 miles
Climb – 1,000m/3,280ft in 7 minutes, 48 seconds

Dornier Do 24

The Do 24 flying boat was produced by Dornier before and during World War II. Originally designed to meet a mid-1930s Dutch Navy requirement for use in the Dutch East Indies (today's Indonesia), the Do 24 was a side-by-side three-engined flying boat intended for military cargo transport and air-sea rescue. Intended to operate far from a home base, the Do 24 had living and sleeping quarters for its then crew of six. Dornier company records claim that up to 12,000 people were rescued by the type in a career that continued through to 1970.

The Dutch specified that, to ease maintenance through compatiblity with other aircraft they operated, the Do 24 was to be engined by Wright Cyclone radials. The prototype flew on July 3, 1937, sea trials followed and the Do 24 soon went into production. Twelve Do 24K-1s were built for the Dutch Navy and then the Dutch began to licence-assemble a further 48 machines that were designated Do 24K-2.

Thirty-seven Dutch and German-built Do 24s had been deployed to the East Indies by the time of the German invasion of Holland in June 1940. Of these machines, six surviving

ABOVE: The Do 24T-2 differed from earlier versions by having a 20mm cannon in the dorsal turret seen here just forward of the cross on the fuselage side.

TOP: This Do 24N-1 was a Do 24K built in the Netherlands and then modified for service with the Luftwaffe. For a large aircraft it presents surprisingly little frontal area. ABOVE: Three prototype Do 24s were built and this aircraft was the Do 24 V3 D-ADLR that was the first to fly on July 3, 1937. Power came from three 890hp Wright Cyclones and the aircraft was delivered to the Dutch for evaluation in late 1937. In Dutch service it was registered as X-1.

aircraft were transferred to the Royal Australian Air Force in February, 1942, when the Japanese overran their bases. The Do 24s served in the RAAF as transports in New Guinea thereby becoming one of the few aircraft types to serve with both Axis and Allied air arms during World War II.

When the Dutch assembly line was captured by the Germans, the Luftwaffe, hitherto disinterested in the Do 24, pressed for production to continue. Eleven aircraft were completed with Wright Cyclone engines already acquired by the Dutch under the designation Do 24N-1 but subsequent machines were built with German BMW Bramo 323 R-2 radials and were designated Do 24T-1.

A further Do 24 production line was established in France during the German occupation. Operated by SNCA, another 48 Do 24s were built there. The factory was abandoned as the Allied liberation forces swept through France but production resumed soon after making a further 40 Do 24s that served in the French Air Force until 1952. A German Do 24 that made a forced landing in neutral Sweden during the war was impounded, then paid for, repaired and remained airworthy in Swedish service until 1952.

The Dornier flying boat served with the Luftwaffe on every front of World War II and was equally adept at troop carrying and air-sea rescue. The type also escorted convoys and carried out maritime reconnaissance and could ship great quantities of supplies. Essential resupply missions during the German defence of the Kuban bridgehead in the Caucasus in 1943 saw 22 of these flying boats deliver 1,000 tons – since airstrips in the region were flooded, the Do 24s were the only lifeline available.

The aircraft's ability to operate in the most hostile of conditions earned it a place in aviation history as one of the greatest ocean-going flying boats. The Do 24 rescued airmen and sailors in the Arctic, the Mediterranean, the North Sea,

the English Channel and the Atlantic. One crew was rescued from the Atlantic 563km/350 miles from the nearest land. The best example of the type's ruggedness is the story of the aircraft that lost its tail on landing but taxied back to shore with crew and rescued survivors safe within the watertight remains of the aircraft.

In June 1944, 12 Dutch-built Do 24s were supplied to Spain apparently on the basis that they would rescue downed airmen of both sides. These Spanish machines were augmented post-war by some French-built examples and some remained in service until 1970.

In February 2004, a restored and re-engined example designated Do-24 ATT, began flying around the world to benefit the UNICEF organization. This sole flying example is now operated as a charter aircraft by South East Asian Airlines.

Between 1937 and 1945 the various factories produced a total of 279 Do 24s.

ABOVE: **The sole flying example, the fully restored Do 24 ATT powered by three Pratt & Whitney Canada PT6A-45 turboprop engines. It is now available for charter and gives the lucky passengers a rare experience of taking off from water in a classic flying boat.**

Dornier Do 24T-1

First flight: July 3, 1937 (prototype)

Power: Three 1,000hp BMW-Bramo 323R-2 9-cylinder radial engines

Armament: One 7.9mm machine-gun in bow and stern turrets and one 20mm cannon in dorsal turret

Size: Wingspan – 27m²/88ft 7in
Length – 22.05m/72ft 4in
Height – 5.75m/18ft 10in
Wing area – 108m²/1,163sq ft

Weights: Empty – 9,400kg/20,723lb
Maximum take-off – 18,400kg/40,565lb

Performance: Maximum speed – 331kph/206mph
Ceiling – 7,500m/24,605ft
Range – 4,700km/2,920 miles
Climb – 2,000m/6,560ft in 6 minutes

Douglas SBD-5 Dauntless

The Douglas SBD Dauntless dive-bomber, a mainstay of the US Navy's World War II air assets in the Pacific, had the lowest loss ratio of any US carrier-based aircraft. The first enemy ship sunk by the US Navy during World War II is credited to a Dauntless from the USS *Enterprise*. The Dauntless went on to destroy 18 enemy warships, including a battleship and six carriers.

The Dauntless had its origins in a 1934 Northrop proposal for a new US Navy dive-bomber, the BT-1, based on the Northrop A-17 light attack bomber. The Northrop machine was the inspiration for Douglas' own XBT-1 which first flew in July 1935. After a series of service trials, an order was placed for 54 BT-1s – the first production examples were fitted with 825hp Wright R-1535-94 engines while the last ones off the production line were fitted with 1,000hp R-11820-32 engines and designated XBT-2. More modifications followed and when the Northrop Corporation became a division of Douglas in August 1937, the aircraft was redesignated XSBD-1.

ABOVE: Unusually for the time, the Dauntless served with the US Navy, Marines Corps and the USAAF, in the latter case as the A-24. The USAAF machines did not have the arrester hook for carrier operations.

ABOVE: Despite its shortcomings, the Dauntless went on to sink more enemy shipping than any other Allied aircraft in the Pacific War. It was the aircraft that won the Battle of Midway and changed the course of the war.

When prototype testing had proved the design to be outstanding in its field, in April 1939 the US Marine Corps and US Navy placed orders for the SBD-1 and SBD-2 respectively. The Navy machine had increased fuel capacity and different armament. Production commenced in 1940, and although the SBD bore a resemblance to its Northrop predecessor, it was a completely different aircraft. The SBD-1 first entered service with the US Marines in mid-1940 when they received a batch of 57 SBD-1s with their distinctive perforated 'Swiss cheese' flaps – dive brakes punched with 7.62mm/0.3in holes so the aircraft could achieve pinpoint accuracy by diving to the target, dropping the bomb and then pulling out of the near-vertical dive.

The US Navy received its first SBD-2s in early 1941, and by the summer of that year had taken delivery of over 400 SBD-3s – this version had self-sealing, larger fuel tanks as well as armour protection, a bullet-proof windscreen and four machine-guns. By the end of 1941, the Dauntless constituted the attack element of the US Navy's carrier-based air group in the Pacific. In 1941, the US Army, aware that it did not have a dive-bomber in the same class as the Luftwaffe's Ju 87 Stuka, ordered the SBD-3 under the designation A-24. This land-based version was identical to the Navy machines but lacked an arrester hook and sported a tailwheel with an inflatable tyre instead of the solid rubber one used on Navy machines. Although it never lived up to its early promise during World War II, the type remained in US Army Air Corps and then US Air Force use for several years after the war.

The SBD-4 featured an improved 24-volt electrical system and some of these machines became SBD-4P reconnaissance aircraft. It was, however, the SBD-5, built at Douglas's new plant in Tulsa, Oklahoma, that was the most widely produced variant. Powered by a 1,200hp R-1820-60 engine, this version could also carry more ammunition for its guns. Over 2,400 SBD-5s were built – some were supplied to, but never used in action by, the Royal Navy's Fleet Air Arm where they were designated Dauntless DB Mk I. Interestingly, Mexico was the other export customer for the SBD-5. The ultimate version was the SBD-6, with an even more powerful engine and greater fuel capacity.

Douglas delivered a total of 5,936 SBDs and Army Air Forces A-24s between 1940 and the end of production in July 1944. In addition to the US Navy, Marine Corps and Army Air Forces, Britain and Mexico, the Dauntless also served with the Royal New Zealand Navy. Free French machines were used against German forces in France post-D-Day.

TOP: **The two-man crew of the Dauntless sat under a continuous 'greenhouse' canopy with a bullet-proof windscreen. The defensive guns in the rear cockpit were effective and one US Navy Dauntless crew is known to have destroyed seven Japanese Zeros in just two days.** ABOVE: **Note the distinctive perforated 'Swiss cheese' flaps visible as this US Navy machine prepares for take-off.**

ABOVE: **Dauntless pilots would typically approach their target at a maximum altitude of 6,100m/20,000ft. When over their objective, they would deploy both upper and lower dive flaps before diving on the target. A telescopic sight, and later a reflector sight, kept them on target.**

Douglas SBD-5 Dauntless

First flight: July 1935
Power: One Wright 1,200hp R-1820-60 Cyclone 9-cylinder radial engine
Armament: Two 0.50in fixed forward-firing machine-guns in the upper part of the forward fuselage; two trainable 0.30in machine-guns in rear cockpit; external bomb or depth-charge load of 1,021kg/2,250lb
Size: Wingspan – 12.66m/41ft 6in
Length – 10.09m/33ft 1in
Height – 4.14m/13ft 7in
Wing area – 30.19m²/325sq ft
Weights: Empty – 2,963kg/6,534lb
Maximum take-off – 4,853kg/10,700lb
Performance: Maximum speed – 410kph/255mph
Service ceiling – 7,780m/25,530ft
Range – 2,519km/1,565 miles
Climb – 457m/1,500ft per minute

Douglas TBD-1 Devastator

The Douglas TBD-1 was the US Navy's first widely used carrier-borne monoplane. The XTBD-1 prototype first flew on April 15, 1935, and was handed over to the US Navy for testing just nine days later.

This large aircraft, with a wingspan of 15.24m/50ft, was designed to carry a heavy torpedo beneath its fuselage. A total of 129 production TBD-1s were delivered to the USN between 1937 and 1939 replacing biplanes in torpedo squadrons on board US carriers *Saratoga*, *Enterprise*, *Lexington*, *Wasp*, *Hornet*, *Yorktown* and *Ranger*.

With a top speed of around 322kph/200mph, the aircraft was fast in its class for the time. The TBD-1 was the first all-metal aircraft in the US Navy, the first with a fully enclosed cockpit and the first with hydraulically folding wings for carrier

operations. With its wings unfolded, the aircraft would take up a lot of room in a cramped carrier hangar so Douglas designed them to fold upwards reducing the span to just 7.92m/26ft. It had a semi-retractable undercarriage and the wheels were designed to protrude 25cm/10in below the wings in the 'up' position to minimize the damage of a wheels-up landing.

A TBD had a crew of three who sat in tandem (pilot, bombardier and gunner/radio operator from front to back) beneath a large greenhouse canopy that ran almost half the length of the aircraft's sleek and curvaceous fuselage. During a bombing run, the bombardier would lay prone having crawled into position beneath the pilot, then aim his weapons (a Mk XIII torpedo or one 454kg/1,000lb bomb) using a Norden bombsight through a window in the bottom of the fuselage.

LEFT: **The TBD's mechanically folded wings was one innovation that made the Devastator possibly the most advanced carrier aircraft in the world for a time.** The fast pace of aircraft development, accelerated by the arms race and political tensions of the time, meant this status was shortlived. By the time of the Japanese attack on Pearl Harbor, the TBD was already outdated. The type did, however, fly on until 1943, albeit in training roles.

The Devastator's defensive armament consisted of one forward-firing 0.30in or 0.5in machine-gun operated by the pilot. The armament can be identified by the presence of a breech fairing blister rear of the starboard air intake – only the Colt/Browning 0.50 calibre M2 required the fairing to be added. The rear gunner also had a 0.30in or a 0.5in machine-gun at this disposal but on a flexible mount.

Around 100 TBD-1s were in service when war broke out, representing the US Pacific Fleet's sole torpedo aircraft for the early stages of the war against Japan. The type served well as a torpedo-bomber and high-level bomber for the first half of 1942 and, on May 7, TBDs were instrumental in the sinking of the Japanese carrier *Shoho* in the Battle of the Coral Sea.

But then the TBD-1 guaranteed its place in history for the worst possible reasons. On June 4, 1942, during the Battle of Midway, three squadrons of TBD-1s made daring but unsuccessful daylight torpedo attacks on the Japanese Imperial Fleet north of Midway Island and lost all but four of the 41 aircraft that began the mission. By then old and slow for the fast-paced air combat environment of the Pacific, with relatively poor defensive armament and no self-sealing fuel tanks, the Devastator was itself devastated by Japanese fighters and anti-aircraft fire. In fairness to the TBD, this was a fate that befell many torpedo-bombers of the time due to the extremely hazardous nature of their mission. Within three years, the TBD-1 had gone from cutting edge to out of date, such was the pace of combat aircraft design performance and tactics.

With the Battle of Midway over, the US Navy had just 39 TBDs left in its front-line inventory and these were rapidly replaced by Grumman Avengers. The surviving TBDs flew on in training units until 1943, or as communication aircraft, and some were used as static instructional airframes through 1944. No TBDs are preserved although an example that ditched in the sea may be recovered for a US museum. Total production was 130 including a floatplane trials aircraft.

ABOVE AND BELOW: **Two 1938 studies of the same aircraft, a TBD-1 from Torpedo Squadron Six (VT-6) operating from USS *Enterprise* (CV-6). The aircraft (Bureau of Aeronautics number 0322) was that of the Torpedo Squadron Six commanding officer and was lost in an accident at sea on March 10, 1939. VT-6 was one of the units mauled during the Battle of Midway due to the lack of co-ordination of fighter escort, as well as attack by numerous enemy fighters.**

ABOVE: **TBD-1 Devastators and Grumman F4F-3 Wildcats parked on the incredibly congested flight deck of the USS *Enterprise*, April 1942. Note the variations in the size of the national insignia on the fuselage sides.**

Douglas TBD-1 Devastator

First flight: April 15, 1935
Power: Pratt & Whitney 900hp R-1830-64 Double Wasp air-cooled radial engine
Armament: Two 0.30in or 0.5in machine-guns plus a Mk XIII torpedo (544kg/1,200lb) or a 454kg/1,000lb bomb
Size: Wingspan – 15.24m/50ft
  Length – 10.69m/35ft
  Height – 4.59m/15ft 1in
  Wing area – 39.2m²/422sq ft
Weights: Empty – 2,804kg/6,182lb
  Maximum take-off – 4,623kg/10,194lb
Performance: Maximum speed – 331kph/206mph
  Ceiling – 6,004m/19,700ft
  Range – 700km/435 miles
  Climb – 222m/720ft per minute

LEFT: **A Fairey IIIB floatplane about to take off. The remarkable longevity of the Fairey III says much about the excellence of the basic design. The IIIB had a larger wing area than the IIIA and was used for mine-spotting from coastal bases.**

ABOVE: **An improved Fairey IIIF Mk IIIB taxis towards a Royal Navy ship.**

Fairey III family

Originally, a World War I twin-float seaplane, the N.10, Fairey converted this general-purpose biplane aircraft into a landplane, the Fairey IIIA, which became one of the company's most successful designs.

This entered Royal Navy service as a two-seat carrier-borne bomber. The IIIB was a floatplane version while the IIIC had a much more powerful engine. The Fairey IIID was the second most numerous variant produced and appeared in RAF landplane but mainly Royal Navy floatplane versions. In the spring of 1926, four RAF Fairey IIIDs carried out a 22,366km/13,900 miles long-distance formation flight from Northolt,

near London, to Cape Town and back through Greece, Italy and France. IIIDs were exported to Australia, Ireland, Chile, Portugal, Sweden and the Netherlands.

The Fairey IIIF, a much-improved development of the IIID was the most numerous variant with 597 aircraft produced. This aircraft, again in landplane and floatplane versions, gave sterling service in the RAF and Fleet Air Arm in Britain and overseas from 1927 until the mid-1930s. The obvious successor to the excellent IIIF was another IIIF, which is what the RAF's Fairey Gordon and Royal Navy Seals were. The two-man Gordon was a IIIF fitted with a different engine and other

minor changes while the Seal was a three-seat naval version with a float conversion option and an arrester hook. Members of this family of aircraft served from World War I through to the early days of World War II – quite an achievement considering the type was thought to be obsolete in 1918.

One complete Fairey III survives, a Mk 2 version of the Fairey III D preserved in the *Museu da Marinha* (Navy Museum) in Portugal. This historic aircraft was involved in a transatlantic crossing attempt by Portugal in 1922.

Fairey III family

First flight: March 19, 1926

Power: One Napier 570hp Lion XIA 12-cylinder V-type engine

Armament: One 0.303in Vickers machine-gun in front fuselage and one 0.303in Lewis gun in rear cockpit, provision for 227kg/500lb bomb load under lower wing

Size: Wingspan – 13.94m/45ft 9in
Length – 11.19m/36ft 8.6in
Height – 4.26m/14ft
Wing area – 40.74m²/439sq ft

Weights: Empty – 1,762kg/3,880lb
Maximum take-off – 2,740kg/6,041lb

Performance: Maximum speed – 193kph/120mph
Service ceiling – 6,700m/22,000ft
Range – 644km/400 miles
Climb – 305m/1,000ft per minute

ABOVE: **A Fairey IIIF Mk IIIB being craned aboard a Royal Navy ship. The service use of this remarkable family of aircraft spanned two World Wars, a rare service record for any aircraft.**

LEFT: Demonstrating just how much space can be saved by wing-folding, this Albacore has it engine run up while deck crew work on the aircraft. ABOVE: The Albacore introduced many 'luxuries' for the three-man crew including an enclosed, heated cabin but it was outlasted by the aircraft it was intended to replace in FAA service. BELOW: From mid-1942, the Fleet Air Arm was operating large numbers of the Fairey biplane from the Mediterranean to the Arctic Circle. In all, 800 aircraft were built but the type was retired from the FAA by the end of 1943.

Fairey Albacore

Designed in response to a British Air Ministry specification S.41/36 for a torpedo/reconnaissance bomber to replace the Swordfish, the single-engine three-seat Albacore was expected to be a great improvement over the earlier Fairey aircraft. Despite having an all-metal fuselage and having features including an enclosed, heated cockpit and automatic emergency dinghy ejection, the Albacore was in fact outlasted in service by the venerable Swordfish. Although more streamlined than the Swordfish and able to reach greater altitudes, the Albacore had lower cruising speed and a shorter range than the older aircraft. To add insult to injury, the Albacore was also used to train Swordfish crews and Swordfish production continued for a year after the Albacore was removed from front-line duties.

The first prototype had its maiden flight in December 1938, the type having been ordered into production from plans 18 months earlier. Production began in 1939 and on March 15, 1940, No.826 Squadron at Ford became the first unit to receive the type. The squadron was in action on May 31 carrying out attacks against E-boats off the Dutch coast as well as inland targets in Belgium. By the end of 1940 there were a further three UK land-based units operating the type carrying out duties from anti-submarine patrols and mine-laying to shipping strikes. Two of the Albacore squadrons, Nos.826 and 829, embarked on HMS *Formidable* in November 1940, and in March 1941 took part in the type's first torpedo strikes in attacks on the Italian battleship *Vittorio Veneto* during the Battle of Cape Matapan.

Fifteen Fleet Air Arm squadrons were equipped with the Albacore by mid-1942 and the type went on to see action in the Arctic, Western Desert, Indian Ocean and the Mediterranean as well as in UK home waters and the Channel. During the Allied invasion of North Africa, Albacores carried out coastal gun suppression and anti-submarine missions. During and immediately after the Allied invasion of Normandy, Albacores operated by the Royal Canadian Air Force were tasked with the suppression of German E-boats attempting to interfere with Allied shipping.

The Albacore was retired before the Swordfish, and from 1942 was gradually replaced by the Fairey Barracuda and Grumman Avenger. One Albacore survives, preserved by the Fleet Air Arm Museum at Yeovilton in the UK.

Fairey Albacore

First flight: December 12, 1938
Power: One Bristol 1,130hp Taurus XII radial engine
Armament: One forward-firing 0.303in machine-gun in starboard wing, two 0.303in machine-guns in rear cockpit plus one 730kg/1,610lb torpedo hung under fuselage or four 227kg/500lb bombs beneath the wings
Size: Wingspan – 15.24m/50ft
　　　Length – 12.14m/39ft 10in
　　　Height – 4.32m/14ft 2in
　　　Wing area – 57.88m²/623sq ft
Weights: Empty – 3,289kg/7,250lb
　　　　　Maximum take-off – 4,745kg/10,460lb
Performance: Maximum speed – 259kph/161mph
　　　　　Ceiling – 6,310m/20,700ft
　　　　　Range – 1,497km/930 miles
　　　　　Climb – 1,829m/6,000ft in 8 minutes

Fairey Barracuda

Fairey's response to the Royal Navy-led specification S.24/37 for a Fairey Albacore replacement was the three-seat Barracuda which had its maiden flight on December 7, 1940. Testing highlighted some shortcomings that were resolved in the second prototype but this did not fly until June 1941 – Britain's aviation industry was focusing on the production of fighters and bombers at the time and the new torpedo-bomber just had to wait. Service trials were consequently not completed until February 1942 after which the more powerful Merlin 32 was fitted. The new engine was required to cope with the increasing weight of the Barracuda due to a beefing-up of the structure and additional equipment that had to be carried. The re-engined Barracuda became the Mk II and was the main production variant of the type. The Mk IIs began to enter service in early 1943, the first Mk IIs

ABOVE: **The design that became Fairey's Barracuda beat off five other proposals that all responded to the request for an Albacore successor. Note the deployed Fairey-Youngman trailing edge flaps that aided the type's all-round performance.** BELOW LEFT: **Looking bug-like with its folded wings, the Barracuda served the Royal Navy in quantity although not all pilots liked the aircraft. Forty-two of these pugnacious aircraft attacked the _Tirpitz_ in April 1944.**

going to No.827 Squadron then re-forming at Stretton. By May 1943, many squadrons of the Fleet Air Arm became fully equipped with Barracuda Mk IIs and then joined carriers of the Home and Far Eastern fleets.

The Barracuda had a number of claims to fame – it was the first British carrier-based monoplane of all-metal construction to enter service with the Fleet Air Arm as well as being the first monoplane torpedo-bomber. A total of 1,688 Barracuda Mk IIs were built by Fairey as well as Westland, Blackburn and Boulton Paul.

The Barracuda Mk III (912 examples built by Fairey and Boulton Paul) was developed to carry ASV (air-to-surface vessel) radar in a radome blister under the rear fuselage, and first flew in 1943. The radar enabled the Barracuda to track its prey much more effectively. In European waters, Mk IIIs, equipped with ASV radar flew anti-submarine patrols from small escort carriers using Rocket-Assisted Take-Off (RATO) to get clear of the short decks.

In April 1944, the carriers _Victorious_ and _Furious_ sent 42 Barracudas to carry out a dive-bombing attack on the German pocket battleship _Tirpitz_ then at anchor in Kaa Fjord, Norway. The Barracudas were part of Operation 'Tungsten', the aim of which was the destruction of the enemy battleship. The Barracudas had practised long and hard for the operation and attacked in a steep dive despite heavy defensive flak. They scored 15 direct hits with armour-piercing bombs for the loss

LEFT: The type was first used operationally in September 1941 in raids launched by HMS *Victorious* on Kirkenes in northern Norway and on Petsamo in Finland. Later, in 1942, Barracudas took part in sweeps over French ports and in the invasion of Madagascar.
BELOW: A formation of Barracudas carrying torpedoes packed a powerful punch but the type could also carry bombs and depth charges.

of only two aircraft. *Tirpitz* was so damaged in the raid that it was out of action for three months and the Navy was able to channel its resources elsewhere, at least for a time.

Nos.810 and 847 Squadrons, Fleet Air Arm, embarked on HMS *Illustrious*, introduced the Barracuda to the Pacific theatre of operations in April 1944 when they supported the US Navy in a dive-bombing attack on the Japanese installations on Sumatra.

In all, 23 operational Fleet Air Arm squadrons were equipped with Barracudas during World War II. Wartime production of the Fairey Barracuda totalled 2,541 aircraft. In 1945 production started on the more powerful Mk V, later designated the TF.5, but only 30 models of this variant were built and were used as trainers during the post-war period.

A total of 2,572 Barracudas of all marks were delivered to the Fleet Air Arm. Barracudas were also operated by the French and Dutch Fleet Air Arms.

ABOVE: Despite its ungainly appearance, the Barracuda could carry out a wide variety of missions well. The high-winged Fairey aircraft was progressively and successfully modified to carry bombs, mines, torpedoes, depth charges, rockets, radar masts and radomes, lifeboats and even containers under the wings for dropping agents into occupied territory.

Fairey Barracuda Mk II

First flight: December 7, 1940
Power: One Rolls-Royce 1640hp Merlin 32 V-12 piston engine
Armament: Two 0.303in Browning machine-guns in rear cockpit; one 735kg/1,620lb torpedo or one 454kg/1,000lb bomb beneath fuselage, or four 204kg/450lb or six 113kg/250lb bombs, depth charges or mines under wings
Size: Wingspan – 14.99m/49ft 2in
Length – 12.12m/39ft 9in
Height – 4.60m/15ft 1in
Wing area – 34.09m²/367sq ft
Weights: Empty – 4,241kg/9,350lb
Maximum take-off – 6,396kg/14,100lb
Performance: Maximum speed – 367kph/228mph
Service ceiling – 5,060m/16,600ft
Range – 1,851km/1,150 miles
Climb – 1,524m/5,000ft in 6 minutes

Fairey Firefly

From 1926, Britain's Fleet Air Arm deployed a series of fast two-seat multi-role fighter reconnaissance aircraft. The Fairey Firefly, designed by H.E. Chaplin at Fairey Aviation in 1940, continued the tradition having been designed to meet Admiralty specification N.5/40. Even before it had flown the design showed enough promise that, in June 1940, the Admiralty ordered 200 aircraft.

The prototype Firefly flew on December 22, 1941, and although it was 2 tons heavier than the Fulmar it was to replace (due mainly to its armament of two 20mm cannon in the wings), the Firefly was 64kph/40mph faster due to a better understanding of aerodynamics and a more powerful engine, the 1,730hp Rolls-Royce Griffon. It was, however, still slower than most contemporary fighters but possessed great low-speed handling characteristics that are vital for a carrier-borne fighter.

TOP: **This Firefly AS.5 served with both the Royal Navy and Royal Australian Navy. It was restored and kept in flying condition but was lost in a fatal crash in 2003.** ABOVE: **The early Firefly production versions had the radiator intake below the engine as can be seen on this aircraft. Notice the four cannon protruding from the wing leading edges.**

The main variant in use during World War II was the F. Mk I, which saw action in all theatres of operations following first deliveries in March 1943 although they did not enter operational service until July 1944 equipping No.1770 Squadron on board HMS *Indefatigable*. The type's first operations were in Europe where Fireflies made armed reconnaissance flights and anti-shipping strikes along the Norwegian coast. Fireflies also provided air cover during the July 1944 sinking of the German battleship *Tirpitz* lying at anchor in Kaa Fjord, Northern Norway.

Firefly night-fighter variants were developed early in production of the type and carried airborne interception radar in small wing-mounted radomes. The associated extra equipment affected the aircraft's centre of gravity and necessitated a lengthening of the fuselage by 45.7cm/18in. This version of the F.1, the N.F.2, was only produced in limited quantities because an alternative means of accommodating the

ABOVE: **In all versions, including this anti-submarine mark, the observer's position was behind the wing while the pilot sat over the leading edge. The Firefly served in the front-line ASW role until the mid-1950s.**

radar equipment was developed that did not require major structural work. Radar was then being fitted as standard to Fireflies and the non-lengthened Firefly N.F.1 was the night-fighter version of the F.R.1 which was itself basically an F.1 fitted with radar. All Firefly night-fighters were equipped with exhaust dampers so that the glowing exhausts of the Griffin would not show up in darkness. During late 1944, Fireflies operated by the Night Fighter Interception Unit based at RAF Coltishall in Norfolk undertook night patrols to counter V1 flying bombs air-launched over the North Sea by Luftwaffe He 111s.

Although the Firefly was never a classic fighter, it excelled in the strike and armed reconnaissance role. Despite this, the first Firefly air combat victory occurred on January 2, 1945, during a Fleet Air Arm attack on oil refineries in Sumatra when a No.1770 Squadron aircraft shot down a Japanese Nakajima Ki-43 'Oscar', a very capable dogfighter.

Throughout its operational career, the Firefly took on increasingly more demanding roles, from fighter to anti-submarine warfare. It was stationed mainly with the British Pacific Fleet in the Far East and Pacific theatres. In January 1945, the first major action by the Fleet Air Arm against the Japanese saw oil refineries in Sumatra set ablaze by rockets fired from Fireflies.

Fireflies entered the history books when they became the first British-designed and built aircraft to overfly Tokyo at the end of World War II. In the weeks immediately after VJ day, Fleet Air Arm Fireflies carried out supply drops to POW camps on the Japanese mainland.

Post-war the Firefly remained in service in the UK, Canada and Australia. The Royal Canadian Navy deployed 65 Fireflies of the Mk AS.5 type on board its carriers between 1946 and 1954. Fleet Air Arm Fireflies carried out anti-shipping missions from aircraft carriers in the Korean War (as did Australian Fireflies) as well as serving in the ground-attack role in Malaya. In 1956, the Firefly's FAA front-line career ended with the introduction of the Fairey Gannet in the ASW role.

ABOVE: **Many types developed in World War II were in action again in Korea including Royal Navy Seafires, Sea Furies and Fireflies (pictured). The Royal Navy only operated propeller aircraft in the war.**

ABOVE: **An ASW Firefly catches the wire. Notice the wing leading-edge radiators that typified the later versions, and the black and white 'D-Day' type stripes applied to all FAA aircraft that fought in Korea.**

ABOVE: **The Firefly was built at two Fairey factories at Hayes in Middlesex and Heaton Chapel on the outskirts of Manchester. General Aircraft were also subcontracted to build the type.**

Fairey Firefly F.1

First flight: December 22, 1941
Power: Rolls-Royce 1,990hp Griffon XII
Armament: Four 20mm cannon in wings
Size: Wingspan – 13.56m/44ft 6in
(4.04m/13ft 3in folded)
Length – 11.46m/37ft 7in
Height – 4.14m/13ft 7in
Wing area – 30.48m²/328sq ft
Weights: Empty – 4,423kg/9,750lb
Maximum take-off weight – 6,360kg/14,020lb
Performance: Maximum speed –
509kph/316mph
Ceiling – 8,534m/28,000ft
Range – 2,092km/1,300 miles
Climb – 4,575m/15,000ft in 9 minutes,
36 seconds

Fairey Flycatcher

The Flycatcher was conceived to meet a 1922 British Air Ministry specification that called for a new versatile single-seat Royal Navy carrier-based fighter that could be configured as a floatplane or amphibian. Power was to be provided by either the Armstrong Siddeley Jaguar or the Bristol Jupiter radial engines. The Flycatcher first flew on November 28, 1922, powered by a Jaguar III engine. After competitive service evaluation trials the Flycatcher was ordered for full production.

The Flycatcher with its fabric-covered mixed wood/metal fuselage was a remarkable aircraft for 1922 as it was one of the first aircraft specifically designed to operate from aircraft carriers. Full length flaps on the wings bestowed great lift so the aircraft only needed 45.75m/150ft in which to land or take off without the need for arrester wires or a catapult. The Flycatcher was also designed to 'break down' easily into sections no longer than 4.11m/13ft 6in for transportation, and the aircraft was already small enough to fit on the aircraft carrier lifts of the time without folding its wings. The undercarriage could be changed for twin floats or even a wheel/float combination for amphibian operations. It was a staggered-wing biplane of unequal span and had a tail skid instead of a tailwheel.

The Flycatcher first entered service with No.402 Flight Fleet Air Arm in 1923 and went on to be flown from all the

ABOVE: **The Fairey Flycatcher was a delight to fly, although it was not a high-performance aircraft. It was, however, versatile.**

British carriers of its era. Some aircraft operated as turret platform fighter floatplanes from capital ships. The type proved to be popular with pilots as they were easy to fly and very manoeuvrable, and they remained in service until 1934 when the last examples, some floatplanes of No.406 flight, were replaced by Hawker Ospreys.

A total of 196 Flycatchers, including prototypes, were produced by Fairey.

ABOVE: **Float-equipped Flycatchers would be fired off rails like this from Royal Navy ships to carry out reconnaissance duties and extend the ship's eyes over the horizon.**

Fairey Flycatcher I

First flight: November 28, 1922
Power: Armstrong Siddeley 400hp Jaguar IV two row, 14-cylinder radial engine
Armament: Two fixed forward-firing Vickers 0.303in machine-guns plus up to four 9kg/20lb bombs under wings
Size: Wingspan – 8.84m/29ft
    Length – 7.01m/23ft
    Height – 3.66m/12ft
    Wing area – 26.76m²/288sq ft
Weights: Empty – 9,24kg/2,038lb
    Maximum take-off – 1,372kg/3,028lb
Performance: Maximum speed – 216kph/134mph
    Ceiling – 5,790m/19,000ft
    Range – 500km/311 miles
    Climb – 3,050m/10,000ft in 9 minutes, 29 seconds

LEFT: **The Fulmar was a large fighter and was an underpowered aircraft for its size. It was 3m/ 10ft longer and had a wing span of 3m/10ft more than the Seafire that replaced it.** BELOW: **Despite its lack of performance compared to land-based single-seat types, Fulmars shot down a number of the more nimble enemy fighters, thanks to their eight guns.**

Fairey Fulmar

The Fleet Air Arm, keen to update its fighter fleet in the late 1930s, nevertheless severely limited designers' imagination by insisting that any new FAA fighter had to be a two-seater. It was felt that the pilot's workload would have been too great, had he needed to focus on controlling the aircraft at the same time as keeping it on course using the new complex navigational aids.

Fairey's proposal was what became the Fulmar, a two-seat reconnaissance fighter developed from their P.4/34 light bomber design. The Fulmar looked very similar to Fairey's Battle but was in fact smaller and lighter – its performance, however, was not much more impressive as the two-seat configuration increased weight thus affecting speed, climb and ceiling. It was clear that the Fulmar was inferior to contemporary single-seat

LEFT: **Crews found the Fulmar comparatively pleasant to fly, and its wide undercarriage track, evident in this photograph, meant it was a good carrier deck aircraft.**

fighters, but it was tough and reliable and packed the same firepower as the RAF's Spitfires and Hurricanes.

The prototype first flew on January 4, 1940, at Ringway (now Manchester International Airport) and 159 production aircraft had been produced for the Fleet Air Arm by the end of the year. The first front-line FAA unit to receive the type was No.806 in June 1940, and in August 1940 the squadron boarded HMS *Illustrious*.

Fulmars fought from the Arctic to the Far East – they defended convoys, took part in attacks on enemy warships and the invasions of North Africa and Sicily, defended Malta and Ceylon, and shot down many enemy aircraft, some of them while serving as night-fighters.

With the Fleet Air Arm in action in the Pacific as well as in European waters the FAA simply had to acquire truly modern carrier-based fighters so the Fulmar was gradually replaced by the Supermarine Seafire in 1943. The type did, however, continue to fly in secondary roles including the training of Barracuda crews.

The Fulmar ultimately equipped 19 Fleet Air Arm squadrons and 1 RAF unit. Of the 601 Fulmars built, only one remains, preserved by the Fleet Air Arm Museum in the UK. This aircraft is N1854, the prototype Fulmar which was the first and is now the last of the type.

Fairey Fulmar I

First flight: January 4, 1940
Power: One Rolls-Royce 1,080hp Merlin VIII engine
Armament: Eight wing-mounted 0.303in machine-guns and one 0.303in machine-gun in rear cockpit
Size: Wingspan – 14.13m/46ft 5in
Length – 12.27m/40ft 3in
Height – 4.27m/14ft
Wing area – 31.77m²/342sq ft
Weights: Empty – 3,187kg/7,026lb
Maximum take-off – 4,445kg/9,800lb
Performance: Maximum speed – 450kph/280mph
Ceiling – 7,925m/26,000ft
Range – 1,287km/800 miles
Climb – 366m/1,200ft per minute

Fairey Swordfish

The Fairey Swordfish holds a remarkable place in aviation history as it is one of the few combat aircraft to have been operational at both the start and end of World War II. This rugged aircraft was also the last British military biplane in front-line service and had the distinction of serving longer than the aircraft intended to replace it in Fleet Air Arm service. The 'Stringbag' was developed from an earlier failed Fairey design and first flew in April 1934 designated TSR II (Torpedo Spotter Reconnaissance II).

After successful service trials, a contract to supply 86 Swordfish Mk Is to the Royal Navy's Fleet Air Arm was signed. The Swordfish entered service with No.825 Squadron in July 1936 and over the next three years a further 600 aircraft were delivered, equipping 13 Fleet Air Arm squadrons. During World

War II another 12 squadrons were formed and equipped with the venerable biplane.

The wartime exploits of this deceptively frail-looking aircraft are legendary. Its first major action was against the Italian naval base at Taranto on November 11, 1940. HMS *Illustrious* launched 21 Swordfish of Nos.815 and 819 Squadrons to make a night attack on the Italian fleet. During the raid the Swordfish destroyed three battleships, two destroyers, a cruiser and other smaller ships for the loss of only two of the attacking aircraft. The attack crippled the Italian fleet and eliminated the opportunity for Italian warships to bolster German naval strength in the Mediterranean.

Other notable actions include the crippling of the German battleship *Bismarck* in May 1941. Swordfish from the Royal Navy carriers HMS *Victorious* and HMS *Ark Royal* were involved in the search for the German battleship. The first Swordfish attack, led by Lieutenant Commander Esmonde, was launched from *Victorious* but none of the torpedoes from the nine aircraft caused serious damage. During the second attack, delivered by 20 Swordfish from the *Ark Royal*, a torpedo severely damaged *Bismarck*'s rudder, greatly limiting the ship's manoeuvrability. The pursuing British task force were then able to catch and finally sink *Bismarck* with naval gunfire.

ABOVE: **A fine air-to-air study of a Swordfish formation. Note the 18in torpedo on the aircraft in the foreground. Note also the bomb shackles beneath the wings that could carry an alternative warload to the 'tin fish'.**

LEFT: **During World War II, Swordfish accounted for the sinking of over 300,000 tons of Axis shipping so were a major contribution towards the Allied victory in the Battle of the Atlantic and in gaining naval supremacy in the Mediterranean.**
ABOVE: **The Royal Navy Historic Flight maintains two of these remarkable aircraft in airworthy condition – a Mk I and a Mk II.**

In February 1942, crews of No.825 Squadron carried out a gallant attack against the *Scharnhorst*, *Gneisenau* and *Prinz Eugen* during which all six aircraft were shot down. Only five of the 18 crew members survived. For his bravery and leadership under fire, Lieutenant Commander Esmonde, veteran of the *Bismarck* mission, and leader of the attack, was posthumously awarded the Victoria Cross, the highest British and Commonwealth military award for gallantry.

While the Mk I was an all-metal fabric covered aircraft, the Mk II Swordfish, which entered service in 1943, had metal-clad lower wings to enable the aircraft to fire rocket projectiles without setting fire to the previously fabric-covered wings. Later the same year ASV (air-to-surface-vessel) radar was installed between the aircraft's fixed undercarriage legs on Mk IIIs while the Mk IV had an enclosed cockpit.

During the desperate Battle of the Atlantic, there were simply not enough aircraft carriers to escort Allied convoys across the ocean. As a stopgap measure to provide some protection for the convoys, Britain converted grain ships and oil tankers to become MAC (Merchant Aircraft Carrier) ships. Grain ships, fitted with a 123m/400ft flight deck, a below-deck hangar and lift, operated four Swordfish. The tankers had a 140m/460ft flight deck but no hangar in which to accommodate their three Swordfish – the MAC Swordfish suffered considerable wear and tear.

In the closing weeks of the war, the Royal Air Force operated a small number of all-black Mk III Swordfish – equipped with ASV radar and operating from landing strips in Belgium, these aircraft were tasked with the destruction of German submarines off the Dutch coast.

From 1940, all development and production of the venerable Swordfish passed from Fairey to the Blackburn Aircraft Company, which built 1,699 (unofficially known as 'Blackfish') of the 2,391 aircraft produced in total.

ABOVE: **Three Swordfish at the time of D-Day in 1944 wearing hastily-applied identification stripes. There were not many biplanes in front-line service at D-Day but the Swordfish was there.**

Fairey Swordfish Mk I

First flight: April 17, 1934
Power: One Bristol 690hp Pegasus IIIM3 9-cylinder air-cooled radial engine
Armament: One fixed 0.303in Browning machine-gun in the nose and one flexible 0.303in Vickers or Lewis machine-gun in the rear cockpit, one 45cm/18in 730kg/1,610lb torpedo or one 680kg/1,500lb mine or bombs
Size: Wingspan – 13.87m/45ft 6in
Length – 10.87m/35ft 8in
Height – 3.76m/12ft 4in
Wing area – 56.39m²/607sq ft
Weights: Empty – 2,132kg/4,700lb
Maximum take-off – 3,407kg/7,510lb
Performance: Maximum speed – 222kph/138mph
Service ceiling – 5,029m/16,500ft
Range – 1,658km/1,030 miles unloaded
Climb – 3,048m/10,000ft in 15 minutes, 2 seconds

LEFT: **While operating from German Navy ships in search of enemy craft, the Fl 282 was setting the foundations for the use of helicopters as naval weapons.** ABOVE: **This prototype was fitted with a largely glazed nose. Note the searchlight under the nose.**

Flettner Fl 282

The Fl 282 *Kolibri* (Hummingbird) was developed by German aeronautical scientist and helicopter pioneer Anton Flettner. Having built his first helicopter in 1930, Flettner produced the Fl 265 that first flew in 1939 and from this developed the Fl 282, designed from the outset for military use. Intended to carry a pilot and an observer, the design was judged to have so much potential for naval use that no fewer than 30 prototypes and 15 pre-production machines were ordered simultaneously to accelerate development and production. The pilot sat in front of the rotors in a typically open cockpit while the observer sat in a single compartment aft of the rotors, facing backwards.

In mock attacks Luftwaffe fighter pilots found it hard to keep the small, fast and agile helicopter in their gunsights. The *Kolibri* could land on a ship, even in heavy seas. Mass production was ordered but Allied bombing of the factories meant that only the prototypes were produced. Nevertheless it was 24 of these aircraft that entered service with the German Navy in 1943 for escort service, flying off the gun turrets of ships to spot submarines, and performing resupply missions in even the worst weather conditions. The Fl 282 was designed so the rotor blades and landing gear could be removed and the helicopter could be stored on a U-boat, although it is not known if this happened. This pioneering military helicopter served in the Baltic, North Aegean and the Mediterranean.

In the clear blue water of the Mediterranean the Fl 282 could spot a submerged submarine as deep as 40m/130ft, mark the enemy's position with a smoke bomb, then radio the position to its home ship while shadowing the submarine – this was groundbreaking use of the helicopter for anti-submarine warfare.

Only three of these helicopters survived the war as the rest of the fleet were destroyed to prevent their capture by the Allies. Two of the surviving machines went to the United States and Britain while the third ended up in the Soviet Union. Anton Flettner moved to the United States after the War and became an adviser to the US military.

LEFT: **The pioneering Flettner machines are often overlooked in aviation history, but the aircraft were true trailblazers. Operational by 1942 on German warships in the Baltic, Mediterranean and Aegean, the type was effectively the world's first military helicopter.**

Flettner Fl 282

First flight: 1941
Power: One Bramo 160hp Sh 14A radial piston engine
Armament: None
Size: Rotor diameter – 11.96m/39ft 2.75in
Length – 6.56m/21ft 6.25in
Height – 2.2m/7ft 2.5in
Weights: Empty – 760kg/1,676lb
Maximum take-off – 1,000kg/2,205lb
Performance: Maximum speed – 150kph/93mph
Ceiling – 3,300m/10,825ft
Range – 170km/106 miles
Climb – 91.5m/300ft per minute

LEFT: **The Fa 330 was the most basic of flying machines but it relied on the forward motion of the 'mother ship' to keep it aloft. This example was captured at the end of World War II and evaluated in the US.** ABOVE: **This photograph, taken during the type's development, shows the extreme vulnerability of the pilot, even without a crash dive by the towing U-boat.** BELOW: **The Fa 330 was made to be carried on U-boats so had to dismantle easily and quickly for stowage in the submarine.**

Focke-Achgelis Fa 330

The Focke-Achgelis Fa 330 *Bachstelze* (Wagtail) was a simple and unusual flying machine – a rotary kite. World War II German submarines sat low in the water and the crew could not see more than a few miles around so they were always at risk from fast-moving enemy destroyers. The Fa 330 was a solution developed to be towed on a winched cable in the air behind U-boats to extend their range of vision. By mid-1942, sea trials proved that the Fa 330 could work but only the Type IX U-boat could tow the Fa 330 fast enough for flight in low wind conditions.

The airframe consisted of two 6.35cm/2.5in diameter steel tubes forming an inverted T. While one tube was the 'fuselage' of the aircraft with the pilot's seat and instruments (altimeter, airspeed indicator and tachometer), the other tube served as the rotor mast. A control stick hung from the rotor blade hub and the pilot simply moved the stick for direct pitch and roll control and used foot pedals to move the large rudder to control yaw. The rotor blades consisted of a steel spar supporting plywood ribs skinned with fabric-covered plywood.

When not assembled, the Fa 330 was stored in two long watertight compartments built into the U-boat's conning tower. One tube contained the blades and tail and the other contained the fuselage. In calm conditions, four crewmen could assemble the entire aircraft on the deck of the submarine in just three minutes.

As the U-boat sped along, the airflow would begin to spin the rotors resulting in autorotation, the movement of relative wind up through the rotor blades which caused them to turn with enough speed to generate lift and carry the craft aloft without an engine. To speed up take-off, a deckhand could pull hard on a rope wrapped around a drum on the rotor hub to spin the rotor.

The craft would be towed by a cable around 150m/492ft long and 'fly' about 120m/393ft above the surface where visibility was 25 nautical miles compared to just 5 nautical miles from the conning tower of a U-boat. Normal flight revolutions per minute (rpm) were about 205rpm at a standard towing airspeed of 40kph/25mph while a minimum speed of 27kph/17mph was required to maintain autorotation. The pilot talked to the submarine using an intercom system via a wire wrapped around the towing cable.

In the event of an attack that would cause the U-boat to dive, both the pilot and craft were expendable although he was equipped with a parachute. Allied

air-cover was so good in the North Atlantic that only U-boats operating in the far southern parts of the Atlantic and the Indian Ocean deployed the Fa 330. Use of the Fa 330 assisted U-boat *U-177* to intercept and sink the Greek steamer *Eithalia Mari* on August 6, 1943.

Several are preserved in museums around the world.

Focke-Achgelis Fa 330	

First flight: 1942
Power: None
Armament: None
Size: Rotor diameter – 7.32m/24ft
　　　Length – 4.42m/14ft 6in
　　　Height – 1.7m/5ft 6in
Weights: Empty – 68kg/150lb
Performance: Airspeed between 27kph/17mph and 40kph/25mph to maintain flight

LEFT: **N5513 was a Sea Gladiator I that served in Alexandria and with HMS *Eagle* before being lost on Crete in May 1941.** ABOVE: **Sea Gladiator N5519, better known as *Charity* of Malta's Hal Far Fighter Flight, one of *Faith, Hope* and *Charity*.**

Gloster Sea Gladiator

The Gloster Gladiator was the RAF's last biplane fighter, and entered service in February 1937, by which time it was already obsolete. Although largely replaced by the start of World War II, the Gladiators of Nos.607 and 615 Auxiliary Squadrons were deployed to France with the Air Component of the Allied Expeditionary Force in November 1939. The squadrons were converting to Spitfires and Hurricanes when the German attack in the West was launched in May 1940, and the Gladiators proved to be no match for the modern Luftwaffe fighters.

The Gladiator had caught the eye of the Admiralty who ordered 60 fully navalized Sea Gladiators. The Sea Gladiator differed from the land-based version, Gladiator Mk II, by being fitted with an arrester hook for deck landings, catapult points for deck launches, and carrying a collapsible dinghy beneath a ventral fairing under the fuselage between the undercarriage legs.

It was Gladiator Mk I K6129 on loan from the RAF that undertook aircraft carrier trials with No.800 Squadron during the summer of 1938 on board HMS *Furious*. As an interim replacement for the Hawker Ospreys and Nimrods the Sea Gladiator was to replace, 38 RAF Gladiator Mk IIs were fitted with arrester hooks for carrier operations and were transferred to the Fleet Air Arm from December 1938 while the fully navalized Sea Gladiators were being developed.

By the start of World War II the carrier-borne Sea Gladiators were, like their land-based cousins, obsolete. The first deliveries had taken place in 1938 with the first Sea Gladiator unit being No.769 Squadron, a training unit. The Navy's first operational Sea Gladiator unit (November 1939) was No.804 Squadron.

It is, however, for the glorious defence of a beleaguered Malta that the Sea Gladiator is best known. From the

aircraft of No.802 Squadron that remained at Malta following the sinking of HMS *Glorious* in 1940, three Sea Gladiators became international legends. *Faith*, *Hope* and *Charity* were part of the Hal Far Fighter Flight, composed of both RAF and FAA personnel. In June 1940, *Faith* alone destroyed two Italian bombers within 24 hours.

Elsewhere, Sea Gladiators undertook less hazardous duties as faster fighter aircraft types entered front-line service. However, the type remained in use until 1944, employed in secondary roles, including communications, liaison and meteorological reconnaissance.

ABOVE: **Having first entered Royal Navy service in 1938, the Sea Gladiator continued to serve until 1944 in secondary roles. In all, 60 aircraft were supplied to the FAA.**

Gloster Sea Gladiator Mk II

First flight: September 12, 1934 (Gladiator prototype)
Power: Bristol 840hp Mercury VIIIA air-cooled radial piston engine
Armament: Two 0.303in machine-guns in nose plus two more mounted in wing
Size: Wingspan – 9.83m/32ft 3in
Length – 8.36m/27ft 5in
Height – 3.15m/10ft 4in
Wing area – 30.01m²/323sq ft
Weights: Empty – 1,692kg/3,730lb
Maximum take-off – 2,449kg/5,400lb
Performance: Maximum speed – 392kph/244mph
Ceiling – 9,700m/31,825ft
Range – 680km/423 miles
Climb – 6,095m/20,000ft in 9 minutes, 30 seconds

LEFT: Grumman's F2F was nicknamed the 'flying barrel' for reasons clear in this port-side view. Note the recess that housed the undercarriage when it was raised. ABOVE: The clearance between the top of the fuselage and the upper wing was negligible, so the pilot usually had to look over the wing instead when in the air.

Grumman F2F-1

Grumman's long association with the US Navy and reputation as naval aircraft specialists began in March 1931 when the US Navy ordered a prototype two-seat biplane fighter, the XFF-1. The all-metal XFF-1 had a top speed of 314kph/195mph and was faster than the US Navy's standard fighter of the time, the Boeing F4B-4.

The Navy ordered the Grumman biplane and it entered USN service as the FF-1 from April 1933. Canadian licence-built versions known as Goblins were supplied to the RCAF and single examples went to Nicaragua and Japan. Spanish Republican forces also acquired 40 aircraft and the two-seaters were in action against Spanish Nationalist forces between 1936–39.

The FF-1 was clearly a fine design and Grumman inevitably began to develop a single-seat version which became the F2F-1. The single-seater was lighter than the FF-1, had a top speed of 383kph/238mph and entered US Navy service during 1935, replacing the F4B. The F2F-1, known as the 'flying barrel', remained in front-line service aboard USS Lexington until as late as September 1940 at which point it became an advanced trainer.

The F2F-1 had exhibited some inherent directional instability which Grumman sought to eradicate in an improved design, the F3F. With a longer fuselage and wings, together with other aerodynamic refinements, the F3F-1 prototype first flew in March 1935 but

crashed two days later killing the pilot when the engine and wings detached themselves from the fuselage in a test dive. Wing and engine fittings were strengthened on the second prototype which itself crashed on May 17 after the pilot was unable to recover from a flat spin. Remarkably, the crashed aircraft was rebuilt and was back in the air after just three weeks, fitted with a small ventral fin beneath the tail to aid spin recovery. The F3F-1 entered US Navy service aboard USS Ranger and Saratoga in 1936. US Marine Corps unit VMF-211 was the last to retire the F3F in October 1941 – by which point it was the last biplane fighter in US service.

LEFT: The Grumman fighter was popular when it joined the US Fleet, but as a biplane entering service in the mid-1930s, its time in the front line was limited.

Grumman F2F-1

First flight: October 18, 1933
Power: Pratt & Whitney 650hp R-1535-72 Twin Wasp Junior radial piston engine
Armament: Two 0.3in machine-guns
Size: Wingspan – 8.69m/28ft 6in
Length – 6.53m/21ft 5in
Height – 2.77m/9ft 1in
Wing area – 21.37m²/230sq ft
Weights: Empty – 1,221kg/2,691lb
Maximum take-off – 1,745kg/3,847lb
Performance: Maximum speed – 383kph/238mph
Ceiling – 8,380m/27,500ft
Range – 1,585km/985 miles
Climb – 939m/3,080ft per minute

Grumman Avenger

Grumman's large single-engine torpedo-bomber was patriotically and appropriately named Avenger on December 7, 1941, the 'Day of Infamy' on which Japan attacked Pearl Harbor. Procured and constructed in great quantities, the Avenger saw action with Allied air arms in virtually all theatres of operation in World War II. Of the 9,836 aircraft produced, 2,290 were built by Grumman (so somewhat confusingly designated TBF) while the General Motors Eastern Division produced the rest which were TBMs, the designation by which all Avengers are sometimes erroneously known.

The Avenger was first flown on August 1, 1941, having been designed in just five weeks – an incredible feat by today's standards when computer-aided designs can take a decade to perfect. The aircraft, designed for a three-man crew, had an internal weapons bay to minimize drag, gun turret, and a rear defensive gun position. A hatch on the right side rear of the wing allowed access into the rear fuselage which was packed with equipment, flares, parachutes and ammunition. On the

ABOVE: **The Avenger was a large, well-armed and hard-hitting carrier-borne warplane that, despite a poor combat debut, made a key contribution to the Allied victory in World War II.**

lower level, the bombardier had a folding seat from which he could either man the lower rear machine-gun, or face forward and aim the aircraft for medium-altitude level bombing. The pilot sat in a roomy and comfortable cockpit above the wing's leading edge and enjoyed excellent visibility.

Only one aircraft returned from the six that made the Avenger's combat debut at Midway in June 1942. Despite this poor start, the Avenger went on to become one of the great naval combat aircraft of World War II, being involved in the destruction of more than 60 Japanese warships. It was the first US single-engined aircraft able to carry the hard-hitting 22in torpedo (as well as depth charges, rockets and bombs) and was also the first to boast a power-operated gun turret. Torpedoes launched by US Navy Avengers were largely

LEFT: **The Avenger became the standard US Navy torpedo-bomber of World War II, and numbered among its pilots a young naval aviator who went on to become President George Herbert Bush.** ABOVE: **In Royal Navy service the Avenger was at first called Tarpon, but was later redesignated Avenger.**

LEFT: **These three Avengers were flying with No.846 Fleet Air Arm when they were photographed in December 1943.** ABOVE: **Even with its folding wings the Avenger was still a large aircraft, due partly to its large internal weapons bay. Ordnance could also be carried externally.**

responsible for the sinking of the large Japanese battleships *Yamato* and *Musashi*.

The Royal Navy received 402 Avengers (designated TBF-1Bs), under the Anglo-American Lend-Lease arrangement – the first unit, No.832 Squadron (on board HMS *Victorious*) being equipped in early 1943. Although originally designated Tarpon Mk Is for British service, they were later redesignated Avenger Mk Is.

Around 330 TBM-1s were also supplied to the Royal Navy and designated Avenger Mk IIs. Delivery of the TBM-3 began in April 1944 with the Royal Navy receiving the 222 TBM-3 aircraft which were designated Avenger Mk III by the British. Torpedo-bomber versions remained in RN service until 1947 and then in 1953, the Royal Navy began acquiring anti-submarine versions designated the Avenger AS Mk IV or AS Mk V. The Avenger finally retired from the Royal Navy in 1962 after almost two decades of service.

In 1951, Royal Canadian Navy anti-submarine units were re-equipped with wartime Avengers, which had been overhauled and updated. In 1955, a further eight Avengers entered Canadian service in the Airborne Early Warning role.

Also during World War II, New Zealand acquired two squadrons of Grumman Avengers which were used as dive bombers by Nos.30 and 31 Squadrons. Secondary roles undertaken by the Kiwi Avengers included target drogue towing and, incredibly, the spraying of Japanese vegetable plots with diesel oil.

Post-war, the type was also adapted to a wide variety of civilian uses including crop-spraying and water-bombing. In New Zealand during 1947 an Avenger was used for trials of aerial seed-sowing and fertilizing. With an additional auxiliary fuel tank converted into a hopper installed in the 'bomb bay', it could carry 1,017kg/2,240lb of fertilizer. A few examples remain in flying condition in Britain and the USA.

ABOVE: **This preserved TBM-3R, with its rear turret position glazed over, was developed to carry seven passengers or cargo on to carriers. The US Navy needed a carrier-capable aircraft for the cargo role, and the tough Avenger was perfect. It removed the need to develop a role-specific type.**

Grumman TBM-3 Avenger

First flight: August 1, 1941
Power: One Wright 1,900hp R-2600-20 radial
Armament: Two 0.50in fixed forward-firing machine-guns in the upper part of the forward fuselage; two trainable 0.30in machine-guns in rear cockpit; external bomb or depth-charge load of 1,021kg/2,250lb
Size: Wingspan – 16.51m/54ft 2in
Length – 12.48m/40ft 11in
Height – 5m/16ft 5in
Wing area – 45.52m²/490sq ft
Weights: Empty – 47,83kg/10,545lb
Maximum take-off – 8,117kg/17,895lb
Performance: Maximum speed – 444kph/276mph
Service ceiling – 7,620km/25,000ft
Range – 1,609km/1,000 miles
Climb – 328m/1,075ft per minute

Grumman F4F Wildcat

With its wing set midway up its stubby fuselage, the Wildcat looks like a biplane missing a set of wings. There is a good reason for that – it was originally conceived as a biplane but was redesigned as a monoplane, the F4F, in 1936. Its industrial appearance, due to the entirely riveted fuselage, masked an aircraft with excellent speed and manoeuvrability.

In early 1939 the French Aéronavale placed the first order for the type with Grumman and this was followed in August that year by an order from the US Navy. After France fell, aircraft destined for the Aéronavale were diverted to Britain where the first examples for Britain's Fleet Air Arm arrived in July 1940. This fascinating time in the Wildcat's history is often overlooked by historians. The British named the F4F the Martlet and put the type into service almost immediately with No.804 Squadron in the Orkneys. In December 1940, two of these Martlets became the first US-built fighters in British

World War II service to destroy a German aircraft. In September 1941, No.802 Squadron became the first FAA unit to go to sea with Martlets, aboard HMS *Audacity*, and on the 20th of the month, two of the aircraft shot down a Focke-Wulf 200 that was shadowing their convoy. Martlets of the Royal Naval Fighter Unit saw action over the Western Desert and shot down an Italian Fiat G.50 on September 28, 1941.

In May 1942, over Madagascar, FAA Martlets saw action against Vichy French aircraft and in August that year during a convoy to Malta, they tackled Italian bombers over the Mediterranean. By now the Martlet/Wildcat was known as a formidable fighter aircraft. Pilots praised its destructive firepower but knew it was a tricky aircraft to fly and handle on the ground too.

ABOVE: Retaining the semi-recessed undercarriage-up arrangement of earlier Grumman types, the Wildcat was derived from a biplane design.

ABOVE: The Fleet Air Arm was first to put the Wildcat into combat as the Martlet Mk I. The aircraft got its first 'kills' in December 1940.

LEFT: The Wildcat was an excellent carrier-borne fighter – small, tough, durable and hard to outmanoeuvre in combat. BELOW: The Wildcat was one of the Fleet Air Arm's primary naval fighters until Wildcat squadrons started to be re-equipped with either the Hellcat or Corsair during 1943. However, many remained in service with the FAA until 1946.

When the USA entered World War II in December 1941, the F4F, by now known as the Wildcat, was the most widely used fighter on US aircraft carriers and also equipped many land-based US Marine Corps squadrons. This tough, hard-hitting and highly manoeuvrable aircraft was the US Navy's only carrier-borne fighter until the 1943 arrival of the Hellcat. Wildcats were central to some of the war's most remarkable heroic actions involving US Navy and USMC pilots.

Marine Corps Wildcats operated extensively from land bases, one of which was Henderson Field on Guadalcanal and it was from here that the Americans mounted their first offensive action of the war in the Pacific. One USMC Wildcat pilot, Captain Joe Foss, a flight commander with Marine Fighting Squadron VMF-121, led his flight of eight Wildcats from Guadalcanal to 72 confirmed aerial victories in a matter of 16 weeks. Foss himself shot down a total of 26 Japanese aircraft, including 5 in a single day, and was awarded the Medal of Honor.

Although in a straight fight Wildcats could not cope well with a Japanese Zero, the Grumman fighter's armour plating and self-sealing fuel tanks together with its pilot's tenacity made it a potent adversary in a dogfight. US Navy Wildcats were phased out in favour of the Grumman Hellcat in late 1943 but Britain's Fleet Air Arm continued to operate the Wildcat until the end of the war. In March 1945, Wildcats (the British abandoned the name Martlet in January 1944) of No.882 Squadron destroyed four Messerschmitt Bf109s over Norway in what was the FAA's last wartime victory over German fighters.

Wildcats manufactured by General Motors were designated FM-1 and -2.

ABOVE: The unusual paint scheme applied to this preserved Wildcat by the US-based Commemorative Air Force did not please the purists but it does remind air show audiences of the type's distinguished FAA service.

Grumman FM-2 Wildcat

First flight: March 1943 (FM-2)
Power: Wright Cyclone 1,350hp R-1820-56 9-cylinder air-cooled radial
Armament: Six 0.5in machine-guns in outer wings plus two underwing 113kg/250lb bombs or six 5in rockets
Size: Wingspan – 11.58m/38ft
Length – 8.80m/28ft 11in
Height – 3.50m/11ft 5in
Wing area – 24.16m²/260sq ft
Weights: Empty – 2,223kg/4,900lb
Maximum take-off – 3,362kg/7,412lb
Performance: Maximum speed – 534kph/332mph
Service ceiling – 10,576m/34,700ft
Range – 1,448km/900 miles
Climb – 610m/2,000ft per minute

Grumman F6F Hellcat

Rightly described as a war-winning naval aircraft, the F6F Hellcat was developed from the F4F Wildcat. Designed and produced in record time, the Hellcat's combat debut in August 1943 firmly swung the air power balance of the war in the Pacific in favour of the United States. From then on, all the major Pacific air battles were dominated by the F6F. In its first big air battle, in the Kwajalein area on December 4, 1943, 91 Hellcats fought 50 Japanese A6M Zeros and destroyed 28 for the loss of only 2. Powered by the Pratt & Whitney R-2800 Double Wasp, the robust Hellcat was credited with 75 per cent of all enemy aircraft destroyed by US Navy carrier pilots with an overall F6F kills to losses ratio in excess of 19:1. The Hellcat was America's all-time top 'ace-making' aircraft with no less than 307 pilots credited with the destruction of five or more enemy aircraft while flying the Grumman fighter. US Navy pilot Lieutenant Bill Hardy became an ace in a day on April 6, 1945, when in a single 70-minute sortie he engaged and destroyed five Japanese aircraft.

TOP: The Grumman Hellcat was the aircraft that the Allies could not have done without in the Pacific War but the Hellcat needed the carriers to operate.

ABOVE: The XF6F-4 was one of a number of prototype 'Hellcats' used to trial engine and armament installations during the type's development.

Effective at any altitude, the Hellcat's unusual features included backwards-retracting landing gear and a distinctive 31.13m^2/335sq ft wing larger than that of any other major single-engined fighter of World War II. The outer sections of the folding wings each contained three 0.5in machine-guns with 400 rounds each.

Night-fighter versions appeared in early 1944 equipped with radar and ensured that the Hellcats were an ever-present threat to their enemies. The Hellcat omnipresence in Pacific combat zones night or day came to be known as 'The Big Blue Blanket'. US Navy ace Lt Alex Vraciu destroyed 19 Japanese aircraft while flying Hellcats, 6 of them in one spectacular 8-minute engagement, and later described the F6F as "...tough, hardhitting, dependable – one hell of an airplane."

From April 1943, Britain's Fleet Air Arm received 252 F6F-3s under the Lend-Lease programme. Initially renamed the Gannet

ABOVE: The Grumman Hellcat was fast and well armed, and was able to claim over 5,000 enemy aircraft destroyed by the end of World War II.

LEFT: **Over 2,500 Hellcats were built during 1943 alone and even the mighty Corsair was not able to displace Grumman's fighter from front-line service.**

ABOVE RIGHT: **The Hellcat was developed with the benefit of air combat experience in both the Pacific and European Theatres.** BELOW: **The all-metal Hellcat had flush-riveted skin and was powered by a mighty 2,000hp Pratt & Whitney engine that helped it outpace enemy aircraft.**

in Royal Navy service, British F6Fs saw a lot of combat in actions off Norway, in the Mediterranean and the Far East, including the final assault on Japan. By late 1945 the Hellcat had been almost completely replaced in Royal Navy service, although a senior Fleet Air Arm officer is known to have had a personal F6F until 1953.

When the last aircraft rolled off the production line in November 1945 it made a total Hellcat production figure of 12,272, 11,000 of which were built in just two years. Swift production of the Hellcat has been attributed to the soundness of the original design, which required few engineering changes while production was underway.

Other nations that operated the Hellcat included France whose Aéronavale used them in Indochina, while the Argentine and Uruguayan navies used them until 1961.

Some US Navy Hellcats were converted into drones packed with explosives and in August 1952, six of these remotely controlled F6F-5Ks were directed on to North Korean targets.

ABOVE: **The Hellcat was for many the ultimate naval fighter of World War II, but the type flew on in front-line service with some air arms into the 1950s and saw action in Korea and Indochina.**

Grumman F6F-5 Hellcat

First flight: June 26, 1942

Power: Pratt & Whitney 2,000hp R-2800-10W 18-cylinder two-row air-cooled radial piston engine

Armament: Six 0.5in Browning machine-guns, plus provision for bombs up to 907kg/2,000lb

Size: Wingspan – 13m/42ft 10in
Length – 10.2m/33ft 7in
Height – 3.96m/13ft
Wing area – 31m^2/334sq ft

Weights: Empty – 4,152kg/9,153lb
Maximum take-off – 6,991kg/15,413lb

Performance: Maximum speed – 621kph/386mph
Ceiling – 11,369m/37,300ft
Range – 1,674km/1,040 miles on internal fuel
Climb – 1,039m/3,410ft per minute

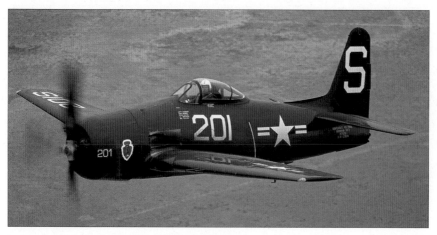

Grumman F8F Bearcat

The Bearcat was the last in the Grumman series of carrier-based fighters that had started back in 1931 with the Grumman FF. It was one of the fastest piston-engined aircraft ever and was built to a US Navy specification calling for a small, light, high-performance naval interceptor.

Grumman's design team aimed to create the diminutive high-performance fighter around the mighty Pratt & Whitney R-2800 Double Wasp that had been used to power Grumman's Hellcat and Tigercat. The Bearcat was 20 per cent lighter than the Hellcat and had a 30 per cent greater rate of climb than its Grumman stablemate as well as being 80kph/50mph faster.

Many features of the Bearcat's design were reportedly inspired by a captured Luftwaffe Focke-Wulf Fw 190 fighter that had been handed over to Grumman. The Bearcat's large 3.76m/12ft 4in four-bladed propeller required long landing gear which gave the Bearcat its characteristic nose-up attitude on the ground. It was also the first US Navy aircraft with a bubble canopy that afforded a clear view for the pilot in all directions. These factors, together with its excellent manoeuvrability and good low-level performance, made it an outstanding fighter aircraft in all respects.

The F8F prototypes were ordered in November 1943 and the type first took to the air on August 21, 1944, only nine months later. The first production aircraft (the F8F-1) were delivered in February 1945, a mere six months after the prototype test flight.

In May 1945, US Navy Fighter Squadron VF-19 became the first unit to equip with the Bearcat and was operational by May 21, 1945, but the type arrived too late to see action in World War II. It is worth noting that in comparative trials at this time, the Bearcat's impressive performance allowed it to outmanoeuvre most of the early jet fighters.

Production nevertheless continued until May 1949 by which time 24 US Navy squadrons were operating Bearcats including the US Navy's Blue Angels team who had re-equipped with the F8F-1 Bearcat on August 25, 1946 – the team used Bearcats until its temporary disbandment during the Korean War in 1950.

The F8F-1B version (100 built), was armed with four 20mm cannon instead of the four 0.5in machine-guns of the F8F-1. Almost 300 examples of the F8F-2 were built with 20mm cannon armament as standard. Radar-equipped night-fighter and photo-reconnaissance versions were also made in small numbers.

Grumman's F9F Panther and the McDonnell F2H Banshee largely replaced the Bearcat in US Navy service, as their performance finally overtook that of piston-engine fighters.

LEFT: The Hellcat remained in service well after the end of World War II, peaking with its equipping of 24 post-war US Navy units. ABOVE: The type was withdrawn from service by late 1952, replaced by jets like the Banshee and Panther.

The Bearcat was phased out of front-line US Navy use by 1952 but around 250 were refurbished and sold as F8F-1Ds to the French Armée de l'Air who used them in action in Indochina. Many of these aircraft were later acquired by the air forces of both North and South Vietnam. The Royal Thai Air Force were also supplied with about 130 Bearcats.

In 1946, a standard production F8F-1 set a time-to-climb record (after a run of only 35m/115ft) of 3,050m/10,000ft in 94 seconds. The Bearcat held this record for ten years until it was broken by a jet fighter which was nonetheless unable to beat the Bearcat's incredibly short take-off run.

The 1946 record-breaking feat led to another career for the Bearcat – air racing. A standard Bearcat won the first of the famous Reno Air Races in 1964, then *Rare Bear*, a highly modified F8F, dominated the air racing scene for decades. *Rare Bear* also set many performance records, including the 3km/1.9-mile world speed record for piston-driven aircraft of 850.26kph/528.33mph in 1989.

In 1972, this souped-up Bearcat had set a new time-to-climb record of 3,000m/9,843ft in 91.9 seconds, breaking the record set by the 1946 Bearcat.

ABOVE: **In service the Bearcat would typically fly with a 150-US gallon droppable auxiliary fuel tank under its centreline to extend its range.** LEFT: **This Bearcat is one of a number of examples of the high-performance Grumman fighter maintained in flying condition either for air racing or for air show participation. Note the long undercarriage legs essential to keep the propeller clear of a pitching carrier deck on landing.**

Grumman F8F-1B Bearcat

First flight: August 21, 1944
Power: Pratt & Whitney 2,100hp R-2800-34W Double Wasp 18-cylinder radial piston engine
Armament: Four 20mm cannon plus provision for two 454kg/1,000lb bombs or four 5in rockets under wings
Size: Wingspan – 10.92m/35ft 10in
Length – 8.61m/28ft 3in
Height 4.2m/13ft 10in
Wing area – 22.67m²/244sq ft
Weights: Empty – 3,206kg/7,070lb
Maximum take-off – 5,873kg/12,947lb
Performance: Maximum speed – 677kph/421mph
Ceiling – 11,795m/38,700ft
Range – 1,778km/1,105 miles
Climb – 1,395m/4,570ft per minute

LEFT: A rare surviving example of a Sea Hurricane. This IB is preserved in the UK in flying condition by The Shuttleworth Collection. The aircraft was built in Canada as a Hurricane I and was converted in the UK to Sea Hurricane standard. ABOVE: A Sea Hurricane on its rocket-powered launch rail on board a merchant ship.

Hawker Sea Hurricane

The Hawker Sea Hurricane was a variant of the famous Hawker Hurricane land-based fighter developed six years after the Hurricane prototype first flew in November 1935. Comparison of the Sea Hurricane/Hurricane and the earlier Hawker Fury's fuselages explains why the embryonic Hurricane was initially known as the Fury Monoplane. The aircraft that only became known as the Hurricane in June 1936 retained the metal-tube construction with fabric covering used by Hawkers since the late 1920s, and not the more modern and complicated stressed-metal fuselage. Stressed-metal-covered wings became standard after early Hurricane models appeared with fabric-covered wings.

It was during the Battle of Britain in 1940 that the Hurricane earned its place in history, accounting for more enemy aircraft than all other defences, ground and air combined. Popular with pilots, the Hurricane was fast, agile and a steady gun platform that could take a lot of punishment. Pilot visibility was better than the contemporary Spitfires as the nose sloped more steeply from the cockpit to the propeller spinner.

The Royal Navy was keen to acquire the Hurricane to help them fight the Battle of the Atlantic which, in early 1940, saw a steep rise in British shipping losses far from shore, away from land-based air cover.

The 'quick-fix' for this was the development of catapult armed merchantmen (CAM ships) from which a fighter could be catapult-launched if enemy aircraft were suspected to be nearby. Hurricanes converted for this role needed only the addition of catapult spools (there was no need for an arrester hook), and 50 Hurricane Mk I landplanes were modified and designated Sea Hurricane Mk IAs.

The 'Hurricat' was mounted on and launched from a rocket-sled catapult on the ship's bows on what was a one-way flight as the aircraft could not land back on board a ship without a carrier deck. Consequently the pilot had to ditch in the sea as near as possible to friendly ships, hoping to be picked up. CAM ship 'Hurricats' alone claimed six enemy aircraft destroyed in the last five months of 1941 with the first victory coming on August 3, 1941, when Lt R.W.H. Everett,

LEFT: Hook deployed, this Sea Hurricane is preparing to catch the wire on a carrier deck. The Sea Hurricane provided the Fleet Air Arm with a much needed fighter stopgap to keep German bombers at bay in the Battle of the Atlantic.

LEFT: **These Packard Merlin 29-engined, Canadian-built Sea Hurricane IIAs were naval conversions of the Hurricane Mk XIIA.**
BELOW: **A 'Hurricat' launches from a CAM ship. This was a last resort due to the almost certain loss of the aircraft, risk to the pilot and the very visible rocket flare caused by the launch.**

protecting a convoy en route to Gibraltar, intercepted and destroyed a Luftwaffe Focke-Wulf Fw 200 Condor.

Later versions, such as the Sea Hurricane IB, operated conventionally from aircraft carriers, fitted with catapult spools and an arrester hook for carrier landings. Initially the IBs were operated from MAC ships which were large merchantmen fitted with small carrier decks from which fighter and ASW aircraft could operate. These aircraft were open to the harshest conditions, since they were permanently stored on the deck as there were no below-deck hangars.

Fleet Air Arm Sea Hurricanes saw action in many theatres but the type's most famous action was fought during August 1942, when aircraft from 801, 802 and 885 Squadrons aboard the carriers HMS *Indomitable*, HMS *Eagle* and HMS *Victorious*, joined with Fairey Fulmars and Grumman Martlets to protect a vital convoy to Malta, in Operation 'Pedestal'. During three days of almost continuous attack by an Axis force of bombers, torpedo-bombers and escorting fighters, 39 enemy aircraft were destroyed for the loss of 8 British fighters.

Sea Hurricanes also hunted and attacked German submarines – in August 1944, three U-boats were attacked in a two-day period.

During World War II the Fleet Air Arm acquired around 600 Sea Hurricanes, 60 of which were built from scratch as Sea Hurricanes while the remainder were conversions from former RAF Hurricanes.

ABOVE: **For a conversion, the Sea Hurricane fulfilled a difficult role well. The non-navalized aircraft suffered from the elements on the Atlantic crossings but gave a good account of themselves when required.**

Hawker Sea Hurricane IIC

First flight: November 6, 1935 (Hurricane prototype)
Power: One Rolls-Royce 1,280hp Merlin XX piston engine
Armament: Four 20mm cannon
Size: Wingspan – 12.19m/40ft
    Length – 9.83m/32ft 3in
    Height – 3.99m/13ft 1in
    Wing area – 23.92m²/258sq ft
Weights: Empty – 2,667kg/5,880lb
    Maximum take-off – 3,674kg/8,100lb
Performance: Maximum speed – 550kph/342mph
    Service ceiling – 10,850m/35,600ft
    Range – 740km/460 miles
    Climb – 6,096m/20,000ft in 9 minutes, 6 seconds

ABOVE: **The He 59 was one of the easier wartime aircraft to identify thanks to its twin-float biplane open-cockpit arrangement.** RIGHT: **Rescue versions were accused of having a clandestine military role and were attacked by British aircraft.**

Heinkel He 59

einkel began to develop a 'reconnaissance-bomber' for the German military in 1930 but, like many other military aircraft under development in the country at the time, the project was presented to the world as a civil aircraft. When the second prototype (the He 59b) of the twin-engine He 59 biplane first flew in September 1931 it was a landplane with a conventional

ABOVE: **Powered by two 660hp engines, the He 59 was a large aircraft but had a range in excess of 1,600km/1,000 miles. Fuel was also carried in the aircraft's twin floats.**

undercarriage. Designed by Reinhold Mewes, it was the first prototype – the He 59a, which, confusingly, was second to fly in January 1942 – that tested a floatplane configuration. It was this version that became the basis for the production machines, 142 of which were built in three main variants.

Evaluation aircraft were designated He 59A (not to be confused with the He 59a) and were followed by a production version, the He 59B-1 armed with a machine-gun in the nose as well as the dorsal position. The He 59B-2 had an all-metal nose with a glazed bombing position and a ventral gun position. The B-3 was a reconnaissance machine while the C-1 was a trainer and the C-2 was a dedicated air-sea rescue aircraft equipped with inflatable dinghies and emergency supplies. The latter variant can be most readily identified by its fixed folding ladder and was used in the English Channel during the Battle of Britain.

The three-man He 59 was of mixed construction. The wings consisted of a wooden frame covered with fabric but with a plywood leading edge while the boxy fuselage was a primarily fabric-covered steel frame. The two floats also served as fuel tanks holding 900 litres/198 gallons each. In addition, an internal

fuselage tank and two extra fuel tanks could also be carried in the bomb bay.

The type saw action with the Condor Legion during the Spanish Civil War, and in the early stages of World War II the He 59 served as a torpedo and mine-laying aircraft. Some were used in a lightning raid operation and landed troops on a Dutch canal to seize a bridge.

The type was gradually relegated to training duties and all were retired by 1944.

The Finnish Air Force operated four of the aircraft for a period in 1943 to transport scouting troops behind enemy lines.

Heinkel He 59B-2

First flight: January 1932 (He 59a)
Power: Two 660hp BMW VI 6,0 ZU piston engines
Armament: Three 7.92mm machine-guns in nose, dorsal and ventral positions plus up to 1,000kg/2,205lb of bombs or a torpedo
Size: Wingspan – 23.7m/77ft 9in
　　　Length – 17.4m/57ft 1in
　　　Height – 7.1m/23ft 3.5in
　　　Wing area – 153.3m²/1,650sq ft
Weights: Empty – 6215kg/13,702lb
　　　Maximum take-off – 9,000kg/19,842lb
Performance: Maximum speed – 220kph/137mph
　　　Ceiling – 3,500m/11,480ft
　　　Range – 1,750km/1,087 miles
　　　Climb – 225m/738ft per minute

LEFT: **Although this version, the He 60D, was armed with a forward-firing machine-gun, the aircraft was easy prey for fast and agile Allied fighters.**
ABOVE: **D-IXES was one of two prototypes of the He 60C – it was this version that served on all major German warships.**

Heinkel He 60

The single-engined Heinkel He 60 biplane floatplane was developed in 1932 as a reconnaissance aircraft to be carried and catapult launched from all large German warships. Designed by Heinkel engineer Reinhold Mewes, the designer of the He 59, the type was also used extensively by sea and coastal reconnaissance units well into World War II.

The prototype He 60a first flew in early 1933 but its original power plant proved inadequate. Upgrading of its engine did little to improve its performance but the He 60, ruggedly constructed to cope with catapult launches and rough seas, still entered service in 1933. Pilots praised the aircraft for its water-handling.

The unarmed He 60A was the first version in Kriegsmarine (Navy) service, then the B model armed with a 7.9mm machine-gun in the observer's cockpit appeared but was soon succeeded by the improved He 60C, which entered service in 1934. The C model was operated from most German warships prior to World War II – the aircraft's multi-purpose floats contained spraying equipment that could either lay down a smoke screen or even spray mustard gas. Like so many other German military aircraft, the type was evaluated during the Spanish Civil War and four examples remained in use in Spain until the end of World War II.

The type was relegated to training duties early in World War II but it continued to serve in the maritime reconnaissance role with shore-based units in the Mediterranean, North Sea, Crete and Greece despite its vulnerability to enemy fighters.

The aircraft was replaced in service first by the Heinkel He 114 and then by the Arado Ar 196 in service. All He 60s were phased out by October 1943.

LEFT: **Demonstrating its original purpose, an He 60 is pictured overflying the German Navy's light cruiser _Köln_. The type extended the ship's view well beyond the sea-level horizon. It served in the shore-based role with the Kriegsmarine until late 1943.**

Heinkel He 60B

First flight: 1933
Power: One 660hp BMW VI 12-cylinder piston engine
Armament: One 7.9mm machine-gun in rear cockpit
Size: Wingspan – 13.5m/44ft 3.5in
  Length – 11.5m/37ft 8.75in
  Height – 5.3m/17ft 4.5in
  Wing area – 56.2m²/604sq ft
Weights: Empty – 2,725kg/6,009lb
  Maximum take-off – 3,425kg/7,552lb
Performance: Maximum speed – 240kph/149mph
  Ceiling – 5,000m/16,405ft
  Range – 950km/590 miles
  Climb – 1,000m/3,280ft in 3 minutes, 12 seconds

353

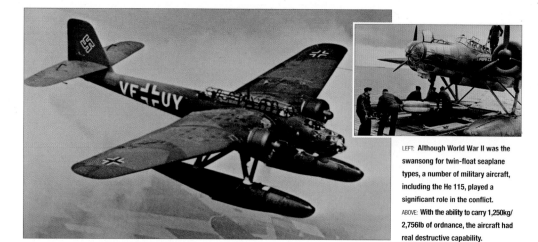

LEFT: **Although World War II was the swansong for twin-float seaplane types, a number of military aircraft, including the He 115, played a significant role in the conflict.** ABOVE: **With the ability to carry 1,250kg/ 2,756lb of ordnance, the aircraft had real destructive capability.**

Heinkel He 115

The largest and most powerful production twin-float seaplane used in World War II, the He 115 was developed in the mid-1930s as a torpedo-bomber, mine-laying and reconnaissance aircraft to replace the company's earlier He 59. Despite the fact that the He 115 was in many ways obsolete at the start of World War II, the type continued in Luftwaffe service almost to the end of the conflict. This was due to the fact that while carrying out its main duty of mine-laying at night, it was able to operate with little interference from Allied aircraft or defences.

The type had a crew of three with the pilot housed in a cockpit over the wing's leading edge. The observer's position was in the glazed nose while the radio operator sat in a separate cockpit positioned over the trailing edge. Defensive armament initially consisted of one forward-firing and one rear-firing 7.9mm machine-gun operated by the observer and

radio operator respectively. In early versions the bomb bay (located in the fuselage beneath the wing) could carry one 800kg/1,763lb torpedo or three 250kg/550lb bombs.

The He 115 V1 (civil serial D-AEHF) prototype made its first flight in 1936 and this robust and reliable aircraft impressed the Luftwaffe sufficiently that 115 were ordered for the air force's *Seeflieger*. In March 1938, after some modifications including a much-streamlined nose, this aircraft set eight speed records over 1,000km/621-mile and 2,000km/1,243-mile courses, carrying payloads up to 2,000kg/4,409lb.

By the third prototype (the He 115 V3), the design had been refined and was very similar to the production versions with the pilot and radio operator cockpits covered and joined by one large 'greenhouse'-type canopy. Production versions also featured a dual-control facility where the essential flying controls were duplicated in the rear cockpit. This would have enabled the radio operator to land the aircraft if the pilot was indisposed. The first production version, the He 115A-1 also featured an underwing bomb rack for two 250kg/550lb bombs.

The He 115 caught the eye of the Swedish and the Norwegians who both placed export orders for the type. Six went to Norway while twelve were ordered for Sweden.

At the start of World War II, 'naval co-operation' unit 1./*Küstenfliegerstaffel* 106 became the first unit to receive the type. Following the completion of the 62nd aircraft in early 1940, the production line at Heinkel's Marienhe plant closed with manufacturing shifting to Einswarden.

The He 115B-1 introduced increased fuel capacity and therefore significantly increased range – up to 3,350km/ 2,080 miles compared to the 2,000km/1,242 miles of the A-series. Large 1,000kg/2,200lb parachute mines could be carried by some B-1s though clearly over a reduced range due to the considerable weight increase.

ABOVE: **At the outbreak of World War II the Luftwaffe had eight He 115s in front-line service on coastal-patrol duties. During the invasion of Norway, German forces were attacked by exported He 115s serving in the Norwegian Naval Air Service.**

The type was used by coastal reconnaissance units of the Luftwaffe and when war broke out dropped parachute mines in British waters. The first such mission on the night of November 20–21, 1939, saw aircraft of 3./*Küstenfliegerstaffel* 906 drop mines off the Essex coast and at the mouth of the Thames.

During the 1940 German invasion of Norway, Norwegian Naval Air Service He 115s (and two captured German machines) were put into action against German forces. Some were subsequently flown to the UK where they were modified and, sometimes sporting German markings, used for clandestine operations. One bright sunny day, one of these landed in Tripoli harbour where it picked up two British agents before flying back to its Malta base, completely unmolested by the Luftwaffe.

The type's success as a mine-layer led to a reopening of production in late 1943 resulting in a total production run of around 500.

ABOVE: **An excellent view of the He 115's large wing area and that of the tail. This is an He 155B taxiing as the radio operator converses with the navigator.**
LEFT: **Notice the large glazed nose on the aircraft, which gave the navigator excellent all-round vision. The sheer size of the aircraft is evident as the crew arms and prepares the aircraft for its next flight while the aircraft's captain looks on.**

Heinkel He 115B-1

First flight: 1936 (prototype)
Power: Two BMW 856hp 132N 9-cylinder radial piston engines
Armament: One fixed forward-firing and one rear-firing 7.9mm machine-guns plus up to 1,250kg/2,756lb of torpedoes, mines or bombs
Size: Wingspan – 22m/72ft 2in
　　　Length – 17.3m/56ft 9in
　　　Height – 6.6m/21ft 8in
　　　Wing area – 86.7m²/933sq ft
Weights: Empty – 5,300kg/11,684lb
　　　Maximum take-off – 10,400kg/22,928lb
Performance: Maximum speed – 353kph/220mph
　　　Service ceiling – 5,500m/18,005ft
　　　Range – 3,350km/2,080 miles
　　　Climb – 235m/770ft per minute

LEFT: **Although the early E7K was virtually obsolete by the start of World War II, many of the machines that survived ended up as kamikaze machines.**
ABOVE: **The E7K was a comparatively large single-engined biplane. With a crew of three the aircraft had an unfortunate reputation for engine unreliability.**

Kawanishi E7K

The Kawanishi E7K was a Japanese three-seat reconnaissance floatplane that was to be given the wartime Allied codename of 'Alf'. The E7K resulted from a 1932 Imperial Japanese Navy (IJN) requirement, which asked the Kawanishi Aircraft Company to produce a replacement for the company's Kawanishi E5K reconnaissance seaplane for IJN service. The proposed replacement, designated the Kawanishi E7K1, was a conventional equal-span biplane powered by a 620hp Hiro 91 engine.

The prototype flew for the first time on February 6, 1933, and after evaluation and competitive trials against an Aichi machine, the type was chosen for production as the Navy Type 94 Reconnaissance Seaplane. The aircraft

could operate from ships or from land bases and was equally adept on anti-submarine patrols and reconnaissance missions. The E7K entered service in early 1935 and though generally liked by its crews, its engine was considered unreliable.

Kawanishi tried an improved Hiro 91 engine but reliability was still an issue. The company later proposed the E7K2 powered by a Mitsubishi Zuisei 11 radial engine and this version had its first flight in August 1938. The IJN were sufficiently impressed by the improved version that they ordered production aircraft under the designation Navy Type 94 Reconnaissance Seaplane Model 2. The E7K1 was meanwhile retrospectively redesignated Navy Type 94 Reconnaissance Seaplane Model 1.

Both versions were in use at the start of the war in the Pacific although the E7K1 was soon removed from front-line duties to assume training and utility roles. The EK72 remained in front-line use until 1943.

Towards the end of the Pacific war, all available examples of both versions were stripped and converted for use on kamikaze missions.

Production consisted of 183 examples of the E7K1 of which 57 were subcontracted to Nippon. A total of 350 of the improved E7K2s were built, with 60 built by subcontractor Nippon.

LEFT: **The Kawanishi E7K, or 'Alf', was able to stay aloft for almost 12 hours – a great performance for a shipborne reconnaissance type, and one that enabled the aircraft to cover great areas of ocean in search of enemy craft.**

Kawanishi E7K2

First flight: February 6, 1933 (prototype)
Power: Mitsubishi 870hp Zuisei 11 radial engine
Armament: One forward-firing 7.7mm machine-gun, one flexible 7.7mm machine-gun in each of the rear cockpits and one downwards-firing ventral position plus up to 120kg/264lb of bombs
Size: Wingspan – 14m/45ft 11in
    Length – 10.5m/34ft 5in
    Height – 4.85m/15ft 11in
    Wing area – 43.6m²/469sq ft
Weights: Empty – 2,100kg/4,630lb
    Maximum take-off – 3,300kg/7,275lb
Performance: Maximum speed – 275kph/171mph
    Ceiling – 7,060m/2,3165ft
    Range – 1,845km/1,147 miles
    Climb – 3,000m/9,840ft in 9 minutes, 6 seconds

LEFT: The Kawanishi H6K was one of the few aircraft to see service in World War II that served in both military and civil roles simultaneously. Japan Air Lines operated the type as well as the IJN. BELOW: The side view shows the type's high parasol wing. The H6K's wing was around 6m/20ft longer than that of the Short Sunderland.

Kawanishi H6K

The Kawanishi H6K was a large Imperial Japanese Navy maritime patrol flying boat with its origins in a 1933 IJN requirement for a high-performance flying boat that could cruise at 220kph/137mph and have a range of 4,500km/2,795 miles.

The four-engined aircraft had a high parasol-type wing with a slight dihedral and was braced by struts connected to the fuselage. The aircraft's distinctive wings had parallel leading and trailing edges for half their length and then tapered at the point where the wing-mounted floats were fitted. The aircraft's shallow hull was all-metal and was modified for better on-water performance following the prototype's first flight in July 1936. The four 840hp Nakajima Hikari radial engines fitted to the prototype did not provide enough power but with more powerful engines,

the Type 97 Large Flying Boat was cleared to enter service in 1938 becoming the Navy's only long-range maritime reconnaissance flying boat in service at the time.

The type first saw action during the Sino-Japanese War and most of the 217 built were used during the Pacific War during which it was codenamed 'Mavis' by the Allies. Its range and endurance (it could fly on 24-hour patrols) made it a key aircraft in the Japanese military inventory – it even undertook long-range bombing missions on targets such as Rabaul.

As the Allies deployed more modern fighters in the Pacific, they started to take their toll on the large slow flying boat so the H6Ks came to be limited to

operations in areas where Allied fighter presence was limited.

The Overseas (Ocean) Division of Japan Air Lines operated 18 examples of the H6K2-L unarmed 18-passenger transport version on Central and Western Pacific routes.

It was Kawanishi's own H8K that replaced the H6K in military service after which the surviving H6Ks were converted for troop carrying. Some H6K2-Ls based in the Netherlands East Indies were seized by Indonesian nationalists and were operated post-war for a time.

Kawanishi H6K4

First flight: July 14, 1936 (prototype)
Power: Four Mitsubishi 1,070hp Kinsei 43 engines
Armament: Total of five 7.7mm machine-guns in open bow, forward turret, side blisters and open dorsal positions, one 20mm cannon in tail turret and up to 800kg/1,764lb of bombs
Size: Wingspan – 40m/131ft 2in
Length – 25.63m/84ft 1in
Height – 6.27m/20ft 7in
Wing area – 170m²/1,830sq ft
Weights: Empty – 11,707kg/25,810lb
Maximum take-off – 21,500kg/47,399lb
Performance: Maximum speed – 340kph/211mph
Ceiling – 9,610m/31,530ft
Range – 6,080km/3,779 miles
Climb – 5,000m/16,400ft in 13 minutes, 31 seconds

ABOVE: Some versions of the Kawanishi H6K were unarmed and were used for transport and communication duties – these were easy targets for Allied aircraft and a number fell to enemy guns.

Kawanishi H8K

The H8K was developed in response to a 1938 Japanese Navy specification for a replacement for its then new H6K, the service's standard maritime patrol flying boat. The new design was to have a 30 per cent higher speed and 50 per cent greater range than the H6K. The requirement also called for a long-range aircraft with better performance than Britain's Short Sunderland or the American Sikorsky XPBS-1. The designers produced one of the finest military flying boats ever built and certainly the fastest and best of World War II.

To give the aircraft the required range, the wings contained eight small, unprotected fuel tanks and a further six large tanks in the fuselage or, more correctly, hull. The hull tanks were partially self-sealing and also boasted a carbon dioxide fire extinguisher system. Ingeniously, the tanks were placed so that if any leaked the fuel would collect in a fuel 'bilge' and then be pumped to an undamaged tank. The aircraft was a flying fuel tank with 15,816 litres/3,479 gallons being a typical fuel load

TOP: **The H8K2-L transport version of this very capable flying boat was modified to carry passengers on an additional upper deck.**

ABOVE: **The H8K was a truly great flying boat that was far from an easy target for enemy fighters thanks to its impressive armament. Nevertheless, on the ground or on water, the large aircraft was easy prey when attacked from the air.**

and accounting for some 29 per cent of the take-off weight. The aircraft positively bristled with defensive armament – a 20mm cannon was carried in each of the powered nose, dorsal and tail turrets with two more in opposite beam blisters. A further three 7.7mm machine-guns were in port and starboard beam hatches and in the ventral position. The crew positions

ABOVE: **This example of an 'Emily' was captured at the end of the war and evaluated by the victors. The Allies were intrigued by the 'Emily', acknowledged as the best flying boat of its class in service at the time, and were keen to learn from the large Kawanishi boat.**

were well armoured – this all ensured that Allied fighter pilots treated the Japanese 'boat' with considerable respect as it was far from an easy 'kill'. It was the most heavily defended flying boat of World War II and one which Allied fighter pilots found hard to down in aerial combat.

The Navy were appropriately impressed with the aircraft, but flight testing of the H8K in late 1940 was far from uneventful and numerous features of the aircraft had to be revised – the heavy aircraft's narrow hull, for example, caused uncontrollable porpoising in the water. When the nose lifted from the water's surface, the whole aircraft became unstable. The design team revised the hull and production of the H8K1 (Navy Type 2 Flying Boat Model 11) began in mid-1941. Total production was a mere 175 aircraft produced in the H8K1, H8K2 (improved engines, heavier armament and radar) and 3H8K2-L (transport) versions.

The H8K was powered by four 1,530hp Kasei 11s or 12s – the latter bestowed better high-altitude performance and powered late-production H8K1s. The aircraft's offensive load, carried under the inner wing, was either two 801kg/1,764lb. torpedoes, eight 250kg/551lb bombs, or sixteen 60kg/132lb. bombs or depth charges.

The H8K made its combat debut on the night of March 4–5, 1942. The night bombing raid on the island of Oahu, Hawaii, was over so great a distance that even the long-range H8K had to put down to refuel from a submarine en route. Although due to bad weather the target was not bombed, the raid showed that the H8K was a formidable weapon of war.

The H8K's deep hull lent itself to the development of a transport version, the H8K2-L with two passenger decks. The lower deck reached from the nose to some two-thirds of the way along the fuselage while the upper deck extended from the wing to the back of the hull. Seats or benches could accommodate from 29 passengers or 64 troops in appropriately differing levels of comfort. Armament was reduced as was fuel-carrying capability with the removal of hull tanks.

ABOVE: From being dangerously unstable in testing, the H8K went on to be among the best military flying boats ever produced. BELOW: The comparatively fast H8K first flew into action in March 1942. Later versions of the H8K2 (the most numerous production model) were fitted with ASV radar that greatly enhanced their capability and threat status to Allied shipping.

ABOVE: Of the 175 aircraft produced, only 4 examples survived after the end of World War II. One was this H8K2 that was captured by US forces at the end of hostilities and taken to the US for evaluation. It was returned to Japan in 1979 and was displayed in Tokyo until 2004, but is now preserved at Kanoya Naval Air Base Museum in Japan. It is a rare example of one of the best military flying boats.

Kawanishi H8K2

First flight: Late 1940
Power: Four Mitsubishi 1,850hp Kasei radial engines
Armament: 20mm cannon in bow, dorsal and tail turrets and in beam blisters plus four 7.7mm machine-guns in cockpit, ventral and side hatches
Size: Wingspan – 38m/124ft 8in
Length – 28.13m/92ft 4in
Height – 9.15m/30ft
Wing area – 160m²/1,722sq ft
Weights: Empty – 18,380kg/40,521lb
Maximum take-off – 32,500kg/71,650lb
Performance: Maximum speed – 467kph/290mph
Service ceiling – 8,760m/28,740ft
Range – 7,180km/4460 miles
Climb – 480m/1,575ft per minute

Kawanishi N1K1-/K2-J

Land-based aircraft have often been turned into floatplanes, but in the case of the Kawanishi N1K1-J *Shiden* (violet lightning) it was, uniquely, a landplane derived from a floatplane fighter. Kawanishi's earlier N1K1 *Kyofu* (strong or mighty wind) was an Imperial Japanese Navy floatplane fighter built to support forward offensive operations in areas where airstrips were not available. However, by the time the aircraft entered service in 1943, Japan was on the defensive and had little use for the N1K1. Codenamed 'Rex' by the Allies, it was no match for US Navy carrier fighters due to the large heavy float it carried.

Two years earlier, Kawanishi engineers had proposed a land-based version without a float and a prototype was produced by Kawanishi as a speculative private venture aircraft. This flew on December 27, 1942, powered by a Nakajima Homare radial engine that replaced the less-powerful Mitsubishi Kasei used

in the N1K1. The aircraft retained the mid-mounted wing of the floatplane version, and this and the large propeller called for long landing gear. The undercarriage proved to be problematic as, due to poor heat-treating, the landing gear would often simply rip off as the aircraft touched down. More were reportedly lost to this fault than to Allied action.

The new version was designated Kawanishi N1K1-J *Shiden*. Codenamed 'George' by the Allies, this Japanese fighter entered service during the last year of World War II, appearing throughout the Pacific from May 1944. It possessed heavy armament and, unusually for a Japanese fighter, could absorb considerable battle damage. In spite of production problems and shortages of parts caused by B-29 raids on the Japanese homeland, over 1,400 were built and were formidable foes. Unique automatic combat flaps that increased lift during

LEFT: **Two N1K1s prepare for flight. It was rare for an effective land-based fighter to be derived from a floatplane design.** ABOVE: **The United States captured and evaluated a number of examples of the type – here US service personnel assess a captured aircraft.**

extreme combat activity dramatically enhanced manoeuvrability. The 'George' proved to be one of the best all-round fighters in the Pacific theatre but it lacked the high-altitude performance needed to counter the devastating B-29 raids. The N1K1-J evenly matched the F6F Hellcat and could win fights with Allied aircraft such as the F4U Corsair and P-51 Mustang. Despite such ability, it was produced too late and in too few numbers to affect the outcome of the war.

Early versions had poor visibility due to the mid-mounted wing and inadequate landing gear and so the N1K2-J version known as the *Shiden-Kai*, 'George 21' to the Allies, was produced. The main difference was the moving of the wing from mid to low position that reduced the need for the troublesome long landing gear. The prototype of this variant first flew in December 1943, and was soon adopted as the standard Japanese land-based fighter and fighter-bomber. The N1K2-J could be built in half the time of the earlier version and

became a truly outstanding fighter aircraft that could hold its own against the best of the Allied fighters. The Homare engine was retained as there was really no alternative even though reliability remained a major problem.

Nevertheless, the *Shiden-Kai* proved to be one of the best fighters operating in the Pacific theatre – it had a roll rate of 82 degrees per second at 386kph/240mph. It was, however, less successful as a bomber interceptor due to its poor rate of climb and poor high-altitude engine performance. Allied bombing raids disrupted production so that only 415 examples were completed.

Total production of all versions reached 1,435, and three aircraft are known to survive in US aviation museums. One is at the National Museum of Naval Aviation at Pensacola, Florida; a second is at the United States Air Force Museum at Wright-Patterson Air Force Base near Dayton, Ohio, while the third is preserved by the National Air and Space Museum.

ABOVE: **Although the type entered service in 1943, the Allies were already well aware of the type, and had even assigned it the codename 'Rex', due to the capture of Japanese documents that spoke of the aircraft and its planned uses. Of the 1,435 built, only 3 survive.**

Kawanishi N1K2-J

First flight: December 31, 1943
Power: Nakajima 1990hp NK9H Homare 21 radial piston engine
Armament: Four 20mm cannon in wings plus two 250kg/551lb bombs under wings
Size: Span – 12m/39ft 4.5in
Length – 9.35m/30ft 8in
Height – 3.96m/13ft
Wing area – 23.5m²/253sq ft
Weights: Empty – 2,657kg/5,858lb
Maximum take-off – 4,860kg/10,714lb
Performance: Maximum speed – 595kph/370mph
Ceiling – 10,760m/35,300ft
Range – 2,335km/1,451 miles with drop tanks
Climb – 1,000m/3,280ft per minute

Martin Mariner

With its history of producing flying boats, Martin began work on a design in 1937 to replace the Consolidated Catalina in US Navy service. Martin's Model 162, naval designation XPBM-1 (Experimental Patrol Bomber Martin 1) had a flat twin-fin tail, inward-retracting wing-floats, a deep hull and shoulder-mounted gull wings. The gull-wing design was used to produce the greatest possible distance between the engines and the surface of the sea water from which the aircraft would operate. An approximately half-scale single-seat version of the design was produced to test the aerodynamics –

ABOVE: **A US Navy PBM-3. Production of this version required the building of a new factory complex. The -3 was powered by improved Pratt & Whitney R-2600-12 engines. Note the flying boat's hull shape.** BELOW LEFT: **A US Navy PBM starts its engine at a Caribbean naval air station as ground crew stand by with a fire extinguisher. Note the large radome aft of the cockpit. The aircraft's all-metal two-step hull can also be seen in this view.**

its success led to the first flight of the full-scale prototype XPBM-1 in February 1939.

The results of test flights called for a redesign of the tail which resulted in the dihedral configuration that matched the angle of the main wings. The aircraft had been ordered before the test flight so the first production model, the PBM-1, appeared quite quickly in October 1940 with service deliveries being complete by April 1941 – impressive even for the uncertain days before the US entered World War II. By now the type was named Mariner, had a crew of seven and was armed with five 0.50in Browning machine-guns. One gun was mounted in a flexible position in the tail, one in a flexible-mount on each side of the rear fuselage; another was fitted in a rear dorsal turret while one was deployed in a nose turret. In addition, the PBM-1 could carry up to 900kg/1,985lb of bombs or depth charges in bomb bays that were, unusually, fitted in the engine nacelles. The doors of the bomb bays looked like those of landing gear but the Mariner did not have amphibian capability at this stage in its development.

In late 1940, the US Navy ordered 379 improved Model 162Bs or PBM-3s although around twice that number were actually produced. This order alone required the US Government-aided construction of a new Martin plant in

Maryland. The -3 differed from the -1 mainly by the installation of uprated Pratt & Whitney 1,700hp R-2600-12 engines, larger fixed wing floats and larger bomb bays housed in enlarged nacelles. This version also featured powered nose and dorsal turrets. Early PBM-3s had three-bladed propellers but production versions soon included four-bladed propellers.

The PBM-3C rolled out in late 1942 as the next major version with 274 built. It had better armour protection for the crew, twin-gun front and dorsal turrets, an improved tail turret still with a single gun, and Air-to-Surface-Vessel radar. In addition, many PBM-3Cs were fitted with an underwing searchlight in the field to assist with the finding of enemy craft at night.

US Navy Mariners saw extensive use in the Pacific, guarding the Atlantic western approaches and in defence of the Panama Canal. It was felt that as most Mariners were not likely to encounter fighter opposition, much of the defensive armament could be deleted – once the guns, turrets and ammunition were removed, the weight saving resulted in a 25 per cent increase in the range of the lighter PBM-3S anti-submarine version. The nose guns were, however, retained for offensive fire against U-boats and other surface targets. Despite this development, a more heavily armed and armoured version, the PBM-3D, was produced by re-engining some 3Cs. Larger non-retractable floats and self-sealing fuel tanks were also a feature of this version.

Deliveries of the more powerfully engined PBM-5 began in August 1944, with 589 delivered before production ceased at the end of the war. With the PBM-5A amphibian version, of which 40 were built, the Mariner finally acquired a tricycle landing gear. The Mariner continued to serve with the US Navy and US Coast Guard (USCG) into the early 1950s and over 500 were still in service at the time of the Korean War. The USCG retired its last Mariner in 1958.

During World War II, 25 PBM-3Bs, designated Mariner G.R.1, were allocated to the RAF under Lend-Lease arrangements. In late 1943, the type was operated for seven weeks from a base in Scotland but never entered front-line RAF service.

ABOVE: **The Mariner had a range in excess of 322km/200 miles and features included a galley, sleeping quarters, sound proofing, heating and a form of air conditioning too. Note the vast radome atop the aircraft.**

BELOW: **A Mariner could land to take surrender of an enemy submarine, having attacked it from the air. The type was developed throughout its production.**

ABOVE: **The Mariner's high wing, with its entire hinged trailing edge, and the aircraft's distinctive dihedral twin-fin tail makes the Martin flying boat very easy to identify.**

Martin PBM-3D Mariner

First flight: February 18, 1939 (XPBM-1)
Power: Two Wright 1,900hp R-2600-22 Cyclone
    radial piston engines
Armament: Eight 0.5in machine-guns in nose
    3,628kg/8,000lb of bombs or depth charges
Size: Wingspan – 35.97m/118ft
    Length – 24.33m/79ft 10in
    Height – 8.38m/27ft 6in
    Wing area – 130.8m²/1,408sq ft
Weights: Empty – 15,048kg/33,175lb
    Maximum take-off – 26,308kg/58,000lb
Performance: Maximum speed – 340kph/211mph
    Service ceiling – 6,035m/19,800ft
    Range – 3,605km/2,240 miles
    Climb – 244m/800ft per minute

LEFT: Mitsubishi's A5M was designed with an increased knowledge of aerodynamics and was created to have minimal drag. Note the streamlined fairings over the fixed undercarriage legs and the guns just forward of the cockpit. BELOW: The enclosed cockpit, welcomed by most fighter pilots, was deleted in later versions of the A5M.

Mitsubishi A5M

The 350kph/217mph top speed specified in a 1934 Imperial Japanese Navy fighter specification seemed to be a tall order at the time. To ease the designers' burden, the need to operate the new fighter from aircraft carriers was not even written into the specification. However, Mitsubishi's offering, the Ka-14, which was first flown in February 1935, showed a top speed of 450kph/280mph that far exceeded the specified speed required.

It was designed with minimum drag in mind – the fuselage had a small cross section, the aluminium skin was flush riveted and the fixed undercarriage had streamlined spats. It was perhaps too complex a design and the inverted gull-wing that caused some handling headaches was replaced with a more conventional low wing. With this change and powered by a 585hp Kotobuki 2-KAI-1 engine, the type was ordered into production as the Navy Type 96 Carrier Fighter Model 1 (Mitsubishi A5M1).

The A5M was the world's first monoplane shipboard fighter and was the direct ancestor of Mitsubishi's later Zero. The type began to enter service in early 1937 and was soon in action in the Sino-Japanese War.

The subsequent A5M2a (basically the same aircraft powered by a 610hp KAI-3) and A5M2b (with the 640hp Kotobuki 3 engine) became the most important Navy fighters during Japan's war with China. Until the A5M2a arrival in theatre, the Japanese were suffering heavy losses but after only a short time the A5M2a achieved total air superiority. Experience of air operations in China speeded up development of the A5M2b with a three-bladed propeller driven by the more powerful engine and the luxury of an enclosed cockpit under a greenhouse-style canopy that in fact proved unpopular with pilots and was omitted on late-build A5M2bs. All had a fixed non-retractable undercarriage with wheel spats for improved aerodynamics. The A5M2s were so effective in China that all Chinese air units were withdrawn out of range of the Japanese fighters.

The final, best known and most numerous production version was the A5M4 that was developed in response to the Chinese withdrawal – greater range was the most important consideration. The A5M4 looked identical to the late production open-cockpit A5M2bs but was powered by the

710hp Nakajima Kotobuki 41 and carried a 160-litre/ 35.2-gallon drop tank. It entered service in China in 1938 and with its longer range greatly extended the area of Japanese air superiority while driving the less able Chinese air units even further away from the battle area.

As some A5Ms were still in service at the beginning of World War II. United States intelligence sources believed the A5M was Japan's primary Navy fighter, when in fact Mitsubishi's much more capable Zero had all but replaced the 'Claudes' on first-line aircraft carriers. It was soon withdrawn for second-line duties (including advanced fighter training) as it was no match for the newer Allied fighters. A dedicated trainer version with twin cockpits, the A5M4-K, was also built – 103 were produced – and continued in use for fighter training long after the regular A5M left front-line service.

As the war in the Pacific approached its desperate end, remaining A5M4s were used in kamikaze attacks against Allied ships off the Japanese coast. Total A5M production numbered 1,094.

TOP: **The 'Claude' was the Japanese Navy's first monoplane fighter and at the start of the war in the Pacific equipped three wings on Japanese light carriers.**

ABOVE: **The Imperial Japanese Navy were early adopters of droppable auxiliary fuel tanks as a means of increasing their aircraft's range. This policy gave the Japanese an early advantage when war broke out in the Pacific.**

BELOW: **The A5M4 was designed in response to a need for increased range to enable its pilots to take the battle to Chinese pilots who were withdrawn beyond the range of earlier versions. Note the guns just forward of the cockpit.**

Mitsubishi A5M4

First flight: February 4, 1935
Power: Nakajima 710hp Kotobuki 41 (Bristol Jupiter) 9-cylinder radial piston engine
Armament: Two 7.7mm machine-guns firing on each side of upper cylinder of engine plus two racks for two 30kg/66lb bombs under outer wings
Size: Wingspan – 11m/36ft 1in
Length – 7.55m/24ft 9.25in
Height – 3.2m/10ft 6in
Wing area – 17.8m²/192sq ft
Weights: Empty – 1,216kg/2,681lb
Maximum take-off – 1,707kg/3,763lb
Performance: Maximum speed – 440kph/273mph
Ceiling – 10,000m/32,800ft
Range – 1,200km/746 miles
Climb – 850m/2,790ft per minute

Mitsubishi A6M Zero-Sen

The Zero is rightly Japan's most famous wartime aircraft and was perhaps most significantly the first shipboard fighter capable of beating its land-based opponents. It had its origins in a 1937 Japanese Navy requirement for a new fighter with a maximum speed exceeding 500kph/310mph to replace Mitsubishi's A5M carrier fighter. The new aircraft had to climb to 3,000m/9,840ft in 3.5 minutes, exhibit manoeuvrability and have range exceeding any existing fighter, and carry the impressive armament of two cannon and two machine-guns. Only Mitsubishi accepted the challenge and design work began under the direction of Jiro Horikoshi.

The prototype was completed on March 16, 1939, first flew on April 1 and was accepted by the Navy on September 14, 1939, as the A6M1 Carrier Fighter. The chosen powerplant was the lightweight Mitsubishi Zuisei, later replaced by the more powerful Nakajima *Sakae* (Prosperity) 925hp radial which was only slightly larger and heavier than the original *Zuisei*. With its

ABOVE: **The Mitsubishi Zero, with its high performance, obsessed the US military, who were keen to understand the enemy aircraft. This example in US markings was assembled in the USA in December 1942 from five captured aircraft.**

new-found power, the fighter amply exceeded the original performance requirements which had been regarded as impossible a few months earlier. At this time, production models of Navy aircraft were assigned type numbers based on the last number of the Japanese year in which production began, and as 1940 was the year 2600 in the Japanese calendar, the A6M series was known as the Zero-Sen (Type 00 fighter).

Even before the final acceptance of the A6M2 as a production fighter, the Japanese Navy requested that a number of machines be delivered for operational use in China to meet growing aerial resistance. Accordingly, 15 A6M2s were delivered for service in China and first appeared over

ABOVE: **Having achieved a high level of success during the war with China, the Zero accounted for over 60 per cent of the Japanese Navy's carrier-borne fighter. It was the first carrier fighter to meet land-based fighters on equal performance terms.**

LEFT: **The Zero epitomized Japanese wartime air power.** ABOVE: **The RAF also evaluated captured Zeros. These aircraft, pictured in 1946, were flown by Japanese pilots under RAF supervision.**

Chungking in August 1940 when the Zeros shot down all the defending Chinese fighters. Washington was informed about the new high-performance Japanese fighter but no heed was taken and so its appearance over Pearl Harbor came as a complete surprise to the American forces. Its subsequent appearance in every major battle area in the opening days of the war seemed to indicate that Japan possessed almost unlimited supplies of the high-performance fighter. In fact, in December 1941, the Japanese Navy had well over 400 Zero fighters. In 1941–42 the Zero certainly got the better of all opposing fighters whether it flew from carriers or had to operate over long distances from land bases. During a Japanese carrier-raid on Ceylon, Zeros easily out-turned opposing RAF Hawker Hurricanes, aircraft that until then had been regarded as outstandingly manoeuvrable.

In mid-1942 the Allies eventually acquired an intact specimen and found that the Zero possessed many shortcomings. It was shipped back to the USA where exhaustive tests revealed the fighter's faults and shattered the myths that surrounded it. The tables were turned at the Battle

of Midway in June 1942 when the A6M5 version came up against a new generation of US Navy and Army fighters, with powerful engines and heavy protection for their pilot and fuel tanks. Against them the Zero, still basically the design which had flown first in April 1939, offered minimal protection for pilot and fuel tanks and from 1943 the Zeros fell like flies. The installation of the 1,560hp Kinsei engine brought the A6M8, the ultimate Zero, closer to the performance of Allied fighters but it was too late. The value of the fighter declined steadily and its lowest point was reached when it was selected as the first aircraft to be used intentionally as suicide attack (kamikaze or divine-wind) aircraft. The outstanding success of this form of attack led to the formation of dedicated kamikaze units, and the bomb-carrying Zeros became the prime suicide attack bombers of the Navy.

More Zero-Sens were produced than any other wartime Japanese aircraft. Mitsubishi alone produced 3,879 aircraft, Nakajima built 6,215 which, together with the 844 trainer and floatplane variants produced by Sasebo, Hitachi and Nakajima, brought the grand total of A6M series aircraft to 10,938.

ABOVE: **This Mitsubishi A6M3 was one of a number taken to the US and thoroughly tested. This aircraft is pictured over the United States on July 1, 1944.**

Mitsubishi A6M5 Zero

First flight: August, 1943

Power: Nakajima 1130hp NK1C Sakae 21 14-cylinder two-row radial piston engine

Armament: Two 20mm cannon in wing, two 7.7mm machine-guns in fuselage, plus two 60kg/132lb on underwing racks

Size: Wingspan – 11m/36ft 1in
Length – 9.06m/29ft 9in
Height – 2.98m/9ft 8in
Wing area – 21.3m²/229sq ft

Weights: Empty – 1,876kg/4,136lb
Maximum take-off – 2,733kg/6,025lb

Performance: Maximum speed – 570kph/354mph
Ceiling – 11,500m/37,730ft
Range – 1,920km/1,200 miles with drop tanks
Climb – 6,000m/19,685ft in 7 minutes, 3 seconds

Nakajima B5N

The Nakajima B5N was designed by a team led by Katsuji Nakamura to a 1935 Imperial Japanese Navy (IJN) requirement for a Yokosuka B4Y replacement. The Nakajima B5N was the IJN's only shipborne torpedo-bomber at the start of the Pacific War, and at that point it was the best carrier-borne torpedo-bomber in the world. Although as the war progressed it was considered obsolete compared to Allied counterparts, the B5N served until the end of World War II.

Internally designated Type K by Nakajima, it successfully competed with the Mitsubishi B5M for a production contract. This low-wing monoplane with its crew of three – pilot, navigator/bombardier/observer, and radio operator/gunner – and powered by a Nakajima Hikan radial engine, first flew in January 1937. Within a year, production versions, now with the full designation Type 97 Carrier Attack Bomber, were operating from Japan's carriers while shore-based units were deployed in China.

Combat experience in the Sino-Japanese War revealed weaknesses in the B5N1, specifically the lack of protection offered to the crew and the aircraft's fuel tanks. The Navy were unwilling to compromise the type's performance by the addition of armour and more defensive guns. Instead, Nakajima sought to improve the aircraft's performance through

ABOVE: **A B5N2. The B5N1 was supposedly refined and improved following combat experience of the type in the war with China, but in reality the later models' performance was little different.** BELOW: **Despite its shortcomings, in 1941 the B5N torpedo-bomber was among the best in the world and went on to inflict great losses on the Allies.**

streamlining and the installation of a more powerful engine which together would hopefully enable the aircraft to outrun enemy fighters. This new version, the B5N2, was in service by 1939 having the more powerful Sakae 11 engine covered with a smaller cowling. Armament and bomb load were unchanged compared to the earlier version (now known as the B5N1), and the B5N2 remained in production until 1943. Performance was only marginally improved compared to the earlier version.

At the time of the Japanese attack on Pearl Harbor in December 1941, the B5N2 had fully replaced the B5N1 with front-line torpedo-bomber units. There were 144 B5Ns (both 1s and 2s) involved in the Pearl Harbor attack, and in the year that followed, the type sank the US carriers *Lexington* at Coral Sea, *Yorktown* at Midway, and *Hornet* at the Battle of Santa Cruz in October 1942.

Allocated the reporting name 'Kate' by the Allies, the B5N was a serious threat – but when carrying a full load, its poor defensive armament of just one machine-gun made it an easy target for Allied fighters. As the Allies gained control of the skies over the Pacific and the B5N2 fleet began to suffer heavy losses, the type was gradually withdrawn as a torpedo-bomber.

Having excellent range, the 'Kate' was then assigned to anti-submarine (some with early radars and magnetic anomaly detectors) and maritime reconnaissance duties in areas beyond the range of Allied fighters. Others were used for training and target-towing while some B5Ns were used as conventional bombers during the unsuccessful defence of the Philippines in October 1944. The B5N also became the basis for the Nakajima B6N Tenzan which eventually replaced it in front-line service with the Japanese Navy.

When production ceased in 1943 a total of 1,149 had been built – Nakajima completed 669, subcontractor Aichi made 200 and the Navy's Hiro Air Arsenal built 280. Of the many produced, no complete examples survive. A partial airframe recovered from Russia may be restored and rebuilt, but until then the replicas based on North American Harvard/Texans made for the 1970 film *Tora! Tora! Tora!* and seen at US air shows continue to be the only flying representations of the type.

ABOVE LEFT: **A Nakajima B5N1 'Kate' taking off from the Japanese aircraft carrier** *Akagi*. Note the size of the torpedo. ABOVE: **A B5N2 pictured over Hickam Field during the Pearl Harbor attack. The caption for this photograph when it was released in Japan read, "Pearl Harbor in flame and smoke, gasping helplessly under the severe pounding of our Sea Eagles."**

ABOVE: **As well as Pearl Harbor, the B5N was also the type that destroyed the USS** *Hornet*, *Lexington* **and** *Yorktown*. BELOW LEFT: **Although the type was withdrawn from front-line service due to increased vulnerability to Allied fighters, their contribution to Japan's war effort was immense.**

Nakajima B5N2

First flight: January 1937 (prototype)

Power: One Nakajima 1,000hp NK1B Sakae 11 engine

Armament: One flexible 7.7mm machine-gun in rear cockpit and up to 800kg/1,764lb of bombs or a torpedo

Size: Wingspan – 15.52m/50ft 11in

    Length – 10.3m/33ft 9.5in

    Height – 3.7m/12ft 1in

    Wing area – 37.7m²/406sq ft

Weights: Empty – 2,279kg/5,024lb

    Maximum take-off – 4,100kg/9,039lb

Performance: Maximum speed – 378kph/235mph

    Ceiling – 8,260m/27,100ft

    Range – 1,990km/1,237 miles

    Climb – 3,000m/9,840ft in 7 minutes, 40 seconds

Nakajima B6N Tenzan

The Nakajima B6N Tenzan (heavenly mountain) was the Imperial Japanese Navy's standard torpedo-bomber for the final years of World War II. Codenamed 'Jill' by the Allies, the aircraft was a development of Nakajima's B5N and replaced it in service. Although the B6N was an effective torpedo-bomber, by the time it got into service the Allied air superiority in the Pacific severely limited its usefulness.

The shortcomings of the B5N were never rectified, but the Japanese Navy had high hopes for a replacement aircraft. Its 1939 specification called to for an aircraft that could carry the same weapon load as the B5N but at greater speed and over a greater range while not being any bigger than the earlier aircraft. The restriction was due to the size of carrier deck lifts. This led the designers to a novel way of creating a rudder of increased area by taking more of the fin and sloping the rudder's front edge forwards, top first.

The aircraft had no internal weapons bay and the torpedo was carried distinctively offset to the right, while the large oil cooler was offset to the left. The type's development was

ABOVE: **The B6N was evidently developed from Nakajima's earlier B5N but brought significant performance improvements for the Japanese Navy. The B6N2 version pictured was powered by the Kasei engine.**

protracted and not easy – there were stability and engine problems (vibration and overheating among others) during the early 1941 testing. This led to a two-year delay in entry to front-line service.

Tenzans went into service for the first time in late 1943, off Bougainville in the Solomon Islands. The B6N1's combat debut in the Battle of the Philippine Sea was a disaster as the US Navy's air superiority meant that the American fighters were able to inflict massive losses while disrupting the B6N1's attacks. The Japanese Navy immediately ordered improvements, the most significant of which was the replacement of the NK7A Mamori 11 engine with the Mitsubishi MK4T Kasei 25, resulting in the improved B6N2 version. The Kasei was slightly less powerful but led to a more streamlined aircraft.

LEFT: **Nakajima's B6N could fly faster and farther than the earlier B5N from which it was developed. Note the unusual and innovative fin shape that gave more control surface area without increasing the height of the fin. Such solutions were – and still are – essential in the creation of carrier-borne aircraft.**

This heavy aircraft could only operate from the largest Japanese carriers, most of which had been destroyed or put out of commission. Accordingly, most B6N2 operations took place from land bases, meaning they failed to make use of this version's improvements and lacked tactical surprise.

Although the Tenzans fought in the Battle of Okinawa, it was also here that the aircraft were used for the first time for kamikaze missions.

Towards the end of the war some were equipped with radar for night-time torpedo attacks on Allied shipping. As the Allies pressed closer to the Japanese homeland, the Japanese Navy's role shifted from attack to one of defence. Accordingly, the final version of the B6N was for land-only use and was much lighter and faster due to the lack of equipment and features previously required for carrier operations. For example, it had a strengthened undercarriage with larger tyres for rough field operations. Two of these B6N3 prototypes were completed, but Japan surrendered before this variant entered production.

A total of 1,268 B6Ns were built, the majority of them B6N2s. Today, only one survives and is preserved at the National Air and Space Museum in the United States.

TOP: **The loss of Japan's larger carriers that could carry the large B6N and the loss of experienced flight crews meant the B6N was never able to demonstrate its improved performance.** ABOVE: **The B6N can be easily identified by the way it had to carry its torpedo offset to the right due to the presence of a large oil radiator protruding under the aircraft belly.** BELOW: **The wartime caption for this photograph taken on December 4, 1943, reads, "A Japanese Nakajima B6N 'Tenzan' torpedo-bomber explodes in the air after a direct hit by a 5in shell from USS *Yorktown* (CV-10) as it attempted an unsuccessful attack on the carrier off Kwajalein."**

Nakajima B6N2 Tenzan

First flight: 1941
Power: One Mitsubishi 1,850hp Kasei-25 14-cylinder two-row radial engine
Armament: One 7.7mm machine-gun, manually aimed, in rear cockpit, one 7.7mm machine-gun, manually aimed by middle crew member, in rear ventral position plus one torpedo or 800kg/1,746lb of bombs carried under fuselage
Size: Wingspan – 14.89m/48ft 10.5in
Length – 10.87m/35ft 8in
Height – 3.8m/12ft 5.5in
Wing area – 37.2m²/400sq ft
Weights: Empty – 3,010kg/6,636lb
Maximum take-off – 5,650kg/12,456lb
Performance: Maximum speed – 481kph/299mph
Ceiling – 9,040m/29,660ft
Range – 3,045km/1,892 miles
Climb – 5,000m/16,400ft in 10 minutes, 24 seconds

LEFT: Another very distinctive and easy to identify aircraft, the N-3PB was the first aircraft produced by the newly formed Northrop. ABOVE: The two large floats gave the aircraft great stability on the water and would be fitted with beaching gear to be manoeuvred on land. BELOW: The N-3PB's achievements were way out of proportion to the tiny numbers of the type that were produced and saw service with Norwegian crews serving in the RAF.

Northrop N-3PB

The Northrop N-3PB was a single-engine low-wing twin-float aircraft with a crew of three. The only customer for this rare aircraft was the Royal Norwegian Navy Air Service (RNNAS) who needed a patrol bomber to protect its waters.

Norway ordered 24 aircraft on March 12, 1940, but before the aircraft could be delivered, Norway was invaded by Germany. As a result, all of the aircraft were delivered to the exiled RNNAS which operated as No.330 (Norwegian) Squadron of RAF Coastal Command based in Reykjavik, Iceland. On May 19, 1941, 18 aircraft arrived in Iceland. Twelve N-3PBs were assembled immediately and divided among the squadron's three flights, based at Reykjavik, Akureiry in northern Iceland and Budareiry in eastern Iceland. Following the loss of ten of the aircraft (due to extreme weather), the remaining aircraft were gradually put into operation. The first operational sortie by an N-3PB was flown from Reykjavik on June 23, 1941.

The squadron moved to Scotland in August 1943 to re-equip with Sunderlands but in their time on Iceland the N-3PBs flew 1,041 operational sorties including 379 convoy-escort missions and 246 anti-U-boat missions. The squadron spotted fifteen U-boats,

attacked nine and damaged seven. N-3PBs were also credited with damage to eight enemy aircraft. These are remarkable results given the very low numbers of aircraft involved and the sheer size of their patrol areas.

On April 21, 1943, an N-3PB, call sign 'U', took off from Budareiry heading for Reykjavik. En route the crew encountered heavy snow showers and were forced to land on a glacier river. The aircraft was wrecked and sank but the crew survived. Thirty-six years later the aircraft was located, removed and restored over a period of a year by Northrop in California. This sole survivor is now preserved and displayed at a museum in Gardermoen, Norway.

Northrop N-3PB

First flight: November 1, 1940
Power: One Wright 1,100hp GR-1820-G205A Cyclone air-cooled radial engine
Armament: Four fixed forward-firing 0.5in machine-guns in wings, one 0.3in machine-gun in dorsal and ventral positions and up to 907kg/2,000lb of bombs
Size: Wingspan – 14.91m/48ft 11in
  Length – 10.97m/36ft
  Height – 3.66m/12ft
  Wing area – 34.93m²/376sq ft
Weights: Empty – 2,808kg/6,190lb
  Maximum take-off – 4,808kg/10,600lb
Performance: Maximum speed – 414kph/257mph
  Ceiling – 7,392m/28,400ft
  Range – 1,609km/1,000 miles
  Climb – 4,572m/15,000ft in 14 minutes, 24 seconds

LEFT: **The Parnall company started as a woodworking business that simply built aircraft for established design companies. The company produced a number of types through to the early 1930s. The aircraft pictured is the Mongoose-powered N181.** ABOVE: **A Peto is shown taxiing away from its 'mother' submarine. The Peto experiment was audacious and high risk.** BELOW LEFT: **A Peto being craned back on to the sub's launch rails for stowage in the hangar.**

Parnall Peto

In 1926, Parnall were approached to produce an unusual aircraft for an even more unusual role. The specification called for a small two-seat floatplane with folding wings that could be carried in a 2.44m/8ft-wide watertight hangar on the deck of the Royal Navy submarine M.2. The project was conceived by submarine commander Sir Max Horton who believed that the future of sea power lay with submarines and aircraft and not ships.

The Peto was made of mixed wood, fabric, aluminium and steel, and had unequal span. One prototype was powered by a 135hp Bristol Lucifer engine while the second had an Armstrong Siddeley 135hp Mongoose. Six production aircraft are believed to have been ordered.

Once the submarine had surfaced, the aircraft was launched by a compressed air catapult along a short length of track. The aircraft was then supposed to scout for enemy ships, note their position, then land back near the submarine. A crane would lift the aircraft back on to its launch rails, then a winch would haul the aircraft backwards, the wings would be folded manually and the aircraft would return to its hangar with two sets of watertight doors closing behind it. The

submarine would then head to the enemy ships and launch an attack. Speed of aircraft deployment was clearly important and the crew were eager to break their 12-minute record.

On January 26, 1932, M.2 was lost with all hands. Divers found the sub on the seabed with both hangar doors and the hatch connecting the hangar to the sub open. It is believed that the crew, eager to improve on the time taken to launch the aircraft, opened the pressure-hull hatch to the hangar as well as the watertight hangar door while the boat was still partly submerged. The water rushed in and the sub sank quickly. The experiment was never repeated and the Peto remains the first and only conventional aircraft to be launched from a British submersible aircraft carrier.

Parnall Peto

First flight: June 4, 1925
Power: One Armstrong Siddeley 135hp Mongoose IIIC 5-cylinder air-cooled radial engine
Armament: None
Size: Wingspan – 8.66m/28ft 5in
    Length – 6.86m/22ft 6in
    Height – 2.71m/8ft 11in
    Wing area – 16.17m^2/174sq ft
Weights: Empty – 590kg/1,300lb
    Maximum take-off – 885kg/1,950lb
Performance: Maximum speed – 181kph/113mph
    Ceiling – 3,447m/11,300ft
    Endurance – 2 hours
    Climb – 183m/600ft per minute

Saro Cloud

The Saro Cloud that entered RAF service in 1933 was a rare bird for the time – not just a monoplane with a fully enclosed cockpit but also an amphibian flying boat.

The Cloud was a scaled up version of the civilian Saro (Saunders-Roe) Cutty Sark flying boat and is worthy of mention because it was used as an advanced trainer for military flying boat crews. While the Cutty Sark was powered by two 150hp engines and seated four passengers, the civil Cloud had two 340hp engines and carried eight.

The Saro A.19 Cloud had first flown at Cowes on July 16, 1930, and was originally designed as a civil aircraft. The RAF called for a modified version that was produced to Air Ministry specification 15/32. The Cloud first entered RAF service in August 1933 with

the Seaplane Training Establishment at Calshot. Trainee pilots first mastered floatplanes, then graduated from Clouds before being trained on examples of large service flying boats attached to the unit. They were then posted to front-line RAF flying boat units.

The Cloud was a novelty in RAF service as it was an amphibian used for the instruction of flying-boat pilots but also served as a flying classroom for training groups of navigators. The large cabin had room for map tables and the excellent view from the cabin made life a little easier for the fledgling navigators as they looked for visual references. The cabin could be configured in numerous

ways, for example eight trainee navigators with basic equipment or six plus wireless and electrical equipment, navigation instruments and signalling apparatus. Sixteen of the amphibians were built by Saunders Roe for the RAF, the last being delivered in 1935. Examples took part in the annual RAF Display from 1933 to 1936 and the Clouds remained in service until being withdrawn early in 1939.

Saro Cloud

First flight: July 16, 1930
Power: Two Armstrong Siddeley 340hp Serval V radial piston engines
Armament: Two 0.303in machine-guns and up to 90kg/200lb of practice bombs
Size: Wingspan – 19.51m/64ft
　　　Length – 15.28m/50ft 1.5in
　　　Height – 5m/16ft 5in
　　　Wing area – 60.39m²/650sq ft
Weights: Empty – 3,084kg/6,800lb
　　　Maximum take-off – 4,309kg/9,500lb
Performance: Maximum speed – 190kph/118mph
　　　Service ceiling – 4,265m/14,000ft
　　　Range – 612km/380 miles
　　　Climb – 229m/750ft per minute

ABOVE: A civil version of the Saro Cloud prepares to leave the water at Cowes. The type remained in RAF service until 1939, having trained many RAF crews who were soon in action.

LEFT: **The shape of the aircraft's hull is clear in this air-to-air study of L7249, one of three prototypes built to prove the design. Sadly, only 21 were built for the Royal Air Force. All that was proved was that the Lerwick was a poor design.**

Saro Lerwick

The Saunders-Roe Lerwick flying boat is of interest because it is a good example of how a respected manufacturer can produce a thoroughly disappointing aircraft that had looked good on the drawing board. Due to pressures of a looming war the aircraft was accepted into service but its service career was short.

The Saro A.36 Lerwick was built to Air Ministry specification R.1/36 and was, after the Sunderland, the second monoplane flying boat to enter Royal Air Force service. These new generation aircraft were intended to replace biplane flying boats like the Stranraer. The Lerwick was a high-winged all-metal monoplane powered by two Bristol Hercules engines and had three powered defensive gun turrets. Armament consisted of a single machine-gun in the nose turret, two in the dorsal turret and four in the tail.

The Lerwick was found to have some fundamental design shortcomings and as a result displayed aerodynamic instability in the most unchallenging flying situations. Its tendency to suddenly and viciously stall did nothing to commend the type to crews who lost many of their comrades in accidents. On water the Lerwick was sadly little better.

Only 21 Lerwicks were built for the RAF. The first entered service in July 1939, the last was delivered in June 1941 and the type was withdrawn from service in October 1942. The first two machines delivered to the RAF were withdrawn in September 1939 only two months after delivery and returned to Saro for remedial works.

The first Lerwick squadron, No.209, carried out its first operational patrol on Christmas Day 1939. Continued problems with the aircraft meant the squadron did not reach full strength until June 1940

but by then the entire fleet had been grounded once, in February 1940. A further grounding kept the aircraft firmly on the water from August to October 1940 at a time when the RAF really needed maritime patrol aircraft to counter a possible German invasion of the UK. Although the aircraft were cleared for operations, a further two were lost in accidents during the winter of 1940–41.

Lerwicks were finally withdrawn in April 1941 but between July and October 1942 they were to fly again as, incredibly, training aircraft for UK-based Royal Canadian Air Force crews. Those fortunate enough to survive the training on Lerwicks went on to Sunderlands.

LEFT: **The service career of the Lerwick was far from auspicious and crews were relieved to see the type's withdrawal despite the wartime need for large military flying boats.**

Saro Lerwick

First flight: November 10, 1938
Power: Two Bristol 1,375hp Hercules II radial piston engines
Armament: Seven 0.303in machine-guns – two in nose, two in dorsal turret and four in tail plus up to 900kg/1,984lb of bombs or depth charges carried beneath wings
Size: Wingspan – 24.7m/80ft 10in
Length – 19.4m/63ft 7in
Height – 6.1m/20ft
Wing area – 78.5m²/845sq ft
Weights: Normal – 12,928kg/28,500lb
Maximum take-off – 15,060kg/33,200lb
Performance: Maximum speed – 344kph/214mph
Service ceiling – 4,270m/14,000ft
Range – 2,478km/1,540 miles
Climb – 268m/880ft in 52 minutes

Saro London

Thirty-one examples of Saro's London biplane flying boat were built for Royal Air Force Coastal Command who operated the type in the front line from 1936 until 1941. The London, with its crew of five, is another fine example of an outmoded aircraft that had to remain in service for much longer than planned as there were simply no more capable, modern aircraft available at the time.

The first flight of the London took place in 1934, the aircraft having been designed to meet a specification calling for a 'general-purpose open-sea patrol flying boat'. The London was in fact derived from Saro's earlier and larger Severn flying boat. The first ten aircraft built were Mk Is with Bristol Pegasus III engines and can be identified by the

powerplants' polygonal cowlings and two-bladed propellers. The definitive Mk II had Pegasus X engines with circular cowlings and four-bladed propellers – construction of this version continued until May 1938 with surviving Mk Is being upgraded to the II standard.

Having first entered service with No.201 Squadron in April 1936, Londons were chosen to represent the RAF on the 150th anniversary of the founding of the State of New South Wales in 1937. Five Londons equipped with auxiliary fuel tanks flew from Britain to Australia demonstrating the type's long-range capabilities over a round trip that covered 48,280km/30,000 miles.

The London was still in service at the start of World War II with Nos.201, 202

ABOVE: **The Saro London served with three RAF Coastal Command squadrons during the early part of World War II.** BELOW: **K3560 was the London prototype built to Air Ministry specification R.24/31 and was later converted to London II standard.**

and 240 Squadrons, carrying out anti-submarine duties and convoy patrols. The type was one of very few front-line biplanes still in the British inventory. It was the aircraft based at Gibraltar that served until April 1941 when they were finally replaced in service by the Consolidated Catalina.

Saro London Mk II	

First flight: 1934 (prototype)
Power: Two Bristol 1,055hp Pegasus X radial piston engines
Armament: Three 0.303in machine-guns in bow and midships plus up to 907kg/2,000lb of bombs or depth charges
Size: Wingspan – 24.38m/80ft
    Length – 17.31m/56ft 10in
    Height – 5.72m/18ft 9in
    Wing area – 132.38m²/1,425sq ft
Weights: Empty – 5,035kg/11,100lb
    Maximum take-off – 8,346kg/18,400lb
Performance: Maximum speed – 249kph/155mph
    Service ceiling – 6,065m/19,900ft
    Range – 2,800km/1,740 miles
    Climb – 360m/1,180ft per minute

LEFT: **Looking like a flying wing on a pair of pontoons, the S.55 was revolutionary in terms of flying boat configuration.** ABOVE: **The 24 S.55s prepare to take off for the Balbo-led transatlantic flight – a remarkable feat of airmanship even by today's standards.**

Savoia-Marchetti S.55

Savoia-Marchetti's S.55 must surely be the most distinctive flying boat in aviation history. The S.55 was proposed to meet an Italian military requirement for a large long-range multi-engine torpedo/bomber flying boat that could carry a substantial bomb load. It first flew in 1924 and encapsulated its designers' daring, ingenuity and advanced understanding of aero- and hydrodynamics. It was a monoplane with twin catamaran-type hulls and two fins and three rudders connected to the rest of the aircraft by two of the stripped-down booms. The two pilots sat side by side in open cockpits located in the leading edge of the centre of the wing. Twin tandem engines, one tractor, one pusher, were mounted on struts over the wing and canted sharply at an upward angle. It must be borne in mind that this aircraft appeared only seven years after the end of World War I in an era dominated by biplanes.

Engine power was gradually increased from the 300hp of the prototype's engines to the 880hp of later versions' engines. However, the Italian Navy were initially unimpressed by the prototype's poor performance and were suspicious of the aircraft's unusual configuration. The manufacturers persevered and developed a civil version, the S.55C which could accommodate five passengers in each of the two hulls. This rekindled the military's interest and the first military orders followed.

The S.55 earned worldwide fame through spectacular long-distance flights. Lt Col the Marchese de Pinedo flew an S.55 named *Santa Maria* from Sardinia to Buenos Aires and then through South America and the USA and back to Italy, covering a distance of nearly 48,280km/30,000 miles. The S.55 will perhaps be best remembered, however, for the remarkable mass formation flights led by the senior Italian Air Force officer Italo Balbo who led fleets of S.55s across the Atlantic. In 1933 he led 24 aircraft all the way to the US and Chicago's Century of Progress International Exposition, flying all the way in a tight 'v' formation.

The type went on to equip numerous Italian long-range maritime reconnaissance/bomber units and some of the machines were still in reserve when World War II broke out. Total production of civil and military versions exceeded 200.

LEFT: **One of the Balbo-flight aircraft being prepared for the transatlantic flight. Note the angle of the engine 'pod'. The flight made the S.55 world famous. Only one example of an S.55 survives, currently under restoration in Sao Paolo, Brazil.**

Savoia-Marchetti S.55X

First flight: August 1924 (prototype)
Power: Two 880hp Isotta-Fraschini Asso 750 Vee piston engines
Armament: Four 7.7mm machine-guns plus one torpedo or up to 2,000kg/4,409lb of bombs
Size: Wingspan – 24m/78ft 9in
　　　Length – 16.75m/54ft 11.5in
　　　Height – 5m/16ft 4.75in
　　　Wing area – 93m²/1,001sq ft
Weights: Empty – 5,750kg/12,677lb
　　　Maximum take-off – 8,260kg/18,210lb
Performance: Maximum speed – 279kph/173mph
　　　Ceiling – 5,000m/16,405ft
　　　Range – 3,500km/2,175 miles

Short Type 184

The Short Type 184 was designed by Horace Short to meet an urgent requirement from the British Admiralty for a torpedo-carrying seaplane. The first example flew at Rochester in early 1915 powered by a 225hp Sunbeam Maori engine. By the end of an impressive production run of 936, involving Short Brothers and nine other aircraft manufacturers, the '184' had established itself as the company's most successful inter-war type.

On August 12, 1915, a Short 184 operating from the seaplane carrier HMS *Ben-My-Chree* in the Aegean became the first aircraft in the world to attack an enemy ship with an air-launched torpedo. Piloted by Flight Commander Charles H.K. Edmonds, the aircraft dropped a 367kg/810lb torpedo against a 5,000-ton Turkish supply ship which

subsequently sank, although a British submarine commander also claimed the victory. On August 17, however, Edmonds torpedoed a Turkish steamer a few miles north of the Dardanelles and on this occasion there was no dispute as to how the vessel had been destroyed.

Another Short 184 from Edmond's flight on the same mission had to put down on the sea due to engine problems. The pilot, Flight Lieutenant G.B. Dacre, spotted an enemy tug nearby and nursed the aircraft engine to give enough power for him to taxi nearer to the tug. Dacre then dropped his torpedo into the sea from zero feet – it ran true and sank the enemy ship.

These early torpedo successes were, however, not typical and the type came to be used more for bombing and reconnaissance. The aircraft went on to

ABOVE LEFT: **The Type 184 is assured of its place in the history books thanks to the August 1915 torpedo attacks by Flight Commander Edmonds.**
ABOVE: **The bravery of the pioneering naval aviators is well illustrated in this study. Note the open cockpit and the exposed construction of the aircraft.**

serve in most theatres during World War I. Wheels could be added to the floats to allow take-off from the decks of carrier aircraft. When the RAF was formed in April 1918 from the RFC and the RNAS, the RAF took over most of the RNAS 184s and the type continued to protect Britain's coastline and its interests overseas into 1920.

A landplane version of the Short 184 was sold to the Royal Flying Corps as the Short Bomber. A forward fuselage section of a Short 184 is preserved by the Fleet Air Arm Museum in the UK.

ABOVE: **HMS *Engadine* was a World War I Royal Navy seaplane tender. Built as a Folkestone-Boulogne ferry, *Engadine* was taken over by the Navy in 1914, and cranes and a hangar were added for operating four Short 184 seaplanes.**

Short Type 184

First flight: Spring 1915
Power: One Sunbeam 260hp Maori Vee engine
Armament: One 0.303in machine-gun in rear cockpit plus one 356mm/14in torpedo or up to 236kg/520lb of bombs
Size: Wingspan – 19.36m/63ft 6.25in
Length – 12.38m/40ft 8in
Height – 4.11m/13ft
Wing area – 63.92m²/688sq ft
Weights: Empty – 1,680kg/3,703lb
Maximum take-off – 2,433kg/5,363lb
Performance: Maximum speed – 142kph/88mph
Ceiling – 2,745m/9,000ft
Endurance – 2 hours, 45 minutes
Climb – 610m/2,000ft in 8 minutes, 35 seconds

Short Singapore III

The Short Singapore was the last of a number of biplane flying boats built by the company and the last use of the name that was first applied to the record-breaking Singapore I of 1926. The Singapore III became a vital element of the Royal Air Force's flying boat force in Britain and overseas in the years leading up to World War II.

The four-engined Short S.12 Singapore II of 1930 was a triple-finned development of the Singapore I but its powerplants were arranged in twin tandem configuration. The four engines were arranged in tandem pairs with two pushing and two pulling. Although this version did not enter production, the Air Ministry was interested enough to order four development flying boats based on the Singapore II. These aircraft, trialled at the Marine Aircraft Experimental Establishment, became the pre-production Singapore Mk IIIs.

The production aircraft that followed were built to Air Ministry specification R.14/34 and the first production example, K3592, first flew on June 15, 1934. Production continued until mid-1937 by which time 37 aircraft had been produced for the Royal Air Force.

The Singapore III, with a crew of six, had all-metal hulls, fabric-covered metal flying surfaces and was powered by four 675hp Rolls-Royce Kestrel IX engines

mounted between the wings. If required, an auxiliary long-range fuel tank could be carried externally on the dorsal hull.

The first RAF unit to operate the type was No.210 Squadron at Pembroke Dock while the first overseas deployment came in April 1935 with No.205 Squadron in Singapore.

By the time this large biplane entered RAF service it was effectively obsolete but it did significantly increase the RAF's flying boat fleet during the mid-1930s arms race. Despite the age of its basic design, 19 Singapore IIIs were still in RAF service when World War II broke out, based in the UK, Aden and Singapore. It was at the latter location that, appropriately, the Singapore III soldiered on until being withdrawn in October 1941. Four of these aircraft were passed to No.5 Squadron of the Royal New Zealand Air Force for use in Fiji and saw action during which a Japanese submarine was destroyed. The Singapores were finally replaced by Consolidated Catalinas.

TOP: **The Singapore III was arrived at through a series of configuration experiments and trials. This aircraft is a Singapore II with a single fin pictured in 1930.** ABOVE LEFT: **This view of two Singapore IIIs show the distinctive triple fin arrangement and the scale of the type. Note the very streamlined engine 'pod' arrangement.** ABOVE: **This enhanced publicity shot from the early 1930s shows a Singapore being put through its paces at low level.**

Short Singapore III

First flight: June 15, 1934 (production Singapore III)
Power: Four Rolls-Royce 730hp Kestrel X radial engines
Armament: Three 0.303in machine-guns in bow, dorsal and tail positions plus up to 907kg/2,000lb of bombs
Size: Wingspan – 27.4m/90ft
Length – 19.5m/64ft 2in
Height – 7.01m/23ft 7in
Wing area – 170.5m²/1,834sq ft
Weights: Empty – 8,360kg/18,420lb
Maximum take-off – 14,300kg/31,500lb
Performance: Maximum speed – 233kph/145mph
Ceiling – 4,570m/15,000ft
Range – 1,609km/1,000 miles
Climb – 213m/700ft per minute

LEFT: **The Short Rangoon prototype, S1433, pictured during its testing, which began in September 1930.** BELOW: **K2134 was a service trials aircraft that at the end of its testing was passed first to No.203 and then on to No.210 Squadron for service use.**

Short Rangoon

The Short Calcutta was a three-engined biplane flying boat developed to meet a civil Imperial Airways requirement for a 'boat' to work the Mediterranean legs of the airline's services to and from India. Derived from the first Short Singapore I military flying boat, the Calcutta first flew in 1928 and was the first stressed skin, metal-hulled flying boat produced in any numbers, although the production run was only five. These durable aircraft were still in service as late as 1939 serving as training aircraft for civilian flying boat crews.

On August 1, 1928, a Calcutta flew to London and was set down at Westminster where the aircraft was moored and inspected by politicians including Winston Churchill. This demonstrated the aircraft's flexibility and gave those in charge of the nation's military budgets the opportunity to see at close quarters how their money could be spent. Also this made it clear that if this large flying boat could land right in the middle of London it could do the same anywhere with the right stretch of water.

It was from the reliable Calcutta that a military version was developed to meet Air Ministry specification R.18/29 – this aircraft became the Short Rangoon having been first known as the Calcutta (Service type). The prototype, registration S1433, first flew on September 24, 1930, with Short's Chief Test Pilot, John Lankester Parker at the controls. The Rangoon differed mainly from the civil version by having military equipment such as gun mounts, guns and bombs, as well as bigger fuel tanks and freshwater tanks to allow the aircraft and crew to operate in tropical conditions.

The Rangoon, like the Calcutta, was able to take off on just two of its three Bristol Jupiter engines. The five-man Rangoon first entered Royal Air Force service in April 1931 with No.203 Squadron in Iraq where the aircraft were used to deter gun-running and any activities counter to Britain's interests in the Persian Gulf. It was aircraft from this unit that made the long flight from Iraq to Australia in September 1934 for the country's 150th Anniversary celebrations. These well-publicized, long-distance flights were carried out to prove the aircraft and show the world that British military aircraft could and would reach all corners of the world if required. The aircraft left Iraq in mid-1935 and were transferred to Gibraltar where they served until

LEFT: **In service with No.203 Squadron RAF at Basra in Iraq, this aircraft, S1435, later had its military equipment removed and was passed to Imperial Airways as a trainer under the civilian identity of G-AEIM.**

July 1936 when they returned to Britain to be retired, although one was demilitarized and passed to Imperial Airways for use as a trainer. Only six Rangoons were supplied to the RAF but the type left an impression well out of proportion to its limited production numbers.

In 1924, a Calcutta had been bought by the French company Breguet who developed a military version of their own for French Navy use. This aircraft was designated the Breguet S.8/2 and was very similar to the Rangoon. Four examples were built for the Aéronavale, as was an improved version known as the Breguet 521 Bizerte.

Shorts also built a military version of the Calcutta for the Imperial Japanese Navy (IJN) – the Short S.15 K.F.1. This was delivered by sea to Japan in 1931 and Kawanishi went on to build four further examples which they designated the H3K. In IJN service the type was known as the Navy Type 90 Model 2 Flying Boat. The H3K gave Kawanishi valuable experience in the production of all-metal military flying boats – this expertise translated directly into the company's later aircraft like the H6K and H8K that the Allies faced during World War II.

ABOVE: **The Rangoon was a design that greatly aided the Japanese in their development of their own flying-boat industry.** BELOW LEFT: **This aircraft, S1434, was the RAF's second example of the type to enter service. Along with the other RAF Rangoons, it flew to Iraq in 1931 and provided an instant, potent and self-sufficient projection of British air power.**

Short Rangoon

First flight: September 24, 1930 (prototype)
Power: Three Bristol 540hp Jupiter XIF radial piston engines
Armament: Three 0.303in machine-guns in nose and midships positions and up to 454kg/1,000lb of bombs
Size: Wingspan – 28.35m/93ft
Length – 20.35m/66ft 9in
Height – 7.19m/23ft 7in
Wing area – 169.9m²/1,828sq ft
Weights: Empty – 6,360kg/14,000lb
Maximum take-off – 10,900kg/24,000lb
Performance: Maximum speed – 185kph/115mph
Ceiling – 3,658m/12,000ft
Range – 1,046km/650 miles
Climb – 168m/550ft per minute

Short Sunderland

The Sunderland is one of only a handful of military aircraft that were developed from an existing civil type. Based upon Shorts' C-Class 'Empire' flying boats operated by Imperial Airways in the 1930s, the Short Sunderland became one of the Royal Air Force's longest-serving operational aircraft over the next two decades. Its service during World War II and, specifically, the Sunderland's decisive role in the defeat of German U-boats in the Battle of the Atlantic, marks it as one of aviation history's finest ever flying boats. Although the first flight of the prototype Sunderland took place in October 1937, the Air Ministry were already familiar with the aircraft's successful civilian counterpart and had placed an order in March the preceding year.

During June 1938 No.230 Squadron, based in Singapore, received the first service delivery of production Sunderland Mk Is. When the Sunderland joined the RAF inventory and replaced the RAF's mixed fleet of biplane flying boats, it represented a huge leap in capability.

TOP: **The very capable Sunderland enabled the wartime Royal Air Force to project its reach over vast expanses of ocean.** ABOVE: **This excellent side view of a 'beached' Sunderland III shows the version's new planing bottom in which the forward step was made shallower. This aircraft, W3999, was the first production example of the Mk III.**

By the outbreak of World War II in September 1939 three RAF Coastal Command squadrons had become operational and were ready to seek out and destroy German submarines. The Sunderland also became a very welcome sight to the many seamen from sunken vessels and the airmen who had ditched out over the ocean. This is best illustrated by the tale of the British merchant ship *Kensington Court*. It had been torpedoed 112km/70 miles off the Isles of Scilly on September 18, 1939, but two patrolling Sunderlands had the entire crew of 34 back on dry land just an hour after the ship sank.

The Sunderland, with its crew of ten, heavily armed and bristling with machine-guns, became known to the Luftwaffe as the 'Flying Porcupine'. Many times during the war a lone Sunderland fought off or defeated a number of attacking aircraft.

Although Sunderlands did engage in many a 'shoot-out' with German vessels, sometimes the sight of the large and well-armed aircraft was enough to have an enemy crew scuttle their boat – such was the case on January 31, 1940, when the arrival

ABOVE: **The Sunderland cockpit area was roomy and offered the aircraft's crew excellent visibility. In hot climates the crew had to be careful to avoid sunstroke due to the cockpit's extensive glazing.**

of a Sunderland from No.228 Squadron prompted the crew of U-Boat *U-55* to do just that.

The Sunderland Mk II was introduced at the end of 1940, powered by four Pegasus XVIII engines with two-stage superchargers, a twin-gun dorsal turret, an improved rear turret and Air-to-Surface-Vessel (ASV) Mk II radar. The most numerous version was the Mk III that first flew in December 1941. This variant had a modified hull for improved planing when taking off. This was followed by a larger and heavier version designated the Mk IV/Seaford. However, after evaluation by the RAF the project was abandoned.

The Mk V was the ultimate version of the Sunderland and made its appearance at the end of 1943. It was powered by four 1,200hp Pratt & Whitney R-1830-90 Twin Wasp engines and carried ASV Mk VI radar. By the end of the final production run in 1945, a total of 739 Sunderlands had been built and after World War II, many continued to serve with the British, French, Australian, South African and New Zealand air forces.

Post-war, RAF Sunderlands delivered nearly 5,000 tons of supplies during the Berlin Airlift, and during the Korean War Sunderlands were the only British aircraft to operate throughout the war. During the Malayan Emergency RAF Sunderlands carried out bombing raids against terrorist camps.

The Sunderland finally retired from the Royal Air Force on May 15, 1959, when No.205 Squadron flew the last sortie for the type from RAF Changi, Singapore, where the illustrious operational career of the Sunderland flying boat had begun over two decades earlier. It was, however, the Royal New Zealand Air Force who in March 1967 became the last air arm to retire the type from military service.

Between 1937 and 1946 a total of 749 Sunderlands were built – this included 240 built at Blackburn's Dumbarton plant.

ABOVE: **The Short Sunderland offered Allied convoys excellent protection within its range, and was a major weapon against the 'U-boat menace' in the war for the Atlantic.**

Short Sunderland Mk V

First flight: October 16, 1937 (prototype)
Power: Four Pratt & Whitney 1,200hp R-1830 Twin Wasp 14-cylinder air-cooled radials
Armament: Eight 0.303in Browning machine-guns in turrets, four fixed 0.303in Browning machine-guns in nose, two manually operated 0.5in machine-guns in beam positions and 2,250kg/4,960lb of depth charges or bombs
Size: Wingspan – 34.36m/112ft 9in
Length – 26m/85ft 3in
Height – 10.01m/32ft 11in
Wing area – 138.14m²/1,487sq ft
Weights: Empty – 16,783kg/37,000lb
Maximum take-off – 27,216kg/60,000lb
Performance: Maximum speed – 343kph/213mph
Ceiling – 5,456m/17,900ft
Range – 4,785km/2,980 miles
Climb – 256m/840ft per minute

Sopwith Camel

The Sopwith Camel, which evolved from the Sopwith Pup and Sopwith Triplane, is the best-known British aircraft of World War I. Credited with the destruction of around 3,000 enemy aircraft, it was by far the most effective fighter of World War I. The aircraft was very easy to turn due to its forward-placed centre of gravity, a result of the concentration of the engine, armament, pilot and fuel in the front 2.17m/7ft of the fuselage. This, coupled with its very sensitive controls, made the aircraft something of a handful for inexperienced pilots but in skilled hands the Camel was an excellent fighter and virtually unbeatable. Like the Pup, the Sopwith Biplane F.1 became better known by its nickname, in this case the 'Camel', and the aircraft's official designation is largely forgotten.

The prototype, powered by a 110hp Clerget 9Z, first flew at Brooklands in February 1917 and was followed by the F.1/3 pre-production model. First deliveries went to Royal Naval Air Service No.4 (Naval) Squadron at Dunkirk who received their new fighter in June 1917. The first Camel air victory occurred

TOP: **The Camel is among the most famous fighter aircraft ever built and its capabilities inevitably led to naval aviation applications.** ABOVE: **HMAS Sydney was attacked by a Zeppelin during May 1917 which escaped unscathed. The Captain was keen to not let an enemy escape again, so a flying platform for launching aircraft was built on the ship. Here a Camel is seen being launched from a gun platform.**

ABOVE: **A Camel being launched from HMS Tiger, which was one of a number of Royal Navy ships modified to launch aircraft. Note the tail's high attitude to ease a swift take-off.**

within days when, on June 4, Flight Commander A.M. Shook sent a German aircraft down into the sea – on the next day Shook attacked 15 enemy aircraft and is believed to have destroyed 2 of them. The Royal Flying Corps' first Camel victory was achieved by Captain C. Collett on June 27.

One manoeuvre, unique to the Camel, was an incredibly quick starboard turn assisted by the torque of its big rotary engine. So fast was the right turn that pilots were able to use it to great advantage in combat, sometimes choosing to make three-quarter right turns in place of the slower quarter turn to the left. It was risky though as during the sharp right turns, the nose tried to go violently downwards due to the torque of the engine. Camels were built with a variety of engines including the Clerget 9B, Bentley BR1, Gnome Monosoupape and Le Rhône 9J.

In the Battle of Cambrai in March 1918, Captain J.L. Trollope of No.43 Squadron used his Camel to shoot down six enemy aircraft in one day – March 24. Later that year, Camels were in the thick of what many historians believe to be the greatest dogfight of World War I. On the morning of November 4, 1918,

LEFT: The Camel was produced as a private venture but went on to become one of the most important British military aircraft of World War I. Around 5,500 examples of the Camel had been built by the time production ended.

Camels of Nos.65 and 204 Squadrons attacked 40 Fokker DVIIs. The pilots of No.56 claimed eight destroyed, six out of control and one driven down, while the pilots of 204 claimed two destroyed and five out of control. Perhaps the most famous single Camel victory is, however, that of Canadian Camel pilot Roy Brown who was credited with the death of Manfred von Richthofen, the Red Baron, on April 21, 1918.

By the end of 1917, over 1,000 Camels were delivered and work began on subvariants including naval versions. Those specially designed for shipboard use were designated the 2F.1 Camel and were the last type of Camel built. The majority were powered by BR.1 rotary engines and most were armed with one Lewis and one Vickers machine-gun – some carried two 22.7kg/50lb bombs on underwing bomb racks. Sea-going Camels had a slightly reduced wingspan and a completely removable tail for easy stowage. They also differed from land-based Camels by having jettisonable tubular-steel landing gear. These versions were flown from Royal Navy aircraft carriers HMS *Furious* and *Pegasus* but were also launched, or more accurately, catapulted, from platforms built on the gun turrets or forecastles of other British fighting ships of the time. In July 1918, 2F.1 Camels took off from HMS *Furious* in the North Sea and flew into the mouth of the River Elbe where they attacked and bombed enemy airship sheds at Tondern. Despite being

fighters, these nimble aircraft became bombers credited with the destruction of Zeppelins *L54* and *L60*. By the Armistice in November 1918, Britain's Grand Fleet had 112 2F.1s in its inventory. Post-war, six Camels that had served with US Navy squadrons in France during hostilities were shipped to the US for platform-launching trials aboard USS *Texas* and *Arkansas*.

In addition to the RFC, RNAS and RAF, Camels were also operated by Belgium, Canada, Greece and the air force of the American Expeditionary Force. Total Camel production was around 5,500.

ABOVE: Camels operating from ships would sometimes have to put down in the water. This was a hazardous operation for the pilot.

Sopwith F1. Camel

First flight: February 26, 1917

Power: Clerget 130hp 9-cylinder air-cooled rotary piston engine

Armament: Two 0.303in synchronized Vickers machine-guns on nose, plus four 11.35kg/25lb bombs carried below fuselage

Size: Wingspan – 8.53m/28ft
Length – 5.72m/18ft 9in
Height – 2.6m/8ft 6in
Wing area – 21.46m²/231sq ft

Weights: Empty – 421kg/929lb
Maximum take-off – 659kg/1,453lb

Performance: Maximum speed – 188kph/117mph
Ceiling – 5,790m/19,000ft
Endurance – 2 hours, 30 minutes
Climb – 3,050m/10,000ft in 10 minutes, 35 seconds

ABOVE: Shipborne Royal Navy Camels carried out audacious and hard-hitting raids that showed, even at this early stage, just how useful and effective shipborne air power could be.

Supermarine Scapa and Stranraer

Supermarine developed the Supermarine Southampton Mk IV – an upgraded, modernized and re-engined version – from the trusty Southampton design in response to Air Ministry specification R.20/31. It first flew on July 8, 1934, with 'Mutt' Summers at the controls and by October the following year it had been renamed the Scapa. While the Scapa was the same size as the aircraft from which it was developed, it contained many changes and modifications. Although the fuselage retained the same broad profile, the Scapa introduced twin fins and rudders in place of the three used on the Southampton. Much to the pilots' delight, the Scapa introduced a side-by-side enclosed cockpit. The all-metal Scapa featured aerodynamically neat, cowled Rolls-Royce Kestrels. Fourteen production aircraft were built for the RAF, the last of which were delivered by July 1936. Nos.202 and 204 Squadrons, operating from Malta and Aboukir/

Alexandria respectively, operated the type on anti-submarine patrols protecting neutral shipping during the Spanish Civil War. The Scapa was able to demonstrate its long-range capabilities on some high-profile publicity flights including a 14,480km/9000-mile return cruise to Africa. The type was gradually replaced in service, the last being retired by the close of 1938.

A related development was the Supermarine Stranraer, originally known as the Southampton V. This was the last biplane flying boat created by R.J. Mitchell and was a larger derivative with a wingspan almost 3m/10ft greater than the Scapa as well as a longer fuselage. It acquired the name Stranraer in August 1935, having first flown in July 1934. This aircraft also differed from the Scapa by having a gun position in the tail for self-defence.

Seventeen Stranraers were ordered by the Air Ministry in August 1935 and the type first entered RAF service with

ABOVE: **The Supermarine Stranraer remained in Royal Air Force service when World War II began.**
BELOW LEFT: **The record-breaking Scapa was aerodynamically refined for its day with its engines in neat 'pods'.**

No.228 Squadron in April 1937. The type was used exclusively around the coast of the UK by RAF Coastal Command. When World War II broke out in September 1939, 15 Stranraers were still in service and continued to serve well into 1941 until being replaced by Consolidated Catalinas.

The Royal Canadian Air Force also operated Stranraers throughout World War II – these 40 machines were licence-built by Canadian Vickers in Montreal, and a number entered civil use after the war's end.

Supermarine Stranraer

First flight: July 27, 1934 (prototype Southampton V)
Power: Two Bristol 875hp Pegasus X radial piston engine
Armament: Three 0.303in machine-guns in nose, dorsal and tail positions
Size: Wingspan – 25.91m/85ft
    Length – 16.71m/54ft 10in
    Height – 6.63m/21ft 9in
    Wing area – 135.36m²/1,457sq ft
Weights: Empty – 5,103kg/11,250lb
    Maximum take-off – 8,618kg/19,000lb
Performance: Maximum speed – 268kph/165mph
    Ceiling – 5,639m/18,500ft
    Range – 1,609km/1,000 miles
    Climb – 411m/1,350ft per minute

Supermarine Southampton

Felixstowe flying boats had been in RAF service since World War I and were rather long in the tooth by the mid-1920s. Their replacement, the Supermarine Southampton, was one of the RAF's most successful ever flying boats. The type was the first flying boat designed after World War I to enter RAF service but was in fact derived from a civilian flying boat, the Supermarine Swan. The success of the Swan gave the Air Ministry the confidence to order six of the military version straight from the drawing board.

It was also the first successful design led by R.J. Mitchell who went on to design the legendary Spitfire which was itself derived from a high-speed floatplane. It was the Southampton biplane that brought to prominence the name of the designer and the company that employed him.

The first production version was the Southampton Mk I, of which 24 were built with wooden hulls and wings. This was followed into service by 41 examples of the Mk II with lightweight metal hulls and the more powerful Lion VA engines. Later Mk IIs had slightly swept-back outer wing sections but all had underwing stabilizing floats and a distinctive tail with three fins and rudders. Its engines were mounted between the wings.

By 1933 the earlier wooden-hulled machines were eventually all reassembled with metal hulls. The duralumin hull was not only structurally lighter than wood but the wooden hull also carried an additional 181kg/400lb in the weight of the water that the wood absorbed. The weight-saving of the metal hull appreciably improved performance, which equated to an additional 325km/200-mile range.

The type first entered RAF service in August 1925 with No.480 Coastal Reconnaissance Flight. The Southampton was soon known as a record-breaker after carrying out a 16,000km/10,000-mile cruise around the British Isles, demonstrating the type's reliability and endurance. In 1926, two aircraft flew from the UK's south coast to Egypt on an 11,270km/7,000-mile round trip.

The Southamptons became synonymous with 'flying the flag' and went on to carry out a four-ship cruise from Felixstowe to Singapore via the Mediterranean and India in 1927 and 1928. This cruise covered no less than 43,500km/27,000 miles.

The popular and reliable Southampton served the RAF for over a decade, retiring in December 1936 – the type was also exported to Argentina, Australia (RAAF), Japan and Turkey.

One Southampton survives, a Mk I, registration N9899, preserved at the Royal Air Force Museum, Hendon.

Supermarine Southampton II

First flight: March 10, 1925 (Mk I)
Power: Two Napier 660hp Lion VA W-12 piston engines
Armament: Three 0.303in machine-guns in bow and mid positions plus up to 499kg/1,100lb of bombs
Size: Wingspan – 22.86m/75ft
  Length – 15.58m/51ft 1.5in
  Height – 6.82m/22ft 4.5in
  Wing area – 134.61m²/1,449sq ft
Weights: Empty – 4,082kg/9,000lb
  Maximum take-off – 6,895kg/15,200lb
Performance: Maximum speed – 174kph/108mph
  Ceiling – 4,265m/14,000ft
  Range – 1,497km/930 miles
  Climb – 186m/610ft per minute

LEFT: **When the Sea Otter was retired from military use, a number passed into civil use around the world – two were operated by the airline Quantas.**

ABOVE: **Royal Navy Sea Otters served until 1952, some years after RAF retirement.**

Supermarine Sea Otter

The Supermarine Sea Otter was a biplane amphibian designed to replace the Supermarine Walrus in reconnaissance and search-and-rescue duties – it became the last front-line biplane in Royal Air Force service. It was also the last biplane to enter RAF service in any capacity. The aircraft was designed to Air Ministry specification S.7/38 and was to be called the Stingray.

The prototype, K8854, first flew on September 29, 1938, and was modified after some service trials. The Sea Otter had a tractor propeller arrangement compared to the pusher configuration of the earlier Walrus. The Sea Otter was faster than its predecessor, could fly farther, handled better on the water and had a metal hull.

Production was carried out by British flying boat pioneers Saunders-Roe who acted as subcontractors to Supermarine for this project. Due to the need to build fighters and bombers first, the first production Sea Otters did not appear until January 1943, but the type did remain in production until July 1946 by which time 290 had been built.

The first Sea Otter unit was No.277 Squadron who received their aircraft later in 1943. Royal Navy Sea Otters entered service a year later and operated from land bases and carriers.

Once the Second World War was over, the Sea Otter was soon retired from RAF service although Fleet Air Arm examples remained in service until January 1952. Of 290 built, 141 served with the Royal Air Force.

Two versions were built – the amphibious Mk I that carried bombs and depth charges, and the Sea Otter ASR Mk II air-sea rescue version of which 40 were built.

The only surviving 'relic' of the type is a nose section of a Sea Otter, a piece of an ex-Royal Australian Navy machine now preserved in an Australian museum.

ABOVE: **Although the Sea Otter was all metal, the aircraft's wing and tail plane surfaces were fabric-covered. Note the small rudder beneath the tail, for additional control on water.**

Supermarine Sea Otter II

First flight: September 29, 1938

Power: One Bristol 855hp Mercury XXX radial piston engine

Armament: Two 0.303in machine-guns in dorsal position and one in the nose

Size: Wingspan – 14.02m/46ft
Length – 11.94m/39ft 2in
Height – 4.93m/16ft 2in
Wing area – 56.67m²/610sq ft

Weights: Empty – 3,087kg/6,805lb
Maximum take-off – 4,912kg/10,830lb

Performance: Maximum speed – 241kph/150mph
Ceiling – 4,877m/16,000ft
Range – 1,167km/725 miles
Climb – 265m/870ft per minute

Supermarine Walrus

The amphibian Walrus was designed in 1933 by the creator of the Spitfire, R.J. Mitchell, as an improved Supermarine Seagull, incorporating a pusher instead of a tractor propeller. The prototype was designated Seagull V (though was little like the earlier Seagulls that served with the Fleet Air Arm except in name) and was built as a private venture which became the production model for the Royal Australian Air Force, the type's first customer, who took the type into service in 1935. The aircraft were to be launched from warships either by catapult or craned into the sea for take-off, then craned back on board on return from reconnaissance or air-sea rescue missions. To save space on deck, the aircraft's wings could be folded on ship reducing its storage width to just 5.5m/17ft 11in.

The Seagull was the first amphibious aircraft with a full military load to be catapult launched so it was very strong. The Walrus was popular with its crews and had a reputation for its ability to absorb battle damage. It could also be looped.

When the type entered Fleet Air Arm service in 1936, it was renamed Walrus Mk I but was better known to its crews by the nickname 'shagbat'. It was in October 1941 that the type began its RAF career as an air-sea rescue aircraft.

The Walrus served widely during World War II in the rescue and reconnaissance roles, and in East Africa as an anti-submarine bomber aircraft fitted with ASV radar. At least five enemy submarines were sunk or damaged by the seemingly harmless Walrus during World War II.

The Walrus had an unusual cockpit arrangement in that the pilot's control column was not fixed in the normal manner but could be unplugged from sockets in the floor, one in front of the pilot and co-pilot positions. Crews often flew with just one control column then unplugged it and passed the column over while in flight. The type was retired from RAF service in April 1946.

A total of 765 Walruses including 26 Seagull Vs were built between 1936 and 1944. Only three Walruses/ Seagulls still exist – one each in the UK's Fleet Air Arm Museum and RAF Museum and a further example in the RAAF Museum in Australia.

ABOVE: **The Supermarine Walrus was a very welcome sight to many hundreds of downed airmen and sailors who found themselves in distress.**

Supermarine Walrus II		
First flight: June 21, 1933 (Seagull V prototype)		
Power: One 775hp Bristol Pegasus VI		
Armament: One 0.303in machine-gun in dorsal and nose position and up to 227kg/500lb of bombs or depth charges		
Size: Wingspan – 13.97m/45ft 10in		
Length – 11.45m/47ft 7in		
Height – 4.65m/15ft 3in		
Wing area – 56.67m²/610sq ft		
Weights: Empty – 2,223kg/4,900lb		
Maximum take-off – 3,266kg/7,200lb		
Performance: Maximum speed – 217kph/135mph		
Ceiling – 5,639m/18,500ft		
Range – 965km/600 miles		
Climb – 320m/1,050ft per minute		

LEFT: **An experimental Spitfire Mk IX floatplane intended for Pacific service but never used.**
ABOVE: **A Mk III Seafire. The Spitfire was not a natural carrier aircraft due to poor pilot visibility and the airframe's comparative weakness.**

Supermarine Seafire

The Supermarine Seafire (initially officially known as the Sea Spitfire) was a naval version of the legendary Spitfire developed mainly for aircraft carrier operations. The sea-going Spitfire differed from its land-based cousin by features including an arrester hook in the tail, carrier catapult attachments and, in later versions, folding wings. The Seafire was not an ideal carrier fighter – it had a short range and landings were particularly challenging for pilots – but its performance, particularly its fast climb, outweighed the shortcomings.

In 1938, with war looking likely, Supermarine proposed a specifically designed naval version of the Spitfire to the Admiralty who instead decided to order the Fairey Fulmar. Three years later in September 1941, and following some disagreements about production priorities between the Admiralty and the Air Ministry, the first order for 250 examples of the most up-to-date Spitfire versions (Mks VA and B) for

the Royal Navy was placed in September 1941, and were renamed Seafire IIs.

Spitfire landing gear, designed for steady, controlled touchdowns on land, frequently collapsed as they thumped down on decks, while bouncing arrester hooks could distort the aircraft's structure. More Seafires were written off by landing incidents than by enemy action.

More ex-RAF machines were converted to improved (although chronologically confusing) Seafire Mk IB standard with naval radios and a strengthened rear fuselage with arrester hooks and slinging points. The first carrier landing of a true Seafire took place on board HMS *Illustrious* on February 10, 1942.

The Seafire F III was the next major production version and began to enter service in November 1943. This was the first Seafire version with a folding wing for easier below-deck stowage. The FIII saw most of its action in the Indian Ocean

LEFT: **Despite the aircraft's shortcomings for carrier-borne operations, the Spitfire's short-range high performance plugged a gap in the Royal Navy fighter inventory until other types were available.**

with the Far Eastern Fleet and in the Pacific with the British Pacific Fleet. It was a Seafire III that became the first aircraft of the Fleet Air Arm to fly over Japan in the summer of 1945. The Mk F IIIs were soon replaced by the low-altitude Mk LIII version powered by the Merlin 55 M engine optimized for low level performance. Fighter reconnaissance versions also appeared armed with cameras as well as guns.

May 1945 saw the service introduction of the first Seafire version powered by the Rolls-Royce Griffon, the Seafire XV, designed from the outset with folding wings. Something of a hybrid, the XV combined the wing of the Seafire III with the fuselage of the Spitfire V and the engine, cowling and propeller of the Spitfire XII. Four Fleet Air Arm squadrons were equipped by this version at the end of World War II but it arrived too late to see action.

The first major combats involving Seafires were Operation 'Torch' in North Africa and Operation 'Husky' in Sicily. During Operation 'Torch' the first Seafire air-to-air victory was achieved by Sub Lt G.C. Baldwin. Operation 'Husky' well illustrates the fragility of the type as over 50 were lost in the first 48 hours in landing accidents.

Around D-Day the Seafire played a major gun-spotting role and subsequently supported the invasion advances. On the other side of the world, a Royal Navy Seafire claimed the last enemy aircraft to be shot down on the very day of the Japanese surrender in August 1945.

The Royal Canadian Navy bought the type as an export and French Seafires of Flotille 1F aboard the *Arromanches* saw action in the Indochina War in 1947–49. It was the ultimate version of the Seafire, the Mk 47, that saw action with the Royal Navy in Korea. The Mk 47s were able to carry three 227kg/500lb bombs or eight rockets and were 160kph/100mph faster and 2,268kg/5,000lb heavier than the first versions of the type.

The Seafire was withdrawn from front-line Fleet Air Arm service in 1951 but continued to serve with the Royal Navy Volunteer Reserve until late 1954.

TOP: **A very rare airworthy Seafire Mk XVII, SX336, is preserved in the UK and makes frequent air show appearances. This particular aircraft first flew in 1946 and was returned to the air 60 years later.**

ABOVE: **Royal Navy Seafire FR.47s saw a lot of action in the ground-attack role in the early stages of the Korean War.**

Supermarine Seafire LF Mk III

First flight: March 5, 1936 (Spitfire prototype)

Power: One Rolls-Royce 1,583hp Merlin 55M piston engine

Armament: Two 20mm cannon, four 0.303in machine-guns and provision for up to 227kg/500lb of bombs or eight 27kg/60lb rocket projectiles

Size: Wingspan – 11.22m/36ft 10in
Length – 9.11m/29ft 11in
Height – 3.02m/9ft 11in
Wing area – 21.46m²/231sq ft

Weights: Empty – 2,472kg/5,450lb
Maximum take-off – 3,900kg/8,600lb

Performance: Maximum speed – 549kph/341mph
Service ceiling – 9,754m/32,000ft
Range – 1,239km/770 miles
Climb – 990m/3,250ft per minute

ABOVE: **A Seafire immediately following a landing accident on a Royal Navy carrier. More of the naval development of the Spitfire was lost this way than to enemy action.**

LEFT: Pictured at a UK air show, this line-up of Corsairs show how many of the high-performance fighters are still preserved in flying condition.
ABOVE: A Royal Navy Corsair about to take off. The designers of the Corsair used the most powerful engine available to them at the time
BELOW: The 'Whistling Death' was the first Allied aircraft with the capability to halt the previously might Zero in combat.

Vought F4U Corsair

The Corsair was not only a great naval aircraft – it was undoubtedly one of the greatest ever fighters. Designers Igor Sikorsky and Rex Beisel used the most powerful engine – a 2,000hp Pratt & Whitney R-2800 Double Wasp – and the largest propeller ever fitted to a fighter aircraft. Accordingly it was no surprise when, in 1940, the prototype Corsair exceeded 640kph/400mph, the first American combat aircraft to do so. It was equipped with a variety of armament over its long career but the Corsair was originally designed to carry two wing and two fuselage guns. Six 0.5in Browning machine-guns became standard, carried in the outer section of the wings, which folded. Cannon and rockets were later added to the weapon options.

ABOVE: The silver XF4U-1 took to the air for the first time on May 29, 1940, at Stratford, with Vought-Sikorsky test pilot Lyman A. Bullard Jr at the controls.

However, despite going on to be one of the fastest and most powerful fighters of World War II, the Corsair was initially rejected by the US Navy who considered it unsuitable for carrier operations. Poor cockpit visibility and a tendency to bounce on landing meant that, in February 1943 over Guadalcanal, the US Marines Corps (USMC) got the first chance to use the formidable fighter in action but as a land-based aircraft. It swiftly established itself as an excellent combat aircraft and the first Allied fighter able to take on the Japanese Zero on equal terms. The Corsair so impressed the USMC that all Marine squadrons re-equipped with the type within six months of its debut. Marine Corsair pilot Major Gregory 'Pappy' Boyington became the Corps' highest scoring pilot, ending the war with a total of 28 victories.

By the end of 1943, the mighty bent-wing fighter, operating purely from land, had accounted for over 500 Japanese aircraft. Japanese troops nicknamed the type 'Whistling Death' as they came to fear the noise made by air rushing through the diving Corsair's cooler vents heralding a deadly attack. By the end of World War II the Corsair's total tally had increased to 2,140 enemy aircraft – an 11:1 'kill' ratio – destroyed in air combat with over 64,000 air combat and ground attack missions recorded.

The Corsair's first use as a carrier fighter was with Britain's Fleet Air Arm who had each of the aircraft's distinctive gull-wings clipped by around 20cm/8in to allow its stowage in the below-deck hangars on Royal Navy carriers. This debut, in April 1944, was an attack on the German battleship *Tirpitz*. The Corsair became the principal aircraft of the FAA in the Pacific and almost 2,000 were supplied to the Royal Navy and the Royal New Zealand Air Force. As FAA Corsair pilot Keith Quilter said, "In dogfights the Corsair could out-turn most contemporary aircraft and in a dive she could outrun anything."

The Corsair's outstanding performance led to extensive post-war use, notably in Korea where they flew 80 per cent of all US Navy and Marine close-support missions in the conflict's first year, 1950. Night-fighter versions were particularly successful during the conflict, and during daytime

engagements, the Corsair even engaged and destroyed Soviet-supplied MiG-15s, demonstrating along with the Hawker Sea Fury that the early jets hadn't quite left the older types behind and they were still a force to be reckoned with.

When production ceased in 1952, over 12,500 had been built giving the Corsair one of the longest US fighter production runs in history. The late F2G version was powered by the 3,000hp Pratt & Whitney R-4350 Wasp Major which was 50 per cent more powerful than the Corsair's original powerplant.

The Corsair continued to serve in the front line for a number of years and French naval pilots operated Corsairs from land bases during the anti-guerilla war against the Viet Minh in Indochina from 1952–54.

Many versions of the Corsair were built from the F4U-1 to the F4U-7. The aircraft designation differed when aircraft were produced by other manufacturers – for example, Brewster (F3A) and Goodyear (FG, F2G).

ABOVE: **Wings folded and being prepared for take-off, these Royal Navy Corsairs crowd the carrier deck. Note how much space is saved by the vertical wing-folding. The Royal Navy were the first to operate the Corsair from aircraft carriers, but the manufacturers of the aircraft had to clip the wings slightly so that they could operate from smaller British carriers.**

F4U-1 Corsair

First flight: May 29, 1940
Power: Pratt & Whitney 2,000hp R-2800-8 18-cylinder Double Wasp two-row air-cooled radial engine
Armament: Six 0.5in machine-guns with total of 2,350 rounds; C model had four M2 cannon
Size: Wingspan – 12.5m/41ft
　　Length – 10.15m/33ft 4in
　　Height – 4.9m/16ft 1in
　　Wing area – 29.17m^2/314sq ft
Weights: Empty – 4,074kg/8,982lb
　　Loaded – 6,350kg/14,000lb
Performance: Maximum speed – 671kph/417mph
　　Ceiling – 1,1247m/36,900ft
　　Range – 1,633km/1,015 miles
　　Climb – 881m/2,890ft per minute

BELOW: **The majority were configured as floatplanes and operated from convoys in the Atlantic and Indian Oceans. Many were also used for training in the West Indies.**

Vought-Sikorsky OS2U-3 Kingfisher

The Vought-Sikorsky OS2U Kingfisher, designed as a more versatile replacement for the O3U Corsair, was the US Navy's first catapult-launched monoplane observation floatplane. Although the aircraft was also built in tail-wheel undercarriage versions, it was mainly produced as a floatplane with one big central float and small stabilizing floats under each wing.

Despite having a comparatively low-power engine, this compact two-man aircraft served as an observation and artillery-spotting platform, anti-submarine aircraft and dive-bomber and also carried out vital rescue missions.

The first landplane and floatplane prototypes flew in March and May 1938 respectively and, following evaluation, the type was put into production in April 1940. The USS *Colorado* was the first US Navy ship to be equipped with OS2Us.

It was an OS2U that rescued US national hero Captain Eddie Rickenbacker when the B-17 in which he was flying had to ditch in the Pacific in 1942. Rickenbacker and two crewmembers were picked up but the over-laden aircraft was unable to take off. Instead the resourceful OS2U pilot taxied the aircraft on the ocean surface over 64km/40 miles to land. In 1944 an OS2U, flying from a battleship, landed in choppy seas to pick up ten downed pilots over a period of six hours, taxiing as far as 32km/20 miles to deliver them to an Allied submarine.

The Fleet Air Arm acquired a total of 100 OS2U-3s under Lend-Lease in mid-1942, designating them Kingfisher Is. These FAA machines were used as catapult-launched observation aircraft and as trainers.

Over 1,500 were built and in addition to US Navy and Royal Navy service, the type was also operated by the US Coast Guard and air arms of Chile, Argentina, Australia, Dominican Republic and Uruguay. Four OS2Us are known to survive today, all in the USA.

Vought-Sikorsky OS2U-3 Kingfisher

First flight: May 19, 1938 (floatplane prototype)
Power: One Pratt & Whitney 459hp Wasp Junior R-985-SB-3 engine
Armament: Two 0.3in machine-guns, one forward-firing, one on mount in rear cockpit plus up to 295kg/650lb of bombs under wings
Size: Wingspan – 10.95m/35ft 11in
 Length – 10.31m/33ft 10in
 Height – 4.61m/15ft 2in
 Wing area – 24.34m²/262sq ft
Weights: Empty – 1,870kg/4,123lb
 Maximum take-off – 2,722kg/6,000lb
Performance: Maximum speed – 264kph/164mph
 Ceiling – 3,960m/13,000ft
 Range – 1,296km/805 miles
 Climb – 3,048m/10,000ft in 29 minutes, 6 seconds

LEFT: **Although it was ultimately a poor combat aircraft, when it was conceived the aircraft was advanced for the time – a largely metal monoplane with a retractable undercarriage and folding wings.** ABOVE: **The Vindicator was known as the Chesapeake in Fleet Air Arm service, and was quickly deemed inferior to the torpedo-bomber types the British could already source.** BELOW: **The crews who trained on the unfortunate Vindicator must have been pleased to survive the experience and move on to aircraft more suited to the task of torpedo-bombing.**

Vought–Sikorsky SB2U Vindicator

The SB2U Vindicator was designed as a carrier-based reconnaissance aircraft/dive-bomber, and combined biplane technology with a monoplane layout configuration. Lacking power and therefore vulnerable, it was not a great success.

In the mid-1930s the US Navy were still hedging their bets on the question of monoplane versus biplane combat aircraft. In late 1934, Vought received a US Navy order for two prototype aircraft, one a monoplane and one a biplane but both built to meet the same requirement for a USN carrier-based scout bomber.

In testing, the XSB2U-1 monoplane proved superior and production began in October 1936. The SB2U-1 had folding outer wings, retractable landing gear, an all-metal structure covered in fabric and metal and an arrester hook for carrier operations. In theory, when it entered service in 1937 the SB2U-1 was a major step forward for the US Navy. However, the addition of essential combat equipment and armour added greatly to the weight thus affecting performance. Although obsolete by 1940, the type did see action in the Pacific (including the

Battle of Midway) with disastrous results – of the SB2Us in USN service some 30 per cent were lost in combat while a further 50 per cent suffered damage or destruction during operational training and carrier deck landing on Lake Michigan. Ironically the only surviving example, currently displayed at the US National Museum of Naval Aviation, was recovered from the bed of Lake Michigan and restored for display. By the end of 1942, US Navy SB2Us had largely been replaced by the Douglas SBD Dauntless.

Between May 1938 and July 1941, 169 SB2Us were produced. Britain's Fleet Air Arm received 50 examples, delivered between June and August 1941, but only one front-line unit, 811 Squadron, was equipped with the type. Named Chesapeake in British service, it proved to be inadequate for its intended torpedo-bomber role, in no small way due to the long take-off run required to get the underpowered aircraft to lift off a carrier deck.

In 1940, French export versions saw some action against invading German forces.

Vought-Sikorsky SB2U-1 Vindicator

First flight: January 4, 1936 (XSB2U-1 prototype)
Power: One Pratt & Whitney 825hp R-1535-96 piston engine
Armament: One fixed forward-firing 0.3in machine-gun and one 0.3in machine-gun in rear cockpit plus up to 454kg/1,000lb of bombs
Size: Wingspan – 12.8m/42ft
　　　Length – 10.36m/34ft
　　　Height – 3.12m/10ft 3in
　　　Wing area – 28.33m²/305sq ft
Weights: Empty – 2,121kg/4,676lb
　　　Maximum take-off – 3,301kg/7,278lb
Performance: Maximum speed – 402kph/250mph
　　　Ceiling – 8,352m/27,400ft
　　　Range – 1,615km/1,004 miles
　　　Climb – 457m/1,500ft per minute

Yokosuka D4Y Suisei

Yokosuka was the location for the Imperial Japanese Navy's First Naval Air Technical Arsenal which in 1938 began to design a carrier-based single-engine dive-bomber. Japan had a good relationship with Germany as both powers were rapidly expanding their military potential in distant parts of the world but with common potential enemies. Co-operation took many forms including some technology sharing.

Japan was allowed to buy one of the Germany's Heinkel He 118 prototypes, the V4, and the rights to develop the He 118 concept. During a test flight the German machine, powered by a Daimler-Benz DB 601Aa, achieved a level speed of 418kph/260mph and so impressed the Japanese Navy they immediately planned for a Japanese carrier-borne version of the He 118. The requirements for this type were laid out in the 1938 Japanese Navy Experimental Carrier Bomber requirement that included a level speed of 518kph/322mph, a range of

2,222km/1,381 miles without a bomb, and a range of 1,482km/921 miles with a bomb load of 250kg/551lb.

Headed by Masao Yamana, the Yokosuka design team created a single-engine, two-seat, mid-wing monoplane dive-bomber with a fully retractable 'taildragger' landing gear. With a wingspan similar to that of the Mitsubishi A6M, the Yokosuka machine did not need heavy, expensive wing-folding gear, thereby reducing maintenance needs too. Designated D4Y1 Suisei (Comet), the aircraft was unusual as it was one of few Japanese combat types to be powered by a liquid-cooled Aichi AE1 Atsuta piston engine, which was the Japanese licence-built derivative of the German Daimler Benz 601.

Although the basic configuration showed a resemblance to the Heinkel machine, the D4Y design was smaller, lighter, stronger and was altogether a more advanced design that benefited from the increasing understanding of aerodynamics.

ABOVE: **The very distinctive nose arrangement of the early D4Ys, reminiscent of a Junkers Ju 87 Stuka, was due to the use of licence-built versions of the German liquid-cooled piston engine. Note the telescope sight in front of the cockpit, for dive-bombing targeting.**

LEFT: **Ground crew await the instruction to remove chocks as this D4Y1 prepares for flight. Note the use of two underwing auxiliary fuel tanks to boost the aircraft's range.** ABOVE: **The D4Y was comparatively slow and was vulnerable to enemy fighters and anti-aircraft artillery.**

The aircraft's main weapon was a 500kg/1,102lb bomb carried internally. The first D4Y1 prototype made its maiden flight in December 1940, and was found to possess an excellent combination of high performance and good handling. Despite this promising start during dive-bombing trials, the wings demonstrated 'flutter', a high-frequency oscillation of the structure, which was sufficient to crack the wing spar. With the aircraft unfit for the task it was designed for, the pre-production version was instead switched to reconnaissance duties, due to its good speed, range and ceiling. The aircraft served in this role from autumn 1942 until the war's end as the D4Y1-C. The dedicated dive-bomber version – the D4Y1 fitted with catapult equipment to operate from smaller Japanese carriers – finally entered service in 1943. The latter version took part in the June 1944 air-sea engagements off the Marianas, becoming the victim in what US pilots named 'The Great Marianas Turkey Shoot'.

Although the Yokosuka dive-bomber generally displayed good performance, excellent range and manoeuvrability, all versions had insufficient armour protection for the crew, and the type's light construction was unable to take much battle damage. These were faults common to many Japanese combat aircraft. The type did not fare well against high-performance Allied fighters, and many fell to their guns – partly due to the lack of self-sealing fuel tanks.

It was the D4Y of Rear Admiral Arima, commanding officer of 26th Koku Sentai, that carried out what is believed to be the first planned suicide kamikaze mission when it flew into the carrier USS *Franklin* on October 15, 1944.

A total of 2,038 were built. The D4Y2 was given a more powerful engine, while the D4Y4 was a bomber version that carried one 800kg/1,764lb bomb and was used in kamikaze missions. The Allied codename allocated to all versions was 'Judy'.

ABOVE: **The D4Y3 was an improved D4Y2 powered by a 1,560hp Mitsubishi radial engine. This required a remodelling of the nose and made the aircraft look very different to the earlier in-line engined versions.**

Yokosuka D4Y2

First flight: November, 1940
Power: One Aichi 1,400hp Atsuta 32 piston engine
Armament: Two 7.7mm forward-firing machine-guns and one 7.92mm rear-firing machine-gun plus up to 800kg/1,763lb of bombs
Size: Wingspan –11.5m/37ft 8.75in
Length –10.22m/33ft 6.25in
Height – 3.74m/12ft 3.25in
Wing area – 23.6m²/254sq ft
Weights: Empty – 2,440kg/5,379lb
Maximum take-off – 4,250kg/9,370lb
Performance: Maximum speed – 550kph/342mph
Service ceiling – 10,700m/35,105ft
Range – 1,465km/910 miles
Climb – 820m/2,700ft per minute

Directory of Modern Naval Aircraft

1945 to the Present Day

Since the end of World War II, naval aviation development has been dominated by high-performance jet-powered carrier-borne aircraft. Jets soon replaced the piston-powered fighters in the post-war front line. The wartime realization that the best naval aircraft were those developed specifically for carrier operations was embraced by aircraft designers.

The fast 'Top Gun' jet-engined types are not, however, the only naval aircraft. Carrier-borne AEW aircraft like the Gannet and Tracker were developed as were incredibly important aircraft such as the Grumman Intruder. Technological developments have seen the introduction, albeit limited, of Vertical/Short Take-Off and Landing (V/STOL) aircraft, namely the Harrier family and the Yak-38. Helicopters have grown in their importance in the period while the large flying boat has all but died out with a few notable exceptions, including the ShinMaywa SS-2.

The next generation of true carrier aircraft will be entering large-scale service soon and they will replace the aircraft developed to fight in the Cold War. The very different world stage demands a different response from the world's naval air arms and the new crop of aircraft like the Lockheed Martin Lightning II will put even venerable types like the F-14 Tomcat in the shade with their integrated applications of the latest technologies.

LEFT: **For many, the definitive modern naval aircraft is the Grumman F-14 Tomcat. However, this high-performance aircraft was just one of many and varied types – both fixed and rotary wing – that comprised late 20th-century naval air power.**

Agusta Westland EH 101 Merlin

The Merlin, one of the world's most capable medium-sized helicopters, resulted from a 1977 Naval Staff requirement describing a new ASW helicopter needed to replace the Westland Sea King in service with the Royal Navy. By late 1977 Westland started work on design studies to meet this requirement. At the same time in Italy, the Italian Navy and Italian helicopter company Agusta were considering the replacement of the Agusta-built Sea Kings then in service. Inter-company discussions led to a joint venture agreement between the companies and the countries. In June 1980 a joint company, European Helicopter Industries (EHI), was set up to manage the project, by then designated the EH 101.

Manufacture of the first parts began in March 1985 at Yeovil and at Cascina Costa near Milan. The first prototype, PP1 (British military serial ZF641), was rolled out at Yeovil on April 7, 1987, and after exhaustive ground testing, first flew on October 9, 1987. The second pre-production example, PP2, flew soon after in Italy on November 26, 1987. Assembly of the Merlin began in early 1995, and the first production example flew on December 6, 1995. The Royal Navy received its first fully operational Merlin HM.1 on May 27, 1997, for trials.

The first of 22 examples for the RAF left the factory in November 1999. Designated Merlin HC.3 and sharing the same RTM.322 engines as the Royal Navy examples, the RAF Merlin is a utility version. The Italian Navy received its first production EH 101 in January 2001.

The Merlin HM Mk 1 has been in service with the Royal Navy, its main operator, since 1998 and although primarily employed as an anti-submarine helicopter, the Merlin can also participate in anti-surface warfare. The Merlin is designed to operate from both large and small ship flight decks, in severe weather and high sea states, by day or night. Overall

ABOVE: **A Royal Navy Merlin in flight. Despite a protracted development programme, the EH 101 is now considered to be one of the world's most capable medium-sized helicopters, and export orders are increasing.**
LEFT: **Perhaps the greatest export achievement was the adoption of a US-built version, the VH-71, as the 'Marine One' Presidential Helicopter Replacement programme aircraft.**

dimensions are less than those of a Sea King, and when embarked at sea, British examples can operate primarily from any ship with a capable flight deck.

Powered by three Rolls-Royce/Turbomeca gas turbines, the rugged, crashworthy airframe is of modular construction and is composed mainly of conventional aluminium-alloy construction with some composite materials in the rear fuselage and tail section. The naval version has powered main rotor blade folding and tail rotor pylon folding. All versions can fly in severe icing and incorporate triple hydraulic systems, three independent alternators and a gas turbine auxiliary power unit.

The aircraft and its mission system are managed by two computers, linked by dual data buses. All crew stations can access the management computers and can operate the tactical displays, fed by the Blue Kestrel radar. Navigation is state of the art with ring laser gyros, inertial reference systems GPS, Doppler and radar altimeters. The avionics include a digital flight control system, a glass cockpit with colour Multi-Function Displays and a comprehensive navigation suite for

RIGHT: **The Merlin HM Mk 1 has been in service with the Royal Navy since 1998. There are five Squadrons, 814 820, 829, 824 and 700, and all are based at the Royal Naval Air Station Culdrose in Cornwall when disembarked.**

FAR RIGHT: **The Canadian Air Force's only dedicated search-and-rescue (SAR) helicopter is the CH-149 Cormorant variant of the Merlin.**

all-weather navigation and automatic flight. Royal Navy Merlins have the Ferranti/Thomson-CSF dipping sonar.

The Merlin's operational debut came in early 2003 when four aircraft from 814 NAS embarked aboard RFA *Fort Victoria* were deployed into the northern Gulf as part of the UK Amphibious Task Group for Operation 'Iraqi Freedom'. With no submarine threat, the helicopters were used in an anti-surface warfare role protecting against swarm attacks by small, fast inshore attack craft. With no ASW requirement, the aircraft's Active Dipping Sonar (ADS) was removed to free up space in the cabin for an extra eight seats to be fitted plus racks for four stretchers. A 7.62mm general-purpose machine-gun was also fitted in the forward starboard window, and a semi-automatic cargo release unit for loading and vertical replenishment or air drops.

As well as Britain and Italy, naval Merlins are also operated by Japan, Portugal and Canada.

ABOVE: **The EH 101 is equipped with chaff and flare dispensers, directed infrared countermeasures infrared jammers, missile approach warners, and a laser detection and warning system.** BELOW LEFT: **It is rumoured that the EH 101 designation was a typing error that stuck as the aircraft was to be called EHI-01.**

Agusta Westland Merlin HM.1

First flight: October 9, 1987 (prototype)
Power: Three Rolls-Royce/Turbomeca 2,312shp RTM.322-01 turboshafts
Armament: Two hard points, one on each side of the fuselage, can carry up to 960kg/2,116lb of homing torpedoes, sonobuoy dispensers or anti-ship missiles
Size: Rotor diameter – 18.59m/61ft
  Length – 22.81m/74ft 10in
  Height – 6.65m/21ft 10in
Weights: Empty – 10,500kg/23,149lb
  Maximum take-off –14,600kg/32,188lb
Performance: Maximum speed – 309kph/192mph
  Service ceiling – 4,575m/15,000ft
  Range – 925km/574 miles
  Climb – 612m/2,008ft per minute

Armstrong Whitworth (Hawker) Sea Hawk

The graceful Sea Hawk is remarkable for three reasons – it was Hawker's first jet fighter, the first standard jet fighter of Britain's Fleet Air Arm and it remained in front-line service long after swept-wing fighters equipped navies elsewhere. Its layout was also unusual in that the seemingly twin-engined type in fact had a single jet pipe bifurcated (split) to feed two exhaust ducts, one at each trailing edge wing root. The leading edge wing roots included the two corresponding air intakes.

The Sea Hawk was derived from the Hawker P.1040, an aircraft built speculatively by the company, which flew in September 1947 and was proposed as a new fighter for both the Royal Navy and the Royal Air Force. Only the Navy placed orders for the Sea Hawk and after only building 35 production Sea Hawk fighters, Hawker transferred production to Armstrong Whitworth, hence the occasional confusion over the Sea Hawk manufacturer's identity. As a design the Sea Hawk certainly looked right, coming from the same team that designed the Hurricane and, later, the Hunter.

The first Royal Navy Sea Hawk squadron, No.806, formed in March 1953 carrying its distinctive ace of diamonds logo on its Sea Hawk Mk 1s. Later that year, one of the squadron's Sea

ABOVE: The Royal Navy Historic Flight's Sea Hawk WV908 was built in late 1954 as an FGA.4 variant and 'joined' the Royal Navy in February 1955. After service with 807 Squadron and then 898 Squadron it embarked on HMS *Ark Royal* and HMS *Bulwark*. BELOW LEFT: Sea Hawks of No.806 NAS.

Hawks, flown by Lieutenant Commander Chilton on to USS *Antietam,* became the first British aircraft to land on a fully angled carrier deck. In February the following year, 806 embarked on HMS *Eagle.* The Mk 2, of which 40 examples were built, had fully powered aileron controls but shared the same Rolls-Royce Nene 101 engine as the Mk 1.

The most widely used Sea Hawk version was the Mk 3 fighter bomber, capable of carrying considerable amounts of ordnance (two 227kg/500lb bombs or mines) under its strengthened wings. The 97 FGA Mk 4 versions built were optimized for the close air support role and could carry four 227kg/500lb bombs or up to sixteen 3in/76mm rocket projectiles with 27kg/60lb warheads. This change in usage was due to the realization that the Sea Hawk's performance could not match that of potential enemies in air-to-air combat. Re-engined (with the 5,200lb thrust Nene 103), Mks 3 and 4 became Mks 5 and 6 respectively. A further 86 Mk 6s were newly produced from the factory.

That said, the Fleet Air Arm's Sea Hawks did see action in the ground-attack role during the 1956 Suez Crisis. On the morning of November 1, 1956, the first Anglo-French carrier-launched attacks against Egyptian airfields began with 40 Royal Navy Sea Hawks and Sea Venoms launched from British carriers. Sea Hawks from HMS *Eagle, Albion* and *Bulwark* all saw action during the politically disastrous 'crisis' during which two were shot down, but the type was proven as a combat-capable ground-attack aircraft.

LEFT: **The straight-winged Sea Hawk flew on in front-line service after being 'reinvented' as a fighter-bomber.** ABOVE: **This Sea Hawk was built as an F.1 by Hawker. Note the folded wings and the auxiliary fuel tanks.**

The type continued in front-line FAA service until 1960, but some continued in second-line roles until 1969. Some ex-Royal Navy aircraft were supplied to the Royal Australian and Canadian navies, but the biggest export customers were the German naval air arm, the Netherlands and the Indian Navy. Dutch aircraft were equipped to carry an early version of the Sidewinder air-to-air missile until their phasing-out in 1964. German Sea Hawks operated exclusively from land bases in the air defence role until the mid-1960s. The Indian Navy's Sea Hawks saw action in the war with Pakistan in 1971 and soldiered on, remarkably, into the mid-1980s when they were replaced by Sea Harriers. The Royal Navy's Historic Flight maintains a lone Sea Hawk FGA Mk 4 in airworthy condition that is much in demand at UK air shows.

ABOVE RIGHT: **VP413 was one of three Hawker P.1040 Sea Hawk prototypes used to test the design and its military potential.** ABOVE: **The sole flying Sea Hawk shows the type's clean lines. Note the arrester hook and the excellent view from the cockpit, essential for deck landings.**

Armstrong Whitworth (Hawker) Sea Hawk F. Mk 1

First flight: September 2, 1947 (P.1040)
Power: Rolls-Royce 2,268kg/5,000lb thrust Nene 101 turbojet
Armament: Four 20mm Hispano cannon beneath cockpit floor
Size: Wingspan – 11.89m/39ft
Length – 12.08m/39ft 8in
Height – 2.64m/8ft 8in
Wing area – 25.83m²/278sq ft
Weights: Empty – 4,173kg/9,200lb
Maximum take-off – 7,348kg/16,200lb
Performance: Maximum speed – 901kph/560mph
Ceiling – 13,170m/43,200ft
Range – 1,191km/740 miles
Climb – 10,675m/35,000ft in 12 minutes, 5 seconds

LEFT: Initially known as the FRS.2, the Sea Harrier FA.2 first flew in 1988 and became the Fleet Air Arm's carrier-borne air defence fighter either as new build or converted from the earlier version.
ABOVE: The FA.2 was preceded by the FRS.1, an example of which is pictured during the 1982 Falklands War.

BAE SYSTEMS Harrier/Sea Harrier

The best illustration of British innovation in the field of aircraft design is the Harrier and Sea Harrier. This truly remarkable aircraft, constantly improved and updated since its first hovering flight in October 1960, is still the only single-engined Vertical or Short Take-Off and Landing (V/STOL) in service. It enables military planners to wield air power without the need for airfields.

During the Cold War it was obvious that the West's military airfields would have been attacked very early in any offensive. Dispersal of aircraft and equipment was one response to this – the other was the Harrier with its ability to operate from any small piece of flat ground. The Harrier is equally at home operating from a supermarket car park or woodland clearing as it is from conventional airfields. The fact that a jet plane can fly straight up with no need for forward movement still leaves spectators stunned almost five decades after the prototype carried out its first uncertain and tethered hover.

The Harrier can take off and land vertically by the pilot selecting an 80 degree nozzle angle and applying full power.

ABOVE: When a mission dictated, the Sea Harrier could have a bolt-on non-retracting inflight refuelling probe fitted.

At 15–30m/50–100ft altitude, the nozzles are gradually directed rearwards until conventional wingborne flight is achieved. The key to the Harrier's vertical take-off lies with the vectored thrust from the Harrier's Pegasus engine, directed by four jet nozzles controlled by a selector lever next to the throttle in the cockpit. The nozzles swivel as one, directing thrust from directly to the rear to just forward of vertical. While hovering or flying at very low speeds, the aircraft is controlled in all lanes of movement by reaction control jets located in the nose, wing and tail. These jets are operated by the Harrier's conventional rudder pedals and control column.

The Harrier's agility is legendary and it is able to make very tight turns by using the nozzles. In air combat the nozzles can be used to rapidly decelerate the aircraft so that an enemy aircraft, previously on the Harrier's tail, shoots by unable to stop, thus becoming the Harrier's prey instead.

The Harrier GR.1 first entered squadron service with the RAF in October, 1969, and early in the Harrier's operational life, the US Marine Corps expressed an interest in the aircraft, leading to more than 100 being built as the AV-8A by McDonnell Douglas in the US. The other customer for the early Harrier was the Spanish Navy, who ordered the US-built AV-8A and subsequently sold some of the aircraft on to the Thai Navy in 1996.

The Harrier's V/STOL capability was not lost on naval strategists and the Sea Harrier's origins go back to February 1963 when an early version of the Harrier landed on HMS *Ark Royal* at sea. The Royal Navy ordered a maritime version in 1975 and the Sea Harrier FRS. Mk 1 flew for the first time in August, 1978. This aircraft was similar to the Harrier GR.3 but had a completely redesigned front fuselage, different avionics and was powered by a special version of the Pegasus engine (104) with improved corrosion resistance. Examples of this version were exported to the Indian Navy as FRS.51s.

LEFT: **Three stages of Sea Harrier training. The two-seat Hunter (bottom) trained in the use of the Blue Fox radar, while the two-seat Sea Harrier trainer (top) helped pilots transition to the single-seat Sea Harrier.** ABOVE: **Sidewinder-armed FRS.1s.**

The Sea Harrier FA.2 was a mid-life upgrade of the FRS.1 with changes to the airframe, armament, avionics, radar and cockpit. The FA.2 was the first European fighter to be equipped with the AIM-120 AMRAAM air-to-air missile. The Royal Navy's FA.2s made their combat debut in August, 1994, over Bosnia, operated by No.899 Squadron from the deck of HMS *Invincible* but early versions of the Sea Harrier had already been in action with the Fleet Air Arm 12 years earlier. In 1982 Britain's task force sailed south on its 12,872km/8,000-mile journey to retake the Falkland Islands but it faced serious opposition. Against considerable odds, the combined Harrier force of RAF and Fleet Air Arm men and machines flew a total of 1,850 missions and destroyed 32 Argentine aircraft, 23 of them in air combat.

Two-seat trainer versions of all marks of Harrier and Sea Harrier have been produced. In 1998, Britain's Strategic Defence Review proposed Joint Force Harrier (JFH), which called for the management and capabilities of the RN Sea Harrier and RAF Harrier forces to be brought together. In 2001, the decision was taken to decommission the FA.2 Sea Harrier and direct available funding into upgrading the Harrier GR7. Accordingly, on March 28, 2006, a ceremony was held at RNAS Yeovilton to mark the Royal Navy Sea Harrier FA.2's withdrawal from service. In its role as part of JFH, the RAF's Harrier GR7 force remains ready to deploy anywhere in the world, in both sea- and land-based operations.

ABOVE: **Joint Force Harrier (JFH) RAF aircraft are able to operate from Royal Navy ships at short notice for rapid deployment anywhere the Royal Navy can reach.**

BAE SYSTEMS
Sea Harrier FA.2

First flight: September 19, 1988 (FA.2)
Power: Rolls-Royce 9,765kg/21,500lb thrust Pegasus 106 turbofan
Armament: Four AIM-120 air-to-air missiles or two AIM-120s and four AIM-9 Sidewinders; two 30mm Aden cannon can also be carried on underfuselage stations, as well as up to 2,270kg/5,000lb of bombs, rockets and anti-ship missiles
Size: Wingspan – 7.7m/25ft 3in
Length – 14.17m/46ft 6in
Height – 3.71m/12ft 2in
Wing area – 18.7m²/201sq ft
Weights: Empty – 6,374kg/14,052lb
Maximum take-off – 11,880kg/26,200lb
Performance: Maximum speed – 1,185kph/736mph
Ceiling – 15,540m/51,000ft
Range – 1,287km/800 miles
Climb – 15,240m/50,000ft per minute at VTOL weight

Beriev A-40/Be-42 Albatross

The Beriev A-40 and Be-42 (search-and-rescue variant) Albatross, designed to replace the Be-12 and Il-38 in maritime patrol and ASW roles, is the largest amphibious aircraft ever built. Although design work on the Albatross (NATO codename 'Mermaid') began in 1983, it was not known to the West until 1988, when the United States announced that one of their spy satellites had taken photos of a large jet-powered amphibian under development in Russia. The Albatross had, in fact, first flown in December 1986, but its first public appearance was not until Moscow's 1989 Soviet Aviation Day Display. The type entered service in limited numbers in 1990, providing access to remote areas in the east of the former Soviet Union, transporting replacement personnel, carrying out anti-submarine operations and Search-And-Rescue (SAR) missions.

The Albatross is a striking aircraft with high, slightly swept dihedral wings and slender fuselage, while booster jet engines are faired in beneath the two main large turbofan engines placed over the wing. Floats are attached at the very end of the wings by short pylons, while the large inflight refuelling probe atop the nose and the high 'T' tail are also key features. The

TOP: **This excellent head-on study of the A-40 shows the engines set high and towards the rear of the wing to protect them from water ingestion. This example has its undercarriage deployed and is taxiing on to dry land.** ABOVE: **Note the rudder at the base of the tail for water taxiing, and the large refuelling probe on the top of the nose.**

take-off run for this vast aircraft is 1,000m/3,281ft on land and 2,000m/6,562ft on water while the landing run on land is 700m/2,297ft and 900m/2,953ft on water. The aircraft had a standard crew of eight consisting of two pilots, a flight engineer, radio operator, navigator and three observers.

The type's ability to land in 2m/6ft swells led to the development of the Be-42 SAR version, designed to take up to 54 survivors of an incident at sea. Equipment included life-rafts, powerboats and a range of specialist medical equipment while the aircraft was also equipped with infrared sensors and a searchlight to find victims in the water.

The Albatross secured over 140 performance records very early in its 1986 testing flights – for example, it had the ability to lift 10 tons of cargo to 3,000m/9,843ft in just 3 minutes. Despite

ABOVE: **The smaller Be-200 was derived from the A-40 and retained the same high tail and high-set engine configuration as the Albatross.**

this, the type has only been produced in small numbers to date because it was entering production as the former Soviet Union was collapsing.

Nervertheless, the aircraft represented a potent anti-submarine weapon system. It can fly far out to sea, perhaps 2,000km/1,250 miles, at high speed, find and attack an enemy sub using depth charges, then land on the water to listen for the enemy craft using a barrage of electronic aids and sensors. The aircraft's endurance and inflight refuelling ability meant it could track a target for days.

The Beriev Be-200, derived from the A-40, is a smaller twin-engine amphibious aircraft available in transport, passenger-carrying, fire-fighting, patrol and search-and-rescue versions. South Korea has expressed interest in a maritime patrol version of this Albatross derivative.

TOP: **The first prototype. Note the aircraft's distinctive planing bottom, very large radome and very long trailing-edge flaps.** ABOVE: **Coming in to land. Note the location of the extended undercarriage, the split rudder and the all-moving tailplane.** BELOW LEFT: **The fillet just forward of the fin housed the aircraft's self-defence chaff and flare dispensers. The port main engine is positioned immediately above the port booster jet.**

Beriev A-40

First flight: December 1986
Power: Two Aviadvigatel 12,016kg/26,455lb thrust D-30KPV turbofans and two RKBM 2,502kg/5,510lb thrust RD-60K booster turbojets
Armament: 6,500kg/14,330lb of bombs, torpedoes or mines carried in internal weapons bay
Size: Wingspan – 41.62m/136ft 7in
Length – 38.92m/127ft 8in
Height – 11.07m/36ft 4in
Wing area – 200m²/2,152sq ft
Weights: Maximum take-off – 86,000kg/189,595lb
Performance: Maximum speed – 760kph/472mph
Ceiling – 9,706m/31,825ft
Range – 5,500km/3,416 miles
Climb – 915m/3,000ft per minute

Beriev Be-12

ABOVE: In addition to its military roles the Be-12 has been developed for a number of other uses including water bombing. Two aircraft were converted to the fire-bomber role, designated Be-12P (*Protivopozarnyi* – Fire protection).

The amphibious twin-engine Beriev Be-12 (NATO codename 'Mail') was one of two large flying boats, previously unknown to the West, that first appeared at Moscow's Soviet Aviation Day flypast of 1961. While Beriev's swept-wing, jet-powered Be-10 attracted a great deal of attention, the turboprop-powered Be-12 drew little. Western analysts believed it to be a one-off experimental turboprop version of the earlier piston-powered Be-6 that first flew in 1949. The Be-12 was in fact a replacement for the Be-6 although it shared the earlier type's twin tails and gull wing – this latter feature led to its name of 'Tchaika' (Seagull) and was necessary to keep the engines and propellers as far as possible from the damaging waves and salt water. The Be-12 went on to become the standard equipment of the Soviet coastal anti-submarine force, entering service in 1964, while the Be-10 was never seen in public again. Over four decades on, the Be-12 was still in service around Russia's coasts, and had earned a reputation for being tough and versatile.

In the late 1950s, the US began development of the first generation Polaris nuclear-missile submarines. Due to the missile's range and accuracy limitations, the launch submarine had to be fairly close to the target country's coastline. In response to this threat, the AV-MF (*Aviatsiya Voenno-Morskovo Flota* – Soviet Naval Air Force) issued a 1956 requirement for an aircraft that could detect and kill enemy nuclear-missile submarines in USSR coastal waters.

The aircraft was developed on the assumption that any threat would first be picked up by shipborne or land-based detection systems and give the search aircraft a fairly accurate location which would then be thoroughly scrutinized by the aircraft's short-range radar, Magnetic Anomaly Detection (MAD) probe and sonobouys. An attack against a 'bogey' would then

LEFT: An excellent study of a Be-12 showing the distinctive glazed nose, the start of the planing bottom and the large radome. ABOVE: A classic Cold War photo taken from a NATO aircraft. If the Cold War had heated up, the Be-12 would have played a key role in reducing the threat from enemy Polaris submarines.

take place, usually in co-operation with surface ships. In contrast, by this time, Western naval air forces were starting to phase out flying boats for maritime patrol duties and were instead turning to long-range landplane types such as the Avro Shackleton and Lockheed P-3 Orion. Soviet plans for high-performance amphibian aircraft in this role had to be shelved when the Be-10 was found to have been built for performance and not its military capability. The Be-10 was cancelled and Tupolev Tu-16 'Badger' bombers were instead adapted for the naval role. However, the Be-12 was retained as its capabilities offered the Soviets true flexibility when policing their home waters.

Be-12s were developed with a weapons bay in the rear hull, as well as external wing pylons for carrying ordnance. Although the first prototype retained the retractable 'dustbin' search radar used on the Be-6, later aircraft had a prominent nose search radar in place of the 'dustbin'. With long endurance and the ability to take over many other roles, the Be-12 was approved for AV-MF service.

Production started in 1963 and continued for a decade during which time 143 aircraft, including development machines, were built. The Be-12 officially entered service with the AV-MF in spring 1964 with the primary role of ASW patrol, operating some 500km/310 miles from shore. By 1967 the Be-12 had replaced the Be-6 entirely for front-line duties and then was used for other duties including coastal surveillance, multi-sensor reconnaissance, anti-shipping patrol, photographic survey, naval co-operation, transport, and search-and-rescue. Over the years, the Be-12 has gained no fewer than 44 aviation world records for its class for time to altitude, speed and payload.

In military service the Be-12's avionics and surveillance was upgraded a number of times to maintain its viability in dealing with the ever-evolving Cold War threat from the West. From 1970, as the US Polaris submarines evolved and could launch

ABOVE: **This photograph shows many of the Be-12s distinguishing features, including the inverted gull wing, twin-fin tailplane and hull.** BELOW: **The name 'Tchaika' (Seagull) came from the aircraft's wing configuration, which allowed engines and propellers to remain far from the water surface, minimizing the danger of water ingestion damage and corrosion. The body of the aircraft housed a weapons bay aft of the hull step.**

from a much greater distance, the coastal ASW patrol role of the Be-12 declined and the type took on more secondary roles. In 1972, some were converted for the high-speed Search and Rescue role, designated Be-12PS. Other roles included fishery protection, transport, mapping and survey, and whaling patrol.

During its career, the Be-12 served with all four of the Soviet Fleet's Naval Aviation forces – Pacific, Northern, Black Sea and Baltic – equipping up to 12 squadrons of 8 aircraft each, as well as a number of independent squadrons. By 2005, the Russian Navy were still operating only 12 Be-12s, but the type is expected to fly on for the foreseeable future.

ABOVE: **Other weapons can be carried on four underwing pylons. The front radome holds a search radar, integrated with a rear-mounted MAD that searched for submarines. The aircraft had a crew of five.**

Beriev Be-12

First flight: October 18, 1960 (prototype)

Power: Two 5,180shp ZMDB Progress Al-20DK turboprop engines

Armament: Up to 3,000kg/6,614lb of depth charges and sonobuoys in internal weapons bay plus mines, bombs, anti-shipping missiles, torpedoes or rockets on underwing hard points

Size: Wingspan – 29.84m/97ft 11in
Length – 30.11m/98ft 9in
Height – 7.94m/26ft 1in
Wing area – 99m²/1,065sq ft

Weights: Empty – 24,000kg/52,910lb
Maximum take-off – 29,500kg/65,040lb

Performance: Maximum speed – 530kph/330mph
Ceiling – 8,000m/26,250ft
Range – 3,300km/2,051 miles
Climb – 912m/2,990ft per minute

LEFT: **An RAF Buccaneer S.2 with its Gulf War nose art. The last RAF front-line Buccaneers were retired in March 1994.** ABOVE: **The Royal Aircraft Establishment at Farnborough operated a number of 'Buccs' as trials aircraft in this distinctive 'raspberry ripple' paint scheme.** BELOW: **This Buccaneer S.2B was one of the Fleet Air Arm aircraft that passed into Royal Air Force use. Note the catapult launch strop falling away from the aircraft. Strop catchers were introduced on HMS *Ark Royal*'s catapults to retrieve the strops for re-use.**

Blackburn Buccaneer

The Buccaneer was the last all-British bomber aircraft design and, in its day, it was the most advanced high-speed low-level strike aircraft in the world. It had its origins in the July 1953 Naval Staff requirement N.A.39, which called for a long-range carrier-borne transonic strike aircraft capable of carrying a nuclear weapon beneath enemy radar cover and attacking enemy shipping or ports.

Blackburn's N.A.39 response, the B-103, was the successful contender and the development contract was awarded in 1955 – the first of 20 pre-production aircraft took to the air on April 30, 1958, and also appeared at that year's Farnborough air show. The B-103 prototype was powered by 3,175kg/7,000lb thrust Gyron turbojets, not the much more powerful Spey of later models. The carrier aircraft elements of the design, such as folding wings, folding nose catapult fittings and arrester hook, were introduced from the fourth aircraft onwards.

The aerodynamically advanced aircraft incorporated many innovations, including a rotary bomb bay door (intended to avoid the drag of conventional bomb bay doors and weapons carried beneath the aircraft) and a vertically-split tail cone which opened to act as airbrakes. The aircraft also had a cutting-edge boundary layer control system in which air from the engines was forced through slits on the wings' leading edges, producing much more lift than that wing would normally give. Increasing the wings' efficiency meant the aircraft could land at lower speed and carry more ordnance – perfect for carrier operations.

The Miniature Detonating Cord (MDC), now standard on most British fast jets, which shatters the cockpit canopy prior to ejection, was pioneered on this Blackburn design. It was actually developed to aid escape in the event of underwater ejection.

Royal Navy carrier trials began in January 1960, and the first B-103 deck landing took place on HMS *Victorious* on the 19th

of the month. Having given the aircraft the name Buccaneer in 1960, the Navy took delivery of the first production version, the S.1, in July 1962. HMS *Ark Royal* sailed with the first operational Buccaneer squadron, No.801, and its anti-flash white (for protection against the nuclear flash of the weapons it used) Buccaneers only six months later in January 1963. The Cold War was at one of its chilliest phases and Britain wanted nuclear-capable aircraft in service as soon as possible.

The S.1 was soon shown to be under-powered and in some conditions the Gyrons could barely lift a loaded Buccaneer off the deck within safety margins. Consequently, Fleet Air Arm Scimitars fitted with inflight refuelling equipment were detailed to refuel the partly fuelled and therefore lighter Buccaneers shortly after they left the deck. Forty S.1s were built before production switched to the next mark. The improved S.2 was the principal production version (84 built) and had a greater range than the earlier version thanks to the more powerful but less thirsty Spey engines. Service S.2s are most easily recognized by the fixed refuelling probe on the nose forward of the cockpit. A retractable refuelling probe proved problematic so instead a fixed probe was introduced, marring the Buccaneer's otherwise clean lines.

The S.2s served in the Royal Navy's front line from January 1967 until the last S.2s left the deck of the *Ark Royal* in November 1978. The Buccaneer's career was, however, far from over as the first of almost 90 aircraft had begun service with the Royal Air Force in October 1969, filling the gap in the RAF inventory left by the scrapping of TSR.2 and the cancellation of the intended F-111 purchase for the RAF. Of the RAF Buccaneers, 26 were new-build, while a further 62 Royal Navy examples were gradually transferred into RAF service. As well as retaining a nuclear strike capability, Buccaneers were also tasked with anti-shipping missions from land bases. RAF Germany, right in the nuclear front line, first welcomed No.15 Squadron's Buccaneers early in 1971. Tornados began to replace the Germany Buccaneers in 1983, but two squadrons tasked with maritime strike remained in service in Scotland. In 1991 some of these aircraft were 'called up' for service in the first Gulf War, where they acted as laser designators for laser-guided bombs dropped by Tornados. To give it even longer range for these special missions, the 'Bucc' was fitted with a 2000-litre/440-gallon fuel tank carried in the bomb bay.

TOP: **The Buccaneer gave the Royal Navy a powerful nuclear punch during some of the most tense years of the Cold War. Note the fixed refuelling probe on these FAA S.2s.** ABOVE: **The Buccaneer's wings were hinged to fold up to 120 degrees.** BELOW: **A Buccaneer S.1, arrester hook deployed, prepares to catch the wire. The paint scheme is extra-dark sea grey on the upper surfaces and anti-flash gloss white on the undersides. Note the tail airbrakes.**

Blackburn Buccaneer S.2

First flight: April 30, 1958 (B-103 prototype)
Power: Two Rolls-Royce 5,035kg/11,100lb thrust Rolls-Royce Spey 101 turbofans
Armament: One nuclear bomb or four 454kg/1,000lb conventional bombs carried internally
Size: Wingspan – 13.41m/44ft
Length – 19.33m/63ft 5in
Height – 4.95m/16ft 3in
Wing area – 47.82m²/515sq ft
Weights: Empty –13,608kg/30,000lb
Maximum take-off – 28,123kg/62,000lb
Performance: Maximum speed – 1,038kph/645mph
Ceiling – 12,190m/40,000ft plus
Range – 3,700km/2,300 miles
Climb – 9,144m/30,000ft in 2 minutes

LEFT: **A heavily laden F/A-18 of VMFA-323 Marine Fighter Attack Squadron 323. Note the large centreline auxiliary fuel tank.** ABOVE: **The F/A-18 pilot has one of the world's most versatile and high-performance military aircraft under his or her control. Note the excellent all-round visibility from the 'bubble' cockpit.**

Boeing/McDonnell Douglas/ Northrop F/A-18 Hornet

The Hornet, today's premier naval fighter, was developed for the US Navy from the YF-17 project proposed for the US Air Force by Northrop. As the company had no experience building carrier-borne aircraft, it teamed up with McDonnell Douglas (now Boeing) to offer a developed F-17. Initially two versions – ground attack and fighter – were proposed, but the two roles were combined in the very capable F/A-18, the first of which flew in 1978. Among the Hornet's features are fly-by-wire, folding wingtips and an advanced cockpit including head-up display and Hands-On Throttle And Stick (HOTAS).

With its excellent fighter and self-defence capabilities, the F/A-18 was intended to increase strike mission survivability and supplement the F-14 Tomcat in US Navy fleet air defence. The F/A-18 played a key role in the 1986 US strikes against Libya. Flying from the USS *Coral Sea*, F/A-18s launched High-speed Anti-Radiation Missiles (HARMs) against Libyan air defence radars and missile sites, thus silencing them during the attacks on military targets in Benghazi.

The F/A-18's advanced radar and avionics systems allow Hornet pilots to shift from fighter to strike mode on the same mission with the flip of a switch, a facility used routinely by Hornets in Operation 'Desert Storm' – they fought their way to a target by defeating opposing aircraft, attacked ground targets and returned safely home. This 'force multiplier' capability gives the operational commander more flexibility in employing tactical aircraft in a rapidly changing battle scenario.

The F/A-18 Hornet was built in single- and two-seat versions. Although the two-seater is a conversion trainer, it is combat-capable and has a similar performance to the single-seat version although with reduced range. The F/A-18A and C are single-seat aircraft while the F/A-18B and D are dual-seaters. The B model is used primarily for training, while the D model is the current US Navy aircraft for attack, tactical air control, forward air control and reconnaissance squadrons.

The improved F/A-18C first flew in 1986 and featured improved avionics, AIM-120 and AGM-65 compatibility and a new central computer.

ABOVE: **The carrier USS *John C. Stennis* embarked Air Wing operates the F/A-18 Hornet, F/A-18E/F Super Hornet, EA-6B Prowler, E-2C Hawkeye and MH-60S Seahawk.**

LEFT: **A missile-armed Hornet of US Navy Attack Squadron 82 (VA-82), operating from the carrier USS *America*. Note the missile carried on the wingtip.**
ABOVE: **An F/A-18C of US Navy Strike Fighter Squadron 86 (VFA-86), the 'Sidewinders', prepares to launch from the deck of USS *Enterprise* (CVN-65) in the Arabian Gulf. This is the eighth US naval vessel to bear the name.**

In November 1989, the first F/A-18s equipped with night-strike capability were delivered to the US Navy, and since 1991, F/A-18s have been delivered with F404-GE-402 enhanced performance engines that produce up to 20 per cent more thrust than the previous F404 engines. From May 1994, the Hornet has been equipped with upgraded radar – the APG-73 – which substantially increases the speed and memory capacity of the radar's processors. These upgrades and improvements help the Hornet maintain its advantage over potential enemies and keep it among the most advanced and capable combat aircraft in the world, not just naval types.

Apart from the US Navy and Marine Corps, the F/A-18 is also in service with the air forces of Canada, Australia, Spain, Kuwait, Finland, Switzerland and Malaysia.

Canada was the first international customer for the F/A-18, and its fleet of 138 CF-18 Hornets is the largest outside the United States. The CF-18s have an unusual element to their paint scheme in that a 'fake' cockpit is painted on the underside of the fuselage directly beneath the real cockpit. This is intended to confuse an enemy fighter, if only for a split second, about the orientation of the CF-18 in close air combat. That moment's hesitation can mean the difference between kill or be killed in a dogfight situation.

Current plans say that F-18A/B aircraft will remain in service with the United States Navy until about 2015 while F-18C/D models will be retired by 2020.

ABOVE: **Two F/A-18s of the US Marine Corps. The aircraft in the foreground is the two-seat combat–capable F/A-18D trainer flying alongside a single-seat F/A-18C.**

Boeing/McDonnell Douglas/Northrop F/A-18C Hornet

First flight: November 17, 1978
Power: Two General Electric 7,721kg/17,000lb thrust afterburning F404-GE-402 turbofans
Armament: One 20mm cannon and up to 7,031kg/15,500lb of weapons, including AIM-120 AMRAAM, AIM-7, AIM-9 air-to-air missiles or other guided weapons such as rockets and tactical nuclear weapons
Size: Wingspan – 11.43m/37ft 6in
Length – 17.07m/56ft
Height – 4.66m/15ft 3.5in
Wing area – 37.16m²/400sq ft
Weights: Empty – 10,455kg/23,050lb
Maximum take-off – 25,401kg/56,000lb
Performance: Maximum speed – 1,915kph/1,189mph
Ceiling – 15,240m/50,000ft plus
Combat radius – 1,020km/634 miles
Climb – 13,715m/45,000ft per minute

Boeing/McDonnell Douglas/ Northrop F/A-18E Super Hornet

The combat-proven F/A-18E/F Super Hornet is the most capable multi-role strike fighter available today or for the foreseeable future. In the words of its manufacturers, "The Super Hornet is an adverse-weather, day and night, multi-mission strike fighter whose survivability improvements over its predecessors make it harder to find, and if found, harder to hit, and if hit, harder to disable."

TOP: **The Super Hornet successfully conducted its initial carrier trials aboard the carrier USS** *John C. Stennis* **(CVN-74) in January 1997. By April 1999, trails aircraft had conducted 7,700 hours of tests.** ABOVE: **A two-seat F/A-18F equipped for 'buddy' refuelling tops up an F/A-18E.**

The F/A-18E/F Super Hornet was devised to build on the great success of the Hornet and having been test flown in November 1995, entered service for evaluation with US Navy squadron VFA-122 in November 1999. The Super Hornet was developed by a team including Boeing, Northrop Grumman, GE Aircraft Engines, Raytheon and more than 1,800 suppliers in the United States and Canada.

The first production model was delivered to the US Navy in December 1998, more than a month ahead of schedule and – after completing the most thorough operational evaluation in US Naval history – the F/A-18E/F Super Hornet entered operational service in November 1999. The first operational cruise of the F/A-18 E Super Hornet was with VFA-115 on board the USS *Abraham Lincoln* (CVN-72) on July 24, 2002, and the type was first used in combat on November 6, 2002, when they participated in a strike on hostile targets – two surface-to-air missile launchers and an air-defence command-and-control bunker in the 'no-fly' zone in Iraq. One of the pilots, Lt John Turner, dropped 907kg/2000lb JDAM bombs for the first time from the F/A-18E in wartime. VFA-115 embarked aboard *Lincoln* expended twice the amount of

bombs as other squadrons in their air wing (with 100 per cent accuracy) and met and exceeded all readiness requirements while on deployment. On September 8, 2006, VFA-211 F/A-18F Super Hornets expended GBU-12 and GBU-38 bombs against Taliban fighters and fortifications west and north-west of Kandahar – the first time the unit had gone into combat with the Super Hornet.

Since its inception, the Super Hornet programme has remained on time, on weight and on cost. In 1999, to acknowledge this acheivement, the F/A-18 programme team was awarded the prestigious Collier Trophy. The award recognizes the greatest achievement in aeronautics and astronautics in the United States, and has been called the greatest and most prized of all aeronautical honours in the United States.

The Super Hornet is 25 per cent larger than its predecessor but has 42 per cent fewer parts. Both the single-seat E and two-seat F models offer increased range, greater endurance, more payload-carrying ability and more powerful engines in the form of two F414-GE-400s, an advanced derivative of the Hornet's current F404 engine family that produces 35 per cent more thrust, a combined 19,960kg/44,000lb. The F414's light yet robust design yields a 9:1 thrust-to-weight ratio, one of the highest of any modern fighter engine. Increased airflow to the engine is provided through the Super Hornet's large, distinctively shaped inlets. A full authority digital electronics control (FADEC) allows for unrestricted engine response in any phase of flight.

Structural changes to the airframe increase internal fuel capacity by 1,633kg/3,600lb, which extends the Hornet's mission radius by up to 40 per cent. The fuselage is 86.3cm/ 34in longer and the wing is 25 per cent larger with an extra 9.3m^2/100sq ft of surface area.

There are 2 additional weapons stations, bringing the total to 11 and bestowing considerable payload flexibility by carrying a mixed load of air-to-air and air-to-ground ordnance. A typical basic load out for a self-escort strike mission starts with an advanced infrared targeting pod, one AIM-120 AMRAAM, two AIM-9 Sidewinder missiles, and an external fuel tank. This leaves six underwing weapon stations available to carry a variety of weapons and other stores.

Two versions of the Super Hornet – the single-seat E model and the two-seat F model – are in production today and in service with the US Navy. Both are true multi-role aircraft, able to perform virtually every mission in the tactical spectrum including air superiority, day/night strike with precision-guided weapons, fighter escort, close air support, suppression of enemy air defence, maritime strike, reconnaissance, forward air control and tanker duties.

The F/A-18E/F has exceptional combat manoeuvrability, an unlimited angle of attack, high resistance to spins, and ease of handling and training. Its reconfigurable digital flight control system can detect damage to or full loss of a flight control and still allow safe recovery. These and other enhancements will ensure that the Super Hornet remains combat relevant well into the 21st century.

TOP: **The F/A-18E is 25 per cent larger than the Hornet and has 11 weapon-carrying stations. Note the variety of munitions carried and the empty pylons.**
ABOVE: **Armourers prepare to load a GBU-12, a 227kg/500lb laser-guided weapon on an F/A-18E.** ABOVE RIGHT: **An F/A-18F goes vertical with a full missile load. The aircraft is from Strike Fighter Squadron 122 (VFA-122), also known as the 'Flying Eagles', a United States Navy F/A-18E/F Super Hornet training or fleet replacement squadron.**
BELOW: **An F/A-18E leaves the carrier deck – note the green 'go' light visible in the bottom left of the photo.**

Boeing/McDonnell Douglas/Northrop F/A-18E Super Hornet

First flight: November 18, 1995
Power: Two General Electric 9,992kg/22,000lb thrust afterburning F414-GE-400 turbofans
Armament: One 20mm cannon, 11 hardpoints carrying up to 8,050kg/17,750lb of weapons including AIM-7, AIM-120 AMRAAM, AIM-9 air-to-air missiles or other guided weapons, bombs and rockets
Size: Wingspan – 13.62m/44ft 9in
Length – 18.31m/60ft 1in
Height – 4.88m/16ft
Wing area – 46.5m^2/500sq ft
Weights: Empty – 13,410kg/29,574lb
Maximum take-off – 29,937/66,000lb
Performance: Maximum speed – 1,915kph/1,189mph
Ceiling – 15,240m/50,000ft plus
Combat radius – 2,225km/1,382 miles

LEFT: **The Breguet Alizé was flying in front-line service over four decades after the prototype first took to the air.** ABOVE: **Wings folded but being prepared for flight, these two examples are pictured on the deck of a French aircraft carrier. Note the weapons hardpoints on the underside of the folded wing on the aircraft shown at the top.**

Breguet Alizé

The carrier-borne anti-submarine Alizé (tradewind) was derived from the Vultur carrier-based strike aircraft that was designed for the French Aéronavale but never produced for service. The Alizé was an extensive redesign of the earlier type and was developed for the anti-submarine role – it had its first flight on October 6, 1956. A low-wing monoplane of conventional configuration, the Alizé carried a radar system with a retractable 'dustbin' radome installed in the belly. The type had a tricycle undercarriage and the main landing gear retracted backwards into nacelles beneath the wings which folded hydraulically. The first production machine was handed over to the French Navy on May 29, 1959.

The cockpit accommodated a crew of three consisting of a pilot seated in front on the right, radar operator in front on the left and the sensor operator sat sideways behind them. The internal weapons bay could accommodate a homing torpedo or depth charges, and underwing stores pylons could carry bombs, depth charges, rockets or missiles. Typical underwing stores included 68mm rocket pods or AS.12 wire-guided anti-ship missiles. The Alizé, powered by the Rolls-Royce Dart RDa.21 turboprop driving a four-bladed propeller, could patrol for over five hours and cover vast areas of ocean thereby providing a valuable defence for French naval assets.

A total of 89 examples of the Alizé were built between 1957 and 1962, including prototypes. The Aéronavale operated 75 from March 1959 on board the carriers *Clemenceau* and *Foch*.

The Aéronavale provided the Alizé with a series of upgrades to ensure the aircraft was able to meet the ever-changing challenges of naval warfare. An early 1980s modernization programme upgraded 28 of the aircraft to Br.1050M standard by the introduction of the Thomson-CSF Iguane radar (as used on Breguet's Atlantique maritime reconnaissance aircraft), new OMEGA radio navigation, and a new ARAR 12 radar and radio location system. Another upgrade programme in the early 1990s fitted 24 of these aircraft with, among other refinements, a new decoy system and a computer-based data-processing system. Later in the 1990s, they were fitted with the Thomson-CSF TTD Optronique Chlio Forward-Looking Infra-Red (FLIR) imaging sensor system.

The Alizé was used in combat during the 1999 NATO air campaign against Serbian forces over Kosovo in the spring of 1999, with the aircraft flying off the French carrier *Foch*.

The last Breguet Alizé was withdrawn from front-line service in 2000 with the retirement of the *Foch*. Despite the many upgrades, by this

ABOVE: **This aircraft, 04, was the first of two pre-production machines built after the three prototypes. It first flew on June 21, 1957, and was used to develop operational procedures and is shown during deck trials at sea.**

time the Alizé was clearly not up to the task of hunting modern nuclear submarines.

The Indian Navy operated the Alizé (around 20 examples) from shorebases and from the light carrier *Vikrant*. The type was used for reconnaissance and patrol during India's 1961 occupation of Portuguese Goa, and was also used for anti-submarine patrol during the Indo-Pakistan War of 1971, during which one Alizé was shot down by a Pakistani F-104 Starfighter in what must have been a most unusual air-combat episode. Numerous Pakistani gunboats were also destroyed by the Alizé in the conflict.

Indian Alizés were gradually relegated to shore-based patrol duties in the 1980s, and were finally phased out in 1992. Like the British Fairey Gannet which they so resembled, the Alizés were replaced by ASW helicopters.

ABOVE: **Aircraft prepare to launch from a French aircraft carrier. The Alizé did not have to use catapults to get airborne, but could just use the whole length of the carrier's deck.** BELOW: **A typical Alizé mission would last for 4 hours, during which the aircraft would consume 2,000 litres/440 gallons of fuel. It would then undergo 30 hours of maintenance to prepare for the next mission.**

ABOVE: **Note the yoke-type arrester hook as this aircraft prepares to land. To help prevent salt-water corrosion each aircraft was thoroughly washed every three weeks while at sea.**

Breguet Alizé

First flight: October 5, 1956 (prototype)
Power: One Rolls-Royce 1,975hp Dart RDa.21 turboprop
Armament: Acoustic torpedo, three 160kg/353lb depth charges housed in internal bomb bay; two anti-shipping missiles carried beneath the folding wings, or a combination of depth charges, bombs or rockets
Size: Wingspan – 15.6m/51ft 2in
Length – 13.86m/45ft 6in
Height – 5m/16ft 4.75in
Wing area – 36m^2/388sq ft
Weights: Empty – 5,700kg/12,566lb
Maximum take-off – 8,200kg/18,078lb
Performance: Maximum speed – 518kph/322mph
Ceiling – 8,000m/26,245ft plus
Range – 2,500km/1,553 miles
Climb – 420m/1,380ft per minute

Dassault Etendard and Super Etendard

Dassault speculatively developed their Etendard (Standard) design to meet the needs of both French national and NATO programmes for new light fighters reflecting the air combat experiences of the Korean War. Various versions did not get beyond the prototype stage but then the Etendard IV multi-role carrier-based fighter drew the attention of the French Navy who for a time had considered the navalized SEPECAT Jaguar for the role. This led to the development of the Etendard IV M specifically for the French Navy – it was the first naval aircraft developed by Dassault.

The Etendard IV M made its maiden flight in May 1958, and from 1961 until 1965 the French Navy took delivery of 69 Etendard IV Ms that served on the French carriers *Foch* and *Clemenceau* – 21 reconnaissance/tanker versions designated Etendard IV Ps also served. The Etendard IV M continued to serve in the French Navy until July 1991 by which time they had logged 180,000 flying hours and made 25,300 carrier landings.

The search for an Etendard replacement led to Dassault proposing the Super Etendard, an updated and much improved aircraft, based on the Etendard IV M but 90 per cent a new design. Designed both for strike and interception duties, it featured the more powerful Atar 8K-50 engine and a strengthened structure to withstand higher speed operations. The weapons system was improved through the installation of a modern navigation and combat management system centered on a Thomson multi-mode radar. The wing had a new leading edge and revised flaps which, with the newer engine, eased the take-off of the heavier Super Etendard.

The Super Etendard prototype made its maiden flight on October 28, 1974, and the first of 71 production aircraft were delivered from mid-1978, again for service on the aircraft carriers *Foch* and *Clemenceau*. One hundred Super Etendards were planned for the Navy but spiraling costs called for a reduction of the order.

ABOVE: **The Etendard IV P reconnaissance version had a fixed refuelling probe and cameras in the nose. Note the arrester hook beneath the tail. The 'blade' aerial under the nose was used to guide the AS.30 missiles launched by the aircraft.**

LEFT: **The Etendard prototype first flew in July 1956 and was designed with the latest knowledge of aerodynamics, including 'area' rule.**

INSET: **The all-French Super Etendard won out as an Etendard replacement over the more advanced Jaguar M which was half British.**

LEFT: **French naval air power, both bought-in and homegrown. Aéronavale Super Etendards and F-8 Crusaders pictured over the French Navy aircraft carrier *Clemenceau*. Note the long length of the Super Etendard's noseleg.**

Armed with two 30mm cannon, the Super Etendard could carry a variety of weaponry on its five hardpoints including two Matra Magic AAMs, four pods of 18 68mm rockets, a variety of bombs or two Exocet anti-ship missiles. A number were also modified to carry the Aérospatiale ASMP stand-off nuclear bomb.

The Argentine Navy's use of the Super Etendard/Exocet combination during the Falklands War of 1982 proved devastating against British ships – Argentina had ordered fourteen Super Etendards from Dassault in 1979 but only five aircraft and reportedly five missiles had been delivered by the time France embargoed arms shipments to Argentina. These five strike fighters, with pilots unwilling to engage the agile British Harriers in air combat, nevertheless proved to be a very potent element of the Argentine inventory.

On May 4, 1982, two Super Etendards took off from a base in Argentina preparing to attack the British task force. After three hours and an inflight refuelling, the aircraft located and launched an attack on the British ships. One of the Exocets

found and severely damaged the frigate HMS *Sheffield* which sank on May 10. On May 25, two Exocet-equipped Super Etendards again attacked the task force, this time sinking the *Atlantic Conveyor* with its cargo of nine helicopters.

A handful of Super Etendards were supplied to Iraq in October, 1983 as the Iraqis were desperate to cripple Iran by attacking tankers in the Persian Gulf with Exocets. Around 50 ships were attacked in the Gulf in 1984, the majority of the actions apparently carried out by Iraqi Super Etendards.

Production ended in 1983 but the Super Etendards underwent continuous modernization through the 1990s to enable them to use the latest laser-guided 'smart' weapons. These updated aircraft, designated Super Etendard Modernisé (SEM), participated in NATO's 1999 operations over Kosovo as well as strike missions over Afghanistan as part of Operation 'Enduring Freedom'.

All remaining Super Etendards are expected to be retired from French service by 2010, their replacement by naval Rafale Ms having begun in 2006.

LEFT: **The Dassault Etendard gave great service to the French Navy for a number of years. Note that only the Etendard wingtips folded since swept wings take up less room on carrier decks.**

RIGHT: **Dassault built 75 Etendard IVMs and 22 IVPs. Three IVMs were converted to Super Etendard standard to test and prove the design.**

Dassault Super Etendard

First flight: October 28, 1974
Power: SNECMA 5,000kg/11,025lb afterburning thrust Atar 8K-50 turbojet
Armament: Two 30mm cannon, plus 2,100kg/4,630lb of weapons including Matra Magic AAMs, AM39 Exocet ASMs, bombs and rockets
Size: Wingspan – 9.6m/31ft 6in
    Length – 14.31m/46ft 11.5in
    Height – 3.86m/12ft 8in
    Wing area – 28.4m²/306sq ft
Weights: Empty – 6,500kg/14,330lb
    Maximum take-off – 12,000kg/26,455lb
Performance: Maximum speed – 1,205kph/749mph
    Ceiling – 13,700m/44,950ft
    Range – 650km/404 miles
    Climb – 6,000m/19,685ft per minute

LEFT: **A French Navy Rafale M from the French carrier** *Charles De Gaulle* **performs a touch-and-go landing aboard the USS** *Dwight D. Eisenhower* **(CVN-69), during the Multi-National Maritime Exercise in May 2005.** ABOVE: **Described by its manufacturers as "omnirole by design", the Rafale was a purely French design and was "provided with distinctive features tuned to worldwide – opposed to strictly West European – market expectations".**

Dassault Rafale

Even as the Mirage 2000 was entering French Air Force service in the early 1980s, a successor was already being sought to be the prime French Air Force fighter. After France withdrew from what became the Eurofighter programme, attention was then focused on Dassault's *Avion de Combat Experimentale* (ACX), which first flew on July 4, 1986, and was later designated Rafale A. This demonstrator aircraft was used to test the basic design including the airframe, powerplant and the fly-by-wire system.

Directly derived from the slightly larger (3 per cent) Rafale A demonstrator, production Rafales appear in three versions – the single-seat air-defence Rafale C (for *chasseur*), the two-seater trainer/multi-role Rafale B (*biplace*) and the single-seat Rafale M (*marine*) fighter for the Navy. The three versions are fitted with the same engines (the SNECMA M88-2), navigation/attack system, aircraft-management system and flight-control systems. The cockpit has Hands-On Throttle and Stick (HOTAS) controls, a wide-angle head-up display, two Multi-Function Display (MFD) monitors showing all flight and instrument information, and a helmet-mounted weapons sight. Voice recognition is planned to feature in future versions so the pilot will be able to issue orders to the aircraft simply by using his or her voice – even in the early 21st century this is a remarkable proposition.

All three versions have the same 213kph/132mph approach speed and a take-off/landing run of less than 400m/1312ft, made possible by complimenting the delta wing with canard foreplanes which together optimize aerodynamic efficiency and stability control without impeding the pilot's visibility. The materials employed and the shapes that make up the aircraft have both been carefully selected to minimize the aircraft's electro-magnetic and infrared signature to make it as 'stealthy' as possible. Carbon and Kevlar composites, superplastic-formed diffusion-bonded titanium and aluminium-lithium alloys have all been used in this aircraft.

The first production aircraft, Rafale B1, flew in December 1998 while the single-seat Rafale C, an air defence fighter with fully integrated weapons and navigation systems, had its first flight on May 19, 1991. Making full use of the latest technology, it is capable of outstanding performance on multiple air-to-air targets.

The two-seat multi-role Rafale B first took to the air on April 30, 1993, and retains most of the elements of the single-seater version, and its weapon and navigation system is exactly the same. The Rafale B can undertake an operational mission with just a pilot as crew or with a pilot and a weapons system operator. In Armée de l'Air service, the B model was chosen to replace the popular ground-attack Jaguar, and can carry up to 8,000kg/17,600lb of weaponry – in the air-to-air role this includes up to eight Matra Mica AAM missiles.

LEFT: **The Rafale's delta wing and close-coupled canards ensure a wide range of centre of gravity positions for all flight conditions, as well as benign handling throughout the flight envelope.**

The Rafale M was ordered to replace the French Navy's ageing fleet of F-8 Crusaders, and is a single-seat fighter modified for seaborne use with a strengthened undercarriage, arrester hook, catapult points for deck launches and a longer nose gear leg to provide a more nose-up attitude for catapult launches. This navalized Rafale first flew in December 1991 and weighs about 500kg/1,100lb more than its land-based cousins. Catapult trials were initially carried out in July and August 1992 at NAS Lakehurst in New Jersey, USA, and Patuxent River, Maryland, USA, as France has no land-based catapult testing facility. The aircraft then undertook trials on the French carrier *Foch*.

The first flight of a production Rafale M took place in July 1999 and, on the same day, a Rafale M prototype landed on France's nuclear-powered aircraft carrier *Charles de Gaulle*. Service deliveries began in 2000 and the type officially entered

ABOVE: **With its versatile weapon-carrying capability, Rafale can combine ground-attack and air-to-air combat missions during the same sortie. It is also capable of performing multiple functions at the same time, such as Beyond Visual Range (BVR) air-to-air firing during the very-low-altitude penetration phase. This gives the Rafale impressively broad multi-role capabilities, along with a high degree of survivability.**

service in December 2000 although the first squadron, Flotille 12, did not actually reform until May 2001. The unit embarked on the *Charles de Gaulle* in 2002 and become fully operational on June 25, 2004. This followed an extended operational evaluation which included flying limited escort and tanker missions in support of Operation 'Enduring Freedom' over Afghanistan. The Rafale M is planned in three versions: the Standard F1, F2 and F3 for fighter, strike and multi-role missions respectively.

LEFT: **The M88-2 is a new-generation engine featuring state-of-the-art technologies, including a non-polluting combustion chamber. It also features the latest advances in reducing electromagnetic and infrared signatures. This very compact powerplant, offering a high thrust-to-weight ratio and exceptional controllability, especially during acceleration, is one of very few military engines with 'green' credentials.**

Dassault Rafale M

First flight: December 12, 1991
Power: Two SNECMA 8,870kg/19,555lb afterburning thrust M88-2 augmented turbofans
Armament: One 30mm cannon plus a mixed weapons load of up to 6,000kg/13,228lb including eight Matra Mica AAMs, ASMP stand-off nuclear missile and other munitions
Size: Wingspan – 10.9m/35ft 9in
Length – 15.30m/50ft 2in
Height – 5.34m/17ft 6in
Wing area – 46m²/495sq ft
Weights: Empty – 9,800kg/21,605lb
Maximum take-off – 16,500kg/36,373lb
Performance: Maximum speed – 2,125kph/1,320mph
Ceiling – 20,000m/65,620ft
Range – 1,850km/1,150 miles with maximum weapon load
Climb – 18,290m/60,000ft per minute

de Havilland Sea Hornet

Following the success of the 'wooden wonder', the Mosquito, the de Havilland design team turned their thoughts to a scaled-down single-seat Mosquito capable of taking on Japanese fighters in the Pacific. To deal with what was anticipated to be an island-hopping war, very long range was a major feature of the design that came to be known as the Hornet. Streamlining was seen as one way of achieving that and Rolls-Royce were involved from the outset and tasked with developing Merlin engines with a reduced frontal area to lessen the drag on the aircraft. Although inspired by the Mosquito, the Hornet was a completely new aircraft – the main similarity between the two types was the plywood-balsa-plywood technique for building the wooden fuselage. The Hornet wing also differed from that of the Mosquito as it was made of wood and metal – the Hornet was the first aircraft in which wood was cemented to metal using the ground-breaking Redux adhesive.

ABOVE: **With a clear family resemblance to the earlier Mosquito, the Hornet and Sea Hornet were developed for Far East combat use. The design was at first worked up as a private de Havilland venture without an official requirement.** BELOW LEFT: **Three Sea Hornet F.20s of No.801 NAS. The Hornet/Sea Hornet pioneered the use of Redux adhesive in aircraft construction.**

Geoffrey de Havilland Jr took the Hornet into the air for the first time in July 1944. Although the first production aircraft were delivered to the RAF in April 1945, the type did not see action in World War II. In fact the first RAF Hornet squadron, No.64, was not formed until May 1946. They defended UK air space until replaced by Meteor 8s in 1951 but from 1949 they were switched from interceptor to intruder duties.

Even before the first Hornet prototype first flew, de Havilland were considering a carrier version for Fleet Air Arm service against the Japanese. In response to the late 1944 specification N5/44, three Hornet F.1s were chosen to be modified to naval standards, with the design work subcontracted to Heston Aircraft.

The first Sea Hornet prototype flew on April 19, 1945, and in common with many navalized landplanes was simply equipped with an arrester hook. In August that year a fully navalized (folding wings, catapult capability and other naval equipment) prototype carried out trial landings and production orders soon followed. The first version produced was the Sea Hornet F. Mk 20, a long-range escort strike fighter that was the Fleet Air Arm's first twin-engine, carrier-based fighter. The production version first flew on August 13, 1946, and retained the four 20mm Hispano cannon and underwing stores of its land-based cousin, although the Royal Navy machines featured half-size drop tanks that could carry an extra 455 litres/100 gallons fuel apiece. Camera windows were included in the rear fuselage to offer FR. Mk 20 (fighter reconnaissance) capability, enabling the aircraft to take oblique aerial photographs.

LEFT: **The ability for the Hornet design to evolve and operate from carriers was an important factor from the outset, hence the excellent cockpit visibility and low-speed handling.** ABOVE: **Close-up of a trial radar nose for the Sea Hornet, containing the rotating ASH radar dish. The aircraft was praised by its pilots for its exceptional performance. Even with one engine feathered, the aircraft could still loop as comfortably as a single-engine fighter.**

The first Sea Hornet F.20 unit was No.801 Squadron which reformed in June, 1947, and the mark remained in front-line service until 1951, the same year that F. Mk 20 production ceased. The type remained in second-line use until 1955.

A total of 78 F.20s were built as well as 43 similar PR.22 photo-reconnaissance Sea Hornets. Very similar to the RAF's Hornet P.R. Mk 2, it featured either two F.52 cameras or a single Fairchild K.19B night-photography camera in the rear fuselage – this version could also carry underwing stores.

In late 1945, the Royal Navy had issued an urgent requirement for a carrier-based, two-seat night-fighter, under the specification N.21/45. Heston Aircraft again modified two Hornet F.3s to meet this specification and created the Sea Hornet NF. Mk 21. This version featured a radar 'thimble' in the nose (making the NF.21 one of the easiest aircraft to identify), exhaust flame dampers, an extra bubble-type canopy on the rear fuselage for a navigator/radar operator position, and an enlarged tailplane to compensate for airflow disruption caused by the second canopy. Although a night-fighter, the NF.21 could carry the same underwing offensive stores as other Hornets and Sea Hornets. The NF.21 entered squadron service in January 1949, and lasted until it was replaced by the Sea Venom in 1954. In all, 78 NF.21s were produced, making a total Sea Hornet production of around 200.

Although the Royal Australian Navy and the Royal Canadian Air Force had one example each, the Royal Navy were the only front-line operators of the Sea Hornet. One notable exception is the Canadian machine, TT193, which passed on to the Canadian civil register and was used for photo survey work.

ABOVE: **PX 239 began life as a Hornet F.1 and became the second NF.21 prototype. It received folding wings and a dorsal fin extension, both standard features on production examples.**

de Havilland Sea Hornet F. Mk 20

First flight: July 28, 1944 (Hornet prototype)
Power: Two Rolls-Royce 2,030hp Merlin 130/131 in-line piston engines
Armament: Four 20mm cannon in nose plus provision for up to 908kg/2,000lb of underwing bombs or rockets
Size: Wingspan – 13.73m/45ft
Length – 11.18m/36ft 8in
Height – 3.97m/13ft
Wing area – 33.54m²/361sq ft
Weights: Empty – 6,041kg/13,300lb
Maximum take-off – 9,493kg/20,928lb
Performance: Maximum speed – 751kph/467mph
Ceiling – 10,670m/35,000ft
Range – 2,414km/1,500 miles
Climb – 1,220m/4,000ft per minute

de Havilland Sea Venom

Proposed by de Havilland as a successor to its Vampire, the RAF's second jet fighter, the Venom was initially designated Vampire FB.8. The design had to be substantially changed to fit the new and more powerful Ghost engine – accordingly the aircraft was given its own identity – the Venom. The first production version, the FB.1, was delivered to the RAF in December 1951 followed by the improved ejection-seat equipped FB.4 version. The Venom ultimately equipped 19 squadrons of the Royal Air Force, with the Germany-based Venoms representing a vital element of the West's Cold War defences at the time.

The naval carrier-borne version, the Sea Venom, evolved from the RAF's Venom NF2 night-fighter. The naval version featured standard 'navalizing' changes, including a tail hook, strengthened and lengthened undercarriage for deck landings, and folding wings to make it suitable for carrier stowage. The first of three Sea Venom prototypes made its first flight in 1951 and began carrier trials on board HMS *Illustrious* in July that year.

The first production version was the Sea Venom FAW. Mk 20 (Fighter All-Weather), which first flew in 1953 and of which 50 were built. Powered by a single de Havilland Ghost 103 turbojet engine, its armament was the same as the RAF version.

The next version was the FAW. Mk 21 which featured changes mirroring the RAF's NF.2A and NF.3 versions including an improved Ghost 104 engine, power-operated ailerons, improved radar, a frameless canopy for better pilot visibility and Martin Baker Mk 4 ejector seats. The most apparent visual difference between the Mk 20 and Mk 21 was the loss of the tailplane extension outboard of the tail fins in the later version. In 1958, seven FAW.21s were modified for electronic countermeasures (ECM) purposes with ECM equipment replacing the cannon.

TOP: **The Sea Venom saw a great deal of action during its time in Royal Navy service and proved itself to be a good combat aircraft. The photo shows an FAW. Mk 22.** LEFT: **A Royal Navy Sea Venom leaves a British carrier deck crowded with other Sea Venoms during the 1956 Suez campaign. Note the catapult strop falling away beneath the aircraft. Sea Venoms of Nos.809, 892 and 893 Naval Air Squadrons based on the carriers HMS *Albion* and HMS *Eagle* saw action during Suez.** ABOVE: **Following trials, later versions of the Sea Venom were equipped to carry the Firestreak, also developed by a de Havilland company. Firestreak was Britain's first effective air-to-air missile and was a passive infrared homing weapon. The aircraft is pictured on board HMS *Victorious* in 1959.**

LEFT: **WM569 was a Sea Venom FAW. Mk 21. This version featured refinements similar to those of the land-based Venom NF.2A and NF.3.** ABOVE: **The first prototype Sea Venom, WK376, did its first carrier take-off on July 9, 1951, from the deck of HMS *Illustrious*. Folding wings did not feature on test aircraft until the third prototype, WK385. Production aircraft differed to the prototypes by having, among other features, permanent wingtip fuel tanks and a windscreen wiper.**

The Sea Venom FAW. Mk 22 was the final version, powered by the 2,400kg/5,300lb thrust Ghost 105 that gave a maximum speed of 927kph/576mph at sea level and a 1135km/705-mile range. Armament consisted of four fixed 20mm guns and bombs or eight rocket-projectiles below the wings. Thirty-nine were built from 1957 to 1958 and some were later equipped with the de Havilland Firestreak air-to-air missile.

In all, 256 Sea Venoms were built for the Royal Navy. From 1959, the type began to be replaced in Royal Navy service by the Sea Vixen, an aircraft that also had the distinctive de Havilland twin-boom tail. The Sea Venom had given the Royal Navy an essential interim radar-equipped all-weather fighter force between the piston-engined Sea Hornet and the appearance of the advanced Sea Vixen.

Royal Navy Sea Venoms, in concert with RAF Venom fighter-bombers, saw action during the Suez crisis in 1956. The aircraft were from Fleet Air Arm 809, 892 and 893 Naval Air Squadrons based on the light fleet carrier HMS *Albion* and fleet carrier HMS *Eagle*. The Sea Venoms saw much action and bombed numerous targets in Egypt. RN Sea Venoms later carried out attacks against Cypriot terrorists and also saw service during the troubles in the Middle East.

From 1956, 39 Sea Venoms were supplied to the Royal Australian Navy (RAN), where they replaced the Hawker Sea Fury in service. The Sea Venom was in turn replaced in RAN service from 1967 by the A-4 Skyhawk. Meanwhile, the French company Sud-Est licence-built 121 Sea Venom FAW. Mk 20s, designated *Aquilon*, for the French Navy, who operated them until 1963.

ABOVE: **The Sea Venom in the foreground shows a number of the type's features – the large hinged cockpit canopy over side-by-side seats, the folding wings and the twin boom tail.**

de Havilland Sea Venom FAW. Mk 22

First flight: April 19, 1951 (prototype)

Power: de Havilland 2,404kg/5,300lb thrust Ghost 105 turbojet

Armament: Four 20mm cannon and provision for two Firestreak air-to-air missiles or 907kg/2,000lb of bombs or eight 27kg/60lb rocket projectiles

Size: Wingspan – 13.08m/42ft 11in
Length – 11.15m/36ft 7in
Height – 2.6m/8ft 6.25in
Wing area – 25.99m²/280sq ft

Weights: Empty – 3,992kg/8,800lb
Maximum take-off – 7,167kg/15,800lb

Performance: Maximum speed – 925kph/575mph
Ceiling – 12,190m/40,000ft
Range – 1,135km/705 miles
Climb – 1,753m/5,750ft per minute

de Havilland Sea Vixen

The Sea Venom's successor in Royal Navy service was the impressive de Havilland Sea Vixen which, when it first appeared in the early 1950s, was a match for any land-based fighter of the time. It gave the Royal Navy its first swept-wing two-seat all-weather fighter and was developed from the 1946-vintage D.H. 110 that was designed to meet the Royal Air Force specification for a land-based all-weather fighter and a Royal Navy requirement for an advanced carrier-borne all-weather fighter aircraft. Naval interest waned and the RAF requirement was ultimately filled by the Gloster Javelin.

Although it followed the Vampire/Venom-type twin-boom configuration, the Sea Vixen was a totally modern aircraft, but development delays following the high profile and tragic 1952 crash of the prototype at a Farnborough air show kept the Sea Vixen from entering Royal Navy Fleet Air Arm service until 1958.

Royal Navy interest in the D.H. 100 was rekindled in 1952 and carrier trials took place in late 1954 – the Royal Navy placed its first Sea Vixen order in January the following year. A partially navalized version first flew in June, 1955 while production of the Sea Vixen FAW. Mk 1 got underway at de Havilland's Christchurch factory – the company's Chester factory was also later involved in Sea Vixen production.

TOP: **At the time of writing this is the only airworthy Sea Vixen, a former No.899 NAS aircraft.** ABOVE: **The Sea Vixen pilot's cockpit and canopy was offset to the port side to make room for the radar operator below.** BELOW: **Showing the aircraft's wing shape to great effect, a Sea Vixen buzzes the island of the British carrier HMS *Hermes*, 1961. The Sea Vixen was the last de Havilland twin-boom type.**

The Mk 1 had a hinged radome which reduced the overall length of the aircraft for carrier stowage, power-folding wings (earlier carrier aircraft had wings folded by hand) and a hydraulically steerable nosewheel – the first production version flew on March 20, 1957. Service trials followed on board HMS *Victorious* and HMS *Centaur* during November 1958 and the type finally became operational the following year. No.892 Squadron FAA was the first Sea Vixen service unit and embarked upon the famous British carrier HMS *Ark Royal* in March 1960. The Sea Vixen was the heaviest aircraft to have entered Royal Navy service.

The aircraft was the mainstay of Royal Navy carrier-borne fighter squadrons for a decade and was the first British interceptor to dispense with guns as it was armed only with air-to-air missiles and rockets – 28 2in rockets were stored in two innovative retractable fuselage containers. For strike missions the missiles could be replaced by up to 900kg/2,000lb of bombs. Sea Vixens could also carry a refuelling pack to enable them to fuel other Sea Vixens, using the 'buddy' system.

The type's remarkable nose arrangement had the pilot's cockpit offset to the port side to provide sufficient working space for a radar operator whose station was below and behind on the starboard side.

The FAW. Mk 2 was an improved version that entered service in December 1963 with No.899 Squadron. Converted Mk 1s were flown in the summer of 1962 to prove the new version and subsequently a number of Mk 1s on the production line were completed as the more advanced Mk 2. A total of 67 Mk 1s were converted to Mk 2 standard, while 29 examples were built from new. More fuel was carried in the forward sections of the tail-booms which were extended forward of the wings, and armament for this model was four Red Top AAMs in place of the Firestreaks carried by the FAW. Mk 1.

Despite the Sea Vixen's late entry into service, the aircraft gave the Royal Navy a formidable all-weather interception and surface attack capability and the type was finally retired from front-line service in 1972.

For two decades after its 'retirement', the type could still be seen flying from some UK military training establishments as Sea Vixen D. Mk 3 drones used to train radar operators by providing high-speed radar targets. 'Flown' by a pilot on the ground, these brightly coloured Sea Vixens with remote control equipment in the observer's position were the last chance to see the ultimate de Havilland twin-boomer in the air, until a privately owned example joined the British civil register and air show circuit in the early 2000s.

ABOVE: **The retirement of the Sea Vixen from the Fleet Air Arm was the end of an era for de Havilland twin-boom types in front-line British military service.**

de Havilland Sea Vixen FAW. Mk 2

First flight: September 26, 1951 (D.H.110)
Power: Two Rolls-Royce 5,094kg/11,230lb thrust Avon 208 turbojets
Armament: Four Red Top infrared homing air-to-air missiles, plus two retractable nose pods with 28 2in rocket projectiles
Size: Wingspan – 15.54m/51ft
Length – 16.94m/55ft 7in
Height – 3.28m/10ft 9in
Wing area – 60.2m²/648sq ft
Weights: Empty – 9,979kg/22,000lb
Maximum take-off – 16,780kg/37,000lb
Performance: Maximum speed – 1,110kph/690mph
Ceiling – 14,630m/48,000ft
Range – 1,287km/800 miles
Climb – 12,190m/40,000ft in 8 minutes, 30 seconds

Douglas Skyraider

The Skyraider can be rightly considered to be one of the greatest combat aircraft ever and one of the most durable to have operated from a carrier deck. A World War II design as a replacement for Douglas' own Dauntless dive-bomber, this rugged aircraft fought in both Korea and in Vietnam. The prototype XBT2D-1 first flew in March 1945, and in February 1946 became the AD-1 Skyraider, the biggest single-seat aircraft in production. Designed around Wright's R-3350 engine, the Skyraider was created with the benefit of considerable combat experience. The designers' aim was to produce a very versatile aircraft which could absorb considerable battle damage and carry the widest range of available weaponry. Built like a big fighter, the Skyraider carried all its weaponry beneath its folding wings.

After carrier trials in early 1946 the Skyraider formally entered US Navy front-line service with VA-19A in December 1946.

Production of consistently improved versions continued and only 4 years into manufacturing, an incredible 22 variants had appeared. Production continued for 12 years and when it ceased in 1957, a total of 3,180 Skyraiders had been delivered to the United States Navy.

Korea is often thought of as a jet war, but the Skyraider's 10-hour loiter capability and great weapon-carrying capacity considerably outclassed any jet that was in service with UN forces at the time. The US Navy were hugely impressed by the performance of the Skyraider.

Among the versions soon appearing were the AD-2 with increased fuel and more powerful engine, and the AD-3

ABOVE: **The combat record of the Skyraider was remarkable. The type saw massive amounts of action both in Korea and during the Vietnam War.** LEFT: **France acquired a number of ex-US Navy Skyraiders, initially to replace the P-47 Thunderbolts they wanted to retire. During operations in Chad, some French aircraft dropped large quantities of empty beer bottles on rebels below. This was considered to be an innovative means of avoiding breaking the ban on non-lethal weapons imposed during the conflict.**

with a revised canopy, improved propeller and landing gear. The AD-4 had the more powerful 2,700hp R-3350 engine and greatly increased load-carrying capacity, the AD-4W was a three-seat Airborne Early Warning variant (used by the Royal Navy's Fleet Air Arm) while the AD-5 was a four-seat multi-role version. The Skyraider was strengthened to carry more and more equipment and ordnance and the AD-5 could operate at all-up weights of 11,340kg/25,000lb. The AD-5 could also be adapted for casualty evacuation or for transporting 12 troops. The AD-6 was a much-improved single-seat attack version while the AD-7 had a 3,050hp engine and even more reinforcement to the wing and undercarriage.

AD-4Ns saw considerable action with the French Armée de l'Air in Algeria and these machines were retired from French service in 1965. By then the United States was embroiled in Vietnam and following trials the Skyraider was found to be the ideal close support aircraft needed for tackling difficult ground targets. Again, the hard-hitting aircraft's loiter capability made it an obvious choice for this type of warfare. The United States Air Force, Navy and Marine Corps all operated Skyraiders in Vietnam, as did the US-trained South Vietnam Air Force. The aircraft also served as Forward Air Control (FAC) platforms, helicopter escort and rescue support missions. Never considered a dogfighter, the Skyraider had four 20mm cannon in the wings and US Navy Skyraider pilots are known to have shot down at least two MiG-17 jets over Vietnam.

In 1962, new tri-service aircraft designations were introduced so all the designations of Skyraiders then in service were changed. The AD-5 was the A-1E, the AD-5N the A-1G while the AD-6 and AD-7 became the A-1H and A-1J respectively.

As well as Britain and France, Skyraiders were also supplied to Chad who was using them in combat up to the late 1970s. The aircraft that had entered service when piston-engined warplanes were thought by some to be obsolete was still fighting more than a quarter of a century after it first entered service.

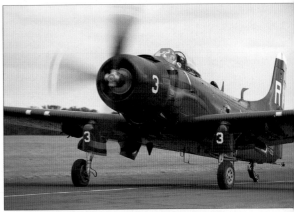

TOP: **The A-1E/AD-5 was a redesigned multi-role version of the Skyraider that had a side-by-side cockpit.** ABOVE: **Although the Skyraider looked like it belonged on a World War II carrier deck, its ruggedness and versatility kept it in use as a front-line aircraft well into the 1970s.**

ABOVE: **An AD-6/A-1H of US Navy Attack Squadron 176. The unit operated the Skyraider from 1955 to 1967, and in 1966 two aircraft from the unit fought and defeated enemy MiGs in air combat.**

Douglas A-1H (AD-6) Skyraider

First flight: March 19, 1945 (XBT2D-1)

Power: One Wright 2,700hp R-3350-26WA radial piston engine

Armament: Four wing-mounted 20mm cannon, up to 3,629kg/8,000lb of ordnance carried under wings and on one fuselage hardpoint

Size: Wingspan – 15.25m/50ft 0.25in
Length – 11.84m/38ft 10in
Height – 4.78m/15ft 8.25in
Wing area – 37.19m²/400sq ft

Weights: Empty – 5,429kg/11,968lb
Maximum take-off – 11,340kg/25,000lb

Performance: Maximum speed – 518kph/322mph
Ceiling – 8,685m/28,500ft plus
Range – 2,116km/1,315 miles
Climb – 870m/2,850ft per minute

LEFT: The Skyray possessed record-breaking speed and climb. Note the small amount of wing folding required for carrier operations. ABOVE: Designed with the benefit of research undertaken by Germany during the war, the aircraft entered US Navy service over a decade after the defeat of Nazi Germany. Even today the Skyray has a futuristic look about it. BELOW: Described by one of its test pilots as a fighter pilot's dream, the aircraft's fundamental instability made it incredibly agile.

Douglas F4D Skyray

Douglas had examined aerodynamic data captured from the Germans at the end of World War II. The data included extensive wind tunnel test findings concerning tailless aircraft designed by Dr Alexander Lippisch, who had developed the tailless Messerschmitt Me 163 rocket fighter. Douglas talked to Lippisch, who had also explored delta wing designs, as the company was interested in the aerodynamic efficiency that the delta configuration offered to compensate for the low power available from jet engines of the time.

In January 1947, a US Navy request for a short-range carrier-based interceptor prompted Douglas to re-evaluate the tailless concept. Their design evolved from a delta flying wing with a tailfin but no pronounced fuselage to a heart-shaped delta with a fuselage. The Navy warmed to the Douglas proposal, and the prototype XF4D-1 made its first flight on January 21, 1951, from Muroc (later Edwards) Air Force Base, with Larry Peyton as test pilot. The aircraft's similarity to the ray fish led to its name.

The F4D-1's capabilities were evident when, on October 3, 1953, the second prototype set a new world air-speed record of 1211.7kph/752.9mph. Deliveries to the US Navy began in April 1956 and 17 front-line US Navy/USMC units, plus three reserve units, were eventually equipped with the Skyray.

The Skyray's deep delta wing roots contained the air intakes feeding the single turbojet, fuel for which was contained both in the wings and the fuselage. Leading-edge slats were fitted for increased lift during take-off and landing.

Known to its crews as the 'Ford' (after the 'four' and 'D' of its designation), this aircraft had a spectacular rate and angle of climb and set five new time-to-altitude records. It saw the

Skyray fly from a complete stop to 15,240m/50,000ft in 2 minutes and 36.05 seconds. This performance led to one Skyray-equipped US Navy unit, VFAW-3 based at Naval Air Station North Island in California, being part of North American Air Defense Command tasked with defending the US from Soviet bombers – the only US Navy unit to do so.

Engine development problems meant that production aircraft were not delivered to the US Navy until early 1956 while the US Marine Corps received their first in 1957. This was an unusually long development period for a time when aerospace innovation was progressing at breakneck speed rendering designs obsolete very quickly.

The production Skyray was fitted with the Aero-13 fire-control system which featured the Westinghouse AN/APQ-50 radar. Impressive for its time, this radar had a normal detection range of 29km/18 miles, and a lock-on range of 20km/12 miles. Pilots admired the Skyray's capabilities. It was very manoeuvrable and possessed an impressive rate of roll but it was a handful for a relatively inexperienced pilot. Keeping the unstable aircraft level was a constant challenge – these days, digital fly-by-wire flight control systems would easily tame the Skyray.

VFAW-3 Skyrays deployed to Florida during the Cuban Missile Crisis in 1962, protecting US air space from Cuban intruders. Radar contact was made with MiGs but no confrontations resulted.

Designed exclusively for the high-altitude interception role, the Skyray was unsuited to the multi-mission capabilities required by the mid-1960s so it had a fairly short service life. The last aircraft were withdrawn from service from 1964, but a single example was used by NASA until 1969, and the US Navy Test Pilots School at Patuxent River in Maryland kept one airworthy to give students experience of how an unstable aircraft flew. In 1962, some Skyrays were fitted out as target drone controllers and redesignated DF-6A.

A total of 420 were built by the time production ended in December 1958. The type was redesignated F-6A when the United States military rationalized aircraft designations in September 1962. A Skyray development, the F5D Skylancer, was designed and prototypes were built, but it was cancelled before production began.

ABOVE: **The aircraft was certainly a handful, and never required more attention than during carrier landings. The mainwheel legs lowered separately, and as the first leg generated drag, the aircraft would start to 'skid' in the air.**

BELOW: **The high angle of attack required on landing meant that the large wing area 'blanked' out the tail from the airflow, which reduced the fin's effect on the aircraft's control. The aircraft was best suited to pilots who liked a challenge every time they flew the type. Today's fly-by-wire technology would have made the Skyray much easier to fly.**

ABOVE: **The Skyray had the Aero-13 fire-control system which featured a Westinghouse AN/APQ-50 radar. Advanced for its time, the radar had a detection range of around 29km/18 miles.**

Douglas F4D Skyray

First flight: January 23, 1951
Power: Pratt & Whitney 6,577kg/14,500lb afterburning thrust J57-P-8B turbojet
Armament: Four 20mm/0.78in cannon, plus up to 1,814kg/4,000lb of fuel or ordnance on six underwing hardpoints
Size: Wingspan – 10.21m/33ft 6in
Length – 13.93m/45ft 8.25in
Height – 3.96m/13ft
Wing area – 51.75m²/557sq ft
Weights: Empty – 7,268kg/16,024lb
Maximum take-off – 11,340kg/25,000lb
Performance: Maximum speed – 1,162kph/722mph
Ceiling – 16,765m/55,000ft
Range – 1,931km/1,200 miles
Climb – 5,580m/18,300ft

Douglas A-3 Skywarrior

By the late 1940s, a whole new class of aircraft carrier was under development by the US Navy, the Forrestal supercarrier class. These enormous carriers would be able to operate large aircraft and give the US Navy the opportunity to take airpower to a new level. The Navy called for a large new strategic bomber to operate from the supercarriers and Douglas came up with the A3D, at 31,750kg/70,000lb the world's largest and heaviest carrier-borne aircraft when it was designed. The nuclear bomb aspect was challenging for the aircraft design team because details of the weapon were top secret, and designers had to guess the appearance and weight of the nuclear bombs to be carried on board. In its vast internal bomb bay, it could carry up to 5,400kg/12,000lb of weaponry. Also, the internal bomb bay had to be accessible from the cockpit, so the crew could arm the nuclear device during flight. The type first flew in October 1952, and went on to become the US Navy's first twin-jet nuclear bomber.

The first production version, the A3D-1 (later redesignated A-3A), with a radar-controlled tail turret and a crew of three, first joined US Navy fleet squadrons on March 31, 1956 when

ABOVE: **The Skywarrior was among the longest serving US Navy strike aircraft; having entered service in the mid-1950s and not being retired until 1991.**
BELOW: **Before the US Navy's Polaris submarines entered service, the Skywarrior was a vital element of the service's nuclear capability.**

five A3D-1s were delivered to Heavy Attack Squadron One (VAH-1) at NAS Jacksonville, Florida. In April 1956, VAH-2 became the Pacific Fleet's first Skywarrior unit.

The first deployment of the A3D-1 was during the Suez Crisis – on November 7, 1956, VAH-1's A3Ds were taken aboard USS *Forrestal* which then sailed for the Eastern Atlantic. The first major depoyment was in January 1957 when VAH-1 took the Skywarrior aboard the USS *Forrestal* on a cruise to the Mediterranean. These aircraft were not, however, combat-ready and were still establishing the parameters for the operation of these large jet-powered aircraft aboard aircraft carriers.

The A3D-2 began to reach fleet squadrons in 1957 and was used to set some impressive records – on March 21, 1957, an A3D-2 travelling west set a US transcontinental speed record with a time of 5 hours, 12 minutes, and a

ABOVE: **For storage below deck, the A-3's wings could fold almost flat, hinged outboard of the engines. Even the tall tail was hinged and would fold to starboard.** RIGHT: **This aircraft is one of 30 A3D-2P reconnaissance variants produced. The weapons bay carried up to 12 cameras plus photoflash bombs and had a crew of three – pilot, co-pilot/photo-navigator and photo technician/gunner/ECM operator. Note the camera fairings on the side of the forward fuselage.**

Los Angeles–New York–Los Angeles speed record of 9 hours, 31 minutes. On June 6, a pair of Skywarriors took off from a carrier off the coast of California, flew across the US and landed four hours later on another carrier stationed off the east coast of Florida. The A3D-1 and the A3D-2 ultimately equipped 13 US Navy VAH squadrons, including two training units.

By the late 1950s, Skywarrior versions included the specialized and primarily land-based electronic reconnaissance A3D-2Q (later known as the EA-3B), the photographic reconnaissance A3D-2P (redesignated RA-3B), and the A3D-2T trainer (TA-3B). The last of 283 Skywarriors left the production line in January 1961 and in 1962 the aircraft was redesignated A-3 by which time, due to its size, it had been christened 'Whale' by its crews.

By 1965 the Skywarrior was in action over Vietnam, initially as a conventional bomber dropping 'iron' bombs, although mining missions were flown later. It was, however, as tanker aircraft that most Skywarriors saw service in South-east Asia.

Eighty-five A-3Bs had their bombing kit removed and permanently replaced by tanker equipment – these aircraft were redesignated KA-3Bs. Later, a number of these were modified for combined electronic countermeasures/aerial tanker use and were redesignated EKA-3B. Tanker Skywarriors, who helped aircraft short of fuel or damaged return to their base or carrier, were credited with saving over 700 aircraft from loss during the course of the Vietnam war.

As advancing technology rendered its old bombing role obsolete, the resilient aircraft's evolution kept it in service for many years. The EA-3B was withdrawn from US carrier use in December 1987 but a few Skywarriors served in the 1991 Gulf War.

A substantially revised US Air Force version of the Skywarrior was named the Destroyer and designated B-66. Douglas built 294 B-66 Destroyers in bomber, photo-recon, electronic countermeasures and weather reconnaissance versions, many of which were active in the Vietnam War.

ABOVE: **The largest and heaviest carrier-borne aircraft of its day – the A-3 Skywarrior. Note the lack of the defensive tail gun, which was deleted in later versions of the A-3.**

Douglas A-3B Skywarrior

First flight: October 28, 1952 (XA3D-1)

Power: Two Pratt & Whitney 4,763kg/10,500lb thrust J57-P-10 turbojets

Armament: Two 20mm cannon in remotely controlled rear turret plus up to 5,443kg/12,000lb of bombs

Size: Wingspan – 22.1m/72ft 6in
Length – 23.27m/76ft 4in
Height – 6.95m/22ft 9.5in
Wing area – 75.43m²/812sq ft

Weights: Empty – 17,876kg/39,409lb
Maximum take-off – 37,195kg/82,000lb

Performance: Maximum speed – 982kph/610mph
Ceiling – 12,495m/41,000ft
Range – 1,690km/1,050 miles
Climb – 1,100m/3,600ft per minute

LEFT: **The unusual and distinctive Fairey Gannet was a vital aircraft in the Royal Navy's Cold War inventory, and provided anti-submarine and then Airborne Early Warning protection across a 23-year period. Note the 'finlets'.**

Fairey Gannet

From hard lessons during World War II, the Royal Navy had learned the value of carrier-based anti-submarine aircraft. For the post-war years the Navy needed a modern aircraft to tackle the submarine threat posed to Britain's navy and its interests by any potential enemy. In 1945 the Fleet Air Arm issued a requirement, GR.17/45, for a carrier-based Anti-Submarine Warfare (ASW) aircraft that could both hunt and kill submarines.

Of two cosmetically similar designs (the other from Blackburn) built to prototype standard, it was the Fairey 17 that ultimately won the contract having flown for the first time on September 19, 1949. The aircraft had a deep barrel-like fuselage to accommodate both sensors and weapons for hunting and killing enemy craft. Power came from an Armstrong Siddeley Double Mamba engine which was actually two turboprop engines driving a shared gearbox, which in turn drove a contra-rotating propeller system. The Double Mamba was chosen as one of the engines could be shut down for more economical cruising flight. Conventional twin-engined

aircraft exhibit problematic handling if one engine fails, resulting in what is known as 'asymmetric flight' when the working engine forces its side of the aeroplane ahead of the other side resulting in a crabbing flightpath as well as major concerns on landing. If 'half' of a Double Mamba failed this would not be an issue for the pilot of the 'single-engined' Gannet.

The Fairey 17 began carrier deck trials in early 1950, and on June 19 that year the aircraft made the first landing of a turboprop aircraft on a carrier – HMS *Illustrious*. The Admiralty then requested that search radar be included as well as a third seat for its operator which resulted in a third modified prototype that flew in May 1951. When Fairey's aircraft won the competition to go into production, the name Gannet was given to the aircraft. The Gannet, brimming with equipment and weapons, was a technically complicated aircraft, an example being the wings that folded not once but twice for below-deck stowage. Due to development delays, the Gannet AS.1 did not enter Fleet Air Arm service until 1955, some ten years after the requirement was first issued.

The Gannet's fuselage had a big weapons bay to accommodate two torpedoes or other munitions, up to a maximum weapon load of 900kg/ 2,000lb. A retractable radome under the rear fuselage housed the search radar. When the extendable 'dustbin' radome was added, it led to lateral instability in flight, which was remedied by the addition of two auxiliary finlets to the horizontal tailplane. Simply raising the height of the vertical tailplane would have had the same effect but would have exceeded below-deck hangar height limits. The Gannet's crew of three sat in

ABOVE: **The Fairey Gannet was a large and tall aircraft and required a complex wing-folding mechanism to enable the aircraft to fit below the decks of Royal Navy aircraft carriers.**

tandem, with pilot, observer/navigator, and radio/radar operator each in their own cockpits, the radio-radar operator's seat facing the tail of the aircraft.

A number of Gannets were operated by foreign air arms. Deliveries to the Royal Australian Navy for carrier operations began in 1955 (phased out in 1967), while the former West German naval air arm operated Gannets from shore bases, phasing them out in 1965. Indonesia obtained refurbished Royal Navy examples.

A total of 181 Gannet AS.1s were built together with 38 Gannet T.2 conversion trainers for training pilots on the idiosyncrasies of the aircraft and its unique powerplant. In 1956, the improved 3,035hp Double Mamba 101 was introduced into Gannets on the production line. Aircraft powered by the 101 were designated AS.4 and T.5 for the trainer version. The Gannet AS.6 was the AS.4 with a new 1961 radar and electronics fit to keep it effective.

Fairey were also contracted to produce an Airborne Early Warning (AEW) Gannet to replace the Douglas Skyraider in

Fleet Air Arm service. Designated AEW.3, these were new-build dedicated early warning aircraft mounting a huge radar installation on the underside of the fuselage beneath the cockpit. This version, which served until 1978, carried a pilot and two radar plotters who were housed in a rear cabin.

ABOVE: **The Gannet AS.1 had a large weapons bay, big enough to accommodate two torpedoes. The version had a retractable 'dustbin' ventral radome that housed a search radar.**

Fairey Gannet AS.1

First flight: September 19, 1949 (prototype)
Power: One Armstrong Siddeley 2,950eshp Double Mamba 100 turboprop
Armament: Up to 907kg/2,000lb of torpedoes, depth charges
Size: Wingspan – 16.56m/54ft 4in
Length – 13.11m/43ft
Height – 4.18m/13ft 8.5in
Wing area – 44.85m²/483sq ft
Weights: Empty – 6,835kg/15,069lb
Maximum take-off – 9,798kg/21,600lb
Performance: Maximum speed – 499kph/310mph
Ceiling – 7,620m/25,000ft
Range – 1,518km/943 miles
Climb – 670m/2,200ft per minute

Grumman A-6 Intruder

Designed for a 1957 US Navy competition, the Grumman A-6 Intruder was a two-seat all-weather, subsonic, carrier-based attack aircraft. While the performance of the subsonic A-6 was not spectacular, it was superbly suited to the particular attack role for which it was carefully tailored. The prototype made its first test flight in April 1960 and was followed by 482 production A-6As delivered to the US Navy from early 1963.

From night flights over the jungles of Vietnam to Desert Storm missions above heavily fortified targets in Iraq, the Grumman A-6 Intruder developed a work-horse reputation and was the subject of many tales of daring aviation during its 34-year career as the US Navy's principal medium-attack aircraft. The aircraft's ruggedness and all-weather mission capability made it a formidable asset to US Navy and Marine Corps air wings throughout its service. The strengths of the Intruder included its ability to fly in any weather and its heavy weapons payload – two traits highlighted on the big screen in the 1991 action film *Flight of the Intruder*. A little-known fact is that the Intruder delivered more ordnance during the Vietnam War than the B-52.

A tough and versatile aircraft, the A-6 was called upon to fly the most difficult missions, with flying low and alone in any weather its specialty. The all-weather attack jet saw action in every conflict the US has been involved in since Vietnam. With the ability to carry more ordnance, launch a wider variety of smart weapons, conduct day or night strikes over greater distances on internal fuel than any carrier-borne aircraft before

TOP: **A US Navy A-6 about to be bombed-up with mines on the deck of a US carrier. The Intruder was capable of carrying a staggering array of weaponry, which made it extremely useful to military planners. Note the folded wings and the integral fold-down ladder beneath the cockpit.** ABOVE: **The Prowler was developed specifically for use over Vietnam.**

or since, and provide mid-air refuelling support to other carrier jets, the Intruder is considered by some to be the most versatile military aircraft of modern times.

In 1986 the A-6E, an advanced upgraded development of the A-6A, proved that it was the best all-weather precision bomber in the world in the joint strike on Libyan terrorist-related targets. With US Air Force F-111s, A-6E Intruders penetrated sophisticated Libyan air-defence systems, which had been alerted by the high level of diplomatic tension and by rumours of impending attacks. Evading over 100 guided missiles, the strike force flew at a low level in complete darkness, and accurately delivered laser-guided and other ordnance on target.

No guns of any kind were carried aboard the A-6, and the aircraft had no internal bomb bay. A wide variety of stores,

LEFT: **Two A-6 Intruders operating from the USS _Constellation_ during the Vietnam War. Note the sheer number of bombs (18 Mk 82 free fall) each aircraft is carrying and the blackened airbrakes under the word 'Navy'.** ABOVE: **The Intruder was finally retired in 1997.**

however, could be mounted externally, including both conventional and nuclear bombs, fuel tanks, and an assortment of rockets and missiles. As with all versatile attack aircraft, many combinations of payload and mission radius were available to the A-6E. For example, a weapons load of 945kg/2,080lb consisting of a Mk 43 nuclear bomb could be delivered at a mission radius of 1,432km/890 miles. For that mission, four 1,136-litre/300-US gallon external tanks are carried. Alternatively, a bomb load of 4,676kg/10,296lb could be delivered at a mission radius of 724km/450 miles with two 1,136-litre/300-US gallon external tanks. Intruders were retired from front-line service in the late 1990s.

The EA-6B Prowlers were developed from the EA-6A which was an Intruder airframe intended primarily to be an electronic countermeasures and intelligence-gathering platform. These aircraft were initially designed to fly in support of the Intruders on Vietnam missions. The EA-6B is, however, a significant

aircraft in its own right and provides an umbrella of protection for strike aircraft (by suppressing enemy air defences), ground troops and ships by jamming enemy radar, electronic data links and communications. At the same time, the Prowler is gathering tactical electronic intelligence within the combat area. The EA-6B has proven itself in Vietnam, the Middle East, South-west Asia and the Balkans, where strike aircraft losses were dramatically reduced when the Prowler was on station.

As a result of 'restructuring of US military assets' in 1995, the EF-111 Raven was retired and the EA-6B was left as the sole tactical radar support jammer in the US inventory. At the time of writing, eight expeditionary squadrons are now available to the US Commanders in Chief – four Navy squadrons with US Air Force aircrews and four US Marine Corps. The United States Department of Defense describes the Prowler as 'a unique national asset' – the type will fly on for the foreseeable future.

ABOVE: **This A-6 Intruder shows the later wing-tip mounted airbrakes deployed. The United States Navy and Marine Corps were the only operators of the type.**

Grumman A-6E Intruder

First flight: April 19, 1960 (YA-6A)
Power: Two Pratt & Whitney 4,218kg/9,300lb thrust J52-P-8B turbojets
Armament: Up to 8,165kg/18,000lb of nuclear or conventional ordnance or missiles
Size: Wingspan – 16.15m/53ft
 Length – 16.69m/54ft 9in
 Height – 4.93m/16ft 2in
 Wing area – 49.13m^2/529sq ft
Weights: Empty – 12,093kg/26,660lb
 Maximum catapult take-off – 2,6581kg/58,600lb
Performance: Maximum speed – 1,035kph/644mph
 Ceiling – 12,925m/42,400ft
 Range – 1,627km/1,011 miles
 Climb – 2,621m/8,600ft per minute

Grumman F9F-2 Panther

The Panther was the US Navy's most widely used jet fighter of the Korean War and the first of the Grumman 'cats' to be jet powered. The Panther was also the first carrier-borne jet to see action. Although it was mainly used in the ground-attack role, it did notch up some air combat successes against North Korean MiGs. On July 3, 1950, a Panther of US Navy unit VF-51 aboard USS *Valley Forge* scored the US Navy's first aerial kill of the Korean war when it downed a Yak-9. By the end of the war the F9F had flown 78,000 combat missions.

Grumman's first jet fighter for the US Navy had its origins in the last days of World War II, when the US Navy Fighter Branch drew up a requirement for an all-weather/night radar-equipped carrier-borne fighter. As originally planned, Grumman's proposed XF9F-1 was powered by no less than four jet engines positioned in the wings. The high number of engines was dictated by the low power output of early

ABOVE: The Panther was operated by the US Navy and US Marine Corps and was the mount of the famous Blue Angels. Reconditioned Panthers were sold to Argentina but were only used from land bases. BELOW LEFT: The wings folded hydraulically from just outboard of the main gear but the wing fold angle was well short of the vertical. Two 454-litre/120-US gallon fuel tanks were permanently mounted on the wingtips of production versions.

turbojets. That many engines called for a wingspan of almost 17m/55.7ft which concerned Grumman – they knew that their twin-engine Tigercat had already proved large for carrier operations.

The US Navy were aware of British jet developments and imported two Rolls-Royce Nenes for testing. They were so impressed that the Grumman design was refined and when the prototype XF9F-2 Panther flew on November 24, 1947, it was powered by a lone Rolls-Royce Nene engine. In the same year, US engine giant Pratt & Whitney acquired a licence and produced their own Nene as the J42 which went on to power a number of US military aircraft. The type's distinctive 454-litre/120-US gallon wingtip fuel tanks were first tested in February 1948 and were adopted as standard to extend the aircraft's range. The straight-wing F9F-2 went into production and was equipping US naval units by mid-1949 having completed carrier trials two months earlier. The type proved popular with pilots who praised its handling, performance and reliability.

The Panther had a large fuselage to accommodate the large diameter engines of the time and two big internal fuel tanks, which enabled the aircraft to carry twice as much as fuel as the Hawker Sea Hawk still on the drawing board at the time. An ejection seat was fitted in the pressurized cockpit while the nose contained radio equipment and four 20mm cannon. Later -2s had underwing racks for two 454kg/1,000lb bombs and six 5in rockets for service in Korea. For a time the attack version of the -2 was designated F9F-2B but as most were modified for attack missions, the B was dropped.

A small number of Panther F9F-3s were built powered by the Allison J33 but these were later converted to -2 standard by the installation of the J42 engine. A total of 109 examples of the -4 were ordered, but powerplant (Allison J33-A-16) issues led to most being completed to -5 standard.

The F9F-5 with its lengthened (by 0.61m/2ft) fuselage and taller fin were powered by the J48 (a licence-built Rolls-Royce Tay) featuring water injection and 3,175kg/7,000lb thrust. Having first flown as the XF9F-5 in December 1949, the longer fuselage could hold a further 2,888 litres/763 US gallons of fuel. This was the most produced Panther, and a number of these machines became F9F-5P reconnaissance versions.

F9F-5 Panthers continued in front-line US Navy service until October 1958, when VAH-7 retired their last machines. The type did, however, continue to equip training units into the 1960s, while the F9F-5KD/DF-9E was used for drone work in missile trials. In 1966 a batch of F9F-2s were reconditioned as fighters, and were supplied to the Argentine Navy.

TOP: **Panthers operating from the deck of the USS *Bon Homme Richard* CV-31. The carrier first deployed to the Western Pacific for actions against targets in Korea in May 1951 and remained on station until December 1951. The carrier and its Panthers returned for the same period in 1952.** ABOVE: **Rocket-armed Panthers from USS *Boxer*, CV-21, over Wonsan in 1951. This was the scene of the large-scale UN landing.** LEFT: **A F9F-2B Panther armed with six 5in High-Velocity Aircraft Rockets (HVARs). On landing approach, the arrester hook would first be extended then lowered, ready to catch the wire.** BELOW LEFT: **An F9F-2B of VF-112 'Fighting Twelve' during the unit's time in the Korean War.**

Grumman F9F-2B Panther

First flight: November 24, 1947
Power: Pratt & Whitney 2,586kg/5,700lb thrust J42-P-8 turbojet (licence-built R-R Nene)
Armament: Four 20mm cannon plus underwing weapon load of up to 907kg/2,000lb
Size: Wingspan – 11.58m/37ft 11.75in
   Length – 11.35m/37ft 3in
   Height – 3.45m/11ft 4in
   Wing area –23.22m²/250sq ft
Weights: Empty – 4,533kg/9,993lb
   Maximum take-off – 8,842kg/19,494lb
Performance: Maximum speed – 877kph/545mph
   Ceiling – 13,590m/44,600ft
   Range – 2,177km/1,353 miles
   Climb – 1,567m/5,140ft per minute

Grumman F9F Cougar

Grumman, aware of wartime German swept-wing research, had considered a swept-wing version of the F9F in December 1945. In March 1950 the company sought official approval for a swept-wing version of the Panther – Grumman was given the green light for this logical and speedy development of an already successful programme. Having been granted a contract in March 1951, Grumman tested the first swept-wing aircraft of the F9F family (still a modified Panther) on September 20, 1951.

It was different enough from the Panther to warrant the new Cougar name but the US Navy really considered it to be just a swept-wing version of the Panther, hence the F9F designation – in fact only the forward fuselage was retained from the original straight-winged aircraft. The wings had 35 degrees sweep and the wingtip fuel tanks were deleted – power was provided by the J48-8 engine with water/alcohol injection giving a thrust of 3,289kg/7,250lb.

An initial production run of 646 F9F-6s were delivered to the US Navy between mid-1952 and July 1954. Armament consisted of four 20mm cannon in the nose while two 454kg/1,000lb bombs could be carried under the wings, as could 570-litre/150-US gallon drop tanks. The Cougar entered US Navy service in late 1952 and, unlike the straight-winged Panther, would not have been outclassed by Russian MiG-15s had it seen Korean War service. Sixty Cougars were built as F9F-6P reconnaissance versions fitted with cameras instead of the cannon in the nose.

The F9F-7 version (later redesignated F-9H in 1962), powered by the 2,880kg/6,350lb J33 engine, reached a production total of 168. The J33 proved to be disappointing and unreliable so almost all were converted to take the reliable J48 engines, thus becoming indistinguishable from the earlier F9F-6s.

The F9F-8 (later redesignated F-9J) was the final production version of the fighter. It featured a 200mm/8in-longer fuselage and bigger, modified wings with greater chord and wing area for better low-speed, high angle of attack flying and to give increased room for fuel tanks. The F9F-8 first flew in December 1953 and in January 1954 exceeded the speed of sound in a shallow dive. A total of 601 of these

ABOVE: The F9F-6 Cougar replaced the Panther in service with the US Navy Blue Angels aerobatics team but these aircraft were withdrawn when problems developed so the team reverted back to the F9F–5 Panther until December 1954 when they acquired the newer F9F-8 model. LEFT: The F9F-8 was in more ways than one the ultimate version of the fighter. This version had six hardpoints for fuel tanks and missiles and is shown here armed with four Sidewinders.

aircraft were delivered between April 1954 and March 1957 – most were equipped for inflight refuelling, and late production examples could carry four AIM-9 Sidewinder air-to-air missiles beneath the wings. Most earlier aircraft were then modified to this configuration. A number of F9F-8s were even fitted with nuclear bombing equipment. F9F-8s were withdrawn from front-line service in 1958–59 to be replaced by the F8U Crusader and F11F Tiger.

The F9F-8B (later the AF-9J) were F9F-8s converted into single-seat attack-fighters while 110 photo-reconnaissance versions, the F9F-8P, were also delivered in 1955–57. The US Navy acquired 377 two-seat F9F-8T (later TF-9J) trainers between 1956 and 1960 for use as advanced trainers and for weapons and carrier training – they served until 1974. Armed with twin 20mm cannon they could also carry bombs or missiles. This was the only version of the Cougar to see action – they were used in the airborne command role during 1966 and 1967, directing air strikes in South Vietnam. After withdrawal from active service, many Cougars were used

as unmanned drones (F9F-6K) for combat training or as drone directors (F9F-6D) – these were later redesignated QF-9F and DF-9F respectively. Two-seat trainer versions of the Cougar were still flying in US Navy service in the mid-1970s.

The only other air arm to use the Cougar was the Argentine Navy who also operated the Panther. An Argentine Cougar was the first aircraft to break the sound barrier in that country.

TOP AND ABOVE: **The F9F-8T was a two-seat carrier-capable trainer version of the F9F-8 that retained some of cannon armament of the single-seat version – the student sat in front, instructor in the rear. The F9F-8T entered service with the Naval Air Training Command (NATC) in 1957 and eventually equipped five squadrons. The F9F-8T (later the TF-9J) played an important role in training most of the pilots who were later to fly combat missions in Vietnam.**

ABOVE: **The Cougar and earlier Panther were powered mainly by engines derived from powerplants developed by Frank Whittle in the UK but it was US engineers who really maximized the output of the licence-built Nene.**

Grumman F9F-8 Cougar

First flight: September 20, 1951
Power: Pratt & Whitney 3,266kg/7,200lb thrust J48-P-8A turbojet
Armament: Two 20mm cannon plus 907kg/2,000lb of underwing weapons
Size: Wingspan – 10.52m/34ft 6in
    Length – 13.54m/44ft 5in including probe
    Height – 3.73m/12ft 3in
    Wing area – 31.31m2/337sq ft
Weights: Empty – 5,382kg/11,866lb
    Maximum take-off – 11,232kg/24,763lb
Performance: Maximum speed –
    1,041kph/647mph
    Ceiling – 15,240m/50,000ft
    Range – 1,610km/1,000 miles
    Climb – 1,860m/6,100ft per minute

Grumman F-14 Tomcat

Despite its age, the swing-wing, twin-engine Grumman F-14 Tomcat remained one of the world's most potent interceptors until its retirement. Its primary missions, in all weathers, were air superiority, fleet air defence and, latterly, precision strikes against ground targets. Continued developments and improvements maintained its capabilities to the extent that it was still a potent threat and an effective deterrent to any hostile aircraft foolish enough to threaten US Navy aircraft carrier groups. Its mix of air-to-air weapons was unmatched by any other interceptor type, and its radar was the most capable long-range airborne interception radar carried by any fighter of the time. With its mix of weapons it could attack any target at any altitude from ranges between only a few hundred feet to over 160km/100 miles away.

The F-14 had its beginnings in the early 1960s when Grumman collaborated with General Dynamics on the abortive F-111B, the carrier-based escort fighter version of the F-111. Even before the F-111B cancellation took place, Grumman began work on a company-funded project known as Design 303, a carrier-borne aircraft for the air superiority, escort fighter, and deck-launched interception role.

Having flown for the first time on December 21, 1970, the first two US Navy F-14 squadrons were formed in 1972 and

ABOVE: **Wings swept back for high-speed flight, the F-14 was at the top of its game for over three decades and posed a major threat to any aircraft foolish enough to engage it.** BELOW LEFT: **On the deck of the USS *Saratoga*, a Tomcat is readied for flight. A Phoenix AAM with a protective shroud over its radome awaits loading on a weapons trolley.**

went to sea in 1974, making the Tomcat the first variable-geometry carrier-borne aircraft in service. Its variable-geometry wings were designed for both speed and greater stability. In full forward-sweep position, the wings provided the lift needed for slow-speed flight, especially needed during carrier landings. In swept-back positions, the wings blended into the aircraft, giving the F-14 a dart-like configuration for high-speed supersonic flight.

The F-14 Tomcat was designed to carry a million-dollar missile, the AIM-54 Phoenix, and was the only aircraft armed with the AIM-54. With a range of over 200km/120 miles, the AIM-54 gave the Tomcat a very long-range punch. Enemy aircraft could be engaged before the Tomcat even appeared on its opponents' radar screens. Less expensive Sidewinders were also carried for close air fighting.

The F-14B, introduced in November 1987, incorporated new General Electric F-110 engines. A 1995 upgrade programme was initiated to incorporate new digital avionics and weapon system improvements to strengthen the F-14's multi-mission capability. The vastly improved F-14D, delivered from 1990, was a major upgrade with F-110 engines, new APG-71 radar system, Airborne Self-Protection Jammer (ASPJ), Joint Tactical Information Distribution System (JTIDS) and Infra-Red Search and Track (IRST). Additionally, all F-14 variants were given precision strike capability using the LANTIRN (Low-Altitude Navigation and Targeting Infra-Red for Night) targeting system, night-vision compatibility, new defensive countermeasures systems and a new digital flight control

LEFT: **The F-14 could carry six examples of the Phoenix and was the only aircraft that carried the 'million-dollar missile' in service.** ABOVE: **An F-14 of US Navy unit VF-103 with its wings spread for lower-speed flight. The type's starring role in the film *Top Gun* suddenly made the Tomcat known to millions the world over.**

system. LANTIRN pods, placed on an external point beneath the right wing, allowed the F-14 to drop laser-guided bombs under the cover of darkness. The improved F-14B and F-14D were built and deployed by the US Navy in modest numbers.

The Tomcat first got to prove itself in combat on August 19, 1981, when two F-14s from the USS *Nimitz* were 'intercepted' by two Libyan Sukhoi Su-22 fighter-bombers. The Libyan jets apparently attacked the F-14s and were destroyed with ease. Again on January 4, 1989, two Libyan MiG-23 'Floggers' were engaged by two F-14s and shot down.

Tomcats also saw combat during Operation 'Desert Storm' providing top cover protection for bombers and other aircraft, and performing TARPS (Tactical Air Reconnaissance Pod System) missions – the TARPS-equipped F-14 was the US Navy's only manned tactical reconnaissance platform at the time. In late 1995 the F-14 Tomcat was used in the bomber role against targets in Bosnia. Nicknamed 'Bombcats', the F-14s dropped laser-guided 'smart' bombs while other aircraft illuminated the targets with lasers.

At one time it was thought that the F-14 would remain in service to at least 2008, but the high cost of upgrades and maintenance finally led to the retirement of the type that epitomized 'Top Gun' in late 2006. The last F-14 combat mission was completed over Iraq on February 8, 2006. During their final deployment on the USS *Theodore Roosevelt*, Tomcat units VF-31 and VF-213 collectively completed 1,163 combat sorties totaling 6,876 flight hours, and dropped 4,300kg/9,500lb of ordnance during reconnaissance, surveillance, and close air support missions in support of Operation 'Iraqi Freedom'. The last flight of the F-14 Tomcat in US service took place on October 4, 2006, when an F-14D of VF-31 was ferried to Republic Airport on Long Island, New York.

A total of 79 of the type were even exported to Iran before the downfall of the Shah and a number were thought to still be in service in 2007, despite having been without the benefit of US technical back-up since 1980.

ABOVE: **The range of weaponry that the F-14 could carry was formidable, and included long, medium and short-range air-to-air missiles, air-to-ground weapons and even mines.**

Grumman F-14 Tomcat

First flight: December 21, 1970

Power: Two Pratt & Whitney 9,480kg/20,900lb afterburning thrust TF30-P-412A turbofans

Armament: One 20mm cannon plus six AIM-7F Sparrow and four AIM-9 Sidewinder AAMs, or six AIM-54A Phoenix long-range AAMs and two AIM-9s, or a variety of air-to-surface weapons up to 6,575kg/14,500lb

Size: Wingspan – 19.55m/64ft 1.5in unswept
Length – 19.1m/62ft 8in
Height – 4.88m/16ft
Wing area – 52.49m²/565sq ft

Weights: Empty – 18,036kg/39,762lb
Maximum take-off – 31,945kg/70,426lb

Performance: Maximum speed – 2,486kph/1,545mph
Ceiling – 18,290m/60,000ft
Range – 725km/450 miles
Climb – 18,290m/60,000ft in 2 minutes, 6 seconds

Grumman F11F Tiger

While the Grumman Cougar was making its first flight, Grumman designers were already hard at work on an aerodynamically advanced supersonic successor (known to Grumman as the G-98) derived from the Cougar/Panther family. It became clear that a simple redesign of the Cougar would not meet the requirements and the G-98 evolved into a completely different aircraft with no resemblance to the Cougar.

The resulting aircraft was the smallest and lightest aircraft that could be designed for the day-fighter mission. The reduced size had another advantage – only the wingtips needed to be folded for carrier handling and storage thus eliminating the need for complex heavy wing-folding gear. The Wright J65 engine, a licence-built version of the British Armstrong Siddeley Sapphire, was fed by a pair of intakes mounted on the fuselage sides behind the cockpit, which was located well forward on the

ABOVE: **Power for the Tiger came from a licensed development of the British Sapphire engine. As well as undergoing some redesign the engine was, in the case of some US Navy examples, fitted with an afterburner too.**
BELOW LEFT: **The second Tiger prototype, equipped with an afterburning engine, became the second supersonic US Navy aircraft to break the sound barrier. Despite early promise, the F11F's front-line career only lasted four years.**

nose and had a rear-sliding canopy. The sloping nose gave the pilot good forward visibility – an important factor when landing on a pitching carrier deck moving in all directions. A retractable tailskid was included to minimize damage to the rear fuselage in the event of a nose-high landing. By now designated the XF9F-9, the aircraft took to the air for the first time on July 30, 1954, with Grumman test pilot 'Corky' Meyer at the controls.

During the long and troubled development period that followed, the aircraft eventually got a new designation – the F11F – and, in keeping with Grumman's feline traditions, the name Tiger. The engine's afterburner problems continued and a de-rated engine was fitted to get the aircraft into service.

The first catapult launchings and carrier landings took place aboard the USS Forrestal in April, 1956. During service trials, the range and endurance of the Tiger were found to be inadequate so the second production batch featured additional fuel tanks built into the engine intake walls and fin, increasing internal fuel capacity from 3,460 litres/914 US gallons to 3,971 litres/1,049 US gallons. A 1.8m/6ft-longer nose was also fitted to later production examples to take the AN/APS-50 radar which was never actually installed.

The first short-nosed F11F-1s were delivered to VX-3 based at NAS Atlantic City, New Jersey, in February of 1957. In service, the Tiger served on the US carriers USS Ranger, Intrepid, Saratoga, Forrestal and Bon Homme Richard.

The Vought Crusader entered Navy service at about the same time as the Tiger and was much faster at altitude. Although easy to maintain, and having pleasant flying qualities, the Tiger was, however, plagued more by engine problems than anything else. Consequently, the US Navy became disenchanted with the Tiger and cancelled contracts for additional machines. Only around 200 F11F-1s were built before production ended with the delivery of the last F11F-1 on January 23, 1959.

The last US Navy Tigers were phased out by April 1961 after only four years of service. Following its withdrawal from fleet service, the Tiger was used primarily as a training aircraft and was retired by VT-26 in mid-1967.

The Tiger was, however, famous as the mount of the Blue Angels US Navy flight demonstration team who operated the type from April 1957 until 1969. During this time, in 1962, the F11F-1 had been redesignated F-11A.

In 1973, two ex-Blue Angels F-11As were taken from 'boneyard' storage at Davis Monthan Air Force Base and were modified by Grumman as testbeds to evaluate inflight control systems. These were the last Tigers to fly and returned to storage in 1975.

LEFT: **The Tiger was swiftly relegated to secondary duties because its performance was inferior to the much more capable and reliable Vought F-8 Crusader and the J65 engine proved unreliable and given to exploding. Note the four Sidewinder missiles under the wings of this Tiger.** ABOVE: **The Tiger's teeth. This publicity shot shows the array of weaponry with which a Tiger could be armed, including cannon, Sidewinder air-to-air missiles and unguided folding-fin rockets.** BELOW LEFT: **A fine example of 'showboating'. Despite the short front-line career, the Tiger was flown by the US Navy's Blue Angels flight team from 1957 to 1969.**

Grumman F11F-1

First flight: July 30, 1954
Power: Wright 3,379kg/7,450lb thrust J65-W-18 turbojet
Armament: Four 20mm cannon and four AIM9 Sidewinder AAMs under wings
Size: Wingspan – 9.64m/31ft 7.5in
Length – 14.31m/46ft 11.25in
Height – 4.03m/13ft 2.75in
Wing area – 23.23m²/250sq ft
Weights: Empty – 6,091kg/13,428lb
Maximum take-off – 10,052kg/22,160lb
Performance: Maximum speed – 1,207kph/750mph
Ceiling – 12,770m/41,900ft
Range – 2,044km/1,270 miles
Climb – 1,565m/5,130ft per minute

LEFT: **Apart from its powerful engines, the slender Tigercat possessed a low frontal area. The combination bestowed an impressive performance on the Grumman fighter.** ABOVE: **Inside the pilot's 'office' of an F7F-3P photo-reconnaissance version. The funnel and hose is the pilot's 'relief tube'.**

Grumman F7F Tigercat

The Tigercat had its origins in 1941, when Grumman began design work on a hard-hitting, high-performance twin-engine fighter to operate from the Midway class of US aircraft carriers. As it developed, it was apparent that the type was going to be heavier and faster than all previous US carrier aircraft. It was also unusual for the time in that it had a tricycle undercarriage although it retained the usual arrester hook and folding wings for carrier operations.

Even before the prototype flew in December 1943, the US Marine Corps had placed an order for 500 of the F7F-1 version. They wanted to use the Tigercat primarily as a land-based fighter operating in close support of Marines on the ground. Although deliveries began in April 1944, the big Grumman fighter arrived too late to be cleared for combat use in World War II.

Wartime production had diversified to deliver the F7F-2N night-fighter, which differed from the F7F-1 by the removal of a fuel tank to make way for a radar operator cockpit and the removal of nose armament for the fitting of the radar.

An improved fighter-bomber version was also developed, the F7F-3, which had different engines for more power at altitude, a slightly larger fin and bigger fuel tanks.

Tigercat production continued after the war's end with F7F-3N and F7F-4N night-fighters, both having lengthened noses to house the latest radar – some of these aircraft were strengthened and equipped for carrier operations. Some F7F-3s were also modified for electronic and photographic reconnaissance missions.

Although it missed action in World War II, the Tigercat did see combat with the Marine Corps over Korea. USMC fighter unit VMF(N)-513 was based in Japan when the Korean War broke out. Equipped with Tigercat night-fighters, they went in to action immediately as night-intruders and performed valuable service.

The US Marines were the only military operators of the Tigercat.

ABOVE: **After their military career, a handful of Tigercats were used for water-bombing forest fires, while others were optimized for air-racing.**

Grumman F7F-3N

First flight: December 1943 (F7F-1)
Power: Two Pratt & Whitney 2,100hp R-2800-34W Double Wasp radial piston engines
Armament: Four 20mm cannon in wing roots
Size: Wingspan – 15.7m/51ft 6in
  Length – 13.8m/45ft 4in
  Height – 5.06m/16ft 7in
  Wing area – 42.27m²/455sq ft
Weights: Empty – 7,379kg/16,270lb
  Maximum take-off – 11,666kg/25,720lb
Performance: Maximum speed – 700kph/435mph
  Ceiling – 1,2414m/40,700ft
  Range – 1,609km/1,000 miles
  Climb – 1,380m/4,530ft per minute

Grumman Tracker

The Grumman G-89 Tracker was a purpose-designed Cold War carrier-borne anti-submarine warfare aircraft that flew for the first time in December 1952. It was built to detect and then destroy fast, quiet deep-diving Soviet nuclear submarines. The aircraft would use both passive and active acoustic search systems, magnetic anomaly detection and powerful searchlights to find the enemy craft. The aircraft could work alone or with helicopters using dipping sonar to complement the Tracker's own sonobuoys. Once located, the enemy sub would be attacked with depth charges, torpedoes, bombs and rockets. Incredibly, one version of the Tracker was capable of carrying a nuclear depth charge.

The Tracker was a large high-wing monoplane with twin Wright Cyclone radial engines. Prototypes and early production aircraft were ordered at the same time in 1950, such was the need to get the type in service and keep Soviet subs in check. The type first entered service in February 1954 – although its early S2F designation was later dropped in favour of just S-2, the aircraft was popularly known as the 'Stoof' (S-two-F) throughout its career. Six military versions from S-2A to S-2G entered service.

The last Trackers in US service were eventually replaced in use by the S-3 Viking in 1976. Trackers, however, continued in service with other naval

air arms for many years. The Royal Australian Navy continued to use Trackers as front-line ASW aircraft until the mid-1980s. The Argentine Navy received its first S-2A models in the 1960s and upgraded these aircraft in the 1990s with turboprop engines.

Grumman produced 1,185 Trackers in the US and a further 99 aircraft designated CS2F were built in Canada under licence by de Havilland Canada for Canadian military use. Other customers for the Tracker included Australia, Holland, Italy, Peru, Japan, Taiwan, Venezuela, Turkey, South Korea, Thailand, Uruguay and Argentina.

From the late 1980s a number of retired US and Canadian Trackers were converted into fire-fighting aircraft called Firecats (or Turbo Firecats for the turboprop-equipped aircraft). Carrying between 800 and 1,200 US gallons of retardant in a tank replacing the military torpedo bay, these aircraft are expected to be in service in North America for years to come.

TOP: **The Tracker could carry torpedoes, depth charges and rockets – versions of the 'Stoof' in US Navy service could even carry a nuclear depth charge.** ABOVE: **A turboprop-powered remanufactured Turbo Firecat of the California Department of Forestry and Fire Protection.**

Grumman S-2E Tracker

First flight: December 4, 1952 (XS2F-1 prototype)
Power: Two Wright 1,525hp R-1820-82WA radial engines
Armament: One nuclear depth charge or homing torpedoes, depth charges or mines in weapons bay plus up to 60 sounding depth charges and 32 sonobuoys carried in the fuselage and the engine nacelles, plus a variety of bombs, rockets or torpedoes carried on underwing hardpoints
Size: Wingspan – 22.12m/72ft 7in
    Length – 13.26m/43ft 6in
    Height – 5.33m/17ft 6in
    Wing area – 45.06m²/485sq ft
Weights: Empty – 8,310kg/18,315lb
    Maximum take-off – 11,860kg/26,147lb
Performance: Maximum speed – 450kph/280mph
    Ceiling – 6,700m/22,000ft
    Range – 2,170km/1,350 miles
    Climb – 425m/1,390ft per minute

LEFT: **An E-2C about to catch the wire on the USS** *Enterprise.* **The distinctive swirl painted on the aircraft's rotodome tells us this aircraft is from VAW-123 'The Screwtops'.** ABOVE: **The C-2A Greyhound is an E-2 derivative that serves in the carrier-borne delivery role. The C-2A has the same tail and wings as the Hawkeye, but has a widened fuselage with a rear-loading ramp.** BELOW: **A French Hawkeye with its carrier,** *Charles de Gaulle.*

Grumman/Northrop Grumman E-2 Hawkeye

The twin turboprop E-2 Hawkeye is the US Navy's current all-weather, carrier-based tactical battle management airborne early warning, command and control aircraft. Having a crew of five, the high-wing aircraft can be most readily identified by the 7.32m/24ft-diameter radar rotodome attached to the upper fuselage containing a radar scanner that rotates several times per minute.

At a unit cost estimated to be $80 million (75 per cent of that being electronics), the Hawkeye provides all-weather airborne early warning, airborne battle management and command and control functions for the US Carrier Strike Group. In addition the E-2 can coordinate surface surveillance and air interdiction, offensive and defensive counter air control, close air support and strike coordination, search-and-rescue airborne coordination and communications relay. An integral component of each US Navy Carrier Strike Group air wing, the E-2C uses computerized radar, Identification Friend or Foe (IFF) and electronic surveillance sensors to provide early warning threat analysis against potentially hostile air and surface targets.

The E-2 Hawkeye was the world's first carrier-based aircraft designed from scratch for the all-weather airborne early warning and command and control mission. Since replacing the Grumman E-1 in 1964, the Hawkeye has been the eyes of the US Fleet. Since its combat debut during the Vietnam War, the E-2 has served the US Navy around the world. E-2s

from VAW-123 aboard the USS *America* directed F-14 Tomcat fighters flying combat air patrol during Operation 'El Dorado Canyon', the two-carrier battle group joint strike against terrorist-related Libyan targets in 1986. In the early 1990s, E-2s provided airborne command and control for Coalition air operations during the first Gulf War. Directing both strike and combat air patrol missions over Iraq, in the early days of the conflict the E-2 Hawkeye provided air control for the shoot-down of two Iraqi MIG-21 aircraft by carrier-based F/A-18. Later during the 1990s, E-2s supported Operations 'Northern' and 'Southern Watch' over Iraq. E-2s also supported NATO operations over the former Republic of Yugoslavia, including Operation 'Deny Flight'. More recently, E-2s have been widely used in Operations 'Enduring Freedom' and 'Iraqi Freedom', directing air strikes.

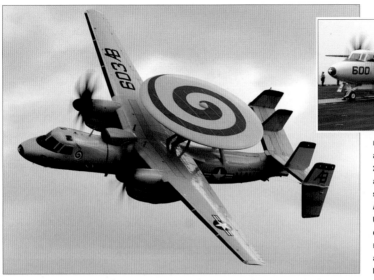

LEFT: **The E-2 Hawkeye is not a small aircraft, and has a wingspan of around 25m/80ft. It is one of the few military aircraft to carry a large radar dome, so it is easy to identify from most angles. Also note the four tail fins.** ABOVE: **The United States Navy quoted the unit cost of each aircraft to be $80 million.** BELOW LEFT: **The E-2 remains a vital aircraft in the US Navy inventory and will be in service for many years to come.**

The original E-2C, known as the Group 0, became operational in 1973 and has been through numerous upgrades since then. The first of these was the E-2C Group I which replaced the older APS-125 radar and T56-A-425 engines with the improved APS-139 radar and T56-A-427. This version was soon followed by the further improved Group II which featured the APS-145 radar. The Group II has been gradually upgraded with new navigation systems, displays and computers culminating in the E-2C Hawkeye 2000 variant. The latest version can track 2,000 targets simultaneously – while at the same time, detecting a further mind-boggling 20,000 targets – to a range in excess of 650km/400 miles while simultaneously guiding up to 100 air interceptions.

The E-2D Advanced Hawkeye (AHE), the newest variant of the E-2, is currently in development and is scheduled to be introduced to the US Fleet in 2011. AHE will feature a state-of-the-art advanced radar and upgraded aircraft systems that will reduce maintenance time and increase readiness. According to the US Navy, this version will "exhibit improved battle space target detection and situational awareness, support of Theater Air and Missile Defense (TAMD) operations and improved Operational Availability. The AHE mission will be to provide advance warning of approaching enemy surface units, cruise missiles and aircraft, to vector interceptors or strike aircraft to attack, and to provide area surveillance, intercept, communications relay, search and rescue, strike and air traffic control."

Variants of the E-2C Hawkeye are also flown by the Egyptian Air Force, Japanese Self Defence Air Force, Republic of Singapore Air Force, Taiwan Air Force and the French Navy.

Grumman/Northrop Grumman E-2C Hawkeye

First flight: October 21, 1960 (prototype)
Power: Two Allison 5,100ehp T56-A-425 or -427 turboprops
Armament: None
Size: Wingspan – 24.58m/80ft 7in
    Length – 17.6m/57ft 9in
    Height – 5.58m/18ft 4in
    Wing area – 65m²/700sq ft
Weights: Empty – 17,090kg/37,678lb
    Maximum take-off – 24,950kg/55,000lb
Performance: Maximum speed – 604kph/375mph
    Ceiling – 9,390m/30,800ft
    Range – 2,583km/1,605 miles
    Climb – 766m/2,515ft per minute

Hawker Sea Fury

The Hawker Fury, inspired and influenced by a captured Focke-Wulf Fw 190, was essentially a lighter, smaller version of the Hawker Tempest. A joint 1943 British Air Ministry and Admiralty specification for a fighter/naval interceptor was written around the project. The land-based Fury first flew in September 1944, but at the war's end the RAF interest in Hawker's ultimate piston-engined fighter ceased. Development of the Sea Fury did, however, continue following the naval version's test flight in February 1945. This aircraft was essentially a navalized land plane, complete with non-folding wings. The second prototype Sea Fury was a fully navalized aircraft with folding wings and an arrester hook, and was powered by a Bristol Centaurus XV.

The production naval version, the Sea Fury Mk X, began to replace Fleet Air Arm Supermarine Seafires in service from August 1947. Meanwhile trials with external stores and RATO (rocket-assisted take-off) equipment led to the development of the Sea Fury FB. Mk 11. It was this aircraft that represented the ultimate development of British piston-engined fighters and the FB.11 proved itself to be an extremely capable combat aircraft. FAA Sea Furies were among the few British aircraft types that saw combat during the Korean War (1950–53) where they were mainly used in the ground-attack role operating from HMS *Theseus*, HMS *Ocean*, HMS *Glory* and HMAS *Sydney*. Korea was the first true jet-versus-jet war but the Sea Fury is known to have destroyed more Communist aircraft than any other non-US type and even shot down a number of North Korean MiGs.

While flying a Sea Fury off HMS *Ocean*, Royal Navy Lieutenant Peter Carmichael destroyed a MiG-15 jet and earned himself a place in the history books. "At dawn on

TOP: **The Sea Fury was widely exported and customers included the Royal Australian Navy who operated 101 examples the type from 1949 to 1962. As the principal fleet defence fighter of the RAN, the type flew off the aircraft carriers HMAS *Sydney* and HMAS *Vengeance*.** ABOVE: **Beneath the cowling, the Sea Fury's mighty Bristol Centaurus radial engine. This excellent engine was first run in July 1938 but was not properly employed for almost four years.**

August 9, 1952, I was leading a section of four aircraft on a patrol near Chinnampo. We were flying at 3,500 feet, looking for rail targets when my Number Two called out 'MiGs five o'clock – coming in!' Eight came at us from the sun. One came at me head on and I saw his tracer coming over. I managed to fire a burst and then he flashed past. I looked over my shoulder and saw an aircraft going down. When all my section called in, I knew I'd bagged a MiG! I believe the Sea Fury is the finest single-seat piston fighter ever built."

The Sea Fury, the last piston-engined fighter in RN front-line service, flew on with Royal Navy Volunteer Reserve units until 1957 and was replaced in FAA service by the jet-powered Sea Hawk.

Although the RAF rejected the Fury design, a little-known contract with Iraq saw 55 land-based Furies and five two-seat trainers delivered to the Iraqi Air Force between 1948 and 1955. The IAF are known to have used the aircraft in the counter-insurgency role. Pakistan also received Furies and used them in action against India until 1973.

Sea Furies were also exported to Egypt, Burma, Canada, Australia and the Netherlands where a number were also licence-built by Fokker. At the time of the Cuban Missile Crisis in 1962, Cuba's fighter defence centred on 15 FB.11s imported during the Batista period.

ABOVE: **Sixty examples of the Sea Fury T. Mk 20 were also produced. These were two-seat tandem trainers with two canopies connected by a Perspex 'tunnel'. The instructor, seated to the rear, could observe the student through a periscope.**
LEFT: **A preserved Sea Fury sporting the D-Day style 'invasion stripes' applied to Royal Navy aircraft during the Korean War. Note the arrester hook.**

After their military service a number of these high-performance piston aircraft were snapped up for air racing in the United States where they set world record speeds. A number remain in flying condition on both sides of the Atlantic.

ABOVE: **On the leading edge of the Sea Fury wing from left to right are two 20mm cannon muzzles (same on far right), a carburettor air intake starboard and port, and the oil cooler air intake.**

Hawker Sea Fury FB.11

First flight: September 1, 1944 (Fury)
Power: Bristol 2,480hp Centaurus 18 two-row sleeve-valve radial engine
Armament: Four 20mm cannon in outer wings plus underwing provision for up to 907kg/2,000lb of bombs or rockets
Size: Wingspan – 11.69m/38ft 4.75in
(4.9m/16ft 1in folded)
Length – 10.56m/34ft 8in
Height – 4.81m/15ft 10in
Wing area – 26.01m²/280sq ft
Weights: Empty – 4,190kg/9,237lb
Maximum take-off – 5,669kg/12,500lb
Performance: Maximum speed – 740kph/460mph
Ceiling – 10,970m/36,000ft
Range – 1,223km/760 miles
Climb – 1,317m/4,320ft per minute

LEFT: **The Seasprite proved to be so capable it was put back into manufacture for the United States Navy.** ABOVE: **The continued upgrade of an essentially 1960s design with 1990s avionics has not been without problems, and in March 2008, the Australian Government cancelled its overrunning contract for SH-2Gs.**

Kaman SH-2 Seasprite

This helicopter originally entered US Navy service as the Kaman HU2K-1 having first flown on July 2, 1959. It was a single-engine helicopter primarily deployed aboard aircraft carriers in the search-and-rescue role. Redesignated UH-2A in 1962, by the end of 1965 the US Navy had received 190 single-engine UH-2A/B utility and rescue versions, most of which were upgraded during the late 1960s and 1970s. A second General Electric-built T58 turboshaft engine, an uprated transmission and a four-blade rotor gave the helicopter substantially increased load-capability and survivability.

The Seasprite was ultimately developed for the United States Navy as a ship-based fighting helicopter with anti-submarine and anti-surface threat capability. The late 1960s' Light Airborne Multi-Purpose System (LAMPS) gave the Seasprite a whole new career. LAMPS centred around the use of a light helicopter to extend the horizon of a warship's sensors and weapons – the Seasprites would track submarines

and attack them with torpedoes, and, in the anti-ship missile-defence role, provide warning of cruise missile attack. LAMPS Seasprites, designated SH-2Ds, were equipped with a search radar, an Electronic Surveillance Measures (ESM) receiver, sonobuoys, torpedoes, an active sonar repeater and a UHF acoustic data-relay transmitter. Secondary missions included medical evacuation, search and rescue, personnel and cargo transfer, as well as small boat interdiction, amphibious assault air support, gun fire spotting, mine detection and battle damage assessment.

The Seasprite SH-2F version had more powerful engines, improved rotors, a towed Magnetic Anomaly Detector (MAD), avionics upgrades, and a tailwheel moved forward to allow operations from smaller ship decks. The SH-2F was even ordered back into production after a 16-year gap, an extremely rare occurrence in aviation history. From 1982, Kaman built 54 brand new SH-2Fs for the US Navy. This

version's operational use included Operation 'Desert Storm' in 1991. The SH-2F was retired from active service in October 1993, after years of hard work. By the time of its retirement, the type was reported to need 30 hours of maintenance for each flight hour – the highest of any aircraft in the US Navy at the time.

The SH-2G Super Seasprite was a remanufactured SH-2F with much greater electronic warfare capability and more powerful engines that gave the type the highest power-to-weight ratio of any maritime helicopter. The type joined the US Navy Reserve inventory in February 1993 and was retired from service in May 2001 but currently remains in use with air arms in Egypt, Poland, Australia and New Zealand.

LEFT: **The Seasprite was used as a search and rescue aircraft throughout the whole Vietnam War. Between 1963 and 1964 the US Army acquired a version designated UH-2 and evaluated its ground support capabilities.**

Kaman Seasprite

First flight: July 2, 1959 (HU2K-1)
Power: Two General Electric 1,723shp T700-GE-401 turboshafts
Armament: Torpedoes, depth charges, anti-ship or anti-tank missiles, air-to-ground missiles or unguided rockets dependent on mission
Size: Rotor diameter – 13.5m/44ft
 Length – 16m/52ft 6in
 Height – 4.57m/15ft
Weights: Empty – 3,447kg/7,600lb
 Maximum take-off – 6,124kg/13,500lb
Performance: Maximum speed – 256kph/159mph
 Service ceiling – 6,218m/20,400ft
 Range – 1,000km/620 miles
 Climb – 632m/2,070ft per minute

Kamov Ka-25

The Ka-25 (NATO designation 'Hormone') was developed to meet the specification of a 1957 Soviet Navy requirement for a shipborne anti-submarine warfare helicopter. In response, Kamov developed the Ka-20 which flew for the first time during 1961 and was the basis for the production Ka-25. Around 460 were produced between 1966 and 1975 during which time the type replaced the Mil Mi-4 as the Soviet Navy's primary shipborne helicopter for killing submarines.

The Ka-25 is one of the easiest helicopters to identify thanks to Kamov's trademark counter-rotating coaxial main rotors, which dispense with the need for a tail rotor. This means the aircraft needs the shortest of tails which saves much needed space during carrier operations. Other distinguishing features include a search radar mounted beneath the nose. Though usually flown unarmed, some

ABOVE: **As well as the large search radar beneath the cockpit, versions of the Ka-25 were equipped with dipping sonar. Note the trademark counter-rotating coaxial main rotors.**

service aircraft were fitted with an internal weapons bay that could carry two torpedoes or depth charges, including nuclear versions for submarine destroying.

Up to 18 Ka-25 variants are believed to have been built, but the major sub-types were the Ka-25PL (NATO Hormone-A), the Ka-25Ts (Hormone-B, used for the guidance and targeting of

ship-launched missiles), the Ka-25PS (Hormone-C, used for SAR) and the Ka-25BShZ. The Ka-25B was the principal anti-submarine variant and was replaced in Russian service by the Ka-27. The Ka-25BShZ was developed to tow mine-sweeping equipment through the ocean.

Kamov Ka-25

First flight: 1961
Power: Two GTD-3F 900hp turboshaft engines
Armament: Torpedoes, conventional or nuclear depth charges
Size: Rotor diameter – 15.75m/51ft 8in
  Length – 9.75m/32ft
  Height – 5.4m/17ft 8in
Weights: Empty – 4,765kg/10,505lb
  Maximum take-off – 7,200kg/15,873lb
Performance: Maximum speed – 220kph/136mph
  Ceiling – 3,500m/11,483ft
  Range – 400km/248 miles

Kamov Ka-27

Kamov began work on a successor for its Ka-25 in 1967, following requests from the Soviet Navy for a helicopter capable of operating night or day and in all weathers. The Ka-27 (NATO codename 'Helix') was an all-new helicopter of similar dimensions to the Ka-25 and featuring Kamov's distinctive counter-rotating coaxial main rotors. The more powerfully engined Ka-27 flew for the first time in 1973 and it is still the

Russian Navy's standard ship-based anti-submarine helicopter.

The standard Ka-27PL anti-submarine version features a search radar mounted under the nose, dipping sonar and disposable sonobuoys and was designed to operate in pairs with one tracking the enemy craft while the following helicopter dropped depth charges. A simpler version, the Ka-28, was exported to India while other

operators of the Ka-27 include Ukraine, Vietnam, South Korea and China.

A civil version of the Ka-27, the Ka-32 exists and though none has been sold to military operators, some Ka-32s in Aeroflot markings have been seen operating off Russian naval ships.

LEFT: **Retaining many of the distinctive features of the earlier Ka-25, design work on the Ka-27 began in 1967. It remains in widespread use today. It has the distinctive Kamov coaxial rotors and twin-fin tailplane of earlier models.**

Kamov Ka-27PL

First flight: 1973
Power: Two Klimov 2,205shp TV3-117V turboshaft engines
Armament: Torpedoes or depth charges
Size: Rotor diameter – 15.90m/52ft 2in
  Length – 12.25m/40ft 2in
  Height – 5.4m/17ft 8in
Weights: Empty – 6,100kg/13,450lb
  Maximum take-off – 12,600kg/27,780lb
Performance: Maximum speed – 250kph/155mph
  Ceiling – 5,000m/16,405ft
  Range – 800km/496 miles
  Climb – 750m/2,460ft per minute

Lockheed S-3 Viking

The versatility of the Viking has led it to be known as the 'Swiss army knife of naval aviation'. The S-3 Viking in service today is an all-weather, carrier-based patrol/attack aircraft, which provides protection for the US fleet against hostile surface vessels while also functioning as the Carrier Battle Groups' primary tanker. The S-3, one of the most successful of all carrier aircraft, is extremely versatile and is equipped for many missions, including day/night surveillance, electronic countermeasures, command and control, and communications warfare, as well as Search-And-Rescue (SAR), a vital naval role.

In the late 1960s the deployment of Soviet deep-diving nuclear-powered submarines caused the US Navy to call for a new breed of carrier-borne US Navy ASW aircraft to succeed the Grumman S-2. Lockheed, in association with Vought Aeronautics, proposed the S-3A which came to be called Viking.

To keep the aircraft aerodynamically clean, as many protuberances as possible were designed to retract so as not to reduce the aircraft's top speed. Thus, the inflight refuelling probe, the Magnetic Anomaly Detection (MAD) boom at the rear of the aircraft and some sensors retracted for transit flight. The small four-man aircraft has folding wings, making it very popular on carriers due to the small amount of space it takes up relative to the importance of its mission. With its short stubby wings, the Viking was something of a wolf in sheep's clothing and could have given a very good account of itself had the Cold War heated up. Carrying state-of-the art radar systems and extensive sonobuoy deployment and control capability, the S-3A entered US Navy service with VS-41 in February 1974. In total, 187 were built and equipped 14 US Navy squadrons.

ABOVE: **This aircraft is pictured when it served with VS-35 the 'Sea Wolves' who were described simply as a 'sea control squadron'. Note the way the Viking's wings fold unopposed for maximum space saving.**
BELOW: **The aircraft's two General Electric turbofans can keep the Viking and its crew aloft for over 3,700km/2,300 miles.**

In the mid-1980s the aircraft were completely refurbished and modified to carry the Harpoon missile, the improved version being designated the S-3B. While the S-3A was primarily configured for anti-submarine warfare, the S-3B has evolved into a premier surveillance and precision-targeting platform for the US Navy and has the most modern precision-guided missile capabilities. It does so many things so well – surface and undersea warfare, mine warfare, electronic reconnaissance and analysis, over-the-horizon targeting, missile attack, and aerial tanking – that its current mission is summed up by the US Navy as being simply 'Sea Control'.

The S-3B's high-speed computer system processes and displays information generated by its targeting-sensor systems. To engage and destroy targets, the S-3B Viking employs an impressive array of airborne weaponry including the AGM-84 Harpoon anti-ship missile, AGM-65 Maverick infrared missile and a wide selection of conventional bombs and torpedoes. Future Viking aircraft will also have a control capability for the AGM-84 Standoff Land-Attack Missile Extended Range (SLAM-ER) missile. The S-3B provides the fleet with a very effective fixed wing, 'over the horizon' aircraft to combat the significant and varied threats presented by modern maritime combatants.

ABOVE: **The Viking has two underwing hardpoints that can be used to carry fuel tanks, general purpose and cluster bombs, missiles, rockets, and storage pods and a 'buddy' refuelling store as in the example shown. Its internal bomb bay stations can carry bombs, torpedoes and special stores.**

On March 25, 2003, an S-3B from the 'Red Griffins' of Sea Control Squadron Thirty-Eight (VS-38) became the first such aircraft to attack inland and to fire a laser-guided Maverick missile in combat. The attack was made on a 'significant naval target' in the Tigris River near Basra, Iraq. VS-38 was embarked on the USS *Constellation*.

One of the most important aircraft in the US inventory, the Viking has proved easy to update with the latest avionics and surveillance equipment. No date has been fixed for its retirement.

ABOVE: **This Viking is fitted for 'buddy' refuelling. The store under the port wing has a drogue which, when let out in flight, is used to pass fuel via the receiving aircraft's probe.**

Lockheed S-3B Viking

First flight: January 21, 1972
Power: Two General Electric 4212kg/9,275lb thrust TF-34-GE-400B turbofan engines
Armament: Up to 1,781kg/3,95lb of ordnance, including AGM-84 Harpoon, AGM-65 Maverick and AGM-84 SLAM missiles, torpedoes, rockets and bombs
Size: Wingspan – 20.93m/68ft 8in
Length – 16.26m/53ft 4in
Height – 6.93m/22ft 9in
Wing area – 55.55m²/598sq ft
Weights: Empty – 12,088kg/26,650lb
Maximum take-off – 23,831kg/52,539lb
Performance: Maximum speed – 834kph/518mph
Ceiling – 12,190m/40,000ft
Range – 3,706km/2,303 miles
Climb – 1,280m/4,200ft per minute

LEFT: **This aircraft was both the X-35A and X-35B. Following its A model testing, it was converted to B standard and had a shaft-driven lift fan fitted that amplifies engine thrust and reduces temperature and velocity during STOVL operations.**
ABOVE: **Pictured on July 7, 2006, the day the Lockheed Martin F-35 Joint Strike Fighter was officially named Lightning II.**

Lockheed Martin F-35 Lightning II

Although the US military's current first-line aircraft remain formidable weapons, their basic designs are decades old, and in the early 1990s a competition was launched to find a more modern aircraft, a Joint Strike Fighter (JSF) to fit their future needs. The two shortlisted designs came from Boeing (the X-32) and Lockheed Martin, whose X-35 was announced as the winner in October 2001. The US Air Force, the US Navy, the US Marine Corps, as well as the Royal Navy and RAF have all committed to buy what is now known as the F-35 Lightning II, the most powerful single-engine fighter in history, to replace the F-16, F/A-18 Hornet, the Harrier, Sea Harrier and the A-10.

The United States and eight international partners are involved in the F-35's funding and development. As well as the UK, Italy, the Netherlands, Turkey, Canada, Australia, Denmark

and Norway are also partners in the programme. Planned production is expected to exceed 3,000, making the F-35 the F-4 of the 21st century. Lockheed Martin is developing the F-35 Lightning II with its principal industrial partners, Northrop Grumman and the UK's BAE SYSTEMS. Two separate, interchangeable F-35 engines are under development: the Pratt & Whitney F135 and the GE Rolls-Royce Fighter Engine Team F136.

First flight of the Lockheed Martin X-35A conventional variant prototype was on October 24, 2000, while the first flight of the X-35C carrier variant took place on December 16, 2000. First flight of the X-35B STOVL variant prototype was in March 2001, with vertical flight testing beginning in June 2001. The first pre-production F-35 took to the air on December 15, 2006, initiating what the manufacturers described as the most comprehensive flight test programme in military aviation history. Three versions of the F-35 are under development: a Conventional Take-Off and Landing (CTOL) variant, a Short Take-Off/Vertical Landing (STOVL) variant for operating off small ships and near front-line combat zones, and a Carrier Variant (CV) for catapult launches and arrested recoveries on board US Navy aircraft carriers.

The F-35B variant, developed for the US Marine Corps, the Royal Air Force and Royal Navy, has a STOVL capability through a shaft-driven lift fan propulsion system. Other than this propulsion system, this variant only differs from the USAF F-35A conventional variant in a few details. The B model has a refuelling probe fitted into the right side of the forward fuselage, rather than the standard US Air Force refuelling receptacle usually located on the aircraft's upper surface. The STOVL variant carries no internal gun, although an external gun pack is an option. The B model shares all the electronic equipment of the USAF variant, and has a virtually identical cockpit layout except for a lever to enable the pilot to switch

ABOVE: **The prototype X-35C carrier version first flew in December 2000. In July 2003 the historic aircraft was officially presented to the Patuxent River Naval Air Museum. The X-35B is preserved in the US by the Smithsonian.**

between hovering and flying modes. The STOVL variant, primarily designed to replace the AV-8B Harrier, has more than twice the Harrier's range on internal fuel, operates at supersonic speeds and can carry weapons internally.

The F-35C is the dedicated US Navy version and most of the differences between the F-35C and the other variants are due to its operation from full-size aircraft carriers. Accordingly the F-35C, the US Navy's first stealth aircraft, has larger wing and tail control surfaces to better manage low-speed carrier approaches. The internal structure of this variant is strengthened to handle the loads associated with catapult launches and arrested landings. The increased wingspan also provides increased range. Like the B model, the F-35C carries a refuelling probe on the right side of the forward fuselage. Weapon loads, cockpit layout, countermeasures, radar, and other features are common with the other F-35 variants but the F-35C's range and payload are superior to the strike fighters it will replace in US Navy service.

Commonality and flexibility are the basis for the F-35 design from the mission systems and subsystems to the airframe. More than 80 per cent of all parts – including the largest and most expensive components, such as the engine and key avionics units – are common on all three variants. The high degree of commonality among the variants of the F-35 and across the total development and production programme is a key to affordability.

A fully integrated weapon system allows F-35 pilots to positively identify and precisely strike mobile and moving targets in high-threat environments, day or night, in all weathers. The F-35 weapon system gives the pilot true multi-role, multi-mission capability.

F-35s are expected to be in service by 2013, and production is expected to last until around 2030.

ABOVE: **The F-35C will be the world's first stealth naval fighter, and the manufacturers state that the aircraft will be able to "endure extreme abuse without degrading its stealth radar-signature performance" on carrier decks.**
BELOW: **The first flight of the Conventional Take-Off and Landing (CTOL) F-35A version took place on December 15, 2006.**

ABOVE: **Although the F-35B can hover like a Harrier, thanks to the computers on board, in terms of pilot workload it is comparatively much easier to fly. The Lightning II will be easier for pilots to learn to fly and to maintain their currency. Compared to the Harrier, now an old design, the F-35's range is also better, the weapons load larger, and the aircraft generally much stealthier.**

Lockheed Martin F-35C Lightning II

First flight: December 16, 2000 (X-35C)
Power: One Pratt & Whitney 15,897kg/35,000lb thrust F135 turbofan
Armament: One external 25mm GAU-12 gun pod, four hardpoints in two internal weapon bays plus six external hardpoints carrying up to 7,710kg/ 17,000lb of air-to-air and air-to-ground missiles or guided munitions
Size: Wingspan – 13.1m/43ft (9.1m/29ft 10in folded)
Length – 15.5m/50ft 10in
Height – 4.7m/15ft 6in
Wing area – 57.6m²/620sq ft
Weights: Empty – 10,885kg/24,000lb
Maximum take-off – 22,680kg/50,000lb
Performance: Maximum speed – Mach 1.5 plus
Ceiling – Unknown
Range – 3,000km/1,863 miles
Climb – Unknown

Martin P5M Marlin

The Martin P5M Marlin (redesignated P-5 Marlin in 1962) was a twin-engined piston-powered flying boat that entered US Navy service in 1951 and served into the late 1960s. It was developed from the company's earlier Mariner flying boat and the XP5M-1 prototype was developed from the last unfinished PBM-5 Mariner. The Mariner's wing and upper hull were married to an all-new lower hull structure and while the Marlin and the Mariner had almost identical cockpits, the Marlin had better engines – Wright R-3350 radials – and a conventional tail. It was a gull-wing aircraft with the engines and propellers kept as far away from the surface of the water as possible. The aircraft had a long hull that rose very gradually towards the tail – with greater contact with the water

the aircraft was less likely to 'porpoise' as it travelled over the water's surface.

The first flight took place in May 1948 and the first of 167 production P5M-1 aircraft appeared in 1949. Changes from the prototype included a raised flight deck for improved visibility, a large radome for the AN/APS-44 search radar in place of the nose turret, the deletion of the dorsal turret, and new, streamlined wing floats. Service deliveries began in 1952.

The P5M-1 was followed into service by 116 P5M-2 versions that had a T-shaped tail, an AN/ASQ-8 MAD boom at the rear of the tail, no tail guns, improved crew accommodation and a refined bow to reduce spray during take-off and landing. United States Coast Guard versions used for air-sea rescue were

designated P5M-1Gs and P5M-2Gs – these machines were later passed on to the US Navy.

The French Navy took delivery of ten ex-US Navy Marlins in 1959 to replace their Short Sunderlands for maritime patrol duties, operating from Dakar, Senegal, in West Africa. These Marlins were returned to the US when France withdrew from NATO.

US Navy Marlins performed coastal patrols in the Vietnam War but were largely out of service by 1965. The last official US Navy Marlin flight was in 1967 and the type was the last flying boat to see US Navy service. A P-5 is preserved at the US Naval Aviation Museum in Pensacola, Florida.

ABOVE: **The Marlin was very well armed. In addition to torpedoes, mines and even nuclear depth charges, the type was also tested with underwing rocket launchers.** LEFT: **Lacking the distinctive T-tail of the later P5M-2, the P5M-1 had a large but conventional tail. The nose housed the AN/APS-44 search radar.**

Martin P5M-2

First flight: May 30, 1948 (XP5M-1)
Power: Two Wright 3,450hp R-3350-32WA radial engines
Armament: Up to 3,629kg/8,000lb of bombs, torpedoes, mines and depth charges, including the Mk 90 nuclear depth charge
Size: Wingspan – 36.02m/118ft 2in
Length – 30.66m/100ft 7in
Height – 9.97m/32ft 8.5in
Wing area – 130.63m²/1,406sq ft
Weights: Empty – 22,900kg/50,485lb
Maximum take-off – 38,560kg/85,000lb
Performance: Maximum speed – 404kph/251mph
Ceiling – 7,315m/24,000ft
Range – 3,300km/2,050 miles
Climb – 365m/1,200ft per minute

McDonnell F2H Banshee

The F2H Banshee, though similar in design and appearance to the company's earlier FH-1 Phantom, was larger and had more powerful twin Westinghouse J34 engines which gave about twice the power of the J30 engines in the FH-1.

Designed to meet the US Navy's exacting requirements for carrier operations, while also satisfying the requirement for high speed and increased rates of climb, the F2H Banshee first flew in January 1947. It became the Navy's standard long-range all-weather fighter and entered US Navy service in 1948 as their second carrier jet fighter, after the FH-1. They served with distinction with the US Navy in Korea from 1950–53 but by the end of the conflict had been superseded by more

ABOVE: **The Banshee had unswept wings and was powered by two low-power early jet engines. The Banshee was, however, one of the USN's primary single-seat fighters during the Korean War.**

advanced designs. That said, Banshees remained in service with US Navy reserve units until the mid-1960s.

McDonnell F2H-3 Banshee	

First flight: January 11, 1947
Power: Two Westinghouse 1,474kg/3,250lb thrust J34-WE-34 turbojets
Armament: Four 20mm cannon plus underwing racks for 454kg/1,000lb of bombs
Size: Wingspan – 12.73m/41ft 9in
  Length – 14.68m/48ft 2in
  Height – 4.42m/14ft 6in
  Wing area – 27.31m²/294sq ft
Weights: Empty – 5,980kg/13,183lb
  Maximum take-off – 11,437kg/25,214lb
Performance: Maximum speed – 933kph/580mph
  Ceiling – 14,205m/46,600ft
  Range – 1,883km/1,170 miles
  Climb – 2,743m/9,000ft per minute

The Royal Canadian Navy acquired 39 ex-US Navy Banshees between 1955 and 1958, operating them from shore bases and from the carrier HMCS *Bonaventure*. The Banshee was the RCN's last fighter and was not replaced when the type was retired in 1962. A total of 805 F2H Banshees were made.

McDonnell F3H Demon

The F3H Demon was the first swept-wing jet fighter aircraft built by McDonnell Aircraft and also the first aircraft designed to be armed only with missiles rather than guns. The carrier-based, transonic, all-weather Demon fighter was designed with the philosophy that carrier-based fighters need not be inferior to land-based fighters. However, the planned powerplant, the new and disappointing J40 turbojet, failed to meet

expectations and left early Demons (designated F3H-1N) underpowered. Production delays were also caused by the US Navy's desire for the Demon to be an all-weather night-fighter. And so, although the prototype had flown in August 1951, the radar-equipped Demon did not enter service until almost five years later in March 1956 as the F3H-2N and then with the Allison J71 turbojet as powerplant.

By the time production ceased in 1959, 519 Demons had been built including the definitive Demon fighter-bomber (F3H-2). At its peak US Navy use, the Demon equipped 11 front-line squadrons.

McDonnell F3H-2 Demon	

First flight: August 7, 1951 (XF3H-1)
Power: Allison 6,350kg/14,000lb afterburning thrust J71-A-2E turbojet
Armament: Four 20mm cannon and four AIM-7C Sparrow AAMs
Size: Wingspan – 10.77m/35ft 4in
  Length – 17.96m/58ft 11in
  Height – 4.44m/14ft 7in
  Wing area – 48.22m²/519sq ft
Weights: Empty – 10,039kg/22,133lb
  Maximum take-off – 15,377kg/33,900lb
Performance: Maximum speed – 1,041kph/647mph
  Ceiling – 13,000m/42,650ft
  Range – 2,205km/1,370 miles
  Climb – 3,660m/12,000ft per minute

ABOVE: **The excellent visibility from its cockpit earned the Demon the nickname 'The Chair'.**

McDonnell Douglas A-4 Skyhawk

An impressive total of 2,960 Skyhawks were built from 1954 by Douglas (and later McDonnell Douglas) in a production run that lasted a quarter of a century. Designed as a small and cost-effective lightweight carrier-borne high-speed bomber, the Skyhawk was affectionately nicknamed 'the scooter' or 'Heinemann's Hot Rod' after the Douglas designer Ed Heinemann. He had been working on a compact jet-powered attack aircraft design which the US Navy ordered for evaluation – this was the XA4D-1 and the first of nine prototypes and development aircraft flew in June 1954. Development progressed quickly and the Cold War US Navy were eager to acquire this new and very capable combat aircraft. Chosen as a replacement for the venerable Skyraider, the Skyhawk provided the US Navy, US Marines Corps and 'friendly' nations with a manoeuvrable and powerful attack bomber that had great altitude and range performance as well as a remarkable and flexible weapons-carrying capability.

Production deliveries of A-4As began in September 1956. The A-4 was first delivered to the US Navy's VA-72 attack squadron on October 26, 1956. Its small size allowed it to fit on an aircraft carrier lift without needing to have folding wings

thus saving time, weight and extra maintenance. The Skyhawk was roughly half the empty weight of its contemporaries and could fly at 1089kph/677mph at sea level. Significantly, the US examples were nuclear capable.

The Skyhawk was progressively developed with more powerful engines – early A-C models had been powered by the Wright J65, a licence-built copy of the British Armstrong Siddeley Sapphire engine. The A-4C was followed by the A-4E, a heavier aircraft powered by Pratt & Whitney's J52 engine. The A-4F was the last version to enter US Navy service and was easily identified by its dorsal avionics 'hump'. The ultimate development of the Skyhawk was the A-4M, known as the Skyhawk II, specifically designed for the US Marines. This model, which first took to the air in 1970, had a larger canopy for better pilot view and had a maximum take-off weight twice that of the early A-4. Power for this 'super' Skyhawk came from a J52-P-408 and the Skyhawk II remained in production until 1979. The US Navy's Blue Angels flight demonstration aerobatics team flew the A-4 Skyhawk II from 1974 to 1986.

The Skyhawk's combat career began on August 4, 1964, with the first American carrier-launched raids on North Vietnam.

ABOVE: **Note the long front undercarriage leg of this A-4, required for carrier operations.** LEFT: **A TA-4J of training wing TW-3 from the auxiliary aircraft landing training ship USS Lexington (AVT-16). The Lexington was first commissioned on February 17, 1944, then in 1963 became a training carrier until being decommissioned in 1991.**

LEFT: **Ed Heinemann** was not widely believed when he first talked of his concept for a light, small and cheap-to-produce jet bomber. This was at a time when aircraft were becoming heavier to become faster. Heinemann stood back, thought around the challenge and his 'hot rod' was still in service half a century after its test flight.

The A-4s were soon performing most of the Navy's and Marine Corps' light air attack missions over South-east Asia.

Skyhawks were also operated by the armed forces of Argentina, Australia, Israel (who used them extensively in the 1973 Yom Kippur war), Kuwait, Singapore, Indonesia, Malaysia and New Zealand, and they remained active with several air services into the 2000s.

Argentina was the first export customer for the Skyhawk, operating A-4Ps and A-4Qs which were modified B and C models respectively. These aircraft, acquired in the mid-1960s, were later complemented by A-4Rs which were ex-USMC A-4Ms. Argentine Skyhawks were the most destructive strike aircraft to engage British Forces during the 1982 Falklands War. Operating from mainland bases, the Skyhawks carried out many attacks against British shipping. On May 12 a Skyhawk raid put HMS *Glasgow* out of action, and on May 21 the Skyhawks attacked the British invasion force landing at San Carlos. On May 25, Argentine Skyhawks attacked and sank HMS *Coventry*. The cost of these actions was high with Argentina losing ten A-4s in a matter of days to anti-aircraft defences and the British Sea Harriers.

ABOVE: **The type was widely exported and even the example that served with the US military often masqueraded as foreign 'bogies' during aggressor training.**

LEFT: **Perhaps the best-known exported examples were those supplied to Argentina, who were the first foreign customers for the type. Flying from mainland Argentina and tanking en route, some of these A-4s were a formidable enemy during the Falklands War.**

McDonnell Douglas A-4M Skyhawk II

First flight: June 22, 1954 (XA4D-1 prototype)

Power: One Pratt & Whitney 5,081kg/11,187lb thrust J52-P-408 turbojet

Armament: Two 20mm cannon in wing roots plus up to 4,155kg/9,155lb of bombs or air-to-surface and air-to-air missiles

Size: Wingspan – 8.38m/27ft 6in
Length – 12.27m/40ft 4in
Height – 4.57m/15ft
Wing area – 24.2m²/260sq ft

Weights: Empty – 4,747kg/10,465lb
Maximum take-off – 11,115kg/24,500lb

Performance: Maximum speed – 1,100kph/683mph
Ceiling – 11,800m/38,700ft
Range – 1,480km/920 miles
Climb – 3,142m/10,300ft per minute

McDonnell Douglas F-4 Phantom II

The F-4, one of the world's greatest-ever combat aircraft, was designed to meet a US Navy requirement for a fleet defence fighter to replace the F3H Demon and to counter the threat from long-range Soviet bombers. The US Air Force also ordered the Phantom when the F-4 was shown to be faster than their high-performance F-104. The F-4 was first used by the United States Navy as an interceptor but was soon employed by the US Marine Corps in the ground attack role. Its outstanding versatility made it the first US multi-service aircraft flying with the US Air Force, Navy and Marine Corps concurrently. The remarkable Phantom excelled in air superiority, close air support, interception, air defence suppression, long-range strike, fleet defence, attack and reconnaissance.

The sophisticated F-4 was, without direction from surface-based radar, able to detect and destroy a target Beyond Visual Range (BVR). In the Vietnam and Gulf Wars alone, the F-4 was credited with 280 air-to-air victories. As a bomber the

ABOVE: **For many, the ultimate carrier-borne fighting aircraft was the F-4 Phantom II. Its versatility, performance and punch raised the bar for all combat aircraft designers.** LEFT: **F-4Js of VF-96, 'The Fighting Falcons'. This unit saw a lot of combat during the Vietnam War.**

F-4 could carry up to five tons of ordnance and deliver it accurately while flying at supersonic speeds at very low level.

Capable of flying at twice the speed of sound with ease, the Phantom was loved by its crews who considered it a workhorse that could do the job and get them home safely. F-4s have also set world records for altitude (30,040m/ 98,556ft on December 6, 1959), speed (2,585kph/1,606mph on November 22, 1961) and a low-altitude speed record of 1,452kph/902mph that stood for 16 years.

Phantom production ran from 1958 to 1979, resulting in 5,195 aircraft. A total of 5,057 were made in St Louis, Missouri, in the US, while a further 138 were built under licence by the Mitsubishi Aircraft Co. in Japan. F-4 production peaked in 1967, when the McDonnell plant was producing 72 Phantoms per month.

ABOVE: **The 'NH' tail code tells us this is an F-4 of VF-114 'Aardvarks', pictured while operating from USS *Kitty Hawk*. Between 1961 and 1976 VF-114 undertook five combat cruises to take part in the Vietnam War, gaining five MiG kills in the process.**

LEFT: **A Phantom of 892 NAS just about to launch from the deck of HMS *Ark Royal*. This was the only unit to operate the type, which had to be heavily modified for the smaller British carrier use.**
ABOVE: **'Cross decking' was and remains an important aspect of training aircrews in the use of friendly nations' ships, facilities and operating techniques.**

The USAF acquired 2,874 while the US Navy and Marine Corps operated 1,264. The F-4 was used extensively by the US in Vietnam from 1965 and served in many roles, including fighter, ground attack and reconnaissance. A number of refurbished ex-US forces aircraft were operated by other nations, including the UK, who bought a squadron of mothballed ex-US Navy F-4Js to complement the Royal Air Force's F-4Ms.

Regularly updated with the addition of state-of-the-art weaponry and radar, the Phantom served with 11 more nations around the globe – Australia, Egypt, Germany, Greece, Iran, Israel, Japan, South Korea, Spain, Turkey and the UK.

Britain's Royal Navy operated Phantoms from 1968 until 1978, mainly as a fleet defence fighter but with a secondary close support and attack role for which it was equipped to deliver nuclear weaponry. However, only one front-line Fleet Air Arm unit, No.892 Squadron aboard HMS *Ark Royal*, was equipped with the Phantom. The Royal Air Force also operated Phantoms from 1968 with the last RAF Phantoms being retired in January 1992.

The year 1996 saw the Phantom's retirement from US military forces by which time the type had flown more than 27,350,000km (around 17 million miles) in the nation's service. Israel, Japan, Germany, Turkey, Greece, Korea and Egypt have undertaken or plan to upgrade their F-4s and keep them flying until 2015, nearly 60 years after the Phantom's first flight.

In 2007 almost 100 Phantoms converted into unmanned QF-4 drones and missile targets were still serving the United States Navy and Air Force, and more than 800 F-4 Phantom II aircraft remained on active duty with the air arms of Egypt, Germany, Greece, Israel, Japan, South Korea, Spain and Turkey. The F-4 is one of the finest-ever combat aircraft.

ABOVE: **Showing signs of wear and tear, this F-4 is pictured on one of its many missions over Vietnam. As well as being used in that conflict by the United States Navy, the US Marine Corps and the US Air Force particularly made extensive use of the type on a variety of missions.**

McDonnell Douglas Phantom F.G.R.2 (F-4M)

First flight: February 17, 1967
Power: Two Rolls-Royce 9,305kg/20,515lb afterburning thrust Spey 202 turbofans
Armament: Eleven 454kg/1,000lb free fall or retarded conventional or nuclear bombs, 126 68mm armour-piercing rockets, one 20mm cannon, all carried externally
Size: Wingspan – 11.68m/38ft 4in
  Length – 17.73m/58ft 2in
  Height – 4.95m/16ft 3in
  Wing area – 49.25m²/530sq ft
Weights: Empty – 14,060kg/31,000lb
  Maximum take-off – 26,310kg/58,000lb
Performance: Maximum speed – 2,230kph/1,386mph
  Ceiling – 18,290m/60,000ft
  Range – 2,815km/1,750 miles
  Climb – 9,754m/32,000ft per minute

LEFT: The MiG-29K – a potent naval fighter.
ABOVE: The naval MiG's nose undercarriage is able to steer through 90 degrees each way and houses a three-colour lamp which indicates the aircraft's position on the glide path and its landing speed to a visual landing signal officer.

Mikoyan-Gurevich MiG-29K

Over 1,200 examples of the very capable, incredibly agile MiG-29 fighter have been built and the type has been exported widely. The type was developed in the early 1970s as a high-performance, highly manoeuvrable lightweight fighter to outperform the best the West could offer. The prototype took to the air for the first time in 1977 but it was a further seven years before the type entered service – ultimately 460 were in Russian service and the rest were exported.

Codenamed 'Fulcrum' by NATO, the aircraft has been exported to Bulgaria, Germany, Cuba, Romania, Poland, Slovakia, Peru, Syria, Hungary, Iraq, India, Iran, North Korea, Malaysia and Moldova among others. It is not widely known, but the US acquired 21 MiG-29s in 1997 from Moldova after Iran had expressed interest in the high-performance fighters. In a unique accord between the US and Moldova, the aircraft were dismantled and shipped to the US.

The MiG 29's radar can track ten targets up to 245km/152 miles away and bestows look-down-shoot-down capability, while the pilot's helmet-mounted sight allows him or her to direct air-to-air missiles wherever the pilot looks.

The MiG is also designed for rough-field operations – special doors seal off the main air intakes to protect against foreign object ingestion during start up and taxiing. Air is drawn in via louvres in the wingroots instead and as the aircraft takes off, the inlet doors open.

The Russians have upgraded some MiG-29s to MiG-29SMT standard by increasing range and payload, replacing cockpit instruments with new monitors, and improving radar and inflight refuelling capability. Daimler Chrysler Aerospace modified a number of Polish MiGs for NATO compatibility after that nation's joining NATO in 1999 just as they did the East German MiG-29s after German reunification.

A navalized version, the MiG-29K with folding wings, fin and radome, was developed but the plans were shelved until the Indian Navy ordered the 'K' to operate from its carrier *Vikramaditya* (formerly the Russian *Admiral Gorshkov*). A $740 million contract was signed in January 2004 to supply the Indian Navy with 16 carrier-based MiG-29K/KUB aircraft (12 single-seat 'K' variants and four dual-seat 'KUB' trainers). The cost also included all training hardware including simulators.

ABOVE: The arrester hook is fitted with lights to indicate when it is lowered. The design had to be considerably strengthened for carrier use.

ABOVE: A Luftwaffe land-based MiG-29 fires an AA-10 Alamo missile. The MiG-29 family equips many of the world's air forces.

LEFT: The aircraft's two Klimov RD-33MK turbofans have smokeless combustors, an anti-corrosive coating to cope with carrier use and a total service life of 4,000 hours with a basic overhaul time of 1,000 hours. BELOW: On November 1, 1989, test pilot Toktar Aubakirov carried out the first landing of a MiG-29K on the aircraft carrier *Tbilisi* that was later renamed *Admiral Kuznetsov*.

The Indian Navy has expressed an interest in having a total of 40 MiG-29Ks. In April 2005 the Indian Navy announced that the MiG-29K's shore base will be INS *Hansa* in Goa and that the unit cost of the aircraft was $32 million. The Indian Navy received the first of its MiG-29Ks in 2007, ahead of the delivery of the carrier INS *Vikramaditya* in 2008 to allow for aircrew and ground crew training.

The export version of the MiG-29K is based on the MiG-29K airframe, but differs in a number of ways. It is lighter and cheaper, partly due to the deletion of high-cost welded aluminium lithium fuel tanks. The export MiG's fuel tanks are located in the dorsal spine fairing and wing leading-edge root extensions which affords a range increase of 50 per cent compared to land-based versions – this can be extended further by the use of the retractable refuelling probe in the port forward fuselage. The MiG-29K take-off run from a 'ski jump' carrier deck is between 125–195m/410–640ft. Extensive use of radar-absorbing materials have reduced the fighter's radar signature by up to a factor of five compared to the standard MiG-29. MiG also developed new anti-corrosion measures to protect the K's

airframe, avionics and engines. The MiG-29K can carry a wide range of weapons including 8 types of air-to-air missiles and 25 air-to-surface weapons on up to 13 hardpoints.

The dual-seat 'KUB' trainer handles almost the same as the single-seat version and the forward nose sections are identical, equipped with similar avionics and able to carry the same armament. In addition to carrying out its primary training role, the trainer has a fully operational capability.

Mikoyan-Gurevich MiG-29K

First flight: October 7, 1977 (MiG-29)
Power: Two Klimov 9,011kg/19,870lb afterburning thrust RD-33MK turbofans
Armament: One 30mm cannon, up to 13 hardpoints carrying up to 5,500kg/12,125lb of weapons, including air-to-air and air-to-surface missiles, rockets or bombs
Size: Wingspan – 11.4m/37ft 5in
Length – 14.87m/48ft 9in
Height – 4.7m/15ft 5in
Wing area – 38m²/409sq ft
Weights: Normal take-off – 18,550kg/40,895lb
Maximum take-off – 22,400kg/49,383lb
Performance: Maximum speed – 2,400kph/1,491mph
Ceiling – 27,000m/88,580ft
Range – 3,500km/2,174 miles with inflight refuelling
Climb – 17,760m/58,260ft per minute

ABOVE: '312 Blue', one of the MiG-29K prototypes, pictured with some of the weaponry it can carry. Note the folded wingtips and extended airbrake forward of the tail as well as the extended refuelling probe.

LEFT: **It was the sea-going Fury that led the way for the land-based Sabre, and it first flew in September 1946.** BELOW: **The swept-wing FJ-2 bore little resemblance to the earlier FJ-1.**

North American FJ Fury

Commonly thought to be a derivative of the famous F-86 Sabre, it was in fact the Fury's initial design that led to the land-based Sabre. In late 1944, the US Navy ordered a number of carrier-based jet fighters that were to be available to take part in the invasion of Japan planned for May 1946 – one of these was a North American design, the NA-134. It was a conventional straight-winged aircraft to be powered by a General Electric J35 axial-flow turbojet fed by a nose intake and having a straight-through exhaust pipe in the tail.

The USAF ordered a land-based version of the Fury designated XP-86. With the benefit of German aerodynamic research data captured at the end of World War II, the XP-86 was redesigned to incorporate swept-tail surfaces and a swept wing which would allow supersonic speeds. The naval aircraft, however, had to retain good low-speed handling capabilities for landings aboard carriers of the time so the US Navy opted to retain the straight-winged design and North American produced three prototypes of the XFJ 1 Fury.

The first XFJ-1 flew on September 11, 1946 (almost a year ahead of the more complex XP-86), and 30 production FJ-1s

were delivered from October 1947 to April 1948. The first and the only US Navy unit to receive the FJ-1 Fury was VF-5A, based at Naval Air Station North Island near San Diego in California. The first Fury deck landing took place on March 16, 1948, aboard USS *Boxer* and the aircraft was shown to be able to take off from the ship under its own power – these trials were the US Navy's first operational jet landings and take-offs at sea. Slow acceleration by these early jets during take-off led to catapulting becoming standard procedure and the greatly increased fuel consumption of the US Navy's new jet fighters demanded increased fuel storage aboard their carriers. Although the aircraft set records, its performance suffered at maximum weight and the pilots were less than impressed with its lack of cockpit temperature control.

The US Navy were aware that swept-wing fighters were essential if their jet fighters were to be a viable defence or threat, as the jet fighter dogfighting in Korea was to prove. In November 1951, the USN issued a contract for prototypes of a navalized F-86E (the FJ-2) complete with arrester hooks, lengthened nosegear (for high angle of attack carrier take-offs and landings) and catapulting capability. Trials of two XFJ-2s, powered by J47-GE-13 engines, began mid-1952. As the Korean War was drawing to a close, production of only 200 of an original order for 300 FJ-2s was undertaken at North American's newly opened Columbus, Ohio, plant. The first aircraft was delivered in October, 1952 and production continued until September 1954. By the time production began, the FJ-2 Fury was, in effect, the US Navy equivalent of the F-86F. Powered by a 2,720kg/6,000lb thrust J47-GE-2 (USN version of the J47-GE-27), the FJ-2 had folding wings, an all-moving tail for increased manoeuvrability, and was armed

LEFT: **One of the XFJ-2 prototypes undergoing carrier qualification trials in December 1952 aboard the USS *Coral Sea*. The tests exposed significant shortcomings, but the US Navy persevered.**

with four 20mm cannon each with 600 rounds. Naval equipment took the take-off weight up to 8530kg/18,810lb compared with 8080kg/17,810lb for the F-86F.

The first squadron to receive FJ-2s was Marine VMF-122 at Cherry Point, North Carolina, in January 1954, followed five months later by VMF-235 aboard USS *Hancock*, a carrier recently equipped with new C-11 steam catapults. By 1955 FJ-2s equipped six Marine squadrons, three with the Atlantic Fleet, and three with the Pacific Fleet.

In March 1952, North American had begun design of the FJ-3 Fury powered by the Wright J65-W-2 Sapphire, built under licence from Britain's Armstrong Siddeley. This version went on to equip 12 US Navy squadrons and on August 22, 1955, an FJ-3 flown by Commander R.G. Dose became the first American aircraft to use the mirror landing system that soon became standard throughout USN carriers. Late-build FJs were equipped to carry Sidewinder heat-seeking missiles. When FJ-3 production ended in August 1956, the US Navy and Marines were operating 23 Fury squadrons.

In the FJ-4 the entire airframe was revised. A thinner wing of greater area and span was used and the addition of a dorsal spine from cockpit to fin makes this version easy to identify. Classified as long-range attack fighters, the FJ-4 carried additional armour in the nose while drop tanks, bombs or Sidewinders could be carried under the wings. The first FJ-4s to enter service joined Marine Squadron VMF-451 in 1956, and by March 1957 152 aircraft were in the inventory.

December 4, 1956, saw the test flight of a new variant, the FJ-4B. Equivalent to the US Air Force's F-86H Sabre, the FJ-4B was fully equipped for low-altitude attack and, apart from being able to carry even more underwing stores, the aircraft could also deliver tactical nuclear weapons.

The 'Bravo Fury' carried inflight refuelling probes beneath the port wing, and in June 1957 'buddy' refuelling was introduced. By the addition of underwing fuel packs, the Fury could take on enough fuel from another Fury to extend its combat radius by around 50 per cent. In October 1958, this technique was used

ABOVE: **The US Navy were slow to adopt swept-wing designs for carrier operations due to required lower stalling speeds and better low-speed handling characteristics. This is why the Navy stuck with straight-wing designs long after the USAF had moved on to swept-wing designs for their front-line fighters. Korean conflicts with faster MiGs persuaded the US Navy they had to change.** BELOW: **Furies went on to equip USMC squadrons too.**

by Marine Squadrons VMA-212 and 214 to complete the first trans-Pacific crossing by single-seat naval aircraft.

Although by the early 1960s Furies were being phased out of the front line, their work was done – from conventional beginnings the Fury helped the US Navy keep pace with fighter technology. In all, North American's Columbus plant delivered 1,112 Furies to the US military.

ABOVE: **From 1962 the FJ-4 was designated the F-1E, and the FJ-4B became the AF-1E. A total of 1,115 Furies were received by the US Navy and Marine Corps – an impressive production run.**

North American Fury FJ-3

First flight: September 11, 1946 (XFJ-1)
Power: Wright 3,497kg/7,700lb afterburning thrust J65-W-2 turbojet
Armament: Four 20mm cannon
Size: Wingspan – 11.3m/37ft 1in
　　　　 Length – 11.3m/37ft 1in
　　　　 Height – 4.17m/13.8ft
　　　　 Wing area – 26.75m²/288sq ft
Weights: Empty – 5,535kg/12,205lb
　　　　 Maximum take-off – 8,573kg/18,900lb
Performance: Maximum speed – 1,096kph/681mph
　　　　 Ceiling – 14,934m/49,000ft
　　　　 Range – 1,593km/990 miles
　　　　 Climb – 2,577m/8,450ft per minute

LEFT: **The reconnaissance mission of the modified Vigilantes served the US Navy well during the Vietnam War and beyond. This RA-5C flew from USS** *Ranger.* ABOVE: **Another RA-5C, this time on the deck of the** *Forrestal.*

North American A3J/A-5 Vigilante

In November 1953, North American Aviation began work on a design project for an all-weather long-range carrier-based strike aircraft capable of delivering a nuclear weapon at speeds of up to Mach 2. To meet the needs of the design, the team proposed an aircraft so advanced in many ways that it is fair to say that when the Vigilante appeared, no other aircraft had incorporated so many technological innovations.

The first prototype, the YA3J-1, was rolled out on May 16, 1958, and was officially named Vigilante. The first flight took place on August 31, 1958, and the aircraft went supersonic for the first time on September 5. A second prototype entered the flight test programme in November that year. The first production A3J-1s soon followed and the sixth Vigilante constructed made 14 launches and landings on the USS *Saratoga* in July 1960.

The demands made on an aircraft flying at twice the speed of sound are considerable and special measures have to be taken to ensure that systems continue to function in this very harsh environment. In the case of the Vigilante, pure nitrogen

was used instead of hydraulic fluid in some of the airframe's hottest areas. The Vigilante was structurally unusual in that major elements were made of titanium to protect against aerodynamic heating while the wing skins were machined as one piece from aluminium-lithium alloy – gold plate was used as a heat reflector in the engine bays.

Advanced aerodynamic features included a small high-loaded swept wing with powerful flaps and a one-piece powered vertical tail. Revolutionary fully variable engine inlets were fitted to slow down supersonic air to subsonic speed before it reached the engine thus producing maximum performance from the engines at any speed. A fully retractable refuelling probe was built into the forward port fuselage ahead of the pilot's cockpit.

The A3J-1 Vigilante also featured some extremely advanced electronics for the time, including the first production fly-by-wire control system, although a mechanical system was retained as back-up. Bombing and navigation computations were carried out by an airborne digital computer, and the

FAR LEFT: **Vigilantes on the deck of the US Navy carrier USS** *Ranger.* **It was from the deck of this carrier that the last Vigilante catapult launch took place on September 21, 1979. The aircraft were all mothballed or scrapped within weeks.** LEFT: **The Vigilante was a large naval aircraft and had a unique means of delivering the nuclear store it was designed to carry. Even when the Vigilante was modified for reconnaissance duties it retained its weapon-carrying capability but was never armed.**

aircraft had the first operational Head-Up Display (HUD). The aircraft's radar had early terrain avoidance features relieving some of the pilot's workload at low-level. In December 1960 the Vigilante set a new world altitude record for its class when it carried a 1,000kg/2,403lb payload to a height of 27,893m/91,451ft, exceeding the then record by 6.4km/4 miles.

The Vigilante's jaw-dropping innovation reached new heights with its weapons delivery. A nuclear weapon was stored in a unique internal weapons bay without bomb bay doors. In the aircraft belly and instead of the nuclear bomb being dropped, the weapon (which was mounted in a long duct that extended back between the two engines) was ejected to the rear during release. This was a complex system and prone to technical problems which kept Vigilante crews appropriately vigilant.

The first squadron deployment occurred in August 1962 aboard the USS *Enterprise* on its first cruise and in September that year, the A3J-1 was redesignated A-5A under the new

ABOVE: **An aircraft of RVAH-3, Reconnaissance Attack Squadron Three, the 'Sea Dragons'. The 'canoe' fitted beneath the aircraft housed much of the type's recon equipment, which included film and stills cameras.**

US Tri-Service designation system. Shortly thereafter, the US Navy's strategic deterrent mission was assumed by nuclear-powered and nuclear missile-equipped Polaris submarines and further procurement of the A-5A was halted after only 59 had been built. Most were returned to North American for conversion to RA-5C standard – 53 were eventually rebuilt as RA-5Cs and were joined in service by 55 new production aircraft. The RA-5C retained the bomber version's very high speed performance and was capable of electromagnetic, optical, and electronic reconnaissance. The type was used to great effect by the US 7th Fleet during carrier air wing operations in the Vietnam War. The US Navy's last RA-5C fleet squadron was disbanded in September 1979.

ABOVE: **When it entered service, the Vigilante was one of the largest and by far the most complex aircraft to operate from United States Navy aircraft carriers. A total of 158 were built.**

North American A-5 Vigilante

First flight: August 31, 1958 (YA3J-1)
Power: Two General Electric 7,326kg/16,150lb afterburning thrust J79-2 turbojets
Armament: One Mk 27, Mk 28, or Mk 43 nuclear bomb in the linear weapons bay, plus one Mk 43 nuclear or a pair of Mk 83 or Mk 84 conventional bombs on weapons pylon beneath each wing
Size: Wingspan – 16.15m/53ft
　　　Length – 23.11m/75ft 10in
　　　Height – 5.92m/19ft 5in
　　　Wing area – 70.05m²/754sq ft
Weights: Empty – 17,240kg/38,000lb
　　　Maximum take-off – 36,285kg/80,000lb
Performance: Maximum speed – 2,230kph/1,385mph
　　　Service ceiling – 20,420m/67,000ft
　　　Range – 5,150km/3,200 miles
　　　Climb – 2,440m/8,000ft per minute

ShinMaywa PS-1/US-1

This aircraft is a rare bird in service these days – a large four-engined (technically, five-engined) amphibian flying boat. Equally rare is the fact that the type re-entered production some years after initial production ceased.

Shin Meiwa were a rebranded Kawanishi company who, during World War II, had demonstrated the ability to build excellent flying boats – the company name later changed again to today's ShinMaywa. Although in the early 1950s Shin Meiwa simply serviced aircraft, the team's flying boat heritage

ABOVE: **In December 2003, the US-1A Kai powered by four Rolls-Royce AE 2100 turboprops completed its first flight in Kobe, Japan. A CTS800-4K engine, produced by Rolls-Royce and Honeywell, was also fitted to the aircraft to drive the boundary layer control system that provides a short take-off and landing capability.** BELOW: **A ShinMaywa PS-1 water-bomber in action.**

and skill pool was not forgotten. In 1959 the company rebuilt a Grumman UF-1 Albatross, which flew in 1960 as an aerodynamically advanced technology demonstrator flying boat, and the company was back in the flying boat business.

The Japanese Maritime Self Defence Force were impressed with the results and in January 1966 awarded a contract to develop the design into a service ASW patrol aircraft. The PS-1 was designed as a high-wing monoplane with fixed floats connected to the underside of the outer wing by struts. A retractable beaching undercarriage enabled this version to taxi on, but not land on nor take off from, land. The nose gear retracted into the hull, while the main wheels pivoted up and into the sides of the fuselage. Flight-testing of two PS-X prototypes began in October 1967 and service evaluation was carried out by the 51st Flight Test Squadron. After testing, the first prototype went on to be converted for evaluation as a firebomber aircraft by Japan's National Fire Agency.

Satisfied by the results of the PS-X programme, the JMSDF ordered the aircraft into production in 1969 as the PS-1 although its makers always knew the aircraft as the SS-2. The aircraft featured an innovative boundary layer control system powered by an independent gas turbine, a 1,400ehp Ishikawajima T-58-1H1-10 carried in the fuselage – this is a means of increasing the lift generated by wings by ejecting high-velocity engine exhaust gases over the wings and control surfaces to generate even more lift. It was this feature that gave the aircraft its good STOL capability. Other innovations

RIGHT: **Note the large nose-radar, the high-set wing and the pronounced hull shape of the flying boat. The recess for the starboard main landing gear can be seen in the fuselage just above and behind the mainwheel. Note also the red danger line painted on the side of the fuselage to warn of the spinning propeller blades.** BELOW: **This PS-1 is preserved at Kanoya Naval Air Base Museum in Japan.**

included a system to suppress spray to ensure that the engines were not flooded with sea water on landings and take-offs.

Sensor systems included search radar with the antenna in a large nose radome, a Magnetic Anomaly Detection (MAD) system with a retractable 'stinger' boom and a passive sonar system with 20 sonobuoys. The aircraft could carry two homing torpedoes each in two pods between the engines on each wing. Four 150kg/330lb depth charges could be carried internally, while wingtip pods could accommodate three 127mm/5in rockets each. No defensive armament was carried.

Twenty-three aircraft – a small, expensive and politically sensitive production run – entered service with the JMSDF between 1971 and 1978, and served until 1989 when they were replaced by the P-3 Orion.

It was not long after the ASW version had entered service that the JMSDF called for the development of a search and rescue version – this led to the US-1. With military armament, equipment and sensor systems removed, the aircraft had a much greater fuel capacity, rescue equipment and full landing gear which made the new version a true amphibian. It first flew on October 15, 1974, and the first of 19 aircraft entered service the following year. Early in production, an uprated version of the original engines was substituted but all of the earlier aircraft were modified to this US-1A standard. Over 23 years of service Japanese US-1s were used in over 500 rescues and saved 550 lives.

Funding would not permit the development of an all new aircraft to replace the aging US-1 fleet so in 1995 ShinMaywa proposed an upgraded version of the US-1A, the US-1A Kai (short for *kaizen* which means modification). This aircraft, now designated US-2, features aerodynamic refinements, more powerful engines and a pressurized hull. Flight testing began with the prototype's maiden flight from Osaka Bay on December 18, 2003.

ABOVE: **The PS-1/US-1 family of flying boats have confounded those who believed the post-war world had no place for large flying boats. Derivatives of these aircraft will be flying for years to come.**

ShinMaywa US-1A

First flight: October 4, 1967 (PX-S prototype)
Power: Four General Electric 3,493ehp T64 (Ishikawajima 10J) turboprops
Armament: None
Size: Wingspan – 33.15m/108ft 9in
　　　Length – 33.46m/109ft 9in
　　　Height – 9.82m/32ft 3in
　　　Wing area – 136m²/1,463sq ft
Weights: Empty – 25,500kg/56,220lb
　　　Maximum take-off – 45,000kg/99,200lb
Performance: Maximum speed – 495kph/310mph
　　　Ceiling – 8,200m/26,900ft
　　　Range – 4,200km/2,610 miles
　　　Climb – 713m/2,340ft per minute

LEFT: **A United States Navy HO3S-1 pictured over the deck of the USS *Kearsage*. The S-51 design was widely used in many forms in Korea, and went on to serve in a variety of roles around the world.**

Sikorsky S-51/Westland Dragonfly

Sikorsky carried out ground-breaking helicopter development work in the early 1940s. Building on the success of this, the company developed the all-new VS-337, a tandem two-seater helicopter powered by a 450hp radial engine – it first flew on August 18, 1943. This design became the R-5 (later the H-5) and was ultimately widely known by Sikorsky's own designation – the S-51. This became the world's first true production military helicopter.

As helicopters became more capable and reliable so their many applications became clear. Early H-5s were fitted on each side with stretcher carriers for casualty evacuation duties and later, rescue hoists. The four-seat version of the S-51 was proposed for civil use and enabled Los Angeles Airways to launch the first scheduled helicopter mail service in October 1947.

In US Army service, the H-5 was used for spotting and communications work, but it is perhaps best known for its

role as a rescue aircraft during the Korean War. It is worth pointing out that until the S-51 there was no production aircraft available to the US military that could take off and land vertically. Short take-off and landing aircraft were in use but could not land in, for example, a jungle clearing. Accordingly, the S-51 afforded the military a new means of extracting personnel from behind enemy lines or from the sea before they could be taken prisoner. The helicopter could also swiftly evacuate wounded personnel from a battlefield and so saved countless lives. Production lasted until 1951, by which time Sikorsky had built 285 machines.

In 1946, UK company Westland had negotiated what came to be a very long-standing licence agreement with Sikorsky – this led to the UK production of a Westland-built S-51 that first flew in 1948. The Dragonfly was a thorough redesign of the S-51 and not just a licence-build – 139 machines were built before production ceased in 1953.

LEFT: **Among the duties at which the S-51 proved most useful was casualty evacuation. The picture shows a USAF H-5H in Korea, 1952, with its external 'casualty pods'. The value of helicopters to the military became clear after World War II but Korea proved them in every way, especially in the rescue of downed aircrew behind enemy lines.**
ABOVE: **The Royal Navy were early adopters of the Sikorsky design but in the form of the Westland Dragonfly.**

Introducing the British Alvis Leonides engine, the Dragonfly was assembled from UK-made components and became the first UK-built helicopter in British military service. The Royal Navy was the first UK military customer with the HR. Mk 1, an air-sea rescue version powered by the Leonides 50. The first RN Dragonfly unit and indeed the service's first helicopter squadron was No.705 Naval Air Squadron formed at Royal Naval Air Station Gosport. Rescue versions of the Dragonfly were equipped with a hoist capable of lifting 170kg/375lb. The introduction of helicopters into the USN and Royal Navy was to transform the services' capabilities not just in ASR but in the ASW mission too.

The RAF's HC. Mk 2 was similar to the Royal Navy version but built for the casualty evacuation role. The Royal Navy's main ASR version was, however, the HR. Mk 3 with 58 machines built. It, like the RAF's HC. Mk 4 again built for the 'casevac' role, differed from the earlier versions mainly by the introduction of all-metal rotor blades and hydraulic servo controls.

RAF Dragonflies served in the anti-terrorist operations in Malaya from 1950 and in three and a half years these helicopters evacuated 675 casualties and carried over 4,000 passengers and 38,100kg/84,000lb of supplies in around 6,000 sorties. Royal Navy Dragonflies operated from aircraft carriers to rescue the crews of aircraft that crashed into the sea.

Proving the type's pioneering position, the world's first regular, scheduled helicopter passenger service was established by BEA (British European Airways) using the S-51 on June 1, 1950, initially between Cardiff and Liverpool.

Westland developed the five-seat Widgeon from the Dragonfly but it only saw limited production as it competed against more sophisticated second-generation helicopter designs.

In addition to operators in the US and UK, the pioneering S-51 and Dragonfly was also exported to Canada, Japan, the Philippines, Thailand, Belgium, Egypt, France, Iraq, Italy, Ceylon and Yugoslavia.

ABOVE: **Just a few years before, the pilot of this ditched F4U Corsair would have had to hope to be picked up by a friendly ship or flying boat or face capture or drowning. Rescues of aircrew downed in the sea rose dramatically thanks to this helicopter, in this case an H-5H variant.** BELOW: **Two classic Sikorsky designs, both of which were taken on by Westlands in the UK and then produced as, top, the Westland Whirlwind (Sikorsky S-55) and below, the Westland Dragonfly. WG722 was a Whirlwind HR. Mk 3.**

ABOVE: **This excellent side view of another Royal Navy HR. Mk 3 shows some of the helicopter's main recognition features including the boxy greenhouse glazed nose and the long and slender tail boom.**

Sikorsky/ Westland Dragonfly HR. Mk 1

First flight: October 5, 1948 (Westland Sikorsky WS-51 prototype)
Power: One Alvis 540hp Leonides 50 radial piston engine
Armament: None
Size: Rotor diameter – 14.63m/48ft
Length – 17.54m/57ft 6.5in
Height – 3.95m/12ft 11.5in
Weights: Empty – 1,986kg/4,380lb
Maximum take-off – 2,663kg/5,870lb
Performance: Maximum speed – 153kph/95mph
Service ceiling – 3,780m/12,400ft
Range – 483km/300 miles
Climb – 244m/800ft per minute

Sikorsky SH-60 Seahawk

The SH-60 Seahawk is a twin-engine medium-lift utility or assault helicopter. It is used for anti-submarine warfare, search-and-rescue, drug interdiction, anti-ship warfare, cargo lift and special operations.

When the US Navy issued a requirement for an updated Light Airborne Multi-Purpose System (LAMPS) helicopter to operate from smaller naval escorts, Boeing and Sikorsky each submitted proposals. Following a 1977 fly-off, the Sikorsky machine, a development of the US Army's Sikorsky UH-60A Black Hawk, was named the winner. While the Seahawk uses the same basic airframe of the UH-60A, the Seahawk is far more expensive and complex due to the addition of extensive avionics and weapons systems. The Navy received the SH-60B Seahawk in 1983.

The SH-60B Seahawk is equipped primarily for Anti-Submarine Warfare (ASW) through a complex system of sensors carried aboard the helicopter including a towed Magnetic Anomaly Detector (MAD), air-launched sonobuoys (sonic detectors) and torpedoes. The SH-60B carries out Anti-Ship Surveillance and Targeting (ASST) operating from cruisers, destroyers, and frigates and can extend the range of the ships' radar capabilities.

ABOVE LEFT: **Described by its manufacturers as the world's most capable maritime helicopter, the Seahawk was created by a team with unparalleled experience in the production of helicopters for maritime missions. With 600 Seahawks in service around the world and 2.5 million flight hours logged, the Seahawk is by any standard an outstanding naval helicopter.**
ABOVE RIGHT: **A Seahawk uses its dipping sonar to listen for submarines under the watchful eye of its carrier.** BELOW LEFT: **Flying the flag – the Seahawk has already served the US Navy for over a quarter of a century.**

Other sensors include the APS-124 search radar, ALQ-142 ESM system and optional nose-mounted Forward-Looking Infra-Red (FLIR) turret. The primary means of attack is with the Mk 46 or Mk 50 torpedo, AGM-114 Hellfire missiles and the capability of a single cabin door-mounted M-60D or GAU-16 machine-gun for defence. A standard crew for a 'Bravo' model is one pilot, one ATO/Co-Pilot (Airborne Tactical Officer) and an enlisted aviation systems warfare operator (sensor operator).

Other capabilities include search and rescue, replenishment, and medical evacuation missions. Due to the success of the original SH-60B variant, the US Navy has also developed the HH-60H special operations model and the improved SH-60F carrier-borne ASW model. All US Navy models will be replaced in time by the MH-60R and MH-60S versions. The US Coast Guard also uses the HH-60J search and rescue version.

The SH-60F 'Foxtrot' is the carrier-based version of the 'Bravo'. It is the primary means of Anti-Submarine Warfare (ASW) and Search-And-Rescue (SAR) for carrier battle group commanders and exists to defend the carrier battle group. It differs from the 'Bravo' in means of submarine detection, utilizing the AQS-13F dipping sonar rather than a MAD detector and carrying fewer sonobuoys

LEFT: **A Seahawk fires a sea-skimming AGM-119 Penguin anti-ship missile. Propelled by a solid rocket engine, the missile performs random weaving manoeuvres as it approaches the target and then hits close to the waterline. The delay fuse causes the warhead to detonate inside the hull of the target ship.** BELOW: **The twin-engine Seahawk is used for anti-submarine warfare, search and rescue, drug interdiction, anti-ship warfare, cargo lift, and special operations.**

(14 rather than the 25 of the 'Bravo'). The 'Foxtrot' is capable of carrying the Mk 46 torpedo and a choice of cabin-mounted guns including the M-60D, M-240 and GAU-16 machine-guns for defence. Standard crew for a Foxtrot is one pilot, one co-pilot, one enlisted Tactical Sensor Operator (TSO) and one enlisted Acoustic Sensor Operator (ASO).

The HH-60H 'Hotel' version is the primary Combat Search-And-Rescue (CSAR), Naval Special Warfare (NSW) and Anti-Surface Warfare (ASUW) helicopter in the US Navy. It carries a variety of defensive and offensive sensors making it one of the most survivable helicopters in the world. Sensors include a FLIR turret with laser designator and the Aircraft Survival Equipment (ASE) package, including the ALQ-144 Infra-Red Jammer, AVR-2 Laser Detectors, APR-39(V)2 Radar Detectors, AAR-47 Missile Launch Detectors and ALE-47 chaff/flare dispensers. Engine exhaust deflectors provide infrared thermal reduction, limiting the threat of heat-seeking missiles. The Hotel can carry up to four AGM-114 Hellfire missiles on an extended wing using the M-299 launcher and a variety of cabin and port window-mounted guns, including M-60D, M-240, GAU-16 and GAU-17 machine-guns. Standard crew for an H model is one pilot, one co-pilot and two 'door gunner' crewmen.

The MH-60S 'Sierra' was developed after the navy decided to phase out the CH-46 Sea Knight helicopter. The 'Sierra' is deployed aboard amphibious assault ships and fast combat supply ships. It has two missions – troop transport and Vertical Replenishment (VERTREP) but can also perform Search-And-Rescue (SAR). The 'Sierra' has no offensive sensors but can carry the ALQ-199 Infra-Red Jammer. However, the Sierra is the first US Navy helicopter with a glass cockpit, in which flight data information is relayed to pilots using four digital screens rather than electromechanical gauges and dials. The primary means of defence is with the M-60D, M-240 or GAU-17, though a 'batwing' in development may be added to accommodate missiles or larger guns and cannon.

In addition to the United States Navy and US Coast Guard, Seahawks were also acquired by Australia, Greece, Japan, Spain, Taiwan, Thailand and Turkey.

LEFT: **Although this SH-60 Seahawk is carrying out cargo duties, note the Forward-Looking Infra-Red (FLIR) turret mounted on the nose. The US Navy's anti-submarine screen has to be able to operate day and night in all weathers to protect the surface ships, and the FLIR makes this possible.**

Sikorsky SH-60B Seahawk

First flight: December 12, 1979 (YSH-60B)

Power: Two General Electric 3,380shp T700-401 turboshafts

Armament: Air-to-surface missile AGM-84 Harpoon, AGM-114 Hellfire, AGM-119 Penguin, Sea Skua, or up to two Mk 46 or Mk 50 ASW torpedoes, Mk 36 mine, Mk 35 depth charge, sonobuoys, dipping sonar, MAD towed array

Size: Rotor diameter – 24.08m/79ft
Length – 19.76m/64ft 10in
Height – 5.8m/17ft

Weights: Empty – 6,190kg/13,650lb
Maximum take-off – 9,909kg/21,845lb

Performance: Maximum speed – 235kph/145mph
Service ceiling – 5,790m/19,000ft
Range – 805km/500 miles
Climb – 214m/700ft per minute

LEFT: The MH-53 Sea Dragon is among the world's largest helicopters but its size hides an impressive flexibility among its special duties.
ABOVE: The large container attached to the port sponson is an auxiliary fuel tank that can hold up to 2,461 litres/650 US gallons of extra fuel. There is another one on the starboard side.

Sikorsky CH-53E Sea Stallion and MH-53 family

The Sikorsky CH-53 Sea Stallion was designed to meet a 1960 US Marines requirement for a new heavy-lift assault transport. Using some systems from their earlier Skycrane, Sikorsky produced a helicopter that remains a key military asset to this day. The first prototype flew in October 1964 and production deliveries of CH-53As began in 1966 – within a year the type was in action in Vietnam. It was at that time that the USAF ordered its first combat rescue version of the CH-53, the HH-52 'Jolly Green Giant', to extract downed pilots from enemy territory.

The CH-53D was a more capable version of the CH-53A. Used extensively both afloat and ashore, the Sea Stallion was the heavy-lift helicopter for the Marine Corps until the introduction of the CH-53E triple-engine variant of the H-53 family into the fleet in 1981. The CH-53D continued in service and performed its multi-role mission lifting both equipment and personnel in training and combat, including Operation 'Desert Storm', the first Gulf War, where the helicopter performed with distinction.

Improvements to the CH-53E included the addition of a third engine to give the aircraft the ability to lift the majority of the US Marines' transportable equipment, a dual-point cargo hook system, improved main rotor blades and composite tail rotor blades. A dual digital automatic flight-control system and engine anti-ice system give the aircraft an all-weather capability.

The CH-53E Super Stallion is designed for the transportation of equipment, supplies and personnel during the assault phase of an amphibious operation and subsequent operations ashore. Capable of both internal and external transportation of supplies, the CH-53E can operate from ships in the most adverse

LEFT: The large, unwieldy yet sophisticated MH-53J is a US Air Force helicopter that is dedicated to rescuing downed pilots and supporting US special operations troops such as the US Navy Seals.

weather conditions, day or night. The three-engine helicopter has external range-extension fuel tanks, 'crashworthy' fuel tanks and defensive electronic countermeasure equipment. The helicopter will carry 37 passengers in its normal configuration and 55 passengers with extra seats installed. The CH-53E can carry external loads at increased airspeeds due to the stability achieved with the dual-point hook system.

The helicopter is capable of lifting 16,260kg/35,850lb at sea level, transporting the load 92.5km/57.5 miles and returning. A typical load would be a 7,250kg/16,000lb M198 howitzer or an 11,800kg/26,000lb Light Armored Vehicle (LAV). The aircraft can also retrieve downed aircraft, including another CH-53E. Equipped with a refuelling probe, the CH-53 can be refuelled in flight, giving the helicopter a technically indefinite range. However, with a typical four and a half hours' endurance, the Super Stallion can move more equipment over rugged terrain in bad weather and at night. During Operation 'Eastern Exit' in January 1990, two CH-53Es launched at sea, flew 857km/532.45 miles at night, refuelling twice en route, to rescue American and foreign allies from the American Embassy in the civil war-torn capital of Mogadishu, Somalia. It was two CH-53Es that rescued Air Force Captain Scott O'Grady following his high-profile downing over Bosnia in June 1995.

The newest military version of Sikorsky's H-53 series is the MH-53E Sea Dragon, the Western world's largest helicopter, used primarily for Airborne Mine Countermeasures (AMCM), with a secondary mission of shipboard delivery. Additional mission capabilities include air-to-air refuelling, hover inflight refuelling, search-and-rescue, and external cargo transport operations over land and at sea.

The MH-53E is heavier and has a greater fuel capacity than the CH-53E but can operate from carriers and other warships. The Sea Dragon is capable of carrying up to 55 troops or a 16,260kg/35,850lb payload but perhaps its most interesting capability is its ability to tow a variety of mine-sweeping countermeasures systems, including the Mk 105 mine-sweeping sled, the ASQ-14 side-scan sonar, and the Mk 103 mechanical mine-sweeping system.

The MH-53J version performs low-level, long-range, undetected penetration into hostile areas, day or night, in adverse weather, to drop, pick up or supply US special forces. This version is the largest and most powerful helicopter in the US Air Force inventory, and is believed to be the most technologically advanced helicopter in the world. Its terrain-following, terrain-avoidance radar and forward-looking infrared sensor, along with a projected map display, enable the crew to follow terrain contours and avoid obstacles, making low-level penetration possible at night in all weathers. The helicopter is equipped with armour plating, and a combination of three 7.62mm miniguns or 0.50 calibre machine-guns. It can transport 38 troops or 14 litters and has an external cargo hook with a 9,070kg/20,000lb capacity.

ABOVE: The MH-53E has enlarged side-mounted fuel sponsons and is configured for towing its mine-sweeping ALQ-166 hydrofoil sled for detonating magnetic mines from high above. BELOW: Some 125 examples of the CH-53D Sea Stallion were delivered to the US Marine Corps between 1969 and 1972.

BELOW: The CH-53E's seven-blade main rotor assembly is powered by three T64-GE-416 turboshaft engines. The downdraft created by the main rotors is enough have earned the CH-53E the nickname of 'the hurricane maker'. Note the protected engine air intakes and the refuelling probe.

Sikorsky CH-53E Super Stallion

First flight: October 14, 1964 (CH-53 prototype)
Power: Three General Electric 4,380shp T64-GE-416/416A turboshaft engines
Armament: Usually none
Size: Rotor diameter – 24.08m/79ft
Length – 30.2m/99ft 1in
Height – 8.97m/29ft 5in
Weights: Empty – 15,070kg/33,226lb
Maximum take-off – 33,340kg/73,500lb
Performance: Maximum speed – 315kph/196mph
Service ceiling – 5,639m/18,500ft
Range – 925km/574 miles with 9,070kg/20,000lb external payload
Climb – 763m/2,500ft per minute with 9,070kg/20,000lb external payload

LEFT: **Derived from the Su-27, the Su-33 differs not only in having navalized features like folding wings and an arrester hook but also by having the ability to refuel in mid-air. Note the Su-33's large canards that shorten the aircraft's take-off distance and improve manoeuvrability.**

Sukhoi Su-33

It was in 1985 that the first outline design for a navalized version of the famous Su-27 fighter was approved to provide the Soviet Navy's new carriers with an air superiority fighter for self-defence. The carrier-borne aircraft was at first designated Su-27K (K for *korabelny* or shipborne) but was later given the Su-33 designation. The NATO reporting name for the new version of the Su-27 was 'Flanker-D'.

The naval version differed from the land-based Su-27 by the addition of canards near the junction of the wing and leading edge extension for better manoeuvrability while generating more lift thereby reducing take-off runs and landing speed. Wing area was increased, although the span remained the same as its shore-based cousin, and the fins were shortened to enable the fighter to fit in the typically crowded hangars of an aircraft carrier.

The Su-33 also featured redesigned power-assisted folding outer wing panels, separately controlled aileron and flaps and an upgraded fly-by-wire control system and hydraulic system. The airframe and landing gear were also strengthened to cope

with the additional stresses of carrier operations as well as being treated for improved corrosion resistance. The nose gear was changed to a twin-wheeled version with a telescopic strut and an additional landing light and three-colour indicator lights for the carrier-based flight controller's visual reference of the approaching aircraft's glide-patch and landing speed. The aircraft was, of course, also equipped with a retractable arrester-hook system. The AL-31F engines were uprated to enable the pilot to recover from a failed hook-up and aborted landing so he had enough power to go around again.

The drag chute was removed from the shortened tail boom and the horizontal stabilizers and nosecone could all fold up with the wings to reduce the aircraft's dimensions onboard ship. Another two hardpoints were added together with a retractable inflight refuelling probe on the port side of the aircraft, forward of the cockpit. The aircraft's navigation, automatic landing and fire-control systems were all upgraded to cope with the very different environment of operating from an aircraft carrier.

ABOVE: **As well as air defence, Su-33 duties were planned to include destruction of enemy ASW, AWACS and transport aircraft.** RIGHT: **The wings were fitted with power-assisted folding, and the vertical tails were shortened compared to the Su-27 to allow the fighter to fit in the hangar of an aircraft carrier. Also the Infra-Red Search and Track sensor was moved forward to provide better downward visibility.**

The Su-33 entered service with the Northern Fleet in 1994, based on the only Russian Navy carrier in service, the *Admiral Kuznetsov*, which sailed with 13 examples on board for the first time in 1995. Before embarking, each pilot made up to 400 landings on a concrete runway training deck painted to match the size and shape of the carrier deck to perfect their technique before being allowed to attempt landings at sea on a deck moving in all planes.

The training of Su-27K pilots is carried out on the Su-27 KUB. This is a combat-capable trainer fitted with a side-by-side cockpit as a tandem cockpit arrangement would not have allowed sufficient visibility for the instructor in the back seat to make a safe carrier landing. The Su-27 KUB also has a larger wing area as well as larger canards, ventral fins, rudders and horizontal stabilizers to enable lower approach speeds and safer landings. The maiden flight, first carrier landing and take-off of the Su-27 KUB all took place in 1999.

ABOVE: **Su-33s and Kamov Ka-27s on the deck of the carrier *Admiral Kuznetsov*. Commissioned in January 1991, the carrier does not have a catapult, which limits the size and weight of aircraft that can be carried.**

The Su-33 can carry a range of guided weapons, including missiles to intercept anti-ship missiles. In addition to the air defence role, the Su-33 can be tasked with the destruction of enemy ASW, AWACS and transport aircraft, anti-shipping strike and support of amphibious landings. Reconnaissance and laying of minefields are also within this very capable aircraft's remit.

Some 24 examples of the Su-33 were built and that seemed to be the end of production for the type. However, in late 2006 the Russian media revealed that talks were underway to supply up to 50 Su-33s to China to operate from the former Soviet carrier *Varyag*, acquired by China from the Ukraine in 1999.

ABOVE: **Sukhoi Su-33s operate from the *Kuznetsov* by using a forward ski-jump pioneered by the British, and then recover using arrester wires.**

Sukhoi Su-33

First flight: April 29, 1999 (Su-27KUB)
Power: Two Lyulka 12,558kg/27,690lb thrust AL-31F afterburning turbofans
Armament: One 30mm cannon and up to 6,500kg/14,330lb of ordnance on 12 external hardpoints, including air-to-air or air-to-surface missiles, bombs, rockets or ECM pods
Size: Wingspan – 14.7m/48ft 3in extended
  Length – 21.94m/72ft
  Height – 5.92m/19ft 6in
  Wing area – 62m²/667sq ft
Weights: Empty – 16,000kg/35,275lb
  Maximum take-off – 33,000kg/72,750lb
Performance: Maximum speed – 2,300kph/1,430mph
  Ceiling – 17,000m/55,770ft
  Range – 3,000km/1,860 miles
  Climb – 13,800m/45,275ft per minute

LEFT: **The straight-winged Attacker was the Royal Navy's first jet fighter and was a 'tail dragger', unusual at a time when most designers were opting for tricycle undercarriages for jets. The use of the Spiteful's wing led to the aircraft's working name of 'Jet Spiteful' before Attacker was applied.**

Supermarine Attacker

The Supermarine Attacker was originally designed to a wartime RAF specification and combined a Nene jet engine with the laminar-flow wing (minus radiators) and landing gear of the piston-engined Spiteful. This simplified approach was taken to get another British single-seat jet fighter in service as soon as possible – the swollen fuselage lines of the Attacker were simply due to the diameter of the centrifugal-flow Nene turbojet. The second and third prototypes had different landing gear and were essentially made to demonstrate carrier capability. Trials on HMS *Illustrious* led to Royal Navy and Pakistan Air Force orders.

Although the prototype first flew in July 1946, the type did not enter service until August 1951 and then with the Royal Navy who maintained interest in the Attacker long after the RAF gave up on it.

The Fleet Air Arm took delivery of 52 Attacker F. Mk 1 interceptors, 8 FB. Mk 1 fighter-bombers (both Mk 1s powered by the Rolls-Royce Nene 3) and 82 FB. Mk 2 fighter-bombers powered by the Nene 102. The FB. Mk 1 could carry two 454kg/1,000lb bombs or four 27kg/60lb rocket projectiles as well as the standard fighter armament of four 20mm cannon. The 36 Attackers supplied to Pakistan were land-based

aircraft – they were basically Attacker Mk 1s but minus folding wings and other naval equipment. The range of the Attacker could be increased by carrying a bulbous belly tank.

The Attacker was in many ways an unremarkable aircraft and the tailwheel made deck landing difficult, but as the first Fleet Air Arm jet fighter in front-line use, the Attacker provided the Royal Navy with its first foothold in the jet age. The type was phased out of front-line use in 1954 after only three years when it was replaced by the Sea Hawk and Sea Venom. Royal Navy Volunteer Reserve (RNVR) units continued to operate the type until 1957.

ABOVE: **Due to the limitations of the early jet engine that powered the Attacker it was felt that the type would not be able to fight above 10,670m/35,000ft. Two examples survive, one in Britain and one in Pakistan.**

Supermarine Attacker F. Mk 1

First flight: July 27, 1946
Power: Rolls-Royce 2,271kg/5,000lb thrust Nene 3 turbojet
Armament: Four 20mm cannon in wings
Size: Wingspan – 11.25m/36ft 11in
Length – 11.43m/37ft 6in
Height – 3.02m/9ft 11in
Wing area – 21m²/226sq ft
Weights: Empty – 3,826kg/8,434lb
Maximum take-off – 5,539kg/12,211lb
Performance: Maximum speed – 950kph/590mph
Ceiling – 13,715m/45,000ft
Range – 950km/590 miles
Climb – 1,936m/6,350ft per minute

Supermarine Scimitar

This large and heavy fighter was the Royal Navy's first swept-wing single-seat jet aircraft, the first RN aircraft equipped to carry an atomic bomb and the last fighter aircraft to bear the famous Supermarine name. Derived from the Supermarine Type 525 that first flew on April 27, 1954, the Scimitar's role evolved from a single-seat fighter to a low-level strike aircraft with nuclear capability. The first production Scimitar flew on January 11, 1957, and production Scimitars were first delivered to the Royal Navy for evaluation in August of that year.

The first front-line Scimitar unit to be formed was 803 Naval Air Squadron. After working up at RNAS Lossiemouth, the unit took part in the 1960 Farnborough SBAC show, before embarking on HMS *Victorious*. Unfortunately, 803's commanding officer was killed when his aircraft went over the side of the carrier due to a failed arrester wire – this happened in front of the press and so the Scimitar's unfortunate reputation was born.

The Scimitar was, at the time of its introduction, the heaviest and most powerful aircraft ever to serve in the Fleet Air Arm. Operating large and fast aircraft from relatively small aircraft carriers made take-offs and landings particularly hazardous. The Scimitar was designed with a tail 'bumper' on which the aircraft would rest for take-off, while the aircraft's nosewheel was high in the air, actually clear of the carrier deck. Launching with this increased angle of attack meant the

catapults on the Royal Navy's carriers could still manage to launch the heavy Scimitar.

Accident rates were high – of the 76 Scimitars produced, 39 were lost in a variety of accidents. The Scimitar was, however, equally at home carrying out low-level bombing attacks, high-altitude interception with air-to-air missiles and long-range fighter reconnaissance – it was a quantum leap on from the Sea Hawk which it replaced as the Navy's standard single-seat strike fighter. Although only produced in small numbers, the Scimitars gave the Royal Navy a nuclear punch.

Mounting losses and the arrival of the Blackburn Buccaneer saw the Scimitar relegated to second-line duties. However, the early Buccaneer's underpowered engines meant that Buccaneers could not take off with a full fuel and weapons load, so Scimitars were configured to provide 'buddy' refuelling – that way the Buccaneers could take off with minimum fuel but maximum weapons load then refuel from a Scimitar immediately. Scimitars were also used as high-speed target banner tug aircraft.

The last front-line squadron (803 NAS) surrendered their Scimitars in October 1966 but the Fleet Requirements Unit flew them for testing and training purposes until the end of 1970.

TOP LEFT: **Although this large, twin-engined fighter was produced in limited numbers it served the Royal Navy well in a variety of roles for a decade.**

TOP RIGHT: **The large wing area is evident in this study of a Scimitar F.1. The dorsal spine extending forwards from the tail had an air intake at the end.**

ABOVE: **The wings' drooping leading edges and large flaps kept carrier handling of this large aircraft within essential limits.**

Supermarine Scimitar F.1

First flight: January 11, 1957
Power: Two Rolls-Royce 5,105kg/11,250lb static thrust Avon 202 turbojets
Armament: Four 30mm cannon; wing pylons for up to 96 air-to-air rockets or a range of other stores
Size: Wingspan – 11.33m/37ft 2in
Length – 16.87m/55ft 4in
Height – 5.28m/17ft 4in
Wing area – 45.06m²/485sq ft
Weights: Empty – 10,869kg/23,962lb
Maximum take-off – 15,513kg/34,200lb
Performance: Maximum speed – 1,143kph/710mph
Ceiling – 14,020m/46,000ft
Range – 2,288km/1,422 miles
Climb – 3,660m/12,000ft per minute

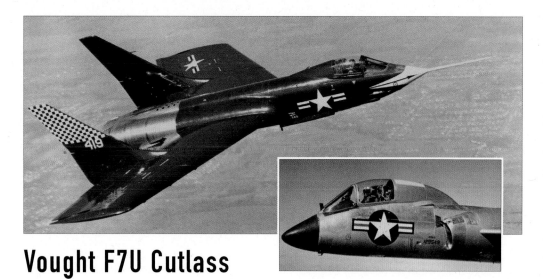

Vought F7U Cutlass

In 1945 the US Navy issued a requirement for a 965kph/600mph carrier-borne jet-powered fighter. German wartime aerodynamic research data proved very useful to US aircraft designers in the immediate post-war years and helped them accelerate many areas of aeronautical development. Vought (or Chance Vought as it was then known) designers were particularly interested in the work carried out by the Arado company on tailless aircraft and this led directly to the highly unusual F7U Cutlass which had a 38 degree swept wing, twin tail fins but no conventional tail surfaces, which together should have given a high-speed aircraft with a great rate of climb. The F7U was the last aircraft designed by Rex Beisel who in 1922 had designed on the first ever fighter made specifically for the US Navy, the Curtis TS-1.

The prototype XF7U-1 first flew on September 29, 1948, piloted by Robert Baker. The Cutlass helped the US Navy break new ground – sadly not always as intended – as it was

TOP: **The F7U was a bold design at a time when experimentation was required. The fact that all three prototypes were lost in testing was a hint of things to come.** ABOVE: **Though helped by wartime German research, Vought were keen to deny the use of Nazi data.**

the first swept-wing and supersonic production aircraft in the US Navy inventory. It featured a pressurized cockpit and tricycle undercarriage before they became the norm. It was also the first production aircraft to use afterburning jet engines.

Despite these innovations, the Cutlass had many shortcomings. Its new J34 Westinghouse engines could not give the aircraft the power necessary to function effectively at all the required levels, earning the type the unfortunate nickname of 'gutless Cutlass'. There were even reports of the engines cutting out in the rain – a serious shortcoming for an aircraft intended to take off and land at sea.

LEFT: **Even on the ground, the pilot sat over 4m/13ft above the ground, and was at the mercy of the frequently malfunctioning nosewheel undercarriage leg, failure of which could prove fatal.**

LEFT: **The Cutlass certainly made the US Navy look very futuristic, but it was the accident and loss rates for the Cutlass that were out of this world.** ABOVE: **An F7U-3 prepares for launch from USS** *Hancock*. **Note the twin fins, the two jet pipes and the cockpit canopy, which is open.**

The F7U-1 was the first version in service but only 14 were built and were used for trials and training. The aircraft was very demanding in terms of maintenance and it also had a high accident rate. Early versions had four 20mm cannon located above the engine air intakes. When fired, the guns created a pressure wave that could cause the aircraft to stall, which led to the loss of a number of aircraft. Early nosewheels were also prone to collapse resulting in the destruction of the cockpit and the pilot. Despite all these problems, pilots who relished a challenge liked the Cutlass and could pull 16g manoeuvres when making use of its excellent aerobatic capability.

The F7U-3 that ultimately equipped 13 US Navy and Marine Corps squadrons ashore and on carriers was not just modified and improved – it was effectively a new design. The F7U-1 version had not been considered robust enough for carrier use so the new model was considerably tougher and was re-stressed throughout. To reduce maintenance time, over 100 extra doors and access panels were added. The nose

was redesigned, twice, to improve pilot visibility and the tricycle undercarriage nose-wheel was both lengthened and strengthened. This new version was introduced into US Navy service from 1954 and the F7U-3M variant was equipped to carry four laser-beam-riding Sparrow air-to-air missiles – it was the first fighter aircraft equipped with air-to-air guided missiles.

The US Navy's Blue Angels aerobatics team flew a pair of Cutlasses as a support act to the main team during their 1952 show season. Although keen to present the fighter in a positive light, the team were not willing to fly the Cutlass en masse in close aerobatics.

Most were withdrawn from service in 1956–57 as new, more capable aircraft became available. The F7U-3 was just as accident-prone as the F7U-1 with an incredible 25 per cent of all built being lost in accidents. Once Vought's F-8 Crusader had flown, all Cutlass development ceased. By the time of its retirement, the Cutlass had claimed the lives of four test pilots and 21 US Navy squadron pilots.

ABOVE: **The old aviation saying, "If it looks right, it is right", could not be applied to this photograph of a Cutlass during a catapult launch. Note the pilot's open cockpit canopy.**

Vought F7U-3 Cutlass

First flight: September 29, 1948 (XF7U-1 prototype)

Power: Two Westinghouse 2,767kg/6,100lb afterburning thrust J46-WE-8A turbojets

Armament: Four 20mm cannon plus underwing attachments for rockets

Size: Wingspan – 12.09m/39ft 8in
Length – 13.13m/43ft 1in
Height – 4.46m/14ft 7.5in
Wing area – 46.08m²/496sq ft

Weights: Empty – 8,260kg/18,210lb
Maximum take-off – 14,353kg/31,642lb

Performance: Maximum speed – 1,094kph/680mph
Ceiling – 12,190m/40,000ft
Range – 1,062km/660 miles
Climb – 3,960m/13,000ft per minute

Vought A-7 Corsair II

Derived from Vought's F-8 Crusader but a completely new aircraft, the single-seat A-7 Corsair II was one of the most successful modern military aircraft. At a unit cost of just over $1 million and the lowest loss rate of any US military aircraft in the Vietnam War, the A-7 gave the US taxpayer outstanding value for money. In over five million flight hours between 1968 and 1991, US Navy and Air Force A-7s were the US military's most cost-effective aerial weapon.

The A-7 resulted from a 1962 United States Navy requirement for an A-4 Skyhawk replacement with improved range and weapon-carrying capability as well as more accurate weapons delivery. The Navy insisted that to keep cost down, all proposals had to be based on existing aircraft designs so Vought's was based on the F-8 Crusader.

The pace of the project was remarkable. Vought's winning response was announced on February 11, 1964, and the YA-7A prototype first flew in September 1965, almost a month ahead

TOP: **This is a Corsair II of VA-12, Attack Squadron Twelve, which operated the A-7E from April 1971. The photo was taken when the unit was part of Carrier Attack Wing Seven.** ABOVE: **Portugal operated a number of ex-United States Navy A-7As (20) and TA-7Cs (6). Deliveries to Portugal began in May 1981, and the aircraft were finally retired in 1999.**

of schedule. By now the aircraft was called Corsair II, reprising the name of the company's famous wartime naval fighter. The first operational US Navy squadron aircraft was delivered in October 1966 and the type first saw combat in December 1967. Twenty-seven front-line US Navy units were equipped with A-7s during the Vietnam war.

The A-7 was shorter than the F-8 but had a bigger span wing, although not of the variable-incidence kind. Power came from the Pratt & Whitney TF30-P-6 turbofan developed for the F-111. The engine did not have an afterburner, as supersonic speed was not a requirement of the early A-7. This power and the fact that the aircraft was much lighter than the F-8 meant that range and weapons load were greatly increased.

The aircraft was equipped with an advanced radar that was integrated with a digital navigation system and a digital weapons computer for increased accuracy from a greater distance, thereby reducing exposure to the risks to be found nearer to targets. The Corsair II was the first US combat aircraft with the now standard head-up display, and also had a projected map display system that accurately displayed the

ABOVE: **Loaded with bombs and missiles this wing-folded A-7 was pictured on the deck of the carrier USS** *John F. Kennedy* **(CV-67), the last conventionally powered aircraft carrier built by the US Navy.**

aircraft's position to the pilot on two different scaled maps. Production of 199 A-7As was followed by 196 A-7Bs and 67 C models – all were basically the same aircraft but with engine updates and modifications.

As they did with the US Navy's F-4, the USAF also ordered the A-7 as a low-cost interim successor to the F-105 until the F-111 was available. The YA-7D prototype with the TF30 flew on April 6, 1968, while the first TF41-powered aircraft took to the air on September 26, 1968. The first USAF version was the A-7D with a fixed high-speed refuelling receptacle behind the cockpit to 'fit' the KC-135 tanker's flying boom instead of the folding refuelling probe of US Navy aircraft. The USAF chose the M61 Vulcan Gatling gun rather than the twin single-barrel 20mm cannon fitted in USN aircraft, and chose a different engine in the form of the Allison TF41-A-1, a licensed version of the Rolls-Royce Spey. This version also had more comprehensive avionics to enable weapons delivery in all conditions, day or night. The US Navy later adopted its own version of this model which was designated A-7E.

United States Air Force A-7Ds flew a total of 12,928 combat sorties during the Vietnam War and were second only to the mighty B-52 Stratofortress in the weight of ordnance dropped on Hanoi. The last shot fired in anger by a United States military aircraft in South-east Asia came from an A-7D of the 345th Tactical Fighter Wing operating from Korat, Thailand, on August 15, 1973.

The A-7E was the final US fleet version and could carry up to 6,800kg/15,000lb of bombs and missiles on eight weapons points. A-7E Corsair IIs were part of the two-carrier battle group that carried out strikes on Libyan terrorist-related targets in 1986. The US Navy flew its last A-7E combat missions during the 1990 Gulf War. During 'Desert Storm', the A-7 achieved 95 per cent operational readiness and did not miss a single combat sortie. The type was fully retired from USN service in 1993. This very capable aircraft became a victim of the US Department for Defense's decision to acquire stealthy,

ABOVE: **The Corsair flew on in US Navy service until 1993 after 27 years of front-line service and a formidable combat record.** BELOW: **The A-7A could carry a fraction of the weapons load later versions were cleared to fly with. Notice the two weapons carrying points under each wing and the rail on the side of the fuselage for carrying Sidewinders.**

multi-role supersonic fighter/attack aircraft that cost 50 times more at new than the single-purpose A-7.

With the exception of some used in deception tactics for the then top secret F-117 programme, most USAF A-7s were phased out by 1991.

The A-7 production line had continued until September 1984 by which time 1,545 examples had been built of which 113 were remanufactured to produce later models. A-7s were also exported to Portugal, Greece and Thailand.

ABOVE: **The Corsair II won its spurs in Vietnam where it served with both the US Navy and later the US Air Force. It is rightly considered to be one of the best ever combat aircraft.**

Vought A-7E Corsair II

First flight: September 27, 1965 (YA-7A)
Power: Allison 6577kg/14500lb thrust
TF41-A-2 turbofan
Armament: One 20mm cannon and up to
6,804kg/15,000lb of missiles, rockets and bombs
Size: Wingspan – 11.81m/38ft 9in
Length – 14.06m/46ft 1.5in
Height – 4.9m/16ft 1in
Wing area – 34.84m^2/375sq ft
Weights: Empty – 8,841kg/19,490lb
Maximum take-off – 19,051kg/42,000lb
Performance: Maximum speed –
1,123kph/698mph
Ceiling – 12,800m/42,000ft
Range – 2,300km/1,430 miles
Climb – 4,572m/15,000ft per minute

Vought F-8 Crusader

The Crusader single-seat naval jet fighter
began as Vought's response to a 1952
US Navy requirement for a carrier-based
supersonic fighter. The prototype first took to
the air in March 1955 and exceeded Mach 1
during this initial flight making it the first aircraft
designed for shipboard operation to fly faster
than sound.

Jet aircraft carrier operations dictate that
aircraft have very robust landing gear, an
arrester hook and folding wings but all these
features add to the overall weight of the aircraft
and can compromise performance. Vought came up with a
brilliant variable-incidence wing which, on take-off and landing,
could be pivoted through seven degrees. This gave the wing
a high angle of attack and so reduced landing approach
speeds. The raised centre section of the wing also acted
as a speed brake to reduce landing speed further.

Armament consisted of four 20mm cannon, two on either
side of the fuselage. Behind the guns, on each side of the
aircraft, was a launch rail for a single Sidewinder missile.
Although the prototype did not have wing stores pylons,
these came on later production models.

The first production version of the F8U-1 Crusader, as it
was then named, flew at the end of September 1955, and the
US Navy accepted its first operational F8U-1 on December 28,
1956. The US Navy was eager to show off their new fighter
and a series of speed and endurance records were set by
Crusaders in 1956–57. On July 16, 1957, an F8U-1 and an
F8U-1P reconnaissance model attempted to set a coast-to-
coast speed record. The pilot of the F8U-1P that landed in
New York after a flight of just three hours and 23 minutes,
was Major John Glenn, who was as a result a celebrity before
his career as a NASA astronaut and later a US senator.

TOP: **The French Aéronavale were the main overseas customer for what
was known in US fighter pilot circles as 'the last of the gunfighters' as it was
the last US fighter designed with guns as its primary weapon.** ABOVE: **The F-8
was among the first supersonic fighters and remained potent for over 40 years.
Notice how long the aircraft is compared to the one-man cockpit.**

The F8U-1E had an improved radar system that gave it
limited all-weather capability while the more powerful F8U-2
incorporated a further improved radar and fire-control system,
as well as an uprated J57-P-16 engine with 7670kg/16,900lb
of afterburning thrust.

The next version was the F8U-2N, with new avionics
including a push-button autopilot, and the uprated J57-P-20
engine, with increased afterburning thrust of 8,165kg/18,000lb.
Yet more versions followed. The first F8U-2NE flew at the end
of June 1961 and carried an improved search and fire-control
radar system for enhanced all-weather operation.

In September 1962 the US Navy introduced an aircraft
designation system in line with US Air Force designations,
so existing Crusader variant designations were changed.
The F8U-1 became the F-8A and the later models changed
from F8U-1E/F-8B, F8U-2/F-8C, F8U-2N/F-8D, F8U-2NE/F-8E,
F8U-1P/RF-8A.

LEFT: **The Crusader's brilliant variable-incidence wing, seen here in use ready for a carrier launch, reduced take-off and landing speeds. US Navy Crusaders were formidable dogfighters during the Vietnam air war and downed at least 18 enemy aircraft.**

ABOVE: **When an aircraft is this good, you are allowed to show off in it sometimes. The Crusader was the first carrier-based aircraft to reach a speed of 1609kmh/1000mph.**

One final new-production model was built – the F-8E(FN), built for the French Aéronavale. However, French carriers were smaller than American carriers, and this dictated new engineering including blown flaps to reduce the aircraft's landing speed.

The Aéronavale operated 42 Crusaders from the carriers *Clemenceau* and *Foch*. The French aircraft also had the capability to carry two Matra R.530 air-to-air missiles and eventually four Matra Magic R.550 heat-seeking missiles, in place of Sidewinders.

The Crusader was used by both US Marine and US Navy detachments during the war in Vietnam, its combat debut coming on August 2, 1964. North Vietnamese patrol boats attacked the US Navy destroyer *Maddox* so four Crusaders from the carrier *Ticonderoga* attacked and sank one of the

patrol boats. The Marines used the aircraft largely in the attack role, but the US Navy used the Crusader as a dogfighter and in the period 1966–68 shot down at least 18 MiGs.

The Crusader proved so effective that in 1966 a re-engineering programme was established to refurbish and improve the type. Stronger wings and main landing gear plus blown flaps (devised for the French Crusaders) were added to a total of 446 rebuilt.

By 1972, fighter versions of the F-8 Crusader were being phased out of US Navy service, but in 1978, 25 refurbished US Navy F-8Hs were sold on to the Philippine Air Force as F-8Ps – they were finally retired in 1986. The Aéronavale Crusaders were the last of the type in service and were replaced by the Rafale from 2000, bringing more than four decades of Crusader service to an end.

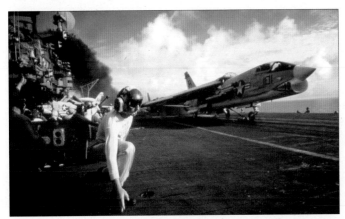

ABOVE: **An F-8 prepares to launch from the USS *Constellation* during Vietnam. Throughout the conflict the aircraft served in photographic, reconnaissance, strike and fighter roles.**

Vought F-8E Crusader

First flight: March 25, 1955

Power: Pratt & Whitney 8,165kg/18,000lb afterburning thrust J57-P-20A turbojet

Armament: Four 20mm cannon, four AIM-9 Sidewinder AAMs, or two AGM-12B Bullpup missiles

Size: Wingspan – 10.72m/35ft 2in
Length – 16.61m/54ft 6in
Height – 4.8m/15ft 9in
Wing area – 32.52m²/350sq ft

Weights: Empty – 9,038kg/19,925lb
Maximum take-off – 15,422kg/34,000lb

Performance: Maximum speed – 1,800kph/1,120mph
Ceiling – 17,983m/59,000ft
Range – 966km/600 miles
Climb – 17,374m/57,000ft in 6 minutes

Westland Lynx

A 1964 British Army requirement calling for a multi-role helicopter able to carry seven fully-armed troops, a 1,360kg/3,000lb load and operate in the casualty evacuation, reconnaissance, or liaison roles led Westland to develop a helicopter that became known as the Lynx. Westland also appreciated the Royal Navy's need for a second-generation helicopter to operate from ships in adverse weather. Meanwhile, France was also looking for an armed reconnaissance and ASW helicopter. The result was an Anglo-French agreement under which Westland would design and produce 70 per cent of a new aircraft while Aérospatiale in France produced the rest. Significantly, the Lynx was the first British aircraft designed using metric and not imperial measurements.

Following design and development, the first prototype Lynx flew in 1971. Of the 13 development machines, the first Royal Navy HAS Mk 2 version flew in 1972. It introduced a lengthened nose for a radar scanner and a wheeled undercarriage as opposed to skids. The first Lynx landing at sea took place on June 29, 1973 aboard Royal Fleet Auxiliary *Engadine*.

ABOVE LEFT: **The Royal Navy's Lynx HMA.8 is a sophisticated, versatile naval helicopter able to carry out anti-submarine, anti-surface and search and rescue missions. The Royal Navy operated HMA. 8s from all their escort ships, destroyers and frigates.** ABOVE RIGHT: **Early in its career the Lynx established itself as the world's best light naval multi-role helicopter.**

In 1972 a Lynx broke the world record over 15km/9.3 miles and 25km/15.5 miles for helicopters by flying at a speed of 321.74kph/200mph. It also set a new 100km/62-mile closed-circuit record flying at 318.504kph/198mph. In 1986 a modified Lynx piloted by John Egginton set an absolute-speed record for helicopters over a 15km/9.3-mile and 25km/15.5-mile course by reaching speeds up to 400.87kph/249.09mph. The Lynx remains one of the most agile helicopters in the world, capable of performing loops and rolls and has equipped the Royal Navy's Black Cats aerobatic display team.

The first production Lynx HAS Mk 2 flew in 1976 and deck-handling trials began on HMS *Birmingham* at sea in February 1977. The first Royal Navy Lynx squadron, No.702 NAS, was commissioned in 1978 leading to the type operating from over 40 ships, mainly frigates and destroyers. The HAS Mk 2 was developed principally for anti-submarine duties, operating from destroyers and frigates. It brought a significant capability to the Royal Navy operating in the air-to-surface search and strike, SAR, troop transport, reconnaissance, fire support, fleet liaison and communication roles. Eighty HAS2s were delivered with the final 20 receiving uprated engines – these machines were designated Mk 3. The French Aéronavale also widely deployed the type.

LEFT: **XX510 was the second naval Lynx prototype and, along with other trials machines, was subjected to tough testing to ensure the design could cope with the harsh carrier environment.**

LEFT: **As well as traditional anti-submarine duties, the Royal Navy's Lynx HMA.8 is used to protect British interests around the world. In 2007, a helicopter operating from RFA *Largs Bay* took parts in an anti-drugs operation in the Caribbean and helped in the seizure of £20 million worth of cocaine.** BELOW: **The French Navy is one of the other prime operators of the Lynx. Usually, naval versions have the tricycle undercarriage while army/utility versions have skids.**

About 25 Royal Navy Lynx took part in the Falklands War and their first action came on April 25, 1982, when a pair of Mk 2s attacked and helped to disable the Argentine submarine *Santa Fe*. Actions on May 3, 1982, best illustrate the capability of the Lynx. HMS *Coventry*'s Lynx launched two Sea Skua missiles at a vessel detected on radar and scored direct hits. Shortly afterwards the Lynx from HMS *Glasgow* was fired at by what it thought to be the same vessel. It launched its missiles from 14.4km/9 miles range, completely destroying the vessel's superstructure. The Navy Lynx went on to see more action in the first Gulf War when the Lynx's Sea Skua was used to devastating effect against the Iraqi Navy.

The Lynx AH.7 currently in service with the Fleet Air Arm operates as an attack/utility helicopter in support of the Royal Marines while the Lynx HMA.8 is an anti-submarine warfare helicopter equipped with the Sea Skua anti-ship missile for Royal Navy warships. The Lynx was back in action during the invasion of Iraq in 2003 – a Lynx from 847 Naval Air Squadron was shot down over Basra, Iraq on May 6, 2006.

Although the Lynx is due to be phased out of service from 2012, the sea-borne Lynx remains possibly the best small ship helicopter in the world.

On June 22, 2006, the UK Ministry of Defence awarded Westland a £1 billion contract for 70 Future Lynx helicopters, described as a new aircraft that builds on the dynamic and vehicle systems of the existing design, incorporating advanced technology and providing increased capability. Future Lynx will feature a redesigned nose and rear fuselage to give greater space and easier access to avionic units. Power will come from two LHTEC CTS800 engines, offering increased power, endurance and economy over existing Lynx powerplants. The Royal Navy variant will be in service from 2015.

As well as Britain and France, Lynx have been operated by the navies of Brazil, Norway, Denmark, Portugal, Germany, Egypt, Argentina, Nigeria, South Korea and the Netherlands.

ABOVE: **The Netherlands acquired a number of versions, including eight for anti-submarine warfare. The entire Dutch Lynx fleet was upgraded in the early 1990s, and fitted with four-bag flotation systems.**

Westland Lynx HAS 8

First flight: March 21, 1971 (prototype)
Power: Two Rolls-Royce Gem 1,135shp 42-1 turboshafts
Armament: Torpedoes, depth charges, anti-ship or anti–tank missiles, dependent on mission
Size: Rotor diameter – 12.8m/42ft
 Length – 15.24m/50ft
 Height – 3.76m/12ft 1in
Weights: Empty – 3,291kg/7,255lb
 Maximum take-off – 5,125kg/11,300lb
Performance: Maximum speed – 232kph/144mph
 Service ceiling – 2,576m/8,450ft
 Range – 275km/171 miles
 Climb – 661m/2,170ft per minute

LEFT: **Flying the flag for the Royal Navy, this Sea King HAS.6 from 816 NAS had its tiger markings applied for the annual Tiger Meet of NATO aircraft.**
ABOVE: **This shot of an 820 NAS Sea King shows a close up of one of the emergency flotation bags in its container above the starboard wheel.**

Westland (Sikorsky) Sea King

The Westland Sea King is a British licence-built version of the Sikorsky S-61 helicopter of the same name, built by Westland Helicopters, now Agusta Westland. Although the aircraft share a name, the British aircraft differs considerably from the American version by having British-built Gnome engines, British anti-submarine warfare systems and a fully computerized control system. The Westland Sea King was also developed for a much wider range of missions than the Sikorsky Sea King.

A 1969 agreement between Westland and Sikorsky allowed the British company to use the Sikorsky Sea King airframe and rotor system to meet a Royal Navy requirement for an anti-submarine warfare helicopter to replace the Westland Wessex, itself a British version of a Sikorsky machine.

The prototype and pre-production machines used Sikorsky-built components but the first Westland-built aircraft and the first production version for the Royal Navy, the Sea King HAS1,

had its maiden flight on May 7, 1969. It was delivered to the Royal Navy in the same year while the last Westland Sea King was built over 20 years later in 1990 – a lengthy production run.

The basic ASW Sea King was upgraded numerous times, becoming the HAS2, HAS5 and HAS6, which was replaced in service by the Merlin. Surviving aircraft are having their mission equipment removed and the aircraft are being used in the utility role.

A troop-carrying version, the Commando, was originally developed for the Egyptian Air Force. Capable of transporting 27 fully equipped troops over 640km/400 miles, it retained the folding rotor blades and tail of the ASW variants. This version is fitted with an external cargo hook capable of carrying underslung loads of up to 2,720kg/6,000lb such as Land Rovers and the 105mm Light Gun. A rescue hoist is fitted as standard. Designated Sea King HC. Mk 4 by the Royal Navy, it remains in service as an important asset for amphibious assaults.

LEFT: **Derived from the export Commando, the Westland Sea King HC Mk 4 is an all-weather, day and night amphibious medium support helicopter. It is cleared for operations from nearly all Royal Navy and many foreign warships, and is equally at home providing support to ground forces when ashore, in all conditions.**

A dedicated search-and-rescue version, the Sea King HAR3, was developed for the RAF, and entered service from September 1977 to replace the Westland Whirlwind and, later, the Wessex, in the search-and-rescue role. These aircraft provide 24-hour SAR cover around the UK and the Falkland Islands. SAR versions of the Sea King were also produced for the Royal Norwegian Air Force, the German Navy, and later for the Belgian Air Force.

The latest variant of the Sea King is the ASaC, formerly known as Airborne Early Warning (AEW). During the Falklands War a number of warships were lost, with casualties, due to the lack of a local AEW capability. Two HAS2 Sea Kings were hastily modified in 1982 to become the Sea King AEW2A. Thirteen Sea Kings were eventually modified, the main difference being the addition of the Thales Searchwater radar attached to the side of the fuselage on a swivelling arm and protected by an inflatable dome. The helicopter lowers the radar in flight and raises it for landing. Further modifications led to the designation AEW7 and then the ASaC7, a further upgrade of the AEW7. The main role of the ASaC Sea King is detection of low-flying attack aircraft. It also provides interception/attack control and over-the-horizon targeting for surface-launched weapon systems. The ASaC7's radar can simultaneously track 400 targets.

Royal Navy Sea Kings proved their remarkable versatility and endurance during the Falklands War of 1982, performing mainly anti-submarine search and attack, also replenishment, troop transport and Special Forces insertions into the occupied islands. During the 1991 Gulf War its roles included air-sea rescue, inter-ship transporting duties and transporting Royal Marines on to any suspect ships that refused to turn around during the enforced embargo on Iraq.

The Sea King participated in the UN's intervention in Bosnia, with Sea Kings operated by 820 Naval Air Squadron and 845 Naval Air Squadron. The Sea Kings from 820 NAS were deployed from Royal Fleet Auxiliary ships and provided logistical support, rather than the ASW role in which the squadron specialized, ferrying troops and supplies across

ABOVE: **The Airborne Surveillance and Area Control (ASaC) – previously Airborne Early Warning – Sea King was rapidly brought into Royal Navy service after the Falklands War, when it became clear that Airborne Early Warning remained an essential part of air power and survival at sea.** BELOW: **A Royal Navy Sea King lowers its dipping sonar to listen for submarines beneath the surface.**

the Adriatic Sea. They performed over 1,400 deck landings and flew in excess of 1,900 hours. The Sea Kings from 845 NAS performed vital casualty evacuation and other tasks and were hit numerous times. In NATO's intervention in Kosovo, ship-based Sea Kings from 814 NAS provided search and rescue as well as transporting troops and supplies. During the 2003 invasion of Iraq the Sea Kings provided logistical support, transporting Royal Marines from their offshore bases on *Ark Royal*, *Ocean* and other ships on to land in Kuwait. In July 2006 Sea King HC.4s from RNAS Yeovilton were deployed to Cyprus to assist with the evacuation of British citizens from Lebanon. Westland Sea Kings were also exported to Australia, Belgium, Germany, Egypt, India and Norway.

ABOVE: **US Navy unit HS-11 'The Dragonslayers' operated the SH-3 Sea King with distinction for a number of years, and played a significant role in astronaut recovery operations following NASA space flights.**

Westland (Sikorsky) Sea King HC.4

First flight: May 7, 1969 (prototype)
Power: Two Roll-Royce Gnome 1,660shp H.1400-1T turboshafts
Armament: Torpedoes and depth charges
Size: Rotor diameter – 18.9m/62ft
Length – 17.02m/55ft 10in
Height – 4.72m/15ft 6in
Weights: Empty – 5,620kg/12,390lb
Maximum take-off – 9,752kg/21,500lb
Performance: Maximum speed – 245kph/152mph
Service ceiling – 3,050m/10,000ft
Range – 1,230km/764 miles (unladen)
Climb – 619m/2,030ft per minute

Westland Wasp

The Westland Wasp was a small, gas turbine powered, shipboard anti-submarine helicopter derived from the P.531 programme that began as a Saunders-Roe design before that company was absorbed by Westland. The same programme also produced the British Army's Westland Scout and at one point the naval aircraft was to be called the Sea Scout. The Wasp differed from the land-based Scout by having a characteristic four-wheeled (quadricycle) castering undercarriage (as opposed to skids) for easy manoeuvring on flight decks, increased fuel capacity for longer over-water operations and a folding tail unit and rotor blades for easy stowage in small hangars on frigates.

The Wasp is a classic Cold War design that met the Royal Navy's Manned Torpedo-Carrying Helicopter (MATCH) requirement for a helicopter small enough to land on the deck of a frigate but able to carry two homing torpedoes. MATCH came about because of the increasing speed and attack range of the Soviet submarine fleet and the increased range at which the enemy subs could be, detected and neutralized. The Wasp was in effect a stand-off weapons system that gave the Royal Navy an anti-submarine reach beyond the range of the weapons it carried on board its warships of the time. However, as the Wasp had no sonar of its own, it had to take its instructions from its parent ship.

The prototype naval P.531 first flew on October 28, 1962, and production followed soon after with 98 Wasps being built for the Royal Navy. The type was in front-line use soon after from mid-1963. Later in its service the Wasp was modified to carry the SS.11 wire-guided missile to target small surface vessels

ABOVE: Deck crew, wearing white to make themselves as visible as possible, and firefighters stand by as a Wasp prepares to start engines and leave the small flight deck of HMS *Nubian*. A Royal Navy Tribal-class frigate launched on September 6, 1960, *Nubian* entered the Reserve in 1979, and was sunk as a target in 1987. RIGHT: A Lynx HAS.1 of 829 NAS with HMS *Aurora* in the background. Note the size of the two torpedoes in comparison to the helicopter itself.

LEFT: **Another shot featuring HMS** *Nubian*, **as a Wasp prepares to land. Note the simple iron-bedstead castering undercarriage which absorbed bumpy deck landings and allowed crews to manhandle and move the small but potent helicopter with comparative ease.** BELOW: **A Royal Navy Wasp armed with two examples of the wire-guided SS.11 missile. This required the fitting of an observer's sight in the cabin roof and the installation of inflatable emergency floats in sponsons on either side of the cabin to prevent capsizing of the top-heavy aircraft in the event of a ditching.**

so an observer's sight was installed in the cabin roof. Also large inflatable emergency floats were added on either side of the cabin to improve survival chances in the event of a ditching.

As the more capable Westland Lynx entered service in the late 1970s, the Wasp was gradually withdrawn from front-line use. That was until 1982 and the Falklands War when seven mothballed Royal Navy frigates and their helicopters were recommissioned for active service in the South Atlantic.

On April 25, 1982, the Argentine submarine *Santa Fe* was spotted and attacked by a Wessex from HMS *Antrim*. HMS *Plymouth* launched a Wasp HAS. Mk 1 and HMS *Brilliant* launched a Westland Lynx to join the attack. The Wasp from HMS *Plymouth* as well as two other Wasps launched from HMS *Endurance* fired AS.12 anti-ship missiles at the submarine, scoring hits that damaged the sub enough to prevent it from submerging thereby making it the first casualty of the sea war during the Falklands War. The Royal Navy Wasp was finally withdrawn from service in 1988 when the last of the frigates for which the helicopter had been designed was decommissioned.

The Wasp did, however, fly on elsewhere entering service with the Royal Malaysian Navy in May 1990, serving with that navy for a decade. The Royal New Zealand Navy acquired the first of its Wasps in 1966 and did not retire the type until 1998. The Wasp was also in service with Holland as well as the Brazilian, Indonesian and South African navies.

LEFT: **A number of mothballed Royal Navy ships and their Wasp helicopters were brought back into service for the Falklands War, thousands of miles from the UK. The Wasp was finally retired, this time for good, in 1988, some ten years after its first retirement.**

Westland Wasp HAS. Mk 1

First flight: October 28, 1962 (naval prototype)
Power: One Rolls-Royce 710shp Nimbus Mk 503 turboshaft
Armament: Torpedoes, depth charges or anti-ship missiles, dependent on mission
Size: Rotor diameter – 9.83m/32ft 3in
Length – 9.24m/30ft 4in
Height – 3.56m/11ft 8in
Weights: Empty – 1,565kg/3,452lb
Maximum take-off – 2,495kg/5,500lb
Performance: Maximum speed – 193kph/120mph
Service ceiling – 3,813m/12,500ft
Range – 488km/303 miles
Climb – 439m/1,440ft per minute

Westland Wessex

In 1955, only a year after the piston-engined Sikorsky S-58 first flew in the US, the Royal Navy had issued a requirement for a turbine-engined ASW helicopter. Westland's submission was a licence-built version of the Sikorsky design already destined for US Navy use but modified for turbine-power. The nose had to be redesigned to accommodate the larger British engine, which exhausted through a pair of bifurcated exhaust pipes port and starboard beneath the front of the cockpit.

The first all-Westland-built machine, by now named Wessex, flew at Yeovil in June 1958, and deliveries to the Royal Navy began in less than two years in April 1960. The helicopter entered RN squadron service with No.815 NAS at Culdrose in July 1961, and a total of 11 squadrons ultimately operated the HAS. Mk 1 version, the first purpose-designed ASW helicopter operated by the Fleet Air Arm. The only offensive weapons carried by this version were torpedoes. Crew included an observer and an underwater control operator who manned the dipping sonar that listened for enemy submarines. The helicopter's tail assembly folded back against the fuselage to save space onboard ship.

The Wessex was also ordered by the RAF as the HC. Mk 2 for use as a troop transport. Seventy-four were built and a number were later converted for SAR duties. These also differed from the HC.1 by having a different engine or rather engines – two Rolls-Royce Gnome engines coupled to a common drive. The HC. Mk 2 could carry 16 troops or 1,814kg/4,000lb slung beneath it with just half of its coupled powerplant operating. The Gnome-powered versions can be readily identified by having just one, bigger, exhaust pipe on each side. A similar version to the HC.2, the HU.5 was ordered for the Royal Marines, with the first being delivered in December 1963, only six months after the prototype first flew. Among the differences was the addition of rapid-inflation flotation bags stowed in drums that extended outwards from the wheel hubs of the main undercarriage legs. These would have been 'fired' in the event of an emergency water landing. Six squadrons operated the HU.5 until 1987 having used the mark in action in Borneo and the Falklands.

Better radar equipment (including a large dorsal radome for a search radar), more engine power and the ability to carry

LEFT: **This SAR Wessex has its flotation bags deployed. Normally stowed in hub-mounted drums on the helicopter's main wheels, the bags would rapidly inflate when required, thanks to a cylinder of high-pressure gas carried on the inside of each wheel assembly.** ABOVE: **Retrieved from the carrier's hangar, this Wessex is being 'unfolded' and readied for flight.**

LEFT: **A Wessex HAS. Mk 3 prepares for take-off. The two exhaust pipes tell us this is a Gazelle-powered example. Note the winch/hoist assembly and the safety covers over the flotation bag stowage drums.** BELOW: **The Wessex HU.5 was an important asset for the Royal Marines who used 100 examples of the tough and reliable helicopter for troop moving and supply as shown here. These machines went wherever the Royal Marines were deployed and so saw plenty of action.**

torpedoes, depth charges and wire-guided missiles were features of the HAS.3, which entered FAA service in January 1967. The radome's position led, inevitably, to this version being called the 'Camel'. Apart from three development aircraft, all HAS.3s were converted or, more accurately, rebuilt HAS.1s and remained in squadron service until December 1982 having had a reprieve for use in the Falklands War earlier that year.

XP142, an HAS. Mk 3 was operating from the Royal Navy destroyer HMS *Antrim* when it reached the South Atlantic before the main British task force in April 1982. On April 22 it rescued an SAS reconnaissance party from a glacier after their own Wessex HU.5s had crashed in a blizzard. On April 25, flown by Lt Cmdr I. Stanley, XP142 attacked, depth charged and helped to disable the Argentine submarine *Santa Fe*. Although the helicopter was subsequently damaged by enemy small-arms fire and bomb splinters, his historic aircraft is now preserved by the Fleet Air Arm Museum at Yeovilton in the UK.

ABOVE: **The tell-tale hump to the rear of the rotor assembly identifies this as a Wessex HAS. Mk 3. The 'hump' was a dorsal radome that housed a rotating search radar scanner that could pinpoint enemy submarines. Inevitably nicknamed 'the camel', this mark of Royal Navy Wessex saw much action in the Falklands War, the most famous being XP142 that attacked an Argentine submarine.**

Westland Wessex HAS. Mk 3

First flight: May 17, 1958 (Westland-rebuilt S-58)
Power: One Napier Gazelle 1,600shp 165 free power turbine
Armament: Torpedoes and depth charges
Size: Rotor diameter – 17.07m/56ft
 Length – 20.07m/65ft 10in
 Height – 4.85m/15ft 11in
Weights: Empty – 3,583kg/7,900lb
 Maximum take-off – 6,168kg/13,600lb
Performance: Maximum speed – 212kph/132mph
 Service ceiling – 3,050m/10,000ft
 Range – 628km/390 miles
 Climb – 503m/1,650ft per minute

LEFT: **XK906 was a Whirlwind HAS.7, the first ever type of British helicopter designed specifically for the anti-submarine role. Of the 129 supplied to the Royal Navy, the Royal Marines took delivery of 12 examples for communications/transport use.**
BELOW: **A Royal Navy Whirlwind gives a demonstration of Search-And-Rescue (SAR) on the deck of a British aircraft carrier. The Whirlwind was a reassuring presence for Fleet Air Arm aircrew as it hovered nearby during take-offs and landings.**

Westland (Sikorsky) Whirlwind

As helicopter design and technology improved after World War II, so the appreciation of the military applications of rotary craft grew. By the early 1950s, helicopters began to be used by the military in greater numbers but Britain's domestic helicopter industry was small and not at the cutting edge of design. Instead, the best way for Britain to quickly acquire a domestically produced helicopter fleet was by building American-designed helicopters under licence. So it was that Westland Helicopters of Yeovil built the Sikorsky S-55 helicopter in the mid-1950s as the Whirlwind. Westland made a number of improvements to the design over the years and the Whirlwind went on to serve in large numbers with the British Army, Royal Navy and Royal Air Force.

Britain's first Whirlwinds were in fact Sikorsky-built models acquired for evaluation. Ten examples of the HAS. Mk 21 rescue versions and twelve HAS. Mk 22 anti-submarine warfare machines were successfully trialled in the UK leading to a licensing agreement. The first British Whirlwind HAR.1 flew on August 15, 1953 powered by the 600shp Pratt & Whitney Wasp. Serving in non-combat SAR roles, it was followed into service by the HAR.3 with a more powerful 700hp Wright R-1300-3 Cyclone 7 engine. It was 1955 before the HAR.5 flew for the first time with a British engine, the Alvis Leonides Major.

The only dedicated anti-submarine Whirlwind, the more advanced HAS.7, first flew on October 17, 1956, and entered Royal Navy squadron service with 845 NAS. in August 1957. This version was equipped with radar and dipping ASDIC for detecting submarines and could carry a torpedo, but could not carry both at the same time. Nevertheless, this aircraft pioneered rotary wing anti-submarine warfare capability for the Royal Navy.

Fleet Air Arm units operating the Whirlwind included Nos.814, 815,

820, 824, 845, 847 and 848 Naval Air Squadrons as well as Nos.705 and 771 Training Squadrons. Surplus HAS.7s were converted for use in the SAR role from 1960 becoming HAR.9s. The HAR.1, HAR.3 and HA.R5 were retired from service by the mid-1960s but the HAS.7 continued in use as a training helicopter until 1975.

LEFT: **The nose of the Westland Whirlwind contained the engines – note the line of engine-cooling air-intake grilles running beneath the helicopter's windscreen. The Whirlwind flew on in Royal Navy service until 1975.**

Westland (Sikorsky) Whirlwind HAR.3 SAR

First flight: August 15, 1953 (HAR.1)
Power: One Wright 700hp 165 R-1300-3 Cyclone 7
Armament: None
Size: Rotor diameter – 16.15m/53ft
    Length – 12.88m/42ft 3in
    Height – 4.06m/13ft 4in
Weights: Empty – 2,381kg/5,250lb
    Maximum take-off – 3,583kg/7,900lb
Performance: Maximum speed – 180kph/112mph
    Service ceiling – 4,815m/15,800ft
    Range – 579km/360 miles
    Climb – 336m/1,100ft per minute

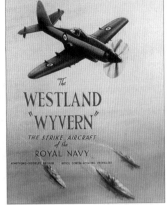

Westland Wyvern

The Westland Wyvern was another British aircraft that began its life with the unfortunate designation 'torpedo-fighter'. Despite the lessons learned during World War II and with aircraft like the Firebrand, some still thought that the two roles of daylight fighter and torpedo-bomber could sit together in one effective aircraft.

And so the Wyvern was proposed in response to specification N.11/44, issued in November 1944, calling for a single-seat ship-based strike fighter powered by a Rolls-Royce Eagle piston engine, but with the flexibility to accept a turboprop. The aircraft had to be carrier-capable, armed with four 20mm cannon, eight rockets, bombs, a mine or a torpedo. The RAF too had considered the same aircraft as a land-based fighter, but the lure of jet fighters proved too great.

Westland's aircraft had a half-elliptical wing similar to that of the Tempest but with an inverted gentle gull-wing configuration that folded for carrier operations. The first flight was made on December 12, 1946, followed by five further prototypes and ten pre-production aircraft. The aircraft were dogged with problems, most of which centred on the Eagle engine which was soon discarded to be replaced by a turboprop. The turboprop route was far from plain sailing and it was not until March 1949 that the first Armstrong Siddeley Python-engined Wyvern TF.2 took to the air.

Carrier trials began on June 21, 1950, and the Wyvern finally entered Fleet Air Arm service with 813 Sqadron in May 1953, replacing the Blackburn Firebrand. The standard service model was the Wyvern S. Mk 4. In November 1956, Nos.830 and 831 Squadrons took part in the Suez campaign, losing 2 aircraft in 79 sorties. No.813, the last front-line Wyvern unit was disbanded in March 1958. The

ABOVE LEFT: **This picture of a Wyvern on the catapult waiting for launch shows many of this aircraft's key features. Note the distinctive cockpit canopy shape and the pilot's field of vision, the large tail, the additional small fin on the tailplane and the turboprop exhaust pipe above the starboard wing fillet. The Wyvern was fitted with a Martin Baker ejector seat which saved the lives of many FAA pilots including one who ejected from underwater when his aircraft went into the sea after a failed catapult launch.** ABOVE: **A contemporary magazine advertisement billing the Wyvern as 'the' strike aircraft of the Royal Navy.**

Wyvern was a powerful, promising and groundbreaking aircraft that packed a punch but its delayed entry into service meant the type lost momentum that was never regained. Total Wyvern production reached 127 and it was the last fixed-wing military type produced by Westland.

Westland Wyvern S.4

First flight: December 12, 1946
Power: One Armstrong Siddeley 4,110ehp 101 turboprop
Armament: Four 20mm cannon, sixteen 27kg/60lb rockets and 907kg/2,000lb of bombs, mines, depth charges or torpedoes
Size: Wingspan – 13.41m/44ft
 Length – 12.88m/42ft 3in
 Height – 4.8m/15ft 9in
 Wing area – 32.98m²/355sq ft
Weights: Empty – 7,080kg/15,608lb
 Maximum take-off – 11,115kg/24,500lb
Performance: Maximum speed – 632kph/393mph
 Service ceiling – 8,535m/28,000ft
 Range – 1,450km/900 miles
 Climb – 2,135m/7,000ft per minute

ABOVE: **During the type's Suez combat use, one Wyvern was hit by Egyptian anti-aircraft fire and glided for three miles out to sea before the pilot ejected near the carrier HMS *Eagle*. The other was lost due to an exploding engine. The Wyvern's combat history is often overlooked.**

LEFT: **The Yak-38 was the world's second operational V/STOL combat aircraft, but its career was comparatively short, while the Harrier that inspired it flourished.**
BELOW: **It was not until 1978 that the Yak-38 entered service.**

Yakovlev Yak-38

Based on the experimental Yak-36M V/STOL research aircraft, Yakovlev developed the Yak-38 which became the first Soviet combat aircraft designed purely for carrier operation to enter series production. The Yak-38 was also the first production vertical take-off/landing aircraft built by the Soviet Union. Though inspired by the British Harrier, the Yak-38 had a completely different configuration to the British jump-jet. While the Harrier had one versatile engine, the Yak-38 had an engine in the rear used for forward flight while two other smaller, less powerful engines housed just aft of the cockpit were used purely for vertical take-off and landing. This added greatly to the aircraft's weight and reduced its fuel capacity.

Designed to perform fleet air defence, reconnaissance and anti-shipping strikes, the first flight of the Yak-36M prototype in conventional mode took place on January 15, 1971. Sea trials are known to have taken place in 1972 aboard the *Moskva* cruiser. A series of pre-production aircraft equipped an evaluation unit that operated from the 'carrier' *Kiev* in the summer of 1976 when the West got its first close look at the type as the *Kiev* entered the Mediterranean via the Bosporus. Six aircraft sat on the deck of the *Kiev* although only three were operational. By the end of the cruise, only one remained serviceable.

It was later in that year that the improved version, the Yak-38, entered production. The Yak-38, codenamed 'Forger' by NATO due to its Harrier inspiration, entered Soviet Navy service in 1978, based on four Kiev-class aircraft carriers, and two years later saw some action in Afghanistan.

LEFT: **The improved Yak-38M first flew in 1982 and featured the new, more powerful Tumansky R-28-300 vectored-thrust engine and the Kolesov RD-38 lift jet, each of which offered around 10 per cent greater thrust than the earlier engines. Despite these improvements, the aircraft remained in service for only a short time.**

The Yak-38's poor performance greatly limited its usefulness. In high temperatures the aircraft reportedly had an endurance of just 15 minutes and could carry only a small payload. The four Yak-38s deployed to Afghanistan in 1980 were operating in 'hot and high' conditions that highlighted the type's shortcomings. A total of 12 combat sorties were flown but the struggling aircraft could only carry two 100kg/220lb bombs each. Even with a greatly reduced fuel and weapons load, the Yak-38 proved incapable of operating during the hot daylight hours so its operations were restricted to pre 05:00 hours. In early hot-weather trials the lift jets refused to start at all and this was remedied by the installation of an oxygen-boosting intake system that was then fitted as standard.

The aircraft was not popular with pilots because of its poor performance and worse safety record. The lift engines had a life of around 22 hours and if one failed (always at low level), the aircraft then experienced a terrifying unrecoverable roll. To protect the pilot in this eventuality (a third of the Yak-38 fleet were lost in accidents), an automatic system ejected the pilot

if it detected an engine failure. A more positive automated system was the Yak-38's hands-free landing capability. On approach, the aircraft could acquire a telemetry link from a computer system on the aircraft carrier which would then guide the aircraft on to the deck while the pilot just monitored the systems. Western observers were unsure of the aircraft's ability to make rolling take-offs but successful trials were carried out in December 1979.

Some 231 Yak-38 aircraft were produced in all, including 38 two-seat trainers (the Yak-38U). The Forger was withdrawn from front-line service in 1992–93, although a few remained in the inventory during 1994 as training aircraft.

This aircraft could not be described as a classic but rather a clear demonstration of the Soviet Union's need to be seen to be able to develop and utilize the same technological developments as the West – the Tupolev Tu-144 'Concordski' being another similar example. Seen as a stopgap aircraft while Soviet V/STOL technology was perfected, the next-generation aircraft never came.

ABOVE: The hinged door that can be seen behind the cockpit was the air intake for the aircraft's lift jets. The 'Forger' was basic, had no radar warning system, and never posed a real threat to NATO.

Yakovlev Yak-38

First flight: January 15, 1971 (Yak-36M)
Power: One Tumansky 6,813kg/15,020lb thrust R-28 V-300 turbofan and two Rybinsk 3,575kg/7,882lb thrust RD-38 turbofans for lift
Armament: Two gun pods and up to 500kg/1,100lb of bombs or missiles
Size: Wingspan – 7.32m/24ft
 Length – 15.5m/50ft 10in
 Height – 4.4m/14ft 4in
 Wing area – 18.5m²/199sq ft
Weights: Empty – 7,485kg/16,500lb
 Maximum take-off – 11,700kg/25,795lb
Performance: Maximum speed – 1,050kph/655mph
 Service ceiling – 12,000m/39,370ft
 Range – 500km/310 miles
 Climb – 4,500m/14,765ft per minute

Glossary

AAF Army Air Forces.

AAM Air-to-Air Missile.

aerodynamics Study of how gases, including air, flow and how forces act upon objects moving through air.

AEW Airborne Early Warning.

AS Anti-Submarine.

ASM Air-to-Surface Missile or Anti-Ship Missile.

ASW Anti-Submarine Warfare.

Accelerator Catapult which accelerates a trolley-mounted aircraft.

Aerostat Tethered, non-navigable lighter-than-air craft, e.g. kite balloon.

afterburner Facility for providing augmented thrust by burning additional fuel in the jet pipe.

ailerons Control surfaces at trailing edge of each wing used to make the aircraft roll.

AMRAAM Advanced Medium-Range Air-to-Air Missile.

angle of attack Angle of a wing to the oncoming airflow.

Anglo-German Naval Agreement (1935) Agreement for German fleet to be built up to fixed proportion of Royal Navy strength. Inter alia, this approved two 22,353-tonne/22,000-ton aircraft carriers for the German Navy.

"Arapaho" Proposed means of deploying V/STOL aircraft from large merchantmen by containerization of all associated services.

Arrester (system) A series of (now) retractable transverse wires, engaged by an aircraft's tailhook to bring it to a halt. Historically also fore-and-aft wires in combination with ramps.

BELOW: **Independence and Essex class carriers .**

ABOVE: **A Sopwith Pup comes in to land.**

ASRAAM Advanced Short-Range Air-to-Air Missile.

ASV Air-to-Surface-Vessel – pertaining to this type of radar developed during World War II.

ASW Anti-Submarine Warfare.

Avgas Aviation fuel.

AWACS Airborne Warning and Control System.

bhp Brake horsepower. Power actually developed by an engine.

Ballast Additional weight put aboard to improve stability, to correct trim or to modify ship movement.

Barrier Flexible entanglement to make emergency arrest of aircraft that has jumped the arrester wires, with minimum damage to aircraft or pilot.

"Batman" See Deck Landing Officer.

Beam Width of hull at the waterline at Standard Displacement.

Belt Heavy vertical side armour designed to defeat low-trajectory gunfire.

biplane An aircraft with two sets of wings.

"Blimp" Non-rigid dirigible. Small airship primarily for coastal duty.

blister A streamlined, often clear, large fairing on aircraft body housing guns or electronics.

Bulge Watertight compartment(s) added and faired to mainly underwater section of hull to increase buoyancy or to improve stability.

Bunkers Compartments for stowage of fuel.

BVR Beyond Visual Range.

C3 (C-3) US Maritime Commission designation for a cargo ship of

between 137–152m/450–500ft waterline length and carrying less than 100 passengers.

C-in-C Commander-in-Chief.

canard wings Two small horizontal surfaces on either side of the front of an aircraft.

CAP Combat Air Patrol. A ship or squadron's organic air cover.

ceiling The maximum height at which an aircraft can operate.

CIWS Close-In Weapon System, e.g. Goalkeeper.

CMB Coastal Motor Boat. The Motor Torpedo Boat (MTB) was a derivative.

CTG Carrier Task Group.

CTOL Conventional Take-Off and Land.

CV Aircraft Carrier.

CVA Attack Aircraft Carrier.

CVE Escort Carrier.

CVL Light Aircraft Carrier.

CVN Nuclear-Propelled Aircraft Carrier.

CVS Anti-Submarine Aircraft Carrier.

Calibre Bore diameter of gun barrel. Also measure of barrel length, e.g. a 3in 70 will be 3 x 70 = 210in in length.

Camber Athwartships curve or rise of a ship's deck.

Cantilever Overhung structure supported at only one side or end.

Casing (funnel) Outer plating surrounding exhaust end of uptake.

Catapult Device to accelerate an aircraft directly.

Deadweight (tonnage) Actual carrying capacity of a cargo ship, expressed in tons of 2,240lb. Abbreviated to dwt.

BELOW: **A Nimitz class carrier.**

500

ABOVE: **A Sangamon class escort carrier.**

Deck Landing Officer (or "Batman") Crew man who guides landing aircraft with visual signals. Largely superseded by Mirror Landing Sight.

delta wing A swept-back, triangular-shaped wing.

Derrick Pivoted spar, rigged with winches, for lifting loads.

dihedral The upward angle of the wing formed where the wings connect to the fuselage.

Dirigible Powered, navigable airship. May be framed (rigid) or unframed (non-rigid).

Displacement, full load or "deep" Weight of ship (in tons of 2,240lb) when fully equipped, stored and fuelled.

Displacement, standard Weight of ship less fuel and other deductions allowed by treaty.

dorsal Pertaining to the upper side of an aircraft.

drag The force that resists the motion of the aircraft through the air.

Draught (or Draft) Mean depth of water in which a ship may float freely.

ECM Electronic Countermeasures.

elevators Control surfaces on the horizontal part of the tail that are used to alter the aircraft's pitch.

ELINT Electronic Intelligence.

eshp Equivalent shaft horsepower.

ESM Electronic Support Measures.

FBW Fly-By-Wire.

Fleet Air Arm (FAA) Air Wing of the Royal Navy.

Fighter Catapult Ship Naval-manned equivalent of Catapult Armed Merchantman (CAM).

fin The vertical portion of the tail.

flaps Moveable parts of the trailing edge of a wing used to increase lift at slower air speeds.

Flare Outward curvature of hull plating.

Fleet Train World War II term for Afloat Support. The assembly of auxiliary vessels which keep a fleet supplied and operational.

Floatplane Same as Seaplane. Aircraft supported on water by external floats.

Flying boat Aircraft supported on water by its own hull, and steadied by wingtip floats.

Freeboard For aircraft carriers, the vertical distance from waterline (at standard displacement) to the flight deck.

g The force of gravity.

Gross registered tons (grt) Measure of volumetric capacity of a merchant ship. One gross ton equals 100cu ft (2.83m3) of reckonable space.

Grand Fleet Title carried by the British battle fleet during World War I.

HAPAG Acronym for Hamburg-America Line.

Heavier-than-air Applied to aircraft supported by lift generated by airflow over horizontal surfaces.

High Sea(s) Fleet Title carried by German battle fleet during World War I.

Horsepower (hp) Unit of power equal to 746 watts.

HOTAS Hands-On Throttle And Stick.

HUD Head-Up Display.

ICBM Intercontinental Ballistic Missile.

IFF Identification Friend or Foe.

ihp Indicated horsepower. Specifically the power delivered by the pistons of a reciprocating steam engine.

jet engine An engine that works by creating a high-velocity jet of air to propel the engine forward.

JMSDF Japanese Maritime Self-

BELOW: **A Mikoyan-Gurevich MiG-29K.**

ABOVE: **A HO3S-1 hovers over the USS *Kearsage*.**

Defense Force.

JSF Joint Strike Fighter.

Kite balloon Aerostat deployed by ships for observation purposes.

LCA Landing Craft, Assault. 12.5m/41.1ft, 35 troops. Carried under davits.

LCAC Landing Craft, Air Cushion. 26.8m/87.9ft, 61 tonnes/60 tons capacity. Carried in well.

LCT Landing Craft, Tank. 58.5m/192ft, 203 tonnes/200 tons capacity. Sea-going.

LCU Landing Craft, Utility. 41m/134.7ft, 145 tonnes/143 tons capacity. Carried in well.

LCVP Landing Craft, Vehicle, Personnel. 10.9m/35.8ft, 35 troops. Carried under davits.

LHA Amphibious Assault Ship.

LHD Helicopter/Dock Landing Ship.

LPD Amphibious Transport, Dock.

LPH Amphibious Assault Helicopter Carrier.

LSD Dock Landing Ship.

Landplane Aircraft with wheeled undercarriage, as opposed to Seaplane with floats.

leading edge The front edge of a wing or tailplane.

Length (bp) Length between perpendiculars. Customarily the distance between forward extremity of waterline at standard displacement and the forward side of rudder post. For American warships, lengths on designed waterline and between perpendiculars are synonymous.

Length (oa) Length overall.

Length (wl) Length, waterline. Waterline length at standard displacement.

Lighter-than-air Applied to aircraft whose lift depends upon the buoyancy of gas.

501

London Treaty (First of 1929–30 and Second of 1935–36) Treaties seeking to reaffirm but to modify the terms of the Washington Treaty (1921–22).

Mach Speed of sound – Mach 1 = 1,223kph/706mph at sea level.

monoplane An aircraft with one set of wings.

NATO North Atlantic Treaty Organization.

NDL Norddeutscher Lloyd, Bremen.

PDMS Point Defence Missile System. Short-range missile system, often on common mount with a rapid-fire gun, for "last-ditch" defence.

Pallisade Windbreak erected to screen launch area on early carriers.

pitch Rotational motion in which an aircraft turns around its lateral axis.

Plan "Orange" American war plan for use against Japan.

port Left side.

Protective deck Either flat, or incorporating slopes or pronounced curvature, the protective deck protects spaces beneath from bombs, plunging fire or splinters.

RAAF Royal Australian Air Force.

radome Protective covering for radar made from material through which radar beams can pass.

RAF Royal Air Force. Unified force created in April 1918 through the amalgamation of the RFC and the RNAS.

RCAF Royal Canadian Air Force.

reheat See afterburner.

RFA Royal Fleet Auxiliary. Afloat support ships of the Royal Navy.

RFC Royal Flying Corps. The army's air wing prior to 1918.

RN Royal Navy.

ABOVE: **A Westland Wyvern S.4.**

RNAS Royal Naval Air Service. The navy's air wing prior to 1918.

roll Rotational motion in which the aircraft turns around its longitudinal axis.

rudder The parts of the tail surfaces that control an aircraft's yaw (its left and right turning).

SAM Surface-to-Air Missile.

SCS Sea Control Ship.

shp Shaft horsepower. Power at point in shaft ahead of stern gland. Does not include frictional losses in stern gland and A-bracket, if fitted.

SLR Side-Looking airborne Radar.

SSBN Nuclear-Propelled, Ballistic Missile Submarine.

SSM Surface-to-Surface Missile.

SSN Nuclear-Powered Fleet Submarine.

starboard Right side.

STOL Short Take-Off and Landing.

STOVL Short Take-Off, Vertical Land.

STUFT Ships Taken Up From Trade. Merchant ships chartered for the support of naval requirements.

Seaplane See Floatplane.

Sheer Curvature of deckline in fore-and-aft direction, usually upward at either end.

Sided Situated toward sides of ship, usually as opposed to centreline location.

Ski-jump A pronounced upward curvature of forward end of flight deck of a V/STOL carrier. Enhances the effect of short take-off run.

Stability range Total angle through which, from a position of equilibrium, a ship is statically stable.

supersonic Indicating motion faster than the speed of sound.

swing wing A wing capable of variable

sweep e.g. on Panavia Tornado.

tailplane Horizontal part of the tail, known as horizontal stabilizer In North America.

TF Task Force, e.g. TF38. A group of warships assembled for a specific purpose.

TG Task Group, e.g. TG38.1, TG38.2 etc. The major components of a Task Force.

thrust Force produced by engine which pushes an aircraft forward.

TSR Torpedo/Spotter/Reconnaissance. Roles for which aircraft such as the Fairey Swordfish were designed.

Trim Amount by which a ship deviates, in the fore-and-aft axis, from her designed draught.

triplane An aircraft with three sets of wings.

TU Task Unit, e.g. TU38.1.1, TU38.1.2. The major components of a Task Group.

Turbo-electric Propulsion system in which a steam turbine drives an electrical generator. This supplies energy via cable to a propulsion motor coupled to the propeller shaft.

UHF Ultra High Frequency.

UN United Nations.

Uptake Conduit conducting products of combustion to the funnel.

USAAC United States Army Air Corps.

USAAF United States Army Air Forces.

USAF United States Air Force.

USCG United States Coast Guard.

USMC United States Marine Corps.

USN United States Navy.

variable geometry See swing wing.

ventral Pertaining to the underside of an aircraft.

VHF Very High Frequency.

BELOW: **A Moskva class carrier.**

BELOW: **Ark Royal (III) with a flight of Fairey Gannets.**

Volume critical A ship whose design is driven by needs of space rather than weight, e.g. aircraft carrier.

Warsaw Pact Eastern military bloc, essentially a counter to NATO.

Washington Treaty (c1921–22) Arms limitation agreement that had a profound effect on the development of the aircraft carrier.

Weight critical A ship whose design is driven by considerations of weight rather than space, e.g. a heavily armoured battleship.

RIGHT: **Fairey III Fs lined up on deck of HMS** *Courageous* **in the 1930s.**

Key to flags

The nationality of each aircraft carrier, carrier class and aircraft is identified in the relevant specification box by the national flag that was in use at the time of its commissioning and service.

 Argentina

 Australia

 Brazil

 Canada

 France

 Germany: WWI

 Germany: WWII

 India

 Italy

 Japan

 Netherlands

 Romania

 Russia

 Spain

 Sweden

 Thailand

 United Kingdom

 United States

 USSR

Acknowledgements

Research for the pictures used to illustrate this book was carried out by Ted Nevill of TRH Pictures. Ted Nevill would like to thank all those who contributed to the research and supply of these images, in particular the staff at the Photographic Section of the Naval Historical Center, Washington, DC, and at Still Pictures at the National Archives at College Park, Maryland, USA.

The artworks used in this book were drawn by Jan Suermondt for Cody Images or supplied by ArtTech. Photographs and other illustrations were supplied by the following. Every effort has been made to acknowledge the pictures properly; however, we apologize if there are any unintentional omissions, which will be corrected in future editions.

(l=left, r=right, t=top, b=bottom, m=middle)

Michael J.F. Bowyer: 281b, 333b, 404tr, 418t, 418bl, 419b, 427m, 427b, 430b, 486b, 487tr.

BELOW: **A Lynx HAS.1 of 829 NAS.**

Francis Crosby Collection:
10t, 11br, 258–9, 263ml, 246b, 265t, 265b, 272t, 272b, 273um, 273bl, 273br, 283bl, 283br, 305bl, 305br, 307t, 308m, 309t, 309m, 310b, 312tr, 324t, 325m, 329tl, 329tr, 329b, 330t, 330b, 331t, 331m, 331b, 332m, 332b, 333t, 333m, 335b, 336t, 336b, 337b, 342bl, 342br, 344bl, 344br, 345m, 346m, 349tl, 350tr, 350b, 351t, 351m, 351b, 353tl, 365m, 366t, 366b, 367tl, 367tr, 367b, 372b, 373tl, 373tr, 382t, 382m, 383b, 385b, 387t, 388tr, 389t, 389m, 389b, 390tl, 390tr, 390b, 391m, 392tr, 392b, 393b, 394tr, 394b, 395tl, 395tr, 395b, 402t, 402b, 403tr, 403m, 405tl, 405tr, 411m, 411b, 424br, 426m, 426b, 427t, 429b, 430tr, 438b, 441b, 446tr, 461b, 463tr, 472br, 480t, 480b, 481tl, 481tr, 487tl, 488b, 490tr, 491m, 494bl, 494br, 495t, 495m, 495b, 496t, 496m, 496b, 497tr.

Chris Farmer: 273t, 308b, 314t, 315t, 325t, 332t, 337tl, 342t, 345b, 410tl, 426t, 428t, 429t, 437b, 447t, 450t, 450b, 455t, 484m, 485t, 486t.

Felicity Forster: 474b.

Brian Marsh: 391t, 403tl.

Geoff Sheward: 410tr, 433tr, 437tr, 447b, 448tr, 452tr,

ABOVE: **US Navy Curtiss BFC-2s fly in formation.**

454t, 455b, 460t, 460b, 461t, 461m, 484t, 485t, 485b, 491b, 494t.

TRH Pictures: 8t, 8m, 9tr, 9tl, 9bl, 10b, 11t, 11bl,14, 16t, 16mr, 17tr, 17mr, 17ml, 17b, 18tr, 18br, 18bl, 19tr, 19mr, 19bl, 20t, 20br, 21tr, 21mr, 21br, 21bl, 22t, 22mr, 22bl, 23t, 23mr, 23bl, 24tr, 24b, 25tr, 25tl, 25mr, 25br, 26t, 26mr, 27tr, 27mr, 27ml, 27b, 28t, 28mr, 29tr, 29tl, 29mr, 29ml, 29br, 30t, 30mr, 31tr, 31tl, 31mr, 31bl, 32t, 32mr, 33tr, 33ml, 33br, 33bl, 34t, 34mr, 35tr, 35tl, 35mr, 36t, 36mr, 37tr, 37tl, 37mr, 37br, 38t, 38mr, 39tr, 39tl, 39mr, 40t, 40bl, 41tr, 41tl, 412br, 41bl, 42t, 42mr, 43tl, 43mr, 43ml, 43br, 44t, 44mr, 45tr, 45tl, 45mr, 45br, 46tr, 46b, 47tr, 47tl, 47mr, 47br, 48tr, 48tl, 48mr, 49tr, 49 2nd from tr, 49mr, 49ml, 49br, 50tr, 50br, 50bl, 51tr, 51tl, 51mr, 51bl, 52tr, 52b, 53tr, 53tl, 53mr, 53br, 54tr, 54tl, 54br, 55tr, 55tl, 55br, 56t, 56mr, 57tr, 57tl, 57mr, 57ml, 58t, 58mr, 59tl, 59m, 59mr, 59br, 60t, 60mr, 61tr, 61tl, 61mr, 61br, 62t, 62mr, 63tr, 63tl, 63mr, 63br, 64t, 64mr, 64b, 65tr, 65mr, 65b, 66tr, 66tl, 66mr, 67tr, 67mr, 67bl, 68tl, 68mr, 68br, 69tl, 69br, 69bl, 70t, 70mr, 71tr, 71tl, 71mr, 71ml, 72t, 72br, 73tr, 73mr, 73br, 73bl, 74t, 74mr, 75tr, 75tl, 75mr, 75br, 76tr, 76tl, 76br, 77tr, 77br, 77bl, 78tr, 78tl, 78mr, 79tl, 79mr, 79br, 80t, 80mr, 81t, 81mr, 81br, 82t, 82mr, 83tr, 83tl, 83mr, 83br, 84t, 84mr, 85tr, 85tl, 85ml, 86t, 86mr, 87tr, 87mr, 87br, 87bl, 88t, 88mr, 89tr, 89tl, 89mr, 90t, 90mr, 91tr, 91tl, 91m, 91br, 92mr, 92b, 93tr, 93ml, 93br, 93bl, 94mr, 95tr, 95tl, 95mr, 95br, 96t, 96mr, 97tr, 97tl, 97ml, 97br, 98t, 98mr, 99tr, 99tl, 99br, 102tr, 102tl, 102ml, 103tr, 103tl, 103bl, 104tr, 104b, 105tr, 105mr, 105ml, 105bl, 106tr, 106tl, 107tl, 107mr, 107ml, 108t, 108mr, 109tr, 109mr, 109ml, 109b, 110t, 110br, 111tr, 111tl, 111mr, 112t, 112b, 113b, 114mr, 114b, 115t, 115mr, 115bl, 116t, 116mr, 117t, 117mr, 117ml, 118t, 118mr, 119t, 119ml, 119bl, 120mr, 120b, 121t, 121bl, 122tr, 122tl, 122mr, 123t, 123ml, 124t, 124mr, 125t, 125mr, 125ml, 126t, 126mr, 127tr, 127tl, 127mr, 127ml, 128tl, 128mr, 128bl, 129tr, 129m, 129bl, 130t, 130mr, 131tr, 131ml, 131bl, 132tr, 132tl, 132mr, 133tr, 133tl, 133bl, 134t, 134mr, 135tr, 135tl, 135mr, 136t, 136mr, 137tr, 137tl, 137ml, 138t,

504

138bl, 139tr, 139tl, 140t, 140bl, 141tl, 141mr, 141bl, 142tr, 142tl, 143tr, 143tl, 144tr, 144mr, 144bl, 145t, 145mr, 145b, 146t, 146bl, 147tr, 147mr, 147bl, 148t, 148ml, 148bl, 149tr, 149bl, 150t, 151t, 151mr, 151bl, 152t, 152mr, 152b, 153tr, 153ml, 153bl, 154t, 154mr, 155t, 155mr, 155bl, 156tr, 156b, 157tl, 157mr, 157bl, 158t, 158mr, 158b, 159tl, 159bl, 160t, 160mr, 161tr, 161tl, 161mr, 161b, 162t, 162br, 163tl, 163mr, 164t, 164mr, 165tl, 165mr, 165ml, 165bl, 166tl, 166mr, 166ml, 167t, 167mr, 167bl, 168t, 168mr, 168br, 169tr, 169tl, 169bl, 170tl, 170mr, 170bl, 171tl, 171mr, 171bl, 172tl, 172mr, 172bl, 173t, 173m, 174tl, 174mr, 175tl, 175mr, 175ml, 175bl, 176tl, 176bl, 177t, 177m, 177bl, 178tr, 178tl, 178mr, 178bl, 179t, 179b, 180tr, 180b, 181tr, 181tl, 181mr, 181bl, 182t, 182bl, 183tr, 183tl, 183br, 184t, 184bl, 185t, 185bl, 186tl, 186tr, 187tr, 187tl, 187mr, 188t, 188mr, 189tr, 189ml, 189bl, 190ml, 191tr, 191tl, 191bl, 194ml, 194bl, 195t, 195ml, 195bl, 196t, 196mr, 196bl, 197t, 197mr, 197bl, 198tr, 198br, 199t, 199m, 199bl, 200t, 200mr, 200bl, 201m, 202tr, 202tl, 202bl, 203t, 203mr, 203bl, 204m, 205m, 205bl, 206t, 206br, 207t, 207mr, 207bl, 208b, 209t, 209m, 209bl, 210tl, 210bl, 211t, 211b, 212tr, 212tl, 212bl, 213tl, 214b,

215t, 215mr, 215bl, 216tr, 216tl, 217bl, 218mr, 219t, 219mr, 220tr, 220tl, 220m, 220b, 221t, 221m, 221bl, 222tl, 222bl, 223tr, 223tl, 223mr, 224tr, 224tl, 224bl, 225tr, 225tl, 225mr, 226tr, 226tl, 226mr, 227t, 227bl, 228tr, 228m, 228bl, 229tr, 229tl, 229bl, 230tl, 230mr, 230bl, 231t, 231m, 232t, 232mr, 233tr, 233tl, 233mr, 233bl, 234tr, 234ml, 235t, 235mr, 235ml, 236tr, 236tl, 236bl, 237t, 237mr, 237bl, 238tl, 238ml, 239ml, 239bl, 240t, 240mr, 240bl, 241tl, 241ml, 242tl, 243t, 243bl, 244tl, 244bl, 245t, 245mr, 245m, 245b, 246tl, 246bl, 247tl, 247bl, 248tl, 249t, 249mr, 249bl, 250tl, 250ml, 250t, 250mr, 250bl, 251ml, 251bl, 252tr, 252tl, 252bl, 253tl, 253bl, 254t, 254bl, 260t, 260b, 261t, 261m, 262t, 262b, 263tl, 263tr, 263b, 264t, 265m, 266t, 266b, 267tl, 267tr, 267m, 267b, 268t, 268b, 269tr, 269m, 269b, 270tl, 270tr, 271tl, 271tr, 271bl, 271br, 274t, 274b, 275t, 275ml, 275mr, 275b, 276t, 276b, 277tl, 277tr, 277m, 277b, 278t, 278b, 279tl, 279tr, 279b, 280t, 280b, 281tl, 281tr, 281m, 282t, 282b, 283tl, 283tr, 283mr, 284t, 284b, 285tl, 285tr, 285mr, 285b, 286t, 286b, 287tl, 287tr, 287bl, 287br, 288b, 289tl, 289tr, 289b, 290t, 290b, 291tl, 291tr, 291m, 291b, 292t, 292b, 293tl, 293tr, 293m, 293b, 296t, 296bl, 296br, 297t, 297m, 297b, 298t, 298b, 299tl, 299tr, 299m, 299b,

ABOVE: **The wreck of the battleship *Arizona* burns at her berth in Pearl Harbor.**

300t, 300b, 301tl, 301tr, 301b, 302t, 302b, 303tl, 303tr, 303b, 304t, 304b, 305t, 305m, 306t, 306b, 307m, 307b, 308t, 310t, 310m, 311t, 311b, 312tl, 312b, 313t, 313b, 314bl, 314br, 315m, 316t, 316b, 317tl, 317tr, 317b, 318t, 318b, 319t, 319b, 320t, 320bl, 320br, 321t, 321m, 321b, 322t, 322m, 322b, 323tl, 323tr, 323b, 324b, 325b, 326tl, 326tr, 326b, 327t, 327m, 327b, 328tl, 328tr, 328b, 334t, 334b, 335t, 335m, 336m, 338tl, 338tr, 338b, 339tl, 339tr, 339b, 340tl, 340tr, 340b, 341tl, 341tr, 341b, 343tl, 343tr, 344t, 345t, 346t, 346b, 347tl, 347tr, 347b, 348b, 349tr, 349m, 352tl, 352tr, 352b, 352tr, 353b, 354tl, 354tr, 354b, 355t, 355m, 355b, 356tl, 356tr, 356b, 357t, 357m, 357b, 358t, 358m, 358b, 359t, 359m, 359b, 360t, 360b, 361tl, 361tr, 361b, 362t, 362b, 363t, 363m, 363b, 364t, 364b, 365t, 365b, 368t, 368b, 369tl, 369tr, 369m, 369b, 370t, 370b, 371tl, 371m, 371b, 372tl, 372tr, 373b, 374t, 374m, 374b, 375t, 375b, 376t, 376b, 377tl, 377tr, 377b, 378tl, 378t, 378b, 379t, 379bl, 379br, 380t, 380b, 381t, 381m, 381b, 382b, 383t, 384t, 384m, 384b, 385t, 385m, 386t, 386b, 387b, 388t, 388b, 391b, 393t, 394tl, 396t, 396b, 397tl, 397tr, 397b, 398–9, 400t, 400b, 401tl, 401tr, 401m, 401b, 404tl, 405b, 406t, 406m, 406b, 407t, 408t, 408bl, 408br, 409t, 409m, 409b, 410b, 411t, 412tl, 412tr, 412b, 413tl, 413tr, 413b, 414t, 414b,

415t, 415ml, 415mr, 415b, 416tl, 416tr, 416b, 417t, 417m, 417b, 419tr, 419m, 420tl, 420tr, 420b, 421t, 422t, 422b, 423tl, 423tr, 423b, 424t, 424bl, 425tl, 425tr, 425b, 430tl, 431t, 431m, 431b, 432t, 432b, 433tl, 433b, 434t, 434b, 435t, 435m, 435b, 436t, 437tl, 438t, 439t, 439um, 439lm, 439b, 440b, 441t, 441m, 442t, 442b, 443tl, 443tr, 443b, 444t, 444b, 445tl, 445tr, 445b, 446b, 448tl, 448b, 449tl, 449tr, 449b, 451t, 452tl, 452b, 453t, 453b, 456tl, 456tr, 456b, 457t, 457m, 457b, 458t, 458b, 459t, 459b, 462t, 462m, 462b, 463tl, 463b, 464tl, 464tr, 464bl, 464br, 465t, 465m, 465b, 466tl, 466tr, 466b, 467t, 467m, 467b, 468tl, 468tr, 468bl, 468br, 469t, 469b, 470t, 470b, 471tl, 471tr, 471b, 472t, 472bl, 473t, 473m, 473b, 474tl, 474tr, 475tl, 475tr, 475b, 476tl, 476b, 477t, 477m, 477b, 478t, 478bl, 478br, 479t, 479b, 481b, 482t, 482m, 482b, 483tl, 483tr, 483b, 484b, 487b, 492t, 492bl, 492br, 493t, 493m, 493b, 497tl, 497b, 498tl, 498tr, 498b, 499tl, 499tr, 499b.

US Navy: 288t.

Nick Waller: 261b, 294–5, 309b, 315b, 337tr, 343b, 347m, 348t, 349b, 350tl, 392tl, 392m, 403b, 404b, 407m, 407b, 418br, 421b, 428b, 429m, 436b, 440t, 446tl, 451m, 451b, 454b, 476tr, 488tl, 488tr, 489t, 489m, 489b, 490tl, 490b, 491t.

BELOW: **The Vought F7U-3 Cutlass.**

Index

ABOVE: **The Grumman F2F entered carrier service in 1935.**

BELOW: **The *Bismarck* under attack from aerial torpedoes.**

BELOW: **The *Illustrious* and the *Invincible*.**

511

ABOVE: **A string of *Bulwark*'s Westland Wessexes positions itself.**